HISTORICAL COMMENTARY
ON THE OLD TESTAMENT

* * *

ISAIAH

HISTORICAL COMMENTARY

ON THE OLD TESTAMENT

Editorial team:

Cornelis Houtman
(Kampen, The Netherlands)

Gert T.M. Prinsloo
(Pretoria, South Africa)

Wilfred G.E. Watson
(Newcastle, UK)

Al Wolters
(Ancaster, Ontario, Canada)

ISAIAH

Part II

Volume 2: Isaiah Chapters 28-39

by

Willem A.M. Beuken

PEETERS - LEUVEN

Dedicated with Gratitude and Esteem
to the Memory of Willem Sterrenberg Prinsloo (1944 -1997)
Who Enriched the International Community of his Colleagues
with his Incisive Scholarship and Academic Endeavours
and Whose Friendship I have greatly Prized

Willem A.M. Beuken
Isaiah II/2
(Historical Commentary on the Old Testament)
Translated from the Dutch by Dr. Brian Doyle
Cover design by Dick Prins
NUGI 632
ISBN 90-429-0813-0
D. 2000/0602/18

© 2000 — Peeters, Bondgenotenlaan 153, B-3000 Leuven (Belgium)

CONTENTS

AUTHOR'S PREFACE: VIEWPOINT AND METHOD

'The moment commentaries became *peri*-literature, innocence took its leave through the back door' (Ferdinand Deist).[1] It was clearly nothing short of inevitable that the broad gamut of exegetical methods which have emerged in the last decades would ultimately lead to a critical examination of the very occupation of explaining the Scriptures. Hermeneutics is now a recognised and necessary component of any exegetical endeavour. Any commentary on the Scriptures is obliged, therefore, to begin with a description and justification of the chosen methodology if it wishes to avoid indoctrination. The problem does not lie with the text but with the interpreters of the text. Even when exegetes profess a high regard for religion and history, a love of literature and an acceptance of the Bible as the word of God, their beliefs and opinions continue to govern their explanation of the text and to limit the Scriptures' almost limitless potential.

The exegetical approach offered by the present commentary is governed by the project proposed for the series *Historical Commentary on the Old Testament*. In the 'Editorial Preface (I)' of *Isaiah Part 3. Volume 1* one can find the main contours of interpretation in so far as they condition the adopted methodology and are designed to serve the intended readership of scholars and educated theologians. The HCOT project proposes to examine the relationship between the genesis of a text and its final form, between the centuries-old history of exegesis of a text and its contemporary expressions, determined as they are by a faith awareness rooted in the Enlightenment, and between the classical literary-historical approach and the methodologically multi-faceted exegesis of the present day. The basic tenet of the project runs as follows:

'The editors are committed to the view that the Old Testament was and is a vehicle of the knowledge of God – a knowledge that was originally imparted at specific times and places within the bounds of human history. In order for people today to recognise and accept the permanent validity of that knowledge, they must realise that the Old Testament originated in a human society which, with respect to the basic realities of the human condition, was not so very different from our own. It was in

---

[1] F. Deist, "Inside a Commentary. Reflections on the Writing of Bible Commentaries", *OTE* 10 (1997), 369-86, esp. 369.

the context of a fundamentally similar society, in the concreteness of ordinary human history, culture and language, that the revelation of God
was received over the centuries. It is only by concentrating on the
specificity of that thoroughly historical revelation (often brought into focus by comparing the traditions of Israel with those of its neighbours),
that we can hope to grasp the uniqueness of the faith of ancient Israel'.

In what way is this fundamental option realised in the present commentary on Isaiah chs. 28-39?

With respect to the *historical explanation* of the text, the fact that several, often contradictory, scenarios have been proposed on the genesis of
the book of Isaiah has not led us to adopt a pessimistic standpoint regarding the possibility of distinguishing oracles of Isaiah ben Amoz
himself, or reports concerning the prophet stemming from his immediate
environment, from new applications thereof provided by the course of
transmission. Similarly, the endeavour to discern the motivations behind
the actualising tradition of Isaiah's prophecies and the redaction thereof
seems, to the present author, far from pointless. Yet the possibility of
describing the genesis of the book of Isaiah, era by era or verse by verse,
does not engender optimism.

It would seem possible in principle, nevertheless, to determine
whether a particular revision dates from before, during or after the exile,
given the fact that the fall of Jerusalem constituted such a profound demarcation between the theological parameters of these periods. Prior to
the exile, God's intervention in the life of his people was coloured by
the threat of judgement while after the exile it was coloured by the
promise of salvation. While this division should not be understood as
exclusive – as if judgement, in the long run, excluded any form of salvation and the new promise of salvation excluded every form of sanction –,
it would seem transparent enough to provide us with dependable points
of orientation.

In this regard, we consider it to be justifiable to accept the existence
of an Assyrian or Josian redaction, in line with the majority of contemporary authors.[2] Scholars assume that this redaction provided an older
collection of the oracles of Isaiah with a new edition in light of the national and religious revival which characterised the reign of king Josiah
(640-609 BC), during which the power of Assyria had begun to wane. It
was this same tendency which transformed the withdrawal of
Sennacherib's army in 701 BC into a paradigmatic narrative concerning

---

[2] Cf. in the Bibliography, under 'Isaiah Chapters 28-39' the studies of Barth 1977;
Vermeylen 1978; Clements 1980; further Sweeney, 57-9.

Zion's inviolability under YHWH's protection. While God had used Assyria as an instrument of punishment and purification for Israel, he had never intended to abandon Zion as his dwelling or to undo his promise to the house of David.

With respect to the *literary explanation* of the text, an assortment of methods has been employed and this has likewise led to a number of choices.

While the *Revised Standard Version* lies at the foundation of the translation, this text has been emended in several places, sometimes based on an alternative linguistic interpretation, sometimes with the intention of preserving the literary form of the Hebrew, and most frequently to allow verbal agreements to emerge with greater clarity. The result is a 'study translation' intended as a support to the exegesis. Besides text-critical information, the 'Notes' also offer a justification of the translational options.

The verse structure (colometry) has also been afforded significant attention. While the text as well as the lay-out of the translation have been divided into two and three part verse lines, the justification thereof has only been possible where the division provided difficulties. At the same time, while it is evident that sentence structure (syntax) and verse structure are closely related, the mutual interplay between both textual structures in the poetic sections of the Old Testament continues to be the subject of current research.[3] Nevertheless, the following option would appear to offer a secure point of departure: the first member (colon) of the verse line enjoys a degree of dominance with respect to the second (and third), to the extent that the verbs of the first colon, according to their position therein, determine the pattern of primary and subordinate clauses, i.e. a syntactic sequence or interruption thereof. The colometry and the syntax thus constitute the basis of the structure. Given the fact that these features serve to clarify the *parallelismus membrorum*, attention can then be focused on the style features which provide the latter with such variety.

With respect to the *semantic explanation* of the text, insight into the literary form thereof constitutes one essential condition for the accurate description of the text's important ideas and concepts. A knowledge of the historical development of the relevant terminology in Israel, in so far as this is reflected in the Hebrew Bible, constitutes a further essential condition. The present commentary endeavours to combine both dimen-

---

[3] Cf. A. Niccacci, "Analysing Biblical Hebrew Poetry", *JSOT* 74 (1997) 77-93, esp. 91: 'Biblical Hebrew poetry remains a mystery from the point of view of the verbal system while prose shows a substantial coherence'.

sions: what is the content of a term in the various literary corpora of the Old Testament (the paradigmatic function) and in what way is that content realised in a determined (con)text in the book of Isaiah (the syntagmatic function)? In addition, attention will frequently be focused on the significance of a term in Isaiah chs. 1-39 since context and historical development (syntagma and paradigma) tend to accompany one another within the limited perimeters of these chapters. First Isaiah constitutes the primary ground of a number of significant terms in chs. 28-39. References to these chapters, therefore, do not intend to imply quoting. Their purpose, rather, is to illustrate relationships within a single literary corpus which may contribute to the content of the term in question.

Regarding reference to *specialist literature*, the agenda of any commentary written in the second half of the twentieth century must consider itself constrained by two determinative facts: its position in the tradition of literary-historical research with its sequential phases of interest, a picture of which can still be formed up to the mid-1970's, and the contemporary explosion of pertinent information and new methodological approaches which has resulted in a vast river of publications. In light of these facts, a commentary can no longer consider itself the proper location for entering into dialogue with other exegetes should it wish to avoid the defeat of its primary object, namely the explanation of the Scriptures. It seems evident, therefore, that selective and representative surveys of the relevant literature will be of greater value to the reader. Only those discussions which are pertinent to the commentary's stated strategy will be treated and only those authors who have shed new light on a particular question will be mentioned. Surveys of exegetical opinion are thus intended to be functional rather than exhaustive.

It is the author's hope that this combination of methods will open a retrospective window on the text: from the significance of the book for the Jewish community around the second temple, living in the aftermath of the exile – to whom the final redaction addressed itself –, up to and including the significance of the oracles for the prophet's audience on the eve of national calamity and ruin. The author is thus convinced that the transmission and redaction have assumed a degree of continuity between the original audience and later readers. Such continuity is not unusual with respect to both religious and secular texts which have enjoyed a degree of ongoing validity from their very conception. The same continuity endures to include the present generation which differs little theologically speaking from those of the past. Indeed the book of Isaiah itself expresses its awareness thereof: 'Bind up the testimony, seal the teaching among my disciples. I will wait for YHWH, who is hiding his face from the house of Jacob, and I will hope in him' (8:16-17).

BIBLIOGRAPHY OF ISAIAH CHAPTERS 28-39

1. Text Editions

Biblia Hebraica Stuttgartensia (ediderunt K. Elliger et W. Rudolph), Stuttgart 1990[4].

The Book of Isaiah (ed. M.H. Goshen-Gottstein), (The Hebrew University Bible Project), Jerusalem 1995.

The Dead Sea Scrolls of St. Mark's Monastery. I. The Isaiah Manuscript and the Habakkuk Commentary (ed. M. Burrows with the Assistance of J.C. Trever and W.H. Brownlee), New Haven 1950.

Isaias (ed. J. Ziegler), (Septuaginta. Vetus Testamentum Graecum Auctoritate Academiae Litterarum Gottingensis editum, XIV), Göttingen 1967.

2. Commentaries on the Book of Isaiah Chapters 1-39

(quoted by the name of the author only; if no page is indicated, *ad locum*)

J.A. Alexander, *Commentary on the Prophecies of Isaiah I-II*, Philadelphia 1875[2] (reprint Grand Rapids 1976).

D. Barthélemy, *Critique textuelle de l'Ancient Testament. 2. Isaïe, Jérémie, Lamentations* (OBO, 50/2), Fribourg – Göttingen 1986.

T.K. Cheyne, *The Prophecies of Isaiah. A New Translation with Commentary and Appendices, I[4]-II[5]*, London 1886-1889.

R.E. Clements, *Isaiah 1-39* (NCeB), Grand Rapids MI, 1980.

A. Condamin, *Le livre d'Isaïe*, Paris 1905.

F. Delitzsch, *Commentar über das Buch Jesaia* (BC, III/1), Leipzig 1889[4].

A. Dillmann, *Der Prophet Jesaja* (für die sechste Ausgabe herausgegeben und vielfach umgearbeitet von R. Kittel), (KEH, V), Leipzig 1898[6].

B. Duhm, *Das Buch Jesaia* (GöHAT, III/1), Göttingen 1922[4] (reprint 1968).

H. Ewald, *Die Propheten des Alten Bundes. Bd. 1. Jesaja mit den übrigen Älteren Propheten*, Göttingen 1867[2].

F. Feldmann, *Das Buch Isaias I (Kap. 1-39)*, (EHAT, 14), Münster / Westf. 1925.

J. Fischer, *Das Buch Isaias I* (HSAT, VII 1/1), Bonn 1937.

G. Fohrer, *Das Buch Jesaja I* (ZBK), Zürich 1964.

W. Gesenius, *Philologisch-kritischer und historischer Commentar über den Jesaia, I/2. (Kap. 13-39)*, Leipzig 1821.

G.B. Gray, *A Critical and Exegetical Commentary on the Book of Isaiah. I. Introduction and Commentary on I-XXVII* (ICC), Edinburgh 1912.

J. Hirsch, *Das Buch Jesaia*, Frankfurt a. M., 1911.

F. Hitzig, *Der Prophet Jesaja*, Heidelberg 1833

Ibn Ezra, *The Commentary of Ibn Ezra on Isaiah* (ed. M. Friedlaender), London 1873.

O. Kaiser, *Der Prophet Jesaja. Kapitel 13-39* (ATD, 18), Göttingen 1973.

R. Kilian, *Jesaja II. 13-39* (NEB.AT), Würzburg 1994.

E.J. Kissane, *The Book of Isaiah I,* Dublin 1941.

A. Knobel, *Der Prophet Jesaia* (KEH, V), Leipzig 1872[4].

E. König, *Das Buch Jesaja*, Gütersloh 1926.

J.B. Koppe, cf. R. Lowth

R. Lowth, *Jesajas neu übersetzt aus dem Englischen mit Zusätzen von J.B. Koppe* (4 Bände), Leipzig 1779-1781.

K. Marti, *Das Buch Jesaja* (KHC, X), Tübingen 1900.

J.A. Motyer, *The Prophecy of Isaiah. An Introduction and Commentary,* Downers Grove IL 1993.

J.N. Oswalt, *The Book of Isaiah. Chapters 13-39* (NICOT), Grand Rapids MI 1986.

A. Penna, *Isaia* (La Sacra Bibbia), Torino 1958.

O. Procksch, *Jesaja I* (KAT, IX), Leipzig 1930.

Rashi, cf. A.J. Rosenberg

A.J. Rosenberg, *Isaiah I. Translation of Text, Rashi and Commentary* (Miqra'ot Gedolot), New York 1982.

E.F.R. Rosenmüller, *Scholia in Jesajae vaticinia in compendium redacta* (Scholia in Vetus Testamentum, II), Lipsiae 1835.

A. Schoors, *Jesaja* (BOT, IX), Roermond 1972.

C.R. Seitz, *Isaiah 1-39* (Interpretation), Louisville KE 1993.

L.A. Snijders, *Jesaja deel I* (POT), Nijkerk 1969.

M.A. Sweeney, *Isaiah 1-39 with an Introduction to Prophetic Literature* (FOTL, XVI), Grand Rapids MI 1996.

C. Vitringa, *Commentarius in librum prophetiarum Jesaiae. Pars Posterior,* Herbornae Nassaviorum 1722.

J.D.W. Watts, *Isaiah 1-33, 34-66* (WBC, 24-25), Waco TX 1985, 1987.

H. Wildberger, *Jesaja. 1. Teilband. Jesaja 1-12. 2. Teilband. Jesaja 13-27. 3. Teilband. Jesaja 28-39* (BK.AT, X/1,2,3), Neukirchen 1972, 1978, 1982.

3. Monographs and Articles

The Book of Isaiah in General and Chapters 28-39 in Particular – Prophetic Topics

P.R. Ackroyd, "Isaiah I-XII: Presentation of a Prophet"; in: *Congress Volume Göttingen 1977* (ed. W. Zimmerli), (VT.S, XXIX), Leiden 1978, 16-48; K.T. Aitken, "Hearing and Seeing: Metamorphoses of a Motif in Isaiah 1-39"; in: *Among the Prophets. Language, Image and Structure in the Prophetic Writings* (eds Ph.R. Davies, D.J.A. Clines), (JSOT.S, 144), Sheffield 1993, 12-41; H. Barth, *Die Jesaja-Worte in der Josiazeit. Israel und Assur als Thema einer produktiven Neuinterpretation der Jesajaüberlieferung* (WMANT, 48), Neukirchen 1977; J. Barthel, *Prophetenwort und Geschichte. Die Jesajaüberlieferung in Jes 6-8 und 28-31* (FAT, 19), Tübingen 1997; J. Barton, "Ethics in Isaiah of Jerusalem", *JThS* 32 (1981) 1-18; U. Becker, *Jesaja – von der Botschaft zum Buch* (FRLANT, 178), Göttingen 1997; U. Berges, *Das Buch Jesaja. Komposition und Endgestalt* (HBS, 16), Freiburg etc., 1998; W.A.M. Beuken, "Women and the Spirit, the Ox and the Ass: The First Binders of the Booklet Isaiah 28-32", *EThL* 74 (1998) 5-26; B.S. Childs, *Isaiah and the Assyrian Crisis* (SBT, II/3), London 1967; B.D. Chilton, *The Isaiah Targum. Introduction, Translation, Apparatus and Notes* (The Aramaic Bible, 11), Edinburgh 1987; R.E. Clements, *Isaiah and the Deliverance of Jerusalem. A Study of the Interpretation of Prophecy in the Old Testament* (JSOT.S, 13), Sheffield 1980; E.W. Conrad, *Reading Isaiah* (OvBTh, 27), Minneapolis 1991; S. Deck, *Die Gerichtsbotschaft Jesajas: Charakter und Begründung* (FzB, 67), Würzburg 1991; W. Dietrich, *Jesaja und die Politik* (BEvTh, 74), München 1976; H. Donner, *Israel unter den Völkern. Die Stellung der klassischen Propheten des 8. Jahrhunderts v. Chr. zur Außenpolitik der Könige von Israel und Juda* (VT.S, XI), Leiden 1964; G.R. Driver, "Isaiah I-XXXIX: Textual and Linguistic Problems", *JSS* 13 (1968) 36-57; S.R. Driver, "Linguistic and Textual Problems: Isaiah I-XXXIX", *JThS* 38 (1937) 36-50; J. Ebach, U. Rüterswörden, "Unterweltsbeschwörung im Alten Testament. Untersuchungen zur Begriffs- und Religionsgeschichte des *'ob* I", *UF* 9 (1977) 57-70; J. C. Exum, "Isaiah 28-32: A Literary Approach"; in: *SBL 1979 Seminar Papers* (ed. P. Achtemeier) (SBL.SPS, 17/II), Missoula MT 1979, II, 123-51; *id.*, "Of Broken Pots, Fluttering Birds and Visions in The Night: Extended Simile and Poetic Technique in Isaiah", *CBQ* 43 (1981) 331-52; J. Fichtner, "Jesaja unter den Weisen", *TLZ* 74 (1949) 75-80; G. Fohrer, "The Origin, Composition and Tradition of Isaiah I-XXXIX", *ALUOS* 3

(1961) 3-38 = "Entstehung, Komposition und Überlieferung von Jesaja 1-39"; in: *id.*, *Studien zur alttestamentlichen Prophetie* (BZAW, 99), Berlin 1967, 113-47; Y. Gitay, *Isaiah and his Audience. The Structure and Meaning of Isaiah 1-12* (SSN, 30), Assen – Maastricht 1991; F.J. Gonçalves, *L'expédition de Sennachérib en Palestine dans la littérature hébraïque ancienne* (ÉtB N.S., 7), Paris 1986; A. Graffy, *A Prophet Confronts His People. The Disputation Speech in the Prophets* (AnBib, 104), Rome 1984; C. Hardmeier, *Texttheorie und biblische Exegese. Zur rhetorischen Funktion der Trauermetaphorik in der Prophetie* (BEvTh, 79), München 1979; J. Hausmann, *Israels Rest. Studien zum Selbstverständnis der nachexilischen Gemeinde* (BWANT, 124), Stuttgart 1987; J.H. Hayes, S.A. Irvine, *Isaiah The Eighth-Century Prophet. His Times and His Preaching,* Nashville TN 1987; H.W. Hoffmann, *Die Intention der Verkündigung Jesajas* (BZAW, 136), Berlin 1974; J. Høgenhaven, *Gott und Volk bei Jesaja. Eine Untersuchung zur biblischen Theologie* (AThD, XXIV), Leiden 1988; F. Huber, *Jahwe, Juda und die anderen Völker beim Propheten Jesaja* (BZAW, 137), Berlin 1976; W.H. Irwin, *Isaiah 28-33. Translation with Philological Notes* (BibOr, 30), Rome 1977; W. Janzen, *Mourning Cry and Woe Oracle* (BZAW, 125), Berlin 1972; H.-W. Jüngling, "Der Heilige Israels. Der erste Jesaja zum Thema 'Gott'"; in: *Gott, der Einzige. Zur Entstehung des Monotheismus in Israel* (eds G. Braulik, G. Hentschel *et al.*), (QD, 104), Freiburg, 1985, 91-114; K. Kiesow, *Exodustexte im Jesajabuch. Literarkritische und motivgeschichtliche Analysen* (OBO, 24), Fribourg – Göttingen 1979; K. Koenen, *Heil den Gerechten – Unheil den Sündern! Ein Beitrag zur Theologie der Prophetenbücher* (BZAW, 229), Berlin 1994; E.Y. Kutscher, *The Language and Linguistic Background of the Isaiah Scroll (1 Q Isaᵃ)* (StTDJ, 6), Leiden 1974; L. Laberge, "The Woe-Oracles of Isaiah 28-33", *EeT(O)* 13 (1982) 157-90; J.A. Loader, "Was Isaiah a quietist?"; in: *Studies in Isaiah* (ed. W.C. van Wyck), (OTSWA, 22-23 [1979-80]), Hercules, RSA 1981, 130-42; H.-M. Lutz, *Jahwe, Jerusalem und die Völker. Zur Vorgeschichte von Sach 12,1-8 und 14,1-5* (WMANT, 27), Neukirchen 1968; W. McKane, *Prophets and Wise Men* (SBT, 44), 1965; M. O'Kane, "Wisdom Influence in First Isaiah", *PIBA* 14 (1991) 64-78; *id.*, Isaiah: A Prophet in the Footsteps of Moses", *JSOT* 69 (1996) 29-51; H.-M. Pfaff, *Die Entwicklung des Restgedankens in Jesaja 1-39* (EHS.T, XXIII/ 561), Frankfurt / Main 1996; J.L. Sicre, *Los dioses olvidados. Poder y riqueza en los profetas preexílicos* (EMISJ, 3), Madrid 1979; H. Spieckermann, *Juda unter Assur in der Sargonidenzeit* (FRLANT, 129), Göttingen 1982; J.F. Stenning, *The Targum of Isaiah,*

Oxford 1949; J. Vermeylen, *Du prophète Isaïe à l'Apocalyptique. Isaïe, I – XXXV, miroir d'un demi-millénaire d'expérience religieuse en Israël I-II* (ÉtB), Paris 1977-1978; A. van der Kooij, *Die alten Textzeugen des Jesajabuches. Ein Beitrag zur Textgeschichte des Alten Testaments* (OBO, 35), Freiburg – Göttingen 1981; J. Vollmer, *Geschichtliche Rückblicke und Motive in der Prophetie des Amos, Hosea und Jesaja* (BZAW, 119), Berlin 1971; W.R. Watters, *Formula Criticism and the Poetry of the Old Testament* (BZAW, 138), Berlin 1976; P.D. Wegner, *An Examination of Kingship and Messianic Expectation in Isaiah 1-35*, Lewiston NY 1992; W. Werner, *Eschatologische Texte in Jesaja 1-39: Messias, Heiliger Rest, Völker* (FzB, 46), Würzburg 1982; J.W. Whedbee, *Isaiah and Wisdom*, Nashville TN 1971; H.G.M. Williamson, *The Book Called Isaiah. Deutero-Isaiah's Role in Composition and Redaction*, Oxford 1994; E. Zurro Rodríguez, "Siete hápax en el libro de Isaías (Isa. 3:18; 9:4; 22:15; 30:24; 32:4; 34:15; 56:10)", *EstB* 53 (1995) 525-35.

Isaiah Chapter 28

S. Amsler, O. Mury, "Yahweh et la sagesse du paysan. Quelques remarques sur Esaïe 28,23-29", *RHPhR* 53 (1973) 1-5; B.A. Asen, "The Garlands of Ephraim: Isaiah 28.1-6 and the *MARZĒAḤ*", *JSOT* 71 (1996) 73-87; K.E. Bailey, "'Inverted Parallelisms' and 'Encased Parables' in Isaiah and their Significance for OT and NT Translation and Interpretation"; in: *Literary Structure and Rhetorical Strategies in the Hebrew Bible* (eds L.J. de Regt, J. de Waard and J.P. Fokkelman), Assen 1996, 14-30; M. Berder, *"La pierre rejetée par les bâtisseurs" : Psaume 118,22-23 et son emploi dans les traditions juives et dans le Nouveau Testament* (ÉtB N.S., 31), Paris 1996; O. Betz, "Zungenreden und süßer Wein. Zur eschatologischen Exegese von Jesaja 28 in Qumran und im Neuen Testament"; in: *Bibel und Qumran (FS H. Bardtke)* (ed. S. Wagner), Berlin 1968, 20-36; W.A.M. Beuken, "Isaiah 28: Is It Only Schismatics That Drink Heavily? Beyond The Synchronic Versus Diachronic Controversy"; in: *Synchronic or Diachronic? A Debate on Method in Old Testament Exegesis* (ed. J.C. de Moor), (OTS, XXXIV), Leiden, 15-38; G.R. Driver, "Another Little Drink – Isaiah 28:1-22"; in: *Words and Meanings: Essays Presented to D.W. Thomas* (eds P.R. Ackroyd, B. Lindars), London 1968, 47-67; J.C. Exum, "Whom Will He Teach Knowledge? A Literary Approach to Isaiah 28"; in: *Art and Meaning: Rhetoric in Biblical Literature* (eds D.J.A. Clines *et al.*), Sheffield 1982,

108-39; J.P. Floß, "Biblische Theologie als Sprecherin der 'gefährlichen Erinnerung' dargestellt an Jes 28,7-12", *BN* 54 (1990) 60-80; K. Fuller-ton, "The Stone of the Foundation", *AJSL* 37 (1920) 1-50; H. Gese, "Die strömende Geißel des Hadad und Jesaja 28,15 und 18"; in: *Archäologie und Altes Testament (FS K. Galling)* (eds A. Kuschke, E. Kutsch), Tübingen 1970, 127-34; M. Görg, "Jesaja als 'Kinderlehrer'? Beobachtungen zur Sprache und Semantik in Jes 28,10(13)", *BN* 29 (1985) 12-6; W.W. Hallo, "Isaiah 28:9-13 and the Ugaritic Abecedaries", *JBL* 77 (1958) 324-38; B. Halpern, "'The Excremental Vision': The Doomed Priests of Doom in Isaiah 28", *HAR* 10 (1986) 109-21; J.F. Healy, "Ancient Agriculture and the Old Testament (with special reference to Isaiah XXXVIII 23-29)"; in: *Prophets, Worship and Theodicy* (ed. A.S. van der Woude), (OTS, XXIII), Leiden 1984, 108-19; S.H. Hooke, "The Corner-Stone of Scripture"; in: *The Siege Perilous*, London 1956, 235-49; K. Jeppesen, "The Cornerstone (Isa.28:16) in Deutero-Isaianic Rereading of the Message of Isaiah", *StTh* 38 (1984) 93-9; L. Koehler, "Zwei Fachwörter der Bausprache in Jesaja 28:16", *ThZ* 3 (1947) 390-93; F. Landy, "Tracing the Voice of the Other: Isaiah 28 and the Covenant with Death"; in: *The New Literary Criticism and the Hebrew Bible* (eds J.C. Exum, D.J.A. Clines), (JSOT.S, 143), Sheffield 1993, 140-62; L.J. Liebreich, "The Parable Taken from the Farmer's Labors in Isaiah 28:23-29", *Tarbiz* 24 (1954-5) 126-8; J. Lindblom, "Der Eckstein in Jesaja 28,16"; in: *Interpretationes ad Vetus Testamentum pertinentes Sigmundo Mowinckel septuagenario missae* (eds N.A. Dahl, A.S. Kapelrud), Oslo 1955, 123-32; O. Loretz, "Das Prophetenwort über das Ende der Königstadt Samaria (Jes 28:1-4)", *UF* 9 (1977) 361-3; R.F. Melugin, "The Conventional and The Creative in Isaiah's Judgment Oracles (Isa 30:15-17; 28:7-13,14-22)", *CBQ* 36 (1974) 301-11; P.G. Mosca, "Isaiah 28:12e: A Response to J.J.M. Roberts", *HThR* 77 (1984) 113-7; D.L. Petersen, "Isaiah 28. A Redaction Critical Study"; in: *SBL 1979 Seminar Papers* (ed. P. Achtemeier), (SBL.SPS, 17/II), Missoula MT 1979, II, 101-22; G. Pfeiffer, "Entwöhnung und Entwöhnungsfest im Alten Testament. Der Schlüssel zu Jesaja 28,7-13", *ZAW* 84 (1972) 341-7; W.S. Prinsloo, "Eighth-Century Passages from the Book of Isaiah? Reflections on Isaiah 28:1-6", *OTE* 1 (1988) 11-9; E. Qimron, "The Biblical Lexicon in Light of the Dead Sea Scrolls", *DSD* 2 (1995) 294-329; J.J.M. Roberts, "A Note on Isaiah 28:12", *HThR* 73 (1980) 49-51; id., "Yahweh's Foundation in Zion (Isa. 28:16)", *JBL* 106 (1987) 27-45; N.A. Schuman, "Jesaja 28:23-29: Een boerengelijkenis als politieke profetie"; in: *Segmenten. Studies op het gebied van de theologie* (eds T. Baarda et al.), Amsterdam 1981, 83-

142; A.C. Stewart, "The Covenant with Death in Isaiah 28", *ET* 100 (1988-9) 375-7; V. Tanghe, "Dichtung und Ekel in Jes xxviii 7-13", *VT* 43 (1993) 235-60; S.C. Thexton, "A Note on Isaiah XXVIII 25 and 28", *VT* 2 (1952) 81-3; K. van der Toorn, "Echoes of Judaean Necromancy in Isaiah 28:7-22", *ZAW* 100 (1988) 199-216; A. van Selms, "Isaiah 28:9-13: An Attempt to Give a New Interpretation", *ZAW* 85 (1973) 332-9; S. Virgulin, "Il significato della pietra di fondazione in Isa 28:16", *RivBib* 7 (1959) 208-20; E. Vogt, "Das Prophetenwort Jes 28:1-4 und das Ende der Königstadt Samaria"; in: *Homenaje a Juan Prado* (eds L. Alvarez Verdes, J. Alonso Hernandez), Madrid 1975, 108-30.

Isaiah Chapter 29

W.F. Albright, "The Babylonian Temple -Tower and the Altar of Burnt-Offering", *JBL* 39 (1920) 137-42; W.A.M. Beuken, "Isa 29,15-24: Perversion Reverted"; in: *The Scriptures and the Scrolls. Studies in Honour of A.S. van der Woude on the Occasion of his 65th Birthday* (eds F. García Martínez, A. Hilhorst, C.J. Labuschagne), (VT.S, XLIX), Leiden 1992, 43-64; E.W. Conrad, "Isaiah and the Abraham Connection", *AJT* 2 (1988) 382-93; S. Feigin, "The Meaning of Ariel", *JBL* 39 (1920) 131-7; A.H. Godbey, "Ariel, or David-Cultus", *AJSL* 41 (1924) 253-66; D.S. New, "The Confusion of *Taw* with *Waw-Nun* in Reading 1QIsa^a 29:13", *RdQ* 15 (1992) 609-10; H. Petzold, "Die Bedeutung von Ariel im Alten Testament und auf der Mescha-Stele", *Theol(A)* 40 (1969) 372-415; T.H. Robinson, "The Text of Isaiah 29:16", *ZAW* 49 (1931) 322; R.L. Routledge, "The Siege and Deliverance of the City of David in Isaiah 29:1-8", *TynB* 43 (1992) 181-90; F. Stolz, "Die Bäume des Gottesgartens auf dem Libanon", *ZAW* 84 (1972) 141-56; J. Werlitz, *Studien zur literarkritischen Methode. Gericht und Heil in Jesaja 7, 1-17 und 29, 1-8* (BZAW, 204), Berlin 1992; H.G.M. Williamson, "Isaiah and the Wise"; in: *Wisdom in Ancient Israel. Essays in Honour of J.A. Emerton* (eds J. Day, R.P. Gordon, H.G.M. Williamson), Cambridge 1995, 133-41; G.C.I. Wong, "On 'Visits' and 'Visions' in Isaiah XXIX 6-7", *VT* 45 (1995) 370-6.

Isaiah Chapter 30

W. Bacher, "Isaïe, XXX, 21", *REJ* 40 (1900) 248-9; W.A.M. Beuken, "What Does the Vision Hold: Teachers or One Teacher? Punning Repetition in Isa. 30:20", *HeyJ* (Issue in Honour of Robert Murray) 36 (1995) 451-66; *id.*, "Isaiah 30: A Prophetic Oracle Transmitted in Two Successive Paradigms"; in *Writing and Reading the Scroll of Isaiah: Studies of an Interpretive Tradition I-II* (eds C.C. Broyles, C.A. Evans), (VT.S, LXX.1-2), Leiden 1997, I, 369-97; O. Borowski, *Agriculture in Iron Age Israel,* Winona Lake IN 1987, 36; M. Dahood, "Accusative *'eṣāh* 'Wood' in Isaiah 30:1b", *Bib* 50 (1969) 57-8; *id.*, "Some Ambiguous Texts in Isaias (30:15; 52:2; 33:2; 40:5; 45:1)", *CBQ* 20 (1958) 41-9; K.P. Darr, "Isaiah's Vision and the Rhetoric of Rebellion"; in: *SBL 1994 Seminar Papers* (ed. E.H. Lovering Jr.), (SBL.SPS, 33), Atlanta GE, 1994, 847-82; J. Day, *Molech: A God of Human Sacrifice in the Old Testament,* Cambridge 1989; J.A. Emerton, "A Textual Problem in Isa. 30:5", *JThS* 32 (1981) 125-9; *id.*, A Further Note on Isaiah XXX 5", *JThS* 33 (1982) 161-2; H.L. Ginsberg,"An Obscure Hebrew Word", *JQR* 22 (1931-2), 143-5; R. Gordis,"Midrash in the Prophets", *JBL* 49 (1930) 417-22; A. Guillaume,"Isaiah's Oracle against Assyria (Isaiah 30:27-33) in the Light of Archaeology", *BSOAS* 17 (1956) 413-5; E. Hertlein,"Rahab", *ZAW* 38 (1919-20) 113-54; B.P. Irwin,"Molek Imagery and the Slaughter of Gog in Ezekiel 38 and 39", *JSOT* 65 (1995) 93-112; W.H. Irwin,"Conflicting Parallelism in Job 5,13; Isa. 30,28; 32:7", *Bib* 76 (1995) 72-4; B.C. Jones, *Howling over Moab. Irony and Rhetoric in Isaiah 15-16* (SBL.DS, 157), Atlanta GE, 1996; B. Kedar-Kopfstein,"Synästhesien im biblischen Althebräisch in Übersetzung und Auslegung", *ZAH* 1 (1988) 47-60, 147-85; S. Kreuzer,"Schubaël – eine scheinbare Ausnahme in der Typologie der israelitischen Namengebung", *ZAW* 93 (1981) 443-5; L. Köhler,"בליל חמיץ Jes 30,24", *ZAW* 40 (1922) 15-7; A. Kuschke,"Zu Jes 30:1-5", *ZAW* 64 (1952) 194-5; L. Laberge, Is 30,19-26: A Deuteronomic Text?, *EeT(O)* 2 (1971) 46-51; R.F. Melugin,"The Conventional and the Creative in Isaiah's Judgment Oracles (Isa 30:15-17; 28:7-13,14-22)", *CBQ* 36 (1974) 301-11; P. Reymond,"Un tesson pour 'ramasser' de l'eau à la mare (Esaie XXX, 14)", *VT* 7 (1957) 203-7; L. Sabottka,"Is 30,27-33: Ein Übersetzungsvorschlag", *BZ* 12 (1968) 241-55; V. Sasson,"An unrecognized 'smoke signal' in Isaiah XXX 27", *VT 33* (1983) 90-5; C. Schedl,"Gedanken zu einem 'Übersetzungsvorschlag' Is 30:27-33'", *BZ* 13 (1969) 242-3; K.-D. Schunck,"Jes 30:6-8 und die Deutung der Rahab im Alten Testament", *ZAW* 78 (1966) 48-56; K.A.D. Smelik,"Ostraca: schrijftafel of boekrol? Jeremia 36, Jesaja 30,8 en twee ostraca uit Saqqara", *NedThT* 44 (1990) 198-207; *id.*,"Moloch, Molech or Molk-Sacrifice? A Reassessment of the Evidence Concerning the Hebrew Term Molekh", *SJOT* 9 (1995) 133-42; R. Tournaire,"Sur des versets ambigus d'Isaïe", *Bulletin de l'Association G. Budé* 1995, 204-

10; G.C.I. Wong, "Faith and Works in Isaiah XXX 15", *VT* 47 (1997) 236-46.

Isaiah Chapters 31:1-32:8

M.L. Barré, "A Note on Is. 31,4-5"; in: *Among the Prophets. Language, Image and Structure in the Prophetic Writings* (eds Ph.R. Davies, D.J.A. Clines), (JSOT.S, 144), Sheffield 1993, 55-9; W.P. Brown, *Character in Crisis. A Fresh Approach to the Wisdom Literature of the Old Testament*, Grand Rapids MI 1996; M.T. Davis, B.A. Strawn, "Isaiah 31:4-5 in the Light of Lion Iconography in the Ancient Near East", *AAR.SBL Abstracts 1996*, 293 (S. 183); G.R. Driver, "Hebrew Notes on Prophets and Proverbs", *JThS* 41 (1940) 162-75; G. Eidevall, "Lions and Birds as Literature: Isa 31 and Hos 11", *SJOT* 7 (1993) 78-87; J.G. Gammie, L.G. Perdue, *The Sage in Israel and the Ancient Near East*, Winona Lake IN 1990; W.H. Irvin, "Conflicting Parallelism in Job 5:13; Isa 30,28; Isa 32:7", *Bib* 76 (1995) 72-4; O. Keel, "Erwägungen zum Sitz im Leben des vormosaischen Pascha und zur Etymologie von פסח", *ZAW* 84 (1972) 414-34; A.F.J. Klijn, "Jerome's quotations from a Nazoraean interpretation of Isaiah (Isa 8: 14,19-9:1; 29:20-21; 31:6-9)"; in: *Judéo-Christianisme: recherches historiques et théologiques offerts en hommage au Cardinal Jean Daniélou* (eds B. Gerhardsson *et al.*), Paris 1972, 241-55; J.W. Olley, "Notes on Isaiah XXXII 1, XLV 19,23 and LXIII 1", *VT* 33 (1983) 446-9; H.M. Orlinsky, "The St. Mark's Isaiah Scroll', *JBL* 69 (1950) 152-5; G. Stansell, "Isaiah 32: Creative Redaction in the Isaian Tradition"; in: *SBL 1983 Seminar Papers* (ed. K.H. Richards), (SBL.SPS, 22), Chico CA, 1983, 1-12; *id.*, "Isaiah 28-33: Blest Be the Tie that Binds (Isaiah Together)"; *New Visions of Isaiah* (eds R.F. Melugin, M.A. Sweeney), (JSOT.S, 214), Sheffield 1996, 68-103; M.A. Sweeney, "Parenetic Intent in Isaiah 31", *PWCJS IX. A: The Bible and its World* (ed. D. Assaf), Jerusalem 1994, 99-106; E. Zurro Rodríguez, "Siete hápax en el libro de Isaías (Isa. 3:18; 9:4; 22:15; 30:24; 32:4; 34:15; 56:10)", *EstB* 53 (1995) 525-35; Z. Weisman, "The Nature and Background of BÂHÛR in the Old Testament", *VT* 31 (1981) 441-50; G.C.I. Wong, "Isaiah's Opposition to Egypt in Isaiah xxxi 1-3", *VT* 46 (1996) 392-401.

Isaiah Chapter 32:9-20

J. Barth, "Eine verkannte hebräische Imperativform", *ZDMG* 56 (1902) 247-8; W.A.M. Beuken, "De os en de ezel in Jesaja literair (Jes. 1:3

en 32:20)"; in: *Herinnering en hoop. Feestbundel Herman Servotte* (ed. R. Michiels), Averbode 1995, 161-83; J. García Recio, "'La fauna de las ruinas', un *topos* literario de Isaías", *EstB* 53 (1995) 55-96; W. Käser, "Beobachtungen zum alttestamentlichen Makarismus", *ZAW* 82 (1970) 225-50; E. Nielsen, "Ass and ox in the Old Testament"; in: *Studia Orientalia Johanni Pedersen septuagenario dicata,* Hauniae 1953, 261-74; J. Reider, "Contributions to the Scriptural Text", *HUCA* 24 (1952-3) 88; R.J. Sklba, "'Until the Spirit from on High Is Poured out on Us' (Isa 32:15): Reflections on the Role of the Spirit in the Exile", *CBQ* 46 (1984) 1-17; B. Stade, "Miscellen. 2. Jer. 3,6-16; 5. Jes. 32. 33", *ZAW* 4 (1884) 151-4, 256-71.

Isaiah Chapter 33

W.A.M. Beuken, "Jesaja 33 als Spiegeltext", *EThL* 67 (1991) 5-35; K. Galling, "Jesaja 21 im Lichte der neuen Nabonidtexte"; in: *Tradition und Situation. Studien zur alttestamentlichen Prophetie (FS A. Weiser)*, (eds E. Würthwein, O. Kaiser), Göttingen 1963, 49-62; H.L. Ginsburg, "Emendations in Isaiah", *JBL* 69 (1950) 57; H. Gunkel, "Jesaja 33, eine prophetische Liturgie", *ZAW* 42 (1924) 177-208; D.R. Hillers, "A Hebrew Cognate of UNUSSU/ 'UNT in Is. 33:8", *HThR* 64 (1971) 257-9; H.R. Holmyard III, "Does Isaiah 33:23 Address Israel or Israel's Enemy?", *BS* 152 (1995) 273-8; D.C. Johnson, *From Chaos to Restoration. An Integrative Reading of Isaiah 24-27* (JSOT.S, 61), Sheffield 1988; R. Murray, "Prophecy and the Cult"; in: *Israel's Prophetic Tradition. Essays in Honour of P.R. Ackroyd* (eds R. Coggins, A. Phillips, M. Knibb), Cambridge 1982; id., "The Origin of Aramaic *'ir*, Angel", *Or* 53 (1984) 303-17; id., *The Cosmic Covenant. Biblical Themes of Justice, Peace and the Integration of Creation* (HeyM, 7), London 1992; D.C. Polaski, "Reflections on a Mosaic Covenant: The Eternal Covenant (Isaiah 24.5) and Intertextuality", *JSOT* 77 (1998) 55-73; J.J.M. Roberts, "Isaiah 33: An Isaianic Elaboration of the Zion Tradition"; in: *The Word of the Lord Shall Go Forth. Essays in Honor of David Noel Freedman in Celebration of His Sixtieth Birthday* (eds C.L. Meyers, M. O'Connor), Winona Lake IN 1983, 15-25; B. Stade, "Miscellen. 5. Jes. 32.33", *ZAW* 4 (1984) 260-6; S.O. Steingrimsson, *Tor der Gerechtigkeit. Eine literaturwissenschaftliche Untersuchung der sogenannten Einzugsliturgien im Alten Testament: Ps 15; 24,3-5 und Jes 33: 14-16* (ATSAT, 22), St. Ottilien 1984; R.D. Weis, "Angels, Altars and Angles of Vision: The Case of *'ärällâm* in Is. 33:7"; in: *Tradi-*

tion of the Text. Studies Offered to Dominique Barthélemy in Celebration of his 70th Birthday (eds G.J. Norton, S. Pisano), (OBO, 109), Freiburg – Götingen 1991, 285-92; R. Weiss, "On Ligatures in the Hebrew Bible (בו=ם), *JBL* 82 (1963) 188-94.

Isaiah Chapters 34-35

W. Caspari, "Jesaja 34 und 35", *ZAW* 49 (1931) 67-86; K. Elliger, *Deuterojesaja in seinem Verhältnis zu Tritojesaja* (BWANT, IV/11), Stuttgart 1933; B. Gosse, "Isaïe 34-35. Le chatiment d'Edom et des nations, salut pour Sion", *ZAW 102* (1990) 396-404; *id.*, "L'emploi de *s's'ym* dans le livre d'Isaïe", *BN* 56 (1991) 22-4; H. Grätz, "Isaiah XXXIV and XXXV", *JQR* 4 (1891) 1-8; A. Mailland, *La 'petite apocalypse' d'Isaïe. Étude sur les chapitres XXXIV et XXXV du livre d'Isaïe,* Lyon 1956; C.R. Mathews, *Defending Zion. Edom's Desolation and Jacob's Restoration (Isaiah 34-35) in Context* (BZAW, 236), Berlin 1995; J.L. McKenzie, *Second Isaiah* (AB, 20), Garden City NY 1968; H.M. Orlinsky, "Studies in the St. Mark's Isaiah Scroll, VI", *HUCA* 25 (1954) 85-92; H.G.L. Peels, *The Vengeance of God. The Meaning of the Root NQM and the Function of the NMQ-Texts in the Context of Divine Revelation in the Old* Testament (ed. J.C. de Moor), (OTS, XXXI), Leiden 1995; M. Pope, "Isaiah 34 in Relation to Isaiah 35, 40-66", *JBL* 71 (1952) 235-43; O.H. Steck, *Bereitete Heimkehr. Jesaja 35 als redaktionelle Brücke zwischen dem Ersten und dem Zweiten Jesaja* (SBS, 121), Stuttgart 1985; C.C. Torrey, *The Second Isaiah. A New Interpretation*, Edinburgh 1928. B.M. Zapff, *Schriftgelehrte Prophetie – Jes 13 und die Komposition des Jesajabuches* (FzB, 74), Würzburg 1995.

Isaiah Chapter 34

J.R. Bartlett, *Edom and the Edomites* (JSOT.S, 77), Sheffield 1989; P.C. Beentjes, "Oracles against the Nations. A Central Issue in the 'Latter Prophets'", *Bijdr* 50 (1989) 203-9; W.A.M. Beuken, "Isaiah 34: Lament in Isaianic Context", *OTE* 5 (1992) 78-102; G. Bickel, *Carmina Veteris Testamenti metrice*, Oiniponte 1882; A. Dicou, *Jakob en Esau, Israël en Edom. Israël tegenover de volken in de verhalen over Jakob en Esau in Genesis en de grote profetieën over Edom*, Amsterdam 1990; *id.*, "Literary Function and Literary History of Isaiah 34", *BN* 58 (1991)

30-45; *id., Edom, Israels Brother and Antagonist in Biblical Prophecy and Story* (JSOT.S, 169), Sheffield 1994; H. Donner, "'Forscht in der Schrift Jahwes und lest!' Ein Beitrag zum Verständnis der israelitischen Prophetie", *ZThK* 87 (1990) 285-98; J.A. Emerton, "A Note on the Alleged Septuagintal Evidence for the Restoration of the Hebrew text of Isaiah 34:11-12", *ErIs* 16 (1982) 34*-6*; S. Erlandsson, *The Burden of Babylon. A Study of Isaiah 13:2-14:23* (CB.OT, 4), Lund 1970; B. Glazier-McDonald, "Edom in the Prophetical Corpus"; in: *You Shall not Abhor an Edomite. Edom and Seir in History and Tradition* (ed. D.V. Edelman), (ABSt, 3) Atlanta GA, 1995, 23-32; B. Gosse, *Isaïe 13,1-14,23 dans la tradition littéraire du livre d'Isaïe et dans la tradition des oracles contre les nations* (OBO, 78), Freiburg – Göttingen 1988; M. Haller, "Edom im Urteil der Propheten"; in: *Vom Alten Testament (FS K. Marti)* (ed. K. Budde), (BZAW, 41), Giessen 1925, 109-17; V. Lauterjung, "Zur Textgestalt von Jes 34,16", *ZAW* 91 (1979) 124f.; J. Lust, "Isaiah 34 and the *herem*"; in: *The Book of Isaiah. Le livre d'Isaïe. Les oracles et leurs relectures. Unité et complexité de l'ouvrage* (ed. J. Vermeylen), (BEThL, 81), Leuven 1989, 275-86; J. Muilenburg, "The Literary Character of Isaiah 34", *JBL* 59 (1940), 339-65; R. Péter-Contesse, "Quels animaux Israël offrait-il en sacrifice? Étude de lexicographie hébraïque"; in: *Studien zu Opfer und Kult im Alten Testament* (ed. A. Schenker), (FAT, 3), Tübingen 1992, 67-78; M. Pope, "Isaiah 34 in Relation to Isaiah 35, 40-66", *JBL* 71 (1952) 235-43; V. Tanghe, "Der Schriftgelehrte in Jes 34,16-17", *EThL* 67 (1991) 338-45; E.J. Young, "Isaiah 34 and its Position in the Prophecy",*WThJ* 27 (1964/5) 93-114.

Isaiah Chapter 35

L. Alonso Schökel, C. Carniti, "'IN TESTA': Is. 35,10", *RivBib* 34 (1986) 397-9; J.A. Emerton, "A Note on Isaiah XXXV 9-10", *VT* 27 (1977) 488-9; W. Harrelson, "Isaiah 35 in Recent Research and Translation"; in: *Language, Theology, and the Bible (Essays in Honour of James Barr)* (eds S.E. Balentine, J. Barton), Oxford 1994, 248-60; F.D. Hubmann, "Der 'Weg' zum Zion. Literar- und stilkritische Beobachtungen zu Jes 35,8-10"; in: *Memoria Jerusalem (FS Franz Sauer)*, (eds J.B. Bauer, J. Marböck), Graz 1977, 29-43; J.K. Kuan, "The Autorship and Historical Background of Isaiah 35", *Jian Dao* 6 (1996) 1-12; A. Marx, "Brève note textuelle sur Esaïe 35,8", *ZAW* 107 (1995) 123-8; A.T. Olmstead, "II Isaiah and Isaiah, Ch.35", *AJSL* 53 (1936-7) 251-3; R.B.Y. Scott, "The Relation of Isaiah, Chapter 35 to Deutero-

Isaiah", *AJSL* 52 (1935) 178-91; P. Wernberg-Møller, "Isa 35:4", *ZAW* 69 (1957) 71-3.

Isaiah Chapters 36-37(39)

(1) Historical Background

A. Alt, "Die territorialgeschichtliche Bedeutung von Sanheribs Eingriff in Palästina"; in: *Kleine Schriften zur Geschichte des Volkes Israel II*, München 1953, 242-9; R.D. Barnett, "The Siege of Lachish", *IEJ* 8 (1958) 161-4; J.A. Brinkman, "Sennacherib's Babylonian Problem: An Interpretation", *JCS* 25 (1973) 89-95; D. Conrad, "Einige (archäologische) Miszellen zur Kultgeschichte Judas in der Königszeit"; in: *Textgemäss: Aufsätze und Beiträge zur Hermeneutik des Alten Testaments (FS E. Würthwein)*, (eds A.H.J. Gunneweg, O. Kaiser), Göttingen 1979, 28-32; P.E. Dion, "Sennacherib's Expedition to Palestine", *EeT(O)* 20 (1989) 5-25; M. Hutter, *Hiskija König von Juda: Ein Beitrag zur judäischen Geschichte in assyrischer Zeit* (GrTS), Graz 1982; A. Jepsen, *Die Quellen des Königsbuches*, Halle 1956²; N. Na'aman, "Sennacherib's Campaign to Judah and the Date of the *lmlk* Stamps", *VT* 29 (1979) 61-86; S. Parpola, "The Murder of Sennacherib"; in: *Death in Mesopotamia: Papers Read at the xxvième rencontre assyriologique internationale'* (ed. B. Alster), Copenhagen 1980, 171-82; H.H. Rowley, *Men of God: Studies in Old Testament History and Prophecy* (Ch.4: Hezekiah's Reform and Rebellion), London 1963; W.H. Shea, "Sennacherib's Second Palestinian Campaign", *JBL* 104 (1985) 401-18; *id.*, "The New Tirhakah Text and Sennacherib's Second Campaign", *AUSS* 35 (1997) 181-7; S. Stohlmann, "The Judaean Exile after 701 B.C.E."; in: *Scripture in Context II: More Essays on the Comparative Method* (eds W.W. Hallo *et al.*), Winona Lake IN 1983, 147-75.

(2) Redaction History

P.R. Ackroyd, "Isaiah 36-39: Structure and Function"; in: *Von Kanaan bis Kerala (FS J.P.M. van der Ploeg)*, (eds W.C. Delsman *et al.*), (AOAT, 211), Neukirchen 1982, 3-21; *id.*, "The Biblical Interpretation of the Reigns of Ahaz and Hezekiah"; in: *In The Shelter of Elyon. Essays on Ancient Palestinian Life and Literature in Honor of G.W. Ahlström* (eds W. Boyd Barrick, J.R. Spencer), (JSOT.S, 31), Sheffield 1984, 247-59 (repr. in: *Studies in the Religious Tradition of the Old Testament*, London 1987, 181-92); *id.*, "Historians and Prophets"; in: *Studies*, 121-51, 278-82; L. Camp, *Hiskija und Hiskijabild: Analyse und*

Interpretation von 2 Kön 18-20 (MThA, 9), Altenberg 1990; A. Catastini, "Le varianti greche di Isaia 36-39",*EVO* 6 (Pisa 1983) 209-34;
R.E. Clements, *Isaiah and the Deliverance of Jerusalem. A Study of the
Interpretation of Prophecy in the Old Testament* (JSOT.S, 13), Sheffield
1980; *id.*, "The Prophecies of Isaiah to Hezekiah concerning Sennacherib. 2 Kings 19:21-34//Isa. 37:22-35"; in: *Old Testament Prophecy.
From Oracles to Canon*, Louisville KY 1996, 35-48; E.W. Conrad,
"The Royal Narratives and the Structure of the Book of Isaiah", *JSOT*
41 (1988) 67-81; J.W. Groves, *Actualisation and Interpretation in the
Old Testament* (SBL.DS, 86), Atlanta 1987; C. Hardmeier, "Die Propheten Micha und Jesaja im Spiegel von Jeremia XXVI und 2 Regum
XVIII-XX: Zur Prophetie-Rezeption in der nach-joschianischen Zeit";
in: *Congress Volume Leuven 1989* (ed. J.A. Emerton), (VT.S, XLIII),
Leiden, 172-89; O. Kaiser, "Die Verkündigung des Propheten Jesaja
im Jahre 701", *ZAW* 81 (1969) 304-15; J. Meinhold, *Die Jesajaerzäh-
lungen: Jesaja 36-39. Eine historisch-kritische Untersuchung*, Göttingen 1898; A. Rofé, *The Prophetical Stories*, Jerusalem 1988, 88-95;
E. Ruprecht, "Die ursprüngliche Komposition der Hiskia-Jesaja-Erzäh-
lungen und ihre Umstrukturierung durch den Verfasser des deuterono-
mistischen Geschichtswerkes", *ZThK* 87 (1990) 33-66; C.R. Seitz,
*Zion's Final Destiny: The Development of the Book of Isaiah. A Reas-
sessment of Isaiah 36-39*, Minneapolis 1991; B. Stade, "Anmerkungen
zu 2 Kö. 15-21", *ZAW* 6 (1886) 156-89; J. Vermeylen, "Hypothèses sur
l'origine d'Isaïe 36-39"; in: *Studies in the Book of Isaiah (FS W.A.M.
Beuken)*, (eds J. van Ruiten, M. Vervenne), (BETL, CXXXII), Leuven
1997, 95-118.

(3) Miscellaneous
E. Ben Zwi, "Who wrote the Speech of Rabshake and When?", *JBL*
109 (1990) 79-92; W. Brueggemann, "Isaiah 37:21-29: The Transfor-
mative Potential of a Public Metaphor", *HBT* 10 (1988) 1-32; K. Budde,
"The Poem in 2 Kings XIX 21-28 (Isaiah XXXVII 22-29)", *JThS* 35
(1934) 307-13; C.F. Burney, "'The Jews' Language'. 2 Kings XVIII
26 = Isa. XXXVI 11", *JThS* 13 (1912) 417-23; M. Burrows, "The Conduit of the Upper Pool", *ZAW* 70 (1958) 221-7; C. Cohen, "Neo-Assy-
rian Elements in the First Speech of the Biblical Rab-Saqe", *IOS* 9
(1979) 32-48; D.N. Fewell, "Sennacherib's Defeat: Words at War in 2
Kings 18.13-19.37", *JSOT* 34 (1986) 79-90; A. Fitzgerald, "*BTWLT*
and *BT* as Titles for Capital Cities", *CBQ* 37 (1975) 167-83; K. Ful-
lerton, "Isaiah's Attitude in the Sennacherib Campaign", *AJSL* 42
(1925) 1-25; G. Götzel, "Hizkia und Sanherib", *BZ* 6 (1908) 133-54;

H. Haag, "La campagne de Sennachérib contre Jérusalem en 701", *RB* 58 (1951) 348-59; J.-G. Heintz, "Lettres royales à la divinité en Mésopotamie et en Israël antiques: esquisse d'un genre littéraire", *RHR* 181 (1972) 111-3; L.L. Honor, *Sennacherib's Invasion of Palestine: A Critical Source Study*, New York 1926; A.K. Jenkins, "Hezekiah's Fourteenth Year: A New Interpretation of 2 Kings XVIII 13 – XIX 37", *VT* 26 (1976) 284-98; S. de Jong, "Het verhaal van Hizkia en Sanherib. 2 Koningen 18,17-19,37 / Jesaja 36-37 als narratieve reflectie op de ballingschap", *ACEBT* 10 (1989) 56-71; H.A.J. Kruger, "'Gods', For Argument's Sake. A Few Remarks on the Literature and Theological Intention of Isaiah 36-37", *OTE* 9 (1996) 52-67, 383-99; H. Leene, "רוח en שמועה in Jesaja 37,7: Een kwestie van verhaalhorizon", *ACEBT* 4 (1983) 49-62; C. van Leeuwen, "Sanchérib devant Jérusalem"; in: כה *1940-1965* (ed. P.A.H. de Boer), (OTS, XIV) Leiden 1965, 245-72; J. Le Moyne, "Les deux ambassades de Sennachérib à Jérusalem: Recherches sur l'évolution d'une tradition"; in: *Mélanges Bibliques (FS A. Robert)*, Paris 1956, 149-53; P. Machinist, "Assyria and Its Image in First Isaiah", *JAOS* 103 (1983) 719-37; A. Murtonen, "The Usage and Meaning of the Words *lebarek* and *beraka* in the Old Testament", *VT* 9 (1959) 158-77; F.H. Polak, "The Messenger of God and the Dialectic of Revelation"; in: *A Light for Jacob. Studies in the Bible and the Dead Sea Scrolls (in Memory of Jacob Shalom Licht)*, Jerusalem 1998, 14*-30*; E.J. Revell, *The Designation of the Individual. Expressive Usage in Biblical Narrative* (CBET, 14), Kampen 1996; K.A.D. Smelik, "Distortion of Old Testament Prophecy: The Purpose of Isaiah XXXVI and XXXVII"; in: *Crises and Perspectives* (ed. A.S. van der Woude), (OTS, XXIV), Leiden 1986, 70-93; *id.*, "King Hezekiah Advocates True Prophecy: Remarks on Isaiah XXXVI and XXXVII / III Kings XVIII and XIX"; in: *id.*, *Converting the Past. Studies in Ancient Israelite and Moabite Historiography* (ed. A.S. van der Woude), (OTS, XXVIII), Leiden 1992, 93-128; W. von Soden, "Sanherib vor Jerusalem 701 v. Chr."; in: *Bibel und Alter Orient* (ed. H.-P. Müller), (BZAW, 162), Berlin 1985, 149-57; A. Strus, "Interprétations des noms propres dan les oracles contre les nations"; in: *Congress Volume Salamanca 1983* (ed. J.A. Emerton), (VT.S, XXXVI) Leiden 1985, 272-85; J. Trebolle Barrera, "La expedición de Senaquerib contra Jerusalén. Reflexiones en torno a un libro reciente", *EstB* 45 (1987) 7-22; C. Uehlinger, "*Figurative Policy*, Propaganda und Politik"; in: *Congress Volume Cambridge 1995* (ed. J.A. Emerton), (VT.S, LXVI), Leiden 1997, 297-350; E. Vogt, *Der Aufstand Hiskias und die Belagerung Jerusalems 701 v. Chr.* (AnBib, 106), Rome 1986; H. Wildberger, "Die Rede des Rabsake vor Jerusalem", *TZ* 35 (1979) 35-47; W. Zimmerli, *Erkenntnis Gottes nach dem Buche Ezechiel* (AThANT, 27), Zürich 1954 (also TB, 19: 41-119).

Isaiah Chapter 38(-39)

P.R. Ackroyd, "An Interpretation of the Babylonian Exile: A Study of II Kings 20 and Isaiah 38-39", *SJTh* 27 (1974) 329-53 (repr. in: *Studies in the Religious Tradition of the Old Testament,* London 1987, 152-71); N. Airoldi, "Nota a Is 38,16", *BeO* 15 (1973) 255-9; R. Althann, "The Sun Reversing its Course: Poetry and Textual Criticism (Is 38:8; 2 Ki 20:11)", *OTE* 1 (1988) 21-7; M.L. Barré, "Restoring the 'Lost' Prayer in the Psalm of Hezekiah", *JBL* 114 (1995) 385-90; J. Begrich, *Der Psalm des Hiskia* (FRLANT, 25), Göttingen 1926; A. Catastini, "Osservazioni filologiche sulla cosidetta 'meridiana di Achaz' (Isaia 38:8 – II Re 20:11)", *Henoch* 5 (1983) 161-78; *id.*, "In margine a Bruno Ognibeni, in *RivBib* 40 (1992), 77-86", *RivBib* 41 (1993) 201-4; R.E. Clements, "The Prophecies of Isaiah to Hezekiah concerning Sennacherib. 2 Kings 19:21-34 //Isa. 37:22-35"; in: *Old Testament Prophecy. From Oracles to Canon*, Louisville KY 1996, 35-48; J.H. Coetzee, "The 'song of Hezekiah' (Isaiah 38:9-20): A Doxology of Judgement from the Exilic Period", *OTE* 2 (1989) 13-26; M. Dahood, "חדל 'Cessation' in Isaiah 38,11", *Bib* 52 (1971) 215-6; P.A.H. de Boer, "Notes on Text and Meaning of Isaiah XXXVIII 9-20", (OTS, IX), Leiden 1951, 170-86; W. Eisenbeis, *Die Wurzel שלם im Alten Testament* (BZAW, 113), Berlin 1969; W.W. Hallo, "The Royal Correspondence of Larsa I: A Sumerian Prototype of the Prayer of Hezekiah"; in: *Kramer Anniversary Volume: Cuneiform Studies in Honor of Samuel Noah Kramer* (ed. B.L. Eichler), (AOAT, 25), Neukirchen 1976, 209-24; M.R. Hauge, *Between Sheol and Temple. Motif Structure and Function in the I-Psalms* (JSOT.S, 178), Sheffield 1995; V. Hoffer, "An Exegesis of Isaiah 38.21", *JSOT* 56 (1992) 69-84; J. Iwry, "The Qumrân Isaiah and the End of the Dial of Ahaz", *BASOR* 147 (1957) 27-33; C. Jeremias, "Zu Jes xxxviii 31f.", *VT* 21 (1971) 104-11; A.H. Konkel, "The Sources of the Story of Hezekiah in the Book of Isaiah", *VT* 43 (1993) 462-82; F. Lindström, *Suffering and Sin. Interpretation of Illness in the Individual Complaint Psalms* (CB.OT, 37), Stockholm 1994; H.-P. Mathys, *Dichter und Beter. Theologen aus spätalttestamentlicher Zeit* (OBO, 132), Fribourg – Göttingen 1994; H.S. Nyberg, "Hiskias Danklied Jes. 38,9-20", *ASTI* IX (FS H. Kosmala) (1974) 85-97; B. Ognibeni, "Achaz o no Achaz: a proposito del testo di Is 38,8", *RivBib* 40 (1992) 76-86; *id.*, "Ombra e sole in Is 38,8. Una risposta ad A. Catastini", *RivBib* 41 (1993) 205-9; A. Rofé, "Classes in the Prophetic Stories"; in: *Studies on Prophecy. A Collection of Twelve Papers* (eds G.W. Anderson *et al.*), (VT.S, XXVI), Leiden 1974, 143-64; K. Seybold, *Das Gebet der Kranken im Alten Testament* (BWANT, 99), Stuttgart 1973; J.M. Watts, *Psalms and Story. Inset Hymns in Hebrew Narrative* (JSOT.S, 139), Sheffield 1992; Y. Zakowitcz, "2 Kings 20:7 – Isaiah 38:21. 22", *BetM* 50 (1972) 302-5.

Isaiah Chapter 39

C.T. Begg, "Babylon in the Book of Isaiah"; in: *The Book of Isaiah. Le Livre d'Isaïe. Les oracles et leurs relectures. Unité et complexité de l'ouvrage* (ed. J. Vermeylen) (BEThL, LXXXI), Leuven 1989, 121-5; J.A. Brinkman, "Elamite Military Aid to Merodach-Baladan II", *JNES* 24 (1965) 161-6; A.D. Crown, "Messengers and Scribes: The ספר and מלאך in the Old Testament",*VT* 24 (1974) 366-70; M. Dietrich, *Die Aramäer Südbabyloniens in der Sargonidenzeit* (AOAT, 7), Neukirchen 1970; P. Höffken, "Zur Eigenart von Jes 39 par. II Reg 20,12-19", *ZAW* 110 (1998) 244-9.

4. Old Testament: General Reference Works and Studies

J. Arambarri, *Der Wortstamm 'hören' im Alten Testament. Semantik und Syntax eines hebräischen Verbs* (SBB, 20), 1990; Y. Avishur, *Stylistic Studies of Word-Pairs in Biblical and Ancient Semitic Literatures* (AOAT, 210), Neukirchen 1984; P.C. Beentjes, "Inverted Quotations in the Bible – A Neglected Stylistic Pattern", *Bib* 63 (1982) 506-23; E. Ben Zvi, "History and Prophetic Texts"; in: *History and Interpretation. Essays in Honour of John H. Hayes* (eds M.P. Graham, W.P. Brown, J.K. Kuan), (JSOT.S, 173), Sheffield 1993, 106-20; Bovati, *Ristabilire la giustizia. Procedure, vocabulario, orientamenti* (AnBib, 110), Roma 1986; M.Z. Brettler, *God is King. Understanding an Israelite Metaphor* (JSOT.S, 76), Sheffield 1989; C. Brockelmann, *Hebräische Syntax*, Neukirchen 1956; E.W. Bullinger, *Figures of Speech Used in the Bible* (London 1898[1]) Grand Rapids MI 1993[17]; B.D. Chilton, "The Isaiah Narrative of 2 Kings 20:12-19 and the Date of the Deuteronomic History"; in: *Isac Leo Seeligmann Volume* (eds A. Rofé, Y. Zakovitch), Jerusalem 1983, 209-20; H.R. Cohen, *Biblical Hapax Legomena in the Light of Akkadian and Ugaritic* (SBL.DS, 37), Missoula MT 1975;

M. Dahood, "Hebrew Lexicography: A Review of W. Baumgartner's *Lexikon*, Volume II", *Or* 45 (1976) 338f.; *id., Psalms III. Introduction, Translation, and Notes with an Appendix: the Grammar of the Psalter* (AB, 17A), Garden City NY 1970; G. Dalman, *Arbeit und Sitte in Palästina I-VII*, Gütersloh 1928-1942, (repr. Hildesheim 1964-1971); R.-F. Edel, *Hebräisch-Deutsche Präparation zu Jesaja*, Marburg 1964[3]; S.J. De Vries, *Yesterday, Today and Tomorrow. Time and History in the Old Testament*, London 1975; *id., From Old Revelation to New. A Tradition-Historical and Redaction-Critical Study of Temporal Transitions in Prophetic Prediction*, Grand Rapids MI, 1995; A.B. Ehrlich, *Randglossen zur hebräischen Bibel. 4. Band: Jesaia, Jeremia*, Leipzig 1912; J.G. Gammie, *Holiness in Israel* (OvBTh, 14), Minneapolis 1989; G. Gerber, *Die Sprache als Kunst I-II*, Berlin 1885[2]; H.W.M. van Grol, "Paired Tricola in the Psalms, Isaiah and Jeremiah", *JSOT* 25 (1983) 55-73; *id., De versbouw in het klassieke Hebreeuws. Fundamentele verkenningen. Deel Een: Metriek*, Amsterdam 1986; W.L. Holladay, *The Root ŠÛBH in the Old Testament. With Particular Reference to its Usages in Covenantal Texts*, Leiden 1958; E. Jenni, *Die hebräischen Präpositionen. Band 1: Die Präposition Beth. Band 2: Die Präposition Kaph*, Stuttgart 1992, 1994; J. Jeremias, *Theophanie. Die Geschichte einer alttestamentlichen Gattung* (WMANT, 10), Neukirchen 1965; O. Keel, *Die Welt der altorientalischen Bildsymbolik und das Alte Testament dargestellt am Beispiel der Psalmen*, Zürich – Neukirchen 1972; E. König, *Hebräisches und aramäisches Wörterbuch zum Alten Testament*, Leipzig 1931; *id., Historisch-kritisches Lehrgebäude der hebräischen Sprache. II.2. Syntax*, Leipzig 1987; J. Krašovec, *Der Merismus im Biblisch-Hebräischen und Nordwestsemitischen* (BibOr, 33), Rome 1977; *id., La justice (SDQ) de Dieu dans la Bible hebraïque et l'interprétation juive et chrétienne* (OBO, 76), Freiburg – Göttingen 1988; E. Kutsch, *Verheißung und Gesetz. Untersuchungen zum sogenannten "Bund" im Alten Testament* (BZAW, 131), Berlin 1973; R. Lowth, *De sacra poesi Hebraeorum praelectiones academicae*, Lipsiae 1815; J.M. Oesch, *Petucha und Setuma. Untersuchungen zu einer überlieferten Gliederung im hebräischen Text des Alten Testaments* (OBO, 27), Freiburg – Göttingen 1979; B.C. Ollenburger, *Zion the City of the Great King. A Theological Symbol of the Jerusalem Cult* (JSOT.S, 41), Sheffield 1987; H.D. Preuß, *Die Verspottung fremder Religionen im Alten Testament* (BWANT, 92), Stuttgart 1971; G. von Rad, *Theologie des Alten Testaments. Band II: Die Theologie der prophetischen Überlieferungen Israels*, München 1965[4]; L.J. de Regt, *Participants in Old Testament Texts and the Translator. Reference De-

vices and their Rhetorical Impact (SSN, 39), Assen 1999; W.G.E. Watson, *Classical Hebrew Poetry. A Guide to its Techniques* (JSOT.S, 26), Sheffield 1984; *id.*, *Traditional Techniques in Classical Hebrew Verse* (JSOT.S, 170), Sheffield 1994; H.W. Wolff, *Gesammelte Studien zum Alten Testament* (TB, 22), München 1964.

ABBREVIATIONS

Abbreviations used in this commentary are borrowed from *Theologische Realenzyklopädie. Abkürzungsverzeichnis* (zusammengestellt von S.M. Schwertner), Berlin – New York 1994[2].

The following abbreviations not contained in *TRE* are also used:

AuS	G. Dalman, *Arbeit und Sitte in Palästina I-VII*, Gütersloh 1928-1942, (repr. Hildesheim 1964-1971).
AV	Authorized Version (King James Version).
BDB	F. Brown, S.R. Driver, C.A. Briggs, *A Hebrew and English Lexicon of the Old Testament*, Oxford 1906.
BJ	*La Bible de Jérusalem*, Paris 1998.
BrSyn	C. Brockelmann, *Hebräische Syntax*, Neukirchen 1956.
M. Buber	*Bücher der Kündung*. Verdeutscht von Martin Buber gemeinsam mit Franz Rosenzweig, Köln 1966.
DCH	*The Dictionary of Classical Hebrew*, eds D.J.A. Clines, Ph.R. Davies, J.W. Rogerson, Sheffield: I 1993, II 1995, III 1996, IV 1998.
DDD	*Dictionary of Deities and Demons in the Bible*, eds K. van der Toorn, B. Becking and P.W. van der Horst, Leiden 1999[2].
GKC	*Gesenius' Hebrew Grammar*, eds E. Kautzsch, A.E. Cowley, Oxford 1910[2].
Ges-B	W. Gesenius, F. Buhl, *Hebräisches und Aramäisches Handwörterbuch über das Alte Testament*, Leipzig 1921[17].
Ges.[18]	*Wilhelm Gesenius Hebräisches und Aramäisches Handwörterbuch über das Alte Testament. 18. Auflage*, eds R. Meyer, H. Donner, Berlin: I 1987, II 1995.
HBS	Herders Biblische Studien.
J-M	P. Joüon, T. Muraoka, *A Grammar of Biblical Hebrew I-II* (SubBI, 14/I-II), Roma 1991.
M. Luther	D. Martin Luther, *Die gantze Heilige Schrifft Deudsch* I-II (eds H. Volz, H. Blanke, F. Kur), München 1972.
NJV	The New Jewish Version.
NAB	The New American Bible.
OvBTh	Overtures in Biblical Theology.
REB	The Revised English Bible.
TOB	Traduction Œcuménique de la Bible.
Zorell	F. Zorell, *Lexicon Hebraicum et Aramaicum Veteris Testamenti*, Roma 1968.

]

INTRODUCTION TO ISAIAH CHAPTERS 28-39

Any introduction to Isaiah chs. 28-39 cannot serve as an introduction to the first half of the book of Isaiah let alone the entire book. Such introductions belong at the beginning of chs. 1-39 or of chs. 40-66 (cf. *Part III. Volume 1: Isaiah 40-48*).

Chs. 28-39 in the Context of the Book

Older opinions concerning the genesis and structure of the book of Isaiah made the writing of an introduction to chs. 1-39 or chs. 28-39 a relatively clear-cut task. The book of Isaiah (henceforth 'BI') was considered to be an amalgamation of three more or less independent literary corpora, each of which, for the most part, had come into existence at a different period of time: chs. 1-39, 'Proto-Isaiah' (henceforth 'PI'), prior to the end of the kingdom of Judah and the destruction of Jerusalem (587 BC), chs. 40-55, 'Deutero-Isaiah' (henceforth 'DI'), towards the end of the exile when the Persian king Cyrus overran the Babylonian empire (roughly 540 BC), and chs. 56-66, 'Trito-Isaiah' (henceforth 'TI'), after the return to the land when the temple had to be rebuilt and social existence around the temple had to take shape once again (from 520 BC). Dominant opinion concluded that the final redaction, without major revision, had unified these three prophetic collections into a single book which it placed under the name of the first prophet, Isaiah ben Amoz. More or less the same opinion existed with respect to the individual genesis of each of these three major segments. Within chs. 1-39, scholars also discerned the presence of a few smaller, and likewise more or less independent literary corpora (chs. 1-12; 13-23; 24-27; 28-33; 34-35; 36-39).

This image of the genesis of BI has undergone thorough revision in recent decades. The conviction that the book consists of three independent corpora has made way for the hypothesis, based on a number of new insights, of a radical redaction which attuned all the smaller collections of oracles to one another and thus provided the book with an elaborate structure. Opinions on the course and development of this process, however, differ considerably.[1] Roughly speaking, two models of explanation can be found in the literature. Some scholars continue to hold to the notion of three major segments which were originally able to develop more or less independently of one another but which were later

---

[1] The literature is immense; for a survey, cf. Berges 1998: ch.1.

subjected to a thoroughgoing harmonisation at the hands of the final redaction. Other scholars maintain that the bulk of chs. 1-39 and the nucleus of chs. 40-55 were combined to form a single prophetic book which later underwent a process of 'Fortschreibung',[2] whereby both parts were profoundly adapted and substantially expanded. With regard to this latter model, the question arises as to whether the inclusive redaction allowed the major theological topics of chs. 1-39 to continue into chs. 40-55(66) or whether chs. 1-39 were rewritten in light of the characteristic convictions of chs. 40-48(55).[3]

While a commentary is not the right place to introduce new insights which have yet to prove themselves in the face of critical assessment, the enduring achievements of recent research clearly do deserve a place in such an endeavour. For the present commentary this implies a number of choices, which, of course, will be necessarily subjective. It continues to be justifiable, for example, to view Isa. 28-39 as a unified whole. Given that chs. 24-27 – the so-called Isaiah Apocalypse – would appear in almost every respect to be a relatively independent textual complex, ch.28 is thus clearly preceded by a caesura, even although this chapter, which commences with a prophecy concerning Samaria, exhibits apparent associations with the large collection of oracles against the nations in chs. 13-23. A caesura is likewise evident after ch.39 since ch.40 transports the reader into a completely different world.

The content of chs. 28-39 also justifies a separate treatment of these chapters. Like the collection chs. 1-12, which has the Syro-Ephraimitic war of 734-732 BC as its background, chs. 28-32 speak of a political situation in which Judah, under threat of an Assyrian invasion, sought help from Egypt, while chs. 36-39 relate how Sennacherib's campaign ultimately did not lead to the fall of Jerusalem, with the consequence that the city and king Hezekiah survived. These events took place between 705 and 701 BC. Chs. 28-39 thus cover the final years of the activities of the prophet Isaiah.

The Structure of Chs. 28-39 from the Redaction-Historical Perspective

In virtually every explanation of the genesis of BI, chs. 28-39 constitute an autonomous segment,[4] made up of three different blocks:

---

[2] This theory is given foundation in the works of O.H. Steck: *Bereitete Heimkehr. Jesaja 35 als redaktionelle Brücke zwischen dem Ersten und dem Zweiten Jesaja* (SBS, 121), Stuttgart 1985; *Studien zu Tritojesaja* (BZAW, 203), Berlin 1991; *Gottesknecht und Zion. Gesammelte Studien zu Deuterojesaja* (FAT, 4), Tübingen 1992.

[3] H.G.M. Williamson, *The Book Isaiah. Deutero-Isaiah's Role in Composition and Redaction*, Oxford 1994.

[4] U. Becker (*Jesaja – von der Botschaft zum Buch* [FRLANT, 178], Göttingen 1997)

(1) From both the literary and the historical perspective, chs. 28-33 constitute the basic text.[5] They consist of six woe cries, the first five directed towards Israel (28:1-29; 29:1-14; 29:15-24; 30:1-33; 31:1-9), the sixth towards the foreign oppressor (33:1-24). Originally, the term 'woe' formed the opening marker of a funerary lament from which it derived the connotation of prevailing death and the mourner's sense of sympathy for the deceased person (1 Kgs 13:30; Jer. 22:18; 34:5; Amos 5:16). It is a conventional term in the prophetic books, not only at the level of the speech genre of accusation, but also at the level of the literary redaction of larger textual units, as can be seen from its occurrence in series (Isa. 5:8,11,18,20ff.; Hab. 2:6,9,12,15,19). It colours the prophetic oracles with the suggestion of death as the inevitable consequence of immoral behaviour (Isa. 1:4 [cf. 5f.], 24; 5:8,11,18,20; 10:1; 17:12; 18,1; 45: 9f.; Jer. 4:13,31; 22:13; 23:1; 48:1,46; Ezek. 13:3,8; 34:2; Hos. 7:13; Amos 6:1; Mic. 2:1; Nah. 3:1; Hab. 2:6,9,12,15,19; Zeph. 2:5; 3:1; Zech. 11:17).[6]

The first five woe cries are concluded by an appeal to go into mourning (32:9-14). This core underwent a threefold expansion. The five woe cries concerning Judah were supplemented by a sixth which announced destruction to the enemy and thereby salvation for Zion (ch.33). The fifth woe cry has an additional promise of righteous leaders (32:1-8) while the appeal to go into mourning is supplemented by a promise of 'the spirit from on high' (32:15-20).

Since ch.33 only comes after the appeal to go into mourning (32:9-14), makes several allusions to texts both preceding and following it in BI and thus fulfils a redactional role, one can justifiably consider the five woe cries together with the call to go into mourning (28:1-31:9 and 32:9-14) as an original literary composition. Given its content, the announcement of disaster, this composition clearly stems from before the exile. The expansion of the fifth woe cry, 32:1-8, refers to the five woe

offers a completely different picture of the redaction history of Isaiah 28-39. In his opinion, chs. 28-31 do not constitute the second collection of the oracles of Isaiah ben Amoz, they are almost entirely the product, rather, of the post-exilic transmission. The 'Fortschreibung' primarily connects with the older (!) source, chs. 36-37, although it is also associated with the 'Denkschrift' of chs. 6-8, the disobedience texts of DI and a collection of prophetic proverbs in the book of Jeremiah. Since Becker's book appeared in print after the present commentary was already complete, we cannot discuss it here, even although it is based on astute analyses. Any discussion, in our view, would have to concentrate on the assumption that the theologoumenon of the miraculous rescue of the city of God during Isaiah ben Amoz' lifetime was not yet in circulation (224).

[5] W.A.M. Beuken, "Women and the Spirit, the Ox and the Ass: The First Binders of the Booklet Isaiah 28-32", *EThL* 74 (1998) 5-26.

[6] *TWAT*, II, 382-8 (H.-J. Zobel). For an extensive description of the form and function of woe cries, cf. Hardmeier 1979.

cries together, sketching a programme of just government in contrast to the policies of the social élite accused therein. The expansion thus appears to have its roots in the first major redaction (the so-called Assyrian or Josian redaction) dating from the seventh century. Both the woe cries and the expansion, therefore, would appear to stem from before the exile.

The appeal to the women to go into mourning (32:9-14) and the promise of 'the spirit from on high' (32:15-19) correspond to the prophecy concerning the women of Zion (3:16-4:1) and the promise of Jerusalem's purification by 'the spirit of judgement and burning' (4:2-6) at the beginning of PI. The macarism concerning 'the ox and the ass' (32:20) likewise refers to the accusation with which BI opens (1:3). These expansions create two distinct ring patterns – one in which the 'women' are related to 'the spirit' and another relating 'the ox and the ass' – around the beginning of BI and ch.32. They leave the literary composition of chs. 28-32 intact while integrating it, together with the other original collection of prophecies of Isaiah in chs. 2-12, into the larger complex of chs. 1-39. This inclusive structure probably dates from the time after the exile.

Besides this redactional expansion, the five woe cries have undergone a tradition-historical, actualising reworking. While this reworking commenced at an earlier stage, it runs parallel in part with the redactional expansion. The significance of this reworking will become more clear in the discussion of the relevant passages.

(2) While chs. 34-35 are also generally considered to be an independent literary unit (the 'minor Isaiah Apocalypse' as opposed to the 'Isaiah Apocalypse' of chs. 24-27), these chapters clearly play a role at the level of the redaction and articulation of PI and BI. Their origin lies at the final phase of the emerging book. Not even the core of these chapters seems likely to hark back to the prophecies of the historical prophet. Ch.34 has a retrospective function, confirming the execution of judgement against the nations announced in chs. 13-23 and now made manifest, by way of example, with respect to Edom. Ch.35 enjoys a prospective function, restoring the connection between ch.33 and chs. 40-48, and announcing anew the dawning of salvation for Zion in terms derived from the preceding chapter.

(3) Chs. 36-39 contain narratives in prose which prepare for the transition to DI. The literary-historical study of these chapters remains unfinished, especially with respect to the question as to whether they are borrowed from 2 Kings 18-20, or visa versa, or whether both texts hark back to an older, independent narrative. Given that the account is

strongly influenced by the so-called Assyrian or Josian redaction of the seventh century (see above), the present commentator is inclined to opt for the latter position. The discussion has led, however, to two insights which will guide our explanation. In the first place, these narratives fit extremely well within the structure of BI, establishing, in their own way, connections between PI and DI. Secondly, even if they stem from different sources, they presently constitute a harmonious narrative.

The individuals who make their entry in chs. 36-37, i.e. the arrogant king Sennacherib, the pious king Hezekiah and the prophet Isaiah, are presented as prototypes against the background of God's promise to stand by Zion: the first is an example of self-exaltation before God, the second an example of pious fidelity, the third an example of well-ordered mediation between YHWH and the king. While the annals of king Sennacherib give witness to the fact that the narrative enjoys a historical nucleus, the latter is clearly subordinate to the plan to show that the one who believes in YHWH's promise to protect Jerusalem and has the courage to resist the godless will not be deceived, as Hezekiah's course of life proves (chs. 36-37).

The narrative of Hezekiah being cured of a deadly illness is a symbol of Israel's salvation from the exile (ch.38) while the narrative of the delegation of Merodach-baladan announces deportation into Babylon (ch.39). This was desirable from the compositional perspective because the following ch.40, the first in DI, heralded the end of the exile. While both narratives are chronologically speaking prior to chs. 36-37, they would appear to have been placed here to facilitate the transition to chs. 40-55(66). In terms of plot, these narratives are legends which have their place in the historical situation of Israel's prophets. In terms of their presentation they are clearly in the service of the spiritual need of the exiles.

The History behind Chs. 28-39

Little data is available to help us discern the historical situation envisaged by these chapters. The collection of woe cries begins with an oracle against 'Ephraim' (28:1-4) which gradually turns into a warning for the leaders in Jerusalem (28:14-22). This transports us to the period before and after the conquest of Samaria by Assyria which was experiencing a second major expansion at the time under the rule of Tiglath-pileser III (745-727 BC). After the defeat of Samaria and the conquest of Damascus in 734-732 BC (Isa. 17:1-6) and after the annexation of the northern kingdom in 722 BC (2 Kgs 18:9-12), Assyria found itself in the heart of

Syro-Palestinian territory and on the border with Judah. In the decades to follow it was to endeavour to bring these territories under its own authority. The controlling policy in Jerusalem at the time was dominated by the question as to whether the Assyrian hegemony could be shaken off with the help of the smaller neighbouring states and, in particular, in alliance with Egypt.

The political themes of the era can be discerned from Isaiah's resistance to such alliances, although the tradition may have influenced the formulation thereof. In the prophet's opinion, Judah would draw no benefit at all from such worthless engagements (30:1-7; 31:1-3). Only the recognition of YHWH as Israel's only God (29:15-16; 30:1-2,9-11,15) and the maintenance of justice and righteousness (28:15,17; 29:13,21; 30:9,12; 31:2) were of any value. Given the fact that these ideals were not being realised, God himself would bring the scourge of destruction upon Judah (28:18-22; 29:1-4; 30:13-17; 32:9-15). The prophet, however, did not only announce the downfall of Judah. YHWH had chosen Zion as his own possession (28:16; 30:19, 29; 31:4-9). He alone could bring the destroyer and he alone could drive him away (29:1-7; 30:18-21, 27-33; 31:4-9). He was to punish Judah and Jerusalem but he would also save his people through judgement (28:23-29). It is the author's hope that the present commentary will succeed in showing that the actual message of Isaiah ben Amoz has to do with this 'wonderful counsel of YHWH' (28:29; 31:5).

History and Explanation

The kings of Assyria and Judah who left their mark on this period in history are not named in chs. 28-35. At the same time, nothing is mentioned of their military campaigns nor the outcome thereof, let alone whether Judah was able to hold firm against the superior might of Assyria. It is only in chs. 36-39 that we are told that the kings in question are Hezekiah of Judah and Sennacherib of Assyria. The same chapters relate how Sennacherib was forced to pay for his attack against Jerusalem with the destruction of his army by the messenger of YHWH and a humiliating withdrawal. It is clear, therefore, that these chapters serve a more ideological purpose than a historical one.

More is known of this period in Israel's history from the annals of the Assyrian kings. Shalmeneser V (727-722 BC) and Sargon II (722-705 BC) conducted a number of military campaigns against the nations of southern Syria and Palestine some of which are mentioned in PI (10:9: against Calno and Carchemis [717 BC]; 10:28-34: against Jerusalem [?];

20:1-6: against Ashdod [712 BC]). Pressure from Assyria, however, reached its high-point under the rule of Sennacherib (705-681 BC). After the death of his father, Sennacherib had to deal with rebellions in Mesopotamia before he was to turn his sights in 701 towards the smaller western states which had been able to shake of the Assyrian yoke with the help of Egypt. According to his annals, he first brought the coastal region, from Sidon in the north to Ashkalon in the south, under control, defeating the Egyptian army at Eltekeh (20 miles west of Jerusalem). Before beginning the more difficult campaign against the mountainous region of Judah, he first took control of Lachish in the Shephelah, the most important city in Judah besides Jerusalem. While he was still engaged in this campaign he sent an army out to demand Jerusalem's surrender or to put it under siege.

It is at this point that the narrative of chs. 36-37 begins. It is also at this point that the Assyrian annals and the book of Isaiah part company. According to the annals, Hezekiah submitted completely to Sennacherib, became a vassal liable to the payment of tribute (cf. 2 Kgs 18:14-16), was forced to hand over most of Judah while being left with little more than Jerusalem and its environs. According to Isaiah, the Assyrian army suffered a major defeat and Hezekiah's trust in YHWH's protection was rewarded (37:36-37). It would appear, however, that Sennacherib's report is more than likely the more accurate of the two. While it is true that, for whatever reason, Jerusalem was not captured, political, military, social and economic life in Judah and Jerusalem alike ultimately fell into disarray as a result of the Assyrian campaign.

The historical situation in which chs. 28-39 are played out does not seem to extend beyond these events. While ch.39 evidently speaks of the Babylonian captivity and the beginning of ch.33 alludes, perhaps, to Persian domination, in so far as the corpus of chs. 28-39 intends to relocate us in a specific period of time, this can only be that of Sennacherib's advance against Jerusalem. As a matter of fact, there is no evidence at our disposal which would lead us to believe that Isaiah ben Amoz continued to preach after the 'liberation' of Jerusalem.

The above leads us to a hermeneutical consideration. It is clearly justifiable to supplement the scarcity of historical information provided by chs. 28-39 with reports from non-biblical sources. One of the primary rules of critical exegesis is that one should lay both sorts of information side by side in an attempt to find out what 'the actual circumstances' may have been, or better still, in an attempt to discover the various perspectives which may have existed with respect to the historical circumstances. What does one do, however, when there appears to be a sharp contrast between the biblical account of the events and that of contemporary historiography? The bible considers Sennacherib's retreat to be proof that YHWH's promise to uphold and defend Jerusalem enjoyed an effective guarantee (chs. 36-38). Historiography maintains that the city's continued existence in conditions of the most extreme destitution for the population of the time must have been evidence either of YHWH's loathing or his impotence. Should one conclude that the Scriptures are guilty of an inaccurate presentation of the events – according to our norms as well as those of the day – in order to salvage YHWH's fidelity?

The question is bound up with the fact that on the redactional level, chs. 28-32 presume the fall of Jerusalem, albeit at the hand of the Babylonians and not of the Assyrians. This calamity is considered to be the consequence of a lifestyle and a politics which took no account of YHWH. While judgement hangs like a sword over the heads of the prophet's audience (28:17-22; 29:1-4; 30:13-17; 31:1-3; 32:9-14), it appears, nevertheless, to be past history in the context of his promises of salvation (28:5-6; 29:22-23; 30:18-26; 31:8-9; 32:15-20). We are left, thereby, with the impression that chs. 28-32 and chs. 36-39 propagate conflicting messages. In the first series of chapters, the fall of Jerusalem constitutes the background against which the rest of the people, in exile and at home, reflect on the significance of this disaster for their future. The second series of chapters contains stories of YHWH's effective fidelity to the city in time of greatest need, whereby destruction and deportation were averted.

Such contradiction between chs. 36-39 on the one hand and chs. 28-32 and contemporary historiography on the other is explained by the fact that the downfall of Israel acquired a theological interpretation. While the first phase of the ruin, submission to the hegemony of Assyria (701 BC), meant that the possession of the promised land had been effectively undone, it was ultimately interpreted as the avoidance of threatening disaster for Jerusalem and as a tangible sign of YHWH's dedication (ch.38). The narrative thus came to serve as both a warning and an encouragement. Yet, wherever there is talk of new salvation, the second phase of the ruin, i.e. the conquest of Jerusalem by the Babylonians (587 BC), is presumed but never related according to the historical facts (cf. 2 Kings 24-25). We do not witness the clash of weapons or the collapse of defences. It is only at the end that we come to hear that the king's sons and treasures had been to be deported to Babylon (39:6-7). In short, while Isaiah ben Amoz announced Assyrian conquest, the fall of Jerusalem to the Babylonians came to be seen as the fulfilment of his prophecy. Given the fact that this event brought about the most serious rupture in Israel's entire history, such an interpretational adjustment is quite understandable.

According to those who passed on Isaiah's oracles, the prophet had also announced that YHWH was resolute in his intention to remain faithful to Zion. For this reason, they expected that after the fall of Jerusalem, God would bring about new salvation (ch.33). Indeed, in the history of the city he had given a foretaste of his fidelity when he had kept her safe because the king and the people had upheld their faith in him alone (chs. 36-38).

THE FIRST WOE CRY:
'WOE TO THE DRUNKARDS OF EPHRAIM' (28:1-29)

TRANSLATION

1   Woe to the haughty crown of the drunkards of Ephraim,
     and to the fading flower of its glorious beauty,
  which is on the head of the fat valley,
     of those overcome with wine!

2   Behold, the Lord has one who is strong and mighty:
     like a storm of hail, a destroying tempest,
  like a storm of powerful, flooding waters,
     he will hurl down to the earth with (his) hand.

3   Under foot will be trampled
     the haughty crown of the drunkards of Ephraim.

4   And the fading flower of its glorious beauty,
     which is on the head of the fat valley,
  will be like a first-ripe fig before the summer:
     whoever sees it, swallows it
       while it is still in his palm.

5   On that day YHWH of hosts will be a crown of beauty,
     and a diadem of glory, to the remnant of his people;

6   and a spirit of (right) judgement to the one who sits in judgement,
     and valour to those who turn back the battle at the gate.

7   These also reel with wine
     and stagger with strong drink.
  Priest and prophet reel with strong drink,
     they are swallowed up by wine,
  they stagger with strong drink,
     they reel with the vision,
       they totter in giving a decision.

8   Truly, all tables are full of vomit,
     of filth with no (clean) place.

9   'Whom will he teach knowledge,
     whom will he cause to understand the message?
  Those who are weaned from the milk,
     those taken from the breast?

10   Truly, *tsaw latsaw tsaw latsaw,*
    qaw laqaw qaw laqaw,
      ze'er sham, ze'er sham'.

11   Truly, with a stammering lip
    and with a foreign tongue
      he will speak to this people,

12   he who has said to them:
      'This is your resting-place; give rest to the weary;
    yes, this is your place of repose'.
      Yet they have been unwilling to listen.

13   So the word of YHWH to them will be:
    '*tsaw latsaw tsaw latsaw,*
      qaw laqaw qaw laqaw,
        ze'er sham, ze'er sham',
    in order that they may go and stumble backward,
      be broken, and snared, and taken.

14   Therefore hear the word of YHWH,
    you swaggerers,
  who rule this people
    which is in Jerusalem!

15   Truly, you have said:
  'We have concluded a covenant with death,
    and with sheol we have made an agreement.
  When the scourge of flooding passes through,
    it will not come upon us.
  Truly, we have made lies our refuge,
    and in falsehood we have hidden ourselves'.

16   Therefore thus says the Lord YHWH:
  'Behold, I myself have laid in Zion for a foundation a stone,
    a massive stone,
  a cornerstone valuable for a sure foundation.
    One who trusts will not shake!

17   I will make righteousness the line,
    and justice the plummet.
  Hail will sweep away the refuge of lies,
    and waters will flood the hiding place.

18   Your covenant with death will be annulled,
    and your agreement with sheol will not stand.
  When the scourge of flooding passes through,
    you will be for it to trample on.

19 As often as it passes through
        it will take you;
    Truly, morning by morning it will pass through,
        by day and by night;
    and it will be sheer terror
        to be made to understand the message'.
20 Truly, the bed is too short to stretch oneself out,
        and the covering too narrow to wrap oneself up.
21 Truly, as on Mount Perazim YHWH will stand up,
        and as in the valley of Gibeon he will rage,
    to do his deed – strange is his doing!
        and to work his work – alien is his work!
22 So now do not swagger,
        lest your bonds be made strong.
    Truly, I have heard a decree of destruction
        from the Lord YHWH of hosts upon the whole earth.
23 Give ear, and hear my voice;
        pay attention, and hear my speech!
24 Is it all day that the plower plows for sowing,
        that he opens and harrows his ground?
25 Does he not, when he has leveled its surface,
            scatter black cummin
                and toss (ordinary) cummin,
    set wheat in rows,
            and barley in plots,
                and spelt at its border?
26 Yes, he instructs him concerning the right order,
        his God teaches him.
27 Truly, black cummin is not threshed with a sledge,
        nor is a cart wheel rolled over (ordinary) cummin.
    Truly, black cummin is beaten out with a stick,
        and (ordinary) cummin with a rod.
28 Is bread grain crushed?
        Not unceasingly does one thresh it.
    One drives one's cart wheel (over it),
        but with one's horses one does not crush it.
29 This also comes from YHWH of hosts;
        he is wonderful in counsel,
            great in wisdom.

NOTES

1 MT is to be maintained. Omission of 'the fat valley' (Wildberger, 1042) or changes in favour of a smoother syntactical parallelism (NRSV: 'those bloated with rich food / those overcome with wine'; cf. Ehrlich 1912: 97f.: read גאה instead of גיא)[1] neglect the meticulous patterns of ballast variants and initial consonant sequence (Irwin 1977: 4-7).

The word ראש is best taken as governing two pairs of nouns in construct state: גיא שמנים and הלומי יין (Oswalt, 507).

12 The words מנוחה ('rest') and מרגעה ('repose') should be interpreted as concrete nouns. The definite article functions as a possessive pronoun and the *waw* at the beginning of v. 12a''' should be parsed as emphatic (Irwin 1977: 24).

13b The Masoretic accentuation recognises the verbs 'that they may go, stumble backward, and be broken' as one semantic sequence (cf. M. Buber), but the metrical scheme imposes a division of 4 + 3. Moreover, the last three verbs are all *niphals*, beginning with ונ.

14 Of old, the verb ליץ has been interpreted as 'to scoff', but the real meaning is 'to swagger', 'to boast' (*TWAT*, IV, 567f. [Ch. Barth]; *HALAT*, 503).

It remains a question whether משלי stems from the root 'to rule' or 'to speak sentences'. At the present time, some scholars prefer the latter interpretation because the prophecy would then be directed not so much at those in power but to the ideologists of foreign policy, the 'speech-makers' (Kaiser, 199; Wildberger, 1064, 1072; Watts, 365f.). The object, 'this people', however, advises against this.

15 Because of the parallel with 'covenant' (cf. v. 18),[2] the translation 'agreement' for חזה is unavoidable, although the corresponding root means 'to see' (for a survey of the question, cf. Wildberger, 1065f.).

16 This verse contains several problems:

(1) The construction הנני with a perfect third person, יסד, instead of a participle, is absolutely unique but can be explained as: 'Behold me who have laid for a foundation' (GKC, §155 f). There is no reason to change the *lectio difficilior* into the participle יוסד (already Duhm, 200) although this form, or a future tense, is found in 1QIs^ab and most of the ancient versions.[3] Changing the reading into: 'Behold, I am laying in Zion for a foundation stone' entails the difficulty that what begins as an act of salvation ends up in chastisement (vv. 17f.). The perfect ought

---

[1] 1QIs^a does not support Ehrlich's emendation (Barthélemy, 196ff.).

[2] Kutsch 1973: 34-9.

[3] For an excellent survey of the question, cf. Gonçalves 1986: 200.

to have a real preterite meaning ('I have laid for a foundation') since the construction הנני with a participle is so common for prophetic announcements of future events (Gonçalves 1986: 196; cf. Edel 1964: 69; Irwin 1977: 30f.; Høgenhaven 1988: 200; *pace* Roberts 1987: 27ff.).

(2) On two occasions in this verse, a word is immediately followed by exactly the same word: אבן and מוסד, constituting either dittography (cf. 1 Pet. 2:6; Lindblom 1955: 125) or the use of *anastrophe*, a literary device of repetition (Irwin 1977: 30; Roberts 1987: 34f.). If we reduce the double occurrences to one, a perfect colometric pattern (3 + 2) arises in vv. 16a´´-17a (Lindblom), but this is a dubious interference. A more nuanced approach involves the deletion of the second מוסד only (participle *hophal*), which in the view of some scholars provides an awkward construction (Wildberger, 1067; Gonçalves 1986: 197). Nevertheless, in a context of sophisticated wording it seems preferable to maintain the two occurrences (Exum 1982: 126; Berder 1996: 124f.; RSV: 'a sure foundation').

(3) The *hapax legomenon* אבן בחן, 'a massive stone', has given rise to a variety of proposals with regard to its origin and meaning. The meaning 'fortress stone' is likely to be original (cf. Isa. 23:13; 32:14; 1 QS 8:7f.; 1QH 6:25ff.; 7:8f.; Roberts 1987: 29-34; *DCH*, II, 137) and makes much sense in the context, but the ancient versions and the history of interpretation show that the word has always been related to the verb בחן, 'to test' (Wildberger, 1066f.). The stone was understood to have been tested for its ability to carry the superstructure.

(4) The prefix in בציון cannot be a *beth essentiae* (*pace* GKC §119 i; Huber 1976: 98; Irwin 1977: 31; Gonçalves 1986: 196), since 'Zion' is not the predicative adjunct but the object (Roberts 1987: 29).

(5) 'A valuable cornerstone'. For יקר in the sense of 'solid, valuable', cf. Irwin 1977: 30f.; Gonçalves 1986: 210; M.J. Mulder, *Koningen Deel I. I Koningen 1-7* (COT), Kampen 1987, 188. According to Berder (1996: 124), however, the first meaning would be 'heavy'.

(6) For חוש as akin to the Accadian *ḫâšu* (*CAD* VI, 147, s.v. *ḫâšu* C) in the sense of 'to waver, shake, quake', cf. Roberts 1987: 36f.; Qimron 1995: 326ff. ['to be undermined']; This interpretation (Tg and 1QS 8:7-8) is preferable to others such as 'to hasten, to flee' (Vg), 'to be anxious' (Syr), or to emendations such as יבוש (LXX), 'to be ashamed' and ימוש, 'to be removed' (Procksch, 356). For a survey of opinions, cf. Wildberger, 1067f.; *TWAT*, II, 820ff. (M. Tsevat); Watts, 367f.

21 'Mount Perazim' and 'the valley of Gibeon' are interpreted by some authors as metaphors for YHWH's action, rather than as adjuncts of place (Irwin 1977: 35f.). Cf. the explanation.

28 The accentuation of MT leads to the rendering: 'One drives one's cart wheel and horses (over it), but one does not crush it' (M. Buber, Hirsch, Hitzig, Delitzsch, Dillmann-Kittel, Feldmann, König, Penna, Kilian; Barthélemy, 201). Besides the colometry and asyndesis of לא ידקנו, the use of the verb המם also pleads against this. With armies and horses as its object, this verb is so closely bound up with the meaning 'to confuse' (Exod. 14:24; 23:27; Judg. 4:15; 10:10; 1 Sam. 7:10; Ps. 18;15; 144:6) that the meaning of 'driving horses for threshing' becomes very unlikely. The use of המם with 'carts' as its object is unique, however, and need not necessarily be understood as 'bringing to confusion'. In this context the meaning 'to drive' is acceptable and can be found as early as Ibn Ezra.

ESSENTIALS AND PERSPECTIVES

Within the redactional unity of ch.28, warranted by the opening expression 'Woe', a variety of sections can be discerned. Opinions are much divided, however, concerning the actual arrangement of the passages. Only vv. 23-29 are generally considered to be a relatively self-contained textual unit, because of their *mashal* form and agricultural imagery. With regard to vv. 1-22 the main point of discussion concerns the question whether vv. 7-13 constitute an originally independent unit (Duhm, Dillmann-Kittel, König, Kissane, Penna, Kaiser, Clements, Wildberger) or whether they should be connected either with the preceding section (vv. 1-6; Schoors, Watts, Oswalt) or the section following (vv. 14-22; Delitzsch, Feldmann; Barth 1977: 10ff.). The former of the last two opinions is based on the common theme of drunkenness (vv. 1,3,7f.), the latter on the fact that vv. 11-13, from a form critical point of view, do not exhibit the usual traits of a judgement oracle (God being referred to in the third person), as is the case with vv. 16-22. Moreover, the word 'swaggerers' in v. 14 seems to aim at the speakers of vv. 9-10.

This commentary favours the very first opinion, i.e. vv. 7-13 constitute an originally independent unit, but for reasons other than those already mentioned. Firstly, vv. 1-6 form a closed textual unit, circumscribed by the 'crown' theme, in which the description of disaster is followed by an announcement of salvation (vv. 1-4, 5-6).[4] Secondly, the

---

[4] Sweeney (359-62) considers vv. 5-6 to be the opening passage of vv. 5-29. It is hard to perceive, however, (1) that v. 5 would not link up with vv. 1-4 since it offers the long-term perspective of the fall of the crown announced therein; (2) that the first words of v. 7, 'these also', would establish a syntactical link with vv. 5-6.

introductory words of v. 7, 'These also', betray a clumsy redactional seam, trying to link up the drunken priests and prophets of v. 7 with the drunkards of Ephraim in vv. 1,3 while by-passing the announcement of salvation of v. 5 and the fig eating theme of v. 4. Thirdly, the internal coherence of vv. 14-22 is so strong in every respect (God's pronunciation of judgement in the first person [vv. 16-17] is often preceded by a prophetic invective [vv. 14-15]) that vv. 7-13 cannot be considered to have originally belonged to vv. 14-22.

We start, therefore, by accepting a fourfold division: vv. 1-6, 7-13, 14-22, 23-29. The explanation below will point to the strong impact of the redactional unity of the passages concerned.

Taking vv. 1-6 as a whole one is impressed by the firm and dogged language of the passage, a result of the 'heavy' rhythm (most cola count four words, some even five) and the paucity of verbal clauses (only vv. 2b″,4a′,5f.) as opposed to the large number of noun clauses created from construct chains, which in some cases are fully repeated (v. 1a-b′ and vv. 3b″-4a). In addition, the rapid change of metaphors ('crown', 'flower', 'drunkard', 'fat', 'trampling') and similes ('storm', 'flood', 'fig'), and the extensive use of word play (in vv. 1,4: 'flower' and 'beauty' [ציץ and צבי]; in vv. 1,3f.: 'haughty' and 'valley' [גאות and גיא], and 'Ephraim' and 'glorious' [אפרים and תפארת/ה]; in vv. 1,4f.: 'head' and 'remnant' [ראש and שאר]; in v. 6: 'to the one who sits' and 'to those who turn' [ליושב and משיבי] [5]) contribute to this impression.

Behind such a shield of unmanageable language some of the actants are forced to exhibit a vagueness of identity.[6] 'The crown of the drunkards of Ephraim' is not a clear figure. The expression may point to the ruling class in the capital, but the name of the city, 'Samaria', in which this group undoubtedly take pride, is apparently not even worth a mention. The instrument by which YHWH will overthrow their power, also remains anonymous. Its identity is built up by a mixture of metaphors: a storm, an army, a glutton (v. 2). If this blend is aimed at Assyria, as it appears to be, then the wording is a verdict on the lasting value of this tremendous world power. The term 'remnant of his people' is less opaque. It is at least determined by the possessive suffix, which refers to YHWH. Moreover, it supposes the great calamity of the exile and its characteristics are the basis for a sound and secure city: the administration of justice and the warding off of enemies. The only person whose proper name is expressed is YHWH. He is the one who presides over the course

---

[5] With double duty suffix. Quite a number of these instances are mentioned by Exum 1982: 115ff.
[6] Exum 1982: 113f.

of history in which arrogance collapses, and justice and security fall to the lot of a suppressed minority. This crown is incorruptible.

With regard to vv. 7-13, the very first words of v. 7, 'These also', give the impression that this passage offers a continuation of what precedes it. It is true that, after the vista of God's salvation (v. 6), v. 7 returns to the topic of alcohol abuse, but the differences between the two passages are such as to create a dynamic progression.

Firstly, this prophecy is outspokenly realistic, as opposed to the pre-dominantly metaphorical character of the preceding prophecy. This is especially apparent from the fact that the actors here, who are identical to those in vv. 1-6, have speaking roles: the drunkards in vv. 9f., YHWH in vv. 12f., and even the enemies (v. 11: 'foreign tongue'), since God speaks partly through their words in v. 13a. Behind this tangible por-trayal of the conqueror, one senses a concrete encounter: YHWH peeks out from behind his meteorological disguise in v. 2 and is presented here as someone who has been and who still is involved in a dialogue with his people (vv. 12f.). Even the prophet himself becomes an actor. While he is not referred to in vv. 1-6, he is mentioned here and quoted by the addressees, his adversaries (vv. 9f.).

Secondly, the impression of a real encounter is mixed with a threaten-ing obscurity. The visions of the prophets and the decisions of the priests, which are normally tools intended to clarify God's will with re-gard to Israel, are made obscure by their drunkenness (v. 7). The actors involved do not understand each other, indeed the denounced classes do not even want to listen (v. 12). The prophet's outburst is not accepted by his audience; his words are even maliciously distorted (vv. 9f.). God's message, so clear in former times (v. 12), will now be clothed in the words of a foreign vanquisher, who speaks the same gibberish as the dis-torted words of the prophet (vv. 11,13, cf. 10).

Thirdly, a striking semantic contrast between vv. 1-6 and vv. 7-13 lies in the obtrusive magnificence of the drunkards in vv. 1-6 (v. 1: 'haughty crown', 'glorious beauty', 'fat valley'; v. 4: 'first-ripe fig') and the tar-nished, almost repugnant appearance of their fellow boozers in vv. 7-13 (v. 7: 'to reel and stagger'; v. 8: 'vomit and filth'; v. 10: cacophonic speaking). In line with this, the sudden ruin of vv. 1-6 (v. 2: 'like a storm'; v. 4: 'while it is still in his palm') is in contrast with the drawn out man-hunt of vv. (7-)13. The end, however, is the same: 'down to earth... under foot' (vv. 2f.) and 'to stumble backward, and be broken' (v. 13).

It follows from all this that vv. 7-13 form a climax vis-à-vis vv. 1-6. The drunken perversion of the priests and prophets, projected against the background of their professional duties and God's earlier benevolent speaking, is perplexing here. Moreover, the punishment comes directly from YHWH, for his word, absorbed in that of the enemies, no longer provides a place of repose but forces flight, a flight which is doomed to fail miserably.

The progressively tragic nature of these verses goes together with the fact that Jerusalem gradually comes into view in the persons of the priests and prophets, and in the reference to 'resting-place'. This prepares the reader for an explicit address of the city at the beginning of the next passage (v. 14). In this way, the succession of the two passages is in agreement with the general prophetic topic: the more intimate with YHWH in time (v. 12: 'He has said to them') and space (v. 12: 'This is your resting-place'), the greater the sinfulness. The perversion of Jerusalem surpasses that of Ephraim (cf. Israel and Judah in Jer. 3:6-11; Ezek. 23:11-19). The judgement cannot but be the same (2 Kgs 21:12f.; 23:27).

The very heart of vv. 14-22 is exposed by the following statement: 'A covenant with death is the ultimate absurdity, since death alone brooks no compromise; yet every post-edenic human endeavour is an attempt to make a deal with death' (Landy 1993: 141). The conflict between Isaiah and his adversaries is not only about their recognition of his authority to deliver them a message from YHWH (v. 9), it is a conflict over life and death. Since they have refused to accept God's word (v. 12) Isaiah announces their downfall (v. 13). The response of the rulers of Jerusalem (v. 14) is to claim that they are immune from destruction because they have made a covenant with death. They at least will not be harmed by the downfall announced by the prophet (v. 15a). It is YHWH himself who reacts against this presumptuousness. The deceit which so characterises their lives will also take hold of the stronghold in which they have entrenched themselves (v. 15b). There is another refuge opposing their stronghold of deceit, the foundations of which YHWH himself has laid: Zion. Only those who trust in Zion will stand firm (v. 16) because Zion's building norms of 'righteousness' and 'justice' are missing from the structure in which Isaiah's adversaries fancy themselves secure. It shall, therefore, be destroyed (v. 17). For 'righteousness' and 'justice' are the only universal powers which can offer any protection against death (v. 18).

Given that obedience to God's word has the very survival and continued existence of the people at stake, the conflict in which Isaiah ben Amoz had become involved transcended its unique, historical context. The tradition was aware that the lesson to be learned from this conflict had validity for the generations to come. It suited its purpose that the judgement could be interpreted as an ongoing threat, a message to be heeded again and again (v. 19). The heart of Isaiah's message was that YHWH himself, who gave victory to David over the Philistines so that he could rejoice in safety in taking possession of the newly conquered Jerusalem (2 Samuel 5), was also able to bring judgement on that city. When his commandments were treated like those of a stranger (cf. Hos. 8:12), those who did so would come to know that he can also act like a stranger; not as Zion's architect but as an outsider, an alien (v. 21). Then the truth of Zion's *Magna Carta* would be known: 'Unless YHWH watches over the city, the watchman stays awake in vain' (Ps. 127:1).

For the understanding of ch.28 as a whole it is crucial that we comprehend the *mashal* of vv. 23-29 as having been designed to help the readers of BI to understand what precedes it. This function has been prepared by vv. 19-22. The direction of speech, while continuing the plural address of the historical audience of Isaiah ben Amoz in vv. 1-4,7-18, enlarges in v. 19 to include the readers of BI of all ages. In this way, vv. 19-22 broaden the judgement, announced in vv. 1-18, in time, and end with an admonition which offers the chance of conversion by declaring the judgement an impending threat. Vv. 23-29 go on to explain the judgement as a process not of annihilation, but of harvesting.

Here we touch upon a fundamental understanding of prophetic oracles as remaining valuable for the generations to come. In the view of the transmitters, the conflict between the prophet and the rulers of Jerusalem is not only an event worth being handed down for the sake of history only, but it is a paradigmatic event. It applies to God's people forever. The judgement which has befallen former generations still overshadows the generations to come. The task 'to make people understand the message' (v. 19) cannot be performed by the prophets only; a disastrous course of history is also necessary to that end. In this way, the judgement functions as a teaching authority and allows for admonition in order to reform religious attitudes.

If the *mashal* does indeed direct itself in this way to the readers of BI, then the farmer has a special significance. He is more than a necessary element in the 'vehicle' of the comparison. V. 26 calls attention to him too explicitly for that: 'Yes, he instructs him concerning the right order, his God teaches him'. There is a relationship between the farmer and '*his* God' in which he accepts God's instruction. Such a relationship is entirely lacking among the 'swaggerers' of vv. 14-22 or among the drunkards of vv. 7-13 for that matter. The audience to which the *mashal* addresses itself is called upon not to follow the way of these adversaries but to take the example of the farmer who lets himself be instructed by God in 'the right order'. The farmer, presented to the readers of BI as an example, is a metaphor for the writing prophet Isaiah, who allowed himself to be instructed by 'his God'. Thus the readers of BI, the successors of those over whom the judgement actually came, are able to learn God's 'wonderful counsel' from the message of Isaiah, the prophet who himself has accompanied the eventful history of his people. By accepting this teaching they will become in the eyes of the nations 'the wise and understanding people, the great nation that has its God so near' (Deut. 4:6f.).

It should be clear from the preceding exposition that the date of ch.28 cannot be determined in one single period. The chapter opens with a prophecy against the Northern kingdom (vv. 1-4) which must stem from before the fall of Samaria (722 BC) and has been reworked as an entrance into a basically original warning for the Southern kingdom (vv. 7-22). Such a construction based on *analogy* would be pre-exilic. The verses in between these two segments contain a reversal of the 'crown' motif in the first segment: from judgement (vv. 1-4) to salvation for 'the rest of his people' (vv. 5-6). This revision based on *contrast* would be exilic, since this reversal interrupts the former connection between vv. 1-4 and vv. 7-22. If v. 19 widens the judgement and presents it as a possible fate for all generations, then the function of the deterrent example which Ephraim had received before the exile, devolves for the post-exilic community upon Jerusalem as this city had not taken the words of Isaiah seriously. These expansions do not necessarily have a function in the redactional genesis of the book. The contrary is true, however, with respect to the reworking of vv. 23-29. This appears to be an original *mashal* of Isaiah ben Amoz concerning the relationship between judgement and salvation but it is now formulated in such a way that 'the farmer' represents the implied prophet who allowed himself to be instructed by 'his God' (v. 24). The actualising reworking results here in a redactional reworking.

SCHOLARLY EXPOSITION

1. Vv. 1-6: 'The Last Act Crowns the Play'

Introduction to the Exegesis: Form and Setting

The opening word, 'crown' (vv. 1,3,5: עטרה), is a structural element in the passage which places the main characters in opposition to one another. Applied to Ephraim it encloses an announcement of judgement (vv. 1-4), applied to YHWH it introduces an announcement of salvation for 'the remnant of his people' (vv. 5f.). The applications vary: the construct chain 'the haughty crown of the drunkards of Ephraim' somehow identifies the people mentioned with their crown (vv. 1,3), while the expression 'YHWH will be a crown to the remnant' (vv. 5f.) seems to underline the distinction between God and those he favours.

The noun 'Ephraim' (vv. 1,3) forms the only historical lead in the passage. It is a poetic term, particularly in the prophetic books, for the Northern kingdom of Israel (Jer. 7:15; 31:9,18,20; Ezek. 37:16,19; Hosea *passim*; Zech. 9:10,13), and also bears this meaning in the preceding chapters of PI (7:2,5,8f.,17; 9:8,20; 11:13; 17:3). The context of doom naturally points to the period of the new rise of Assyria's power in the West which, after some revolts, eventually led to the downfall of the city-state of Samaria (722 BC).

This era certainly forms the background of the prophecy, but we cannot go so far as to state that it dates from that time.[7] We must take the literary context into account, especially the contrast between Ephraim (vv. 1,3) and 'the remnant of his people' (v. 5). Because the latter term nowhere means the remnant of the Northern tribes but, in the (post)exilic comprehensive sense, the remnant of all Israel (cf. 11:11,16), the passage as a whole must stem from that period. It opposes the tragic destiny of Ephraim to the felicitous perspective for what remains of God's people.[8]

One may argue that vv. 5f. forms a later addition, in view of the connecting expression 'On that day', but this does not mean that vv. 1-4 in their present form stem from the eighth century, the period of confrontation with Assyria. They may have undergone some adjustments at the time of the final redaction. The original wording is impossible to recover although the text contains a good number of characteristically Isaianic terms. In other words, the post-exilic redactor looks back upon a prophecy of Isaiah ben Amoz from the Assyrian period which was originally destined for the people of the Northern kingdom but was still significant for the time in which he was living, be it, first of all, as a contrast.

Underneath this contrast, however, there is an older theological intention, i.e. the desire to convey the notion that Judah has gone the same unwholesome way as Ephraim. The Southern kingdom should have learned from the fate of the Northern kingdom but it did not (cf. the re-

---

[7] Prinsloo 1988; *pace* Hayes, Irvine 1987: 323: 'late in 727 or early in 726'.
[8] Hausmann 1987: 156ff., 199f.

markable correspondences between Isa. 28:1-4,9,12,14,19,23 and 2 Kgs
17:7-23; 21:10-15).[9] Once it had been struck by God's judgement, however, it was destined to meet his particular favour.

The structure of the passage is simple. The announcement of judgement (vv. 1-4) and the salvation oracle (vv. 5-6) are connected by the
prophetic redactional formula 'On that day' (v. 5). The first section consists of two elements which are introduced by a deictic term: 'Woe' (v.
1: הוי) and 'Behold' (vv. 2-4: הנני). The former functions as an accusation, the latter speaks exclusively of judgement and mirrors the classical
diptych of God's intervention (vv. 2-3: 'Behold') and its consequences
(v. 4: '[It] will be' [והיתה]). An elaborate comparison in a tricolon closes
the judgement oracle (v. 4b). The second section (vv. 5-6) consists of
one clause. The opening verb form 'YHWH will be' (v. 5: יהיה) creates a
contrast with the last element of the first section: 'The fading flower will
be' (v. 4: והיתה).

This results in the following schema:
1-4 woe oracle
    1   accusation against 'the crown' of Ephraim
    2-4   announcement of judgement
        2-3   God's intervention
        4   consequences
5-6 salvation oracle
    5   YHWH will be a crown to the remnant
    6   YHWH will be a spirit of right judgement and valour

Exegesis by Verse

1 The 'woe' (הוי) cry gains emphasis because of its extra-metrical position (*anacrusis*). It is the first of six (28:1; 29:1,15; 30:1; 31:1; 33:1)
and provides the basic division of chs. 28-33 (cf. 'Introduction to Isaiah
Chapters 28-39'). Here, an overtone of moral indignation prevails because of the charges of pride and drunkenness which, in the view of the
sages, lead to ruin (Prov. 20:1; 23:20f. 29-35; 31:5; Sir. 31:29f.; 3
Apoc.Bar 4:17; T.Judah 16:2ff.). The connotation of death remains
present, however, in the image of the 'fading flower'.

The syntactical structure of v. 1 is curious: an accumulation of nouns,
interrupted only by a relative pronoun, and not a single finite verb form
in sight. Some scholars avoid the allegedly clumsy build-up of construct
states by supposing a sequence of appositions (Exum 1982: 112) or by
interpreting v. 1a″ as a nominal sentence (Kissane, 310: 'faded flowers

[9] O'Kane 1996: 41f.

is his splendid adornment'). It seems preferable, though, to consider the
linguistic awkwardness as a literary device, the bombastic expression
adding to the evocative description of the drunkards in the capital
(Delitzsch, 312; Duhm, 194f.).

The metaphor which dominates the whole passage is the term 'crown'
(עטרה). As a distinctive ornament, a crown can play a number of roles in
the royal panoply (2 Sam. 12:30; Isa. 62:3; Jer. 13:18; Ezek. 21:31;
Ps.21:4), the liturgical attire of the high-priest (Zech. 6:11,14; Sir.
45:12), the wedding ritual (Ezek. 16:12; 23:42; Cant. 3:11) and other
acts of honouring people (Job 19:9; 31:36; Prov. 4:9; 12:4; 14:24;
16:31; 17:6; Lam. 5:16; Esth. 12:30). It also occurs in geographical
names (Num. 32:3,34f.: Atroth[-shophan]; Josh. 16:2,5: Ataroth[-
addar]; 1 Chr. 2:54: Atroth-beth-joab).[10] All these connotations fittingly
direct the metaphor to the capital of the Northern kingdom, i.e. to
Samaria. This town was founded by king Omri in about 880 BC, on a
high and isolated hill in Ephraim, overlooking a rich valley (1 Kgs
16:24). His son Ahab enlarged it with palace buildings and a temple for
Baal (1 Kgs 16:32) which somehow crowned the hill, turning the city
into a symbol for idolatry and sumptuous living (Jer.23:13; Ezek. 23:4-
7; 16:51; Hos. 7:1; 8:5f.; 10:5f.; Amos 3:9,12; 4:1ff.; 6:1ff.; Mic.
1:5ff.). It should be noted, however, that the name of the city, Samaria,
is not mentioned. The impact of this concealment, a figure of speech
called *aposiopesis*, is twofold. Firstly, the inhabitants of the city, 'the
drunkards', get more attention than the capital itself. Secondly, the accusation is ready to be contrasted with the promise for the city which, likewise nameless, will be evoked in vv. 5-6. For a correct understanding of
the prophet's accusation, however, it is necessary to note the fact that he
denounces the same evil among his own people in Jerusalem, in the
same context of excessive revelry and judicial injustice (שכר ['drunkards']: 5:11,22; 19:14; 24:9; 28:3,7; יין ['wine']: 5:11,22; 22:13;
24:9,11; 28:7). This has made it easy for the redaction of the chapter to
connect this oracle against Samaria with a salvation oracle for the remnant of Israel, i.e. in a setting directed to a Judean public.

The attributive adjunct 'haughty' (גאות means both 'lifting up' and
'pride'; cf. Isa. 9:17; Ps. 89:10 and Ps. 17:10) lends the word 'crown'
its metaphorical function. This evocative description of Samaria agrees
with what we know about the city from elsewhere, its high location be-

---

[10] *TWAT*, VI, 30 (D. Kellermann). Some scholars take the view that the Hebrew term
עטרה can also mean a 'garland of flowers' (cf. Ezek. 23:42; Prov. 4:9). If such is the
case, it could apply to 28:1 (*HALAT*, 771; Wildberger, Watts, Oswalt, Irwin 1977;
TWAT, VI, 1030 [G.Steins]).

ing symbolic of the pride of its inhabitants. The prophet connects this arrogance with the abuse of wine, one of the luxurious products which were guaranteed by the fertility of the plain overlooked by the city (for 'fat' [root שמן] as a quality of the soil, food and people cf. Isa. 5:1; 10:16; 25:6; 30:23). By locating the drunkards in 'Ephraim' rather than in 'Samaria' he brands them as the ruling class of the country. Their splendid capital is not a centre of righteous government but a carousal of drunkards.[11]

The word parallel to 'crown' is 'fading flower'. The term ציץ means both single flowers and the blossom of a plant (Num. 17:23; Isa. 40:6ff.; Ps. 103:15; Job 14:2), but can also signify a head ornament with a floral design (Exod. 28:36; Lev. 8:9; 1 Kgs 6:18,29,32,35). By itself the word is an appropriate equivalent for 'crown', but its traditional symbolic value for human transitoriness is made explicit by the adjunct 'fading' (נבל; cf. Isa. 1:30; 24:4; 34:4; 40:7f.; 64:5; Jer. 8:13; Ez. 47:12; Ps. 1:3; 37:2). This renders it even more fit to match the word 'crown', against which the 'woe' has been announced.

The double adjunct 'glorious beauty' adds to the impressive character of the capital. The word for 'beauty' (צבי) has a broad spectrum of meaning:[12] it may refer to the landscape (Jer. 3:19; Ezek. 20:6,15), to the architectural vista of a city (Isa. 4:2; 13:19; 23:9; Ezek. 25:9; Dan. 8:9; 11:16,41), to persons (2 Sam. 1:19) or simply to jewelry, in this case the head ornaments of the prominent people (cf. Ezek. 7:20).[13] The adjunct 'glorious' (תפארה) sets an Isaianic tone. The word embodies the contrast between the 'glory' that will perish in the judgement (3:18; 10:12,15; 13:19; 20:5; 28:4) and 'the glory' of God's salvation (4:2; 28:5). In the latter context the term occurs in DI and is especially important in TI.[14]

2 With regard to syntax, the question arises as to how we should interpret the *lamed* in לאדני: as datival ('Belonging to the Lord') or emphatic ('Strong and mighty is surely the Lord')?[15] The former, more traditional explanation seems preferable since it implies a military force by means of which YHWH will act against Ephraim (cf. Isa. 2:12; 22:5). This agrees with the Isaianic theme of Assyria being an instrument in God's hands (5:25,30; 7:20; 8:5-8; 10:5f.). The name of the world power in question is avoided but its real existence is suggested, as is the case with

---

[11] For the banquet background as symbolic for Israel's corruption, cf, Asen 1996.

[12] *TWAT*, VI, 896ff. (H. Madl).

[13] M. Gilula, "צבי in Isaiah 28,1 – A Head Ornament", *Tel Aviv* 1 (1974) 128; M. Görg, "Die Bildsprache in Jes 28,1", *BN* 3 (1977) 17-23.

[14] W.A.M. Beuken, *Jesaja deel IIIA* (POT), Nijkerk 1989, 169.

[15] Irwin 1977: 8. For a survey of other explanations, cf. Alexander, 445.

the passive form 'will be trampled' of v. 3 and the indeterminate form 'whoever sees it, swallows it' of v. 4 (cf. the nameless mention of a people in 5:26; 8:7; 10:28).

'Behold' (הנה) often introduces the prophetic announcement of God's intervention. In PI this occurs not only in constructions with God as subject (3:1; 8:7; 10:33; 13:17; 19:1; 22:17; 24:1; 26:21; 28:16; 29:14; 30:27; 35:4; 37:7; 38:5,8) but also where some person or object embodies God's activity (5:26,30; 6:7; 7:14; 8:18; 13:9; 17:14; 32:1; 34:5). To what or whom does the expression 'one who is strong and mighty' refer: to a concept of time, i.e. 'day', to a wind in relation to the following comparison, to an army or to a person, i.e. the king of Assyria? A military reference seems more probable. The combination of the roots in question (חזק and אמץ) occurs frequently in military contexts, more particularly the wars of YHWH (Deut. 31:5f., 23; Josh. 1:6f., 9,18; 10:25; Isa. 35:3; Amos 2:14ff.; 1 Chr. 22:13; 28:20; 2 Chr. 32:7f.).[16] The hidden reference includes, therefore, both the king of Assyria and his army.

That strength can only be derived from God is one of the themes of PI (8:11; 27:1,5; 35:3f.). In this context the title 'Lord' (אדני)[17] is most fitting. While its origin may still be obscure,[18] it is a characteristic term of PI (34 times, while almost absent from chs. 40-66 [only in 49:14]) and is basically used in the context of judgement (3:17f.; 6:1,8,11; 9:7,16; 21:6,8,16; 22:5,12,14f.,18; 29:13; 30:20; by means of Assyria: 7:20; 8:7; 10:12,23f.) It is sometimes used in an accusation (3:15; 7:14), and only rarely in a post-exilic context of salvation (4:4; 11:11; otherwise in 37:24; 38:14,16). The title portrays God's transcendence in history: he is the one who really disposes of all human authority and might.

The 'one who is strong and mighty' is compared with 'a storm of hail, a destroying tempest' and 'a storm of powerful, overflowing waters'. 'Storm' (זרם) is a rare word, almost confined to PI. It belongs to the vocabulary of theophany (Hab. 3:10), connected either to judgement (Isa. 28:2; 30:30) or salvation (Isa. 4:6; 25:4; 32:2). The word for 'hail' (ברד) is primarily known from the plagues of Egypt (Exod. 9-10; Ps. 78:47; 105:32), but also has theophanic connotations (Isa. 30:30; Ps. 18:13f.). Furthermore, it plays a role in the punishment of Israel's enemies and the wicked (Josh. 10:11; Isa. 28:17; 32:19). Some other

---

[16] Laberge 1982: 164.

[17] The reading of 1QIs[a], יהוה, is a harmonisation; cf. Wildberger, 1043.

[18] *THAT*, I, 36ff. (E.Jenni): perhaps from the cult in Jerusalem; otherwise *TWAT*, I, 75-8 (O. Eißfeldt).

terms add to the evocation of divine judgement: 'tempest' (שַׂעַר; cf. Ezek. 32:10; Nah. 1:3; Job 9:17) and 'destroying' (קֶטֶב; cf. Deut. 32:24; Hos. 13;14). The metaphor 'powerful, overflowing waters' has already been used by PI for the invading Assyrian army (8:6ff.; 17:12f.; cf. 30:28).

Commentators disagree with regard to the question whether the subject of the sentence 'he will hurl them down with (his) hand' is still 'the strong and mighty one' (the majority) or 'the Lord' (Rashi; Wildberger, 1048). From a merely syntactical point of view the former interpretation is correct since the subject of the nominal sentence of v. 2a' has not been replaced. The logical subject of v. 1, 'the Lord', however, might be evoked by the expression 'with (his) hand' (בְּיָד), in light of the well-known idiom that God acts 'with a strong hand' or 'with an elevated hand' (Exod. 13:9; Deut. 26:8; Ps. 136:2). Moreover, the concept of the hand of God occurs frequently in PI (1:25; 5:12,25; 8:11; 9:11,16,20; 10:4,10; 11:11,15; 14:27; 19:16; 23:11; 25:10; 26:11; 31:3). Only the form is unique here, thus adding further ambivalence to the sentence (יָד without article, adjective or suffix).

The term 'to hurl down', literally 'to lay down forcibly' (נוח hiphil B), occurs in a number of judgement oracles (Lev. 24:12; Num. 15:34; 32:15; Isa. 65:15; Ezek. 16:39; 22:20; Hos. 4:17).[19] The basis of this meaning is a negative application of the concept 'to rest', which we also find elsewhere in PI (7:2,19; 30:32). Since it lacks an object, the sentence focuses on the invading strong-man, although the annihilation of the object, the elaborate subject of the 'woe' of v. 1, is mentioned in the next verses, split up into two sentences with different imagery (vv. 3-4).

3 The vivid sketch of the punishment switches from meteorological metaphors to a metaphor for military operation ('to trample' [רמס]: 2 Kgs 7:17; 9:33; Isa. 10:6; 16:4; 26:6; 28:18; 41:25; Ezek. 26:11; Mic. 7:10; Nah. 3:14; Dan. 8:7; otherwise in Isa. 5:5; 63:3; Mic. 5:7).[20] As a compound nominal clause the sentence is subordinate to that preceding it: the violence of the storm turns into the violence of an army. The passive verb form 'will be trampled' fittingly suggests an anonymous mass. The stylistic collision of 'with (his) hand' (ambivalently applicable to God) and 'under foot', respectively the last word of v. 2 and the first of v. 3, does not require that God be the implicit acting subject of 'to trample' as he is ambivalently of 'to hurl down'. Al-

---

[19] TWAT, V, 303 (H.D. Preuß).

[20] TWAT, VII, 532ff. (G. Waschke). The plural form תרמסנה betrays either a collective understanding of 'the haughty crown of the drunkards of Ephraim' or should be changed into the forma energica of the feminine singular (Irwin 1977: 10; BHS, HALAT).

though the anthropomorphism of God's 'feet' does occur in the Bible, this applies only to theophanies and the topic of his dwelling place (Exod. 24:10; Hab. 3:5; Zech. 14:4; Ps. 18:10 and Isa. 60:13; 66:1; Ezek. 43:7; Ps. 99:5; Lam. 2:1).[21] The reference here is to the feet of the Assyrian infantry. 'Just for a moment God has been visible as the acting subject of history. Again he disappears behind those who are charged with the enforcement of his verdict on earth' (Wildberger, 1048).

4 The imagery of 'a first-ripe fig' carries something of a contradiction. The term 'fading flower' suggests some elapse of time but the comparison with a first-ripe fig swallowed 'while it is still in his palm' suggests untimeliness ('before the summer') and excludes any time interval. The impact of the contrast is twofold: the excessive attractiveness of the early fig (cf. Hos. 9:10; Mic. 7:1) underlines the wealth of 'the head of the fat valley', but its fast consumption symbolises the weakness of the capital, its innate transitoriness, like that of a flower, but overlooked by the haughty drunkards.

5-6 The salvation oracle links up with the preceding announcement of judgement, in the first place with v. 4 by means of the time category 'on that day' and the opening verb form 'will be' (v. 5: יהיה; v. 4: והיתה), and in the second place with v. 1 by means of common semantics ('crown', 'beauty' and 'glory').

The expression 'on that day' (ביום ההוא) has a multiple function. Taken by itself it would point to the simultaneity of events which follow one another, but its use in the prophetic literature, however, points rather to a literary and theological coincidence. Its main duty is redactional, i.e. connecting prophetic oracles (Isa. 3:18; 4:2; 7:18,20; 11:10,11; 12:1,4; 17:7; 19:19,21; 22:25; 26:1). This is only possible, firstly because the notion of the specific duration of a 'day' got lost while the substrate meaning of time remained, and secondly because a salvation historical understanding of the course of time had arisen. The expectation of a decisive appearance of YHWH who would put the world in order (Isa. 2:11,17,20; 5:30; 10:27; 22:20; 29:18), entailed the projection of all particular divine interventions into one unknown moment in the proximate future. The expression 'on that day', therefore, does not so much announce the coincidence of the restoration of God's remnant with the destruction of Samaria, but rather counterbalances both events at an unknown future time, that of God's intervention.[22] In this sense the notion

---

[21] *TWAT*, VII, 342f. (F.J. Stendebach).
[22] De Vries 1995: 121.

is open to an eschatological interpretation, depending on both its semantic implantation in the oracle to which it belongs (24:21; 25:9; 27:
1,12,13), and the viewpoint of the reader.[23]

The salvation to come is not simply a return to the previous state of
well-being with new and corrected moral standards, it is something
wholly new, although partly formulated in the language of the announcement of judgement. Firstly, the 'crown' is no longer a city, not
even a point on earth, but God himself, or better, it serves as God himself. This means that all the negative elements in the description of the
'crown' city which was the subject of 'woe', 'drunkards', 'haughty',
'fading flower' and the location 'on the head of the fat valley', have disappeared (cf. v. 5 and v. 1). Instead, a new, almost unique word is introduced: 'diadem (of glory)' (v. 5: צפירה[24]). Its uniqueness eminently
suits the promise that 'YHWH of hosts' himself will be the glory of his
people.

The title 'YHWH of hosts' (יהוה צבאות) would have been at home in the
cult of YHWH in Jerusalem (Psalms 24; 46; 48; 84).[25] PI uses it with distinct preference (cf. v. 29), probably for no other reason than that the
word 'hosts', whatever its etymology, evoked the idea of overwhelming
might. As such the term was able to carry a very important aspect of the
prophet's concept of God: YHWH's power rises above all earthly forces,
be it Israel's stubbornness (3:1; 5:7,9,16,24; 8:13; 9:12,18; 29:6) or
the armies of hostile nations (1:9; 10:26,33; 13:4,13; 14:22ff.; 17:3;
19 passim; 23:9). In short, YHWH's power rises above all human haughtiness (2:12; 6:3,5). Sion's hope is ultimately founded on this strength
(8:18; 9:6; 10:16; 31:4).

The persons for whom salvation is destined have changed. It is no
longer 'the drunkards of Ephraim' (v. 1) but 'the remnant of his people'.
The context warrants the post-exilic meaning of the term 'remnant'
(שאר), i.e. those who have come through the great calamity and consider
themselves to be the legitimate progeny of the old Israel of the twelve
tribes, bound to the uncompromising confession of the one God and the
fulfilment of the law of Moses, in anticipation of the restoration of Israel
before the eyes of the nations, as the prophets had foretold. The use of
the term here forms the end of a development from a context of warning

---

[23] *TWAT*, III, 569f, 585f. (M. Sæbø).

[24] The word also occurs in Ezek. 7:10 in the sense of a 'braided net'; cf. M. Masson,
"ṢᴱPĪRÂ (Ezéchiel VII 10)", *VT* 37 (1987) 301-11.

[25] Whether the title originally belonged to the theology of the ark of YHWH or was
based in the Jebusite cult, remains a point of discussion; cf. *TWAT*, VI, 881f. (H.-J. Zobel); Wildberger, 28, 1608.

to one of promise as can be read from its assorted applications in PI
(from 7:3 over 10:20-22 to 11:11,16 and 4:3).[26]

While the referent(s) of the 'crown' in the 'woe' oracle are puzzling,
its application in the salvation oracle is quite clear. V. 6 explains the
word pair 'crown / diadem' by a second word pair: 'spirit of (right)
judgement / valour'. The mention of the beneficiaries of these gifts, 'the
one who sits in judgement / those who turn back the battle at the gate',
reveals that God's presence to his people will be manifest in the administration of justice and the defense of the city.

The concept 'spirit' (רוח) as a term, among others, for the active influence of God upon his people is quite Isaianic (4:4; 11:2,4; 19:14;
29:10; 30:1; 32:15; 34:16). The same holds true for the following concepts.

The term 'justice, judgement' (משפט) is of great importance in the
three main parts of BI. In PI it occurs in different historical layers, i.e. in
oracles generally ascribed to the prophet himself and in passages ascribed to the Isaianic tradition. Since this classification remains subject
to discussion, it is more valuable to note that BI starts with the accusation that 'justice' has disappeared from God's people and Zion (1:17,21,
27; 3:14; 5:7,16; 10:2; 32:7; 34:5) but that it is expected to return as
the fruit of God's salvific action (4:4; 9:6; 16:5; 26:8f.; 30:18;
32:1,16; 33:5).

The word 'valour' (גבורה), although less prominent, is, nevertheless,
also an Isaianic term (3:25 [concrete meaning]; 11:2; 30:15; 33:13;
36:5; cf. 'valiant' [גבור]: 3:2; 5:22; 9:5; 10:21). Like 'justice', it belongs to God and will be imparted by him at the time of the great rescue.

Seen against the background of these two terms, the salvation oracle
(vv. 5-6) displays a thoroughly Isaianic character. The redactors who
added this to the judgement oracle against the capital of Ephraim (vv. 1-
4) adopted language akin to that of the prophet so as to promote the actualisation of the eighth century oracle for their exilic audience. Some
scholars relate this redaction more closely with the milieu from which
passages like 9:1-6 and 11:1-5 stem: the former shares the theme of
trampling warriors (9:4) and the terms 'valiant (God)' and 'justice'
(9:5f.) with 28:3,6, while the latter shares the concepts of God's 'spirit',
'valour' and 'right judgement' (11:2f.) with 28:6.[27] Our passage, however, unlike these texts, does not focus the new era in a descendant from
the house of David. It focuses rather on some beleaguered city, not as

[26] *TWAT*, VII, 940-3 (R.E. Clements).
[27] Vermeylen 1977: 388f.

the object of God's revenge but as the beneficiary of his gifts. The passage is open ended, therefore, in that it raises the question: which city is ultimately intended? Is it still the capital of Ephraim? Behind this city Jerusalem begins to loom up although the name does not occur prior to v. 14.

2. Vv. 7-13: 'Pride Comes before a Fall'

Introduction to the Exegesis: Form and Setting

The passage exhibits the general topics of accusation (vv. 7-8), ending with a quotation from the accused (vv. 9-10), and a proclamation of judgement (vv. 11-13).[28] The latter, however, is devoid of the usual form-critical characteristics: a messenger formula, an introductory 'Behold, me...' and the dual pattern of God's action and its consequences ('I' and 'you' or 'they'; cf. vv. 16-19). Instead, there is a digression on the strange manner of God's speaking (v. 11), an allusion to what he said earlier (v. 12a), an accusation that 'they' have not listened (v. 12b), a verdict but not in the first person (v. 13a), and a reference to the consequences in metaphorical language. These anomalies can be explained by the fact that accusation and verdict are connected by the rare theme of unintelligible words. This is in keeping with the fact that the passage has no semantic affinity with what follows and therefore contains a quite independent prophecy. It is only on the redactional level that there are connections with the surrounding oracles.

Its structure appears as follows:

7-10	accusation of priests and prophets	
	7-8	their improper behaviour
	9-10	their taunting questions
11-13	God's reaction	
	11	his strange manner of speaking now
	12a	his former words: gift and command
	12b	accusation: they have not listened
	13a	his verdict
	13b	its disastrous consequences

Three questions dominate the broad interpretation of the passage. The first concerns its dating in relation to its addressees. Scholars who take

---

[28] Sweeney (359, 362f.) offers a different structure: vv. 7-8 indictment; vv. 9-13 consequences. This is based on the contrast between the gibberish talk of the incompetent leaders (v. 10) and that of the foreign conqueror (v. 11).

the passage as forming one original unity with vv. 1-6 consider it directed towards the priests and prophets of Ephraim.[29] They look for an historical situation of an impending Assyrian invasion of the Northern kingdom and adopt the same epoch as for the previous section (see above). Others consider the beginning of v. 7 ('These also...') as a literary-historical seam and find it unlikely that Isaiah would denounce the apostate priestly and prophetic circles of Samaria. They expect him rather to urge the religious leaders of Jerusalem to behave correctly. Moreover, v. 12 also has a Jerusalemite background, and an address to the rulers of Jerusalem becomes explicit in v. 14. In this case there are two possibilities, depending on how one interprets the gist of the passage. If it contains an attack against necromancy, it may date from any pre-exilic period when political instability encouraged magic cults to thrive (Van der Toorn 1988). If the politics of the aristocracy in Jerusalem with regard to the threat coming from Assyria are being denounced, we have to look for a moment in the history of Judah when an Assyrian attack was immanent, i.e. during the Syro-Ephraimitic war (734-732 BC) or Sennacherib's march on Jerusalem (701 BC). This is a touchy matter, however, since Jerusalem is not pointed to directly. We would be better to ask which date is more important for understanding the prophecy in its present form and context: that of its origin in the ministry of the prophet Isaiah or that of its insertion into the present redactional unity? Since the text may have been adapted for its insertion (cf. the introductory words of v. 7: 'These also'), the former date would be hard to establish. The latter is likely to be any time at which the fate of Ephraim at the hands of Assyria might have served as an example for Juda. In our opinion, therefore, the period after the fall of Samaria (722 BC) prior to the decline of Assyria as a world power (630 BC) and the so-called Assyrian redaction of PI under king Josiah is eligible for the historical frame within which we ought to interpret the passage (Barth 1977).

The second broad question, on which there is much diversity of opinion (for surveys see Rosenmüller, 419; Alexander, 450f.), runs as follows: who is the speaker of vv. 9-10 and who is the subject of the sentence: 'Whom will *he* teach knowledge, whom will he make to understand the message?':

(1) 'He' refers to Isaiah. The adversaries of the prophet, the denounced priests and prophets, are quoted as they make a stand against him and reject his accusation. They protest against his sermonising manner on the grounds that they are not little children. The word of God is

---

[29] Tanghe 1993: 240ff.: after the court in Samaria now the priesthood in Bethel.

linked to this protest (v. 13). Opposition between a quotation of the addressees and a formal oracle of YHWH also occurs in 28:14-18 and 30:15-17 (although there with a quotation formula). This interpretation is widely supported (first proposed by Jerome, taken over by critical exegesis since Lowth[30]).

(2) 'He' refers to God. Some scholars point to the fact that the teaching of YHWH is an important theme by which the redactor has joined the separate prophetic oracles of the chapter culminating in vv. 23-29. In this case it would be Isaiah himself who speaks here. If this is correct then the prophet is suggesting either that the drunkards are like little children, unable to receive God's teaching, or that no other persons except little children are left to be taught by God. YHWH, therefore, will have to adapt his vocabulary to their mental grasp (v. 11) which he does in v. 13.[31]

(3) The first 'he' refers to the 'priest', the second to the 'prophet'. They are denounced here by Isaiah as he denounced them in v. 7 (in the singular). This disjunction is argued on the basis of the fact that the objects, 'knowledge' and 'message', also refer to the specific tasks of priests and prophets. The inebriety of these officials renders them unfit to instruct even little children.[32]

The text itself does not give decisive indications. The suggestion of a confrontation between the prophet and those accused would really be evident in the case of an address in the second person singular ('Whom will *you* teach?'), but this is not apparent. The passage as a whole avoids the impression of a direct clash between the prophet and his audience (v. 7 is also in the third person), perhaps in order to focus upon God's speaking to 'this people' (vv. 11,13) as it also reports an earlier direct contact between the same actants (v. 12). In addition, the use of the third person expresses distance and contempt (Procksch, 354). Just the same, we opt for the first interpretation considering that the wickedness of the denounced is rendered more salient if they not only lead a life of debauchery but also defy God's messenger. Moreover, the link between the verdict (v. 13) and the accusation (vv. [9-]10) is stronger if YHWH repeats the obtuse words which Isaiah's adversaries have ascribed to the latter, and turns them into a announcement of disaster.

[30] Lowth 1815: 468f.

[31] S.D. Luzzatto, XVI (published in Rosenmüller, *Scholia*); Van Selms 1973: 332f.; Petersen 1979: 109; Exum 1982: 111, 120f., 131-5; Deck 1991: 87f., but already Vitringa, 131.

[32] First proposed by J.A. Dathius, *Prophetae majores ex recensione textus Hebraei et versionum antiquarum Latine versi notisque philologicis et criticis illustrati*, Lipsiae 1779, quoted by Rosenmüller, 419; further Watts, 363; Tanghe 1993: 236-9, 245f.

In close connection with the previous question, the third focuses on the words *tsaw latsaw tsaw latsaw, qaw laqaw qaw laqaw ze'er sham ze'er sham* (vv. 10,13). If 'he teaches / he will cause to understand' refers to the denounced priests and prophets (the third opinion mentioned above), then Isaiah is imitating the unintelligible jabber of these drunkards. If these sentences refer to YHWH (the second opinion), then, in the prophet's view, God has only little children to instruct because the priests and prophets are drunk and his words are nonsensical to them.[33] If the accused priests and prophets are quoting Isaiah (the first opinion), then they are imitating his childish way of speaking which, while intelligible, is nevertheless not at their level of understanding.[34]

From the ancient versions on, translators and scholars have surmised that the words are not totally unintelligible but allude to cognate roots (צוה, 'to command' or צור, 'to afflict'; קו, 'measuring line', or קוה, 'to hope for'). Hence translations like: 'Expect affliction upon affliction, hope upon hope' (LXX), and the most frequent: 'For it is precept upon precept, line upon line' (RSV). One argument in favour of this interpretation is that the last clause certainly makes sense: 'A little here, a little there'. If this is so then why not the preceding clauses? The deciding factor here is that v. 11 characterizes the disputed words as 'foreign tongue'. The cheeky reproach of the adversaries will turn against themselves: God will indeed speak to them, not in the language of children, however, but in the tongue of a foreign conqueror. Thus, because of the comparison involved in the relation between v. 11 and v. 13, the difficult words must be understood perhaps as gibberish at first sight, but ultimately full of threat.

Exegesis by Verse

7-8 The perspective of salvation (vv. 5-6) abruptly gives way to a scene of intoxication which looks like a continuation of vv. 1,3 but differs from those verses in several respects. Firstly, the opening words 'These also' draw our attention to a new group which in the following line appears to consist of the priests and prophets.[35] It is not uncommon

---

[33] Wildberger, 1053, 1059; Petersen 1979: 108f.; Exum 1982: 121f.; Watts, 363.

[34] A special form of this interpretation considers the words as referring to the alphabet (the letter *q* does indeed follow the *ts*). The adversaries feel themselves treated in a schoolmasterly manner as if they were little children (Procksch, 354; Hallo 1958). There are many other, highly imaginative interpretations (for surveys, cf. Alexander, 451f.; Wildberger, 1053f.; Oswalt, 512).

[35] According to König (250f.), 'These also' refers to 'the remnant of his people' (v. 5), in the sense that there are also persons among them to be found who abuse their status. The literary genre of an announcement of salvation (vv. 5f.), however, supposes the end of all evil doing. Instead of an anaphoric use of the demonstrative pronoun a cataphoric use is more likely (J-M, §143 b).

to find these categories mentioned together (2 Kgs 23:2; Jer. 2:8,26; 6:13; 8:10; 14:18; 18:18; 23:11; 32:32; Ezek. 7:26; Mic. 3:11; Zeph. 3:4; Zech. 7:1ff.; Lam. 2:20), but in this instance it is not clear whether or not they are found within Ephraim, in addition to the group mentioned in vv. 1,3. Secondly, vv. 1,3 offer a drunken scene in which hardly anything hapens. The drunkards, moreover, are only vaguely identified with the ruling class by means of the metaphor 'crown'. In vv. 7-8, on the other hand, it is precisely the responsible classes of priests and prophets who are portrayed as taking part in a banquet of excessive drunkenness, perhaps even in the temple itself[36] (for similar invectives against the abuse of wine cf. 5:11ff.,22f.; 22:13; 28:1; 29:9f.; for accusations against the leading classes, cf. Jer. 2:8; 4:9; 5:31; 23:9ff.; Mic. 3:5ff.). Thirdly, priests and prophets are presented as failing in their public and professional duties (v. 7), something which is completely absent from vv. 1-4. While they should provide 'vision' and '(judicial) decision',[37] which would be the appropriate function of prophets and priests (cf. respectively Jer. 23:16ff.; Hab. 2:1,3 and Isa. 16:3; cf. Exod. 31:22; Deut. 17:8ff.; 19:17; 21:5; 32:31; Ezek. 44:24; Hos. 4:4ff.),[38] their output consists of nothing but loathsome vomit and filth (v. 8).

The coarse language of the scene is paradoxically worded in a sophisticated literary pattern,[39] further adding to the sense of moral decay. The climactic progression from 'to reel' and 'to stagger' to 'to totter' reflects increasing levels of misbehaviour: not only do the priests and prophets quaff wine, forbidden for priests (Lev. 10:8f.; Ezek. 44: 21; Hos. 4:11), they are themselves 'swallowed up by wine'.[40] The result is a disgusting spectacle of regurgitation. There is also a supporting literary side effect. By means of assonance, the Hebrew words for 'vomit' and 'filth', קיא and צֹאָה, anticipate the enigmatic words צַו and קַו of vv. 10,13.

These verses evoke a scene which is described in more detail and carries a different intention to that of vv. 1,3. This endorses the hypothesis

[36] According to some commentators, the term 'tables' would point to temple furniture (cf. Ezek. 40:38-43; Ps. 23:5; Wildberger, 1057; Tanghe 1993: 245), but the basis for this supposition is rather feeble (Alexander, 449f.; Feldmann, 329).

[37] Since the words for 'vision' and 'decision' are parallel to 'strong drink', some scholars interpret these terms as alternative words for specific sorts of drinks (cf. the survey of Watts, 361), It would be too rigid, however, to abandon the traditional explanation for this reason alone.

[38] For 'teaching' the commandments as another task of the priests, cf. Deut. 24:8; 33:10; 2 Kgs 17:27f.; Jer. 2:8; Ezek. 22:26; Mic. 3:11; Zeph. 3:4; Mal. 2:6-9.

[39] The three lines of v. 7 exhibit the syntactical sequence: S[ubject] M[odifier] V[erb] / M V; S V M / V M; V M / V M / V M. Moreover, the verbs rhyme with one another.

[40] There is no reason to suppose here a root different from בלע, 'to bewilder' (*pace* HALAT, 129; Wildberger, 1052f.; cf. TWAT, I, 659 [J.Schüpphaus]; Ges.[18], 153f.).

that the opening words 'These also', and perhaps even v. 7a as a whole, form a secondary seam which aims at linking this passage with what precedes. Meanwhile, the readers are invited to ask themselves where this tableau is to be located since there is not a single geographical indication.

9-10 The priests and prophets respond by simply denying Isaiah's right to read them a lesson. The terminology is quite specific. To supply 'knowledge' which stems from God (דעה: 1 Sam. 2:3; Isa. 9:11; 28:29; Ps. 73:11; Job 36:4; Prov. 24:14; Sir. 51:16)[41] is the privileged field of the priests just as it is the unique task of the prophets to inform the people about what they have 'heard' (שמועה: Isa. 53:1; Jer. 49:14; Ezek. 21: 12; Obad. 1; cf. the terms 'vision' and 'decision' for the same professional objectives in v. 7). The defence, however, centres neither on the question of Isaiah's right to hurl reproaches nor on their appropriateness, but on the question whether priests and prophets have to accept instruction ('to teach / to cause to understand') about the consequences of their religious expertise. This comes down to claiming that their special status within Israel dispenses them from responsibility in matters of moral behaviour.

V. 9b ('Those who are weaned from the milk, those taken from the breast') forms an apposition to 'Whom..?' in v. 9a and can be taken as either a question or an exclamation.[42] In the former case the addressees refuse to be treated like little children, in the latter they refer Isaiah to a kindergarten class as the appropriate audience for his lessons. In Ancient Near Eastern cultures the age of weaning was rather late, coinciding more or less with school age (1 Sam. 1:23f.).[43] The difference between a question and an exclamation has no bearing on the meaning of the verses. In both cases the prophets and the priests haughtily reject not only Isaiah's invective but also his authority.

As we explained above, we consider v. 10 to be a parody of Isaiah's 'knowledge / message' (v. 9) put forward by the priests and prophets. By means of strange words they ridicule his outburst against them (vv. 7f.). From the rhetorical point of view, v. 10 is a *reductio ad absurdum* that renders the questions of v. 9, by which the speakers reject Isaiah's invective, as not destined for them.[44] The parody implies that the words reflect something of the speaker and his message. They set the prophet up

---

[41] The appropriate term for 'the knowledge (of God)' which the priests are supposed to communicate is not דעה, but דעת (Isa. 11:2,9; 33:6; Hos. 2:22; 4:1; Jer. 2:8; 31:34; cf. *TWAT*, III, 507-10 [J. Botterweck]).

[42] Alexander (450f.) and some of his predecessors.

[43] Wildberger, 1059; Oswalt, 511.

[44] Van Selms 1973: 332f.: 'a motivated interrogative sentence'.

as a schoolmaster rattling off his lesson. The message is presented as poor language, hardly understandable because of its simplicity and consisting of nothing but a few catchwords.

In sharp contrast to the intention of Isaiah's adversaries, exegetes through the centuries have given full reign to their imagination and ingenuity in order to find all sorts of hidden meanings and allusions behind the words *tsaw latsaw tsaw latsaw, qaw laqaw qaw laqaw, ze'er sham ze'er sham*![45] Since these are presented as distorted language one can only look for the semantic content that offers itself at first hearing.

The first combination, *tsaw latsaw*, is commonly understood as alluding to the root צוה, 'to command'.[46] In this case it would mean something like 'precept upon precept' and expose the prophet's constant desire to control and find fault. The second, *qaw laqaw,* is more difficult. It is often considered as being on the same wavelength as *tsaw* if *qaw*, which means 'measuring line', can be understood as 'norm' (NAB: 'rule upon rule'). This is questionable, however, since the metaphoric use of the word occurs in oracles of judgement and salvation where it serves as God's instrument of destruction or rebuilding (cf. respectively 2 Kgs 21:13; Isa. 28:17; 34:11,17; Lam.2:8; [other word in Amos 7:7ff.] and Jer. 31:39; Ezek. 47:3; Zech. 1:16).[47] The meaning, therefore, would tend rather towards a threat of punishment. The third word-group, *ze'er sham,* does not constitute scrambled speech and is mostly translated even when the other terms are simply recorded in transliterated Hebrew. This last word-group, however, is open to a variety of interpretations and thus also carries the stigma of unclear language. It should, therefore, be treated in the same way as the two preceding word groups. Its ambiguity lies in the question whether *ze'er* applies to what is taught or the one being taught. In the former case, it can have a spatial or a temporal meaning, i.e.: 'Here a trifle, there a trifle' or 'Now a trifle, then a trifle'. In the latter case the schoolmaster might use it to call to his pupils: 'Little one, here! Little one, there!'. This explanation, however, is less probable since the word *ze'er* is never applied to persons. In any event, the tendency remains the same: Isaiah's jabbering is exposed as proof of his meddlesomeness and sermonising.

---

[45] For a survey of far-fetched interpretations, often based on changes in the text or the alleged use of cognate languages cf. Wildberger, 1053ff.; Oswalt, 512; Tanghe 1993: 246ff.; for a survey of the ancient versions, cf. Procksch, 355.

[46] The word occurs in one other place, Hos. 5:11, where it is also controversial; cf. F.I. Andersen, D.N. Freedman, *Hosea* (AB, 24), Garden City NY 1980, 409f.; *HALAT*, 946.

[47] *TWAT*, VI, 1223f. (K.-M. Beyse).

In summary, we may state that the strange words of v. 10 and v. 13 evoke something like 'precept upon precept, measuring line upon measuring line, here a trifle, there a trifle'. If translated this way, however, the words completely lose their character of stupid language. The paraphrase of REB, therefore, deserves serious consideration: 'A babble of meaningless noises, mere sounds on every side'.

11-12 These verses contain the introduction to God's verdict (v. 13) and are tuned in to the priests' and prophets' offensive caricature of Isaiah in v. 10. The opening particle כי of v. 11 adversatively links up with the same particle in v. 10 and twists the mockery into menace.[48] YHWH will speak in the same way as they have imputed of his prophet: 'with a stammering lip and with a foreign tongue'. The first phrase, לעגי שפה, refers primarily to backward language, but has the connotation of 'mocking' language since לעג means both 'to stammer' (Isa. 33:19; Hos. 7:16) and, more frequently, 'to mock' (Isa. 37:22; Jer.20:7; Ezek. 23:32; 36:4; Ps. 2:4; 35:16; 44:14; 59:9; 79:4; 123:4; Job 34:7).[49] The second phrase, לשון אחרת, bears upon the unintelligible speech of foreign nations (cf. the same topic, although not the same term, in Deut. 28:49; Jer. 5:15; Ezek. 3:5).[50]

From the background of PI as a whole we may infer that the words 'with a foreign tongue' are aimed at the Assyrians (33:19; 36:11). Their political and military power is the instrument by which God will punish Israel for its own good (8:1-10; 10:5-19; chs. 36-39). What we know from the larger context, however, should not be inferred too quickly and thereby spoil the proper dynamics of the narrower context, i.e. its more allusive than explicit character. By not mentioning the Assyrians the prophet creates a sort of taboo and enhances the ominous impact of the announcement.

The direction of speech widens from the priests and prophets to include 'this people', although this change does not necessarily point to the beginning of a new literary unit. The term 'this people', often used negatively, applies in Isaiah to the people of Judah (6:9f.; 8:6,11f.; 9:15; 28:11,14; 29:13f.). It may serve, therefore, as the first indication that the denounced classes of v. 7 are to be located in Jerusalem. Their

[48] Rosenmüller, 415; Oswalt, 512.

[49] Already Hitzig, 341. Some scholars assume two different roots, others one root לעג. Interference of the two meanings, however, is most probable here; cf. respectively *TWAT*, IV, 583 (Ch. Barth) and *HALAT*, 506; *TWAT*, IV, 602 (B. Kedar-Kopfstein). According to Tanghe (1993: 248f.) only 'to mock' applies here.

[50] The interpretation of Tanghe (1993: 249f.), 'a different meaning', in the sense of ambiguity, relies too much on the parallelism with 'a mocking lip' and on the use of לשון in the Babylonian Talmud.

perversion is only symptomatic of that of the population as a whole, and the verdict on their rejection of Isaiah's message will fall upon the entire people (cf. v. 14: 'you, who rule this people in Jerusalem').

The primary point of interest, however, is not the verdict as such or the impending invasion by a world power, but the relation between 'this people' and their God (v. 12). What YHWH has already said is once again called to mind. As with the Assyrians in v. 11, he is not mentioned by name but referred to by a relative sentence: 'he who has said to them'. (Only in v. 13 does his proper name, YHWH, occur.) While this construction, with the rather prose-like relative particle אשׁר, leads one to suspect that the verse forms a later insertion, it still has quite a definite impact: before recording the verdict the prophet reminds his audience of the history of God's words to Israel. From God's side it was an act of benevolence which called upon Israel for an act of commitment but his people's response was sheer lack of commitment.[51]

God's earlier message to Israel is enclosed by the antithetical clauses: 'he who has said to them'[52] and 'Yet they would not hear'. The direct speech itself contains a commandment: 'give rest to the weary', enclosed by two formulas of allocation: 'this is your resting-place' and 'this is your place of repose'.[53] The focal points of these formulae are the entry of Israel into the land and the dedication of the temple in Zion. When YHWH assigned his people the place where they would find rest after their wanderings, he had fulfilled his promise. The full realisation of the promise would only come when he himself set up his abode among his people in Jerusalem (1 Kgs 8:56; cf. Deut. 12:10; Josh. 21: 44f.). The retrospective nature of v. 12, therefore, is paramount to a reminder of God's faithfulness to his people, from the allocation of the land to his choosing Zion as his dwelling.

With regard to the oracle itself, the question arises as to what the demonstrative pronouns in 'This is your resting-place... this is your place of repose' refer: intratextually to the command 'give rest to the weary'

---

[51] Tanghe's remark (1993: 252) that v. 12 interrupts the connection between v. 13 and v. 11, and therefore must be considered as a deuteronomistic homiletic insertion, does not recognise its appropriateness for locating the addressee, 'this people'.

[52] Either the relative at the beginning of v. 12 has its antecedent in the immediately preceding 'this people' ('to whom he has said') or it is used absolutely ('he who has said to them'; cf. Gen. 15:4; Numb. 22:6; Josh. 10:11; BrSyn, §151; J-M, §145 a). The latter interpretation is to be preferred since only then is the subject of v. 11 ('he will speak') determined.

[53] The parallelism of v. 12 would be perfect if the clause 'this is your place of repose' were followed by a clause like 'let the needy repose' (הרגיעו לאביון), parallel to 'give rest to the weary' (Roberts 1980). There is, however, no text critical evidence whatsoever for such a reconstruction (Mosca 1984).

(Redaq, Hitzig, Alexander, Duhm, Feldmann, Procksch) or extratex-
tually to the territory in which the addressees are living (Ibn Ezra,
Dillmann-Kittel, König, Fischer)? The former interpretation supposes a
metaphorical use of the concept 'rest' ('Your rest will consist in giving
rest to the weary') whereas the latter understands it geographically
('Since this place of rest has been given to you, you should give rest to
the weary'). The metaphorical interpretation brings the text to bear upon
the political situation of Judah under the threat of an Assyrian invasion:
the people will gain rest, i.e. political security, by not imposing war contributions on the poor. In a geographical explanation the oracle would
point to social ethics in general. It is a fact that the concept 'rest' (מנוחה)
is basically connected to a concrete location (Gen. 49:15; Num. 10:33;
Deut. 12:9; 1 Kgs 8:56; Isa. 11:10; 32:18; Mic. 2:10; Zech. 9:1; Ps.
23:2; 95:11; 132:14).[54] It is more likely, therefore, that the text intends
to draw our attention to the place to which God has led and settled his
people.[55] The term 'weary' (עיף) confirms this view since it carries the
connotation of being on a (military) march (Deut. 25:18f.; Judg. 8:4f.; 2
Sam 16:14; Isa. 5:27; 46:1) and in need of refreshments (Gen. 25:29f.;
2 Sam. 17:29; Isa. 29:8; Jer. 31: 25; Job 22:7; Prov. 25:25).

In this way, the oracle in question presents YHWH as he spoke to Israel
at the moment of entry into Canaan, when he attached a social code to
his handing over of the promised land. The tranquillity and prosperity of
this land (cf. 1 Kgs 5:5) excludes no one from a share in its benefits.[56]
Nevertheless, the history of this programme can be summed up in one
sentence which hails from the theology of the covenant: 'They have
been unwilling to listen' (לא אבוא שמוע: Lev. 26:21; Isa. 1:19f.; 30:9;
Ezek. 3:7; 20:8; Ps.81:12).[57]

13 The past entails the future. Since Israel has refused to take to heart
the quite comprehensible message by which God admitted them into the
land (v. 12), the word of God will now come upon them in the shape of
the same distorted and barely comprehensible terms by which the prophets and the priests render Isaiah's indictment: *tsaw latsaw tsaw latsaw,
qaw laqaw qaw laqaw ze'er sham ze'er sham* (cf. the explanation of v.
10). These words will now be spoken by a 'foreign tongue' (v. 11).
What the leaders have taken as mumbling incompetence will turn out to
be the effective instrument of the nation's destruction (Watts, 364).

[54] Also the rare parallel term מרגעה is connected to a concrete location (cf. Jer. 6:16;
31:2).
[55] *TWAT*, V, 304ff. (H.D. Preuß): The Old Testament concept of rest is not only connected to the promise of land and temple but also to God's guidance through the desert.
[56] Gonçalves 1986: 193.
[57] Arambarri 1990: 283-8.

In the classical structure of a judgement oracle the element of God's initiative is followed by its consequences. Here, the former, v. 13a, is expressed in veiled terms, leaving the latter, v. 13b, to bear the full weight of the necessary information. We can hardly deny its originality, although its likeness to 8:15 suggests that it might be a redactional addition.[58] Moreover, v. 13b combines two metaphors, to collapse and to be captured, which are in keeping with the passage as a whole. The topic 'to stumble backward, and be broken', brought about by God's intervention, is in line with the heavy drinking which made the prophets and priests totter (v. 7).[59] The topic 'to be snared, and taken' (cf. 8:14f.) builds on the threat of foreign invasion (v. 11). Both stand in meaningful contrast to the theme of rest (v. 12). As a whole, therefore, v. 13b is worded in terms which specifically aim at the denounced socio-religious classes of v. 7 and suggests that any attempt to escape from captivity will fail.

Which power will bring about this ruin? It follows from vv. 11,13 that, on the initiative of YHWH, a people 'with a foreign tongue' will form the threat behind the abortive flight. The first metaphor, 'to go, and stumble backward, and be broken' does not necessarily suggest a cause (שבר niphal with persons as subject: 1 Sam. 4:18; Isa. 8:15; Jer. 48:25; Ezek. 29:7; 30:22; Ps.34:21; 37:17; Job 31:22; Dan. 8:25).[60] The second metaphor, 'to be snared, and taken' (יקש and לכד: 8:14f.; 24:18; 29:21; Jer. 5:26; 50:24; Ps.9:16; 35:8; 124:7; Prov. 6:5; 9:16;12:13) does suppose a cause, in first instance a trap or snare (8:14) and in the second a catcher or trapper who is more a human being than God. The over-all suggestion of the combined metaphors is that the people to whom God's word is addressed are themselves heading for a fall.

The similarity of v. 13b with 8:15 raises the question of the literary-historical interdependency of these verses.[61] A comparison of the two

---

[58] Gonçalves 1986: 192. Petersen (1979: 101) confounds mysteriousness with unintelligibility in arguing that v. 13b forms an attempt on the part of a redactor to make intelligible what was intended to be unintelligible (v. 13a).

[59] Exum 1982: 122. Starting with Ibn Ezra (129) some scholars explain the verb 'to go' as 'to go to Egypt for help' (30:2; 31:1). This would strengthen the political background of the passage. The language as a whole, however, is too metaphorical to make this plausible.

[60] TWAT, VII, 1034 (B. Knipping): The undetermined nature of the verb form leaves it to the reader to connect the fate of 'being broken' with an action of God (cf. Ezek. 26:2; 27:34).

[61] According to Vermeylen (1977: 227, 390) 28:13b forms the necessary conclusion of the whole oracle, whereas 8:15 is a secondary explanation of v. 14, giving the perspective of the redactor. According to Petersen (1979:110), however, 28:13b draws upon the language of 8:15.

lines reveals that in 8:15, the combination of 'to stumble and fall' and 'to be taken' logically follows from the metaphors 'stone and rock' and 'trap and snare' in the preceding verse. In 28:13 the semantic link with the context is less evident although vv. 11ff. ('foreign tongue', 'resting-place' and 'weary') may function as a source of the flight imagery. The first word, therefore, 'that they may go', which is lacking in 8:15, is most appropriate, in the sense of 'to set out', in 28:13. Likewise, the ex-pression 'to stumble backwards' (כשל אחור is a *hapax legomenon*), as opposed to the combination 'to stumble and to fall' in 8:15, fits better in the context of 28:13, since it evokes falling into the hands of a foreign enemy which is made explicit in 'to be snared, and taken'. As a result, there is no need to consider v. 13b a redactional conclusion.

3. Vv. 14-22: 'Absurdly in Love with Death'

Introduction to the Exegesis: Form and Setting

Classical prophetic literary forms determine the structure of the pas-sage. It opens in v. 14 with the messenger formula and a direct address, the first in the chapter: 'you swaggerers, who rule this people in Jerusa-lem'. The indictment, v. 15, is couched in a quotation from the address-ees, and the judgement in a divine oracle which covers vv. 16-19, the 'I' in vv. 16f. referring to God, and the direct address continuing into v. 19. The semantic correspondences between these two forms bear the inten-tion of the passage. The divine oracle moves from a retrospective glance at God's election of Zion (v. 16) to the announcement of a juridical in-quiry (v. 17a) and a punishment by means of a calamity (v. 17b). It is followed by a refutation of the addressees' proud statement of self-assur-ance (v. 18, cf. v. 15).

At the same time, vv. 15-18 exhibit an evident, tightly concentric pat-tern (A-B-C-D-C'-B'-A'), built by a large number of recurring words in the corresponding segments v. 15a-b' and v. 18, v. 15b'' and v. 17b, v. 16a-b'' and v. 17a, which has the statement: 'One who trusts will not shake' (v. 16b''') as its core.[62]

Vv. 19-22, as a whole or in part, are generally considered an inser-tion.[63] Indeed, v. 19 broadens the effect of the punishment in time while,

---

[62] Bailey (1996: 16ff.) speaks of 'the parable of the two builders'.

[63] According to Vermeylen (1977: 396-9) and Gonçalves (1986: 200), the whole pas-sage is secondary, according to Wildberger (1070, 1078) only v. 19 and v. 22. Melugin (1974: 309f.) deemed v. 19 to be part of the original oracle and considered vv. 20-22 to be an addition. – Sweeney (360, 363) includes v. 20 in the oracle of YHWH but the lack of

according to vv. 17f., this punishment is radical and does not bear repeating. Yet, v. 19 is not necessarily a post-exilic creation. In this metaphorical language, the time adjuncts 'morning by morning' and 'by day
and by night' can also indicate that when the destruction comes there
will not be a single moment of relief.[64] One can only say that it perfectly
fits in the post-exilic perspective. With regard to v. 20, it is hard to tell.
The verse contains a proverb which does not continue the topics of vv.
15-19, yet this would be a feeble argument for a later origin. Although
YHWH is referred to in the third person in v. 21, the first half of the verse
belongs to the same Davidic tradition as the Ariel song (29:1-8) which is
certainly Isaianic, and the second half contains the very Isaianic theme
of YHWH's 'strange work' which anticipates the conclusion of the chapter concerning the wonderful counsel of YHWH (v. 29). V. 21, therefore,
must be Isaianic by origin or a perfect imitation.

In v. 22 ('do not swagger') we again find the prophet addressing the
same audience as in v. 14 ('you, swaggerers') with an admonition and a
resumé of his revelation. Some scholars consider v. 22 also as an interpolation from the same 'apocalyptic' writer who added 10:23. The announcement of judgement, however, does not necessarily exclude an admonition, at the level of either the prophet or the final redactor. Furthermore, the extended parable by which this composite chapter ends (vv.
23-29), highlights the wonderful counsel of YHWH, which is certainly not
a *Chiffre* for lasting disaster.

These considerations lead to the following structure:

14-15   speech of the prophet
     14   call to listen and address
     15   indictment: quotation as proof of culpable self-confidence
16-19   oracle of YHWH
     16   - messenger formula
           - retrospective of God's founding Zion
     17   announcement of juridical inquiry and chastisement
     18   refutation of self-exaltation
     19   chastisement extended in time
20-22   confirmation by the prophet
     20   proverb
     21   comparison from Israel's history
     22   conclusion

a direct address and the literary genre of a proverb recommend to take v. 20 with vv. 21-
22 as prophetic speech.

[64] Courtesy Roy F. Melugin in his paper "Understanding Isaiah 28-32", read at the
International Meeting of the Society of Biblical Literature in Cracow (July 1998).

A too rigid form critical approach would tend to obstruct the discovery of the passage's intention. The beginning of the divine oracle (v. 16: 'Therefore') looks like an announcement of judgement. Instead of the usual present tense, however, we find a preterite: 'Behold, I myself have laid for a foundation a stone' (cf. 'Notes'). Many scholars change this into: 'Behold, I am laying' but without sufficient reason. It is a unique feature of this oracle that the announcement of doom is projected against a salvific act in the past, i.e. God's founding of Zion.

Exegesis by Verse

14 The passage is linked to that which precedes it by way of a redactional 'Therefore' (לכן), the call to listen referring especially to the accusation that 'they have been unwilling to listen' to God's command (v. 12), and to the announcement of a strange sounding word of YHWH (v. 13). From now on the shroud of secrecy covering this word will be lifted. The addressees who up to this point have lurked in the shadows now come to the fore. For the first time in the chapter, they are spoken to directly and characterised as 'swaggerers' (אנשי לצון), a phrase which in Hebrew has assonance with 'Zion', and as 'rulers in Jerusalem' (מֹשלי), which in Hebrew can mean also 'derisive proverb-makers' (Num. 21:27; Ezek. 16:44; Joel 2:17; Sir. 44:4).[65] The negative content of these titles can only refer to the arrogance with which the opponents in the previous passage have ridiculed the words of the prophet (v. 10). Finally, the phrase 'who rule this people in Jerusalem' suggests that the leading classes have deluded the people. This accords with the smooth transition from 'priest and prophet' in v. 7 to 'this people' in v. 11. It follows, therefore, that v. 14 as a whole brings about the identification of the drunken priests and prophets in the previous passage with the addressees here. This literary process is similar to the assimilation of the priests and prophets in v. 7 to the drunkards of Ephraim in v. 1. In other words, the three categories are placed on a par in such a way that the rulers in Jerusalem, the only ones to be directly addressed, form the climax. By avoiding explicit mention of the geographical location of the second group the alignment of the three is facilitated. Thus, the prophecy against them which follows has to be seen against the background of the preceding oracles.

15 The quotation here serves as an accusation. It describes the rulers from the vantage point of the prophet, at least in as far as they speak

---

[65] Wildberger, 1063, 1072; Exum 1982: 124; *HALAT*, 611; *pace* Gonçalves 1986: 203. The parallel occurrence of the nouns מֹשל and מליצה in Hab. 2:6 is a strong argument in favour of the negative aspect presupposed in 'rulers'.

highly of their reliance on 'lies / falsehood', but probably also in as far as they vaunt their bond with 'death / sheol'. What can this mean?

The metaphorical character of the latter statement is obvious: the speakers claim to have safeguarded themselves against ultimate evil. Does this point to the political reality of Judah's alliances with neighbouring peoples, especially Egypt, or to the worship of chthonic deities? The former case would present Isaiah as satirically characterizing the allies as pernicious forces for Judah, together with a possible hidden reference to their veneration of Moth and Osiris, the Syrian and Egyptian gods of death and the underworld.[66] The latter case would imply that the addressees themselves openly confessed their devotion to the underworld deities following an ancient Canaanite tradition which had tenaciously survived in the Israelite popular religion of the 8th and 7th centuries. It is indeed reported that the kings of Judah, from Solomon to Manasseh, took the initiative of setting up cults to foreign gods (1 Kgs 11:1-13; 2 Kgs 21:1-11; Zeph. 1:5). Given the fact that in vv. 7-22, priests and prophets as well as the rulers of Jerusalem are accused, a more specific explanation of 'the covenant with death' might imply that Isaiah is referring here to the practice of necromancy (cf. 1 Samuel 28; 2 Kgs 23:24).[67] After all, BI itself bears witness to the fact that the topic of consulting the dead concerning the future played a role in the controversy between the prophet and his adversaries (8:19; 19:3; 29:4). For these, the practice was perfectly consistent with belief in YHWH (Mic. 3:6f.,11), even though it was severely condemned by the law under priestly and prophetic inspiration (Lev. 19:31; 20:27; Deut. 18:10-14).

The frequent problem of calling upon the socio-religious context of prophetic oracles is that the textual data are too scant for the purpose. In the present case both hypotheses are plausible: an attack against the foreign policy and an accusation of necromancy. Neither is strong enough to exclude the other. The prophecy may indeed be a fitting condemnation of the necromancy perpetrated and propagated by syncretistic circles in Jerusalem, since the terms 'covenant' and 'death' are quite exceptional for PI (respectively 24:5; 33:8 and 25:8; 'sheol' occurs more often: 5:14; 7:11; 14:9,11,15; 38:10). At the same time, however, the quotation is fully moulded to Isaiah's own subsequent rejection. It is at least striking that the wording is not syncretistic at all, rather it presents the situation of the speakers as aberrant. Any mention of YHWH (cf. Mic.

---

[66] Fischer, 188; Kissane, 306f.; Snijders, 284.
[67] Duhm,174f.; Dillmann-Kittel, 252f.; Wildberger, 1073ff.; F. Stolz, "Der Streit um die Wirklichkeit in der Südreichsprophetie des 8. Jahrhunderts", WuD 12 (1973) 9-30, esp. 24; Van der Toorn 1988.

We prefer to interpret the terms in connection with the immediately following v. 16. The refuge chosen by the speakers will turn out to be deceitful, in contrast to the trustworthiness of the edifice founded by YHWH.[76] The terms כזב and שקר differ only in that the former refers more to deceit by means of words, 'lies', while the latter includes treachery by way of deeds, 'falsehood'.[77] In this way, the self-accusing character of the quotation is stronger. On the one hand, the speakers proclaim their blatant preference for the deceptive, deified powers of destruction instead of trustworthy YHWH, while on the other hand, they fully ignore the absolute obligation of social justice as the one ground of salvation, so much so that they have to be confronted with that ever valid standard by YHWH himself in the following verdict (v. 17).

16 The messenger formula carries the title 'Lord' (אדני), which is quite characteristic of PI (Wildberger, 1637f.). In connection with 'YHWH' it occurs mostly in the context of judgement (3:15; 7:7; 10:23f.; 22:5,12,14f.; 25:8; 28:16,22; 30:15). It embodies, therefore, God's dominion over Israel as it is evident in her history.

The topic of trustworthiness continues to be the subject matter, while a new metaphor serving it enters the field: 'foundation stone'. God refers to the fact that he himself has founded Zion, indeed on a valuable stone, in opposition to the deceitful refuge which the accused have chosen through their covenant with death (v. 15).[78] The terminology is akin to that of the narrative of the construction of Solomon's temple (1 Kgs 5:31; cf. 7:9-12). YHWH's involvement with Zion, therefore, is presented as reliable grounds for security.

The terms for 'stone' are problematic. Generally speaking, both from a literary and an archaeological point of view, it remains doubtful that they refer to the stone used during the first stone laying ceremony or to the bedrock of Mount Zion.[79] If 'stone' is to be understood in a collective sense (Gen. 3:11; Deut. 8:9; 2 Sam. 5:11; 1 Kgs 6:7; 2 Kgs 12:13; Jer. 51:26; Job 28:2), then any basis for a specific stone is lacking.

More important than architectural evidence, however, is the question of what the stone symbolises. A messianic interpretation reaches back to

---

[76] M.A. Klopfenstein, *Die Lüge nach dem Alten Testament. Ihr Begriff, ihre Bedeutung und ihre Beurteilung*, Zürich 1964, 147-52, 234f. esp. 151: 'כזב und שקר sind theologische Urteile Jesajas über eine falsche religiöse Haltung des judäischen Volkes in einer Zeit äußerster Bedrängnis durch die Assyrermacht'; Wildberger, 1073; *TWAT*, IV, 121 (R. Mosis).

[77] *THAT*, II, 1011 (M.A. Klopfenstein).

[78] Lindblom 1955: 126f.

[79] Gonçalves (1986: 212f.) offers a good survey of the opinions involved.

the ancient versions (LXX: 'Who believes *in him*'; Tg) and the New Testament (1 Pet. 2:6; Rom. 9:33), and still finds followers among ecclesiastical exegetes. Closely related to this is the explanation that the Davidic kingship is meant, especially in the person of king Hezekiah. A different current of thought considers the faithful community or the remnant which survives the exile as the well founded stronghold against the calamities of politics. Thirdly, from a specific understanding of Israelite prophecy, the ethical programme of this movement is conceived as the tested stone. Finally, some interpreters, building on the affinity of v. 16b'' with 7:9b and 8:14, see YHWH himself as the cornerstone.[80]

It is evident that all these explanations depart from some extratextual concept, most being based on the interpretation that God is establishing something new: 'Behold, I am laying'. In a past tense interpretation of the opening words 'Behold, I myself have laid', the foundation stone cannot but refer to YHWH's election of Zion as his abode. The cultic language of v. 15b'' admits this specific understanding of 'Zion', and there is no reason to regard this understanding of the temple as contrary to prophetic preaching.[81] According to PI's inaugural vision, YHWH's dominion over Israel's history is founded on his kingship as he resides in the temple (Isa. 6; 24:23). Moreover, in the true Yahwistic understanding proclaimed by PI, God's presence in Zion is essentially bound to an ethical programme: 'YHWH has founded Zion, and the needy among his people will find refuge in her' (14:32). It is an on-going theme of PI that God dwells on Zion (8:18), but his protective presence there is indissolubly bound to the observance of righteousness (1:27), and if need be, will only continue after a painful judgement (4:4f.; 10:12,24f.,32; 12:6; 29:8; 30:19; 31:4f.,9; 33:14, 20).

V. 16b'' ('One who trusts will not shake') has been divorced from its context in the theological discussion concerning the nature of faith or confidence. Here, the verse line must be explained against its textual background and in connection with 7:9, a strongly cognate statement of the same prophet. Seen syntactically, the saying is a compound nominal clause which should clarify specific elements of the preceding verbal clause. It is striking, however, that not a single component of v. 16b'' refers syntactically to anything in the foregoing clause. Nevertheless, the very first word, the participle המאמין, 'one who trusts' (literally 'one who takes a stable stand, gains stability for himself'[82]), is semantically

---

[80] Surveys in Alexander, 454f.; Lindblom 1955; Wildberger, 1076f.; Berder 1996: 129-33.

[81] J.D. Levenson, "The Temple and the World", *JR* 64 (1984) 275-98.

[82] For the problem of how to ascertain the basic meaning of the verb, cf. *TWAT*, I, 313-33 (A. Jepsen).

related to the preceding noun group, 'a cornerstone, valuable for a foundation', so much so that the lack of an element which refers to 'cornerstone' is quite striking. This leads the reader to fill in as the object of trust not the cornerstone itself which is not mentioned, but the whole founding act of YHWH. By means of this *ellipsis*, the verb becomes an explicit theological term (as is the case in other instances where the verb, אמן *hiphil*, is used absolutely: Exod. 4:31; Isa. 7:9; Ha. 1:5[83]; Ps.116:10).

It is remarkable that the subject is in the singular, is not specified and implies a condition ('if one trusts'). The sentence sounds, therefore, like a motto or a proverb, and aims at a larger group than the plural addressees of v. 15.[84] This has led scholars to assume that it forms, or refers to, the inscription on the cornerstone,[85] since stones such as these were placed *on*, not *under* the ground,[86] and we know from Ancient Near Eastern texts that large monuments received a foundation inscription.[87] A different interpretation presents itself from recent research on levels of communication in literary texts: the direction of speech can change without a formula to mark the change.[88] In this sense, the specific character of v. 16b´´ can also be explained as due to the author presenting God as expressing himself about the individual mentioned in the preceding verses, i.e. the person who has been attacked and mocked by the addressees in v. 9: 'Whom will he teach knowledge, whom will he make to understand the message?'. After all, it is for this reason that God pronounces judgement upon these people (cf. v. 14 and the messenger formula in v. 16). Moreover, there are other texts in which God encourages his prophet who suffers from the lack of confidence of his fellow countrymen (8:11-18; cf. 6:5ff.).

This explanation is in line with what scholars lately recognise as one objective of the final redactor of BI: to present the prophet Isaiah as an example of someone who obediently accepted the message of salvation

[83]   A.S. van der Woude, *Habakuk. Zefanja* (POT), Nijkerk 1978, 20f.

[84]   According to Gonçalves (1986: 216), v. 16b´´ is directed to the rulers mentioned in v. 14, the singular participle expressing only the condition which restricts the validity of the cornerstone promise.

[85]   Procksch, 358; S. Mowinckel, *He That Cometh*, Oslo 1956, 135; M. Tsevat, *TWAT*, I, 591f.

[86]   K. Galling, "Serubbabel und der Wiederaufbau des Tempels in Jerusalem"; in: *Verbannung und Heimkehr. Beiträge zur Geschichte und Theologie Israels im 6. und 5. Jahrhundert v. Chr. (FS W. Rudolph)* (ed. A. Kuschke), Tübingen 1961, 67-96, esp. 72ff.

[87]   *ANET*, 499ff.

[88]   A similar phenomenon has been observed with regard to the related text Isa. 7:9; cf. C. Hardmeier, "Gesichtspunkte pragmatischer Erzähltextanalyse", *WuD* 15 (1979) 33-54.

through judgement and was saved for that reason. By means of this presentation, then, the final author addresses himself to the audience to
whom he transmits the prophecies of Isaiah, in short the readers of BI.[89]

The prospect which God holds out to the person who meets this condition is that 'he will not shake'. This negative term (חוש *hiphil*; cf.
'Notes') says little about the political consequences of what apparently
is a promise of salvation. As a metaphor it is in line with the preceding
metaphor of a solid foundation and can be compared with the boast of
the ruling class: 'The scourge of flooding will not come upon us' (v.
15). In other words, the expression does not describe what trust in God
in general will yield in psychological or spiritual terms, but only what
can be expected with regard to the concrete calamity of a foreign invasion which even the prophet's opponents are awaiting (v. 15): whoever
trusts in YHWH's commitment to his dwelling place Zion, will find out
that this place does not topple down.

Another text of PI in which the same verb 'to trust' occurs, sheds
more light on v. 16b˝. It runs: 'If you will not believe, surely you shall
not be established' (7:9 RSV), literally: 'If you do not take a stable
stand, i.e. trust, you will have no stability' (אם לא תאמינו כי לא תאמנו; the
verb אמן occurs here in the *hiphil* and the *niphal*). Here, the condition is
explicitly worded, and the *hiphil* verb form is again used absolutely.
This allows us to take the whole political situation in which the house of
David finds itself, described in 7:1-6, as the subject matter of the act of
trust, against the background of God's promise to David: 'Your house
and your kingdom shall have stability (נאמן) forever' (2 Sam. 7;16).[90]
The analogies between the context of 7:9 and that of 28:16 are mani-
fold. Against the background of the threat of a foreign invader (in ch.7
Aram and Ephraim, in ch.28 'the scourge of flooding', i.e. Assyria), the
opponents of the prophet (in ch.7 Ahaz and the house of David, in ch.28
the rulers in Jerusalem) are warned that only trust in God's earlier
salvific activity on behalf of his people (in ch.7 the election of David, in
ch.28 the foundation of Jerusalem) will help them to escape ruin. Does
this imply that the prophet is taking a concrete political stand? For both
chapters, it can hardly be argued that the call to trust involves a political
programme nor does the verb 'to trust' include some concept of God or
a specific religious attitude other than taking God's promise and his loy-

---

[89] Ackroyd 1978: 16-48; Conrad 1991. A consistent approach to BI along this line
comes to the fore in the studies of Seitz 1991 and 1993.

[90] E. Würthwein, "Jesaja 7,1-9. Ein Beitrag zu dem Thema: Prophetie und Politik";
in: *Theologie als Glaubenswagnis (FS K. Heim)* (ed. Evang.-Theol. Fakultät Tübingen),
(Furche-Studien, 23), Hamburg 1954, 47-63.

alty throughout history seriously and acting on the basis of this assurance.

17-18 These four lines resume the three lines of the quotation by repeating many of the terms used therein: v. 17/v. 15b´´, v. 18a/v. 15a, v. 18b/v. 15b´ (according to the pattern ABC / CAB). The first three lines (vv. 17-18a) open with future tenses (*w^eqatal*). Syntactically, these continue the opening formula of v. 16 ('Behold, I myself have laid a stone') as if the latter had opened with the same time perspective ('Behold, I am laying') by means of the usual form (הנני with the participle יוסד).[91] The first line announces God's intervention (v. 17a: 'I will make'), the second and third its consequences (vv. 17b-18a: third person). In this way, the past founding act (v. 16) and the present establishment of a measuring line (v. 17a) can be seen as forming the one building activity of YHWH.

The terms used for the measurement in v. 17a do not necessarily refer to the construction of a monument, they can also refer to its inspection ('line / plummet': 2 Kgs 21:13; cf. 1 Kgs 7:23; Amos 7:7ff.; Lam. 2:8). In reply to the claim of the rulers of Jerusalem that they rely on 'lies / falsehood' (v. 15b´´), God proclaims that he will use the measuring instruments of 'righteousness / justice' to test the building he has founded. The presupposition of the metaphor which links this answer to the quotation is that the rulers had been given the task of finishing the building. YHWH comes to test the result of their work and disapproves. In this way, God's authority is brought to the fore together with the recklessness of the leaders.

'Righteousness / justice' (משפט / צדקה) is a word pair (or adjacent pair) which runs throughout PI and TI (56:1; 58:2; 59:9,14). The two words, while jointly expressing the order of social justice, differ in that 'righteousness' (משפט) points to judiciary and legislative decisions (v. 6) and 'justice' (צדקה) to concrete acts of just behaviour.[92] In PI the pair occurs both in texts commonly ascribed to the prophet himself (5:7,16; 16:5) and in texts of which the authorship is disputed (1:21,27; 9:6; 26:9; 32:1,16; 33:5).[93] Since v. 17, as the counterpart of v. 15b´´, is

---

[91] For הנני with participle followed by *w^eqatal*, cf. Isa. 13:17-19; 29:14; 37:7; for הנה with separate subject and participle followed by *w^eqatal*, cf. Isa. 3:1-4; 8:7f.; 10:33f.; 17:1; 19:1; 24:1; 26:21; 39:6.

[92] *TWAT*, VI, 905-8 (B. Johnson). For an extensive survey of the semantic content of this word pair and its history, cf. H. Niehr, *Herrschen und Richten. Die Wurzel špṭ im Alten Orient und im Alten Testament* (FzB, 54), Würzburg 1986, 179-306, 358-61. Krašovec (1988: 82ff.), on the contrary, interprets the word pair as referring to qualities of God.

[93] Watters 1976: 156, nr. 36.

strongly anchored in the structure of the context, the occurrence of the word pair here is likely to be original. It is here, therefore, that we meet the ethical message of the historical Isaiah expressed in words which were considered worthy of constituting a refrain throughout the book. Its value lies in the fact that it opposes ethics to the manipulation of transcendent powers (v. 15: death and sheol) as the one guarantee for the unassailability of the place chosen by YHWH.

V. 17b describes the consequences of God's measuring as a countering the initiative taken by his adversaries to secure a place of protection from the flood. The word pair 'refuge of lies / hiding place' takes up the terms of v. 15b″ (only 'falsehood' is left out). The calamity itself is painted in the same terms, 'hail / flooding waters' (ברד / מים ישפטו), that were used for the calamity which will come over Ephraim (v. 1). The depiction of the calamity here is less elaborate, making this verse a sort of quotation or reference. Its impact, however, should not be underestimated: 'the rulers of Jerusalem' will be struck by the same dire fate as 'the drunkards of Ephraim'. The latter have behaved as happy-go-lucky people, the former have boasted of their cunning dexterity. Their stronghold, however, is no better than 'the haughty crown'.

According to v. 18a, not only the actual shelter will collapse, the transcendent powers on which it is based will also be overruled: 'your covenant with death / your agreement with sheol'. The term 'to be annulled' (כפר pual) does not involve forgiveness or atonement as is the case in texts of the priestly tradition. It is rather the basic meaning of the root which applies here: removing the tension between two partners – here the rulers of Jerusalem and YHWH who has laid its foundation stone – by removing the cause of the outrage.[94] The parallel expression 'will not stand' (לא יקום) conveys the association of utter failure. The term has a wisdom overtone. It is a topic of the sages borrowed by the prophets that human plans do not come to fruition unless they agree with God's counsel which alone will endure (Job 8:15; 22:28; Prov. 19:21; Isa. 7:7; 8:10; 14:24; 32:8; 40:8; 46:10; Jer. 44:29; 51:29).[95]

In v. 18b, the self-assurance of the addressees, in view of 'the scourge of flooding' (v. 15b′), is countered a second time. The proud statement 'it will not come upon us' is flatly substituted by the threat 'you will be for it to trample on' (והייתם לו למרמס; cf. Isa. 5:5; [10:6]; Mic. 7:10; Dan. 8:13). This expression is peculiar since the metaphor 'to trample' does not fit the subject, i.e. a storm. There is no other occurrence where

---

[94] *TWAT*, IV, 306f. (B. Lang).
[95] *TWAT*, VI, 1261f. (J. Gamberoni).

the root is thus improperly used: the subject is always a being which moves on the ground (2 Kgs 7:17; 14:9; Isa. 1:12; 26:6; 41:25; 63:3; Ezek. 26:11; 34:18; Mic. 5:7; Ps. 7:6; 91:13; Dan. 8:7).[96] It appears likely, therefore, that the wording refers to the judgement pronounced against Ephraim by means of the same term in the beginning of the chapter: 'Under foot will be trampled the haughty crown of the drunkards of Ephraim' (v. 3: תרמסנה). Once again, the rulers of Jerusalem are ranked with the detested renegades of Samaria. In the judgement of YHWH all sinners are alike.

19 While the oracle so far speaks about the judgement as an unexpected, once-only calamity, this verse presents it as a recurrent event and an ongoing process. 'Morning by morning' (Exod. 16:21; 30:7; 36:3; Lev. 6:5; 2 Sam. 13:4; Ezek. 46: 13ff.; Zeph. 3:5; 1 Chr. 23:30; 2 Chr. 13:11), meaning 'every day' (as in Isa. 50:4),[97] and 'by day and by night' it will pounce on the addressees (v. 19a). It cannot be denied that the direction of speech, while continuing the plural address, is extended to include the readers of BI of all times. Here we touch upon the fundamental understanding of prophetic oracles as retaining their value for the generations to come. The conflict between the prophet and the rulers of Jerusalem is not only worthy of being transmitted for the sake of history, but is an exemplary event which will repeat itself. The wording of the prophecies, therefore, is always in need of being adjusted to changing circumstances.

V. 19b involves the following questions:

(1) Has the expression הבין שמועה a transitive ('to get to know the message') or a causative ('to make [people] understand the message') meaning? In view of v. 9 ('Whom will he make understand the message?'), most interpreters prefer the latter explanation.[98] What the prophet has not been able to bring home to his audience, will be impressed upon them by 'the scourge of flooding'. It is a painful teaching experience.

(2) Is 'sheer terror' the subject or the subject complement of the sentence? The common interpretation takes it as the latter: 'It will be sheer terror to understand the message' (RSV). In the former case, terror is the teaching event, not the result of the information: 'Terror alone shall convey the message' (NAB; cf. Procksch 359, 362). The common interpretation seems preferable. Nowhere else does the term 'terror' point to an

---

[96] TWAT, VII, 532ff. (E.-J. Waschke).

[97] TWAT, I, 751 (Ch. Barth).

[98] Delitzsch, Dillmann-Kittel, Feldmann as opposed to König; Irwin 1977:34; HALAT, 118.

active force; it is rather an emotion provoked in people by some hostile event (Jer. 15:4; 24:9; 29:18; 34:17; Ezek. 23:46; 2 Chr. 29:8).[99] The instructive aspect alone should be brought to the fore, hence our translation: 'It will be sheer terror to be made to understand the message'.

In v. 19, the perspective moves slightly towards apocalyptic in the sense that the calamity simply swallows time. While v. 19a by itself can still be interpreted as a metaphoric exaggeration, v. 19b might bear apocalyptic overtones: history and disaster are seen as coinciding. The task 'to make people understand the message' is something which is performed not by the prophets but by the ongoing disastrous course of history.[100] Nevertheless, since the subject is that of v. 18b, 'the scourge of flooding', the extension is strongly anchored in the context.

20-21 Two statements, both beginning with 'truly' (כי), serve to confirm the preceding announcement of judgement. The first contains an implicit comparison (v. 20), the second an explicit one (v. 21).

The first comparison (v. 20) presents an experience from daily life as can be found in wisdom literature. It would be improper to call it a proverb, however, since it deviates from descriptive proverbs by not drawing or suggesting a lesson (cf. Prov. 13:4; 14:28; 15:22; 17:8; 18:11; 20:14; 25:25; 26:13). It may be borrowed from a wisdom context but it is made to fit this prophetic context in order to illustrate the nature of the disaster. The association of 'bed' with 'night' (v. 20) carries it along. Formally, it provides the vehicle of the comparison while the tenor has to be invented by the audience, e.g.: 'You will be looking for rest (cf. v. 12), but the available means do not suffice' (Duhm, 202; Kissane, 319) or: 'You have miscalculated the protection which your self-made hiding place offers you' (Delitzsch, 318: cf. vv. 15,17).[101] The incompleteness of the comparison engages the audience.

---

[99] The position of רק זועה immediately after the verb והיה does not necessarily make it the subject of the sentence, it can also be the subject complement in emphatic position (cf. BDB, 956b: רק emphasizing single words', with היה in Deut. 28:13,33; with other verbs 1 Kgs 14:8; 2 Kgs 22;16; Job 1:15-19; 2 Chr. 18:15). In the latter case, the term היה רק forms a sort of superlative of היה ל.

[100] Moreover, the term 'terror' (זועה) is at home in the later Jeremian tradition: 15:4; 24:9; 29:18; 34:17; cf. H.Weippert, *Die Prosareden des Jeremiabuches* (BZAW, 132), Berlin 1973, 187-91.

[101] Some commentators explain the comparison as a dialectic aporia. If one stretches oneself the bed is too short, if one pulls up one's knees the covering is too narrow (Ehrlich 1912: 101; Feldmann, 335). A quite distinct interpretation recognises here the topic of the bed in sheol (cf. Isa. 14:11; Ezek. 32:25; Job 17:13; Ps. 139:8; N.J. Tromp, *Primitive Conceptions of Death and the Nether World in the Old Testament* [BibOr, 21], Rome 1969: 156f.; Irwin 1977: 34ff.). In view of the context of vv. 15,17, this interpretation seems plausible, but the concomitant notion of wrapping oneself contradicts an association with the underworld.

The second comparison (v. 21a: 'Truly, as on Mount Perazim YHWH will stand up, and as in the valley of Gibeon he will rage')[102] takes two connected episodes from Israel's history as an example to illustrate the nature of YHWH's imminent intervention. The first refers to the story of David's victory over the Philistines near Baal Perazim (2 Sam. 5:17-21). Certain elements in the narrative support the comparison. Firstly, in v. 20 David interprets the name of the place as 'YHWH bursts forth (פרץ) against my enemies before me, like a bursting flood' (כפרץ מים). It goes without saying that the element of the invading flood connects the prophecy of Isaiah (v. 17) with this story. Secondly, David's victory puts an end to the idolatry of the Philistines (v. 21) which matches the false trust of Jerusalem's rulers in their covenant partners, death and sheol (vv. 15,18). Most important, however, is a third, contrasting point of contact: in 2 Sam YHWH waged a holy war to support Israel and the city over which David had become king (2 Sam. 5:9). Here, however, he rises up to fight his own people and to bring total devastation to the same city. In this way, Isaiah contradicts the popular understanding of YHWH as a God of unconditional alliance and raises questions with regard to his works (v. 21b).

According to some scholars, the second story referred to in v. 21a ('like in the valley of Gibeon he will rage') points to the defeat of the Amorites near Gibeon, when YHWH came to rescue Joshua's army by throwing huge 'hail stones' on the enemy (Josh. 10:11; cf. Isa. 28:17). It is more likely, however, that we are being reminded of a second battle of David against the Philistines which took place some time after the one mentioned earlier (2 Sam. 5:22-25). Here, David strikes the enemies down 'from Geba all the way to Gezer' (v. 25) or, according to the parallel version, 'from Gibeon to Gezer' (1 Chr. 14:16).

In this way, the two stories form one example from the history of David and Jerusalem which testifies to YHWH's former willingness to strike down hostile armies in order to rescue his people. Again, according to Isaiah, YHWH will 'rise and rage' (קום / רגז), i.e. he will take the initiative to appear (cf. 2 Sam. 5:24) and reveal his sovereign might (רגז is a theophanic term both where God himself is the subject ['to rage':

---

[102] Some scholars explain כעמק בגבעון / כהר פרצים not as adjuncts of place (J-M, §133 h: 'After כ the expected preposition – here ב – is often omitted') but as the vehicle of the comparison: 'Like Mount Perazim YHWH will stand up, and like the valley of Gibeon he will quake' (Irwin 1977: 35: cf. Jer.46:18; Exum 1982: 123, 128; Hirsch, 195: 'wie ein hervorbrechender Berg' [פרצים is not a proper name, but a common noun plural]). In this way, the cosmic dimension of God's intervention, 'the grandeur of Yahweh's action in terms of height and depth' (Irwin) would come to the fore The reference to the two stories of 2 Samuel 5 would, however, be distorted.

Hab. 3:2; Job 37:2; Sir. 5:6] and where he makes others 'quake' [Isa.
13:13; 23;11; Jer. 50:34; Job 9:6).[103] Against whom? In the same way
as the prophet left the application of the metaphor of the bed to the audience (v. 20), so too he leaves it to them to raise the question against
whom YHWH will direct his attack, and then answer it.

V. 21b postpones the answer to this crucial question by focusing on
the exasperating nature of YHWH's 'doing/work' (roots עשׂה / עבד). The
topic of what YHWH has done and will be doing is extraordinarily important in BI (only the root עשׂה plays a charateristic role in this theme). It
covers what we call God's rule over history. Here, for the first and last
time, the prophet announces that God's activity will be 'strange / alien'
(נכריה / זר), but the basis for this prophecy has been laid in the parable of
the vineyard. The baffling message regarding what the owner 'will do'
to his beloved plantation for which he 'has done' so much, is that he will
destroy it because of its poor vintage (5:4-6). From this chapter on, the
prophet continually blames the people for their lack of attention to what
YHWH, the 'Maker' of Israel (עשׂה: 17:7; 27:11; 29:16), 'is doing'
(5:12; 22:11; 33:13), indeed for their challenging him to speed up 'his
work' (5:19). In the announcement of judgement, it is said that YHWH
will use Assyria as his instrument in order to execute 'his work' of punishment (10:12,23). It is only after this calamity, which Israel deserves
so much, that YHWH will return to perform 'deeds' of salvation for which
his people will praise him (9:6; 12:5; 25:1,6; 29:23).

The perplexing character of YHWH's dealings with Israel, therefore,
does not stem from his inconstancy but corresponds to Israel's behaviour
in relation to him: formerly they proudly claimed to 'have made an
agreement with sheol' (v. 15: the same verb עשׂה). It appears that the
conflict is rooted in Israel's attitude toward foreign nations. 'They clasp
hands with foreigners' (2:6: נכרים; cf. 17:10: 'you set out slips of an
alien [זר] god') so that their land is filled with treasures and idols, 'the
work of their hands' (2:7f.). Therefore, their punishment by YHWH will
consist in the tyranny of 'alien' rulers (זר: 1:7; 25:2; 29:5). What the
prophet has announced before fits this larger context: 'With a foreign
tongue (לשׁון אחרת) YHWH will speak to this people' (v. 11).

22 Some interpreters regard this verse as stemming from the final
redaction of BI. In their view, a call to repentance cannot follow an announcement of judgement. Moreover, the second half seems to quote
10:23 and speaks of a judgement 'upon the whole earth' whereas the
whole chapter is only interested in the land of Judah.[104] The majority,

---

[103] *TWAT*, VII, 330 (G. Vanoni).
[104] Wildberger, 1071, 1080; Kilian, 113.

however, consider the imperative 'do not swagger', which links up with the address 'you swaggerers' (v. 14), the theme of fatal 'bonds', which could refer to 'the covenant with death' (v. 15), the theme of 'to hear' and 'message' (vv. 9,12,14,19) and 'the decree of destruction' so much in line with the whole passage that they maintain the verse as authentic. In between these opposing tendencies, a third reduces the eschatological character of the verse by taking only the last words 'upon the whole earth' as an addition[105] or by translating them as 'upon the whole land'.[106]

In view of all this, we consider at least v. 22a as integral to the passage. The verse line is wholly geared to the specifics of the previous segment. Moreover, it is neither exceptional for PI to end an oracle in a conclusion with 'So now' (ועתה: 5:3,5; 16:14) nor are negative imperatives uncommon in PI (6:9 [also followed by 'lest', פן]; 7:4; 10:24; 16:3; 22:4).[107] Last but not least, v. 22a is connected to the preceding verse by means of a sophisticated rhetorical manoeuvre. In v. 21, Isaiah's listeners certainly have the essential keys at their disposal for interpreting 'the strange work' which YHWH will perform as a threat to themselves, since they are familiar with the background of his preaching (see above). Nevertheless, while leaving it to their initiative to draw this perilous conclusion, the prophet goes on to invite them explicitly to turn back from their arrogance towards YHWH (v. 22a). In other words, before the judgement theme has reached its end, it is superseded by another, that of conversion. From our modern, logical point of view it is hard to understand that an announcement of judgement can be followed by a call to repentance. (Hence many scholars regard v. 21 as a later addition.) These general categories, however, do not fit the intricate rhetoric of prophetic preaching. There is a growing insight that logic cannot account for the relationship between admonition and verdict in Old Testament prophecy.[108] They do not appear to be mutually exclusive. The ruin of Israel and the possibility of a return to God are, in the prophetic vision, on the same level of feasibility.

Thus, the imperative 'do not swagger', together with the statement 'I have heard', takes up the address of v. 14: 'hear... you swaggerers'. The

---

[105] Duhm, 202; Procksch, 363.

[106] RSV, TOB; Watts, 371; Oswalt, 520.

[107] Barth (1977: 43) appropriately points to the fact that the sentence 'lest your bonds be made strong' may reflect the worry of the 'swaggerers', not that of the prophet.

[108] The literature is simply immense. Suffice to note: E. Oßwald, "Aspekte neuerer Prophetenforschung", ThLZ 109 (1984) 641-50, esp. 645f.; W. Houston, "What Did The Prophets Think They Were Doing? Speech Acts And Prophetic Discourse In The Old Testament", BI 1 (1993) 167-88, esp. 179-84.

confrontation between YHWH and the ruling class in Jerusalem, who taunt him shamelessly, may inevitably lead to an outburst that will annihilate them. The way of repentance, however, remains open till the last moment. The warning 'lest your bonds be made strong' may refer to their entanglement with sin (the topic is found in 5:18f.; 8:13ff.),[109] to the ties of dependency which bind them to the political power Assyria (cf. 10:27; Nah. 1:13)[110] or to the complacency of the addressees concerning their alliance with death and sheol.[111] In the given socio-religious situation these allusions may have been effective at the same time. Israel has recourse to sinful magic because politically it is tied hand and foot to the foreign oppressor.

The infrequently denotative character of the Hebrew language, especially in poetry, leaves it open as to whether these bonds should not become 'strong at all' or 'stronger' (Wildberger, 1071). Nevertheless, the term 'strong' (חזק) recalls v. 2, where the audience are confronted with 'a strong and mighty one', most probably Assyria, who will be the instrument of YHWH's anger. As a whole, however, PI calls YHWH the one who is truly 'strong' (8:11), to whom it is worth clinging for protection (27:5: חז hiphil) and who ultimately will bestow 'strength' upon his faint-hearted people (35:3f.).

In v. 22b ('Truly, I have heard'), the prophet returns explicitly as the speaker (prepared by the third person for YHWH in v. 21). He concludes his tirade by appealing to what he 'has heard' from God. In this way, he confirms his divine call and mission against his contestants (vv. 9,12,14,19). It is not uncommon for the prophet to do this, mostly at the beginning of his oracles (5:9; 6:8-12; 8:11-18; 30:8-11), but also once at the end (22:14). In v. 22b, he summarises his message as 'a decree of destruction' (ונחרצה כלה is a *hendiadys*). Authors discuss the Isaianic authenticity of this expression in connection with that of 10:23: 'For the Lord YHWH of hosts will make a full end, as decreed, in the midst of all the earth'. It seems defensible that the latter verse stems from the Isaianic tradition, which builds on the previous verse, an authentic word of the prophet: 'Destruction is decreed [כליון חרוץ], overflowing with righteousness' (10:22; cf. 10:25). Later on, the expression found its way into apocalyptic vocabulary (Dan. 9:27; 11:36). In any event, the concept 'to destroy' is too common to PI on all its literary-historical layers for us to deny it to the prophet in any responsible way (כלה: 1:28; 10:18; 15:6; 16:4; 21:16; 24:13; 27:10; 29:20; 31:3; 32:10; 33:1).

---

[109] Duhm, Watts.

[110] Alexander, Dillmann-Kittel, Feldmann, Procksch, Penna; Barth 1977: 43.

[111] Irwin 1977: 37; Exum 1982: 128.

The prophet traces his message back to 'the Lord, YHWH of hosts'. This designation of God combines the titles used already in the chapter: 'the Lord' (v. 2), 'YHWH of hosts' (v. 5) and 'the Lord YHWH' (v. 16) so as to form a climax and to enclose vv. 16-22 as one divine oracle. Both epithets, 'the Lord' and 'YHWH of hosts', are characteristic of Isaiah, the 8th century prophet who acted in Jerusalem (cf. vv. 1,5). Whatever their origin may be, it is certain that he has adopted them. By using them in formulaic and non-formulaic language, he has made them into important divine titles which embody his understanding of God. The full combination occurs at the beginning, in the middle and the end of prophecies (1;24; 3:15; 10:23f.; 22:5,12,14f.). The way it is used here does not argue against Isaianic authenticity.

The question of Isaianic authenticity recurs for the last words על כל הארץ in connection with the question whether this expression means 'upon the whole earth' or 'upon all the land'. (The former meaning is dominant, the latter is found in Gen. 13:9,15; Deut. 19:8; 34:1; *passim* in the books of Joshua, Judges, 1-2 Samuel, Jeremiah and Zecheriah.) In PI, the meaning 'the whole earth' is most frequent (6:3; 10:14,23; 12:5; 13:5; 14:7,26; 25:8; 'the whole land' is valid for 7:24). In light of the textual affinity of v. 22 with 10:23, therefore, the same meaning is plausible here. The dynamics of ch.28, however, in which the judgement goes from Ephraim to Jerusalem, leaves the way open for the other interpretation. Since v. 22b reflects the interest and the language of both the prophet Isaiah and the Isaianic tradition, intentional ambiguity may be at stake. The prophet has announced that the calamity will affect not only Ephraim but also Judah, in other words 'the whole land'. The tradition projects this judgement against the course of history which it expects to be a judgement 'upon the whole earth'. In so doing, the Isaianic school does not deviate from the prophetic view, it only makes it more explicit. The judgement upon Israel signifies a radicalisation of God's dealing with the world, it involves an ultimate reckoning with all the powers opposing the realisation of YHWH's counsel.[112]

4. Vv. 23-29: 'Strange is God's Work but for the Wise'

Introduction to the Exegesis: Form and Setting

The final passage of the 'woe' section is distinguished by its unique character: it is a sapiential comparison or *mashal*. While it contains sev-

---

[112] H.Wildberger, "Jesajas Verständnis der Geschichte"; in: *Congress Volume Bonn 1962* (ed. M. Noth), (VT.S, IX), Leiden 1963, 83-117, esp. 111-7.

eral terms which are characteristic of Isaiah ben Amoz (v. 26: 'the right order' [מִשְׁפָּט] and 'to teach' [ירה hiphil]; v. 29: 'YHWH of hosts', 'wonderful' [פלא] and 'counsel' [עצה]), exegetes still have difficulty situating it within the preaching of the prophet, since the topic of wisdom, that God's decrees go beyond and above human understanding (Prov. 10:22; 16:1,9,33; 20:24; 21:30f.), is far too general to fit the context. Is the prophet contesting with the worshippers of Baal who call on the gods as lords of the harvest to acquire secret knowledge of fertility?[113] Is he responding to the taunt of his adversaries who claim that in spite of his preaching YHWH will not execute judgement (Duhm, 203)? Is he pointing out to his disciples or to rigidly dogmatic wisdom circles that in God's plan, judgement and salvation go hand in hand in a mysterious and incomprehensible way?[114] Is he proclaiming salvation at the precise moment when it is most needed (cf. 17:12-14; 29:1-7; Wildberger, 1090)? The latter two explanations are a more or less accurate reflection of the tenor of the passage but they do not do justice to the fact that it is unclear who is being addressed here. It cannot be the 'swaggerers, who rule in Jerusalem' (vv. 14,22). How could a radical judgement over them (vv. 14-21), combined with a warning for the same group of people (v. 22), be followed by an appeal to wonder at YHWH's wise governance (vv. 23-29)? The situation of oral preaching does not provide an explanatory framework.

Opposite attempts to situate this comparison in the preaching of the prophet there are others which try to explain it on the level of the redaction as a reflection on the three oracles in this chapter, designed by the transmitters in the language of Isaiah and destined for the readers of BI (Kaiser, 209). This reflection would have the following purpose: the last word concerning God's actions is not the downfall of his people, but his 'wonderful counsel and great wisdom' (v. 29).[115] The passage links up with what precedes it by means of some topics and catchwords. The 'wonderful counsel' stands in one single line with the theme of God's strange actions (v. 21) and his speaking in unintelligible language (v. 11). At this point the isotope concerns precisely the relationship between judgement, salvation and admonition. If we take seriously the fact that the judgement, in both its announcement and execution, has affected Is-

---

[113] *La Bible. L'Ancient Testament* (Bibliothèque la Pléiade), Paris 1959, *h.l.*

[114] Procksch, 368f.; G. von Rad, *Old Testament Theology. Volume II: The Theology of Israel's Prophetic Traditions*, Edinburgh 1965: 'Isaiah only once spoke in a very fundamental and theoretically didactic fashion about Jahweh's action in history, namely in 28:23-29'; Amsler 1973.

[115] Exum 1982: 130-4; Petersen 1979: 115-9.

rael's understanding of YHWH, including that of the exilic community who look with hindsight upon the judgement, then a concluding passage for the readers of BI is appropriate. This conclusion should point to the punishing action of God in the past as 'the right order' (v. 26: מִשְׁפָּט), comparable with the right order in agriculture which involves plowing, planting and harvesting. In recognizing this 'wonderful counsel and great wisdom' (v. 29) there remains room, after the judgement, for a life in obedience to God's teaching.

This purpose is served by the *mashal* throughout the chapter and even in its parts. It opens with a call to listen (v. 23), as is characteristic not for a prophet, but for a wisdom teacher (cf. 1:10; Ps. 49:2; Job 33: 31; Prov. 4:1; 7:24).[116] The two stanzas, each with a conclusion, describe the process of sowing and reaping (vv. 24-26, 27-29). Sowing consists of two actions, plowing and planting, each of which must take place at the appropriate time (vv. 24-25). The manner of reaping varies according to the type of crop: the use of too much strength is thereby avoided (vv. 27-28). Here also the aspect of time has a role to play (v. 28: 'not unceasingly does one thresh it'). If we take account of the fact that the semantics of these verses allude to military campaigns (cf. 'Exegesis by Verse'), then it becomes clear that the *mashal* does not only speak about agriculture but also refers metaphorically to the judgement over God's people. Time and manner of plowing, sowing and reaping comply with the 'right order' and serve the harvest. This is the way YHWH handles Israel.

The structure of the passage appears as follows:

23   call to listen to the teacher
24-29   *mashal*
        24-26   the farmer prepares the land
            24   the plowing
            25   the planting
            26   conclusion: God instructs him
        27-28   the farmer reaps the harvest
            27   the wrong and the right way of reaping cummin
            28   the wrong and the right way of reaping bread grain
        29   final conclusion:
            - knowledge about reaping comes from YHWH of hosts
            - praise of his counsel and wisdom

---

[116] Wildberger, 35, 1090: 'Lehreröffnungsformel'.

Exegesis by Verse

23 The appeal to listen, served by the repetition of the verb 'to hear'
(שמע) in relation to 'to give ear' (אזן *hiphil*; cf. 1:2,10) and 'to pay attention to' (קשב *hiphil*; cf. 34:1; 49:1; the last two verbs also in 51:4), is
the most emphatic to be found in BI. It can be distinguished from other
similar appeals by the fact that the addressees are not named.[117] This
confirms our hypothesis that it is not an audience of the historical
prophet which is being addressed here but the readers of BI who are the
heirs of the preceding oracles. The thematic word 'to hear' embodies
this historical continuity at the level of the audience throughout the entire chapter.[118] The observation 'they have been unwilling to listen' (v.
12) has led to an appeal to listen to the word of YHWH which announces
downfall (vv. 14, 17-19). The new appeal to listen, v. 23, in this case to
God's strategy (v. 23: 'right order'; v. 29: 'counsel'), is directed to
those for whom the whole course of events, from accusation to judgement, in vv. 1-22 is not simply historical in significance. For them it also
has topical value, in the first place because it defines their situation, and
secondly because therein YHWH is a source of instruction for them, revealing himself as 'wonderful in counsel, great in wisdom' (v. 29). One
can only agree with the remark: 'The emphasis in vv. 23-29 is not only
on YHWH's wisdom but also on YHWH's *teaching*'.[119] By this call to listen, the passage is strongly affiliated with v. 9 where the adversaries reject 'the teaching of knowledge' (ירה *hiphil*; cf. v. 26) and 'the understanding of the message' (שמועה; cf. v. 23).[120]

The speaker is clearly the prophet himself, there being no reference to
a word of YHWH nor does he refer to God (vv. 26,29). He draws attention
not only to his message but also to the fact that he speaks, precisely because the terms 'voice' (קול) and 'speech' (אמרה) nowhere else refer to
the prophet himself (except in 32:9).[121] The speaker in v. 23 is the continuation of the speaker in v. 22 and in fact of the entire chapter. Due to
the absence of an addressee, the historical prophet flows over unnoticed
into the prophet presented by BI ('the implied prophet').

[117] Elsewhere the addressees are mentioned, including places where the imperative of
שמע has no parallel verb form (6:9; 7:13; 28:14).

[118] Aitken 1993: 19-21, 26-8.

[119] Exum 1982: 131f. In this author's strictly synchronic outlook, v. 23 is addressed to
'all'.

[120] The traditional explanation at this point is followed, not that according to which
God or the prophet is the speaker in v. 9. Cf. the 'Introduction to the Exegesis' of vv. 7-
13.

[121] This does not prove the Isaianic authenticity of v. 23, only the use of Isaianic terms
by the redaction (pace Wildberger, 1090f.).

24-25 From a syntactic perspective, the first half of the *mashal* consists of two rhetorical questions, the first expecting a negative answer (v. 24), the second a positive one (v. 25). The 'plower' is the subject of both sentences. This creates a clear contrast between the right and the wrong way of working the land. In the former situation, the farmer wrongly devotes all his time ('all day') to preparing the soil. In the latter situation the farmer's preparatory work is only the first phase ('when he has leveled its surface'); there follows a second phase in which he plants various kinds of crop.

There are a number of linguistic and lexical problems in vv. 24-25 (Wildberger, 1083f.; Healy 1984: 114f.):
(1) In v. 24, the word 'for sowing' is questionable from a metrical point of view. Furthermore, it makes mention of the precise activity which is supposed to be absent in the wrong way of working the land. While the translation 'to harrow' (שׂדד; cf. Hos. 10:11; Job 39:10) is traditional, it might perhaps be out of place in a description of the agricultural techniques of the day in Palestine since it implies a second, deeper level of plowing. Nevertheless, the context seems to support it as meaning 'to harrow', in preparation for sowing and planting (*HALAT*, 1218).
(2) In v. 25a, the translation 'dill' for קצח is also traditional, but 'black cummin' appears to be a more accurate botanical term term (*HALAT*, 1047; for the crop terminology used here, cf. Rosenmüller, 429-32).
(3) In v. 25b, some commentators interpret the words for 'rows' (שׂורה) and 'plots' (נסמן) as names of crop species (as early as Aq and Theod: κένχρος, 'millet') and translate: 'two-rowed barley' and '*nisman*-seed'. In this case, however, the term 'border' is left without a parallel in the verse line. The triad 'rows', 'plots' and 'border' stands appropriately for the concretisation of 'right order' (v. 26). We remain, therefore, with the usual translation (confirmed by *HALAT*, 717, 1224f.; Barthélemy, 198ff.).

26 The conclusion comes as something of a surprise, though not in the sense that agricultural life corresponds to the 'right order' as established by God (cf. Job 39:10-12,17 [RSV: 13-15,20]), since the myth of the deity as the teacher of agricultural techniques was widespread through the ancient Mediterranean world: Enlil in Sumer, Isis and Osiris in Egypt, Demeter in Greece and Ceres in Rome (Wildberger, 1091f.). The surprise lies in the fact that 'God' only comes to be mentioned in the second part of the verse line and is presented as 'his God' rather than 'God' as such. In this way, the suggestion is made that the farmer is related to God in a special way (cf. 'God' with singular suffix: Isa. 7:11,13; 8:21; 17:10; 25:1; 37:4,10,38).

The farmer accepts the teaching of the one who regulates the process of fruitful nature upon which humanity depends. Within the boundaries of the *mashal*, מִשְׁפָּט, translated here as 'the right order', can extend to signify even the created order to which the agricultural cycle belongs, together with the regularity that flows from it (מִשְׁפָּט as 'order' in the non-juridical sense: Gen. 40:13; Exod. 26:30; Judg. 13:12; 18:7; 1 Kgs 18:28; 2 Kgs 17:26f.; Jer. 8:7; Eccl. 8:6). In the application of the *mashal*, the concept refers to YHWH's policy concerning Israel, as proclaimed by the prophet. Even here the activities of plowing, sowing and planting follow each other, everything bent on the harvest. The farmer is presented as an example of a person who has been instructed about the process through which Israel is going. In other words, he symbolises Isaiah.[122]

The audience is called upon to take that example and to let itself be instructed by God in 'the right order' of judgement and salvation. This means that they will have to turn aside from those who have been accused in this chapter of refusing to accept YHWH's strategy ('to instruct' [יסר] can be found in one other place in PI with the same prophetic meaning: 'YHWH instructed me not to walk in the way of this people' [8:11]). Only thus they will escape the fate which has befallen these people.

27-28 The second part of the *mashal* deals with threshing. As was the case with plowing, a right way and a wrong way are presented in contrast, both of which are applied to two types of crop: '(black and ordinary) cummin' (v. 27) on the one hand and 'bread grain' (v. 28) on the other. 'Bread grain' (לחם), emphatically placed at the beginning of the verse line in order to set up the contrast, combines 'wheat, barley and spelt',[123] which function next to 'cummin' in the plowing example of v. 25b, into one word. The effect of this change is twofold:

(1) Attention is shifted from the orderly setting of 'wheat, barley and spelt' to the correct way of threshing, this theme being present in each half of the verse lines. The various instruments and procedures used for threshing constitute a mounting opposition: not with a 'sledge / wheel' (v. 27a), but with a 'stick / rod' (v. 27b); not 'crushed / unceasingly threshed' (v. 28a), but with a 'cart wheel', yet not 'crushed by horses' (v. 28b).[124] Nevertheless, this opposition is not absolute since the inappropriate instrument used for threshing 'cummin', namely the 'cart wheel' (v. 27a), is appropriate for threshing 'bread grain' (v. 28b). The correct instruments, therefore, are the 'stock / rod' for 'cummin' and the 'cart wheel' for 'bread grain'. In PI the first word pair 'stock / rod' is

---

[122] Fohrer, 69f.; Snijders, 289; Schoors, 170f.
[123] Bread' (לחם) is mainly made from wheat but also from barley and spelt (*TWAT*, IV, 539 [W. Dommershausen]).

characteristic of the semantic field of judgement: YHWH uses Assyria as as 'stock / rod' (שבט / מטה) to punish his people (together in 9:3; 10:5,15,24; 14:5 [Babylon]; 30: 31f. [inversion]; apart in 10:26; 11:4; 14:29). In this way the intent of the *mashal* comes into view: the manner and duration of Israel's judgement.

(2) The term 'bread grain' (לחם; cf. 36:17) stands for the product of the threshing process. At the same time it is the main ingredient of 'bread', which in PI is listed among the necessities of life along with 'water' and 'clothing'. The word is powerfully reminiscent of attack by hostile troops and exile (Isa. 3:1,7; 4:1; 21:14; 30:20,23; 33:16; 36:17) and in this sense it also facilitates the application of the *mashal* to the judgement of Israel.

A number of semantic elements reinforce this application. This is true to a certain extent for the term '(cart) wheel' (גלגל; cf. 5:28; 17:13[125]). The term 'horses' (פרשים) has military connotations both in PI (21:7,9; 22:6f.; 31:1; 36:9), and in general biblical language usage (Gen. 50:9; Exod. 14 *passim*; Josh. 24:6; 1 Sam. 13:5; 2 Sam. 1:6; 8:4; 10:18; 1 Kgs 10:26; 2 Kgs 18:24; Ez. 26:7; 38:4; Hos. 1:7; Dan. 11:40; Ezr. 8:22)[126]. Furthermore, elsewhere the terms 'to thresh' and 'to crush' form images for the destruction of lands and peoples or horrifying acts of war (דוש: Isa. 21:10, 25:10, Judg. 8:7,16; 2 Kgs 8:12; 13:7; Amos 1:3ff., Mic. 4:12f. [127]; דקק: 2 Sam. 22:43; Mic. 4:13) and even for God's judgement (Isa. 41:15; Hab. 3:12). Finally, the term '(not) unceasingly' (לנצח) is to be found primarily in contexts referring to the way God punishes people (in BI almost exclusively in PI: 13:20; 25:8; 33:20; 34:10; 57:16; Jer. 15:18; 50:39; Am. 1:11; Ps. 9:7; 44:24; 49:20; 74:10,19; 77:9; Job 4:20; 14:20; 20:7; 34:36.[128]

It would appear, therefore, that the second half of the *mashal*, in contrast with the first, encourages and promotes its application to God's intention in judging Israel in and through its semantic components.

29 This verse not only concludes vv. 27-28 but also the entire *mashal*. The opening words 'This also' turn the verse line into a counterpart of

---

[124] The history of technology's mistrust of the idea of 'threshing with horses' and the emendation of פרשיו ('one's horses') to פרש ('one spreads, winnows it') fail to appreciate the style figure of an argument *per absurdum* (Wildberger, 1085; pace Duhm, Schoors, *BHS*, Healy 1984: 116).

[125] The meaning 'wheel' is alluded to in 17:13: 'like a tumble-weed before a storm wind' (Wildberger, 674).

[126] *TWAT*, VI, 785f. (H. Niehr): 'The majority of occurrences of פרש are in a military context'.

[127] *TWAT*, II, 197ff. (H.F. Fuhs).

[128] *TWAT*, V, 567f. (G.W. Anderson).

the conclusion in v. 26, although the phrase: 'This comes from YHWH of hosts' creates ambiguity (cf. the use of the same verb 'to come from' [יצא] in 2:3; 51:4). Does 'This' (זאת) refer to the correct way to thresh? Elsewhere in PI the demonstrative frequently refers to an intervening act of God (9:6; 12:5; 14:26; 23:8; 27:9; 28:12; 37:32). The parallelism makes clear that the word refers to 'counsel / wisdom'. Elsewhere in PI the term 'counsel' (עצה) signifies the opposition between God's govern-ance of history and the futile attempts of his adversaries to push through their own schemes and designs (cf. 5:19; 11:2; 14:26; 19:17; 25:1 and 8:10; 19:3,11; 29:15; 30:1; 36:5). The word translated here by 'wis-dom' (תושיה) is unique for BI. It has its roots in wisdom literature and means something like 'sound, efficient prudence' (Job 5:12; 11:6; 12:6; 26:3; Prov. 3:21; 8:14; 18:1; *HALAT*, 1579). In this sense it fits well in the isotope of 'wisdom' (חכמה), a word which also functions in PI to mark the opposition between YHWH and his adversaries (11:2; 31:2; 33:6 and 5:21; 10:13; 19:11; 29:14). In the context of PI, there-fore, both terms, 'counsel' and 'wisdom', imply something which tran-scends agricultural insight, namely YHWH's governance of Israel. The actions of the farmer who is subject to God's teaching lead *per analogiam* to a conclusion concerning the actions of YHWH (Wildberger, 1089). The phrases 'he is wonderful in counsel / he is great in wisdom' are a rendering of divine characteristics which arise from these divine actions.[129] The first verb, פלא *hiphil*, refers as a rule to the works of God in the sense that they are beyond human imagination (Isa. Judg. 13:19; Joel 2:26; Ps. 17:7; 31:22; 2 Chron. 26:15).[130] The second verb, גדל *hiphil* (with God as subject: Gen. 19:19; Joel 2:20; Ps. 18:51; 138:2; 126:2), has a role to play in the theme of God's power over history (Ps. 48:2; 96:4; 104:1; 145:3).[131] Moreover, in PI the roots in question characterise the actions of YHWH ('wondrous': 9:5; 25:1; 29;14; 'great': 12:6; 27:1; 29:6; 34:6).

Even the divine title, 'YHWH of hosts', breaks through the chokmatic framework of the *mashal*. This title, which is the most characteristic at-tribute used for YHWH in PI,[132] embodies not only his uniqueness (6:3; 37:16), but also his actions concerning Israel and the nations with refer-ence to election (5:7; 6:5; 8:18; 24:23; 25:6; 28:5,22), admonition and accusation (3:15; 5:24; 8:13; 9:12), judgement (1:24; 2:12; 3:1; 5:9;

---

[129] BDB, 152, 810: 'he makes counsel wondrous / he makes wisdom great'; *HALAT*, 172, 876; König, Rosenberg, Kilian.

[130] *TWAT*, VI, 574f. (J. Conrad).

[131] 105*TWAT*, I, 942-7 (R. Mosis).

[132] יהוה צבאות can be found 56 times in Isaiah 1-39 and only 6 times in Isaiah 40-66.

9:18; 10:16,23,26,33; 13:4,33; 14:22ff.,27; 17:3; 19:4,12,16f.; 21:10; 22:5,12,14,25; 23:9; 29:6; 39:5) and salvation (1:9; 9:6; 10:24; 18:7; 19:18; 20,25; 28:29; 31:4f.; 37:32). In relation to this divine title 'counsel / wisdom' point beyond the order of creation, in which agriculture is to be found, to YHWH's actions in the history of Israel. In addition, there is evidently a refrain at work with regard to v. 22: 'Truly, I have heard a decree of destruction from the Lord YHWH of hosts upon the whole earth'. The reference in v. 29, 'This also', does not only point to the first half of the *mashal,* i.e. the process of plowing and planting (vv. 24f.), but also to the conclusion of the previous prophetic oracle. It is not only 'a decree of destruction' that comes from 'YHWH of hosts', but also his wonderful governance in which bread grain is indeed threshed but not crushed. God's governance punishes Israel but never to the point of total destruction.

THE SECOND WOE CRY: 'WOE, ARIEL' (29:1-14)

1   Woe, Ariel, Ariel,
        the city where David encamped!
    Add year to year,
        let the feasts run their round.

2   Yet I will distress Ariel,
        and there shall be moaning and lamentation,
            and she shall be to me like an Ariel (altar hearth).

3   And I will encamp against you round about,
        and I will besiege you with a mound,
            and I will raise ramparts against you.

4   Then prostrate you shall speak from the earth,
        from low in the dust your speech shall come.
    Your voice shall be like a ghost's from the earth,
        and from the dust your speech shall whisper.

5   But the multitude of your invaders shall be like fine dust,
        and the multitude of the ruthless like passing chaff.
    And it shall be in an instant, suddenly:

6   there will be a visit from YHWH of hosts,
    with thunder and earthquake
        and with great noise,
    with whirlwind and tempest,
        and with the flame of a devouring fire.

7   And it shall be like a dream, a vision of the night:
    the multitude of all the nations that fight against Ariel,
        and all that war upon her, and the siege-works against her,
        and those who harass her.

8   And it shall be as when a hungry man dreams,
        and behold, he is eating,
            and he awakes, the hunger not satisfied;
    or as when a thirsty man dreams,
        and behold, he is drinking,
            and he awakes, and behold, he is faint, the thirst not quenched,
    so shall be the multitude of all the nations
        that fight against Mount Zion.

9   Tarry and be astounded!
          Delight yourselves and be blind!
     They are drunk, but not from wine;
          they stagger, but not from strong drink!
10   Truly, YHWH has poured out upon you
          a spirit of deep sleep.
     He has closed your eyes, the prophets,
          and covered your heads, the seers.
11   The vision of all this has become to you
          like the words of a writing that is sealed.
     When they give it
          to one who can read,
     saying: 'Read this',
          he says: 'I cannot,
               for it is sealed'.
12   And when the writing is given
          to one who cannot read,
     saying: 'Read this',
          he says: 'I cannot read'.
13   The Lord has said:
     'Because this people has drawn near with its mouth
          and honoured me with its lips,
               but has kept its heart far from me,
     and their fear of me has been
          a human commandment, a thing learned,
14   therefore, behold, I go on doing wonderful things
          with this people, wonderful and shocking.
     The wisdom of its wise shall perish,
          and the discernment of its discerning shall be hidden'.

NOTES

   2 Many authors read 'and you shall be' in v. 2b˝ (cf. 1QIsᵃ: והייתה).
Such a reading continues Ariel's direct address from v. 1 while MT
('she shall be') continues the discourse concerning Ariel in v. 2a. From a
text critical perspective there appears to be no urgent reason to opt for
one or the other (Werlitz 1992: 264ff.; Barthélemy [202f.] does not
even discuss the variant). From a stylistic perspective the MT reading
seems to make more sense: the discourse concerning Ariel marking the
triple 'against you' of v. 3 more distinctly.

3a The reading of LXX: ὡς Δαυιδ should not be preferred to that of MT: כדור ('round about'), in spite of the mention of David in v. 1 (Barthélemy, 202f.; *pace* Gonçalves 1986: 225). It remains an exegetical interpretation (Van der Kooij 1981: 67).

3b From within the context and in agreement with LXX (χάρακα), the *hapax legomenon* מצב should be interpreted as 'siege-works' (Werlitz 1992: 311f.). The frequently followed reading 'guard posts' has its roots in Ges-B but cannot be maintained from a lexical perspective (Wildberger, 1098f.; *HALAT*, 587).

4 The term אוב is more likely to refer to a tool for consulting the dead, frequently a hole in the ground, than 'spirit of a dead' or 'excorcist' (cf. Ebach, Rüterswörden 1977: 64-7). Reference to the 'spirit of a dead person', however, should not be dismissed outright.[1]

5 The choice between the reading of the MT: זריך ('your foreigners', i.e. 'your foes') and that of 1QIs^a: זדיך ('your insolent ones') is of great importance for our interpretation of the passage as a whole (cf. 'Essentials and Perspectives'). While we cannot reiterate the detailed discussions of Wildberger (1099) and Barth (1977: 185f.) who follows 1QIs^a, and of Barthélemy (203f.) and Werlitz (1992: 277f.) who follow MT, it would seem that priority should be given to the MT for the following reasons: (1) The reading of LXX (ὁ πλοῦτος τῶν ἀσεβῶν) does not necessarily refer to זד and does not, therefore, contradict that of MT; (2) Elsewhere, זרים, עריצים and גוים constitute a trio (Ezek. 28:7; 31:12; Irwin 1977: 52). The reading of MT does not present any problems if one considers the following: (1) In the exile, the term זר also came to mean 'invader'; (2) זריך can also be understood as a participial form of the root זרה, 'to winnow', and bear the meaning 'dispersers', next to that of 'foreigners'.

6 It is better to explain תפקד in line with LXX (ἐπισκοπὴ ἔσται) as a third person feminine and not as a second person masculine, as most commentators are wont to do, since the latter form does not recur in what follows. The feminine verbal form does not refer back to Ariel (*pace* Sweeney, 382) but is in fact neuter since the enemy has already emerged as the object of God's judgement from v. 5 on (for a *femininum pro neutro* in passive verb forms cf. Isa. 1:6; Ps. 50:3; Prov. 15:6; GKC, §144 b; König, 264, 269: 'eine Heimsuchung wird veranstaltet werden'; Oswalt, 525; REB: 'Punishment will come'). The passive of מעם, moreover, never expresses the acting person (*HALAT*, 749f.).

---

[1] K. Spronk, *Beatific Afterlife in Ancient Israel and in the Ancient Near East* (AOAT, 219), Kevelaer – Neukirchen 1986, 252-6.

7 From the metrical perspective this verse is very long, the repetition of the root 'to fight' (צב[א]), among other things, giving the impression of a certain excess. Nevertheless, there is enough parallelism present for us to speak of poetry. Reconstructions remain doubtful. The term מצדתיך, however, does tend to refer to offensive rather than defensive siege-works (cf. Vg: qui militaverunt et obsederunt). Does the MT employ the style figure of 'a noun instead of a verb variation' including rhyme (-מצ-, cf. -ה-)? The translation 'siege-works against her' fits better in the context (as early as Redaq; cf. Barthélemy, 205f.).

9a Almost every commentator accepts that this verse line consists of four imperatives. Rashi and Qimchi, however, consider the imperatives of v. 9a″ to be *qatal*, an interpretation which is grammatically possible and inspired perhaps by the *qatal*-forms in v. 9b and the equally negative meaning of 'to be blind' and 'to be drunk' (Rosenberg, 235: 'Stop and wonder. They became blind and they blinded'). We would then be left with the explanation that the inhabitants of Judah during the time of Ahaz were invited to reflect on the false prophets. V. 9a″ is absent from LXX although Tg, Vg and Syr do offer translations of the words in question using imperatives. Parallelism and colometry also constitute an indication that v. 9a′ and v. 9a″ employ the same verbal forms. The majority of modern commentators (since J.B. Koppe, the translator of R. Lowth's commentary) accept that the same verb in two imperative forms (*hithpael* and *qal*) can be found both in v. 9a′ and v. 9a″ (cf. RSV: 'Stupefy yourselves and be in a stupor, blind yourselves and be blind!'). A number of unresolved problems remain:

(a) In v. 9a′ the first verb form, strictly speaking, goes back to the root מהה, 'linger, tarry' (*hithpalpel*), while the second refers to the root תמה, 'be astounded' (*qal* and *hithpael*). Had the first verb stemmed from the same root as the second then the form would have to be הִתַּמְּהוּ (cf. *BHS* which proposes an amendment along these lines with reference to Hab.1:5; also Wildberger, 1112: 'nach Analogie von 9ab sind zwei Formen desselben Verbs zu erwarten'; *HALAT*, 523; *TWAT*, IV, 710 [H.-J. Fabry]; VIII, 672 [U. Berges]). The versions (LXX, Vg, Tg, Syr), however, presuppose two different roots for the imperatives of v. 9a′ (also Vitringa, 174; Delitzsch, 325; König, 265). From a text-critical point of view there are no pressing reasons to apply the usual emendation (Barthélemy does not discuss this matter either).

(b) Then the question remains as to whether two forms of the same root (שעע) are to be found in v. 9a″. Two homonyms exist with respect to the root שעע: I. 'be smeared over, be blind' (*qal* and *hithpalpel*); II. 'take delight in' (*pilpel* and *hithpalpel*; cf. *HALAT*, 1489f.; *TWAT*, VIII,

356ff. [J. Hausmann]). Gesenius (854) considers it possible that v. 9a´´
does indeed play with two homonyms, in the same way as v. 9a´ plays
with similar sounding forms of two different roots. He thus translates
v. 9a´´: 'seyd nur lustig und verblendet'. Such an interpretation would
imply that in both v. 9a´ and v. 9a´´ the second action is the consequence
of the first one which we might render as follows: 'Simply hesitate to
believe, you will be all the more astonished. Furnish yourselves with
nothing but pleasures, they will only make you blind'. Alexander (465)
follows a similar line: 'Waver and wonder! Be merry and blind!' (*pace*
Hoffmann 1976: 51f.).

This apart, the majority of commentators assume the grammatical datum that where two imperatives are connected with w^e the former functions conditionally (GKC, §54 e; Wildberger [1114] even offers a form-
critical explanation of the conditional connection, suggesting that it provides a combination of accusation and announcement of judgement: 'If
you continue with your corrupt behaviour you will have to bear with the
consequences'). The same grammatical datum applies whether one assumes two forms of the same root or two similar sounding and homonymous roots. In contrast to this, an alternative explanation suggests that
the imperatives simply reinforce one another: 'Falter in your stupor; go
blind, all blind' (Irwin 1977: 55).

9b Several translations and commentaries read imperatives here also
(cf. 1QIs[a], LXX and Vg; Tg is ambiguous, Syr follows MT; Wildberger,
1112). In most cases this is based on the fact that the 2nd person plural
found in v. 9a and v. 10 is also postulated for the verse line in between.
Barthélemy (207f.), however, sees no basis for such an interpretation
and explains the alternation in the direction of speech in v. 9b as follows: the prophet shows the one to whom he has been speaking to the
audience (cf. Vitringa, 175f.; Rosenmüller, 439).

Other commentators achieve their desire for a single direction of
speech in a different manner. According to them, the perfects of v. 9b
constitute relative clauses which function as vocatives: 'You who are
drunk but not with wine, who stagger but not with strong drink' (Irwin
1977: 55f., in line with Ehrlich 1912: 104).

10b A substantial number of authors consider the words 'the prophets' and 'the seers' as a late gloss. Oswalt (529f.), however, corrects this
notion, proposing that the words in question are not later glosses but integrated glosses formulated by the Isaianic redaction on the basis of
28:7f.. It is striking that the *nota accusativi* is missing before 'the seers'.
According to Ewald (427, 430) this is an indication that glossing is not
evident for the second part of the sentence. He therefore retains the sec-

ond word and translates: 'he has closed your eyes [...] and covered your seeing heads'.

From a semantic perspective glossing seems probable nevertheless. The expression 'your seeing heads' is somewhat strange given that the function 'to see' is generally reserved for the eyes. Moreover, the verb כסה, 'to cover', with body parts as its object, implies precisely that their proper functioning is obstructed (Gen. 9:23; Exod. 28:42; Isa. 6:2; Ezek. 1:11,23; 12:6,12). With persons as object the verb suggests 'being covered' (Gen. 24:65; 38:14; 1 Kgs 1:1; Isa. 51:16; 60:2), 'being hidden' (Judg. 4:18f.) or 'being clothed' (Deut. 22:12; 1 Kgs 11:29; 2 Kgs 19:1f.; Isa. 58:7; Ezek. 16:8; 18:7,16; Hos. 2:8; Jonah 3:6,8; *TWAT*, IV, 278 [H. Ringgren]). Glossing is also probable since the following verse restores the 'blinding' to the addressees ('to you') and not to the prophets. In addition, the accents of MT propose an alternative clause division: 'He has closed your eyes; the prophets and your heads who stargaze, he has covered' (Rosenberg, 236). Such a division, however, does not take account of the parallelism and appears to be an endeavour to syntactically integrate the glosses (not appositions but objects).

11 We consider the expression חזות הכל to be an objective genitive: 'the vision of all this'. The suggestion that הכל, as a subjective genitive, refers to the aforementioned 'prophets / seers' is somewhat laboured (*pace* BDB, 482b; Irwin 1977: 57). The subject of 'the vision' is included in להם (cf. 'your eyes / your heads' in v. 10). Moreover, the words for 'vision' taken from the root in question never appear with a subjective genitive, only with a genitive of authorship (Num. 24:4,16) or an objective genitive (Ezek. 13:7).

13 It has become the custom to translate the verb forms of the divine locution in the present (probably under the influence of Mark 7:6 par.). The Hebrew (*qatal* and *wayyiqtol*), however, offers no support for such an interpretation (Dietrich 1976: 174; Wildberger, 1118f.; NJV; Rosenberg, 237). The *piel* רחק is sometimes understood as intransitive (*HALAT*, 1139f.; Kaiser, 217), but it is transitive in every other occurrence (Isa. 6:12; 26:15; Ezek. 43:9; BDB, 935; Wildberger, 1118). The parallelism also supports a transitive interpretation.

The Masoretic accents do not treat מלמדה as an adjectival participle but as an apposition (*participium femini pro neutro*) with respect to מצות אנשים: 'a thing learned' (Alexander, 466).

14 Certain authors consider the repetition of העם הזה as a gloss for reasons of the colometry and the forced placement of the expression as object of להפליא (Duhm, 211; Procksch, 378; Wildberger, 1118; *BHS*).

If we drop these words, however, the singular suffixes of v. 14b would lack an antecedent and one would expect plural suffixes after יראום in v. 13. This apart, 1QIsᵃ reveals a tendency to normalise the alternation between singular and plural in v. 13 (Irwin 1977: 58f.).

ESSENTIALS AND PERSPECTIVES

Vv. 1-8 prevail as the verses in which the central exegetical problems of PI are most clearly marked. Salvation and doom run seemlessly into one another without reason being given for the turn about in Jerusalem's fortunes. A number of experts are of the opinion, therefore, that it is possible to ascribe these two perspectives to one single author, Isaiah ben Amoz. For him, the relationship between salvation and doom rests on the divine assurance of Zion's invincibility, a traditional topic of the cult (v. 8). On the basis of this and other passages, therefore, the authors in question explain the unity of judgement and salvation as part of the paradigm of Isaiah's own preaching. Moreover, they tend to situate these verses among the prophet's own words, preached at a time when Jerusalem was under military threat. The period of Sennacherib's campaign against Palestine (705-701 BC) is the most frequently proposed context although the revolt of the Northern Kingdom against Assyria (724-721 BC) has also been suggested (Sweeney, 380-3). In contrast, other exegetes understand the relationship between salvation and doom to be a theological creation of the Isaiah tradition, particularly of the so-called Assyrian redaction, rooted in the historical event of Sennacherib's sudden withdrawal from the siege of Jerusalem in 701 BC (cf. Isaiah 36-37).[2]

Although disaster and relief are closely connected to one another in this passage, it is not so easy to point out exactly where that connection lies. V. 8 certainly speaks of the endangered expectations of Zion's enemies, but expressions of salvation may go back as far as v. 7 if we can understand this verse as meaning that the enemy armies are only a bad dream for the population of Ariel. There might also be evidence of a reversal of fortunes as far back as v. 6 if we give a positive interpretation to God's 'visit', and perhaps even to v. 5 if we understand it as a reference to the transitory nature of the adversary. The latter suggestion is supported here. Of course, the literary-historical explanation of vv. 1-8 also changes in line with the textual location of the reversal of fortunes.

---

[2] The hermeneutical techniques are clearly presented in Werlitz 1992: esp. 253.

The problem of the relationship between salvation and doom returns in vv. 9-14. V. 8 does promise the failure of the enemy siege, but how do the present verses connect with the preceding passage? Perhaps the relationship is a weak one and vv. 9-14 constitute an originally independent prophetic oracle in which the prophet broadly censures the religious dispositions of his audience? Perhaps they speak of the negative attitude with which the population of Zion received the Ariel prophecy; in other words, does 'the vision of all this' (v. 11) refer to vv. 1-8 (cf. v. 7: 'a vision of the night')? The latter interpretation is followed here. The insincere attitude of 'this people' leads to an accusation in v. 13 which forms the basis of the announcement of YHWH's continuing intervention, one which is not exclusively salvific (v. 14).

Discussion with regard to the question whether the announcement of salvation and doom in Isa. 29:1-14 constitutes a variety of literary-historical layers is based on the fact that certain exegetes tend to isolate vv. 1-8 from vv. 9-14. Redaction critics, however, tend to steer us clear of such procedures since the context of the 'woe cry', so evidently the structuring pattern of Isaiah 28-33, makes vv. 1-14 into an interpretative unity (Sweeney, 376-80). This does not deny that the verses in question may have undergone a process of growth which we can endeavour to reconstruct, but vv. 1-14 taken as a whole remain the primary interpretative context for the relationship between disaster and salvation.

The closer we relate vv. 1-8 with vv. 9-14 the more we relativise the notion that salvation and doom in the present woe cry ought to be understood as absolutely distinct literary-historical genres. Within the context of the whole, judgement and salvation are simply different dimensions of God's 'wonderful' deeds (three times in v. 14). Similarity with the conclusion of the previous woe cry (28:29), in which the announcement of YHWH's 'wonderful counsel' constitutes the crown of a prophecy which likewise relates salvation (vv. 5-6) and doom (vv. 18-22), is quite remarkable. In terms of literary genre, only the final verse of 29:1-14 contains an announcement of God's pending intervention in the characteristic terminology: 'Therefore, behold, I go on doing wonderful things'. Indeed, while this verse does look forward it also looks back to the salvation and doom spoken of in the Ariel oracle. It announces further disaster, in particular for 'the wise', but leaves room via the notion of 'wonderful things' for a change in God's behaviour, perhaps the return of his salvific acts. Doom and salvation are not successive acts of YHWH, but facets of his engagement with his people.

Our separate discussion of vv. 1-8 and vv. 9-14, in line with the majority of commentators, would appear to be something of a contradiction. The split is based on the literary genre and is supported by the Hebrew text divisions.[3] Vv. 1-8 describe a future event in which Ariel constitutes the central focus (3rd pers. fem. sing. in v. 2 and v. 7, 2nd pers. fem. sing. in vv. 3-5). In vv. 9-14 the situation is different; the play on the word Ariel is concluded. This passage is only barely narrative (v. 10 refers to God's past actions, v. 14 to his future deeds). The second person plural dominates and the tenor is one of accusation. From the perspective of content, vv. 9-14 constitute a *metatext* with respect to vv. 1-8. The way in which the audience receives the previous prophecy is the object of discussion.

If we accept that 29:1-14 is a historically formed, literary complex then the Ariel oracle constitutes its oldest core (vv. 1-7). In these verses the prophet proclaims disaster for the city, but both the siege of the city (v. 1-4) and its relief (vv. 5-7) are the work of YHWH. For the contemporaries of Isaiah ben Amoz, talk of God himself turning against Ariel as an enemy must have been unheard of. An interpolated comparison, perhaps intended for a later generation, sketches the disappointment of the besiegers and identifies Ariel with Zion (v. 8).

In vv. 9-14 the Isaiah tradition (or the redaction of BI) presents the prophet in confrontation with the audience of the preceding oracle. He challenges them to disregard this prophecy (v. 9: 'tarry... delight'), but also to accept the consequences of so doing ('be astounded... be blind'). He interprets their indifference as a punishment from YHWH who has turned their unwillingness to accept the message into an inability to do so (v. 10). In an aside, the prophet points out to other unnamed addressees that the irresponsible behaviour of his audience has a specific origin (v. 9b: 'They are drunk, but not from wine'). A new audience thus appears in the background as witness to the controversial reception of the Ariel oracle.

A comparison follows, detailing the consequences of God's intervention: the vision has become inaccessible like a 'sealed writing' (vv. 11-12). The vehicle of the comparison, a 'writing', reveals something about the background audience: they are the later audience who possess the prophecies of Isaiah in written form. In this way, they are involved in the controversy with the original, direct addressees. The negative reception of the prophecy is also a matter for the following generations: is it possible that the blinding endures?

In the form of an authentic announcement of judgement, the final oracle provides YHWH's reaction to the sceptical reception of the Ariel

---

[3] After v. 8, 1QIs[a] has a *petucha*, codex L (and others) a *setuma*.

prophecy (vv. 13-14). Since no one is directly addressed in this reaction, the divine utterance should not only be understood as a matter for the original audience who rejected the prophecy but also for the background audience, the generation of 'the writing'. Both are simply referred to as 'this people' and they are told that YHWH's involvement in their affairs is ongoing. One of the consequences of that involvement will be the humiliation of 'the wise' (v. 14b) which refers to those who did not take the Ariel prophecy to heart. Further consequences of God's intervention depend on the reaction of those who are witness to the prophecy's sceptical reception. Perhaps they will learn something from what they have seen.

It is understandable, therefore, that the two dimensions of this narrative concerning the future, salvation and doom (v. 1-8), are summed up in the discursive text under the aspect of God's 'wonderful deeds' (v. 14).

SCHOLARLY EXPOSITION

1. Vv. 1-8: City Lost, City Regained

Introduction to the Exegesis: Form and Setting

The explanation of the so-called Song of Ariel is dominated historically by the question concerning which verses or parts thereof can be ascribed to the prophet. Within this context there are authors who consider only the announcement of punishment to be authentic, while other commentators maintain in principle that the expectation of salvation also belongs to the original message of Isaiah, even although they consider that message to have been expanded during and after the exile. It would be impossible to examine all the positions and the arguments on which they are based in the present commentary.[4]

Since it is not clear where the transition from doom to salvation actually takes place (cf. 'Essentials and Perspectives'), opinions concerning the extent of the original oracle are divergent, even among those who restrict the so-called authentic text to a judgement oracle. Most commentators in this category consider v. 5a-b′ and vv. 7-8 to be an announcement of doom for the enemy (and thus salvation for Ariel) while they interpret vv. 5b″-6 as disaster for Ariel. In such an event, the origi-

---

[4] For overviews, cf. Wildberger, 1100ff.; Gonçalves 1986: 225f.; Werlitz 1992: 259-6.

nal oracle would consist of vv. 1-4, 5b´´-6. For different reasons, doubts have been raised as to the authenticity of v. 2b and v. 4b (cf. 'Exegesis by Verse').

The alternative position, which would ascribe the connection of salvation and doom to the prophet himself,[5] is not too far in fact from the position which would consider such a relationship to be an original theme of the cultic tradition.[6] Both explanations do not necessarily exclude the possibility that the passage has undergone a process of growth. Almost every commentator who takes this possibility into account considers v. 8 to be an addition to an already rounded-off text, and this for the following reasons. Firstly, the language type lies between that of prose and that of poetry. There is a strong external parallelism between the two elements of comparison, hunger and thirst, but the meter reveals an unusual pattern (Werlitz 1992: 259f.). Secondly, the tenor of the foregoing verse is found to have been altered (Schoors, 173f.). The dream of v. 7 is that of the population of Ariel: after God's 'visit' (v. 6) it appears that the threat of capture by the besiegers was only a nightmare. In v. 8, however, it is the dream of the besiegers themselves which turns out to be deceptive: they cannot satisfy themselves on the spoils of Zion. Thirdly, while v. 7 takes up the word 'Ariel' from vv. 1f., thereby enclosing vv. 1-7, v. 8 seems to want to interpret Ariel as Mount Zion via the repetition of the words: 'the multitude of all the nations, that fight against...' (Werlitz 1992: 259ff.). From this perspective, v. 7 leans heavily on v. 5b´´-6a´: 'And it shall be in an instant, suddenly' (both lines begin with והיה). The sudden arrival of YHWH turns the threat of downfall into nothing more than a dream. There is no reason, therefore, to consider v. 7 as an interpolation. The opposite is true, however, with respect to v. 8.

The discussion of the authenticity of v. 2b provides a useful point of access to the structure of the passage. V. 2b has been called into doubt on account of the break it introduces in a series of 1st pers. sing. verbal forms (vv. 2a,3), the apparent tautology of v. 2b´´, and the anticipation of the end of the siege (Ariel as an altar hearth for the enemy) which does not in fact take place until v. 3 (Procksch, 369-72). The removal of v. 2b, however, would only serve to introduce further tensions into the context (Werlitz 1992: 264ff.; cf. 'Notes'). It would be more meaningful, therefore, to identify v. 2 as a prior summary of the three events which will be further elaborated in vv. 3-7: YHWH's siege of Ariel, lamentation and the effects of the altar hearth. The elaboration contains a

---

[5] Schoors, 171: a conditional salvation oracle; Barth 1977: 189 (with emendation of זריך in v. 5 to זדיך; cf. 'Notes'); Wildberger, 1100ff.

[6] Kaiser, 210-3.

surprisingly new element which comes only gradually to the fore: the attacking army disappears before YHWH's visit (vv. 5-7).

This provides us with the following outline:

1   woe cry
    1a   addressee: Ariel
    1b   call to intensify cultic celebrations / prophetic critique of the cult
2   announcement of what lies in store for Ariel: siege
    2a   YHWH lays siege to Ariel (1st pers. and 3rd pers.)
    2b´   lamentation
    2b´´   altar hearth
3-7   elaboration of what lies in store for Ariel: siege and relief
    3   YHWH lays siege to Ariel (1st pers. and 2nd pers.)
    4   lamentation
    5-7   altar hearth
        5a-b´   the fate of the invaders
        5b´´-7   theophany
            5b´´-6   YHWH's visitation
            7   those besieging Ariel vanish like a dream
8   appended comparison: Zion is like a deceptive dream for the besiegers

Exegesis by Verse

1 In many respects, the woe cry 'Woe, Ariel!' (הוי) is employed here in an unusual fashion (cf. 'Introduction to Isaiah Chapters 28-39'). Firstly, it is immediately followed by a proper name, 'Ariel', the only other instance of which being Isa. 10:5 ('Woe, Assyria!'),[7] although 'woe' is exclaimed elsewhere also over an entire population (Isa. 1:4; Zeph. 3:1). The word 'Ariel' can be found in the Scriptures as a personal noun (Ezr. 8:16) and as a common noun meaning 'hearth', i.e. the upper part of the altar of burnt offering (Ezek. 43:15f.).[8] The idea of YHWH's altar hearth, if not the word itself, also occurs elsewhere in the present collection of woe oracles (30:33; 31:9).

There remains little point in trying to establish whether 'Ariel' as a place name for Jerusalem alludes to an ancient tradition.[9] Given the

---

[7] In Jer. 48:1 a preposition precedes the proper name.

[8] Cf. also, according to some, the difficult word אראלם in Isa. 33:7. The word can be found with this meaning on the Mesha stele, l.12 (*KAI*, II, 169, 175): 'I brought back from there the altar hearth (אראל) of its DWD'. In addition, it is employed as a special, technical term for a 'leader / hero' or a 'priest' in 2 Sam. 23:20 / 1 Chron. 11:22 (*Ges.*[18], 99 and *DCH*, 377f. respectively).

[9] The origin of the proper name 'Ariel' remains shrouded in mystery. Reduction to ארי, 'lion', and translation as 'lion of God' can already be found in the Midrash (Exod. R

term's unicity and the metaphorical function, one would be better advised to understand it as a creation of Isaiah himself, designed for the present context (Hardmeier 1978: 227f.). The rhetorical process in which the prophet develops the term from a place name to a common noun (vv. 1-2) invites the reader to further reflection. The cultic meaning 'altar hearth' is of some assistance in this regard. It characterises the city as the location where YHWH is worshipped, evoking his right to recognition and his obligation to afford shelter. The second characterisation, 'city where David encamped', is in keeping with the first. The reference here is not to David's siege of the Jebusite Jerusalem (2 Sam. 5:7-9; *pace* Procksch, 371) but rather to the fact that he once brought his army into the city, thereby providing it with protection (Gonçalves 1986: 227f.). The Davidic tradition plays a further role elsewhere in PI (7:2,13; 9:6; 22:9; 28:21). Against this background, the question arises as to the identification of the offering for which Jerusalem will serve as the altar hearth.

Secondly, the present 'Woe' appears to lack the essential element of a clear accusation or charge. Indeed, the prophetic woe cry is an advance application to the living of a ceremonial lament usually reserved for the dead, an anticipation based on behaviour which has delivered the individual in question into the power of death (cf. the texts mentioned under 28:1; Werlitz 1992: 298f.). This aspect of the woe cry is worked out later in v. 4b. Nevertheless, the notion of accusation or charge is not completely absent from v. 1 (Werlitz 1992: 300). Assuredly, according to some, v. 1b ('Add year to year, let the feasts run their round') is only a specification of the temporal period within which the judgement will strike.[10] The conjunction w^e of the following v. 2, however, may have an adversative significance (König, 263) and need not necessarily have a consecutive function (Feldmann, 343). V. 1b has a strong literary structure (*asyndeton*, chiastic arrangement, inclusive rhyme: ‏ספו‎... ‏קפו-‎) which underlines the irony of the content. The addressees are encouraged to attend to their festive cycle year after year, but YHWH will react

29,9), although it is rejected by Ibn Ezra (133). The last century saw a revival of support for such an etymology (cf. the authors mentioned in BDB, 72). It remains a popular etymology (Wildberger, 1104f.), however, and cannot be defended on a contextual basis. As such it has been dropped from modern dictionaries. Feigin (1920) provides the material on the basis of which the discussion was pursued but his own explanation of the word as *necropolis* remains speculative. Cf. also Penna, 266f.

[10] A somewhat literal exegesis of v. 1b leads Hitzig (335f.) to suggest a period of two years, with Delitzsch (323) and Irwin (1977: 47) proposing one year. Dillmann-Kittel (260) has pointed out, however, that the absence of the definite article with 'year' suggests that no specific time – such as the new year feast – is implied here (cf. Duhm, 206).

to this by bringing distress upon Ariel. They are apparently unaware of what lies in store for them and consider the celebration of the liturgy to be a guarantee of their safety. We acknowledge the prophetic attitude of distance and aloofness with respect to the cult, although it would be going too far to suggest that here Isaiah is criticising the practice of offering sacrifice while social justice is being neglected as he does in 1:10-17.

2 By way of a double contrast, the woe cry of v. 1 is further elaborated in an announcement of what YHWH is going to do to Ariel. He will not provide the protection which the altar of burnt offering and the significance of David for the city have led the people to expect; instead, he will bring 'distress'. Thus their festivities will have to make way for 'moaning and lamentation'. The first term, 'distress' (צוק *hiphil*), stands for physical violence and the accompanying feelings of anxiety and sorrow (Deut. 28:53; Isa. 8:23; 51:13; Jer. 19:9; Zeph. 1:15; Ps. 25:17; 107:6; 119:143).[11] The latter element is immediately brought to the fore in 'there shall be moaning and lamentation'. This short sentence (note the impressive rhyme: וְהָיְתָה תַאֲנִיָּה וַאֲנִיָּה) calls to mind the cultic lament over the fall of the city as found, for example, in Lam. 2:5 (with the same word pair). Just as the latter text expressly mentions YHWH as the perpetrator of the city's distress, so does the present verse (v. 2b´´): 'She shall be to me like an Ariel' (altar hearth as common noun). At the same time, the element of violence in the term 'to distress' is thereby brought into greater relief. The frequently occurring expression 'to be for a person like...' (כ+ ל+ היה) stands for the value or function which is rightly or wrongly meted out to something or somebody by another (Exod. 22:24; Lev. 15:26; 19:34; Judg. 17:11; 2 Sam. 12:3; Jer. 12:8; 15:18; Ezek. 21:28; 33:32; 47:22; Ps. 35:14; 71:7).[12] This means that YHWH is employing the altar hearth in a new manner in his service (Dillmann-Kittel, 260). The details of YHWH's plan remain to be seen. The fact that they are not to the city's advantage, however, is already quite evident.

3 The use of military terminology is quite striking in the development of v. 2a (cf. Deut. 20:20; 2 Kgs 25:1-4; Ezek. 4:2; 21:22; Hab. 2:1). At the same time, the triple 'against you' (על in the hostile sense), connected with three verbs in the 1st pers. sing. for God, sharply underlines the fact that conflict is determinative of the relationship between YHWH and Ariel. It is a source of further distress that God himself is the one who is waging war and that there is no mention of an army fighting on his behalf as is often the case elsewhere (Isa. 7:18ff.; 8:7f.; 9:10;

---

[11] *TWAT*, VI, 963-6 (H. Lamberty-Zielinski).
[12] Jenni 1994: 119f.

10:5f.; 28:2). Moreover, the repetition of the verb 'to encamp' from v. 1 suggests that David's protection is no longer operative (cf. Psalm 132 as contrast). Contemporaries of the prophet, nevertheless, will have recognised the image of an Assyrian siege in these prophetic words. The following text from a report of king Sennacherib concerning his expedition against Jerusalem serves as an illustration:

'As to Hezekiah of Judah, he did not submit to my yoke, I laid siege to 46 of his strong cities, walled forts and to the countless small villages in their vicinity, and conquered them by means of well-stamped earthramps, and battering-rams brought thus near to the walls, combined with the attack of foot soldiers, using mines, breeches as well as sapper work... I surrounded him with earthwork in order to molest those who were leaving his city's gate'.[13]

4 The 'moaning and lamentation' announced in v. 2b″ is elaborated here in two verse lines which are strongly connected to one another from the stylistic perspective via external parallelism and chiasm as is evident from the following literal rendering of the textual sequence:

Then prostrate / from the earth / you shall speak,	A B C
and from the dust / shall come low / your speech	B¹ A¹ C¹
(It) shall be like a ghost's / from the earth / your voice,	D B C²
and from the dust / your speech / shall whisper.	B¹ C¹ D¹

It is not easy to determine the predominating imagery in v. 4a. The topic of war in v. 3 might lead one to imagine an individual who has been brought down in battle (שפל: Isa. 2:9,11f.,17; 5:15; 10:33; 32:19), who speaks as he lies prostrate on the ground (שחח: Isa. 25:12; 26:5; 51:23; 60:14), like a defeated warrior begging for mercy. Ancient Near Eastern iconography supports such an interpretation.[14] According to other commentators, the feminine forms of address are reminiscent of daughter Jerusalem lamenting as she sits in the dust (Isa. 3:26; 47:1; Jer. 6:26; 48:18; Mic. 1:10; Lam. 1:2; 2:10).[15] A third explanation suggests we are dealing here with a flight into the caves as an attempt to find cover against the victorious enemy.[16] The latter explanation is in line with Isaiah's own *Chiffre* according to which all those who vaunt their pride before YHWH will be forced into humiliation in the dust (cf. Isa. 2:10-17 – the principal text in this regard).[17]

---

[13] *ANET*, 288.
[14] Kissane, 325; Kaiser, 213; Keel 1972: 276.
[15] Hitzig, 352.
[16] As early as Josephus, *De Bello Judaico*, VII, 14; Vitringa, 169f.
[17] *TWAT*, VII, 1212f. (L. Ruppert).

The authenticity of v. 4b has frequently been called into doubt, partly on account of the introductory word 'and it shall be' (וְהָיָה) which is considered redactional, but primarily because of the fact that the line itself introduces nothing new.[18] There are reasonable grounds, however, for envisaging a progression and even a climax at this point, v. 4a presuming a fall to the ground and v. 4b a descent into the underworld (Werner 1982: 181; Werlitz 1992: 262ff.). The comparison with a 'ghost' introduces the element of 'death', something not entirely unexpected after the woe cry over the (presumed) dead Ariel. Related texts (Isa. 8:19; 19:3) reveal that Isaiah was familiar with the topic of speaking ghosts who make a sound like that of birds (צפף *pilpel*: Isa. 10:14; 38:14). Nothing can be deduced from this, however, regarding Isaiah's position on life after death. Death itself is the message.

5a-b' The change of subject here draws our attention to some new actants: 'your invaders / the ruthless' (MT; cf. 'Notes'). Although implicitly present in the military operations of v. 3, they have not been directly mentioned until now. 'Your invaders' (זָרָיִךְ; actually 'foreigners') refers to subjugation by alien forces (Isa. 1:7; 25:2; 61:5; Jer. 30:8; Ezek. 11:9; 28:7; 30:12; Hos. 8:7; Joel 4:17; Ps. 109:11; Lam. 5:2). The aspects of violence and terror associated with the abuse of power predominate with regard to the term 'ruthless' (עָרִיצִים) (Isa. 13:11; Jer. 15:21; 20:11; Ps. 37:35; 54:5; 86:14; Job 6:23) although the notion of foreign tyranny is not completely absent (Isa. 25:3ff.; 49:25; Ezek. 28:7; 30:11; 31:12).[19]

The primary question remains whether this verse is a continuation of the description of the judgement facing Ariel or a first announcement of the downfall of the enemy.[20] Does the comparison with 'dust / chaff' stand for the overwhelming numerical might of the enemy and their unstoppable advance[21] or, according to the accepted interpretation, for their mortality? 'Chaff' would certainly point to the latter interpretation (Isa. 17:13; 41:15; Hos. 13:3; Zeph. 2:2; Ps. 1:1; 35:5; Job 21:18). 'Dust' (אָבָק) as such is less unequivocal. While it bears the connotation of mortality in Isa. 5:24, elsewhere it refers to useless material which can be easily whirled around in the wind (Ezek. 26:10; Nah. 1:3). It is true that, in the context of God's judgement, 'dust' can be understood as an instrument of punishment (Exod. 9:9; Deut. 28:24) but the adjective

---

[18] Duhm, 184; Childs 1967: 54; Dietrich 1972: 189.

[19] *TWAT*, VI, 404 (B. Kedar-Kopfstein).

[20] Werlitz' well founded explanation (1992: 276-82) is followed here with some supplementation.

[21] Kaiser, 213; Exum 1981: 345; Werner 1982: 181.

'fine' (דק) employed here adds the nuance of 'powerlessness' and 'in-significance' (Isa. 40:15; Gen. 41:3-7,23f.; Lev. 13:30; 21:20; 1 Kgs 19:12).[22] It would appear, therefore, that v. 5a-b´ does not portray the enemy as dangerous. Indeed, if that were the case one would have expected their mention prior to v. 4. It seems clear that a reversal of fortunes from doom to salvation is being announced in v. 5a-b', although by means of a comparison which is not immediately clear. The ambiguity of v. 2 – whether Ariel will be an altar hearth for her inhabitants or for the enemy – continues in the present verse although it is beginning to lean towards the latter interpretation.

5b´´-6 These verse lines are recognisable as the announcement of a theophany in which YHWH advances against his enemies via the phenomena surrounding a storm.[23] God's intervention in a conflict is frequently compared with such phenomena. In the iconography of the Ancient Near East, the god of the storm is also the god of war (Keel 1972: 192-7).

The terms employed here can be found elsewhere in the context of theophany: 'thunder', רעם: Ps. 77:19; 81:8; 104:7; Job 26:14; 'earthquake', רעש: 1 Kgs 19:11f.; Ezek. 3:12f.; 38:19; '(great) noise', (גדול) קול: Deut. 5:22; Jer. 10:13; Amos 1:2; Ps. 18:14; 29:3ff.; 46:7; 68:34; 77:19; 104:7; 'whirlwind', סופה: Isa. 17:13; Amos 1:14; Nah. 1:3; Ps. 83:16; 'tempest', סערה: Isa. 40:24; Jer. 23:19; 30:23; Ezek. 1:4; Zech. 9:14; Job 38:1; 40:6; 'flame', להב: Isa. 30:30; 66:15; '(devouring) fire', (אוכלה) אש: Exod. 3:2; 19:18; 24:17; Deut. 4:11,24; 1 Kgs 18:24,38; 2 Kgs 1:10-14; Isa. 66:15; Nah. 1:6.

It goes without saying that the purpose of the theophany is to root out the adversary but whether this applies to Ariel or to the advancing enemy remains a question. According to v. 7, the siege of Ariel will turn out to be no more than a bad dream. Implicitly, therefore, v. 7 promises salvation for the city, but is this also the implication behind vv. 5b´´-6?

The explanation of these verse lines is indeed dominated by the question whether 'there will be a visit from YHWH' implies a saving or punishing action. The usual answers fit appropriately within the variety of interpretation of the intention and literary-historical articulation of the passage as a whole. Only in the *qal* do we find the verb 'to visit' (פקד) with a positive meaning 'to be concerned for' (with God as subject in Gen. 21:1; 50:24f.; Exod. 4:31; 1 Sam. 2:21; Ps. 8:5; 65:10; Job 7:

---

[22] The verb דקק almost always means 'to pulverise something so that it can no longer accomplish anything': Exod. 32:20; Deut. 9:21; 2 Sam. 22:43; 2 Kgs 23:6,25; Isa. 28:28; 41:15; Mic. 4:13; 2 Chron. 15:16; 34:4,7. The root is only found with a positive meaning in Exod. 16:14; 30:36; Lev. 16:12.

[23] Jeremias 1965: 73f.

17f.; Ruth 1:6), otherwise it bears the meaning 'to condemn' (with God as subject in Exod. 32:34f.; Isa. 10:12; 13:11; 24:21; 26:14,16,21; 27:1; Jer. 11:22; 23:2; 29:32; 46:25; Hos. 4:9; Amos 3:14; Zeph. 1:13).[24] The rare occurrences of the verb in the *niphal* imply an order (Ezek. 38:8) or judgement by God (Num. 16:29; Isa. 24:22; Prov. 19:23) but never salvation (Werlitz 1992: 284). Such facts make the negative interpretation of the phrase 'there will be a visit from YHWH' as punishment all the more probable.

The temporal indicator 'in an instant, suddenly (לפתע פתאם) serves to underline this probability. While the double expression is very rare it does occur in the context of divine punishment (Num. 6:9; Isa. 30:13). In the prophetic literature the second word characterises the sudden, un-expected nature of God's judgement both over his own people (Isa. 48:3; Jer. 4:20; 6:26; 15:8; Mal. 3:1) and over the nations (Isa. 47:11; Jer. 18:22; 51:8; Ps. 64:5,8).

There appear to be strong arguments, therefore, to interpret vv. 5ab″-6 as an announcement of judgement and not salvation.[25] Such an expla-nation does not create a problem after v. 5a-b′, which refers to the mor-tality of the enemy and places salvation on the horizon, if one under-stands the verb form תפקד not as a 2nd pers. masc. but as a 3rd pers. fem. and thereby as impersonal (*femininum pro neutro*; cf. 'Notes'). In-deed, v. 6 does not mean that YHWH himself intends to visit someone, i.e. the addressee, because the term מעם never designates the 'acting person' with respect to a passive.[26] The expression implies that a 'visit' will go out from YHWH ('from YHWH' or 'from God' [מעם]: Gen. 41:32; 2 Sam. 3:28; 1 Kgs 2:33; 12:15; Isa. 8:18; 28:29; Ps. 121:2; Ruth 2:12; 2 Chron. 10:15). For this reason, the notion of a visit has been given an almost abstract theological significance. In the classical theophany texts YHWH himself appears accompanied by various natural phenomena which signify his sovereignty (Ps. 18:8-20). The expression employed in v. 6 replaces his arrival with his authoritative initiative; thereby the ac-companying phenomena actually become the subject of the 'visit'. Seen in this way, v. 6 need not be in conflict with v. 5a-b′. After the enemies are described as mortal (v. 5a-b′), YHWH's initiative to reveal his might can only be directed at these enemies, although they are not mentioned directly (likewise those who stand to benefit from it: the people of Ariel).

---

[24] *TWAT*, VI, 713-19 (G. André).

[25] *pace TWAT*, VI, 819f. (W. Thiel).

[26] In the other texts with פקד *niphal*, the 'acting person' is not explicitated (Num. 16:29; Isa. 24:22; Ezek. 38:8; Prov. 19:23).

7 The literary genre of the theophany exhibits its basic twofold pattern: the coming of God and the world's reaction to his coming (cf. the reaction of the cosmos: Judg. 5:4f; Mic. 1:3f.; Ps. 68:8f.; of the inhabitants: Isa. 19:1; 30:27-31; Ps. 76:5-10; of both: Isa. 63:19-64:2; Hab. 3:3-6; Ps. 144:5-8).[27] V. 7 together with v. 6 corresponds to such a pattern. It speaks of enemies, the besiegers of Ariel, and we are left to expect the declaration that the fate of God's adversaries will overcome them. This does indeed happen, but not directly. There is no announcement of the enemies' military defeat but we are told, rather, how their victims shall experience the end of their aggression: they will turn out to be of no real substance, nothing but a dream in the night (cf. Isa. 17:14).

The significance of this verse depends on the value of 'a dream/vision of the night' (חזון לילה / חולם) in the Scriptures as a human phenomenon (not as a place of revelation as, *e.g.* in Gen. 28:12; I Kgs 3:5; Joel 3:1; and Gen. 15:1; 1 Sam. 3:1; Ps. 89:20). The dream sometimes stands for transitoriness and lack of real substance (Zech. 10:2; Ps. 73:20; Job 20:8; Eccl. 5:2,6). In the present verse, the metaphor appears to have a purpose similar to that of v. 5 where the enemies of Ariel are referred to as 'fine dust / passing chaff', the main difference between the two being the climactic shift from transience to unreality.

Thus the passage as a whole reaches a surprising culmination in v. 7. Where Ariel was still the object of God's subjugation in v. 2a, now all hostility against her is silenced at the initiative of YHWH himself (v. 6). Ariel's name resounds once again but this time in the context of salvation. The puzzling nature of the expression in v. 2b ('and she shall be to me like an Ariel') is thereby resolved

8 The aforementioned dream comparison has attracted yet another dream although this time the besiegers do not form the content, they are themselves the dreamers. Several commentators do not appear to evaluate the line of thought they assume to be behind this interpolation very highly, nor do they show much appreciation for its literary form.[28] The suggestion, however, that the poetic form of the text is interrupted by prose at this point cannot be maintained. Indeed, external parallelism between the line referring to the hungry and that referring to the thirsty is sustained with care and enriched with a number of climactic elements (Hitzig, 354), to the extent that one has to accept the presence of a different sort of (non-metrical) poetry (Werlitz 1992: 259f.).[29]

[27] Jeremias 1965.

[28] Duhm, 208; Procksch, 374f.; Wildberger, 1102, 1110.

[29] Even the element from the 'thirst' line which has no parallel in the 'hunger' line ('and behold, he is faint' [והנה עיף]) can be seen as compensation for the extra element at the beginning of the 'hunger' line, והיה.

V. 8 is likewise not redundant. Given that v. 7 sketches the end of the siege in the experience of those besieged, its makes sense that v. 8 sketches the same end in the experience of the besiegers. While some commentators find the somewhat measured, double comparison a little heavy and boring, others point to the element of sarcasm contained therein: normally those besieged are the ones who suffer hunger and thirst but here it is the besiegers who are thus afflicted.

Finally, v. 8 has the function of explaining the name 'Ariel' as 'Mount Zion'. In terms of meaning and style, the verse links up well with vv. 1-7 but this fact does not yet imply that it constitutes an original unity together with these verses. It is quite possible that in the prophet's oral preaching the fascinating efficacy of the strange term 'Ariel' did not require clarification but that at one or other stage in the formation of BI, the redactors considered some kind of explanation necessary. If that were the case, then they have passed on the song of Ariel as a sort of parable, together with an explanation, to future generations.

2. Vv. 9-14: The Writing Sealed, yet Wonders to be Expected

Introduction to the Exegesis: Form and Setting

A number of scholars consider these verses to be a different prophetic oracle added on to that of vv. 1-8 without much intrinsic relationship between the two.[30] Most of them, however, tend to side with the quest for a reasonable connection. Thus some have assumed a pause in the actual situation of prophetic preaching after v. 8 during which the prophet observes his audience's astonishment at the Ariel prophecy, particularly with respect to its sudden switch from doom to salvation, and then responds to it in vv. 9-14.[31] Such an explanation, however, is based on emendations made to the text of v. 9a (cf. 'Notes'). If the MT of v. 9 is left unemended then the text does not only speak of surprise but also – and more incriminatingly – of tardiness in accepting the prophecy as well as blinding self-indulgence. For this reason it would not be advisable to view vv. 9-14 as concurrent with vv. 1-8.

Still other authors rightly search for the connection between these two textual units at the level of redaction. Some suggest, for example, that an 'eschatological redactor' has expected vv. 1-8 to be fulfilled in a manner different from that of Sennacherib's siege in 701 BC and the fall of Jeru-

---

[30] Duhm, 209; Cheyne, 165; Schoors, 174.

[31] Ibn Ezra, 135; Hitzig, 354; Delitzsch, 324f.; Dillmann-Kittel, 202; Feldmann, 345; König, 265f.; Procksch, 375; Penna, 268f.

salem in 587 BC. Thus the same redactor added two authentic prophetic oracles, vv. 9-10 and vv. 13-14, together with his own words in vv. 11-12, in the form of a commentary after vv. 1-8 so that later readers of the Ariel prophecy would take it to heart as still effective.[32] Such an approach, however, too easily assumes that vv. 11-12 are 'eschatological' (i.e. very late), although it does explain how vv. 9-14 can be ascribed to the redaction of BI in its plan to actualise the 'political' oracles of Isaiah ben Amoz with the help of other prophecies in which he berates the spiritual attitudes of his contemporaries.[33]

The suggestion that vv. 9-14 constitute a text about a text, i.e. a *metatext*, is founded on the fact that vv. 13-14 consist of a commentary of YHWH, in solemn style, on the preceding verses. Such a proposal tends, in addition, to do justice to the unity of the woe cry as well as to the fact that an abrupt accusation follows after the (indirect) proclamation of salvation of vv. 7-8. While it is true that vv. 9-14 are complex in structure it is equally unmistakable that they thematise the Ariel prophecy. 'The vision of all this' (v. 11) refers to 'a vision of the night' (v. 7), whereby the definite article and the additional 'of all this' also designate the two dreams (vv. 7f.), and indeed the entirety of vv. 1-8, as a 'vision' (Exum 1981: 349). The expression 'a deep sleep' (v. 10) is also isotopically linked to the two dreams. An important connection between text and metatext can be seen in the notion of 'wonderful things' (v. 14). After the accusation of v. 13 one is left to expect a punishment of the people in the form of a disaster of some sort (cf. 1:11-20; 58:3-20) rather than God's continued 'doing of wonderful things'. V. 14 seems better understood, therefore, as a reference to the Ariel prophecy and its astonishing swing from doom to salvation. Finally, the change of speech direction from 2nd pers. fem. sing. (vv. 3-5; cf. 3rd pers. fem. sing. in v. 7) to 2nd pers. masc. plur. (vv. 9-11) constitutes a persuasive indication that vv. 9-14 are directed towards a different audience than that of vv. 1-8, no matter how far the former is drawn into the preceding prophecy.

The question remains, however, whether the actual situation of the prophetic preaching is not enough to explain the relationship between vv. 1-8 and vv. 9-14. In that case Isaiah ben Amoz is speaking for his contemporaries alone in vv. 9-14. What indications are there to suggest that a double 'audience' was intended, indications which might prove that the tradition intended the prophet to speak to his readers over the

---

[32] Kaiser, 214-8; Vermeylen 1977: 404-7.

[33] The suggestion that vv. 1-8 contain a *iudicium temporale* and vv. 9-14 a *iudicium spirituale* (Vitringa, 163; Alexander, 460f., 465) is evidently present here.

heads of his contemporaries? In our opinion, the most persuasive indication appears to be the accusation in the 3rd pers. plur. in the concluding
prophecy (vv. 13f.). After the incriminating direct address of vv. 9-11
one would also expect a 2nd pers. plur. in vv. 13f. In principle, it is possible to envisage 'this people' as the inhabitants of Ariel (vv. 1-6) but
the reference would then extend over a rather long portion of text. It
would seem more logical, therefore, to understand the addressees of
vv. 9-11 as 'this people'. In this event, the 3rd person establishes distance and 'this people' becomes the object of attention for others. Indeed, something similar takes place in v. 9b: 'They are drunk / they
stagger'. Thus the passage contains, both at its beginning and its end, an
aside to addressees who are not further identified. We assume the implied third party to refer to the readers of BI.

If vv. 9-14 constitute a metatext then one has to assume their *functional* unity in relation to the question of their internal structure, even
although vv. 9-10 and vv. 13-14 probably date back to the prophet himself while vv. 11-12 stem from a later period.

The first part, vv. 9-10, cannot be accommodated in one particular
literary genre. It is in fact a mixed form which includes a moral evaluation, an ironic exhortation and a look back at a judgement. One can
primarily identify in these verses a characteristic topic and passage
from Isaiah's call vision: the so-called 'benumbing order' (6:9-10).
The points in common with this text are strong: the topic that God
himself desires and, indeed, brings about the blindness of his people,
the pairs of imperatives which are related to each other as cause and
effect (6:9; 29:9) and the use of the verb שעע (6:10 *[hiphil]*: 'besmear
its eyes'; 29:9 [*qal*]: 'be blind'). What is brought up by the prophet in
the present text (29:9-10) is in fact a part of the task given him in 6:9-
10.

The second part consists of a twofold comparison, vv. 11-12, which
objectively elaborates the consequences of God's intervention for the
Ariel prophecy. It has become a closed book waiting in vain to be
opened because the two groups (v. 11: 'one who can read'; v. 12: 'one
who cannot read') which constitute the people as a whole cannot read it
through their own fault.

The third and final part, vv. 13-14, constitutes a classical prophetic literary genre: an accusation and an announcement of God's intervention.
The form employed here is only found in chs. 1-39 of BI: a subordinate
clause introduced by יען כי and followed by a main clause (3:16; 7:5;
8:6 [here also with לכן הנה]; 30:12; 37:29). The form in question,
therefore, points to Isaianic usage.

What then is the relationship between these three individual segments? From a macro-syntactic perspective v. 11 and v. 13 are closely
linked to v. 10 (twice *wayyiqtol* after *qatal*). For a start, therefore, one
can consider vv. 11-12 as a consequence of v. 10. Since YHWH has obstructed any possibility 'to see', the vision itself has become a sealed
and inaccessible book. It does not matter if one can read or not, any possible communication between the audience and God by way of the vision has been interrupted. The link to v. 13 is less simple. Does the oracle contain an explanation for YHWH's actions in v. 10 as the accusation
suggests: the people did not seek sincere contact with God (v. 13)? Such
behaviour, however, is presented as an argument for further action on
YHWH's behalf: 'doing wonderful things' (v. 14) which will not lead to
the downfall of 'this people' but to the confusion and humiliation of the
wise. Added to the status of vv. 13-14 as an oracle, such facts lead us to
assume that v. 14 does not only contain a different expression for God's
actions in v. 10 but also, in fact, announces their consequence. YHWH is
going to do something about the arrested communication. In principle,
the idea of 'doing wonderful things' can mean more than the humiliation
of the wise. Whether it also includes salvation, it does not say. The fact
that God intends to do wonderful things is the woe cry's final word.

The following schema reveals the structure of the argumentation:

9-10   moral screening
    9   ironic exhortation
        9a   command to disregard the prophecy
        9b   observation of behaviour: drunkenness and its cause
    10   the real cause: YHWH's blinding
    10a   on the people: stupor
    10b   on the prophets: blindness
11-12   simile: the vision as a sealed book
    11   the reaction of those who can read
    12   the reaction of those who cannot read
13-14   announcement of judgement
    13   accusation: a false relationship to YHWH
    14   judgement
        14a   YHWH will go on doing wonderful things
        14b   consequences: the wisdom of the wise will perish

Exegesis by Verse

9 After the usual emendation of MT (cf. 'Notes') which results in the
translation: 'Stupefy yourselves and be in stupor, blind yourselves and

be blind' (RSV), v. 9a forms a summons to two different activities, each in the form of two imperatives of the same verb, the first of which invites the subjects to perform the activity in question upon themselves ('stupefy yourselves / blind yourselves'), the second being an invitation to carry the consequences of the first as a personal characteristic ('be in a stupor / be blind'). According to the reading of MT followed here it is a question of *two times* two different actions, the second of which being the external consequence of the first and being emphasised by the conditional function of the first: 'If you go on to tarry, you will be astounded. If you go on to delight yourselves, you will be blinded'.

The negative sense of 'to tarry' (מהה) involves to hesitate in making a decision which one is being urged to make on religious grounds (Gen. 19:16; Ps. 119:60: 'I hasten and do not delay to keep your commandments'). The term appears to express here the reluctance with which the Ariel prophecy is being received. Such hesitation will result in astonishment. The root 'to be astounded' (תמה) stands for human reaction to a visual observation of what has been brought about by God (Gen. 43:33; Deut. 28:28; Isa. 13:8; Hab. 1:5; Ps. 48:6; Eccl. 5:7; Zech. 12:4).[34] Thus, an unexpected event is supposed to take place between 'to tarry' and 'to be astounded', an event we can reasonably assume to be the fulfilment of the Ariel prophecy.

The first imperative of the second colon, 'delight yourselves', can sometimes imply the carefree attitude of children (root שעע II: Isa. 11:8; 66:12; Jer. 31:20; Prov. 30:8),[35] an aspect which fits well with the negative reception of the Ariel oracle suggested in the first colon. If the addressees are only concerned about their own pleasure and are not interested in the prophecy then persistent 'blindness' shall be their lot. With the imperative 'be blind' (שעע I, a homonym of שעע II, 'to delight') we meet a very important theme from Isaiah's call vision: '...shut their eyes (ועיניו השע), lest they see with their eyes, and understand with their hearts, and turn and be healed' (6:10). The use of this term here indicates, according to some authors, that the passage stems from the prophet himself. Strictly speaking, however, such usage in fact says nothing more than that we should understand this text, at the level of redaction, against the background of Isaiah 6, especially since the root in question only appears in PI (further in 32:3). Moreover, besides noting the agreement with 6:10 we should also pay attention to the differ-

---

[34] *TWAT*, VIII, 672f. (U. Berges).

[35] The term can also stand for religiously inspired joy: Ps. 5:7; 94:19; 119:16, 24,47,70,77,92,143,174. The aspect of nonchalant behaviour is also present in the rather difficult passage Sir. 13:6: 'When he needs you, he will deceive you'.

ence: in 6:10 it is the prophet who has to cause blindness (*hiphil*), in 29:9 it is the audience itself (*qal*). [36]

The semantic word-game being played with these four verbs is highly intricate. The audience is accused of not taking the message concerning Ariel seriously due to a lack of decisiveness and self-absorption with its own pleasure. It is warned that events will overtake it and that it will find itself in a self-elected and permanent blindness. Accusation and announcement of judgement are closely connected here in the sense that unbelief continues as mischief: those who no longer wish to see shall no longer be able to see (Hoffman 1974: 52). The literary style of the passage supports the message, the first two imperatives being consonant, the latter pair being homonymous.

It also makes sense to maintain the *qatal* forms of MT in v. 9b since they describe the current situation of the audience and explain the ironic imperatives 'tarry' and 'delight yourselves' to which they are chiastically linked: 'they are drunk' with 'delight yourselves' and 'they stagger' with 'tarry'. Drunkenness (root שׁכר) is considered negatively in the Scriptures because of its associations with social disintegration (1 Sam. 25:36; 1 Kgs 16:9f.; 20:16-21; Ps. 69:13; 107:27; Jer. 48:26; Prov. 31:4f.; 20:1; 26:9; for PI, cf. 28:7). The term 'to drink', however, also functions as a metaphor in the context of God's judgement, in as far as this confronts Israel or the nations (Isa. 19:4; 49:26; 51:21f.; Jer. 25:27f.; 48:26; 51:7; Ezek. 23:33; Job 12:25) or is preceded by a carefree attitude towards it (Isa. 24:9; Joel 1:5).[37] 'To stagger' (נוע) means to move around without intention or purpose (Gen. 4:12; Num. 32:13; 2 Sam. 15:20; Jer. 14:10; Ps. 109:10; Job 28:4; Lam. 4:14), often in the context of overwhelming events (Exod. 20:18; Isa. 7:2; 19:1; 24:19f.; Amos 4:9; 8:12; Ps. 107:27).[38]

The metaphorical charge of the terms 'to be drunk' and 'to stagger' is brought to the fore in the denial of the usual cause of such states: 'not from wine / not from strong drink'. Given the imperative 'delight yourselves', actual drunkenness need not be completely ruled out.[39] It remains mere speculation, nevertheless, to suggest, via a reference to 22:13, that this prophetic word had its origin in a drinking-bout which took place after the sudden departure of Sennacherib's army in 701 BC.[40] As a matter of fact, the literary form of antithesis, which is not in-

---

[36] *TWAT*, VIII, 355ff. (J. Hausmann).
[37] *TWAT*, VIII, 3-5 (M. Oeming).
[38] *TWAT*, V, 316f. (H. Ringgren).
[39] Delitzsch, 325; *pace* Duhm, 209; Dillmann-Kittel, 263.
[40] Hoffmann 1974: 55f.; Dietrich 1976: 181.

frequent in this part of PI (30:1-2, 6-8; 31:1-3), implies a climax (Rosenmüller, 439). The non-material cause predominates herein: 'The divine judgement imprisons them in their situation of drunkenness and vacillation over which they no longer have any control whether they drink or not. The cause of their drunkenness is now something other than drink; it is the spirit of stupefaction' (Hoffman 1974: 53). There may also be a climax at work, at the redactional level, vis-à-vis 28:1: the inhabitants of Samaria were 'only' drunk as a consequence of affluence and pleasure-seeking, the audience here is 'under the influence' of YHWH himself (Oswalt, 531).

10 Mention here of the more profound cause of the audience's drunkenness: 'YHWH has poured out upon you a spirit of deep sleep', sets up an isotopic link with the theme of drinking in vv. 8-9 via the term 'to pour out' (with 'spirit' as object only here), and with the dreams of vv. 7-8 via the notion of 'sleep'.[41] We are dealing here, however, with different actants, the new direction of speech of v. 9 being confirmed by the emphatic 'upon you' (placed before the subject). This fact and the mention of YHWH as acting subject (cf. v. 6) clearly mark this passage off as a metatext, a commentary on vv. 1-8 in which God moves against people other than those mentioned therein. From the perspective of logic, the song of Ariel which announces the punishment of Zion's enemies (vv. 6-8) also implies salvation for Zion's inhabitants. YHWH, however, does not work according to such logic. The audience, who may have expected a logical outcome, is informed that God is acting upon them in a different and direct manner. The salvific meaning of the Ariel prophecy will elude them because YHWH has poured out a 'spirit of deep sleep' upon them. 'Deep sleep' (root רדם) suggests that every form of observation and activity has been interrupted, even the primitive urge to preserve one's own life (Judg. 4:21; 1 Sam. 26:12; Jonah 1:5f.; Ps. 76:7). Sometimes God himself brings about such deep sleep in order to create something out with or beyond human beings (Gen. 2:21: woman; 15:12: covenant) or to initiate them in knowledge they could not otherwise attain (Job 4:13; 33:15; Dan. 8:18; 10:9). The question remains as to how this background feeds into our text. It is probable that a contrast is being established: 'deep sleep' does not lead to something new or to new insight – as one might expect – but rather to complete ignorance with respect to the meaning of the song of Ariel (vv. 10-11).

V. 10b further elaborates the image of 'sleep'. Persons who sleep close their eyes and place a blanket over their head (similar image in

---

[41] Fohrer 1967: 130; Exum 1981: 348.

28:20).[42] Since the sleep we are dealing with in our text comes from YHWH, he is thus the one who performs these actions on his audience. It is probable that the text confines itself to the imagery of sleep ('eyes / heads') while two explanatory glosses, 'prophets / seers', introduce the theme of prophets not doing their job (cf. Isa. 3:2). The theme in question is in widespread use: the prophets fall short because their message does not help Israel (Isa. 30:10; Jer. 5:13; Hos. 9:7; Amos 2:12; Mic. 2:6-11) or because of their own misbehaviour (Isa. 28:7; Jer. 14:13f.; 23:9-32; 29:14; Ezek. 13:2; Mic. 3:5-8; Zeph. 3:4). The present text, however, does not elaborate these elements further (thus supporting the surmise of glossation), the following verses speaking only of the audience itself (v. 11: 'you'; v. 13: 'this people').

11-12 The comparison employed in these verses must originate from a later period than that of the prophet's preaching. The content of the vision is available in written form while the phrase 'the vision of all this' presumes a point in time when prophetic oracles had been collected. 'Sealing' likewise suggests the preservation of a written document because of its consequences for the public (cf. Jer. 32:10-14). As a juridical metaphor it is not infrequently applied to prophecies, with the element of preservation until the time of their fulfilment often playing an important role (Isa. 8:16; Dan. 9:24; 12:4,9).

A good understanding of the comparison is not easy to achieve. Broadly speaking it implies that the vision is inaccessible to everyone, the learned and the unlearned alike, because a higher instance has 'sealed off' its written form (cf. 1 Kgs 21:8; Esth. 8:8-10; Dan. 6:18; Neh. 10:1f.). In this sense, the comparison is an elaboration of v. 10 ('He has closed'). At the same time, however, it contains an element of a false exoneration and thus sets the stage for the indictment of v. 13 ('this people'). The prophets often employ quotations to expose guilt. This is very clear in the response of the unlearned who admits that he is unqualified (v. 12: 'I cannot read') but says nothing of the fact that the 'writing' is sealed and thus fails to appreciate its nature and background. Does this mean that the response of the learned is correct (v. 11)? It would appear so at first sight since the 'writing' is indeed sealed and is therefore inaccessible, even for a person who can read. It would be strange, however, if the comparison were to declare the first person correct and the second person not, all the more so given that the following verse (v. 13) constitutes an accusation against all the people.

---

[42] Delitzsch, 325; Feldmann, 346.

The ingenuity of the present comparison lies in the fact that we can only look back and realise that something is wrong with the first person after we have heard about the second person. Clearly, the learned does not seem to be interested in the content of the writing nor does this person ask whether it can be opened or not (Qimchi), although the invitation 'read this' implies that the content is important for the addressee.[43] In our explanation both the learned and the unlearned are open to censure: both persons lack any interest and the second person is even indifferent with respect to the provenance of the seal, and, thus, with respect to the authority from which the 'writing' stems. Any effort to further identify the learned and the unlearned as, for example, 'the educated leaders' and 'the masses', would simply overburden the comparison (*pace* Penna, 270). Together they represent the entire people in ascending order (Feldmann, 346: v. 11 to v. 12 constitutes a climax). As a whole they are unable to understand the message, because God has prevented this. They do not even want to understand it and are disinterested in its origin. It would appear, therefore, that communication between God and his people has not unilaterally been broken off by God alone, the rupture has also been endorsed by the people.

13-14 An utterance by 'the Lord' himself (אדני; cf. 28:2) ratifies the prophet's accusation and brings the woe cry to its climax. The last time God himself spoke was in vv. 2-3 but without the accompanying introductory formula. The present utterance possesses a recognisable, compact literary form: a subordinate clause introduced by יען כי together with a main clause mostly introduced by a conjunction, in this case לכן. Such a structure is characteristic of 'an oracular pronouncement of exceptional solemnity' which explains people's past behaviour as the reason for God's future behaviour (cf. יען כי: Num. 11:20; 1 Kgs 13:21f.; 21:29; Isa. 3:16; 7:5; 8:6f.; יען only: Num. 20:12; 1 Sam. 15:23; 1 Kgs 14:13; Isa. 30:12; 21:29; Ezek. 5:11; 24:13 [44]; לכן הנני with respect to God: 1 Kgs 14:10; 2 Kgs 22:20; Jer. 16:21; 23:30,39; Ezek. 13:8; 16:37; 22:19; 25:4,7,9; 28:7; 29:10; Hos. 2:8). The present oracle, moreover, is clearly distinguished by a number of chiasms.[45]

---

[43] The comparison assumes that the undetermined individual who offers the 'writing' to be read does not know who can and who cannot read. The passive form used in v. 12 underlines this fact.

[44] D.E. Gowan, "The Use of יען in Biblical Hebrew", *VT* 21 (1971) 168-85, esp. 174f.; M.J. Mulder, "Die Partikel יען"; in: *Syntax and Meaning. Studies in Hebrew Syntax and Biblical Exegesis* (ed. A.S. van der Woude), (OTS, XVIII), Leiden 1973, 49-83, esp. 69f., 76, 82f.

[45] V. 13a: ABC / C´A´ / C´´A´´B´; v. 13b: ABC / B´C´A´; v. 14b: ABC / B´C´A´.

It is possible, on the one hand, to view the divine oracle as an original and independent prophecy of Isaiah ben Amoz, although it is clear, on the other hand, that it is neatly woven into its present literary context. The formulation is markedly Isaianic, not only from the perspective of form – an accusation and announcement of God's intervention linked via יען כי and (הנה) לכן (8:6f.; 30:12f.) – but also in view of terminology such as 'this people' (v. 13; cf. 28:11), 'to do wonderful things' (root פלא in 25:1; 28:29), 'wisdom, wise' and 'discernment, discerning' in the specific sense of political leadership (v. 14; cf. root חכם in 3:3; 5:21; 10:13; 11:2; 19:11f.; 31:2; 33:6; root בין in 1:3; 3:3; 5:21; 6:9,10; 10:13; 11:2; 27:11; 28:9,19; 29:16,24; 32:4; 33:19), and the antithesis style figure (v. 13; cf. 1:3,18,21; 2:4; 3:5,24; 5:2,7,20; 6:9; 7:11,23; 8:9f.,12f.,23; 9:1,9,19; 11:6ff.; 22:9ff.,12f.,22). From thematic perspective, moreover, it is easy to recognise the prophetic critique of the cult (cf. 1:11-17; Jer. 7:21-23; Amos 5:21-26; Mic. 6:6-8; Ps. 50:8-15). On the basis of its evidently Isaianic character, exegetes have endeavoured to explain the oracle from the historical context of the prophet's own preaching. Isaiah would be taking a stand here against a liturgical service which took place around the time of Sennacherib's siege of Jerusalem in 701 BC (cf. vv. 1-8). The topic of one's correct disposition before God, together with appropriate terminology, such as 'to draw near', 'to honour', 'mouth', 'lips' and 'heart', 'to fear' and 'to do wonders' all tend to fit well in a cultic context.[46] At the same time, the threats aimed at 'the wise / the discerning' might actually be directed towards the ruling classes (cf. 28:23-29; 31:2; Jer. 18:18; Prov. 21:30f.).[47]

While such an explanation is indeed plausible, it does not explain the function of vv. 13-14 within the woe cry as a whole. The verb form ויאמר ('He said') is on a par with ותהי ('The vision has become to you') in v. 11 (both wayyiqtols). Since we are dealing with a framing formula which serves to introduce a divine utterance, vv. 13-14 should not be seen as a description of what follows after vv. 11-12 but as commentary on vv. 10-12 as a whole. The 'hardening' of the people complies with what YHWH had predicted. This is given admirable stylistic expression: the chiastic parallelism in v. 10b and v. 14b establishes an *inclusio* which also involves isotopic associations – 'prophets / seers' is in bal-

---

[46] Dietrich 1976: 173f.; Wildberger, 1119-22.

[47] Fichtner 1949; McKane 1965. Williamson (1995) points to the fact that, on the one hand, Isaiah ben Amoz' clash with the political leaders demonstrates a common thought world, on the other hand, it shows a growing opposition between prophecy and wisdom.

ance with 'wise / discerning' and 'eyes / heads' with 'mouth / lips / heart' (v. 10 and v. 14; Exum 1981: 348).

Nonetheless, the function of this oracle does not limit itself to offering an explanatory commentary on what YHWH has done (vv. 10-12), it also announces the continuation of God's involvement: 'Behold, I go on doing wonderful things' (v. 14; for the root פלא, cf. 28:29). In other words, 'YHWH has poured out upon you a spirit of deep sleep' (v. 10) is not his final act, but a part, rather, of a more inclusive 'to do wonderful things'. A door is thereby left open for future (different) divine actions: 'Behold, I...'. This fact is underlined by the division of the recipients of such actions into two: 'this people' and 'its wise / its discerning' (v. 14). Of course, where the latter category are concerned, God's wonderful deeds have negative connotations (v. 14: 'the wisdom... shall perish). It remains possible, however, that the future holds something different for 'this people'.[48] It thus becomes evident once again that labels such as 'announcement of judgement' or 'salvation oracle' are too unrefined to be used to characterise the passage.

The change from 2nd pers. plur. (vv. 9f. and v. 11) to 3rd pers. sing. ('this people': vv. 13f.) is not inappropriate in the context. It is possible to explain it by ascribing a different *Sitz im Leben* to the concluding verses, but in its literary context, it functions as a means to broaden the target audience of the woe cry. The accusation does not only apply to those who reacted wrongly to the siege of Ariel and its sudden end (vv. 9f), nor to those for whom the vision has become a written document which they cannot and will not understand (vv. 11f.), but in the broadest sense to 'this people' as a whole.

The accusation which is intended for everyone is no longer formulated in terms of a reaction to the Ariel oracle but in general, cultic terms used in relation to one's disposition towards YHWH, terms which can be found elsewhere in the Old Testament in similar circumstances. 'Honour', which comes from the heart, and 'fear', which God himself teaches, have been withheld from YHWH.

'To honour God' (כבד *piel*) is an all-inclusive human disposition in response to God's favour, a disposition which expresses itself in prayer, liturgy and the fulfilment of the commandments (Deut. 28:58; Isa. 24:15; 25:3; 26:15; 58:13; Jer. 25:3; Ps. 15:4; 50:23; 86:9; Prov. 3:9; 14:31).[49] Such recognition has its roots in the human heart (לב[ב]), the seat of religious and ethical living (Isa. 1:5; 6:10; 9:8; 10:7,12;

---

[48] The suffixes in v. 14b make it impossible for 'wise / discerning' to coincide with 'this people' (Dietrich 1976: 173, n. 222).

[49] *TWAT*, IV, 20 (P. Stenmans).

14:13; 32:4,6; 38:3; Deut. 8:14; 29:18; 30:14; 1 Kgs 9:4; Jer. 4:14,18; 7:24; 31:32; Ezek. 36:26f.; Hos. 13:6; Ps. 28:3; 73:1; 81:13; Job 27:6; Prov. 23:12). 'The fear (יראה) of YHWH (God)' is an all-embracing concept determined by exclusive worship of YHWH and faithful adherence to the provisions of his covenant. This too is frequently localised in the heart (Deut. 5:29; Jer. 5:24; 32:39; Ps. 86:11; Prov. 23:17; Sir. 7:29; 40:26; 45:23).[50] In PI the fear of God tends to be reserved for the so-called 'end-time' (11:2f.; 25:3; 33:6; 35:4; 36:6). At the moment, Israel is accused of harbouring fear for those who are not worthy of it (7:4; 8:12; 10:24; 18:2; 21:1).

The claim that such fear is merely 'a human commandment, a thing learned' implies, on the one hand, that its origin as a commandment of God is not appreciated (cf. למד, to learn from God: Deut. 4:1,10; 5:31; 6:1; 14:23; 17:19; 31:13; Jer. 32:33; Ps. 25:4f.; 34:12; 51:15; 71:17; 94:10,12; 119:7,71; to learn from people: Deut. 18:9; Jer. 2:33; 9:13; 10:2; 12:16), and, on the other, that it is an acquired fear. The fundamental meaning of the verb למד is evident here: 'to drill, to impose something from the outside by way of habituation, discipline or negative experience' (Judg. 3:31 ['ox-goad']; 2 Sam. 22:35; Isa. 26:9; Jer. 9:19; 31:18; Hos. 10:11; Ps. 144:1).[51] It would appear, therefore, that the phrase 'a thing learned' refers to worship with 'mouth' and 'lips' (cf. the negative connotation of these terms in 6:7 and 36:5). What lies in the heart of the worshippers is pointedly left unspoken. The negative connotation of the term 'human' is apropos within Isaianic vocabulary (אנשים: 2:11,17; 5:22; 7:13), as is the fact that the verb צוה is only found in Isaiah with God as subject (5:6; 10:6; 13:3; 23:11; 34:16).

---

[50] *TWAT*, IV, 438-47 (H.-J. Fabry). The same article includes further specification of the concept within the various types of Old Testament literature.

[51] *TWAT*, IV, 577-82 (A. Kapelrud).

THE THIRD WOE CRY:
'WOE TO THOSE WHO, AWAY FROM YHWH, HIDE DEEP THEIR COUNSEL' (29:15-24)

15 Woe to those who, away from YHWH, hide deep (their) counsel!
Their deeds are in the dark,
    and they say: 'Who sees us? Who knows us?'.
16 You turn things upside down! Shall the potter be regarded as the
          clay?
    Truly, should the thing made say of its maker: 'He did not make me';
        or a thing formed of clay of him who formed it: 'He has no un-
                derstanding?'.
17 Is it not yet a very little while
until Lebanon shall turn back to a fruitful field,
    and the fruitful field shall be regarded as a thicket?
18 On that day the deaf shall hear the words of the writing,
    and out of gloom and darkness the eyes of the blind shall see.
19 The meek shall increase joy in YHWH,
    and the poor among men shall exult in the Holy One of Israel.
20 Truly, the ruthless shall be no more
    and the arrogant shall cease,
        and all who take care to do evil shall be cut off,
21 who, in a lawsuit, make a man out to be an offender,
    and lay a snare for him who reproves in the gate,
        and with an empty plea turn aside him who is in the right.
22 Therefore, thus says YHWH – who redeemed Abraham -
concerning the house of Jacob:
'Jacob shall no more be ashamed,
    no more shall his face grow pale.
23 Rather, when he sees his children, the work of my hands, in his
          midst,
he will sanctify my name;
they will sanctify the Holy One of Jacob,
    and will stand in awe of the God of Israel.
24 And those who err in spirit will come to understanding,
    and those who murmur will accept instruction'.

NOTES

15 The inversion of מיהוה ('away from YHWH') makes this adjunct of place refer not only to the object עצה ('counsel') but also to the subject המעמיקים ('those who hide deep'; Vitringa, 181).

16a Numerous far-reaching emendations have been proposed with respect to the difficult הפככם (survey in Wildberger, 1125f.).[1] LXX and Syr offer no equivalent. 1QIsᵃ (הפך מכם; according to Kutscher [316] a *lectio facilior*) and Tg (הלמהפך; Stenning [94]: 'Do you seek to pervert?') vary only slightly from MT, they are certainly familiar with the word הפך. The problem disappears if one avoids the postulation of a verbal form for the word in question and one considers it to be a substantive (הֶפֶּךְ; cf. Ezek. 16:34) in exclamation: 'O, your turning (things) upside down!' or 'O, your perversity!' (cf. as early as Rosenmüller [442], who also points to the accent *zaqef qaton*; Alexander, 467: 'perversion' rather than 'perverseness'; Wildberger, 1126; J-M, §162 c; HALAT, 243; DCH, II, 582; Schoors [175f.] follows 1QIsᵃ: 'Zo keert men de zaken om').

The Masoretic accents regard כחמר היצר as construct state: 'Surely your turning of things upside down shall be esteemed as the potter's clay' (AV); or: 'Your perversions. Do you know this, that it is like the potter's clay? Just as the clay cannot say of its maker: "He did not make me", so you cannot say that I do not understand your deeds' (Rashi [Rosenberg, 238f.]). There is hardly an author nowadays who still follows this interpretation (even Vitringa [181], Rosenmüller [442] and Alexander [467] do not).

16b 1QIsᵃ reads חמר instead of אמר, a root which is already present in the first colon. Preference is given to this reading (Kutscher, 505f.; Wildberger, 1126; Watts, 387f.).

18 We translate דברי ספר with 'the words of *the* writing' since the term in question appears to refer to the same term in 29:11 (Hitzig, 358; Alexander, 468; König, 268). Older translations render ספר as 'the Scripture' for which reason they employ the definite article (AV). Certain authors propose the collective term 'Scriptures' (Wildberger, 1140: 'canonical Scripture in the making').

19 Some commentators translate אביוני אדם as a superlative: 'the poorest (among) men' (J-M, §141 d: cf. Ezek. 7:24; Wildberger, 1134; Ges.[18], 15b; but not TWAT, I, 86 [F. Maass]; DCH, 125a). The parallel

---

[1] The reading הכפכים, 'as flasks' (reversing two letters), suggested by BHS, goes back to Robinson 1931.

texts mentioned in *DCH* might lead us to suspect an elative: 'very poor men'. One should not be tempted to apply the present phrase to humanity in general. The term says nothing more than that the poor constitute a special category. The same term אדם also has an impersonal meaning in v. 21.

21 Recent research considers the terms employed here to be juridical. Thus the word דבר is recognised as a term for a 'lawsuit' (*TWAT,* II, 115 [W.H. Schmidt]; *Ges.*[18], 240a; as early as Alexander, 469; Wildberger, 1134; NJV; NRSV). Likewise חטא *hiphil*: 'to declare an offender' (*Ges.*[18], 338: 'jem. als schuldig hinstellen', although not yet in *HALAT,* 293: 'zur Sünde verführen'). Koenen (1994: 21, n.7) maintains the older interpretation, since, in his opinion, the present text would then constitute the only place where a juridical meaning would have any validity. The argument from the context, however, is a great deal stronger.

23 LXX translates כי with αλλά (likewise Duhm, 214: 'sondern'). Following the negative clause in v. 22 such an adversative is indeed quite probable (*HALAT,* 448: *sub voce,* 3: cf. Isa. 7:8).

ילדיו is often considered to be a gloss *(BHS)*. Interpreted as a subject, the word corrects the suffix of בראתו: 'when he, that is to say his children, see(s)...' (cf. LXX; Delitzsch, 328; Duhm, 214), although in a rather wooden and syntactically unlikely manner. If one interprets the word as the object of בראתו, with מעשׂה ידי as an appositional clause, (Hitzig, 359f.; Alexander, 470), then one is obliged to read יקדישׁ as singular (Wildberger, 1135). Such an interpretation is probably the least radical. The word ought to be maintained, however, because it offers a bridge between 'Jacob', understood as singular, in v. 22b and the plural subject 'they' in vv. 23b-24, which represents 'Jacob / Israel', understood collectively.

ESSENTIALS AND PERSPECTIVES

The woe cry exclaimed in the present text is rarely considered a literary unity.[2] This is especially so if one does not accept v. 15 as a new opening but places vv. 15-16 with the previous passage, as many scholars are indeed inclined to do (Sweeney, 373-85). By doing so, however, one creates an obstacle in the path of understanding the particular purpose of this woe cry. We consider the woe cries of Isaiah 28-33 as formal elements which mark the major redaction-historical composition of this larger complex, the present case being no exception (cf. 'Introduc-

---

[2] Feldmann, 351f.; Penna, 270f.; Oswalt, 535f.

tion to Isaiah Chapters 28-39'). Moreover, the internal unity of 29:1-14, as we have seen, vouches for the redactional independence of this passage.

Historical-critical research has been unable to reach a consensus with respect to the disputed authenticity of a number of these verses.[3] Doubts with regard to the literary unity of the piece are indeed suggested by the fact that the connection between the four major segments (vv. 15-16, 17, 18-21, 22) is unclear at the outset. The direction in which we will look for an answer lies on the semantic level. Two biblical terms of major importance form an interrelated couple: 'You turn things upside down!' (v. 16) and 'Lebanon shall turn back to a fruitful field' (v. 17). It is apparent here that there is talk of reversion for evil, expressed by the term 'to turn upside down' (הפך) and of reversion for the good, expressed by the term 'to turn back' (שוב). These two reversions, however, also appear at the statement level. To the first category belongs the fact that the artefact denies its maker and the pot the potter as their origin (v. 16). To the second category belong the hearing of the deaf and the seeing of the blind (v. 18), the joy of the poor (v. 19) and the ruin of the oppressors (v. 20f.), the end of Jacob's shame (v. 22) and the fact that those who err in spirit will come to understanding (v. 24).

Hidden beneath these surface facts lies a subtle rhetorical development concerning the 'reversion' theme. The woe cry itself already discloses an absurd reversal of affairs. Reality is turned around when people think that they can keep their counsel 'hidden' from God. History is pre-eminently defined by God's 'counsel' (Isa. 5:9; 11:2; 14:24,26f.; 19:17; 23:8f.; 25:1; 28:19), and human plans only have real worth if they are in agreement with that 'counsel' (Isa. 7:5; 8:10; 16:3; 19:3,11f.; 30:1; 36:5). The attempt to keep God out of humanly devised plans, however, contains something more. It implies a withdrawal from YHWH (v. 15a), to such an extent that one expects to fall outside his field of vision, witness the quotation: 'Who sees us? Who knows us?' (v. 15b). It is followed immediately, therefore, by the direct accusation: 'You turn things upside down!' (v. 16).

This accusation is then substantiated with a double appeal, to the clear difference between 'clay' and 'the potter' on the one hand, and to the fact that no one ever hears from the mouth of an artefact: 'He did not make me' (v. 16) on the other. This fictitious quotation thus clarifies the absurd but real attitude of those who would make their own plans to the

---

[3] According to Duhm (212) and Kilian (169ff.), only v. 15 is authentic, according to Kaiser (187f., 222f.), Wildberger (1126f., 1137f.) and Barth (1977: 292ff.) only vv. 15-16, according to Procksch (379) vv. 15-16, 19-20, 22-24.

exclusion of God (cf. the double verb 'to say' in vv. 15f.). The last sentence of v. 16: 'He has no understanding' points back in particular to: 'Who knows us?'. For if the paralellism between v. 16b´ and v. 16b´´ were completely synonymous, the latter would run: 'He did not form me'. Thus, vv. 15-16 sketch a situation in which the real relationships between maker and artefact are turned on their head. They do this in such a rhetorical way that the accused, who in v. 16 also happen to be the audience, are forced to agree.

Who is the prophet addressing in v. 17? Given the encouraging content of this verse it would seem unlikely that he is still speaking to the same individuals he addressed in v. 16. More appropriate candidates would be the people spoken of in vv. 18-21 who, it is predicted, will receive the prophetic message with joy. The prophet appeals to foreknowledge, but the question as to where this information previously arose depends on the correct interpretation of v. 17b: '...until Lebanon shall turn back to a fruitful field, and the fruitful field shall be regarded as a thicket' (cf. 'Exegesis by Verse'). The prophet is not simply referring to a change in the landscape, he is simultaneously using metaphorical language to indicate what is about to happen, i.e. a change in human society: 'On that day the deaf shall hear... the blind shall see... the meek shall obtain joy... the poor shall exult' (vv. 18f.).

The text builds on the Ancient Near Eastern myth of an endangered garden and refers to another realisation thereof, namely that found in Isa. 10:34: 'He will cut down the thickets of this forest with an axe, and Lebanon with its majestic trees will fall'. In contrast to the announcement of Lebanon's restoration in the present text, Isa. 10:34 announces judgement for Lebanon. The two passages are connected by the word pair 'thicket / Lebanon', the sequence found in 29:17 being the reverse of that found in 10:34. Such phenomena occur with reasonable frequency in the case of quotations or a references to other texts (Beentjes 1982: 506-23).

A second striking fact is that the only other parallel in BI for the introductory clause of 29:17 ('Is it not yet a very little while until...') occurs in the very context of 10:34, namely in 10:25: 'Truly, in a very little while the indignation will come to an end, and my anger will be directed to their destruction'. This text announces the end of the Assyrian oppression and a turn for the good for Israel. Given the number and variety of literary correspondences between the contexts concerned (cf. 'Exegesis by Verse'), we assume that 29:17, a rhetorical question, intentionally calls 10:25 to mind.

If we are to do justice to these facts then we are likely to arrive at the following position with regard to the passage: with an appeal to a prophecy of imminent judgement against Assyria (10:25; 29:17: 'in a very little while'), those overconfident individuals who work out their own 'counsel' to the exclusion of God (vv. 15f.) together with those who commit injustice in Israel (vv. 20f.) are notified of the impending reversion of relationships. In this way the negative content of the idea 'Assyria' is projected in all its fullness against this domestic class of people. The reference text itself offered the possibility of broadening the application of the prophecy since we find therein that Assyria, Midian and Egypt have already been lined up together as Israel's oppressors, against whom God's wrath is directed (10:24-27).

Vv. 18-21 focus on those who are to be the beneficiaries of the expected reversal: 'the deaf / the blind' (v. 18) and 'the meek / the poor' (v. 19). From a tradition-historical perspective, this implies a number of different groups who are set to encounter various different forms of good fortune. 'The poor' shall be liberated from their oppressors (v. 19f.), and the perversion of justice will come to an end (v. 21). Such a theme is broadly represented in the accusations and future expectations of the prophets, Isaiah included (Isa. 1:16-23; 5:7f., 23; 58:4-7; Jer. 9:1-7; Ezek. 18:5-13; Amos 2:6f.; 5:10f.; 8:4ff.; Mic. 2:8f.; 3:2f.,9ff.). For this reason we can view vv. 19-21 as belonging to the original woe cry.

The implied identity of 'the deaf / the blind' (v. 18) is difficult to establish since the terms employed for both groups appear here for the first time in BI. One might read the text against the background of the widely held expectation that the great reversal of fortunes also included the healing of physical defects (Isa. 32:3; 35:5f.; Jer. 31:8; Ps. 146:8; Penna, 272). At the same time, however, the promise expressed in these verses was intended for a particular group of people in Isaiah's purview (Oswalt, 538). 'The deaf / the blind' in the present context are handicapped in a quite unique sense, since 'the deaf' are promised that they will hear 'the words of the writing'. The fact that a deaf individual is unable to understand a text when it is read out is not likely to be his or her most essential loss.[4] With this in mind, therefore, the promise need not be understood in a purely physical way, but rather with the fuller meaning of 'being instructed'. This is precisely the case whenever the verb 'to hear' (שמע) has the term 'word(s)' (דברים) as its object.[5]

---

[4] Cf. NJV: 'The deaf shall hear *even* written words, and the eyes of the blind shall see *even* in darkness and obscurity'.

[5] Arambarri (1990: 200f.) offers the complete list of texts.

Furthermore, the expression 'out of gloom and darkness' (מֵאֹפֶל
וּמֵחֹשֶׁךְ) is evidently metaphorical in content. Nowhere else do we find
this word pair signifying the physical condition of blindness. It refers
rather to the profound unhappiness brought about by 'the day of YHWH'
or by his judgement (Amos 5:20; Joel 2:2; Zeph. 1:15 and Isa. 8:22;
58:10; 59:9; Job 3:4ff.; 23:17 respectively; in Exod. 10:22 it means
physical darkness). V. 18b, therefore, should be understood in this non-
physical sense, as is the case with v. 18a. The darkness out of which the
blind shall escape is not one of failing eyesight but has to do with their
inability to recognise a certain cognitive content. Blindness here is the
result of YHWH's judgement.

Since 'the deaf / the blind' do not simply imply physical handicaps, a
significant number of commentators are tempted to view the promise
made to them as a redactional allusion to the preceding woe cry, the expression 'the words of the writing' constituting a literal reference to the
sealed document which cannot be read out (29:11f.) and 'the blind' being reminiscent of the eyes which YHWH closed in a spirit of deep sleep
(29:10). It is here, however, that we encounter the heart of the problem.
Does v. 18 speak of the same people who were accused in 29:9-14 of
not taking the prophecy concerning Ariel seriously (29:1-8)? Does v. 18
herald the end of the judgement announced against them?[6] If so, we are
left with the problem that a promise of salvation offered to these individuals, who coincide, in fact, with those 'who hide deep their counsel
from YHWH' (v. 15), appears to overturn the woe cry too early.

The allusion to v. 11 most probably goes hand in hand with a change
of tenor (Dillmann-Kittel, 265). In the present context, 'the deaf / the
blind' are considered to be the victims of YHWH's judgement more than
guilty offenders. Such a view is made possible by the fact that the distinct responsibilities of the adressees in 29:10-12 '(you') and 'the prophets / the seers' are not clearly demarcated. One might interpret the verses
in question as implying that the addressees are being forced to bear the
consequences of the fact that YHWH had deprived the guilty prophets of
the ability to see.

Bearing this interpretation in mind, 'the deaf / the blind' constitute a
unique category of people within the wider audience addressed by BI:
they are distinct from those against whom the woe cry is uttered (v. 15),
and from the social perspective they are considered to be among the 'the
meek / the poor' (v. 19). They too have suffered at the hands of those

---

[6] This, in fact, is Rashi's position (Rosenberg, 239f.); also Hitzig, 358; Alexander,
468.

'who, away from YHWH, hide deep their counsel' (v. 15). From a tradition-historical perspective, however, they are also to be distinguished from the oppressed in the context of the administration of justice.[7] In the unique world of BI, they embody the victims of the judgement which YHWH was obliged to bring. In short, the double perspective of address which we established with respect to the preceding woe cry is also present here. The obvious beneficiaries of the 'reversion' (v. 17) are clearly 'the meek / the poor' (v. 19). The redaction, however, has placed those who suffered under the judgement intended for the godless, i.e. the exile, on a par with the oppressed on whose behalf the prophet Isaiah spoke. When the former group hear 'the words of the writing', they emerge 'out of gloom and darkness', i.e. from the sufferings of the exile, and the salvation promised in 'the writing' is thereby fulfilled in them (this is in line with Redaq's interpretation [Rosenberg, 239f.]).

Of course we are left with the question as to why the redaction placed v. 18 before v. 19 if, from a tradition-historical point of view, vv. 19-21 constitute the initial realisation of v. 17. From the literary perspective, however, the verse sequence as it now stands is quite plausible. In its metaphorical sense, Lebanon's 'return to a fruitful field' (v. 17) is realised in the transformation of 'the deaf / the blind' and their liberation from 'gloom and darkness' (v. 18). The restoration of judicial order, in contrast, is not the subject matter of metaphorical language. Moreover, v. 19 with its topic of recognition of 'YHWH / the Holy One of Israel' constitutes a climax with respect to v. 18. Finally, the present sequence of verses has the advantage that the restoration of judicial order becomes a prospect for 'the deaf/the blind'.

The woe cry concludes with a divine utterance (vv. 22-24). Commentators have traced evidence of a later re-working (later than the primary redaction itself) in the prose character and the awkward syntax of v. 22a and v. 23a and, in particular, in the interpolations 'who redeemed Abraham' and 'his children'. From a form-critical perspective, the verses in question do not reveal the classical pattern of elements: 'God's intervention' and its 'consequences'. Nevertheless, the fact that the segment does not include an announcement of judgement against the perpetrators of injustice mentioned in v. 20f is not sufficient reason to call it an interpo-

---

[7] Such an explanation is in line with the tendency evident in a number of commentaries to envisage the presence of three distinct groups in this passage: v. 15 focuses on the godless, v. 18 on those who believe but lack proper insight (in which context reference is made to v. 24), and v. 19 on the devout believers who already live according to their faith and who will one day experience the joy of having their faith confirmed (Duhm, 213; Wildberger, 1140). According to other commentators, the second group are lacking in eschatalogical expectation (Kaiser, 221f.).

lation (*pace* Wildberger, 1135f., 1143), since these individuals are not the primary focus of the present woe cry but rather 'the deaf / the blind' and 'the meek / the poor'. The reversal announced in v. 17 shall be realised in the transformation to be experienced by Jacob. Vv. 22-24, therefore, constitute the passage's natural conclusion.

It is clear that the audience is being addressed in relation to its patriarch Jacob whose name occurs three times in vv. 22-23, with the expression 'the Holy One of Jacob' (a variant of 'the Holy One of Israel') constituting an imposing climax, given its unique appearance here in the Scriptures. The phrase 'the house of Jacob' (v. 22) is quite appropriate as a succinct and comprehensive reference to the opposing groups of 'the deaf / the blind', 'the meek / the poor' on the one hand (vv. 18f.) and 'those who, away from YHWH, hide deep their counsel' on the other (v. 15). Both groups are thus reduced to their common origin, since, among the prophets, the name of 'Jacob' constitutes a *Chiffre* for Israel's journey from election through a rift in the covenant to ultimate restoration. Moreover, 'Jacob typifies God's faithfulness toward his people, a source of comfort in deepest depression'.[8]

It would appear, therefore, that even those to whom the woe cry is addressed in v. 15, 'those who, away from YHWH, hide deep their counsel', fall under this promise to the house of Jacob since one can interpret v. 24 in every respect as referring to them. Both verses contain wisdom terminology: 'counsel' (v. 15) and 'understanding / instruction' (v. 24). The expression 'those who murmur' (v. 24) might be interpreted as referring to 'they say: "Who sees us? Who knows us?"' (v. 15), while the sentence 'those who err in spirit will come to understanding' (v. 24) might refer to the distorted order of creation in the expression: 'He has no understanding' (v. 16). Moreover, it is not a change of fortune (as in v. 17) which is being announced to 'the house of Jacob', but a change in morality. Expressions such as 'to be no more ashamed' (v. 22), and 'when he sees... the work of my hands' (v. 23) are indicative of this. In short, the sentence 'they will sanctify my name' (v. 23) is in contrast with the behaviour which constituted the subject of complaint in v. 15.

Both groups, the ruling class of political and social pragmatists for whom YHWH's name has taken on a perspective of inconvenience (v. 15 and vv. 20f.), and their victims – originally those who suffered from repressive social injustice (vv. 19-21), but also those who, because of YHWH's judgement, have remained cut off from the prophetic vision contained in 'the writing' (v. 18) –, together make up 'the house of Jacob'.

[8] *TWAT*, III, 770-4, esp. 773 (H.-J. Zobel).

(v. 20). The ruin of the latter group is secondary to the recovery and joy of the former (vv. 18f.). The needy, therefore, will ultimately have something to do with 'the house of Jacob', for whom the announcement of salvation of vv. 22-24 is intended. Thus, the mention of this target group has a retroactive function in that those who can identify themselves with the needy in vv. 18-21 may consider vv. 22b-24 as intended for them.

Consequently, in the one piece of direct speech in the passage (v. 16a: 'You turn things upside down!'), the actual party concerned is not exposed. On the contrary, in the presence of the implied audience of the passage, the prophet turns, for a moment, directly to the guilty party. In vv. 17-24 these overconfident individuals remain the subject matter of discussion. As such they return as part of the promise regarding 'the house of Jacob' (v. 24). By their conversion to 'understanding/ instruction', however, they will ultimately join the implied audience of the passage, namely 'the needy'.

The question as to the historical identity of the accused group has to be answered in a twofold fashion. On the one hand, given the signficance elsewhere in PI of the key word 'counsel' (vv. 15f.; cf. 5:19; 8:10; 11:2; 14:26; 16:3; 19:3,11,17; 28:29; 30:1; 36:5), the text appears to point to those who were in control of foreign policy and who tried to establish alliances with Egypt (28:14f.; 30:1-7; 31:1-3). On the other hand, it would appear that they were in a position to get their own way in matters of justice (vv. 20f.; cf. 28:12; 30:12; 32:6-8; 33:15). Such a bi-directional reference need not be seen as strange, given that both these topics are combined in the overall accusation of chs. 28-33. Since v. 22 speaks of the liberation of Abraham and the end of Jacob's shame, it is also possible to consider the accusation as a judgement directed against the foreign invaders with which Israel was confronted during the exile (Kilian, 170f.). In this way, the twofold perspective of the tradition manifests itself.

Commentators *date* the woe cry according to their literary-historical division of the text. The majority ascribe vv. 15-16 to the historical prophet himself and situate the verses in question in Jerusalem at a time when the inhabitants were preparing the rebellion against Assyria which would ultimately lead to Sennacherib's campaign against Judah (705-701 BC).[13] Since vv. 17-24 are often considered proto-apocalyptic, this segment is dated in the 5th century (Wildberger, 1127,1134). In recent

---

[13] R.Martin-Achard, "Esaie et Jérémie aux prises avec les problèmes politiques", *CRThPh* 11 (1984) 306-22, esp. 306-18.

years, scholars have been better able to distinguish the concern for the landscape of Northern Israel and the restoration of Jacob in these verses as well as the absence of the Zion theme. As a consequence, there is a tendency to situate the core of the passage long before the exile, after the invasion of the Northern Kingdom by Tiglath-pileser (734-732 BC; 2 Kgs 15:27-31), at a time when the inhabitants were once again occupied with the preparation of a rebellion, a situation which in Judah stimulated the expectation of a restored single Davidic kingdom (724-721 BC; 2 Kgs 17:1-3; Sweeney, 380ff.).

Such a correction with respect to the usual dating of these verses may be correct but it remains to be seen if one can establish the years of their genesis with any real accuracy. The prophecy as such is directed at a group of individuals who had attempted to reinforce their foreign policy as well as their social position with no regard for God or commandment. The situation in which Isaiah preached is evident here, a situation in which interest in the restoration of Jacob would not have been out of place (chs. 8-11). Beyond this, there are traces in the text of a post-exilic re-working, at a time when the social opposition between 'the devout' and 'the godless' had taken on a more radical perspective (vv. 18-21; cf. chs. 56-66).[14] The re-working in question knew the prophecies of Isaiah in written form and considered them equally applicable to later generations (v. 18). It understands the inheritence of Isaiah ben Amoz as a promise of swift restoration (v. 17) after which the poor would no longer be oppressed (vv. 19f.) and the leading classes would achieve wisdom (v. 24). It would be a restoration in which the prophet's major concern, the recognition of 'the Holy One of Israel', would come to fulfilment (v. 23). A more precise dating of the verses in question would appear to be impossible.

Given the passage's literary genre and direction of speech, it is clear that *the structure*, taken as a whole, is dialogical. There are three macrosyntactic words which have a discourse function: הוי (v. 15), הלוא (v. 17) and לכן (v. 22). Each of these three has a word with a deictic function nearby which produces a subordinate clause: הפככם (v. 16a: 'You turn things upside down!'; the word being an answer to the quotation: 'Who sees us? Who knows us?' in v. 15b´´) and three times the word כי (vv. 16,20,23). The fact that in each case the particle in question establishes a subordinate clause is apparent from what follows: v. 16b is an elaboration of v. 16a, v. 20 begins the description of the sec-

---

[14] As far as Vermeylen (1977: 407f.) is concerned, this is a sociological fact. Koenen (1994: 18-22) sees it more as a theological topic.

ond category of people who are subject to the time adjunct: 'Shall it not be a very little while until...' (v. 17), and in v. 23 the particle is followed by an infinitive construct, and not a finite verb.

These observations lead to the following arrangement:[15]

15-16 woe oracle

    15   woe cry and accusation with a quotation (third person)

    16   accusation / disputation

        16a'   exclamation (second person)

        16a''-b rhetorical questions with a simile (third person)

17-21 announcement of a general reversion

    17   rhetorical question with an appeal to a former prophecy

    18-21 dyptich: the lot of the just and the godless will change

        18-19 the just

            18 the deaf and the blind

            19 the meek and the poor

        20-21 the godless

            20 the end of the wicked

            21 catalogue of social offences

22-24 word of salvation to Jacob

    22a   messenger formula elaborated

    22b-24 divine oracle: the consequences of God's intervention

        22b   no longer shame for Jacob

        23   recognition of Israel's God

        24   understanding for those who err

Exegesis by Verse

15 The present woe cry (cf. 'Introduction to Isaiah Chapters 28-39') can be distinguished from the two preceding it on the basis of the fact that it does not included a proper name (cf. 28:1 and 29:1, which do), but employs, rather, a common noun as do the woe cries which follow (30:1; 31:1f.; 33:1). With the latter group it shares the presence of a substantival phrase following on the word 'woe': 'those who hide deep their counsel' (cf. 30:1: 'the rebellious children'; 31:1: 'those who go down to Egypt'; 33:1: 'destroyer / treacherous one').[16] The woe cry here in 29:15 is unique, however, in that it does not introduce an announcement of judgement as is elsewhere the case (28:2; 29:2; 30:3f.; 31:2; 33:1), but an accusation. From the very start, therefore, the present woe cry is oriented towards the promise of salvation found in vv. 22-24.

[15] Partly according to Sweeney 1996: 374f.
[16] Hardmeier 1979: 239-43, 274ff.

On the one hand, the accusation exhibits similarities with the description of the godless in the lament psalms (cf. Ps. 64:6f.; 88:7; 94:7;
Wildberger, 1128f.), on the other hand it is formulated in language characteristic of PI (cf. 5:18f.). 'To hide' plays a role in the relationship between God and human beings (סתר: 4:6; 8:17; 16:3f.; 28:15,17; 32:2)
and in the present context can even be seen as an evidently contrastive
hinge term in relation to the conclusion of the preceding woe cry (v. 14:
'the discernment of its discerning shall be hidden'). Metaphorically
speaking, the concept 'deep' (עמק) portrays the impenetrability of both
God's deeds and human depravity (respectively Isa. 7:14; 30:33; cf.
Ezek. 23:32; Ps.92:6 and Isa. 31:6; Hos. 5:2; 9:9; Ps. 64:7; Prov.
22:14; 23:27). With respect to the term 'counsel' (עצה), the first woe
cry already established that only YHWH's 'counsel' would persist (cf.
28:29). Finally, the idea of movement 'away from YHWH' in Isaiah is
usually prompted by respect for his might (מן + [an attribute of] 'God' or
'YHWH': 2:19,21; 7:1; 19:1,16,17 [with עצה]; 26:17; 30:31; 36:10;
38:6; negative meaning in 29:13; 30:11).

What follows the woe cry also includes an accumulation of concepts
characteristic of PI, although not exclusively so (v. 16b). 'Darkness' is
considered to be a place in complete opposition to the good (root חשך:
5:20,30; 9:1; 13:10; 29:15,18). The dispute concerning what people
'do' (root עשה: 2:8,20; 3:11; 10:3,13; 17:8; 22:11; 26:12,18; 28:15;
29:15; 30:1; 31:7; 32:6; 37:11,19,31; 38:3), in contrast to what YHWH
does (28:21 see there; 37:16,26,32; 38:7,15), is also a recurring theme
in PI. In addition, it is among PI's favourite procedures to illustrate the
sinful (sometimes also faithful) nature of people with a quotation (אמר,
'to speak', as introduction to a negative quotation: Isa. 5:19f.; 7:5,12;
8:12; 9:8; 10:8,13; 14:13; 19:11; 28:15; 30:10; 36:4; 37:24). Both
words, 'to do' and 'to speak', also constitute supplementary concepts to
the idea of 'counsel' (עצה; cf. 2 Sam. 16:20; Isa. 16:3; 25:1; 46:10 and
Isa. 44:26 resp.).[17] With regard to the actual content of the quotation,
questions with 'Who?' tend to be numerous in discussions between God
and human persons as well as between human persons concerning God
(1:12; 10:3; 14:27; 22:16; 23:8; 28:9; 33:14; 36:5,20; 37:23). The
verb 'to see' often functions in descriptions of Israel's distorted relationship with God (ראה: 5:12,19; 6:9f.; 17:7f.; 22:11; 26:10; 30:10). Indeed, Israel's denial in the present context that YHWH can even see her
constitutes something of a climax. The same can be said for 'to know'

---

[17] Also with synonyms: גבורה in 2 Kgs 18:20; Isa. 11:2; 36:5, צליליה in Jer. 32:19,
דבר in Isa. 8:10.

(ידע). At the very beginning of BI, YHWH already complains that Israel has no 'knowledge' of her master (1:3). Such ignorance is so pervasive that Israel ultimately turns the tables, thereby laying the foundations for the accusation which follows.

16 This verse consists of an exclamation and two rhetorical questions. The exclamation ('You turn things upside down!') includes a terse accusation expressed in a single word. In a chokmatic context such as this, the root הפך connotes ways of thinking or acting which are counter to wisdom (Amos 5:7; 6:12; Prov. 6:14; 8:13; 10:31; 16:30; 21:8; 23:33). The same root is also characteristic of the downfall of Sodom and Gomorrah ('to overthrow': Gen. 19:21,25,29; Deut. 29:22; Isa. 1:9; 13:19; 34:16; Jer. 20:16; 49:18; Hos. 11:8; Amos 4:11; Lam. 4:6).[18] The exclamation thus combines elements of both accusation and judgement.

The accusation proper consists of two rhetorical questions, both of which are ingeniously structured in the service of the course of the discussion. The passive verb form of the first question ('Shall the potter be regarded as the clay?') leaves the subject of such foolish argumentation unmentioned while the second question makes the subject explicit: 'the thing made', with 'a thing formed of clay' in the parallel colon forming a climax. In this way, 'those who, away from YHWH, hide deep their counsel' (v. 15) are put firmly in their place.

The discussion als provides an answer to the questions stated in v. 15: 'Who sees us? Who knows us?', it is namely 'the maker / he who formed'. Both words are trade related (Isa. 5:5; Jer. 18:3 and Isa. 30:14; 41:25; Jer. 18:6; Lam. 4:2 respectively) as well as names for the Creator (together elsewhere in 27:11; 'the Maker' in 17:7, parallel with 'the Holy One of Israel'; 'he who forms' in 22:11; 37:26). The first term (root עשה) is comprehensive and draws more attention to the product: 'He did not make me'. The second term (root יצר) is the proper term for the manufacture of pottery and focuses more on the care and effort involved in the procedure: 'He has no understanding'. The latter term links up with the woe cry: those who think they can hide their 'counsel' from YHWH, envisage YHWH as one inferior to themselves.

Thus the audience is reminded that they are created beings and that they ought not to reverse their relationship with YHWH. The argumentation is based on the Ancient Near Eastern[19] and Old Testament notion

---

[18] TWAT, II, 456-9 (K. Seybold).

[19] Cf. an ancient Babylonian text concerning the creation of man by the mother goddess: 'Let Lullu appear! He who shall serve all the gods, let him be formed out of clay, be animated with blood!' (ANET, 99). For Ancient Near Eastern parallels, cf.

that God formed (יצר) human persons and other living beings out of clay in the same way as the potter fashioned his pots (cf. 'clay' [חמר] in the present context: Isa. 45:9; 64:7; Jer. 18:4ff.; Job 10:9; 33:6; in Gen. 2:7f.,19 'of dust from the ground'; without mention of the material employed: Isa. 43:7; 49:5; Amos 7:1; Ps. 104:26). The notion was later expanded to include the creation of the cosmos (Isa. 45:18; Amos 4:13; Ps. 95:5). The metaphor led to YHWH as Creator being given the title יוצר ('He who forms / has formed'), a title which was then applied to the creation of Israel, particularly by DI (Isa. 43:1,21; 44:2,21,24; 45:11; Jer. 10:16; 51:19).

The belief that God created human persons is thus given a characteristic application in v. 16. It not only provides an answer to the question of human origins but also places our daily activities in the presence of YHWH. Those who think they can organise their lives without God foolishly deny the very one whose hands formed and created them. We encounter here what for Isaiah constitutes the very foundation of the moral order. No matter how concrete he was as a prophet in his indictment of unethical behaviour, he still enjoyed the opportunity to hark back to the human attitude which is the source of all sin: the failure to appreciate reality as a well-ordered whole in which God as Creator and the human person as creature each have their own place, the failure to recognise, in a certain sense, the 'natural law' (cf. 1:2f.; 2:6-22; 5:20; 8:19; 31:3).[20]

17 We already argued above (cf. 'Essentials and Perspectives') that the adjunct of time, 'Is it not yet a very little while'..?, refers to 10:25: 'Truly, in a very little while the indignation will come to an end, and my anger will be directed to their destruction'.[21] This verse belongs to a passage which announces the end of Assyrian oppression and a turn for the good for Israel (10:5-34). It serves its purpose in a striking way in that 'the indignation' spoken of concerns Israel while 'my anger' concerns Assyria (cf. 26:20).[22] The only difference between the two texts lies in

Th.C. Vriezen, *Onderzoek naar de paradijsvoorstelling bij de oude semietische volken,* Wageningen 1937, 87f., 91-4, 129f. (which nuances the development of the concept 'potter' into the divine title 'Creator'); Wildberger 1129ff.; G. Pettinato, *Das altorientalische Menschenbild und die sumerischen und akkadischen Schöpfungsmythen,* (AHAW.PH, 1), Heidelberg 1971; C. Westermann, *Genesis. 1. Teilband Genesis 1-11* (BKAT, I/1), Neukirchen 1974, 276-82.

[20] Barton 1981.

[21] Modern commentators agree in recognising Isa. 10:5-34 as a redactional unity, entitled 'Woe, Assyria' (v. 5), which deals with the role and fall of Assyria (Oswalt, 260-76; Kilian, 80-7; for Watts [154f.] 10:24-12:6 forms such a unity).

[22] A suggestion exists that we change the MT reading in 10:25b: ואפי על תבליתם into ואפי על תכל יתם 'my anger will be wholly brought to an end' (S.R. Driver 1937: 39). Reading the text this way means that God's wrath is directed to only one nation, namely Israel. A number of authors have adopted the emended reading (Wildberger, 417, 420).

the fact that 10:25 is introduced by an emphatic particle (כי) and 29:17
by an interrogative particle (הלוא). We are led to conclude, therefore,
that the latter text, a rhetorical question, is reminiscent of the former. It
may seem pretty unlikely that 10:25 constitutes the reference text of
29:17 given that 29:15-24 is not dealing with a foreign enemy (cf. the
sort of crimes in vv. 20-21). Yet, there are clearly a number of striking
agreements in word usage and style between the two passages:

(1) The introductory 'woe' (הוי:10:5 and 29:15)
(2) The end or new shape of 'Lebanon' (10:33f. and 29:17) and the words
'fruitful field' (כרמל) and 'thicket' (יער: 10:18f. and 29:17)
(3) The proper names 'the Holy One of Israel' (10:17,20 and 29:19,23) and
'(the house of) Jacob' (10:20f. and 29:22f.)
(4) The theme 'the work of God' (10:12,23 and 29:23) as opposed to the
work of Assyria and human work (10:11,13 and 29:16)
(5) The terms 'to cease' (כלה: 10:18 and 29:20), to (be) cut off (כרת hiphil
and niphal: 10:7 and 29:20) and 'reversion' (שוב: 10:21f. and 29:17)
(6) Quotations which expose arrogance (10:8-11 and 29:16) and an appeal to
the natural order in the form of a question (10:15 and 29:16).

Such a harvest of agreements ultimately leads us to the conclusion
that, with an appeal to a prophecy against Assyria (10:25), the addressees of vv. 18-21 are being reminded of an imminent reversion of relationships. In this way the negative content of the idea 'Assyria' is projected against their godless oppressors.[23]

The prophet's reference to 10:5-34 raises the question of the correct
interpretation of v. 17b: 'until Lebanon shall turn back to a fruitful field,
and the fruitful field shall be regarded as a thicket'. Some difficulties
present themselves at this point.

The opinion that the change in landscape should be seen as a metaphor for a change in human society (vv. 18ff.) has a great measure of
probability because we would expect a more elaborated text if a change
in the countryside itself was the only intention (cf. 33:9; 35:1f.; 51:3;
55:12f.). Moreover, the verb ושב ('shall return') is difficult to understand here without viewing it as part of a metaphorical statement. The
root שוב almost invariably means 'to turn back to a point of departure'.
The idea that Lebanon would *turn back* to the landscape condition of 'a
fruitful field' in a purely literal sense is difficult to accept since nowhere

---

[23] We find a similar phenomenon of interpretation in the other reference text, 10:34:
'He will cut down the thickets of this forest with an axe, and Lebanon with its majestic
trees will fall'. Originally, vv. 33f. were directed to a party in Jerusalem who were in favour of a political alliance with Ashdod against Assyria. The final redactor of 10:5-34,
however, intended 'Lebanon' to be the Assyrian world power, which God would destroy
(Schoors, 91f.; Wildberger, 427f., 433ff.).

in the Scriptures do we find the idea that Lebanon in older times was not a wood but 'a fruitful field'.[24] In the Psalms and the prophetic literature, however, Lebanon has a metaphorical significance. Renowned for its imposing cedars (Judg. 9:15; 1 Kgs 5:13; 2 Kgs 14:9; 19:23; Isa. 60:13; Ezek. 17:3; Ps. 29:5; 37:35; 92:13; 104:16) and its lofty mountain peaks (Jer. 18:14; 22:6), Lebanon was also a symbol for those who opposed YHWH in their arrogance, those who would ultimately taste humiliation (Isa. 2:13; 10:34; 14:8; 33:9; 37:24; Jer. 22:23; Ezekiel 31; Zech. 11:1-3; Nah. 1:4f.).[25] It has been conjectured, in this connection, that a number of these texts build on the Ancient Near Eastern (Mesopotamian and Canaanite) myth of an endangered garden on mount Lebanon. With the reception of this idea in Israel, Jerusalem could be conceived of as Lebanon, her inhabitants as trees of the forest and YHWH as their, sometimes defied, owner.[26] Among the texts quoted, those from Isaiah (especially 10:33f.) are considered strong evidence of the influence of such a mythologoumenon.[27]

In this way, the term 'to turn back' (שוב) in v. 17 becomes comprehensible. On the level of the original myth it implies the recovery of an original, unsullied condition, while on the level of the context it suggests the recovery of the correct attitude and behaviour, i.e. the end of the abuses described in vv. 15f. 'Lebanon' is a metaphor for those who have raised themselves up in their pride against YHWH, as is the case elsewhere in PI (cf. the texts quoted above). The general meaning of the verb, 'to turn back', properly applies here, but it need not imply a return to a past situation or condition as much as to a *normal and normative* attitude.

The use of the phrase 'fruitful field' (כרמל) in BI supports this interpretation. It arises in the context of concern either for what people experience of God (10:18; 16:10; 32:15f.), or the way they behave towards him (37:24). Even when the word functions as a proper name, mount 'Carmel', it still has to do with the notion of empathising with God's works (33:9; 35:2).

---

[24] Some dictionaries seem to have adopted the non-metaphorical, physical interpretation since they suggest that in this verse alone the meaning 'to turn back' does not hold good and that the term here means something similar to 'to become like'; cf. J. Fürst, *Hebräisches und chaldäisches Handwörterbuch zum Alten Testament II*, Leipzig, 1876, 416a; BDB, 998a; *HALAT*, 1328; Holladay 1958: 55. Most translations and commentaries follow this interpretation, LXX: μετατεθήσεται; cf. AV, RSV, NJV, StV, TOB, EÜ. Only M. Buber, REB and BJ form an exception.

[25] *TWAT*, IV, 466-9 (M. J. Mulder).

[26] Stolz 1972.

[27] Barth 1977: 71f.

The second half of v. 17b ('and the fruitful field shall be regarded as a thicket') raises further difficulties. Are we talking here of a change for the good, as was the case in the first half of the verse, or a change for the worse, paraphrased: 'The proud forest becomes a garden, the garden a proud forest'? The latter position seems to be ruled out because the result of the change is not 'Lebanon' but יער. The word יער is not the equivalent of 'forest' but implies a terrain which, due to its luxuriant though not very useful bushes, is difficult to get at and to cultivate ('thicket'; NJV: 'mere brush').[28] As a consequence, the verb used here is not 'to turn back' (שוב) or 'to become like' (היה ל) but 'to be regarded as' (חשב niphal). This does not mean that the qualitatively higher landscape, 'the fruitful field', shall degenerate into the qualitatively lesser one, 'thicket', but that 'the fruitful field' – normally an exception in the landscape and brought about by careful cultivation – shall pass for the normal form of the landscape, as the thicket does now.[29]

Thus the verb 'to be regarded as' functions in the two 'reversions' which form the main theme of the passage. A negative reversion of values takes place when the potter is esteemed as clay (v. 16) and a positive reversion takes place when 'the fruitful field' is regarded as if it were mere steppe with its copse. V. 17b′′ is not, therefore, antithetically parallel with v. 17b′[30] but progressively parallel.[31]

18 The expression 'on that day' is in the second position here. As such, it partly lacks the characteristics of formulaic usage. At the same time, it does not function to unite independent prophetic sayings in a secondary relationship (cf. Exod. 8:18; Deut. 31:17; 1 Sam. 8:18; 1 Kgs 13:3; 22:25; Isa. 3:7; 5:30; 19:21; 30:23; Jer. 25:33; Hos. 2:20; Zech. 2:15; 6:10; 12:8). While the phrase evidently refers to some undetermined time in the future, its connection here with v. 17 ('Is it not yet a very little while...') suggests 'immediate future' rather than that of 'the end-time'.[32]

We have already noted that the healing of 'the deaf / the blind' should not be understood in exclusively physical terms (cf. 'Essentials and Per-

[28] C. Houtman, "De jubelzang van de struiken der wildernis in Psalm 96:12b"; in: *Loven en geloven (Feestbundel N.H. Ridderbos), Amsterdam 1975, 151-74, esp. 168; TWAT*, III, 783-7, esp. 786 (M.J. Mulder).

[29] In itself, the root חשב does not have any negative connotations; cf. *TWAT*, III, 248: 'Tätigkeit und Vorgang sind wertfrei bezeichnet, wenn sich חשב auf ein gegenständliches Objekt bezieht' (K. Seybold). Accordingly Houtman (*ibid.;* my translation): 'The fertility would be so immense that even plantations would serve as firewood'.

[30] *pace* Redaq (cf. Rosenberg), Vitringa, Watts, Fohrer, *ad locum.*

[31] Thus, in principle, the Targum: 'Lebanon shall again be as a fruitful field, and the fruitful field shall cause many cities to be inhabited' (Stenning, 94; cf. Schoors, 176).

[32] De Vries 1975: 311, 342: 'just over the horizon of the morrow'; De Vries 1995: 39.

spectives'). '(Not) hearing', often coupled with '(not) seeing', as the (un)willingness or (in)ability to receive and understand God's word, is an important theme in PI. YHWH himself has given a mission to the prophet which envisages that Israel shall not hear and shall not understand (6:10; cf. 1:19; 7:13; 28:9,12,14; 32:3,9; 33:13). If we apply this to v. 18 and take the connection with vv. 11-12 seriously, then 'the deaf' come to mean those who cannot take cognisance of any message. They are the victims of the fact that, according to vv. 11f., there is no one to be found who can 'read' (קרא) the book. It should be noted that the verb 'to read' dominates vv. 11f., while 'to hear' is absent.

Due to the parallelism, therefore, the verb 'to see' has 'the words of the writing' from the first half of the verse as its object. At first glance this would seem problematic. Nevertheless, the 'writing' mentioned in vv. 11-12, is a report of 'the vision of all this', a phrase which in turn harks back to 'the vision of the night' (v. 7). Indeed, blindness is an important topic in the immediate context of vv. 11-12. The addressees are sarcastically summoned: 'Delight yourselves and be blind... For YHWH has closed your eyes, the prophets' (vv. 9-10). In other words, blindness with respect to the vision goes hand in hand with the sealed book from which no one is able to read so that the words may be heard. It is God's one punitive measure against his people.

Interpreted thus, v. 18a and v. 18b are in harmony with the not-purely-physical meaning of 'to hear' and 'to see'. Such an explanation, which is supported in fact by several commentators, has the advantage that it does justice to the connection with vv. 11f. while revealing simultaneously which 'writing' is being referred to in v. 18. In addition, it clarifies the identity of the deaf and the blind. They are not to be viewed in general terms as the physically and therefore socially deprived nor should they be interpreted as people with a hardened heart who refuse to accept God's word. There is clearly a difference between those who cannot read (vv. 11f.) and the deaf who will 'hear the words of the writing' (v. 18), as there is between those who, under God's punishing hand, are to strike themselves with blindness (vv. 9f.), and the blind who will 'see out of gloom and darkness' (v. 18).[33] The latter are the victims of the former. They are suffering from the consequences of the judgement which YHWH, in the form of 'blinding' and a 'closed book' (vv. 9-12), has been forced to bring upon his people. For this reason, the change of fortune spoken of in v. 18 does not concern those to whom the woe cry

---

[33] The use of different words for 'blind' functions well here (in v. 9 the root שעע, in v. 18 עורים).

is announced in v. 15; it concerns, rather, the victims of the judgement that such individuals have called down upon Israel. While the former group perform their deeds 'in the dark' (v. 15), the latter group will be allowed to leave their 'gloom and darkness' (v. 18).

19 The terms 'the meek / the poor' (אביונים / ענוים) usher the well-known biblical category of the needy into view (both terms in the plural: Isa. 41:17; Ps. 12:6; 69:33f.; Job 24:4; Prov. 30:14; one in the plural, one in the singular: Isa. 32:7; Amos 8:4; Ps. 9:19; 72:4; both in the singular: Deut. 15:11; 24:14; Jer. 22:16; Ezek. 16:49; 18:12; 22:29; Ps. 35:10; 37:14; 40:18; 70:6; 74:21; 86:1; 109:16,22; Job 24:14; Prov. 31:9, 20). Israel generated a legal system for the protection of the weakest members of society and a correlative social ethics and 'theology of the poor' which developed significantly throughout the course of history.[34] It is often difficult, therefore, to establish the precise meaning of specific terms in individual texts. In light of the accompanying concept 'joy in God', the term ענוים in v. 19 appears to refer more to the spiritual attitude of 'the poor of YHWH' than to a social class of less well-off individuals and for this reason it is usually translated 'the meek'. What follows in vv. 20f., however, also seems to suggest an element of juridical-social content. The use of the term elsewhere in PI reveals a similar ambiguity, a fact which need not be considered unusual given that a special relationship between God and the underprivileged can be detected in even the oldest layers of the Scriptures. The poor thus enjoy YHWH's special protection and their fellow human beings are obliged to assist them (Exod. 23:1-3,6-12; Amos 2:6f.; 4:1f.; 8:4-7; Jer. 22:16; Prov. 14:31; 19:17; Job 31:13-23). The social, ethical and theological dimensions of the term have scarcely known any form of independent existence. The present passage is a good illustration of the fact that the conflict between YHWH and his adversaries (vv. 15f.) in Israel is usually played out in the territory of the socially powerless. God affirms his divine rectitude in his defense of the poor.

Although the term 'men' (אדם) in the expression 'the poor among men' might appear a little unusual (cf. 'Notes'), this need not necessarily be the case if one is aware of the fact that it plays a noteable role in PI in the topic of the opposition between God and human persons, in which contexts God's holiness is sometimes under discussion in the same way as it is here (2:9,11,17,20,22; 5:15 [cf. 16]; 6:11f. [cf. 3]; 13:12; 17:7;

---

[34] The amount of literature on this topic is overwhelming. Useful surveys can be found in *TWAT*, I, 28-43 (G.J. Botterweck); VI, 247-70 (E. Gerstenberger); cf. also F. Crüsemann, *The Torah: Theology and Social History of Old Testament Law*, Edinburgh 1996 (German edition: München 1992).

31:3,8 [cf.1]; 37:19; 38:11). The accompanying terms are to be found
in texts which can be ascribed to both the prophet himself as well as to
the tradition ('meek' [ענו or עני]: 3:14f.; 10:2; 11:4; 14:32; 26:6;
32:7; 'poor' [אביון]: 14:30; 25:4; 32:7). There appears to be insufficient reason, therefore, not to ascribe v. 19 to the original prophecy of
Isaiah ben Amoz (*pace* Wildberger, 1137).

On the day of 'the reversal', YHWH will reveal himself as 'the Holy
One of Israel'. The significance of this divine title, and particularly of its
relational content, is generally recognised.[35] 'Holy' might even be considered a primary feature of YHWH in PI (1:4; 5:16,19,24; 6:3;
10:17,20; 12:6; 17:7; 30:11f.,15; 31:1; 37:23; also in the rest of BI)[36]
and it is certainly characteristic of these chapters that the denial of
YHWH's holiness is not only a cultic matter but also an ethical one (1:4;
5:16,18ff.; 6:5,7; 10:20f.; 30:11f.; 31:1f.).[37] God's holiness can be discerned in the context of the offence he has endured because of his rejection by Israel (1:4; 5:18f.,24; 30:8-14; 31:1; 37:23ff.). At the same
time, however, it reveals itself in the fact that God inspires people to
deeds of righteousness (5:16; 17:7f.). God's holiness, therefore, is not
only disciplinary, it is also orientated towards the purification of his people (6:3; 10:17,20; 12:6; 30:15).

Those who have suffered because of others who, in their arrogance,
reject God's concern (v. 15), shall ultimately derive joy from his superior might. Terms for 'joy' can also be found elsewhere in PI: 'joy' [root
שׂמח]: 9:2,16; 14:8,29; 16:10; 22:13; 24:7,11; 25:9; 35:10; 39:2; 'to
exult' [root גיל]: 9:2; 16:10; 25:9; 35:1f. Only in 9:2; 25:9; 35:10,
however, is there mention of the joy which God has prepared for Israel
persecuted, here at the hands of alien oppressors. As is always the case,
'joy' does not only express a feeling or sentiment, it also constitutes the
articulation of that feeling or sentiment in expressions of gratitude towards God who has brought an end to affliction (Isa. 51:3,11; 55:12;
66:8; Jer. 33:6,11; Joel 2:23; Zeph. 3:14; Zech. 2:14; 8:9; 10:7; Ps.
14:7; 68:4; 97:1,8,12; 126:3; 149:2).[38]

20-21 The joy of the poor lies in the cessation of the injustice they
have been forced to endure, as part of the downfall of *every* oppressor.
V. 20 has an unusual form, the subjects constituting a climax: 'the ruthless', 'the arrogant', 'all who watch to do evil'. The verb forms appear to

[35] Gammie 1989. Cf. the same author for a survey of how the interpretations of the
concept in question have developed.
[36] Jüngling 1985: 97-101; Gammie 1989: 71-96.
[37] *TWAT*, VI, 1193f. (H. Ringgren).
[38] *TWAT*, VII, 812f.: 'שׂמחה ist kein reines Abstraktum' (G. Vanoni).

be in reverse order. The sequence: 'to be cut off', 'to cease', 'to be no more' might have been more logical but in connection with v. 19, the development most closely related to the joy of the poor is mentioned first: the oppressors are no more. Thus a contrast also emerges between the two verses: in v. 19 the poor are aware that YHWH is on their side; in v. 20 the evildoers are alone in their downfall. Supported by all the aformentioned semantic elements, the portrayal of the needy and their oppressors rises above any specific, historically demonstrable group and establishes a picture of a sort of final judgement over the just and the godless.[39] The downfall of the latter is described partly in wisdom terminology as a process which brings about its own inevitable end ('to be no more', 'to cease'), partly as a sentence or penalty ('to be cut off'), although without mention of God as the one who will carry it out. The expression 'to be cut off' (כרת *niphal*) is characteristic of prophetic utterances against the nations as well as being distinctive of the theme of the righteous in their struggle against those who do evil.[40] All this is clearly part of the present context, given that the passage concludes with the mention of 'the righteous' (צדיק), who also constitute a topic within the purview of PI (3:10; 5:23; 24:16; 26:2,7).

In v. 21, the announcement of the downfall of the godless switches over to a summary depiction of their wicked deeds. In what might be considered predominantly juridical language – language which, for the most part, can be found elsewhere in PI –, the present violation of the juridical order ('in a lawsuit / in the gate') is roundly denounced.

What follows is a review of the most significant terms found in vv. 20-21 as they are employed in PI and elsewhere:

V. 20 - 'to be no more' (אפס): Isa. 16:4; 34:12; 40:17; 45:14; 47:10; Amos 6:10; Zeph. 2:15; the synonym אין is more frequently encountered in PI with the same meaning: 1:30; 5:9; 6:11; 14:31; 17:2,14; 19:7; 33:19; 34:12.
- 'to cease' (כלה): Isa. 1:28; 10:18; 15:6; 16:4; 21:16; 31:3; Jer. 16:4; 44:27; Ezek. 5:12; 13:14; Ps. 39:11; 71:13; 73:26; 90:7; Job 4:9; 33:21; Prov. 5:11.
- 'to be cut off' (כרת *niphal)* in oracles against the nations: Isa. 14:22; Jer. 47:4; 48:2; 51:62; Ezek. 21:8f.; 25:7, 13,16; 29:8; 30:15; 35:7; Amos 1:5,8; 2:3; Ob 14; Zech. 9:6; in the context of the struggle of the righteous: Ps. 12:4; 34:17; 37:9,22,28,34,38; 109:13,15; Prov. 2:22; 10:31; further in Gen. 9:11; Isa. 48:19; 56:5; Hos. 8:4; Dan. 9:26.
- 'ruthless' (עריץ): Jer. 15:21; Job 6:23; 15:20; Ps. 37:35; Prov. 11:16; elsewhere in PI the word refers to foreign enemies: 13:11; 25:3-5; 29:5.
- 'arrogant' (לץ): Ps. 1:1; Prov. 3:34; 9:8; 15:12; 21:24; absent elsewhere in PI.

[39] Koenen 1994: 18-22.
[40] *TWAT*, IV, 360f. (G.F. Hasel).

- 'all who watch (to do) evil' (שֹׁקְדֵי אָוֶן) may constitute a superlative variant of the well-known expression 'workers of iniquity' (פֹּעֲלֵי אָוֶן): Isa. 31:2; Hos. 6:8; Ps. 5:6; [+ 15 times in Ps.]; Job 31:3; Prov. 10:29. The concept 'evil' is many-sided, mostly including an aspect of 'social evil': Isa. 1:13; 10:1; 31:2; 32:6; 55:7; 59:6f.; 58:9; Ezek. 11:2; Hos. 12:12; Zech. 10:2; Ps. 10:7; 36:4; 41:7; 55:11; Job 22:15; 34:36; Prov. 6:12; 11:7; 17:4.

V. 21 - 'to make a man to be an offender', literally 'to bring into sin / guilt or condemnation or punishment' (חטא *hiphil): Deut. 24:4; Eccl. 5:5; the root is fairly frequent in PI (although not always with juridical implications): 1:4,28; 3:9; 5:18; 6:7; 13:9; 27:9; 30:1; 31:7; 33:14; 38:17.

- 'lawsuit' (דבר): Exod. 18:16,19,22,26; 22:8; 23:8; 24:14; Deut. 1:17; 16:19; 17:9; 19:15; Judg. 18:7,28; 2 Chron. 19:6.

- 'to lay a snare' (קוֹשׁ, mostly יקשׁ) is often used for the wicked plans of the evil doers and for the consequences of involvement therewith: Ps. 64:6; 69:23; 124:7; 140:6; 141:9; Prov. 6:2,5; 12:3; 29:6,25 and Exod. 23;33; Deut. 7:16; Judg. 2:3; 1 Sam. 18:21; in PI the term relates to God's judgement: 8:15; 28:13.

- 'to reprove' (יכה *hiphil) has a variety of forensic meanings which can be found in Gen. 21:25; Lev. 19:17; Jer. 2:9; Hos. 4:4; Mic. 4:3; Job 6:25; Prov. 9:8; 15:12; 19:25; 24:25; the participial form employed here appears to be a term for a judicial function: Ezek. 3:26; Amos 5:10; Prov. 9:7; 25:12; 28:23; Job 9:33; 32:12; 40:2; the root has a less specific content in PI: 1:18; 2:4; 11:3f.; 37:4.

- 'to turn aside' (נטה *hiphil) also has a variety of juridical meanings; with a person as object it means 'to deny someone just and due process': Isa. 10:2; Amos 5:12; Mal. 3:5; Job 24:4; Prov. 18:5.[41]

22-24 A divine utterance concludes the passage. Although no one is directly addressed (2nd pers.) herein and the utterance refers to Jacob, God does, however, speak of himself (1st pers. in v. 23a). For whom is this divine utterance intended?

The mention of 'the house of Jacob' in the messenger formula (v. 22a) and the double appearance of the name 'Jacob' in the ensuing message (vv. 22b-23) are sufficient proof that the name itself must be of interest to those who stand to gain from the message as such. What does the name 'Jacob' call to mind in PI? (The name mostly occurs several times in one particular context: Isa. 2:3,5f.; 10:20f.; 14:1; 27:6,9; further in 8:17; 9:7; 17:4; 'the house of Jacob' in 2:6; 8:17; 10:20; 14:1; the word pair 'Jacob / Israel' in 9:7; 14:1; 27:6.) It is striking that the context frequently has to do with Israel's sins or the law which should be the norm for her behaviour (2:3,5f.; 8:17; 9:7; 10:20f.; 27:6,9).

---

[41] Bovati 1986: 171ff. Besides the usual translation of בתהו with 'with an empty plea' (ב *pretii;* cf. Amos 2:6: 'for a pair of shoes'), Bovati (172, n. 51) suggests the possible interpretation of the term as a sarcastic adjunct of place: 'in an empty place', parallel to 'in the gate' (ב *loci;* cf. Prov. 18:5; Isa. 45:19; 59:4).

What we probably have here is a continuation of the tradition concerning Jacob with whom the prophets above all have identified Israel, the Northern kingdom (Isa. 43:27f.; Jer. 9:3; Hos. 12:4; cf. also Deut. 32;14f. [cf. LXX]; Ps. 85:30).[42] This might also be the case in vv. 22f. The announcement that 'Jacob shall no more be ashamed' (v. 22) leads us to suspect that the cause of this shame lies in the Northern state's unwarranted trust in political alliances (cf. the meaning of 'to be ashamed' [בושׁ] in Isa. 1:29; 20:5; 26:11; 30:3, 5; 37:7).

If the name 'Jacob' arouses this kind of association, the question arises whether the new situation, as announced in these verses (cf. twice 'no more' in v. 22), describes a turn-about among the wayward 'makers of plans' (vv. 15f.) rather than a reversal of fortunes for the oppressed (vv. 18-21). At first glance it is perhaps tempting to equate those who will sanctify YHWH (v. 23) with those who will rejoice in him (v. 19), but such an identification depends entirely on the two related terms 'the Holy One of Israel' (v. 19) and 'the Holy One of Jacob / the God of Israel' (v. 23b). At the same time, we must give due weight to the differences between the two groups: the needy in v. 19 shall 'increase joy / exult', the people in v. 23 shall 'sanctify / stand in awe'. Furthermore, it is not a change of fortune which is being announced to the 'house of Jacob' (as is the case in vv. 18-21) but a change in morality. Expressions such as 'to be no more ashamed' (v. 22b), 'when he sees... the work of my hands' (v. 23) and 'to come to understanding' (v. 24) are indicative of this. For this reason it is not recommended that we equate '(the house of) Jacob' with the needy in vv. 28-21. The sentence 'when he sees... the work of my hands' (v. 23: מעשׂה ידי) points precisely in the direction of 'the makers of plans' in vv. 15-16. Where these individuals are concerned, the deeds of YHWH are up for discussion both thematically (v. 16: 'He did not make me' [לֹא עֹשׂני]) and practically in that they try to hide their own deeds from him (v. 15: מעשׂיהם). Thus the expression 'the work of my hands' will not have originally referred to 'his children', but rather to YHWH's deeds in the history of his people (Wildberger, 1144).

In this regard, the transition from singular (vv. 22-23a) to plural (v. 23b) is significant. The present form of the text leads us to suspect that the tradition wanted to focus on the continuation of the generations, drawn by the fact that the text it had at its disposal already made allusion to the sins of the patriarch (v. 22b) and to the development of 'Jacob' into 'Israel' (v. 23b). To this end, it added the words 'who redeemed Abraham' to the beginning of v. 22 and then inserted the term 'his chil-

---

[42] *TWAT*, III, 771f. (H.-J. Zobel).

dren' which it made the subject of the sentence: 'They will sanctify the
Holy One of Jacob and will stand in awe of the God of Israel' (v. 23b;
cf. 'Notes'). In this way, an unbroken line was established from Abraham to Jacob, from the patriarch (singular) to 'his children' (plural).
Jacob's sense of shame with regard to his sins is justified, but in spite of
his failures, YHWH has remained faithful to the redemption of Abraham.
Thus in the midst of Jacob, YHWH has performed deeds for which Jacob's
children sanctify his name. The use of the term 'children' (ילדים) instead
of 'sons' (בנים) supports a non-historical interpretation: not only Jacob's
own sons but also future generations will sanctify YHWH.[43]

The phrase 'who redeemed Abraham' acquires its meaning
against such a background. The patriarch in question is not mentioned
elsewhere in PI (although he does appear elsewhere in the prophets: Isa.
41:8; 51:2; 63:16; Jer. 33:26; Ezek. 33: 24; Mic. 7:20). It is only in
the book of Jubilees (mid 2nd century BC) that God is called upon 'to
redeem' Abraham, namely in the specific context of his prayer for liberation from the service of the idols in Ur and from the hostility of the
idol worshippers in his own family: 'Save me from the hands of evil
spirits which rule over the thought of the heart of man, and do not let
them lead me astray from following you, O my God' (12:20).[44] This late
text can hardly be the source of Isa. 29:22 but it does allow us a glimpse
into the way in which the course of Abraham's life eventually came to
be interpreted. The verb פדה, employed here for 'to redeem', connotes
liberation from the binding claims or persecution of a third party for
which God demands nothing in return (in earlier texts: Exod. 13:13;
21:8,30; 34:20; 1 Sam. 14:45; 1 Kgs 1:29; Hos. 7:13; 13:14; Mic.
6:4; in later texts: Isa. 1:27; 35:10; 50:2; 51:11; Num. 3:45; Deut.
7:8; 9:26; 21:8; Jer. 15:21; 31:11; Ps. 25:2; 49:9,16; 69:19; 78:42;
130:8).[45] The same continues to hold in v. 22. Just as YHWH redeemed
Abraham on his own initiative from a situation in which his claim upon
the patriarch was not recognised, thus shall he liberate his descendant
Jacob from the arrogance of those who endeavour to determine the
course of social existence without heed to YHWH (vv. 15,20f.; cf. Hitzig,
359; Delitzsch, 328).

The expression 'they will sanctify my name' is set in contrast, therefore, with the behaviour complained about in v. 15. The only other text

---

[43] Alexander (470) notes the particular use of 'children' in the present text but explains this as 'children (not by nature, but) created such by me'.

[44] The Old Testament Pseudepigrapha. Volume 2, ed. James H. Charlesworth, London
1985, 81.

[45] TWAT, VI, 516-21 (H. Cazelles).

in PI where the expression 'to sanctify God' occurs, points to a specific *Sitz im Leben*: 'But YHWH of hosts, him shall you sanctify; let him be your fear, and let him be your dread' (8:13: קדשׁ *hiphil* with God as object, also parallel to a term derived from the root ערץ). Here the addressees are people in Jerusalem who show themselves receptive to the preaching of the prophet. They stand in opposition to 'this people' who are busy with things other than their relation with YHWH (vv. 11f.; Wildberger, 337). The affinity between the two texts makes it probable that v. 23 creates a similar opposition to vv. 15f. A group of socially powerless believers in YHWH, 'the meek / the poor' of v. 19, are promised that the ruling class of political and social pragmatists, for whom YHWH's name has taken on a perspective of inconvenience, will one day recognise him as 'the Holy One of Israel' (for this title cf. v. 19). This shall take place when Jacob 'sees the work of my hands' (v. 23), in contrast to the denial that YHWH is able to see them (v. 15). Here too we encounter PI's characteristic vocabulary (ראה in this sense cf. 5:19; 17:7, also in connection with 'the Holy One of Israel'; cf. also 5:12; 22:11; cf. 26:10).[46]

The intention behind v. 24 ('And those who err in spirit will come to understanding, and those who murmur will accept instruction') seems also to be to identify those who from now on will sanctify YHWH with the self-willed policy makers of vv. 15f., who themselves are like the fools of vv. 13f. By denying 'understanding' to God (v. 16: לא הבין), they have demonstrated the inferiority of their own 'understanding' (v. 14: בינת נבניו תסתתר). By sanctifying God's name, these people will make room for genuine 'understanding' (v. 24: וידעו בינה). Likewise, the 'instruction' which they will receive (v. 24: ילמדו לקח) is set in contrast to the previous false 'instruction' (v. 13: 'a human commandment, a thing learned [מלמדה]'). These chokmatic terms appear elsewhere in PI in accusations and proclamations of judgement concerning the ruling classes ('to err' [תעה]: 3:12; 9:15; 19:13f.; 28:7; cf. Ps. 119:110,176; 'in spirit' (רוח): cf. 'spirit of deep sleep' in v. 10; for 'coming to understanding' cf. ידע: 1:3; 5:13; 6:9; 28:9; 32:4; בינה: 11:2; 27:11; בין: 1:3; 5:21; 6:9f.; 28:9,19; 32:4).

We must conclude, therefore, that the liberation of 'the house of Jacob' will bring an end to the shame which 'the makers of plans' (vv. 15f.) have brought upon it. The new situation is described in language

---

[46] In BI, the adjunct of place 'in the midst of' (בקרב), only occurs in chs. 1-39 (with one exception in 63:11), and is often accompanied by an action of YHWH (5:25; 6:12; 10:23; 12:6).

which is characteristic of Isaiah's preaching against the ruling classes and is accordingly not from the point of view of the policy makers themselves but from that of the needy who suffer under their oppressive activities (vv. 19ff.) and under the shame of Jacob. The same God in whom they will rejoice (v. 19: 'the Holy One of Israel') will also be sanctified and respected by the policy makers (v. 23: 'the Holy One of Jacob / the God of Israel'). Both groups together will make up the new 'house of Jacob'.

THE FOURTH WOE CRY: 'WOE TO THE STUBBORN CHILDREN' (30:1-33)

1   Woe to the stubborn children, oracle of YHWH,
who carry out a plan, but without me,
    who make an alliance, but without my spirit,
        so that they add sin to sin.

2   Who set out to go down to Egypt,
    without asking for my word,
to take refuge in the protection of Pharaoh,
    and to seek shelter in the shadow of Egypt.

3   Yet the protection of Pharaoh shall become your shame,
    and the shelter in the shadow of Egypt your humiliation.

4   For though his vassals are at Zoan
    and his envoys reach Hanes,

5   all come to shame
    on account of a people that cannot profit them,
that brings neither help nor profit,
    but shame and disgrace.

6   The oracle / burden of the animals of the Negeb,
    in a land of trouble and anguish.
Lioness and lion belong there,
    viper and flying serpent.
They carry their riches on the back of donkeys,
    and their treasures on the humps of camels.
to a people that cannot profit them.

7   For Egypt's help is worthless and empty.
Therefore I call her:
    'Rahab – who sits still'.

8   And now, go,
    write it before them on a tablet,
        and inscribe it in a record.
so that it may be for a later day
    a witness for ever.

9   Truly, they are a rebellious people, faithless children,
    children who will not hear the instruction of YHWH.

10   Who say to the seers: 'Do not see',
     and to the prophets: 'Do not envision for us what is right.
 Speak to us smooth things,
     envision illusions.
11   Depart from the way,
     turn aside from the path,
        remove from our sight the Holy One of Israel'.
12   Therefore thus says the Holy One of Israel:
 'Because you reject this word,
     and put your trust in oppression and deceit,
     and rely on them,
13   therefore, this iniquity shall become for you
     like a breach about to collapse, bulging out in a high wall,
       whose break comes suddenly, in an instant.
14   It breaks like one breaks a potter's vessel,
     - once it is smashed, one has no regret for it –
       and among its fragments not a sherd is found
 for taking fire from the hearth
     or scooping up water from a pool'.
15   Truly, thus says the Lord YHWH,
     the Holy One of Israel:
 'In returning and rest you shall be saved,
     in quietness and trust
       shall be your strength.
 But you have refused
16   and you have said: "No, for sure!
 We will fly upon horses"-
     therefore you shall flee!
 and: "We will ride upon swift steeds" -
     therefore your pursuers shall be swift!
17   One thousand shall flee at the threat of one,
     at the threat of five you shall (all) flee
 until you are left
     like a flagstaff on the top of the mountain,
       like a signal on the hill'.
18   And therefore YHWH waits to be gracious to you,
     and therefore he will rise up to show mercy to you.
 Truly, a God of justice is YHWH.
     Happy are all those who wait for him.
19   Truly, a people shall dwell in Zion,
     in Jerusalem you shall weep no more.

He will surely be gracious to you at the sound of your cry.
    When he hears it, he will answer you.

20 The Lord will give you
    the bread of adversity and the water of affliction,
and your teachers shall not be pushed aside any more,
    but your eyes shall be looking upon your Teacher.

21 And your ears shall hear a word
    behind you saying:
'This is the way, walk in it',
    when you turn to the right or when you turn to the left.

22 Then you will defile your silver-covered idols
    and your gold-plated images.
You will scatter them like filthy rags,
    you will say to them: 'Away with you!'.

23 He will give rain for your seed
    with which you sow the ground,
and grain, the produce of the ground,
    which will be rich and plenteous.
Your cattle will graze, on that day,
    in broad pastures.

24 The oxen and donkeys that till the ground
    will eat silage,
        which has been winnowed with shovel and fork.

25 There will be, on every lofty mountain
    and every high hill,
        brooks running with water,
on the day of the great slaughter,
    when the towers fall.

26 It will be that the light of the moon is like the light of the sun,
    and the light of the sun will be sevenfold,
        like the light of the seven days,
on the day when YHWH binds up the injuries of his people,
    and heals the wounds inflicted by his blow.

27 Behold, the name of YHWH comes from far away,
    his nose is burning, and what it exhales, is heavy.
His lips are full of indignation,
    and his tongue is like a devouring fire.

28 His breath is like an overflowing stream
    that reaches up to the neck,
to sift the nations with a deceptive sieve,
    and to place on the jaws of the peoples a bridle that leads them
                                            astray.

(BHS) consider the entire clause in v. 17a´ to be redundant because in the second colon there would then appear to be five enemies rather than only one necessary to bring about the flight (an anticlimax). Hitzig (366f.) has shown, however, that the text makes good sense if one takes v. 17b to be a subordinate clause of v. 17a´´ alone: one enemy will set a thousand to flight, but five enemies will make sure that hardly anyone is left. In this case אחד can stay as it is. The word as such underlines the asymmetry of the numerical relationship (Barthélemy, 214f.; *pace* Wildberger, 1182).

18 Procksch (394f.) was the first to suggest that in the present context יחכה ('to wait for') would not mean 'to look out for, to long for', but rather 'to delay, postpone'. In this event, one can no longer understand v. 18a as an announcement of salvation, but rather as a penalty clause thus allowing one to read the verse alongside v. 17 (Vitringa, 211; Dillmann-Kittel, 274; König, 275; Oswalt, 557; Sweeney, 400). This approach, however, cannot be defended from the lexical point of view (already refuted by Alexander, 479; Schoors, 183). The meaning 'to wait for' (certainly not 'to postpone') is to be found where the verb is used in its absolute form (2 Kgs 9:3; Dan. 12:12) or with the preposition עד (2 Kgs 7:9). In association with ל, the meaning is invariably 'to long for' (Isa. 8:17; 64:3; Hab. 2:3; Zeph. 3:8; Ps. 33:20; 106:13; Job 3:21; *TWAT*, II, 917 [C. Barth]; *Ges.*[18], 348; *DCH*, III, 218).

19 The beginning of the verse line is commonly changed into: 'Yea, O people in Zion, who dwell in Jerusalem' (RSV; participle of ישׁב instead of the imperfect), but this is inspired by the supposition that v. 19 forms the *incipit* of a new prophetic oracle. From the context of the chapter, however, it is clear that 'those addressed are the remnant in exile, and not the people actually in Zion' (Kissane, 346, 338; cf. König, 275). Moreover, a new vocative, after the third pers. plur. of v. 18b, would open with a personal pronoun (Delitzsch, 335; Oswalt, 557; cf. LXX).[1]

20a Many authors understand v. 20a to be an announcement of punishment which they consider out of place here. In so doing, they interpret the verb form ונתן as a preterite ('he was given') or emend the text to read 'bread without adversity and water without affliction' (haplography of מ; *BHS;* Wildberger, 1190f.). Even a concessive interpretation of v. 20 (RSV: 'though the Lord give you') is not needed if one considers the gift of bread and water to be the beginning of salvation (cf. Delitzsch, 335: 'verheißend, mit zurücktretender Drohung'; cf. Alexander, 481; Dillmann-Kittel, 275; Feldmann, 365).

---

[1] Cf. the discussion with Rosenmüller, 455; Alexander, 480; Delitzsch, 334f.; Laberge 1971: 40f.; Wildberger, 1190.

20b The question whether the double מוריך constitutes a singular or a plural can be answered by viewing it as a play on words or a 'punning repetition': it is plural in the first instance and singular in the second (Beuken 1995). This results in the translation: 'Your teachers shall not be pushed aside anymore, but your eyes shall be looking upon your Teacher'. Such an interpretation is based on the particular features of the verbs related to מוריך, in the first instance as subject and in the second as object. The first verb לא יכנף ('shall not be pushed aside') can hardly refer to the mysteriousness of God nor can the second expression והיו עיניך ראות ('your eyes shall be looking upon') refer to Israel's new found obedience, in contrast to its former arrogance, with regard to the prophets (cf. v. 10: 'Who say to the seers: "Do not see", and to the prophets: "Do not prophesy to us what is right. Speak to us smooth things, prophesy illusions"').

24 The meaning of בליל המיץ remains unclear, although the interpretation 'salted food' has been abandoned (Köhler 1922). The expression may refer to ensilaged vegetation, 'silage' (*DCH*, III, 254: 'fodder of sorrel'), or mixed vegetation (*Ges.[18]*, 365: 'Sauerfutter [mit Salzkräutern untermischt]'). A recent interpretation suggests 'yellow peas' (Borowski 1987: 36; *ZAH* 4 [1991] 205).

27 The translation of v. 27a′′ is based on the realisation that the word אפו, 'his nose', constitutes the only subject in the sentence. The term has two predicates: בער ('burning') and כבד משאה ('heaviness of exhalation'; Barthélemy, 218f.).

32a The common emendation of מוסדה ('staff of appointment, destiny, doom'; Alexander, 487) to read מוסרה ('staff of punishment'; Wildberger, 1209) is rarely called upon in current exegesis because the concept of 'punishment' implies correction while, in the case of Assyria, one expects destruction (Ehrlich 1912: 111; Barthélemy, 219f.; Watts, 403; Oswalt, 568; *pace TWAT*, III, 673 [R. Mosis]; *HALAT*, 528).

32b The difficult expression ובמלחמות תנופה is almost impossible to explain. LXX drops the first word while 1QIs[a] does not. The term is clearly recognisable in Vg and Syr while in Tg it is actually the only word one can recognise (Chilton, 60, footnote). In light of this, the emendation במחלות ('with war dances'), which goes back to H. Greßmann, should not be maintained (*pace* Procksch, 402; Wildberger, 1209; Kilian, 180; *BHK, BHS*). Other commentators interpret מלחמות as a *nomen concretum* for either weapons (cf. Isa. 3:25; 21:15; 22:2; Hos. 1:7; 2:20; Ps. 76:4; BDB, 632a; Zorell, 441; *HALAT*, 557f.), or musical instruments (NEB: 'with shaking sistrums'; cf. G.R. Driver 1968: 51), or, by metonymy, 'war songs' or 'war dances' (Irwin 1977: 103). With respect to the first interpretation, the second word, תנופה, raises no difficulties since one need not attach cultic significance to the term when one is aware that it does not have such significance in Isa. 19:16 (מפני תנופת יד יהוה, 'before the hand which YHWH shakes over them'; cf. the use of הניף in 10:15; Feldmann, 371; Schoors, 186f., and the extensive discussion in *HALAT,* 1622f.).

ESSENTIALS AND PERSPECTIVES

Opinions on the redaction-historical composition of Isaiah 30 and the dating of the individual prophetic oracles which make up the chapter are in partial agreement. This has primarily to do with the hypothesis that vv. 1-17 can be traced back to an authentic statement of Isaiah ben Amoz,[2] and that vv. 18-26 constitute an early post-exilic written composition. Theories on vv. 27-33, however, are quite diverse. Some continue to hold that the basic core of this announcement of judgement against Assyria stems from Isaiah himself and that it refers solely to a theophany. Due to the addition of v. 29 and v. 32, perhaps at the time of Josiah, it became a word of salvation for Zion.[3] On the basis of this the idea of a sacrificial feast was introduced.[4] This position distinguishes itself from that which refuses to ascribe the entire passage to the historical Isaiah but contends that it belongs to the so-called Assyrian redaction at the time of Josiah.[5] Such a late dating of vv. 27-33 has persevered, indeed even later datings have been proposed.

Werner (1982: 183-90) places the passage in and around the time of Trito-Isaiah, based on its eschatological elements and its relationship with ch.34. Kaiser (240-4) identifies an Isaianic text in vv. 9-17, which has undergone Deuteronomistic revision, and as a consequence he places vv. 27-33, together with vv. 19-26, during the religious persecution of Antiochus IV Epiphanes (175-164 BC; 'Assur' in v. 31 standing for Syria). A fourth perspective is presented by Watts (353-7). Although he refrains from making any redaction historical divisions, he places the entire chapter in a period when the fall of Nineveh would have been expected, probably during the early part of the reign of Josiah (640-633 BC). Other exegetes more or less concur with one or other of the positions presented above.

In relation to the aforementioned discussion, the question of the internal cohesion of this fourth woe-section arises. The purpose of vv. 27-33 composes the primary issue therein. Since this passage, which pro-

---

[2] Wildberger (1150, 1160f., 1169, 1176, 1183f., 1193ff.) substantiates this opinion from sub-division to sub-division. For him, the date of origin of the prophecies in question ought to run from the beginning of the rule of Sennacherib (705 BC) to immediately after the battle of Eltheke at which the Egyptian army was defeated (701 BC).

[3] Wildberger, 1210, 1215, 1568.

[4] Fohrer, 111-5.

[5] Barth 1977: 97-103.

claims judgement against Assyria, immediately follows on the promise of salvation for Zion in vv. 18-26, it is difficult to see how the chapter as a whole displays any form of purposive development. Nevertheless, against the background of recent research into BI which makes it plausible that the redactors created well-wrought constructions between mutually related passages,[6] it would be pertinent to see if vv. 18-26 and vv. 27-33 offer a worthy continuation of vv. 1-17 and to establish whether the woe-section of ch.30 forms a meaningful literary unity.

The first passage, vv. 1-7, presents Israel on a journey into Egypt in search of protection. The expedition, however, is a result of lack of confidence and trust in YHWH: 'Woe to the stubborn children... who set out to go down to Egypt, without asking for my word' (vv. 1-2). The journey as such is the dominating concern of the entire passage. Reference is made to pointless negotiations with envoys in the Egyptian cities of Zoan and Hanes (vv. 4-5) and to the transportation of expensive gifts through the dangerous Negeb region which are equally useless at securing tangible assistance (vv. 6-7). In contrast to Israel's impious mobility Egypt is static: 'I call her: "Rahab – who sits still"' (v. 7). It would seem permissible to interpret the last word of this sentence, שֶׁבֶת, 'to sit still', as a pun on the word בֹּשֶׁת, 'shame', which is used twice in the passage to characterise the outcome of the expedition to Egypt (vv. 3,5b; cf. v. 5a: 'all come to shame').

The second passage (vv. 8-17) exhibits a semantic shift within the theme of movement from place to place. We hear for the first time that those accused in the previous passage, 'the rebellious people, faithless children, children who will not hear the instruction of YHWH' (v. 9; cf. v. 1: 'Stubborn children'), invite the prophet to: 'Depart from the way, turn aside from the path, remove from our sight the Holy One of Israel' (v. 11), thereby introducing the metaphorical connotation of the phrase 'to go one's way'. While it is true that the metaphor in question is used throughout the Scriptures, it also fits extremely well into the context of our chapter. The very 'rebellious people, faithless children' who have followed the path towards Egypt (v. 9; cf. vv. 1-2) now encourage their prophets to abandon the way of YHWH and stop confronting them with 'the Holy One of Israel' (v. 11). If we consider the fact that the exhortation 'Leave' (סורו) is a cognate of the negative qualification 'stubborn children' (v. 1: סוררים), then it becomes clear that the addressees are actually branding their own expedition to Egypt as a departure from the way of YHWH.

The topic 'to go' comes to the fore once again in the concluding verses of the passage, in this case forming the climax to an argument between the

---

[6] This is the dominant opinion in contemporary research (Williamson 1994).

addressees and YHWH which results in an announcement of judgement (vv. 15-17). The first word in fact resumes the metaphorical meaning of 'path' which has been developed in the chapter: 'In returning (בשׁובה) and rest you shall be saved' (v. 15). There is no doubt that the term is used here in its religio-ethical sense (cf. Isa. 1:27; 6:10; 9:12; 10:21f.; 19:22; 29:17; 31:6; 35:10). The core of the argument, however, is that the audience refuse to accept 'returning and rest' as a guiding principle: 'No, for sure! We will fly... we will ride' (v. 16). They do this by disregarding the metaphorical meaning of 'to return', taking it literally as 'to return (home)' (cf. Isa. 21:12; 37:7f.,29,34,37; 38:8), and announcing a conflicting course of action in its place: 'to fly / to ride'. At the same time the addressees propose fast movement 'upon horses / upon swift steeds' as their ultimate value in contrast to the concept of 'rest'.

The argument is not over yet. YHWH provides an alternative interpretation for the term 'to run fast' (נוס), which had already been used by his adversaries when they said: 'We will fly upon horses', fielding their arrogance by using it in its more common meaning 'to flee' in his answer: 'Therefore you shall flee'. In this way the topic of 'movement' is brought to a temporary close. There will be no swift military campaign, supported by Egypt, against the might of Assyria (still unnamed) as the opponents have been preparing (vv. 1f.). There will only be humiliating flight. The term 'flight' is the focal point of our passage, being fully elaborated in v. 17: 'One thousand shall flee at the threat of one, at the threat of five you shall flee'. Thus, Isaiah ben Amoz' own prophecy concludes with an announcement of judgement in the form of a universal flight and complete desolation 'on the top of the mountain / on the hill' (v. 17).

The tradition history, however, has provided for a double expansion in vv. 18-26 and vv. 27-33 whereby the original oracle (vv. 1-17) maintains its applicability to the (post-)exilic situation. In which way are the lines of thought contained in the prophetic oracle moved forward in these two expansions?

The major division of the first expansion, vv. 18-26, is clear from the sequence of personal verb forms in the first position at the level of clause connection. The clause 'YHWH waits to be gracious' (יחכה לחננכם [*yiqtol*]) in v. 18 is taken up by 'He will surely be gracious' (חנון יחנך [*yiqtol*]) in v. 19b and continued, first, by a twofold 'he will give' (ונתן [*weqatal*]) in vv. 20,23, secondly, by a twofold 'It will be' (והיה [*weqatal*]) in vv. 25,26. (The other verse lines are subordinate to these main clauses.) Thus, the repetition of 'He will give' structures the passage as a twofold promise according to the schema 'solicitous guidance during the wandering' and 'a felicitous sojourn in the land', with two consequences with regard to the day of the judgement.

The foundation for this expansion is laid in v. 18˝: 'And therefore YHWH waits to be gracious to you, and therefore he will rise up to show mercy to you. Truly, YHWH is a God of justice. Happy are all those who wait for him'. By way of the inclusive concept 'to wait for' (חכה) which is applied both to YHWH and to Israel, the transmitters have created a vision of a new era, a time of 'grace' and 'mercy'. The judgement that has passed, therefore, should no longer be considered the last chapter in the history of Israel's relationship with God. From a formal perspective, the relationship between judgement and salvation is established by the phrase 'And therefore' (v. 18). It is difficult to see, however, to what extent this word might exercise a logical function. It is more probable that it is introducing an *ellipsis*: 'because this has actually happened', in other words, 'because the proclamation of judgement of v. 17 has come true'. After the judgement had been executed, the Isaianic tradition could consider nothing other than the expectation of God's benevolence. The language itself betrays theological diffidence in grounding this renewed salvation. In contrast to the fact of total destruction, God's compassion is proclaimed, a compassion based neither on the magnitude of the disaster nor on the conversion of those involved, but in YHWH himself. As v. 18b points out: 'YHWH is a God of justice'. The concept of 'justice' (משפט), which in allegedly Isaianic texts provides an ethical motivation for God's acts of judgement (1:27; 3:14; 28:17), is used here and elsewhere by the Isaianic tradition as an ethical foundation for YHWH's expected saving intervention (4:4; 9:6; 26:8f.; 28:6; 32:16; 33:5).

It is of essential importance that the addressees in vv. 18-26 are a continuation of the audience in vv. 1-17. They can be identified with 'the children who will not hear the instruction of YHWH' (v. 9), who were forced into a humiliating flight in their search for a refuge (v. 17). An initial indication in favour of this is the fact that they are addressed as lamenters (v. 19: 'you shall weep no more... at the sound of your cry'; v. 20: 'the bread of adversity and the water of affliction'). Furthermore, the position YHWH intends to take constitutes a response to a situation of need (vv. 18-19: 'to be gracious', 'to show mercy', 'to hear'). These lamenters are now recognisable as the addressees of the preceding announcement of judgement, i.e. as the persons who have been forced to flee. It is important to recognise the significance of v. 19a here: 'Truly, a people shall dwell in Zion'. It is this verse that announces a reversal of the flight scene of vv. 16-17. The 'flagstaff / signal' left behind denotes the abandoned nature of 'the mountain / the hill'. In contrast to this, God promises in v. 19 that 'Zion / Jerusalem' will be inhabited once again. By means of an alternating plural and singular address in vv. 18-23, the passage continues to address itself to the same group as before – those who have been forced to flee – while at the same time identifying the addressees with the 'people' who will once again inhabit Zion according to God's promise (v. 19a, taken up in v. 26).

A passage in which 'the way' constitutes the central theme (vv. 20-22) follows on YHWH's promise that Zion will once more be inhabited. In a schematic and undetailed fashion we are confronted with the image of a journey, a journey, moreover, which finds its roots in the will of YHWH and not in Israel's former stubbornness. The context invites us to interpret this journey as a return to Zion. At first glance, v. 20 ('The Lord will give you the bread of adversity and the water of affliction') seems to be an announcement of punishment but this would be rather strange in a context of pardon and blessing. On the contrary, the future tense of the verb (וְנָתַן) indicates the beginning of a gradual change from distress to salvation. Therefore, we have to understand the verse to mean that YHWH will provide the necessary means of survival in the present situation of need, no matter how sparingly (cf. 1 Kgs 22:27 / 2 Chr. 18:26; Isa. 3:1).

If we can interpret v. 20 in this way then vv. 20-21 form a rather unusual introduction to the theme of 'return'. At first sight, the promise 'your eyes shall be looking upon your Teacher' does not initially evoke the idea of a journey, but in relation to 'and your ears shall hear a word behind you saying: "This is the way, walk in it"', the Teacher is given the features of a shepherd or guide on the road.

The command: 'This is the way, walk in it' is by itself an expression from the genre of torah preaching in the broadest sense of the word (Isa. 42:16; 48:17; 65:2; Jer. 31:21; 42:3; Ps. 25:8,12; 32:8; 101:6; 139:24; Prov. 1:15; 16:19). In the Scriptures, the concept 'way' (דֶּרֶךְ) encompasses both Israel's salvation history from the exodus out of Egypt to the entry into the land, and the lifestyle which YHWH holds up to his people as a guarantee to happiness in the land.[7] This dual horizon of meaning is also present in v. 21. It is precisely the phrase 'behind you' which introduces a geographical connotation and transforms 'the way' into something more than a metaphor for ethical behaviour. The term is in the first place a declaration of loyalty, to be found in late biblical and post-biblical parlance in the expression 'to turn aside from behind' (with different verbs; with God as subject: Deut. 23:15; Jer. 32:40; with God as object: Isa. 59:13; 1 QS 1:17; CD 6:1). Nevertheless, after the promise 'your eyes shall be looking upon your Teacher', which suggests face to face contact, it has a rather surprising effect. Together with the concept 'the way', the localisation 'behind you' transforms the Teacher into a shepherd.[8] It is true that some

[7] *TWAT*, II, 309f. (K. Koch).

[8] Other explanations, 'as a teacher or father follows behind his children' (Rosenmüller, 456; Duhm, 223) and 'as a farmer drives his cattle' (Dillmann-Kittel, 75; König, 276) are not supported by biblical usage.

consider it unlikely that a shepherd would guide his flock from behind.[9] In the Near East, however, it is quite common for a shepherd to guide and lead his flock from behind, an idea, moreover, to be found in a number of folk tales.[10]

The localisation 'behind you' not only provides the term 'the way', next to its metaphorical meaning of ethical behaviour, with a second significance, that of a 'real' way, a way to be travelled (cf. Isa. 48:17), it has another marked influence on the context. As a consequence, the Teacher whom the addressees will see with their own eyes, i.e. in front of them, and whose voice they will hear behind them, takes on the likeness of the Messenger of God at the exodus from Egypt: 'Then the Messenger of God who went before the host of Israel moved and went behind them; and the pillar of cloud moved from before them and stood behind them' (Exod. 14:19; cf. 13:21f.). Those who consider it far-fetched that Isa. 30:20-21 might be making such a reference ought to realise that the same idea is to be found at work elsewhere in BI: 'You shall not go out in haste, and you shall not go in flight, for YHWH will go before you, and the God of Israel will be your rear guard' (52:12; cf. also 58:8). Moreover, the allusion fits extremely well in ch.30 as a whole which begins with the accusation that Israel has gone for help to Egypt (vv. 1-5). According to vv. 20-21, the guidance which the Teacher will provide transforms the way taken 'without asking for my word' (v. 2) into a way in agreement with God's will, and the dangerous way through 'a land of trouble and anguish' (v. 6) into a safe way to a blessed sojourn in the land.

The ethical and geographical significance of 'the way' is further expressed in the phrase: 'when you turn to the right or when you turn to the left' (v. 21). This expression occurs in the first place with its literal meaning (Num. 22:26; 1 Sam. 6:12; 2 Sam. 2:19, 21). As such it has a role to play in the context of Israel's strategy in relation to the nations, when the people pass through their territory on the way to the land (Num. 20:17; Deut. 2:27). At the same time, it carries a figurative significance in the context of the way of the commandments (Deut. 5:32; 17:20; 28:14; Josh. 1:7; 2 Kgs 22:2; 1 Macc. 2:22). The text of Josh. 23:5-7 is noteworthy in this regard: 'YHWH, your God, will push them back before you, and drive them out of your sight; and you shall possess their land, as YHWH, your

---

[9] This leads to the emendation of 'behind you' (מאחריך) to read 'your Guide' (מארחך; Kissane, 341, 346). The reading מאשרך had already been proposed (cf. 3:12; Feldmann, 365f.).

[10] Dalman, *AuS*, VI, 249f.: guiding from behind primarily takes place in the evening, as the flock returns to the fold, in order to avoid the theft of stragglers. Likewise Hitzig, 368; Delitzsch, 335; Schoors, 184.

God, promised you. Therefore, be very steadfast to observe and do all that is written in the book of the law of Moses, turning aside from it neither to the right nor to the left, so that you may not be mixed with these nations left here among you, or make mention of the names of their gods, or swear by them, or serve them, or bow yourselves down to them'. The warning contained in these verses connects both the contexts outlined above: Israel must not deviate from the law of Moses and by so doing associate herself with the nations and their worship of foreign gods. Isa. 30:21f. functions in much the same way: not deviating from the path, neither to the left nor to the right, must result in the removal of idols.

The following scene, 'the defilement of the idols' (v. 22), is thus provided with the exodus from Egypt as its background. The destruction of the idols is often illuminated by texts which show that the worship of images remained a point of complaint for the prophets before, during and after the exile (before: 2 Kgs 23:8,10,13; Isa. 1:29; 2:8,18ff.; 10:11; 31:17; Hos. 8:4; Amos 5:26; during: Isa. 42:6f.; 44:17ff.; 45:20; 46:6f.; Ezek. 8:10; 18:6,11,15; after: Deut. 27:15; Isa. 27:9; 57:5-9; 65:3,11; 2 Chr. 29:5). The technical construction of idols with a gold or silver covering does indeed point to the craftsmanship of a more settled Israel (Preuß 1971: 191). In prophetic critique, the 'covers' stand for Israel's inclination to covetousness and greed (Deut. 7:25). By use of the phrase 'you will scatter them' (תזרם), the text itself points to the destruction of the golden calf at the foot of Mount Sinai: 'And he (Moses) took the calf which they had made, and burnt it with fire, and ground it to powder, and scattered (ויזר) it upon the water' (Exod. 32:20).[11] In this way, the proclamation of salvation in Isa. 30:22 portrays the defilement of the idols as an act of obedience to the Teacher, in imitation of Moses.[12]

In what follows, vv. 23-26, the 'journey' theme does not have a role to play. It would seem that the addressees have arrived in the land and are living there under the blessing sent out by God over field and flock (vv. 23-25a). It has been pointed out that there is a thematic affinity between this passage and the Deuteronom(ist)ic literature (cf. Deut. 11:8-17; Laberge 1971). It offers a vision of life in the land in line with the ancient promise which declared the renunciation of the worship of idols as the basis for a happy life (cf. Joshua 24). There is still no question of eschatol-

---

[11] For the technical problems associated with this ritual of destruction cf. S.E. Loewenstamm, "The Making and Destruction of the Golden Calf", *Bib* 48 (1967) 481-90; *id.*, "The Making and Destruction of the Golden Calf. A Rejoinder", *Bib* 56 (1975) 330-43.

[12] For an explanation of the LXX reading of vv. 20-22, which differs much from that of MT, cf. Tournaire 1995. There is no reason, however, to assume that the LXX reading would be older because the MT version would be less logic (209).

ogy at this point. Rather, reference is made to 'the day when YHWH binds up the injuries of his people and heals the wounds afflicted by his blow' (v. 26b). The term 'injuries' (שֶׁבֶר) refers here to the 'break / breach' which has befallen the people (cf. שׁבר three times in vv. 13ff.).

With regard to vv. 1-26, we can tentatively conclude that a prophecy of Isaiah ben Amoz announcing that a diplomatic mission to Egypt from among Judah's politicians would result in a disastrous flight of the entire people (vv. 1-17),[13] has been expanded by the tradition in the addition of a passage concerning a return to Zion (vv. 18-26) and thereby actualised. In so doing, it makes use of the ancient paradigm of a 'journey' under YHWH's leadership leading to a blessed life in the land. Obedience to God's word and renunciation of the worship of idols now characterise the new relationship between YHWH and his people.

The Isaiah tradition, however, did not confine itself to the expansion of the prophetic oracle according to the first paradigm (vv. 18-26). The question arises as to whether the second expansion (vv. 27-33) was in fact necessary. Which aspects of the oracle called for further actualisation? Does the second expansion also correspond to a tradition-historical paradigm?

A correct explanation of this passage demands that we ascertain the precise location where Assyria's punishment will take place (vv. 30-33), which is basically the same as ascertaining the location of the theophany since this event dominates the text up to the last verse. Such is apparent from the encompassing concept 'the breath of YHWH' (different words in v. 28 and v. 33) with its accompanying terms: 'burning', 'to kindle', 'fire' (vv. 27,33) and 'stream' (vv. 28,33) together with the role of YHWH's 'voice' (vv. 30f.) in the middle of the passage, likewise accompanied by theophanic terms: 'nose, anger' and 'devouring fire' (vv. 27,30). Where does the 'name of YHWH' come from and where is it leading?

According to most commentators, the place where YHWH is coming to, and where the punishment of Assyria will occur, is Zion (Wildberger, 1216f.; Kaiser, 244). This is based primarily on the fact that they consider the 'burning place' (v. 33) to be the Topheth located in the Ben Hinnom Valley next to Jerusalem (Procksch, 403; Schoors, 186; Kilian, 181). The suggestion that YHWH is coming to Zion does not have to be in contradiction with the biblical belief (Isaiah included) that he already lived there (cf. Isa. 8:18 with 31:4). However, in contradiction to the dominant explanation of v. 27 that YHWH is coming to Zion, there is the suggestion that

---

[13] With regard to Isaiah's own stand as far as a revolt against Assyria is concerned, cf. F.J. Gonçalves, "Isaïe, Jérémie et la politique internationale de Juda", *Bib* 76 (1995) 282-98, esp. 283-91.

YHWH is going from Zion to Assyria and that it is in Assyria that he intends to ignite a funeral pyre for this hostile power. Indeed, it is maintained that within the Isaianic tradition, it is precisely Zion which is described as the dwelling place of YHWH. From Zion he goes forth to other countries to punish them, as he does to Egypt in 19:1. Consequently, the 'burning place' in v. 33 is taken to be a place in Assyria dedicated to the god Moloch (Barth 1977: 98ff.). In spite of these arguments, however, the context points to Zion as the location of God's theophany, as may appear from what follows.

The question of the place where the judgement against Assyria will come about is not unrelated to the meaning of v. 28a´´-b since YHWH's initial actions are directed against the nations in general: 'to sift the nations with a deceptive sieve, and to place on the jaws of the peoples a bridle that leads them astray'. The word pair 'nations / peoples' does not necessarily exclude the Assyrians since they are presented elsewhere in PI as a conglomeration of nations (17:12; 29:7).[14] Nevertheless, the word pair 'nations / peoples' encountered here refers throughout the Bible to the world of the nations as a whole.[15] Therefore, the purport of v. 28b is that none of the nations will escape humiliating defeat. The phrase 'a bridle that leads them astray' suggests their withdrawal from the place in which they had unlawfully set themselves up.

Consequently, this verse-line promises the withdrawal of the nations and by so doing focuses on the importance of the verbs 'to come' and 'to go' in this passage. Although most exegetes easily consider v. 29 as a poorly fitting addition, the *inclusio* formed by the verb 'to come' in v. 27a and v. 29b proves that the redaction has tried, nevertheless, to create a meaningful connection. There is a movement in vv. 27-29 by which the *coming* of '(the name of) YHWH' (v. 27a) brings about the *departure* of the nations (v. 28b) and the *coming* of the addressees (v. 29b). Three other words confirm the theme 'to come': the comparison of 'God's breath' with 'an overflowing stream' (v. 28), the comparison of the addressees with 'one who sets out to the sound of the flute' (v. 29b) and the 'wandering about' (תעה *hiphil*) of the nations (v. 28). The movement continues further in a meeting between YHWH and the addressees, if we take the so-

---

[14] This is in line with historical reality. The Assyrian army consisted of an assortment of auxiliary troops drawn from among the peoples under Assyrian rule who assisted the Assyrian army as such (Wildberger, 671f.).

[15] Gen. 17:16; Deut. 4:27; 7:16f.; 20:15f.; 28:64f.; 32:8; Isa. 2:2f.; 14:6; 25:6f.; 33:3; 49:22; 61:9; Jer. 10:2f.; Ezek. 11:16f.; 20:41; 25:7; 26:2f.; 28:25; 29:12f.; 32:2f.,9f.; 36:15; 38:15f., 22f.; 39:27; Joel 2:17; Mic. 4:1f.,3; 5:6f.; Hab. 2:5,8; Zeph. 3:8f.; Zech. 8:22; Ps. 33:10; 47:9f.; 66:7f.; 67:3f.; 96:3,10; 106:34f.; 1 Chr. 16:24. The military and universal meaning are combined in Ezek. 38:15f.,22f..

phisticated parallelism between 'the mountain of YHWH' and the 'Rock of Israel' seriously (further only in 2 Sam. 23:3). In BI and elsewhere 'rock' stands both for Mount Zion (Isa. 17:10; 27:5; 61:3) and for YHWH (Isa. 8:14; 26:4; Ps. 18:3, 32,47; 31:3; 62:3; 71:3; 94:22; 144:1f.).[16] While everything in v. 28 is in motion and the nations have nothing to hold on to, the addressees in v. 29 find firm ground in 'the Rock of Israel'. There is a clear and significant thematic opposition between both verses.

In this way, the theme of theophany provides vv. 27-29 with a coherent image of place. YHWH comes 'from far away' (v. 27) to an unnamed location, from which he removes the nations (v. 28). The addressees go up to 'the mountain of YHWH' and encounter there 'the Rock of Israel' (v. 29). The identity of the location in question is only disclosed when the nations are removed and Israel meets its God. Since v. 30 ('YHWH will cause his majestic voice to be heard') from a syntactic perspective (by means of $w^e qatal$) is directly linked to v. 27 ('Behold, the name of YHWH comes'), then Zion must also be the place where YHWH will carry out his judgement against Assyria (vv. 30-33).

We conclude that the paradigm of the journey (vv. 18-26) left room for and even called for a further expansion of the prophetic oracle (vv. 1-17) in the form of a paradigm of theophany (vv. 27-33), either because the prophecy in the journey passage was felt to be insufficiently actualised or because traditional elements from the journey paradigm were missing. Indeed, arguments can be found to support both perspectives.

The prophecy itself (vv. 1-17) has concluded with the announcement of a flight which can be understood as a complete depopulation against the metaphorical background of the abandoned 'flagstaff on the top of the mountain' (v. 17). The journey passage, in contrast, presents the outlook of renewed habitation of Zion (v. 19) and a blessed existence in the land (vv. 23-25). No answer is provided, however, to the unavoidable question: How can the exiles return to a land that the Assyrian super-power, and other nations in its wake, has taken in possession? Indeed, the journey passage does not state that YHWH has driven these enemies out of the land. The paradigm at the basis of these verses does not permit such a thing, at least as far as the journey itself is concerned. According to the Pentateuchal narratives, YHWH did not destroy the nations Israel encountered on the way but led Israel safely through their midst (Exod. 15:14ff.; Deut. 2:4-18; Josh. 24:17). It is true that he did consign the peoples in Canaan itself to destruction (Num. 33:50-56; Deut. 4:38; 7:1-6; 9:1-5; Ps. 78:55; Neh. 9:24f.), and that such a topic would have been fitting in the description of

[16] *TWAT*, V, 879 (E. Haag); VI, 980 (H.-J. Fabry).

the fruitfulness of the land (vv. 23-25). Nevertheless, the paradigm of theophany was apparently more appropriate for the task. Indeed, the destruction of God's enemies constitutes a classical element of such a paradigm (Exod. 15:9f.; Isa. 59:15-19; 66:15f.; Jer. 25:30-33; Nah. 1:2, 8-13; Hab. 3:13-16; Ps. 18:18ff.; 46:7-12; 48:1-8; 68: 22ff.; 76:6-13; 97:1-3). In short, by linking the fall of Assyria to the appearance of YHWH and not to the renewed possession of the land, the Isaianic tradition has branded this world power as an enemy of God himself. An additional factor might be seen in the fact that Assyria bore more of the features of an invader and conqueror than one of the peoples inhabiting Canaan which had to make way for Israel. For that matter, the journey passage does anticipate the fall of Assyria in its announcement of 'the day of great slaughter, when the towers fall' (v. 25).

The mention of a theophany might also be inspired by the fact that the paradigm of the journey through the wilderness has the appearance of YHWH on Mount Sinai as its central episode. The title 'Teacher' used for YHWH makes us expect something similar in vv. 18-26 as the Sinai narrative itself gives witness: 'YHWH said to Moses: "Come up to me on the mountain, and wait there; and I will give you the tablets of stone, with the law and the commandment, which I have written for their instruction"'[17] (Exod. 24:12; for God as subject of teaching cf. Exod. 15:25; 1 Kgs 8:36; Ps. 25:8,12; 32:8; 27:11; 86:11; 119:33). The Isaianic tradition was able to supplement the absence of a theophany with what BI itself states in its opening vision: 'Many peoples shall come, and say: "Come, let us go up to the mountain of YHWH, to the house of the God of Jacob; that he may teach us his ways and that we may walk in his paths". For out of Zion shall go forth the law, and the word of YHWH from Jerusalem' (Isa. 2:3). It is true that the nations in this case are the ones who benefit from God's instruction, but the tradition that YHWH teaches on Mount Zion cannot be anything other than an extension of what God's own people can expect there, all the more so when we consider that Israel, according to the introduction to BI itself, has urgent need of 'the teaching of our God' (1:10; cf. 30:9). A theophany of YHWH as Teacher stands in line with the paradigm of the journey. That the theophany will take place on Mount Zion comes up to the expectations already stirred in BI. YHWH's appearance on Mount Zion *after* the return to the land replaces that on Mount Sinai *during* the journey. The redaction of Isaiah 30 has linked these elements with the judgement of Assyria. This nation shall be overcome with fear at the voice

---

[17] The formulation does not exclude the possibility that Moses is God's mouthpiece, but YHWH is ultimately the logical subject of this teaching; cf. *TWAT*, III, 926f. (S. Wagner).

of YHWH (v. 31), having misunderstood, in its arrogance, its God given
role as an instrument in the punishment of Israel (Isa. 10:5-19).

The paradigm of theophany offered the chance to introduce a further
topic, that of a cultic celebration (v. 29). While the first expansion speaks
of 'Zion / Jerusalem' as the place where the people shall live (v. 19) and
the blessing of the land conjures up the image of the residential area surrounding the city (vv. 23-25), the theophany and the meeting with the
addressees take place on 'the mountain of YHWH / the Rock of Israel' (v.
29). These terms refer to the place within Jerusalem where YHWH himself
lives (cf. Exod. 15:17; Mic. 4:2; Zech. 8:3; Ps. 24:3).[18] In this way the
journeying movements of the first and second expansion fall in line with
each other: the addressees turn back from their flight (v. 17) to live in Zion
once again and to cultivate the land (vv. 19-24). At the same time, however, they make a pilgrimage to the mountain of YHWH to celebrate a 'holy
festival' there (v. 29; Wildberger, 1221). For this purpose, it is necessary
that the nations be removed (v. 28) and the judgement of Assyria be completed (vv. 32f.).

The celebration is intensified by the fact that YHWH will carry out his
judgement against the great enemy in 'the burning place', a place similar
to Topheth (v. 30) which witnessed the dreadful cult of child sacrifice and
bore the marks of idol worship (Lev. 18:21; 2 Kgs 23:10; Jer. 7:31f.;
19:6,11ff.; 32:35). The king of the super-power under whose authority
the anti-YHWH liturgy was introduced in the vale of Ben Hinnom is himself
put to death in the oven which once symbolised his invincible power in its
technical construction and richly available fuel.[19]

Against this background, v. 27: 'The name of YHWH comes from afar'
can be seen in a new light. It does not refer to his journey from Zion (or
Sinai) to Assyria but to his return to Zion. In the eyes of the tradition, the
place which Assyria and the nations had occupied and in which the Topheth
was raised as a sign against YHWH, had, of course, to be deprived of his
presence. (The sudden closure of Isaiah's prophecy in v. 17 said nothing
about this.) Now that the people are returning, under YHWH's leadership, to
live in Zion (vv. 18-26), 'the name of YHWH' also returns to carry out
judgement against Assyria (and the nations) who had occupied Zion as the
seat of their dominion.

In summing up, we can establish that the Isaianic tradition has further
actualised the prophecy of Isaiah ben Amoz by way of a second expansion

---

[18] *TWAT*, II, 480 (S. Talmon): In the course of time, sanctuary and mountain have become identical.

[19] It is tempting to interpret the word מלך in v. 33 as a play on the name of the god
Molech, but the question as to whether there are traces of a cult to this god still present in the
Scriptures remains extremely obscure; cf. *AncBD*, IV, 895-8 (G.C. Heider).

which rests upon the paradigm of YHWH's appearance on Mount Zion (vv. 27-33). The coming of YHWH, apparently to his own mountain (vv. 27ff.), forms the sequel to the journey of the refugees back to Jerusalem and the land (vv. 19-22). The terrifying phenomena which always introduce a theophany, embody the judgement. The nations are removed (v. 28) and the great enemy Assyria comes to its end on a bonfire similar to the Topheth, the symbol of a cult directed against YHWH (v. 33). The people who once again inhabit Zion go up to the mountain of YHWH and celebrate a holy festival (vv. 29,32). In this way, the paradigm of theophany created the possibility for the tradition to answer questions unanswered in the preceding paradigm of the journey.

It would appear from our study so far that vv. 18-26 and vv. 27-33 deserve separate discussion. In addition, we distinguish vv. 1-7 from vv. 8-17 because the verses in question give the impression that what were once original and independent oracles have been harmonised with one another by the redaction (cf. 'Scholarly Exposition').

SCHOLARLY EXPOSITION

1. Vv. 1-7: Descent into Egypt for Help without YHWH

Introduction to the Exegesis: Form and Setting

With the exception of v. 1, in which a monocolon and a tricolon counterbalance one another, the colometry of this segment is made up entirely of bicola.

The passage derives its relative independence from its distinctive theme: the initiative to seek help from Egypt does not come from YHWH and as such must ultimately lead to disappointment (cf. 31:1-3) The remaining verses of ch.30 do not return to these events (implicitly, perhaps, in v. 12 and v. 16).

The literary genre of the passage is only partly verifiable. The woe cry itself consists of an addressation which is simultaneously an accusation (vv. 1f.), and an announcement of disaster (v. 3). The addressation is in two parts, v. 1 and v. 2, both of which are constructed in a similar fashion: (1) an address in noun phrases: 'the stubborn children' (v. 1) and 'who set out' (v. 2); (2) an accusation in construct infinitives: 'who carry out... who make an alliance... that they may add sin to sin' (v. 1) and 'to go down to Egypt... to take refuge... to take shelter' (v. 2). The first segment describes the attitude of the accused towards YHWH, the second their political initiative. Both are related to one another, however, via the parallel expressions 'without me', 'without my spirit' (v. 1) and 'without asking my word' (v. 2). The announcement of disaster is associated with the accusation (v. 3) via the *weqatal* and is significant in itself because it is here that YHWH addresses the accused directly for the first time, something which does not recur until v. 12.

Vv. 4-5 constitute an expansion and do not fall within the genre-critical parameters of the rest of the segment. Having stated the political fact that Pharaoh's representatives are in the border cities of Zoan and Hanes, apparently in order to negotiate with Judah's representatives who have 'gone down to Egypt' (v. 4 constitutes an informative mirror image of v. 2), the prophet then announces that the negotiations will come to nothing. The word 'shame' (v. 3) is paired with 'no profit' (v. 5a) and then further elaborated in v. 5b: 'no help' explains 'no profit' and 'disgrace' explains 'shame' (v. 5b).

There is evidently a caesura between v. 5 and vv. 6-7, especially if one considers v. 6a to be the superscription to a prophecy (RSV translates משא with 'oracle', NJV with 'pronouncement'; cf. 'Notes'). The fact that v. 6a is not syntactically linked with the verses preceding it supports this. In addition, the first two verse lines of v. 6 stand apart from the third ('They carry their riches...'). In opposition to this division of the text, certain commentators insist that one cannot understand vv. 6-7 without vv. 1-5. Taken together, both sets of facts give the impression that v. 6a constitutes a 'synthesising' prophetic superscription (cf. 13:1; 15:1; 17:1; 19:1; 21:1,11, 13; 22:1; 23:1), whereby the word משא has a double meaning: 'burden' in line with its thematic context and 'pronouncement' in line with its syntactical context. Once again we are confronted with ambiguous verbal usage (Sweeney [399f.] speaks of a 'pun').

The connection between vv. 6-7 and v. 5 is to be found primarily on the thematic level. The diplomatic mission to Egypt did not only yield nothing ('no profit' / 'no help' in vv. 6 [end], 7a repeats the qualification of v. 5b´ in reverse order), there remains a heavy price to pay for it: the ambassadors (v. 2) 'carry a burden' (two times the root נשא) of treasures with them and, in addition, they must pass through dangerous territory (v. 6). The word pairs 'riches / treasures' and 'worthless / empty' establish a contrast thereby.

Examined on their own, vv. 6-7 do give a strong impression of being an independent prophetic oracle. Having realised the worthlessness of Egypt (v. 7a), the explanation YHWH provides of her epithet Rahab sounds like a judgement, especially since it is introduced with the characteristic 'Therefore' (v. 7b). The judgement itself, 'I call her Rahab – who sits still', however, has to do with the addressees of the woe cry, the people who sought an alliance with Egypt (v. 2). All they will find in Egypt is a lack decisiveness and energy. In addition, the explanation of the name, 'who sits still' (שֶׁבֶת), also contains an allusion to the 'shame' (בֹּשֶׁת) which Egypt shall bring about. This appears to confirm the suggestion that vv. 6-7 were composed with a view to vv. 1-5 from the very beginning.

As far as dating is concerned, most commentators locate the passage between 705 and 701 BC, the period when Hezekiah forged a number of alliances in support of his rebellion against Assyria (Sweeney, 397-9). V. 7 allows us to be more precise, locating the passage either before or after the battle of Eltheke at which Sennacherib defeated the Egyptians (Wildberger, 1150, 1160f.).

We propose the following division:

1-3   woe cry
    1-2   address and accusation
           1   stubbornness: disdain for YHWH
           2   going down to Egypt: trust in Egypt
    3   verdict: disillusionment in Egypt
4-5   elaboration
    4   the apparent success of Egypt's willingness to negotiate
    5   Egypt's failure to bring help
6-7   pronouncement concerning the journey to Egypt
    6   description of the caravan
           6a-b´   the dangers on the road
           6b´´   the price of the request for help
    6b´´´-7a   evaluation of the journey: of no use
    7b   explanation of Egypt's name / verdict on the journey

Exegesis by Verse

1-2 For the form and function of this woe cry, cf. 29:15 and 'Introduction to Isaiah Chapters 28-39'. The addressation 'children' (literally 'sons') locates the entire woe cry in the context of the unique relationship between the people of God and YHWH as a father / child(ren) relationship (Exod. 4:23; Deut. 14:1; 32: 5,19; Isa. 43:6; 45:11; 63:8; Jer. 31:9; Hos. 2:1; 11:1), even when the stipulation of negative behaviour constitutes a necessary part thereof (Deut. 32:20; Isa. 1:2,4; 30:9; Jer. 3:14,22; 4:22; Hos. 13:13). This is evidently the case here. The qualification 'stubborn' (סוֹרֵר) underlines the aberrant behaviour of these children with respect to the dedication and authority of their parents. Israelite law had regulations for dealing with such abusive situations (Deut. 21:18-21). It would appear that Hosea was the first to apply the term 'stubborn' to Israel

(Hos. 4:16; 7:14; 9:15; Isa. 1:5,23; 31:6; 65:2; Jer. 5:23; 6:28; Zech. 7:11; Ps. 78:8; Neh. 9:29).[20]

The woe cry lays the foundation of the accusation to follow. Israel is not free to establish alliances with earthly powers because her history bears witness to the fact that she is already in a covenant relationship with her God. The expressions 'without me / without my spirit' pointedly reflect the absurd nature of such political manoeuvring (cf. 29:15).[21] Indeed, the assumption of an existing relationship with YHWH resonates throughout the chapter (vv. 9,11, 18ff.,26,29).

Israel's transgression is thus a political one, made concrete in her efforts to establish alliances beyond her alliance with YHWH (for 'plan', עצה, cf. 28:29; 29:14; for 'alliance' cf. 'Notes'). By characterising this policy as 'sin' (root חטא: 1:4,18,28; 3:9; 5:18; 27:9; 31:7; 33:14),[22] Isaiah is playing on a characteristic prophetic theme: politics in itself is not neutral, it has to do with YHWH (Isa. 8:3f.; 10:5f.; 11:11f.; 20:1-6; 22:11; 31:1f.; 45:9-13; Jer. 22:21; 26:8f.; Amos 7:10-17).

Having introduced the theological qualification of 'stubbornness' in v. 1, the prophet goes on in v. 2 to reveal the concrete political deeds which are at the roots of this attitude.[23] 'To go down to Egypt' is clearly reminiscent of Jacob's initiative in Genesis 46 but the additional expression 'without asking my word' here pointedly highlights the difference between to two 'descents'. Jacob consulted the God of his father Isaac and received the command from YHWH himself to go down to Egypt together with the promise that he would guide Israel (Gen. 46:1-4). It is no longer possible to recover the kind of consultation Isaiah had in mind here; perhaps a more institutional inquiry made by temple functionaries or even prophetic intervention on his own behalf (cf. Isa. 7:10f.; 8:19; Jer. 23:33; 37:17; 38:14,27).[24] Whatever the original significance might have been, the in-

---

[20] *TWAT*, V, 960 (L. Ruppert).

[21] Commentators frequently interpret 'without my spirit' as 'in conflict with the word of God's divinely inspired prophets', but in this instance the term 'spirit', which is parallel with 'me' (double duty prefix), is more evidently an anthropological term applied to God (*pace* S. Tengström [*TWAT*, VII, 398], who understands 'spirit' to be an equivalent of 'plan' [cf. 40:13]).

[22] The expression 'to add sin to sin' (v. 1) should not be interpreted literally as if 'to carry out a plan' constituted the first sin and 'to make an alliance', i.e. 'to pour a libation' for a foreign god, the second (*pace* Vitringa, 198). The expression, rather, should be understood as having the value of a superlative (cf. Num. 32:14; Isa. 26:15; 29:1, 19; Jer. 7:21; 45:3; 2 Chr. 9:6). For that matter, the preposition למען has a consecutive rather than final significance at this point (J-M, §169 g).

[23] Huber (1976: 113-7) has demonstrated how the language of this passage alternates from theological to empirical-historical.

[24] According to H.-F. Fuhs the expression 'without asking for my word' means nothing more than that those involved were simply not concerned about YHWH's word as it was announced by the prophet (*TWAT*, VII, 922).

different behaviour of the accused here clearly stands in stark contrast to the care with which Israel's leadership sought the will of God in military matters or matters of government policy in the past (שָׁאַל ביהוה / באלהים: Judg. 18:5; 1 Sam. 10:22; 14:37; 22:10,13,15; 23:2,4; 28:6; 30:8; 2 Sam. 2:1; 5:19,23).

V. 2b formulates the purpose of the political mission in the language of prayer. Israel's policy makers sought from Pharaoh and Egypt what the psalmist sought only from God: protection ('refuge', מעוז: Isa. 17:10; 25:4; Ps. 27:1; 31:5; 37: 39; 43:2; 52:9; Jer. 16:19; Joel 4:16; 'to seek shelter', root חסה: Isa. 4:6; 14:32; 25:4; 28:15,17; Ps. 5:12; 7:2; 16:1; 18:3; 25:20; 31:20; 34:9,23; 37:40; 57:2; 64:11; 71:1; 118:8f.; 141:8; 144:2; 'shadow', צל: Isa. 4:6; 25:4; Ps.17:8; 36:8; 57:2; 63:8; 91:1; 121:5). Israel's political initiative is thus given a flavour of idolatry.

3 In his judgement, YHWH directly addresses the very policy makers who have been trying to avoid him (v. 1f.). The prophet thus establishes the expectation of confrontation. This judgement concerning Israel's foreign policy is also formulated in the language of prayer. 'Shame / humiliation' lies in wait for sinners who have placed their trust in something other than God (both roots, בוש and כלם, are frequently found together: Ps. 35:4,26; 40:15f.; 69:7f.; 70:3f.; 71:13; 109:29; בוש can be found in PI in 20:5; 29:22; כלם is not found elsewhere in PI).

4-5 In contrast to the expected humiliation, however, we find a temporary outcome, namely that Pharaoh's envoys have come to the border towns of Zoan and Hanes, apparently intending to enter into negotiations with a delegation from Judah. Given that Pharaoh ruled in the land directly under his control by way of messengers and in the dependant border territories by way of vassal princes, the suffixes of the MT ('his vassals / his envoys') are easy to explain (Kuschke 1952). Zoan (Greek 'Tanis') was located in the north east of the Nile Delta (it is also mentioned in Num. 13:22; Isa. 19:11; Ezek. 30:14; Ps. 78:12, 43). Commentators have frequently identified Hanes, which is found nowhere else in the Old Testament, with modern day *ahnas* (Herakleopolis Magna) to the south of the Delta. On the basis of a list of princes dating from the time of Assurbanipal, however, more recent scholarship tends to identify it with modern day *hnes* (Herakleopolis Parva), a little to the east of the Delta.[25] From the historical perspective, it seems quite acceptable that the two delegations met one another in the border territory between Egypt and Palestine. Against the background of the fact that the tradition places the exodus from Egypt in 'the fields of Zoan' (Ps. 78:12,43), however, this information is somewhat ironic.

[25] Wildberger, 718f., 1154f. The details are clearly described in *AncBD*, III, 49f. (H.O. Thompson), although preference is given to identification with the more southern Herakleopolis Magna.

V. 5 further elaborates the judgement already announced in v. 3. The prophet returns to the concept of 'shame' (בשׁת) and in so doing he establishes an *inclusio* (the second word in the first colon, the second last in the fourth colon). A new element is introduced in the expansion of the meeting between the delegations to include the relationship between their respective peoples: the 'shame' will have its effect on 'all' in Judah, its cause being 'a people that cannot profit them'. The combination of the theme of 'shame' with the negative propositions 'no profit' (twice) / 'no help' (v. 5a″-b) is also new and constitutes a return to the political reality in which people take initiatives and calculate their potential outcome ('no profit' [יעל]: Isa. 44:9f.; 47:12; 57:13; Jer. 2:8; 7:8; 12:13; 16:19; 23:32; Hab. 2:18; 'no help' [עזר]: 2 Kgs 14:26; Isa. 10:3; 20:6; 30:7; 31:1ff.; Ps. 22:12; 107:12; Lam. 1:7; Dan. 11:45). The influence of chokmatic thinking is recognisable in the expression 'no profit' (Job 15:3; 21:15; 30:13; 35:3; Prov. 10:2; 11:4) and that of political-military terminology in the expression 'no help' (Josh. 1:14; 10:6,33; 2 Sam. 8:5; 21:17; 1 Kgs 1:7; Isa. 37:7; 41:10,13f.; Ezek. 12:14; Lam. 4:17; Ezra 8:22; 1 Chr. 12:21; 2 Chr. 20:23; 26:13).

6-7 There follows a somewhat picturesque segment which is only related to the preceding verses by way of topics and key words. The first word משׂא, 'oracle', presents the segment as a prophecy against a foreign nation similar to those in chs. 13-23 (cf. 'Notes'),[26] but the addressation 'the animals of Negeb' immediately raises doubts as to whether the term should be understood as 'oracle' in the present context. Indeed, if one reads a little further one has the feeling that a *double entendre* is at work, the term simultaneously and concisely rendering the content of the prophecy, namely 'burden', and providing thereby a sarcastic evaluation of the diplomatic mission to Egypt. In order to get to Egypt one must pass through the inhospitable Negeb region and in order to secure its support one must bring 'riches / treasures'. The term 'burden' serves as a metaphor for the costs and exertions involved in the operation. It would appear from the superscription that 'the animals' carry the burden – clearly not a reference to the dangerous animals 'lion / snake' mentioned immediately hereafter although anticipating the 'donkeys / camels' which follow – but in the only verbal clause of the entire scene it is the travellers themselves who are the subjects of the verb 'to carry' and there is clear mention of '*their* riches / *their* treasures'.

The locative expression 'a land of trouble and anguish' can refer to a variety of afflictions, although evident associations with 8:22 ('They will

---

[26] The genre is described by Jones 1996: Ch.2. *"Characteristics of OAN and* משׂא *Texts"*, 53-88.

pass through the land... they will look to the earth, but behold, trouble and darkness, the gloom of anguish') suggest the image of a journey through hostile territory ('trouble' [צרה], brought about by human agents: Gen. 42:21; Ps. 22:12; 120:1; 138:7; by natural disaster: Jer. 14:8; Jonah 2:3; Ps. 46:2; Prov. 17:7; 'anguish' [צוקה], before an enemy: Deut. 28:53,57; Isa. 29:2,7; Jer. 19:9; Zeph. 1:15).[27] The danger which stems from the animals is in part real ('lion[ess]': 1 Kgs 13:24; 20:36; Amos 3:4; Prov. 22:13; 'viper': Isa. 59:5; Job 20:16), and in part fable ('flying serpent': Num. 21:6,8; Deut. 8:15; Isa. 14:29). The latter might constitute a literary convention borrowed from Ancient Near Eastern descriptions of military campaigns as is evident, for example, in a report detailing the tenth campaign (also against Egypt) of king Esarhaddon (680-669 BC):

'A distance of four double-hours I marched over a territory covered with alum and *mûsu*-stone. A distance of four double-hours in a journey of two days, there were two-headed serpents whose attack spelled death – but I trampled upon them and marched on. A distance of four double-hours in a journey of two days there were green animals whose wings were batting' (*ANET*, 292).

The end of v. 6 and v. 7a together repeat the theme of 'neither help nor profit' from v. 5 (in reverse order) while expanding it to include the name 'Egypt' and the value judgement 'worthless and empty'. The first of these two terms, הבל, connotes the idea of 'being in conflict with general values and expectations' (Prov. 31:30; Eccl. 11:10; Lam. 4:17), while the second, ריק, points more to the effort involved (Lev. 26:16; Deut. 32:42; 2 Sam. 1:22; Isa. 49:4; 65:23; Jer. 50:9; Hab. 2:13; Ps. 73:13; Job 39:16).

V. 7b reveals the specific function of biblical name-giving. Although YHWH's action is a performative one (קראתי *[qatal]*: 'I call'), the name Rahab itself is not new nor, perhaps, is its application to Egypt. What is probably new is the explanation of the term 'who sits still', but this does not depend on the etymology of the word Rahab, as is often the case elsewhere (Gen. 2:23; 3:20; 31 *passim*; Exod. 2:10; Isa. 8:1-4; Hosea 1 *passim*), but rather on word-play. The 'shame', *boshet* (בשׁת), which Judah will experience as a result of her diplomatic offensive (vv. 3,5) will ultimately be due to Egypt's inertia, *shabet* (שׁבת; the verb ישׁב in this sense: Judg. 5:17; Jer. 8:14). The name-giving itself contains no explanation of the name Rahab as such nor of Egypt's character. Rather, it presents the disappointment Judah can expect as a deed of YHWH, an act of divine judgement over Judah (commonly introduced with the term 'Therefore').[28]

---

[27] Huber (1976: 118f.) explains the associations between v. 6 and 8:22 in such a way that v. 6 appears to refer to the situation in Judah during Sennacherib's military campaign.

[28] Huber 1976: 119f.

Which elements or associations are contained in the name 'Rahab' which allow for the explanation 'who sits still' when tonal effects and etymology are to be ruled out? It is probable that the application of the name has to do with the role played by Rahab in a specific biblical presentation of the creation, one of Canaanite origin, in which the name refers to the chaos monster, defeated but not destroyed by YHWH, which lives in the primal sea (Isa. 51:9; Ps. 89:11; Job 9:13; 26:12). The continued existence of creation depends on the ongoing subjection of such elementary powers. In its present use, Rahab may have constituted an emblematic name for Egypt because of its associations with power and water. From the mythological perspective, the monster embodies strength and violence, from the theological perspective, subjection by YHWH.[29] Isaiah thus applies a creation theme to the political situation, and thereby to the history of Israel (cf. Jer. 7:32; 19:6; 20:3; 46:7).[30]

2. Vv. 8-17: The Flight from the Mountain

Introduction to the Exegesis: Form and Setting

On the understanding that it is possible to have verse lines which are longer than usual and providing that the parallelism draws the cola together, the second part of the woe cry remains unproblematic from the perspective of colometry. Such long verse lines are to be found in vv. 9, 10a, 12a''-b, 14a-b' and 17a. Tricola are evident in vv. 8a, 11, 12a''-b, 14a-b', 15a'' and 17b. It is significant that tricola enclose the larger units which run from vv. 8-11 and from vv. 15a''-17. The messenger formula in v. 12a' constitutes a monocolon. Absence of parallelism in v. 13 suggests that one should consider it a prose line.

The messenger formula ('Therefore, thus says'), which is found twice in the passage – both occurrences accompanied by the divine title 'the Holy One of Israel', the second reinforced by the parallel title 'the Lord YHWH' (v. 12 and v. 15) – provides clear points of articulation. The portion of text which precedes the first messenger formula consists of a command to write down the words of the prophet (v. 8), followed by the reason for doing so, an accusation (vv. 9-11). The latter concludes with the same divine title 'the Holy One of Israel' and is thus connected to the announcements of punishment which follow, via the style figure *anadiplosis*. The

[29] *TWAT*, VII, 375ff. (U. Rütersworden).
[30] Whether Isaiah was the first to apply the name Rahab to Egypt or whether he was in line with an already customary usage remains difficult to determine. Hertlein 1919/20 defends the latter position.

first divine oracle is also otherwise related to the aforementioned accusation ('this word' in v. 12 refers to vv. 8-11). At the redactional level, therefore, the classic prophetic schema of accusation and announcement of punishment is realised.

The function of v. 8 in the first segment is the subject of dispute. Does the command 'write it / inscribe it' refer to the name alluded to in v. 7 and as a consequence 'before them' to the emissaries who are on their way to Egypt in v. 6? From the perspective of syntax, the latter is unlikely: 'before them' has to apply proleptically to the people in v. 9 who are referred to as 'rebellious'. With regard to the content, the name given to Rahab remains indeed the most natural reference for what the prophet is commanded to write (cf. the feminine object suffixes of the imperatives). Indeed, that will ultimately serve as a witness (cf. 8:1f., 16ff.).[31] This includes a judgement for the audiences of both vv. 1-7 and vv. 8-17 since they are of similar temperament in both segments: 'stubborn children' (v. 1) and 'faithless children' (v. 9). They are of the opinion that the continued existence of Judah can be maintained with YHWH at arm's length (Barth 1977: 279ff.). The connective function of v. 8 thereby becomes evident (Kaiser, 234).

Both oracles (vv. 12-14,15-17) consist of an accusation and an announcement of punishment. In the first segment these are clearly delineated: 'because' (v. 12: יען) and 'therefore' (v. 13: לכן). In the second segment, the announcement of punishment is deployed twice as a response to the citation which is intended to prove the guilt of the addressees: 'therefore you shall flee... therefore your pursuers shall be swift' (v. 16). The announcements of punishment lack the classical two-part structure, God's intervention ('I') and its consequences ('they'); only the consequences are described in any detail.

Our examination of the text provides us with the following structure:

8-11   YHWH's instruction for the prophet
    8a   command to write the prophecy down
    8b   purpose: a witness for later days
    9-11   argument / accusation
        9   basic indictment
        10-11 evidence: quotation of the people
12-14 first accusation and announcement of judgement
    12   messenger formula and indictment

---

[31] It is striking that it is not the 'tablet / record' (masculine nouns) which will serve as a witness (ותהי is a feminine verb form), but that which is written (feminine object suffixes), which connects with '(I call) her' in v. 7.

13-14   punishment in two similes
    13   as a breach in a wall
    14   as a broken potter's vessel
15-17 second accusation and announcement of judgement
    15a   messenger formula and escape clause
    15b-16 indictment / evidence: two quotations and YHWH's responses
    17   punishment: total annihilation

A broad consensus exists with respect to dating this passage in favour of the period prior to Sennacherib's expedition when Judah and Egypt turned to Assyria for support (705-701 BC). Indeed, vv. 15f. imply that there were high hopes for a military victory. As a matter of fact, the language usage contains a number of terms which are considered characteristic of Isaiah ben Amoz. Nevertheless, some commentators consider the hand of a Deuteronomistic redactor to be present in vv. 8-17 (Kaiser, 233ff.; Vermeylen 1977: 412-6). While elements of language and thematic features do appear to suggest a degree of truth in such a proposal, modern insights tend to support a fairly autonomous and highly complex genesis for BI, one in which the first collection of oracles in the 8th century BC and a radical redaction thereof during the period of Josiah's kingship in the 7th century constituted the primary driving forces (Sweeney, 394-400). A cross-connection with the Deuteronomistic movement, itself an extremely complicated event, says more about the network of tendencies related to languistic performance within the biblical transmission than about the period of origination of textual complexes.

Exegesis by Verse

8 From the redaction-historical point of view, this verse and the passage which it heads, vv. 8-14, clearly contribute to depicting the prophet Isaiah as 'a prophet in the footsteps of Moses' who also was instructed to write his teaching down as a lasting, admonitory document for a rebellious people and who also was rejected by them in the course of history (cf. Deut. 31:16-24,24-29).[32]

From the religion-historical point of view, this verse has become something of a focal point in the discussion surrounding the manner in which the prophetic oracles ultimately came to be written down. Together with Isa. 8:16f., Jeremiah 36 and Hab. 2:2 it has prevailed as evidence that the prophets themselves progressed to a written form of

---

[32] O'Kane 1996: 38-41.

their words when they realised that the majority in Israel were not taking their announcement of a complete, universal judgement seriously. Later generations would be able to discern from their written prophecies that the fall of Israel was not a result of YHWH's unwillingness to stand by his people or any inability on his part to do so but of Israel's disobedience to his law.[33]

In the meantime, however, it would be wrong to ignore the intent of the verse in its present context. The temporal indicators in the second half of v. 8 do not necessarily refer to a period later than that in which the address-ees now live ('for a later day' [ליום אחרון]: Prov. 31:25; Neh. 8:18; 'for ever' [עד עולם]: Exod. 14:13; 21:6; Deut. 15:17; 1 Sam. 1:22; 27:12; 1 Kgs 1:31; Job 40:28).[34] They refer rather to the moment at which the prophet's prediction that Egypt's help is worthless (v. 7) will be realised. The formulation designates the audience as those for who the written form of the prophecy is intended. The verb 'to go' (בוא) also does not mean that the prophet is being told to go home (pace Duhm, 218f.), but rather that he should not allow himself to mix with his audience (Ibn Ezra, 139: he fears confrontation). 'Before them' (אתם) he is told to write his words down and for them this command will ultimately serve as evidence of their authenticity.

Little further information can be derived concerning the shape of the written form of the prophecy since it is associated with the style figure of inversion. The correct expression would be: 'to write in a record' (ספר stands for soft material) or 'to inscribe on a tablet' (to engrave [חקק] in hard material [לוח]). It makes little sense, therefore, to presume the existence of two written forms of the prophecy: 'on a tablet' for the purpose of public proclamation and 'in a record' for archival purposes (cf. Exod. 24:12; 1 Kgs 8:9; Jer. 17:1; Hab. 2:2 and Gen. 5:1; Exod. 17:14; Deut. 24:1; Jer. 32:11f.; Ps.139:16 respectively).[35]

It will not be an extensive collection of prophecies, certainly not chs. 28-30 which will serve as a 'witness' but rather that which precedes this

[33] Von Rad 1965[4]: 41-133, esp. 47-53; Wolff 1964: "Hauptprobleme alttestamentlicher Prophetie" (206-31) and "Das Geschichtsverständnis der alttestamentlichen Prophetie" (289-307). In the same context, Procksch (390) even speaks of the ageing prophet wishing to preserve his words for generations to come.

[34] TWAT, V, 1148ff. (H.D. Preuß). More than the expression 'for a later day', the term 'for ever' can express the unlimited progress of time, particularly where this is related to the succession of the generations (Gen. 13:15; Exod. 12:24; Deut. 12:28; 28:46; Josh. 4:7; 1 Sam 13:13; 2 Sam. 7:16; 1 Kgs 9:3; Isa. 9:6; 32:14,17; 34:17; Jer. 7:7; 17:4; 35:6; Ezek. 27:36; THAT, II, 232f. [E. Jenni]).

[35] In order to avoid such duplication some authors have related ספר to the Akkadian siparru, 'bronze', (cf. Exod. 17:14; Job 19:23; König, 272), but such an approach is no longer accepted today (HALAT, 724).

verse, namely the title which YHWH has given to Egypt together with the explanation thereof (v. 7: 'Rahab – who sits still').[36] The term עֵד, 'witness' (cf. 'Notes'), which is borrowed from the world of jurisprudence (Lev. 5:1; Num. 5:13; Deut. 17:6; Jer. 32:10; Prov. 21:28; Ruth 4:9), also has a role to play elsewhere in BI. In PI it functions in the discussion surrounding the credibility of the prophet and of the one whose message he bears, namely YHWH (8:2; 19:20). In DI it functions in the so-called lawsuits against the gods (43:9-12; 44:8f.). Two particular questions emerge from the very nature of the concept: what is the 'witness' expected to confirm and against which adversary is he being deployed? The 'witness' in the present context is a written inscription which states that in applying the epithet Rahab to Egypt ('who sits still'), YHWH has established the political worthlessness of this nation prior to the course of events which would make it evident (the feminine verb form of v. 8b, ותהי, refers to v. 7). The people against whom the 'witness' is deployed are those in whose presence the prophet is being called upon to write ('before them'). This interpretation requires further explanation: why are these people considered adversaries and is a witness against them necessary? The explanation follows in v. 9.

Even if we are to search for the meaning of v. 8 more in the social situation of the time than in the impulse towards a religious tradition, the initiative to establish a particular political standpoint in writing is of unique significance. In the context of his faith in YHWH, the prophet actuates what one might refer to as Israel's specific form of historiography: not a chronicle of its victories but a 'report' on the conflicts which arose concerning public values. The people's memory is thereby mobilised as the very foundations of their religious and cultural identity [37]. What would later become political reality was to be measured against the motivations of times gone by. By linking YHWH's blessing to a programme of foreign policy, i.e. no reliance upon military allances, the confession of his name acquired an ineradicable place at the heart of the society and its self-awareness.

9 Of necessity, we are now informed of the identity of those against whom the 'witness' is intended to function. The fact that the term 'children' is repeated from v. 1 suggests that the accusations in both places are

---

[36] The notion that the writing in question here contains the core of the second collection of prophecies (chs. 28-33) already has a long pedigree (Duhm, 218f.) and continues to find some support (Barth 1977: 280f.; Oswalt, 550f.). Most commentators, however are inclined to reject it (Dillmann-Kittel, 271; Feldmann, 360; Kilian, 175).

[37] J. Assmann, *Das kulturelle Gedächtnis. Schrift, Erinnerung und politische Identität in frühen Hochkulturen,* München 1992; W.C. Smith, *What is Scripture? A Comparative Approach,* London 1993.

to be understood as one and the same. The descriptive terms 'faithless' and 'who will not hear the instruction of YHWH', however, are additional and new. Moreover, given that the designation 'children' is in parallel with 'a rebellious people', we are reminded of the opening of BI where we encounter a number of terms from the same word-field: '*Children* have I reared and brought up, but *they have revolted* against me... Israel *does not know, my people does not understand*. Woe, sinful nation, *a people* laden with iniquity, offspring of evildoers, *children* who deal corruptly! They have forsaken YHWH, they have despised *the Holy One of Israel*' (1:2-4). From the historical perspective, such terminological similarity might constitute an argument for suggesting that both passages stem from Isaiah ben Amoz. At the redactional level, it creates a consistent image of the audience with whom the prophet is confronted throughout the book. These are not his personal adversaries, but those rather who have fallen away from their faith in YHWH.

With regard to the Isaianic background of the terms used, confer:
- 'people' (עם) with a negative modification in PI: 1:10; 6:5; 8:6,12; 10:6; 27:11; 29:13.
- 'rebellious' (מרה) is almost a technical term, especially in Deuteronom(ist)ic literature, for Israel's recalcitrant behaviour in the desert: Num. 17:25; 27:14; Deut. 1:26; 9:7,24; 31:27; Ps. 78:8,17,40,56; 106:7.43; Neh. 9:26; among the prophets, the terms characterises Israel's unwillingness to live according to the commandments: Isa. 1:20; 3:8; Jer. 4:17; 5:23; Ezek. 20:8,13,21; Hos. 14:1; cf. the term 'rebellious house' (בית [ה]מרי) for Israel, which occurs 16 times in the book of Ezekiel.
- 'faithless' (NJV; כחש), in a religious context, means 'to renounce YHWH by one's actions' (Josh. 24:27; Isa. 59:13; Jer. 5:12; Hos. 10:13; 12:1; Job 31:28; Prov. 30:9). The translation 'lying' (RSV) might imply that the term has a profane content (Lev. 19:11; Hos. 4:2; 1 Kgs 13:18; Ps. 18:45f.; Job 8:18), but such an interpretation seems inappropriate at this juncture (*TWAT*, IV, 143f. [K.-D. Schunck]).
- 'who will not hear' (לא אבו שמוע) in BI is related to the threat of judgement (1:19; 28:12; without 'to hear' in 30:15) and the retrospective perception thereof (42:24).
- 'the instruction (תורה) of YHWH' in PI does not mean the law in its entirety but God's concrete instruction given through the prophets (parallel with 'word': 1:10; 2:3; 5:24; parallel with 'testimony', תעודה: 8:16,20).

10-11 The rebellious attitude of the people towards YHWH is given concrete form in the detailed quotation of statements addressed to the prophets (cf. 28:9,15f.; 29:15; 30:16) who are the apparent bearers of 'the instruction of YHWH' (v. 9). The quotation consists of two parts: what the prophets should and should not say (v. 10) and what they must do (v. 11). As always, it is formulated from the perspective of the addressee, i.e. the prophet.

The prohibition in v. 10a is limited to visionary experience: 'do not see / do not envision'.[38] This carries a degree of irony, given the fact that in the narratives concerning prophetic revelation the prophets were overcome by their experience and had no say in the contents thereof (Isaiah 6; Jer. 1:11,13; 24:1; Ezek. 1:1-4; 2:9; 8:1-4; 37; Amos 7:1,4,7; 8:1). The parallelism supports the evident irony since, in contrast to 'do not envision for us what is right', the command 'do not see' does not have an object.[39] It would appear that the very act of seeing itself is being forbidden, but the supplementary 'what is right' (נכחות) in the second colon limits the absolute nature of the prohibition. This term is borrowed from the topic 'walking along the way' (Isa. 57:2; 59:14; Sir. 6:22) and introduces an ethical perspective (2 Sam. 15:3; Isa. 26:10; Amos 3:10; Prov. 8:9; 24:26) which serves to oust that of foreign politics.

The command in v. 10b continues this ethical stance. The sequence of the imperatives 'speak / envision' is not the logical sequence associated with the prophet's mission in which vision normally precedes proclamation. The reverse order discloses the true interests of the speakers. They are not concerned with what YHWH has revealed to the prophets but rather with what the prophets themselves say: 'smooth things / illusions' (חלקות / מהתלות). The first term implies 'agreeable words' but Isaiah attaches a further connotation: 'at the cost of the truth' (Ps. 12:3f.; Ezek. 12:24; Prov. 26:28; Dan. 11:32).[40] The second term (a *hapax legomenon*) stems from a root (תלל [or התל]) which basically means 'to cheat / to deceive' (Gen. 31:7; Exod. 8:25; Judg. 16:10,13,15; Isa. 44:20; Jer. 9:4).[41] The quotation thus reaches a climax: the speakers not only want to be deceived objectively, they insist also on being subjectively deceived. At this point it becomes evident that they have lost all sense of reality

In v. 11, the degree of self-deception increases, revealing, at the same time, its true nature: the prophets are ordered to depart from the right path and to confront their 'audience' with the God of Israel no longer. The first half of the verse returns to the perspective of ethical behaviour in general (the word pair 'way / path' [דרך / ארח] is at home in this domain: Isa. 2:3;

---

[38] Several translations render the verb חזה by 'to prophesy ' (RSV). Although the term is also employed in reference to the reception of verbal revelation (Isa. 2:1; 13:1; Mic. 1:1; Nah. 1:1; Hab. 1:1; Job 27:12; Lam. 2:14; Sir. 15:18), it is not used for the transmission thereof.

[39] It is true that 'do not see' cannot have an object *metri causa* and the parallel object of 'do not envision for us what is right' fulfils a 'double duty' just as 'who say' in the first colon governs the second colon by way of double duty. Nonetheless, the poetic form's striking use of the absolute 'do not see' does suggest that it enjoys a special significance.

[40] B. Kedar-Kopfstein, "Synästhesien im biblischen Althebräisch in Übersetzung und Auslegung", *ZAH* 1 (1988) 147-58, esp. 148.

[41] *TWAT*, VIII, 662 (verbal form), 667-9 (semantics) (H. Irsigler).

3:12; Mic. 4:2; Ps. 25:4; 27:11; 139:3; Job 22:15; Prov. 2:8,13,20; 3:6; 4:14; 9:15; 12:28; 15:19; separately in Isa. 8:11; 26:7f.). With renewed sarcasm, we are introduced to the word 'to depart' (סור) which is specifically employed elsewhere for the removal of alien gods (Gen. 35:2; Josh. 24:14,23; Judg. 10:16; 1 Sam. 7:3f.; 1 Kgs 15:2) and the abandonment of a sinful existence (Isa. 1:16,25; 6:7; 27:9; 36:7). In the second half of the verse the speakers' shamelessness reaches its summit in the demand that the prophet bring an end to the presence of their own God, 'the Holy One of Israel' (see 29:19; 'to remove', literally 'cause to cease' [שבת] *hiphil*). Given the fact that it is precisely God himself who promises an end to the godless (Deut. 32:26; Isa. 13:11; 14:4; 17:3; 21:2; Ps. 89:45; 119:119), such a demand is clearly blasphemous. It is striking that the name 'YHWH' is also missing here, the very name under which God revealed himself to his people!

12-14 The first announcement of judgement begins with an accusation which takes up the thread of the chapter by labelling the preceding challenge to the prophets as 'rejecting his word', an expression which can refer to nothing other than the explanation of Rahab's name in v. 7. The rejection of YHWH, his word and his gifts, threads its way continually throughout Israel's history (מאס: Exod. 20:24; Num. 11:20; 1 Sam. 8:7; 10:19; 2 Kgs 17:15; Isa. 5:24; 8:6; Jer. 8:9; Hos. 4:6; Amos 2:4).

The other side of such rejection is expressed by the term 'to trust' (בטח) in false certainties (Isa. 31:1; 32:9ff.,17) rather than in God (Isa. 12:2; 26:3f.). More than virtually any other term, 'trust' embodies the exclusiveness of YHWH as the source of Israel's profound need of secure existence. In the final chapters of PI this same trust in YHWH is elevated to the level of a theme (36:4-9,15; 37:10). Where the threat of destruction at the hands of the superpowers presents itself with such urgency, the temptation to seek security where it cannot be found (Deut. 28:52; Isa. 42:17; 59:4; Jer. 2:37; 5:17; 7:4,8,14; 28:15; Ezek. 29:16; Hos. 10:13; Amos 6:1; Hab. 2:18; Ps.44:7) instead of in the One who created Israel and cares for her (2 Kgs 18:5; Isa. 50:10; Zeph. 3:2; Ps. 78:22; 115:9ff.) becomes all the more apparent. The false security of which the speakers are accused here consists of 'oppression' (עשק) and 'deceit' (נלוז). The first word can imply an unethical attitude and practice (Isa. 54:14; 59:13; Jer. 6:6; Ezek. 18:18; 22:29; Ps. 73:8; 119:134; Eccl. 5:7) as well as an unjustly acquired good in itself (Lev. 5:23; Jer. 22:7; Ps. 62:11; Eccl. 7:7).[42] The second word is once again a metaphor for 'following crooked paths', a way of life which is contrasted with respect for God (Prov. 2:15; 3:32;

42 *TWAT*, VI, 445 (E. Gerstenberger).

14:2).[43] The parallel colon makes use of a different verb, 'to rely' (שׁען), in order to modify the accusation of searching for false security. While the alternative term carries a different metaphorical content than 'to trust', it would appear that both terms have received the same theological content from Isaiah ben Amoz (Isa. 3:1; 10:20; 31:1; 32:9,11; 36:6; 50:10; Ezek. 29:6f.; Mic. 3:11; 2 Chr. 16:7f.; 13:18).[44]

The two comparisons (vv. 13,14) are related to one another via words from the root 'to break' (שׁבר) at the end of the first and the beginning of the second (anadiplosis).[45] This word plays a role in descriptions of judgement found in PI (8:15; 21:9; 24:10; 28:13). Each comparison has its own point of focus. The first pictures the sudden collapse of a wall, an image used elsewhere in PI as a metaphor for self-reliance or trust in God (2:15; 22:10; 25:12; 26:1; 36:12), but lacks any element of intention. The second presumes a fully conscious act ('one breaks... one has no regret') and thereby suggests a punitive response (the broken pot is also found elsewhere as a metaphor for judgement: Jer. 19:10f.; Ps. 2:9). In addition, this comparison serves to illustrate the complete uselessness of the broken potsherds after the pot has been smashed.[46]

A number of difficulties are evident from the linguistic perspective:

(1) On strictly logical premises, the term פרץ in v. 13 would have to be understood as the fallen debris from the wall rather than the breach therein (Wildberger, 1174f.). On the other hand, one might also interpret the flash image of the breach as 'falling', i.e. beginning high in the wall and widening as it 'falls' until it smashes to the ground (Oswalt, 549, 554). Both explanations are simpler than that which interprets פרץ as a 'torrent' (cf. Hitzig [365] via a dubious appeal to 2 Sam. 5:20; Job 30:14; cf. also Alexander, 477).

(2) The first word of v. 14, ושׁברה, is a verb form. The feminine object suffix must refer to חומץ in v. 13 (cf. the possessive suffix in שׁברה at the end of that verse), the subject may be either 'a breach' (v. 13) or undefined (cf. Vg: comminuetur).

15-17 The second oracle consists of an accusation and an announcement of judgement, and constitutes a climax with respect to the first. The climax is evident in the more solemn messenger formula: 'the Lord YHWH / The Holy One of Israel' (see at 28:2 and 30:11), and consists of the fact that the primary topic of the present woe cry, 'to move to Egypt and – hopefully with results – back', takes a major turn. V. 15a finally fills in the information gap which was carefully constructed in the preceding

[43] TWAT, IV, 494f. (H. Ringgren).

[44] TWAT, 353f. (U. Dahmen).

[45] Others consider the repetition to be an example of dittography (Wildberger, 1175).

[46] The more precise translation 'to scoop up water from a pool' (Reymond 1957) aptly renders this aspect of the comparison.

discussion: if there is no help to be found in Egypt, where then can one expect to find salvation? The term 'to be saved' (root ישע) introduces the topic which is inherent to the name Isaiah itself and has become programmatic of this prophetic book at the conclusion of the initial collection (ch.12; cf. Ackroyd 1977). The concept 'salvation' spans the entirety of PI: running from the first song of thanksgiving (12:2f.) through the second (25:9; cf. 26:1,18) to the first conclusion (33:2,6,22), to the transitory chapter (35:4) and to the concluding narrative (37:20,35; 38:20). At the same time, it runs parallel with the question as to where Israel's 'strength' (גבורה) lies, the answer, of course, being 'in YHWH' (10:21; 33:13). According to the final redaction, a son, born of the house of David, will mediate this 'power / strength' (9:5; 11:2).

The way to salvation is indicated via two word pairs: 'returning / rest' and 'quietness / trust'. The first concept, 'return' (שוב), already received programmatic significance in the opening chapter of BI (1:27; also in 6:10,13; 9:12; 10:21f.; 19:22; 29:17; 31:6). Within the inclusive theme of the present chapter – turning to Egypt for help – and given the context of the following verses, there are evident echoes of the literal, geographical meaning of 'return' (cf. 35:10; 37:7f.,29,34,37; 38:8). The term 'rest' (root נוח) in PI has the occupation and inhabitation of the land as its background (11:10; 14:1; 28:12; 32:18). In terms of meaning, the second word pair is related chiastically with the first: 'quietness' (השקט; cf. 7:4; 32:17) being a synonym of 'rest', the theological term 'trust' (cf. v. 12) complying with 'to return'. While 'rest' and 'quietness' require no further explanation, 'returning' and 'trust' lack an object. The subject of the messenger formula fills the gap: 'Thus says the Lord YHWH, the Holy One of Israel'.[47] In this way it becomes evident that YHWH himself is the alternative for Egypt.

It becomes clear in vv15b-16a' just how far Israel has cut herself off from YHWH: 'You have refused... and said: "No, for sure!"'.[48] Any possible compromise has been lost. As in v. 10 ('they say'), the accusation is illustrated with a quotation although the present verse employs direct addressation (v. 16: 'You have said'). In opposition to the warning to observe 'rest / quietness' (v. 15), the accused declare their intention to undertake a swift military campaign (v. 16). Given the fact that horses and chariots were not a feature of Israel's military potential (Isa. 31:1-3), however, such a campaign would demand an alliance with Egypt. The two part quotation is interrupted by God's response to the first part, giving rise to a fast

---

[47] For the details and purport of the ensuing chiastic structure, cf. Wong 1997.

[48] The *wayyiqtol* ותאמרו forces us to translate the *qatal* ולא אביתם as past tense in contrast to the *qatal* לא אבו in v. 9.

moving debate based on word-play. In the first half (v. 16a) the same word
נוס means 'to move fast, to fly' on the lips of the audience while on God's
lip it means 'to flee'.[49] In the second half (v. 16b) the root of 'we will ride'
(רכב) rhymes with that of 'your pursuers' (רדף), so that while the audience use the term 'swift' (קל) for their horses, God applies it in contrast to
their pursuers.

The terms associated with the imagery employed here are also to be found
elsewhere in PI: 'horses' (סוס): 2:7; 5:28; 31:1,3; 36:8; 'to flee / to fly' (נוס):
10:3; 13:14; 17:13; 20:6; 24:18; 31:8; 35:10; 'to ride' (רכב): 19:1; 21:7,9;
22:6f.; 31:1; 36:8f.; 37:24; 'to pursue' (רדף): 17:13.

V. 17 takes us a step further than the sparring match of vv. 15f., the
announcement of judgement leaving the adversaries with no further say.
While their bragging will fall silent (v. 16), the hostile army will rise in
tumultuous revolt (the term 'threat' also contains the idea of 'tumult'; cf.
the root גער meaning 'to blast explosively': Isa. 17:13; 50:2; 51:20; 54:9;
66:15; Jer. 29:27; Nah. 1:4; Ps. 18:16; 80:17; 104:7; Job 26:11; Ruth
2:16).[50] In terms of content the difference between this and the previous
segment is considerable. What was a discussion concerning the possible
fortunes of war has now become a prediction of total annihilation. By way
of a climax, the prophet develops the notion that a small number of enemy
pursuers is enough to put the entire Israelite army to flight, so much so that
no one will remain (cf. 'Notes'). Indeed, similar numerical descriptions of
uneven military proportions are far from unusual (Lev. 26:8; Deut. 32:30;
Josh. 23:10; Amos 5:3).

A powerful metaphor with an ambiguous character is used to describe
this final scene: 'until you are left like a flagstaff on the top of the mountain, like a signal on the hill'.[51] Detailed and exhaustive discussion on 'the
remnant' in BI has resulted in an almost universally accepted proposition
that Isaiah himself only used the concept negatively. Only an insignificant
remnant shall remain after the judgement (1:8; 7:3,22b; 17:6). In the prophet's preaching, the remnant is not seen as a sign of hope or the beginning
of a restoration. Such an understanding is the work of the tradition in BI

[49] The play on the word 'swift' in v. 16b, together with the context, does not allow for the
suggestion that Isaiah's adversaries are announcing their own flight. In the mouth of the
speakers, the verb נוס must mean 'to run fast' (Wildberger, 1182; TWAT, V, 312 [J. Reindl]).
RSV translates the word-play by: 'We will speed upon horses' and 'You shall speed away'.

[50] J.M. Kennedy, "The Root G'R in the Light of Semantic Analysis", JBL 106 (1987)
47-64, esp. 59.

[51] It is possible that the definite articles in the word pair 'the mountain / the hill' are
already a reference to 'Zion / Jerusalem' in v. 19. In a context like this, determination as such
would be appropriate since Hebrew uses it frequently in comparisons; cf. J-M, §137 i. In PI,
'Zion / Jerusalem' is qualified as 'the mountain / the hill' par excellence (cf. 2:2; 10:32;
31:4).

(1:9; 4:2f.; 6:13; 10:20ff.; 11:10-16; 24:6,12; 28:5f.).[52] It is clear that in v. 17 the radical nature of the judgement would not permit a positive interpretation of 'until you are left'.

This is confirmed by the metaphor of the 'flagstaff / signal' which is closely related to what precedes it, since the terms 'to flee' (נוס) and 'signal' (נֵס) are homonyms and the terms 'you are left' (נוֹתַרְתֶּם) and 'flagstaff' (תֹרֶן) are significantly assonant. It should be noted that the terms 'flagstaff / signal' do not refer to a portable military banner (such a thing was unknown in the Ancient Near East), but to a fixed identification mark set up in some high place. It consisted of a piece of cloth ('signal') which was attached to a pole ('flagstaff'; cf. 33:20) as an indication of the place were people were supposed to gather, either for the sake of safety (Isa. 11:10,12) or to assemble as armed forces (Isa. 5:26; 13:2; 18:3; 31:9). In light of this description, the metaphor in v. 17 becomes all the more meaningful. Since the poetic parallelism dissociates 'flagstaff' and 'signal' somewhat, the impression is created that while there will be time to erect the 'flagstaff' there will not be enough time to attach the 'signal', the necessity for flight being so great. As a consequence, the sign around which people were to gather now finds itself reversed: an unadorned stick, a silent witness to presence transformed into abandonment.[53]

3. Vv. 18-26: The Journey through the Desert and Life in the Land

Introduction to the Exegesis: Form and Setting

The colometry of the third segment is quite uniform, being dominated by bicola of three or four beats. Tricola are to be found in v. 24 (otherwise one would be left with the impression of excess), v. 25a and v. 26a.

The speaker remains the prophet throughout. He addresses himself to an audience which has already experienced the announced disaster, an audience which is to be identified as the people who will once again inhabit Zion. This is clear from the combination of a plural and a singular address. The plural address of vv. 12-17 continues in v. 18, but changes in v. 19 to a singular address, referring to 'a people shall dwell in Zion'. This singular address then dominates vv. 19b, 20b and 21a, but changes again

---

[52] U. Stegemann, "Der Restgedanke bei Isaias", *BZ* 13 (1969) 161-86; G.F. Hasel, *The Remnant. The History and Theology of the Remnant Idea from Genesis to Isaiah* (AUM, 5), Berrien Springs MI, 1972; J. Hausmann, *Israels Rest. Studien zum Selbstverständnis der nachexilischen Gemeinde* (BWANT, 124), Stuttgart 1987, 139-70. Pfaff (1996: 209f.), however, ascribes Isa. 30:17 also to the postexilic redactors.

[53] B. Couroyer, "Le NES biblique: signal ou enseigne?", *RB* 91 (1984) 5-29, esp. 11ff.; *TWAT*, V, 468-73 (H.-J. Fabry).

to a plural address in v. 21b and the verb form of v. 22a. By v. 22b 'my people' is once again the focus of attention.

The macro-syntactic division of the passage is clearly determined by a series of six primary clauses: two *yiqtols* in v. 18a and v. 19b, followed by four *weqatals* in vv. 20a,23a,25,26. The *yiqtol* clauses and the first two *weqatal* clauses have YHWH as actant: *yiqtols* in v. 18a and v. 19b with verbs belonging to the topic 'to be gracious' (יחכה לחננכם and חנון יחנך), *weqatals* in v. 20a and v. 23a with the root 'to give (ונתן). The final two *weqatal* clauses involve the verb 'to be' (היה).

In the first segment, vv. 18-19, two verbal clauses which have 'to be gracious' as their theme (*yiqtol* in v. 18a and v. 19b) surround two subordinate כי-clauses which provide more specific detail with respect to God and people: a nominal clause in v. 18b and a compound nominal clause in v. 19a respectively. This gives rise to an ABBA pattern. The second segment, vv. 20-22, which deals with YHWH's first gift, is articulated by two consecutive verb forms in the first position, each of which have a subject other than YHWH: in v. 20b ולא יכנף ('shall not be pushed aside') and in v. 22a וטמאתם ('you will defile'). The said verb forms introduce distinct themes: guidance on the road and the renunciation of alien gods. In the third segment, vv. 23-24, which describes YHWH's second gift, a *yiqtol* in the first position (ירעה: 'will graze') marks the transition from the theme of 'soil' (v. 23a) to the theme of 'cattle' (vv. 23b-24). The fourth and fifth segments begin with 'will be' (והיה) for the first line (vv. 25a,26a) and 'on the day of' (ביום) for the second (vv. 25b,26b; Motyer, 251).

In light of the above observations we can now propose the following division:

18-19   announcement of mercy
    18a   YHWH is eager to extend mercy
    18b   he is a God of justice
    19a   people will dwell in Zion
    19b   YHWH will favourably answer the outcry
20-22   YHWH's first gift: protection on the journey
    20a   livelihood in need
    20b-21 instruction concerning the road
    22   repudiation of the idols
23-24   YHWH's second gift: fertility of the land
    23a   of the soil
    23b-24 of the cattle
25   the first consequence:
    water on the heights on the day of the slaughter of the enemies

26   the second consequence:
      increase of the light on the day of YHWH's healing of his people.

With respect to dating, the present passage stems from the situation of the exile in which the judgement announced prior to this has become reality. The people look forward to a time of blessing (v. 18), hoping to re-populate Zion once again (v. 19) after their return under God's guidance (vv. 20-22), and to live in a fertile land (vv. 23-24) where the enemy's strongholds have collapsed (v. 25) and YHWH is a source of healing for his people (v. 26). It is difficult to find a commentator for whom even a por-tion of this passage goes back to Isaiah ben Amoz himself. (Procksch [394-9] is unique in suggesting that vv. 18,19,20b,21,23a are original.) Basing themselves on a difficult to defend interpretation of v. 18 ('YHWH will delay showing favour to you'; cf. 'Notes') and on the so-called 'early Deuteronomistic' terminology and language, some authors ascribe the passage to a 6th century redaction of BI under king Josiah (Sweeney, 396f., 400). Others, in contrast, consider these elements to be Deuteronomistic and conclude that they have a late exilic origin.[54] Others still consider vv. 25-26 at least to be early apocalyptic (Kilian, 178). A definite answer on the question seems to be beyond our reach. As a matter of fact, it is more important that we recognise the salvation historical period within which the text relocates the readers, a period which presumes that the announce-ment of judgement found in vv. 1-17 has reached fulfilment. The readers who are subject to this judgement come to learn that YHWH is looking for-ward to a time when he can bestow his grace just as much as they them-selves are.

Exegesis by Verse

18-19 In its ABBA pattern (see above), the first segment exhibits a stimu-lating semantic constellation of new and traditional terms. In the first place, it is striking that the logical sequence of 'hearing' and display of mercy is reversed (v. 18a and v. 19b). Partly due to the term 'he will rise up' in v. 18a´´, emphasis is placed on the salvific initiative of the one who stands above all earthly powers (רום with reference to God: Isa. 6:1; 26:11; 57:15; Ps. 18:47; 46:11; 57:6,12; 99:2; 113:4). Secondly, our attention is drawn to the fact that YHWH himself 'waits (to be gracious)', since throughout the Scriptures there is no reference to YHWH as the subject of the verb 'to wait

---

[54] Laberge (1971: 53f.): post-exilic Jerusalemite priests took care of collecting the ora-cles of the prophets; Watts (401f.): 'The implied hearers... are despondent pilgrims in Jerusalem'.

for' (חכה) whereas expressions referring to human beings waiting for God's salvific action are quite common, witness the end of the present verse: 'Happy are all those who wait for him' (elsewhere in Isa. 8:17; 64:3; Hab. 2:3; Zeph. 3:8; Ps. 33:20; Dan. 12:12). In this way, a common term used to describe the human act of waiting in anticipation for God's benevolent intervention is transferred to YHWH in order to create a theological point of departure for the proclamation of renewed salvation after judgement. By way of the word pair 'to be gracious / to show mercy' (רחם / חנן), the text takes up a strongly traditional element from the so-called 'formula of grace' which establishes the unique nature of YHWH for Israel in terms he himself has employed, rather significantly, after the incident with the golden calf: 'YHWH, a God merciful and gracious, slow to anger, and abounding in steadfast love and faithfulness' (Exod. 34:6; Joel 2:13; Jonah 4:2; Ps. 86:15; 103:8; 145:8; Neh. 9:17; the word pair can be found elsewhere in Exod. 33:19; 2 Kgs 13:23; Isa. 27:11; Ps. 102:14).[55] The fact that the term 'to be gracious' (חנן) is expressly repeated in v. 19b suggests that it should be given special attention. This entire verse is constructed from the terminology of the lament psalms, more particularly from the aspect of 'hearing' (שמע, קול and חנן: Ps. 27:7; קול, זעק and חנן: Ps. 142:2; שמע and ענה: Ps. 4:2; 27:7; 30:11).

The expressions concerning God's display of mercy frame two כי-clauses, the first constituting motivation (v. 18b), the second consequence (v. 19b). Both the initial words of each line, 'God' and 'people' (אלהים and עם) call to mind the covenant and imply the restoration thereof (Exod. 4:16; Isa. 8:19; 40:1; 51:22; Jer. 7:23; 30:22; Hos. 2:25; Joel 2:26; Zech. 8:8). Important concepts support this idea. It is precisely because 'justice' (משפט) is secure with YHWH (Deut. 1:17; Mal. 2:17; Ps. 76:10; 105:7) that his people will have a dwelling on Zion. It goes without saying that the final topic is firmly represented in the lament and promise of the exilic literature (Isa. 10:24; 12:6; 44:26; Jer. 6:8; 9:10; 17:25; 33:10; 44:2; Ezek. 12:9; Zech. 8:4; 12:5f.; Ps. 69:36; 137:1-4; Ezra 10:9; Neh. 11:1f.). Combined with the promise 'in Jerusalem you shall weep no more', the assurance of a new inhabitation of Zion announces the end of the exile (Ps. 137:1).

20-22 The first segment dealing with what God will give as a result of his mercy exhibits a degree of independence since the subject is mentioned once again: 'the Lord' (אדני; see 28:2). It is characteristic of BI

---

[55] H. Spieckermann, "'Barmherzig und gnädig ist der Herr...'", *ZAW* 102 (1990) 1-18. The roots as such are not particularly characteristic of PI (חנן in 26:10; 33:2; רחם in 9:16; 13:18; 14:1).

that God 'gives' or 'offers', particularly in a salvific context (נתן with God as subject: 3:4; 7:14; 8:18; 9:5; 22:21f.; 33:16; 34:2; 37:7; 40:23,29; 41:2,19,27; 42:1,5f.,8,24; 43:3f.,16,20,28; 45:3; 46:13; 47:6; 48:11; 49:6,8; 50:4; 55:4; 56:5; 61:8; 62:7). God's generosity encompasses three distinct themes: sustenance (v. 20a), teaching focused on 'the way' (vv. 20b-21) and the removal of idols (v. 22). Since we have already discussed these themes in some detail in 'Essentials and Perspectives' what follows are mainly supplementary remarks, especially concerning their place in BI.

The promise of 'the bread of adversity and the water of affliction' (v. 20a) does not constitute a punishment but describes, rather, God's concern for the vital needs of oppressed people (cf. 1 Kgs 22:27; 'bread' in BI: 3:1,7; 21:14; 33:16; 51:14; 55:10; 58:7; 'water': 36:16f.; 41:17; 43:20; 44:12; 48:21; 49:20).[56] Indeed, precisely the word 'affliction' in BI often suggests a degree of need brought about by the enemy ([צר[ה: 5:30; 8:22; 25:4; 26:16; 30:6; 33:2; 37:3; 63:9; 65:16).

The pledge of 'your Teacher' as opposed to 'your teachers' (vv. 20b-21) is replete with topics which are characteristic for PI and which establish a connection with the second half of BI ('to see' and 'to hear' in combination: 6:9f.; 29:18 [see 'Exegesis by Verse']; 32:3; 42:18,20; 52:15; 64:3; 66:8,19; 'to teach' [root ירה and תורה]: 1:10; 2:3; 5:24; 8:20; 24:5; 28:9,26; 30:9; 42:21,24; 51:4,7).

The expectation that the idol images will be defiled (v. 22; טמא *piel* with cultic matters as object: Lev. 15:31; 20:3; Num. 19:13, 20; 2 Kgs 23:16; Jer. 7:30; 32:34; Ezek. 5:11; 9:7; 23:38; Ps. 79:1), is characteristic of BI's concern that the sacredness of YHWH be respected (טמא: 6:5; 35:8; 52:1; 52:11; 64:5), together with its plan to denounce idolatry (פסל[י[ל and מסכה: 10:10; 21:9; 40:19; 42:8,17; 44:9f.,15,17; 45:20; 48:5), which includes a critical attitude with respect to 'silver (and gold)' (2:7,20; 13:17; 31:7; 39:2; 40:19; 43:24; 46:6; 52:3; 55:1f.).

23-24 The second segment dealing with what YHWH will 'give' depicts the blessing of the land and its organic (v. 23a) as well as animal husbandry (vv. 23b-24), flowing naturally from the preceding verses: after a journey under the leadership of the Teacher and the removal of idols, Israel's obedience will result in residence in a prosperous land. This theme is in line with the tenor of the book of Deuteronomy, especially with respect to the topic that YHWH will provide rain which is the foundation of all fertility. Given such a background, it is possible to set out a number of

---

[56] Laberge 1971: 43f. – Wildberger (1189ff.) emends to: 'Brot ohne Not / Wasser ohne Bedrängnis'; Kaiser (238) scraps the words 'adversity' and 'affliction' as glosses.

points of agreement between the present passage and, for example, Deut. 11:8-17,[57] but the conclusion that these verses constitute a Deuteronom(ist)ic interpolation is a little rash. From a tradition-historical perspective, the theme of fertility in the land as a divine provision has widespread connections (Gen. 49:25f.; Deut. 8:6-14; 28:11f.; 33:13ff.; Jer. 2:7; Hos. 2:10f.,23ff.; 6:3; 10:12; Ps. 65:10-14).[58] Furthermore, the topic of God as provider of the rain does not give evidence of a strictly Deuteronomi(sti)c distribution (Deut. 11:14; 28:12,24; 1 Sam. 12:17f.; 1 Kgs 8:36; 18:1; Zech. 10:1; Job 5:10). Moreover, an explicit call for obedience to the commandments, which in Deuteronomy would constitute a prior condition to the granting of fertility, is absent. In the final analysis, the portrayal of the salvific era in the present verses takes on a somewhat unrealistic character, one which only increases in the verses to follow: e.g. in the attention given to the food provided for the oxen and donkeys and its unique preparation (Wildberger, 1201). Characterisation as 'Deuteronomi(sti)c' or 'early apocalyptic' helps little in establishing the meaning of these verses and their function in the context. It seems better to understand this language as realistic, in so far as it portrays a blessed existence in the land, but with exaggerated features which serve to express the consummate nature of the expected salvation (Oswalt, 562).[59]

25-26 It is generally accepted that these verses are early apocalyptic and as such should be considered late. There is evidence, nevertheless, of formal stylistic features. In the first place, the first and the third lines constitute tricola, while the second and fourth lines constitute bicola.[60] Secondly, both verses open with the same words: 'it will be' (והיה) in v. 25a and v. 26a, 'on the day of' (ביום with infinitive construct) in v. 25b and v. 26b. Finally, the mention of YHWH in v26b forms an *inclusio* with the beginning of the passage, v. 18a (each time the third word in the line). The divine name is significantly absent from v. 25b, 'the slaughter' not being ascribed to YHWH. Clearly such careful composition suggests that a later redaction was concerned with the relation of this segment with its context.

---

[57] Laberge 1971: 51.

[58] C. Gottfriedsen, *Die Fruchtbarkeit von Israels Land. Zur Differenz der Theologie in den beiden Landesteilen* (EHS.T, 267), Frankfurt a.M., 1985.

[59] This does not prevent us from treating v. 24b as an explanatory gloss on the difficult term 'silage'. The interpolation is unsuccessful to the extent that the term has to do with the harvesting of grain. Moreover, the sequence 'shovel / fork' is also incorrect, since one first removes the straw with the 'fork' and then one winnows the grain with the 'shovel' (Wildberger, 1202).

[60] Although the third colon of v. 26a ('Like the light of seven days') is absent from LXX, one cannot consider it a gloss simply on account of the version (Laberge 1971: 48; Irwin 1977 [96] defends it on metrical grounds).

V. 25 continues the theme of vv. 23f. The land will be granted so much rain that her wells will be filled to overflowing, even in her mountain territories, where one would normally expect it to seep away (for fertility in mountainous regions, cf. Amos 9:13; Joel 4:18; Ps. 72:16). While the contrast between this salvific perspective and 'the great slaughter / when the towers fall' is somewhat unusual, it can be explained against the background of the function of the word pair 'mountain / hill' in BI. It is on the 'mountain / hill' that the sin of pride followed by judgement first manifested itself (Isa. 2:14; 10:32; 30:17; 41:15; 42:15; 65:7), to be followed later by salvation (Isa. 2:2; 31:4; 40:4,12; 54:10; 55:12). It is probable that the redaction of BI is falling back at this point on 2:10-12 where it is announced programmatically that 'The haughtiness of people shall be humbled, and the pride of everyone shall be brought low, and YHWH alone will be exalted on that day' (2:11,17). In this regard, the discussion as to whether the term 'towers' signifies the power of the godless Jews (Oswalt, 562f.) or that of Assyria (Feldmann, 367; Penna, 283) is redundant (Dillmann-Kittel, 276; survey in Alexander, 489), since the source text of the reference constitutes an announcement of the universal power of YHWH himself over every form of human self-satisfaction.

In v. 26 the salvific era takes on a cosmic character which fits well with the mythical world-view of the preceding verse: mountains and heavenly lights together with water and light constitute the dimensions of the universe. Thus, the national, ethical and religious restoration of Israel (vv. 19-24) goes hand in hand with cosmic renewal (vv. 25-26). The expression 'like the light of seven days' clearly points to the seven days in which God created the world (Genesis 1). The reference is not solely numerical, however, in that it implies more than the observation that the amount of light in one day of the new order will be equal to that of seven days of the old. Such intensity of light means that the sun, moon and stars, the lights created on the fourth day (Gen. 1:14-18), will have ceased to exist (Delitzsch, 337). Similarly, the continuous inter-change of day and night (Gen. 1:3,8,13,19,23,31: 'and there was evening, and there was morning, a....day') which so determines our existence will come to an end. In short, only light will remain (cf. Isa. 4:5; 60:19-20; Zech. 14:7).[61]

This hitherto unknown outburst of light goes hand in hand with an almost humble deed on the part of YHWH, namely that he himself will attend to and heal the wounds of his people ('to heal' [רפא] with God as subject:

---

[61] *TWAT*, I, 174 (S. Aalen); Laberge 1971: 50: 'an allusion to the perfection of illumination'. According to Gordis (1930: 421f.) this passage is based on the midrash that God hid 'the primal light' of the first day behind the lights of the fourth day because he foresaw the sinfulness of the generations to come (bHagigah 12a).

Exod. 15:26; Deut. 32:39; Isa. 19:22; 57:18f.; Jer. 8:22; 30:17; 33:6; Hos.6:1; 11:3; Ps. 30:6; 'injuries' [שבר]: cf. vv. 13f. and 1:28; 51:19; 60:18). The prophecy makes no effort to conceal the fact that the God whose 'mercy' is the very source of the new era (v. 18) is the same God who once chastised Israel ('blow' [מכה] of God: Deut. 28:59,61; 29:21; Lev. 26:21; 1 Sam. 4:8; Isa. 1:6; 10:26; 27:7; 30:26; Ps. 64:8; the root נכה hiphil with God as subject in BI: 1:5; 5:25; 9:12; 11:15; 27:7; 30:31; 37:36; 53:4; 57:17; 60:10). Thus, in the new order, the memory remains of this feature of YHWH, not in order to belittle Israel, but to strengthen the image of the One whose fidelity might lead him to punish but only with an eye to salvation.

4. Vv. 27-33: The Theophanie on the Mountain of YHWH

Introduction to the Exegesis: Form and Setting

With the exception of the three last verse lines (vv. 32a´´-b,33), the colometry of this passage is composed exclusively of bicola. Scholars suspect the interpolation of a third colon in the two penultimate verse lines: 'he will fight against him' (v. 32b´´) and 'yea, this has been prepared for the king' (v. 33a´´).

The establishment of the text-grammatical composition of these verses can be useful since the assumption exists that they have been revised by a variety of different hands. At first sight, the passage seems to be disorganised but closer inspection shows it to be more systematic. In any event, there is evidence of a clear *inclusio* with rhyme: 'the name of YHWH' (beginning of v. 27: שם יהוה) and 'the breath of YHWH' (beginning of v. 33: נשמת יהוה).

The opening clause: 'Behold, the name of YHWH comes' (v. 27a: הנה שם יהוה בא) is taken up twice at an equivalent level of syntax in: 'YHWH will cause his majestic voice to be heard' (v. 30: והשמיע יהוה את הוד קולו) and in: 'Every stroke of the appointed staff will be' (v. 32: והיה כל מעבר מטה מוסדה). This text structure is an example of the classical pattern of הנה with a subject and a participle followed by w[e]qatals.[62] The intervening clauses are subordinate to these main clauses. These data suggest a division of the passage into three segments: vv. 27-29, 30-31, 32-33.

The first segment, vv. 27-29, consists of the announcement of YHWH's coming (v. 27a') with two subordinate parts each of which concludes with an infinitive of purpose (vv. 27a´´-28 and v. 29). The first part is articu-

---

[62] J-M, §119 n.

lated by a description of three bodily attributes of YHWH: 'his nose', 'his lips' and 'his tongue' (vv. 27a´´, 27b, 28a), and the purpose of his coming: 'to sift the nations' (v. 28b: להנפה גוים). The second part is articulated by two activities of the congregation: 'singing' and 'rejoicing' (v. 29a.b´), and the purpose of this festival: 'to come to the mountain of YHWH' (v. 29b´´: לבוא). Since v. 29 introduces a new logical (not syntactic) subject, i.e. the addressees ('Singing shall be yours'), the two infinitives of purpose mark out their subjects as the two primary actants of vv. 27b-28 and v. 29 respectively, namely 'YHWH' and 'you'.

The second and third segment, vv. 30-31 and vv. 32-33, also give evidence of an equivalent articulation formed by a main sentence (w^{e}qatal; v. 30: והשמיע; v. 32: והיה) and a component introduced by the particle כי (vv. 31,33: 'truly'). After the verbal sentence with YHWH as subject (v. 30a: 'YHWH will cause his voice to be heard'), the second segment contains two subordinate clauses which describe bodily attributes of YHWH: 'the descending blow of his arm' and 'the fury of his nose' (v. 30a´´-´´´).[63] The כי-clause (v. 31) constitutes an elaboration of the main clause in v. 30, 'the voice (of YHWH)' (קול) forming the link word.

The structure of the third segment (vv. 32-33) is clear for the main sentence (v. 32), but less orderly for v. 33. Three noun clauses clearly stand out here: 'A burning place has long been laid out' (v. 33a), 'Fire and wood are in abundance' and 'The breath of YHWH, like a stream of sulphur, kindles it' (v. 33b). The intervening words, however, are difficult to resolve into clause types as the old assumption that we are dealing with glosses testifies. If we consider the clause: 'Yea, this has been prepared for the king', as an interpolation, then two asyndetic perfects remain: 'One has deepened, widened' (העמיק הרחב). Their object, 'its pit' (מדרתה), refers, by means of the suffix, to the subject of the first noun clause: 'a burning place' (תפתה).[64]

From this survey we can conclude that vv. 27-33 possess a balanced text-grammatical composition. Only v. 33 shows some traces of ambiguous clause formation. This leads us to the following structure:

27-29 the encounter of YHWH and the congregation on his mountain
    27-28 announcement of a theophany
        27a´   the coming of YHWH from afar
        27a´´-28a´´ description of his appearance:
                - his nose

---

[63] We have noted the same articulation in the first segment (vv. 27-28a).

[64] The use of the feminine suffix remains an inexplicable anomaly, given the fact that תפתה in v. 33a counts as a masculine noun (הוכן, ערוך; Feldmann, 372; Wildberger, 1210).

                                    - his lips and tongue
                                    - his breath
                28a‴-b   purpose: the expulsion of the nations
        29   result of the theophany: festival of the congregation
                29a   singing in the night
                29b′   rejoicing during the procession
                29b″   purpose: to come to the mountain of YHWH
30-31 YHWH's victory over Assyria
        30   the manifestation of YHWH's voice
        31   the downfall of Assyria
32-33 the celebration of Assyria's execution
        32   flagellation
        33   burning at the stake

Opinions concerning the date of the passage have already been discussed in 'Essentials and Perspectives'. Although the idiom exhibits indisputably Isaian characteristics in a number of places (vv. 28,30f.; Wildberger, 1210-5), the all-inclusive paradigm is typical of the redaction of PI during the exile. Throughout PI, the restoration of God's inhabitation of his mountain, the tribute paid to him by the community and the destruction of Assyria (and Babylon) are the topics *par excellence* which, spread all over PI, have introduced a degree of unity to the variety of textual data (2:2-5; 4:2-6; 10:12-19; 24:21-23; 25:6-12; 31:8-9).

The way we have discussed the succession of the paradigms might have given the impression that we would date the second expansion, vv. 27-33, later than the first, vv. 18-26. Such an impression would nevertheless be incorrect. It would only be possible to give a verdict on the historical relationship between these expansions on the basis of a comparative study of further passages which use both paradigms, within the Isaianic tradition and perhaps elsewhere in the prophetic literature. Here we can go no further than the statement that the theophany of YHWH to destroy Assyria is organically linked to the return journey of God's people to Zion.

Exegesis by Verse

27-28 Many exegetes consider 'the name of (YHWH)' in v. 27 to be an addition. It is true that the Scriptures never say that 'the name of YHWH comes' (שֵׁם יהוה with בוא; only Isa. 59:19 bears any comparison). The reason for the addition would have been that it was preferable to have God's coming to destroy the enemy presented under the attribute of his name rather than in person. From a text-critical point of view, however, there is no reason to presume an addition here. The concept 'name of YHWH', moreover, is not the exclusive property of the Deuteronom(ist)ic theology (Werner 1982: 186).

The abrupt reference to YHWH's coming betrays a redactional seam. Perhaps this arrival serves as an explanation for the overpowering light alluded to in the preceding verse (cf. Isa. 60:1-3), but a theophany frequently has the destruction of YHWH's enemies as its primary purpose (Isa. 31:4; 42:13; 59:19; 66:15f.; Jer. 25:30f.; Zech. 9:14). In the present text, YHWH's appearance is elaborated in the form of a judgement concerning Assur consisting of a terrible storm (cf. Isa. 28:2,15,18; 29:6; Exod. 15:7-12; Judg. 5:4; Nah. 1:3-5; Psalm 29; 50:3). The contrast with the preceding verses is evident: overpowering light (v. 26) set against fire and thick smoke (v. 27a; Barthélemy, 219); water which brings fertility (v. 25) set against an overflowing stream which endangers life itself (v. 28). Although the language is archaic and anthropomorphic (cf. Habakkuk 3; Psalm 18; 68), the utilisation of various terms is nevertheless characteristic of PI both in passages which are generally ascribed to the prophet and those ascribed to the Isaianic tradition. From a semantic perspective, therefore, this second expansion constitutes an integral part of the fourth woe cry.

- 'the name (שֵׁם) of YHWH' is a concept which belongs to the later parts of PI (12:4; 18:7; 24:15; 25:1; 26:8,13; 29:13). It occurs always in the context of the recognition of YHWH's sovereignty.
- 'from far away' (ממרחק) signifies the place where the judgement of YHWH originates (10:3; 13:5) as well as its ultimate outreach (8:9; 17:13).
- 'nose' (אַף)[65] in PI is a term exclusively used with regard to YHWH (5:25; 9:11,16, 20; 10:4,5,25; 12:1; 13:3,9,13). The same holds true of 'indignation' (זעם), even in the whole of BI (10:5,25; 13:5; 26:20; 66:14).
- 'to be full of' (מלא) with regard to parts of the body: 1:15; 21:3.
- 'the breath (רוח) of YHWH' occurs both as bodily phenomenon (11:15; 27:8; 34:16) and as mental principle (11:2; 30:1; 32:15).
- A number of terms occur frequently in the context of judgement: 'burning' (בער: 4:4; 5:5; 6:13; 10:17; 34:9); 'lips' (שׂפתים: 11:4); 'fire' (אשׁ: 1:7; 5:24; 9:4,17; 10:16f.; 26:11; 29:6; 30:14,27,30,33; 33:11f.,14; 37:19); 'overflowing' (שׁטף: 8:8; 10:22; 28:2,15,17f.); for 'devouring fire' (אשׁ אכלת) see 29:6.

Exegetes have explained the expression 'from far away' (ממרחק) as belonging to the storm imagery which accompanies a theophany (Feldmann, 368; Oswalt, 566), or as a theophanic term in itself meaning 'from the heavens' (Isa. 26:21; 63:19; Mic. 1:3) or 'from the mountain of God in the wilderness' (Deut. 33:2; Judg. 5:4; Hab. 3:3)[66] or 'from Zion', i.e. on

---

[65] For the translation 'nose' rather than 'anger' cf. Barth 1977: 93; Barthélemy, 218f.
[66] Jeremias 1965: 58.

the way to Assyria (cf. 'Essentials and Perspectives'). It remains a question, however, whether we have to interpret 'from far away' as a *specific* place. It is quite possible that the expression is simply saying that God has bridged the gulf which prevents him from acting personally on the spot where his people is oppressed by enemies (Duhm, 225; Wildberger, 1216f.).

The group of terms for cosmic phenomena – 'burning', 'heavy exhalation', 'devouring fire' and 'overflowing stream' – can be reduced to two distinct domains: fire and water. The middle point of this semantic constellation, however, is formed by the single word 'indignation' (זעם) which, although it is often synonymous with 'anger' (אף: cf. the texts in PI mentioned above, also Lam. 2:6), does not in itself possess an anthropological substratum. The word זעם has become a characteristically prophetic term for judgement.[67] It occurs in BI in the context of God's wrath both against Israel, using Assyria as an instrument (10:5, 25; cf. Ezek. 22:24,31), and against the foreign nations and the world (13:5; 26:20; 66:14; cf. Jer 10:10; 50:25; Ezek. 21:36; Ps. 78:49). Characteristic of the term is that it frequently alludes to a 'selektives Gerichtshandeln': the enemies of YHWH are struck by his 'indignation' but there is salvation for his own people (Isa. 26:20f.; 66:14ff.; Nah. 1:6f.; Hab. 3:12f.; Zeph. 3:8f.). This specific feature of the term זעם makes it appropriate for laying the connection with v. 29 in which the addressees are promised salvation.

Although the topic of YHWH confronting his enemies belongs to the theophany genre, it is expressed here in a rather unusual form: 'to sift the nations with a deceptive sieve, and to place on the jaws of the peoples a bridle that leads them astray' (v. 28a‴-b). While the practice of deporting the vanquished into exile constitutes the evident background to the phrase, one does not have to explain the metaphor 'a bridle on the jaws of the peoples' literally, as a cruel form of carrying off into imprisonment. In the Scriptures, acts of violence in which the victims are struck in the jaw, imply intentional acts of humiliation (1 Kgs 22:24; Isa. 50:6; Ezek. 29:4; 38:4; Mic. 4:14; Ps. 3:8; Job 16:10; Lam. 3:30).

A number of linguistic difficulties deserve our attention:
(1) Does the second verse line of v. 28 consist of two images, 'to sift' and 'to bridle' (following the usual explanations and translations) or should we interpret the word נפה not as 'sieve' but as 'yoke', an equivalent of 'bridle'? In this case the first colon would also refer to the carrying off of exiles: 'to yoke the nations in a yoke of error'.[68] The most important objection to such an explanation lies in the

[67] *TWAT*, II, 623-6 (B. Wiklander).
[68] Ginsberg 1931-2: 143ff. This explanation is adopted by Barth 1977: 93f.; Gonçalves 1986: 297, in contrast to *HALAT*, 669; *TWAT*, V, 319 (H. Ringgren): 'Schwinge'.

fact that we are obliged to interpret the word (הנפה(ל as a denominative verb, and a *hapax legomenon* at that, since the usual reduction to the root נוף, 'to move back and forth above something',[69] hardly describes the activity of placing animals under a yoke.[70]

(2) Another explanation of v. 28a‴: 'to signal nations with a signal for destruction' (Watts, 402), associates the colon with related texts in PI where the expression הניף יד על, 'to wave the hand threateningly against...', is to be found (10:32; 11:15; 13:2; 19:16; cf. Job 31:21; Zech. 2:13). The word גוים in v. 28, however, is an object. Without the drastic addition of על the presence of such an expression cannot be assumed.[71]

The 'sieve' (נפה),[72] with which the judgement against the nations will be brought about, is accompanied and further determined by the word שוא which is translated as 'falsehood' or 'destruction', the former referring to the occasion or reason for the punishment[73] and the latter referring to its execution.[74] Nevertheless, the explanation that שוא defines the word נפה, with which it is connected, remains closer to the text. Such an explanation does justice to the parallelism with 'a bridle that leads astray' (רסן מתעה). In short, the 'sieve' functions in a deceptive way: instead of separating the grits from the flour it lets everything through so that nothing remains in the sieve. The parallelism between the two verse halves is progressive: none of the nations are spared; they will all meet with the misfortune of going astray (תעה, 'to go astray, to wander about', as ruin: Isa. 3:12; 9:15; 63:17; Jer. 42:20; Ps. 107:40; Job 12:24; Prov. 10:17).[75] The punishment in question forms a contrast with the promise made to the exiles: 'A people will dwell in Zion' (v. 19) since the verb 'to go astray' does not only mean 'to miss the correct path', but also 'to lose the place where one lives' (תעה with this meaning: Gen. 20:13; 21:14; Exod. 23:4; Isa. 35:8; Jer. 50:6; Ps. 107:4; Prov. 21:16).

Vv. 27-28, taken together, exhibit a striking semantic pattern, the core of which is formed by a continuous succession of anthropological terms.

[69] *HALAT*, 242, 644; *TWAT*, V, 320f. (H. Ringgren). The Aramaicising form of the *hiphil* infinitive (הנפה(ל seems to have been chosen to accomplish assonance with בנפת (Dillmann-Kittel, 277; Wildberger, 1208).

[70] Even Sabottka's explanation that 'to move back and forth' is the same as 'to startle' is not based on parallel references; cf. Sabottka 1968: 241ff.: 'auf daß er die Nationen schrecke mit vernichtendem Schrecken'.

[71] *TWAT*, V, 319 (H. Ringgren). It is true that על is also missing from Isa. 10:32 but in this case 'the mount of the daughter of Zion' must be seen as an accusative (Feldmann, 148).

[72] The word does not appear elsewhere in the Old Testament (except in the geographical term נפת דור: Josh. 11:2; 12:23; 17:11; 1 Kgs 4:11) but is well known from post-biblical Hebrew; cf. Dalman, *AuS* III, 258ff.

[73] *TWAT*, VII, 1113 (F.v. Reiterer).

[74] Wildberger, 1207ff., 1218f.

[75] The metaphor of the 'sieve' is extremely rare in the Scriptures, cf. Amos 9:9; Sir. 27:4. In both texts the word כברה is used for 'sieve'.

Four of these terms refer to God: 'his nose', 'his lips', 'his tongue' and 'his breath'. The following term, 'the neck' does not refer to God[76] but has to do, rather, with those against whom the judgement is to come and as such anticipates the 'nations / peoples'. The latter are referred to once again under a final anthropological term: their 'jaws'. In this way, a sequence of six anthropological terms, which concern almost every part of the head, evokes the confrontation between YHWH and the nations.

29 The theophany results in a festival of YHWH's people. Taken as a whole, this verse sets the destiny of the nations over and against that of the addressees. Indeed, 'singing shall be yours'[77] and 'to the sound of the flute' in v. 29 do not introduce something strange but constitute a meaningful contrast with v. 28 since the nations, muzzled as they are, cannot react to their removal by complaining, for example. Moreover, while the nations in v. 28 are prey for the 'devouring (אכל) fire', the addressees in v. 29 are anticipating a festival (חג), a word which, due to its semantic field, conjures up images of 'eating' (חג and אכל in the same context: Exod. 12:14f.; 13:6; 23:15; 34:18; 32:5f.; Lev. 23:6; Num. 28:17; Hos. 9:4f.).[78] Finally, the comparison with 'the night (when a holy festival is kept)' links well with the natural phenomena which introduce the theophany, namely 'fire' and 'smoke', which suggest darkness ('darkness' [ערפל or ענן, חשך] is mentioned in the following theophanic texts: Exod. 20:21; Deut. 5:22; 1 Kgs 8:12; Joel 2:2; Nah. 1:8; Ps. 18:10,22: 97:2).[79]

Which feast is being referred to in v. 29: Passover or Tabernacles? Exegetes in favour of the former refer to the nocturnal celebration and the theme of liberation,[80] while those in favour of the latter point to the absolute use of the term for 'festival', חג, and the accompaniment of musical instruments (vv. 29, 32).[81] The facts, nevertheless, are too few to lead to a responsible choice (Wildberger, 1220). Moreover, efforts to establish the festival do not account for the fact that the schematisation of Israel's feasts

[76] Cf. Isa. 8:8. Nowhere in the Scriptures do we find talk of God's 'neck', as opposed to other ancient religious texts; cf. the Prayer of Lamentation to Ishtar: 'How long, O my Lady, wilt thou be infuriated so that thy spirit is enraged? Turn thy neck which thou has set against me; set thy face [toward] good favour' (*ANET*, 385, ll.94f.). Courtesy Alphonso Groenewald, Fakulteit Teologie B, Universiteit van Pretoria, RSA.

[77] השיר is highlighted by its position at the beginning of the clause. For the collective meaning of this word cf. 1 Kgs 5:12 and König, *Lehrgebäude, II/2*, §255 b. The construction היהwith possessive ל is not rare in PI (3:6; 5:1; 11:16; 19:15,19).

[78] In many other texts, the theme of eating but not the word 'to eat' is connected with the term 'festival'.

[79] Light and fire, on the one hand, and darkness and dark clouds, on the other, are not mutually exclusive in the context of a theophany; cf. *TWAT*, III, 275 (H. Ringgren); VI, 273 (D.N. Freedman – B.E. Willoughby), 399 (M.J. Mulder).

[80] Procksch, 400: after Hezekiah's reformation of the cult, Passover became a temple feast (Werner 1982: 187f.).

[81] Jeremias 1965: 57f.

in the three well-known calendar celebrations is a post-exilic objective (Exod. 23:14-17; Deut. 16:1-17). Older texts do not always lend themselves to such schemas (Isa. 29:1 speaks in general about 'feasts'). It is true, however, that from the history of religions' perspective the elements which characterise a חג are present here: a festival journey to the sanctuary, joyful song and thanksgiving, offerings and a festive meal.[82] Such an insight raises doubts concerning the traditional opinion that vv. 27-33 constitute a 'rag bag' of unrelated topics. The theophany and the festival serve to structure this passage into a unity.

The announcement of a religious feast is not at odds with the rest of PI, especially if one is aware of what it implies here: 'to come (לבוא) to the mountain of YHWH, to the Rock (צור) of Israel' (v. 29b). In the introduction to BI, the attitude with which one comes (בוא) into the presence of YHWH is already presented as a norm of religious piety (1:12) while the final verdict against those who exalt themselves before YHWH is described as the ultimate contrast to such an ascent: 'Enter into the rock (בוא בצור), and hide in the dust from before the terror of YHWH' (2:10,19,21). Further on, the ascent to YHWH in Jerusalem is taken up as a theme by the redaction of BI (26:2; 27:13; 35:10) which also uses the term 'Rock' as a divine title (17:10; 26:4; cf. its unique usage in 8:14). A number of subordinate terms support the Isaianic character of this theme. The fate of the nations under YHWH's judgement or mercy is also connected elsewhere in PI with 'singing' (שיר) or the absence thereof (5:1; 23:15f.; 24:9; 26:1), while salvation is received with 'gladness (of heart)' (שמח: 9:2; 25:9; 29:19; 35:10; the absence of 'gladness' constitutes a theme in 24:7,11, likewise false gladness in 22:13). Thus the festival constitutes the antithesis of the feasting of the godless so denounced by Isaiah ben Amoz, feasting which he believed must ultimately lead to exile (5:12f.: 'flute').

30-31 The second segment resumes the topic of theophany while focusing itself on the manifestation of YHWH's 'voice / arm' (v. 30a). Given that the term 'voice' is repeated in v. 31 in parallel with 'rod', however, it is clear that primary emphasis belongs with this word. A number of elements from vv. 27f. recur here, namely YHWH's 'anger (nose)', 'a devouring fire' and, more explicitly, the element of storm. While the latter is only present in v. 28 in the form of 'an overflowing stream', it is represented here in the three weather phenomena: 'cloudburst and tempest and hailstones' ('tempest' [זרם] elsewhere in 4:6; 25:4; 28:2; 32:2; 'hail' [ברד] in 28:2,17; 32:19). Both the differences and the similarities indicate that the second

---

[82] *TWAT*, II, 736-44, esp. 736 (B. Kedar-Kopfstein). The author also notes that the term חג cannot refer to Passover, although it might refer to Unleavened Bread (739).

act of the theophany is commencing here, namely the destruction of Assyria which is interpreted as a revelation of YHWH who will let his power be 'heard / seen' (שמע / ראה). This word pair subsumes the downfall of that world power into one of the primary themes of BI. While the prophet's task is to prevent Israel from hearing and seeing (6:9f.), future salvation will restore her capacity to hear and see (29:18; 32:3; 42:18,20; 64:3; 66:8), and even the nations will have a part therein (52:15; 66:19). Against this background it is significant that Assyria only experiences the revelation of God's sovereignty as a punishment.

Natural phenomena and articulated speech are sometimes difficult to distinguish in the expression 'the voice of YHWH' (vv. 30f.: קול) since the ancients believed that the divinity spoke in the very thunder itself (Jer. 25:30; Amos 1:2; Joel 4:16; Ps. 18:14f.; 29:2-9; 68:34ff.; 77:17ff.; Job 37:2-5; 38:33ff.). For this reason, 'the voice of YHWH' is often used as the equivalent of his judgement (Joel 2:11; Mic. 6:9; Hab. 3:16; Zeph. 1:14; Ps. 46:7).[83] The concept as such exhibits a consistent pattern in BI: YHWH's voice manifests itself in the commissioning of the prophet (6:8) and in the disruption of the hostile siege of Jerusalem (29:6; 33:3; 66:6). The notion 'arm of YHWH' (זרוע) corresponds in v. 30 to that of his 'voice' and again, both terms appear together in the context of the deliverance of Jerusalem (cf. 33:2f.). The texts in question function as a prior announcement of the important role which 'the arm of YHWH' will play in chs. 40-66 (40: 10f.; 48:14; 51:5,9; 52:10; 53:1; 59:16; 62:8; 63:5,12). The other term set in parallel with 'voice', namely 'rod', i.e. of YHWH,[84] is found elsewhere in explanations of God's intentions with respect to Assyria (שבט: 10:5,15,24; 11:4; 14:5,29; 28:27).

The announcement that 'Assyria will be terror-stricken' proclaims that the mightiest nation of the Ancient Near East is to suffer the same fate as she herself once imposed on the nations around her (חתת: 7:8; 8:9; 20:5; 31:9; 37:27), and is in conformity with a prophecy of Isaiah himself (9:3), the outcome of which continues in DI as a lesson (51:6f.). The parallel concept, '(he) shall smite (with the rod)' (נכה hiphil), is reminiscent of the fact that YHWH does not deal with his own people any differently than he does with Assyria (v. 26: 'the wounds inflicted by his blow' [מכתו]). Where Israel is concerned, however, the ultimate outcome is restoration while for Assyria there is only downfall.

[83] TWAT, VI, 1249f. (B. Kedar-Kopfstein).

[84] A number of older commentaries consider Assyria to be the subject of v. 31b and translate 'when he smites with his rod'. In other words, at the very moment Assyria attempts to strike, she is paralysed by YHWH's voice (RSV?; cf. Alexander, 486f.). The logical subject of v. 31a, however, is probably also to be understood as the subject of the compound nominal clause in v. 31b (Delitzsch, 340).

32-33 Commentators show little appreciation for the religious ideas lying behind these verses nor for the apparently cultic celebration of Assyria's
downfall (v. 32) nor for the evident pleasure with which the destruction of
Israel's arch-enemy is proclaimed (v. 33).[85] The alien culture which is
evident here, however, is no reason to ascribe this segment to a very late
redaction.[86] It would be more realistic to ask whether these verses are at
home in the semantic and metaphoric ambience of PI.

The segment consists of two scenes: a sort of flogging scene (v. 32) and
a burning at the stake which exhibits characteristics of a ritual sacrifice,
perhaps to Molek (v. 33).[87] Neither scene is totally out of place in the
context. The flogging is related to v. 30a´´ ('the descending blow of his
arm') and at the same time contains a reference to, and inversion of,
10:5,15,24. (The word pair 'rod / staff' [מטה/שבט] can be found in each of
these texts [as they occur in sequence in 30:31b-32a], the verb הניף moreover in 10:15.) The flogging scene is accompanied by musical instruments,
reminiscent of the celebration referred to in v. 29. The burning of corpses
appears to be a dimension of the theophany (vv. 27f.), since the last line, v.
33b´´, refers back to it, thereby creating a sort of inclusion: cf. 'the breath
of YHWH' [88] with 'the name of YHWH' in v. 27a, 'like a stream of sulphur'
with 'like an overflowing stream' in v. 28a, 'kindles it' with 'burning'
(בער) in v. 27a, 'fire' in v. 27b and v. 30b.

Although the description of the 'burning place' has no direct affinities
with what precedes it or with PI as such, it seems possible that the relationship between the flogging and the burning constitute a loose rendition of
10:15-17. This woe cry (v. 5) speaks first of the arrogance of the 'rod /
staff' (v. 15) and then goes on to announce that 'the light of Israel will

---

[85] Duhm, 228; Marti, 230; Wildberger, 1222f.

[86] According to some, the redactor of v. 32 transformed the burning of corpses in v. 33
into a sacrifice to Molek (Wildberger, 1223). – A number of explanations exist which attempt to play down the rather repulsive character of the passage. YHWH, for example, comes
across as less of a tyrant if one translates v. 32a as follows: 'Every passage of the rod of
doom, which YHWH will lay upon him', whereby the relative clause refers back to 'doom'
and not to 'rod'. Alternatively, one might interpret 'passage' as a *nomen loci* such that the
sentence can be interpreted as follows: 'In every place through which the rod of the oppressor had passed before, there should now be heard the sound of joyful music' (Alexander,
487). A Jewish translation takes things a step further: 'Every place where the established
staff shall pass, upon which the Lord shall grant peace (יניח), shall be with drums and harps'
(Rosenberg, 255).

[87] Day 1989: 17; B.P. Irwin 1995: 93ff.

[88] In its negative sense, 'the breath of YHWH' (נשמה) is only found elsewhere in Ps. 18:16
and Job 4:9 (also theophanic texts). In PI, 2:22 is the only other location where the term
נשמה appears, although human beings constitute its subject: '...mortals in whose nostrils is
breath, of what account are they?'. The contrast between 30:33 and 2:22 is significant in
light of the apparently implied associations between the passages to which these verses
belong.

become a fire' and shall burn Assyria (v. 17). These events are described in terms also found in 30:31-33 (besides 'rod / staff' also 'fire', 'flame', 'burning' and 'devouring'). The statement that there is 'wood in abundance' (v. 33), may refer to 'the glory of his forest' (10:18), in which case the sentence 'fire and wood are in abundance' is the height of sarcasm: the former is supplied by YHWH, the latter by Assyria! It is possible, finally, that the comment clause: 'Yea, this has been prepared for the king' may be the result of a redactional intervention which considered a separate mention of the king of Assyria lacking in v. 33 in contrast to its presence in 10:12: 'When YHWH has finished all his work on Mount Zion and on Jerusalem, I will finish the arrogant boasting of the king of Assyria' (it is precisely the locatives in the latter text which support the connection with our passage [v. 29]). The king's blasphemous arrogance consisted of the fact that he had equated himself with YHWH (v. 13).[89] The expression 'for the king' (למלך), moreover, may be interpreted as an allusion to the god Molek, especially in the context of the 'burning place' (תפתה; cf. 2 Kgs 23:10).[90]

In v. 32b the reader tends to spontaneously ascribe different subjects to the adjuncts 'with timbrels and lyres / with brandished weapons': the former to Israel, in particular the celebrating community of v. 29, the latter to YHWH, even although they appear to be equivalent stipulations (with ב). The position of the *atnach* supports this. Some commentators find this illogical and ascribe the use of musical instruments to YHWH also (or to his heavenly army; Duhm, 228; Wildberger, 1222f.). Others change the word for 'weapons' (מלחמות) in the word for 'dances' (מחלות), thus making it possible to have one subject, the celebrating community, for both terms (cf. 'Notes'). Instead of forcefully creating one subject by artificial explanations or literary-critical surgery, one might equally view the text as an example of poetic *ellipsis*. Perhaps the rather lame third colon 'he will fight against him' is indeed an interpolation intended to show that YHWH himself is the bearer of the 'brandished weapons'. The suggestion that YHWH sets upon the subjection of Assyria to the accompaniment of musical instruments provided by Israel corresponds, in the first place, to the dramatic pattern which associates these three actants with each other in PI. Assyria seemed to be stronger than the God of Israel but Isaiah has insisted again and again that this world power was merely an instrument in YHWH's hands. The destruction of Assyria is evidence thereof, as well as of YHWH's fidelity towards his people. Against such a background, it would

---

[89] S.A. Irvine, "Problems of Text and Translation in Isa.10:13bb"; in: *History and Interpretation. Essays in Honour of John H. Hayes* (eds M.P. Graham, W.P. Brown and J.K. Kuan), (JSOT.S, 173), Sheffield 1993, 133-44.

[90] B.P. Irwin 1995: 95.

be impossible for Israel to be anything less than an active witness to the fulfilment of God's judgement against Assyria (cf. the musical expressions of joy after Israel's victory in Exod. 15:19-21 and 1 Sam. 18:6f.).

It would appear from what we have said thus far that the highly unusual scene depicting the burning of corpses does not only have its roots in the historical fact of the Topheth (cf. 'Essentials and Perspectives') but also exhibits a literary, inner-Isaianic background. From the hermeneutical perspective, therefore, it would be wrong to characterise this prophecy as an expression of political emotionality or ideology of hatred hiding behind the flag of religion. The fact that the terminology refers to older prophecies, probably to be ascribed at their core to Isaiah ben Amoz himself, yet treats them freely and creatively, suggests the activity of a critical mind which transcends the need for retribution or magical manipulation and approaches a 'second naivete' in which terms and metaphors are employed with full awareness of their limited value in expressing the contemporary view of God and world. In this regard, it is striking that we do not find the usual term Topheth here but rather the similar term *tophteh*. Should the latter word be a common noun derived from the former, a proper noun,[91] then it would suggest that the tradition intended to remind its audience of the historical Topheth while avoiding the identification of this particular funeral pyre – on Mount Zion no less! – with such a contemptuous place. Should one still be tempted to judge a passage which gives evidence of so much literary refinement as naive religiosity or unsavoury literature then one would be guilty of defending stereotypes which the texts themselves are ultimately unable to support.

---

[91] König, *Wörterbuch*, 55; adopted in *TWAT*, VIII, 742-6 (M.J. Mulder; with survey of opinions). The suggestion of Procksch (403) that we interpret the ה as a suffix with dative force, which would lead to the translation 'a burning place for him', has received limited approval (cf. Wildberger, 1207, 1209f.; Irwin 1977: 105).

THE FIFTH WOE CRY:
'WOE TO THOSE WHO GO DOWN TO EGYPT FOR HELP' (31:1-32:8)

TRANSLATION

31:1 Woe to those who go down to Egypt for help,
    and rely on horses,
who trust in chariots because they are many,
    and in horsemen because they are very strong,
but do not look to the Holy One of Israel
    or consult YHWH!

2 And yet he is wise and brings evil,
    he does not withdraw his words.
So he will arise against the house of the evildoers,
    and against the help for those who work iniquity.

3 The Egyptians are men, and not God,
    and their horses are flesh, and not spirit.
Yet YHWH stretches out his hand:
    the helper will stumble, and he who is helped will fall,
      and they will all perish together.

4 Truly, thus YHWH has said to me:
'As a lion growls,
    or a young lion, over his prey,
- when is called forth against him
    a band of shepherds -
he is not terrified by their shouting
    or subdued by their noise,
so YHWH of hosts will come down
    to fight upon Mount Zion
      and upon its hill.

5 Like birds hovering,
    so YHWH of hosts will protect Jerusalem.
He will protect and deliver (it),
    he will repel and rescue (it)'.

6 Turn to him from whom they have radically withdrawn,
    O children of Israel.

7 'Truly, on that day
they shall cast away, every one, his idols of silver and his idols of
gold,
which your hands have sinfully made for you.
8 Then the Assyrian shall fall by a sword, not of man,
and a sword, not of man, shall devour him.
And he shall flee from the sword,
and his elite troops shall be put to forced labour.
9 His rock shall pass away in terror,
and his officers desert the standard in panic',
says YHWH, whose fire is in Zion,
and whose furnace is in Jerusalem.
32:1 Behold, for righteousness will reign a king,
and indeed, princes will rule for justice.
2 Each will be like a hiding place from the wind,
a covert from the tempest,
like streams of water in a dry place,
like the shade of a great rock in a weary land.
3 Then the eyes of those who see will not be blinded,
and the ears of those who hear will hearken.
4 The heart of the rash will have good judgement,
and the tongue of the stammerers will eagerly speak genuine
words.
5 The fool will no more be called noble,
nor the villain said to be honourable.
6 Truly, the fool speaks foolishness,
and his heart plots iniquity,
to practice ungodliness,
and to speak error against YHWH,
to leave the craving of the hungry unsatisfied,
and to deprive the thirsty of drink.
7 The villainies of the villain are evil,
he devises wicked plans,
to ruin the poor by lying words,
and by charging the needy with a judgement.
8 But he who is noble devises noble things,
and by noble things he stands.

NOTES

31:1-2 The chain of verb forms in v. 1 does not comply with the rules
of syntax because *yiqtol* (ישעו) is followed by *wayyiqtol* (ויבטחו) and

twice w^e + negation + *qatal* (וְ...לֹא דָרְשׁוּ וְלֹא שָׁעוּ). It is probable that v. 1a expresses the current situation ('who go down... and rely') while v. 1b relates the process which led up to it and is still going on. This past that continues in the present is best translated by present verb forms ('who trust... but do not look... or consult'). Something similar can be found in v. 2: the nominal clause הוּא חָכָם is followed by a *wayyiqtol* (וַיָּבֵא) and w^e + negation + *qatal* (וְ...לֹא הֵסִיר). Some explain these forms as a sort of *habitualis* (Feldmann, 374: 'חכם [samt Kopula] dürfte den Sinn eines aoristus gnomicus haben, dem sich dann das konsek. Imperf. und das Perf. als Ausdruck erfahrungsmäßiger Tatsachen anschließen'). Others consider the w^e*qatal* form (וְקָם) in v. 2b to have a past meaning because it follows a *qatal* (Wildberger, 1227f.), or view it as present on the basis of its content (RSV, NJV; Feldmann, 374; Kaiser, 247; Sweeney, 402f., 406). We consider v. 2a as a description of the process which YHWH has set in motion and v. 2b as a statement of the expected consequences thereof. V. 1b and v. 2a thus exhibit the same temporal perspective (past that continues in the present) while v. 1a and v. 2b express incomplete time which connects fittingly with v. 3. The translation follows this interpretation.

1 Both in general and in the present context, besides 'horsemen', פָּרָשִׁים can also refer to 'steeds' (Wildberger, 1226; *HALAT*, 919a; *TWAT*, VI, 783f. [H. Niehr]). Given that the context is suggesting that Judah had placed her trust more in human allies than in YHWH, the translation 'horsemen' is given preference.

2 While the translation of the RSV ('against the helpers of those who work iniquity') interprets עֶזְרָה as a *nomen agentis*, i.e. the Egyptians, it seems probable that YHWH does not turn, in the first place, against these but against 'those who work iniquity' themselves. The compact poetic expression indicates that YHWH is attacking Jerusalem's political leaders while simultaneously making any assistance from the Egyptians pointless (König, 279).

3b The clause type, a compound nominal one, prevents us from assuming a temporal sentence here (*pace* RSV: 'When YHWH stretches out his hand').

4 G.R. Driver's suggestion (1940: 163) that we interpret עָנָה on the basis of the Arabic as 'to be troubled' has found its way into many English translations (RSV: 'he is not daunted'). From a lexical perspective, however, this is unacceptable. The ordinary meaning ('to be subdued, to abase oneself') is sufficient.

5 In the present context, the verb פָּסַח has always caused a degree of surprise. The translation 'to spare' (RSV) is based entirely on the specific use of the term in the law concerning Passover (Exod. 12:13,

23,27). Likewise, the translation 'to hobble' as birds do (Keel 1972: 430: 'Hüpfen und Springen beim Landen und Starten'; cf. Deut. 32:11), is rooted in the acceptance of a basic meaning which is not always appropriate to each of the difficult cases (1 Kgs 18:21,26). Recent research appears to have found a way of explaining both the literal and the apotropaic applications of the term: 'to repel, to knock against' (*TWAT*, VI, 664-6 [E. Otto]; *pace* Irwin 1977: 114: 'to stand guard'; cf. 'Exegesis by Verse').

6 Since the imperative 'turn' (שׁוּבוּ) is followed by a relative clause with a verb form in the third person (הֶעֱמִיקוּ), some commentators are reluctant to treat בְּנֵי יִשְׂרָאֵל as a vocative, preferring to see it as the subject of the verb: 'Turn to him from whom the children of Israel have radically withdrawn' (Duhm, 232; König, 280; Schoors, 189; Kaiser, 250; Wildberger, 1237; Watts, 408; Irwin 1977: 115). A vocative seems necessary, however, since it would otherwise be impossible to derive the imperative's addressee from the context. Therefore, the emendation of RSV ('Turn to him from whom you have deeply revolted, O children of Israel') would appear to be a reasonable one. However, since the person of the primary clause and that of the relative clause need not be one and the same (J-M, §158 n: cf. Isa. 54:1; Jer. 5:21; Ezek. 26:17; 29:3; Mic. 3:3,9), we opt for a different interpretation, one in which הֶעֱמִיקוּ is considered to render an impersonal subject: 'Turn to him from whom they have radically withdrawn, O children of Israel' (Alexander, 491; Delitzsch, 343; Dillmann-Kittel, 282; Feldmann, 374; Oswalt, 573). Viewed thus, 'they' can refer back to the accused of vv. 1-2: 'those who go down to Egypt... the evildoers'. In this case, v. 6 clearly makes a distinction between the people, 'the children of Israel', and their leaders, those who rebel against YHWH. Similar shifts in addressation, either widening or narrowing the focus, can also be found elsewhere in PI (1:29; 5:8; 29:13; 30:9).

8 Oswalt (576) rightly takes 'the opening *waw* as resumptive, expressing an apodosis flowing from vv. 6-7'.

32:1 Some exegetes do not interpret הֵן as a presentative ('behold') but consider it to be a conditional ('if') conjunction (Fohrer, 123; Snijders, 317; Schoors, 190; Irwin 1977: 120; Watts, 410f.). While this is possible from a lexical perspective, it nevertheless invalidates the passage as an announcement of salvation, a fact we are obliged to assume from the context.

The preposition לְ prefixed to שָׂרִים is often considered a scribal error (Schoors, 190; Wildberger, 1250; Oswalt, 577) or understood as meaning 'with regard to' or as emphatic or asseverative.[1] The latter meaning, balancing with 'behold' in the first colon, fits well and is accepted here (also Wegner 1992: 279; Watson 1994: 386). A number of Jewish commentators, however, are inclined to interpret the expression as a reference to Hezekiah and his court which leads them to translate: 'Behold for righteousness shall a king reign, and over princes who rule with justice' (Rosenberg, 260).

3 Strictly speaking the verb תשעינה is a *qal* form of שעה, 'to see', but the expression 'eyes will not see' in parallel with 'ears will hearken' is strange. It is generally accepted, therefore, that a form of the root שעע, 'to be smeared over, blinded' is intended (*qal* or *hophal*; cf. as early as Rashi, Redaq and Ibn Ezra [Rosenberg, 260f.]; *BHK, BHS*; BDB, 144a; *HALAT*, 1489b; Wildberger, 1250; Wegner 1992: 280; only *TWAT*, VIII, 355 [U. Dahmen] remains undecided). If one wishes to maintain the root שעה, 'to see', then one is obliged to view the negation לא in the first half of the verse as doing double duty for the second half of the verse ('will not see... will not hearken'; Sweeney, 410f.) or to emend it to לו, 'if' (with reference to הן understood conditionally in v. 1; Irwin 1977: 121; Watts, 411). Such explanations, however, do not account for the possibility that this verse may be a reversal of Isa. 6:10. We accept the root שעע, 'to be blinded', to be present here.

4 While the second half of the verse is generally understood as a promise of eloquence for those who lack linguistic skill, the context undermines such a reading and demands a religio-ethical interpretation (Ibn Ezra, 149; Alexander, 2; Dillmann-Kittel, 285). The problem lies primarily with the difficult word צחות which is only found elsewhere in the physical sense of 'clear, dazzling' (Isa. 18:4; Jer. 4:11; Cant. 5:10). It remains possible, however, that the verb מהר, in the sense of 'to exert oneself / do one's best' (BDB, 555; *HALAT*, 524f.), shares a degree of its ethical content with צחות: 'genuine words'.

5 M. Dahood semantically resolves the *hapax legomenon* כילי into כליה, 'innards' and translates v. 5: 'The knave will no longer be called noble, nor his sentiments pronounced generous' but the parallelism suggests otherwise.

6 Several exegetes and translators emend יעשה to read יחשב on the basis of 1QIs[a] (חושב) and LXX (νοήσει), Syr and Tg (Th, Sym and Vg

---

[1] F. Nötscher, "Zum emphatischen Lamed", *VT* 3 (1953) 372-80, esp. 380: within parallelism, the *lamed* can join the first (Jer. 30:12) or the second member (Jer. 9:2; Ezr. 6:7). *HALAT* (485f.) and *DCH* (IV, 484) also recognise the possibility of an asseverative function for *lamed*.

follow MT). LXX, however, always translates the root with λογίζομαι, and Syr and Tg follow suit (Orlinsky 1950; Kutscher, 239f.). It seems unlikely, therefore, that they read חשב here. Rather, it would appear that they have rendered עשה as an action of 'the heart' in their own manner (Wildberger, 1250; Barthélemy, 221f.; Watts, 411; Oswalt, 578).

7 From an ethical perspective, the usual translation of v. 7b″: 'even when the plea of the needy is right' (RSV) is somewhat problematic (for a survey of the solutions, cf. Wegner, 283). The difficulty has its roots in the parallelism of the verse: is לחבל עניים parallel with בדבר אביון or are the latter words parallel with באמרי שקר? In the first instance scholars reduce בדבר to a different root meaning 'to destroy, to subdue' (*DCH*, II, 396: cf. *piel* in Prov. 21:28; 2 Chr. 22:10; *hiphil* in Judg. 18:7; Ps. 18:48; 47:4).[2] This implies that the prefix of באמרי שקר also governs the word משפט (*double duty*): 'to destroy the needy by a judgement'. In the second instance, בדבר is understood in its usual meaning as a *verbum dicendi*, either in the sense of 'to speak' with משפט as object – leaving the syntactic function of אביון difficult to determine ('by pronouncing judgement on the needy'; Irwin 1995: 74) –, or in the unique forensic sense of 'to charge' (cf. Deut. 22:14,17,20; 1 Sam. 22:15) or 'to slander' (cf. Ps. 41:7), once again with the prefix of באמרי שקר serving double duty for משפט (Irwin 1977: 125f.). An objection against the second solution lies in the fact that באמרי שקר would have a fully fledged pendant in בדבר while simultaneously providing a double duty parallel to משפט. This problem can be met by viewing משפט as an *accusativus instrumenti*. Consequently, we ascribe a negative forensic significance to the verb דבר. The resultant translation: 'by charging the needy with a judgement'.

ESSENTIALS AND PERSPECTIVES

The fifth woe cry (31:1-32:8) appears to stem from two distinct periods. The woe cry itself (ch.31) has its roots in the same situation as the preceding woe cry, at the moment when the political leaders in Jerusalem sought to establish an alliance with Egypt in order to break the siege of the Assyrian king Sennacherib (705-701 BC). In contrast to that which precedes it, however, the present woe cry appears to have been less drastically re-worked. The oracle of Isaiah ben Amoz announces both doom and salvation. While Jerusalem's unacceptable foreign policy

---

[2] *DCH* distinguishes six roots under the lemma דבר, included among which is another root with hostile significance: 'to drive, out, pursue' (IV). *Ges.[18]* is aware of only one root, 'to speak'.

will ultimately lead to the downfall of Egypt and the leading classes in Judah (vv. 1-3), YHWH will not let himself to be deprived of his city (vv. 4-5) and Assyria is destined for defeat (vv. 8-9). An expansion introduces the promise of a just king and of righteous leaders (32:1-8). Given that the terms 'righteousness / justice' played a primary role in the ideological programme of Jerusalem's royal house, it is probable that the expansion has its origins in the late 7th century redaction of PI, the so-called Assyrian or Josian redaction. The years during which the power of Assyria started to wane and Judah enjoyed a political and religious revival under Josiah constitute a ready background. The expansion in question can be found both at the tradition-historical level of ch.31 and the redactional level of chs. 28-32.

Commentators rarely associate 32:1-8 with ch.31, preferring as they do to see ch.32 as an independent, albeit composite, literary complex having its own place between the fifth (ch.31) and the sixth woe cry (ch.33). It is further assumed that the tradition inserted a perhaps original Isaianic oracle, a summons to mourn addressed to the 'women at ease', into a context of salvation between vv. 1-5(8) and vv. 15-20. That the text underwent such a process seems unlikely, however, given that a command to mourn would clearly lack any meaning within such an all-inclusive promise of just governance (vv. 1-3) with peace and prosperity (vv. 15-20). The summons to lament over the destruction of the land and the city can only be justified if one assumes a strong caesura between v. 8 and v. 9 of ch.32 (Delitzsch, 311, 346).[3]

The suggestion that one ought to interpret 32:1-8 more in relation to the preceding woe cry than to 32:9-14 finds its primary support in the semantic relationship between the two passages. The 'princes' of the king who reigns with justice stand in contrast to the 'princes' of Assyria (31:9; 32:1), a hinge concept which is further strengthened by the parallel term 'rock' (as metaphor for the king of Assyria in 31:9 and for the 'princes' in 32:2).

Nevertheless, the fact that the king and the princes who govern with justice constitute the antithesis of Jerusalem's leaders against whom the prophet has taken a stand in the preceding woe cries remains more significant. It is evident that 32:3-5 do not describe the consequences of just governance for the people but rather the disposition of the leaders themselves. They are the ones who will see and hear, judge justly and not stammer (Barth 1977: 214). A large number of topical and verbal agreements between 32:1-8 and the woe cries gives their relationship a

---

[3] It should be noted that such a caesura is clearly bridged by the hinge word 'to rise' (קום; v. 8: 'by noble things he stands'; v. 9: 'Rise up, you women').

more visible profile. Such an anthological style also characterises the description of the behaviour of the fool in 32:6-8, a segment which commentators have always considered secondary.

While the fifth woe cry is evidently compositional in character, the interpolation in 32:1-8 is clearly of a different order to those found in the preceding woe cries. On the one hand, 32:1-8 has close connections with 31:1-9 while on the other, it shows evidence of association with all the preceding woe cries in that it formulates a contrasting image to the political leaders who are denounced therein. In a certain sense, therefore, 32:1-8 constitutes an actualising conclusion to the entire collection of five woe cries in chs. 28-31 with respect to the accusations they contain.

SCHOLARLY EXPOSITION

1. 31:1-9: YHWH Alone Bent on his Prey

Introduction to the Exegesis: Form and Setting

In its endeavour to reconstruct the original Isaianic shape of the passage, literary-historical exegesis has designated vv. 6-7 in particular as a later addition. A call to conversion (v. 6) would have been unusual for Isaiah ben Amoz and out of place alongside the promise of assistance in vv. 4b-5, and under normal conditions, it would not have consisted of the removal of idols (v. 7).[4] Recent research has shown, however, that for Israel's prophets, the relationship between punishment, salvation and conversion follows a different logic to that which we have assumed up to now.

In addition, those who have interpreted the lion allegory as an announcement of judgement against Jerusalem and translated v. 4b accordingly ('… YHWH of hosts will come down to fight *against* Mount Zion'), have tended to explain the second comparison which clearly promises salvation (v. 5: 'Like birds hovering, so YHWH of hosts will protect Jerusalem') either in part or in its entirety as an addition.[5] Careful analysis of the two comparisons has shown, however, that both have the same point: YHWH is defending Jerusalem, his prey.[6] The lion allegory makes it clear that YHWH is engaged in a struggle, not against Mount Zion but

---

[4] Duhm, 229; Feldmann, 377; Schoors, 189; Kaiser, 253f.; Wildberger, 1239f.

[5] Feldmann, 376; Procksch, 406ff.

[6] Davis, Strawn 1996.

rather on Mount Zion, a struggle against those who would rob him of his prey, i.e. the military power against whom the leadership in Jerusalem turned to Egypt for help, the as yet unnamed Assyria (vv. 1-3,8).

Other commentators have assumed vv. 8b-9a to be an addition, insisting that falling by the sword, fleeing from the sword and the forced labour endured by prisoners of war cannot all be the result of the same struggle at the same time. Such an argument, however, is restricted by a contemporary understanding of logic. All three consequences simply constitute possible outcomes of a military defeat.[7]

The question remains as to whether one can reduce a text which was constructed as a literary unit to its probable constituent parts in oral preaching and whether one can determine the meaning thereof out of the context.[8] If one gives recognition to the paraenetic intent of the entire text then several so-called tensions therein appear to be quite meaningful (Sweeney, 401-20). Firstly, while the cry 'Woe' itself is directed to a particular political grouping (v. 1) and announces their downfall (v. 3), this does not exclude the possibility that YHWH will protect Zion as his own property (v. 4f.) or that the people should change their ways (v. 6f.). Likewise, the announcement that Egypt will perish together with those who depend on her for support (v. 3) does not exclude the possibility that the one who will conquer them, i.e. Assyria, will ultimately be ousted by YHWH because God has attached himself to Zion (vv. 8-9). Secondly, if one admits both aspects of YHWH's involvement with Israel – he punishes yet remains faithful – there is no contradiction between the lion and the bird comparison (vv. 4-5). Thirdly, the various different addressations in the text fit appropriately in such parenetic intent. The third person in vv. 1-3 establishes the political classes as the object of discussion, providing better preparation for the call to conversion addressed to all Israel (v. 6), together with the promise that Assyria will fall (vv. 8-9), than any direct addressation would have done. Similarly, the personal addressation in the messenger formula underlines the fact that YHWH's attachment to Zion has continued legitimacy which is evident from the prophet's own words (v. 4: 'YHWH has said *to me*').

As a consequence, it would appear to be more useful to take the unity of the passage as a point of departure. The generally recognised authentic Isaianic character of most parts of the text in question, the solidly Isaianic vocabulary, the thematic alignment of vv. 8-9 with vv. 4-5, the terminological associations between vv. 8-9 and vv. 1-3 and the pres-

---

[7] Schoors, 189; Wildberger, 1239; *pace* Duhm, 232f.; Kaiser, 253.

[8] Kilian (181-5) offers a recent, strictly literary-critical interpretation of the passage in which vv. 1,3 alone are considered as authentically Isaianic with any certainty.

ence of typical style figures such as antitheses (vv. 3,8) and word-plays (vv. 4,8-9) present the passage as a coherent prophecy of Isaiah ben Amoz announced to his contemporaries. In contrast to the preceding woe cries, however, his message is not really actualised for future generations. The literary structure itself is intended for the original audience.

The absence of any radical redaction is not without explanation. It is probable that the promise of help for Zion (v. 5) and the call to conversion (v. 6) possessed a timeless value. The same is even more evident for the image of YHWH which emerges from the text as a whole. Such a God could punish yet at the same time exhibit unconditional solidarity with his people and thus demand their conversion. Indeed, while every historical power would be forced into defeat before such a mighty God, those among his people who do not put their trust in him would likewise perish. Thus YHWH was to put every form of human self-sufficiency to shame.

The passage is clearly divisible into three parts: a woe cry (vv. 1-3), an oracle addressed to the prophet (vv. 4-5) and a call to conversion with a promise of salvation (vv. 6-9).

The woe cry as such describes the false confidence of the leading classes (v. 1), sets it in contrast to YHWH's policy (v. 2) and confronts both actants according to their nature and capability (v. 3). The last line constitutes a tricolon which provides a suitable conclusion to the preceding series of bicola.

After the messenger formula, the divine oracle consists of two comparisons. The first (with lions) is comprehensively formulated in three or four lines (v. 4), the second (with birds) more succinctly in two lines (v. 5). The final line of the first comparison and the first line of the second are tricola and thereby establish a chiastic colometric pattern.

The actual call to conversion consists of a pithy monocolon containing an accusation (v. 6). The salvation oracle is introduced by a temporal formula (v. 7: 'on that day') and is made up of a chain of verbs forms (vv. 7-8: *yiqtol* and twice *wᵉqatal*). As such, the removal of idols is not set up as a precondition for the defeat of the Assyrian army but both events are placed on the same level as gifts of YHWH. The final line (v. 9a: compound nominal clause in the first colon) exposes the Assyrian king (together with his 'princes') in his arrogance ('rock') and downfall and, at the same time, creates an appropriate contrastive image of YHWH in the concluding framing formula (v. 9b: 'says YHWH, whose fire is in Zion, and whose furnace is in Jerusalem'). This makes it clear that the entire segment from vv. 6-9 should be understood as a divine oracle and reveals the basis upon which the fall of Assyria's might is founded.

We can thus establish the structure of the passage as follows:

1-3 woe oracle

    1a   woe cry proper

    1b   accusation

          1b´   false trust in military aid

          1b´´   no thought for YHWH

    2   YHWH's attitude

          2a   his policy so far: he has brought disaster

          2b   his further policy: will take action against evil doers

    3   Egypt and YHWH compared

          3a   Egypt has no divine status

          3b   YHWH is able to destroy both helper and helped

4-5 oracle of YHWH for the prophet

    4a´   messenger formula

    4a´´-b first comparison: YHWH is as a lion

          4a´´   vehicle: a lion keeps guard over his prey

          4b   tenor: YHWH will fight on Mount Zion

    5   second comparison: YHWH is as birds

          5a´   vehicle: birds hover over their prey

          5a´´-b tenor: YHWH will protect Jerusalem

6-9 call to return to YHWH

    6   call proper to 'the children of Israel' with accusation

    7-9   salvation oracle

    7a´   temporal formula

    7a´´-b first promise: abandonment of idols

    8-9a   second promise:

          8   defeat of Assyria's army

          9a   dethronement of Assyria's king and princes

    9b   concluding oracular formula:

          Zion is the place of YHWH's powerful appearance

Exegesis by Verse

1 The actual woe cry (cf. at 29:15 and 'Introduction to Isaiah Chs. 28-39') has to do with a delegation sent to Egypt to obtain military assistance (עזר, 'to help', in the diplomatic and military sense: Judg. 5:23; 2 Sam. 8:5; 21:17; Isa. 20:6; Jer. 37:7; Ezek. 32:21; Ps. 35:2; 2 Chr. 28:16). The situation is the same as that of 30:1f.,16 (cf. the corresponding terminology) but the present text focuses more on the fact that Judah has already experienced the negative consequences of her foreign policy

(v. 2a). The verb forms (present in v. 1a and past in v. 1b) show that the current initiative is the fruit of a process which had already begun. It is possible that this prophecy stems from the time referred to by Sennacherib in his annals:

'He (Hezekiah) had become afraid and had called (for help) upon the kings of Egypt (and) the bowmen, the chariot(-corps) and the cavalry of the king of Ethiopia, an army beyond counting – and they had (actually) come to their assistance. In the plain of Eltekeh, their battle lines were drawn up against me and they sharpened their weapons. Upon a trust(-inspiring) oracle (given) by Ashur, my lord, I fought with them and inflicted a defeat upon them' (*ANET*, 287).

Three lines provide us with the motif of seeking military assistence: Egypt possesses a powerful army with chariots and horses. They also sketch the religious attitude which lies behind it: Judah can expect nothing from YHWH. Word-play between 'to rely on' (שׁען על; cf. 10:20; 30:12) and 'to look to' (שׁעה על; cf. 17:7f.) establishes a connection between politics and religiosity. The usual sequence of the divine names 'the Holy One of Israel' followed by 'YHWH' is reversed, thus emphasising the people's failure to understand God's solidarity with Israel (1:4; 5:24; 10:20; 17:7; 29:19; 30:15; 37:23f.). The final words of the accusation, 'who do not consult YHWH' (דרשׁ), constitute a significant theme in the preaching of the prophet (1:17; 8:19; 9:12; 11:10; 16:5; 19:3; 34:16).

Three words epitomise the military power of Egypt: horses, chariots and horsemen (Isa. 2:7; 5:28; 22:6f.; 30:16; 36:8f.; 37:24). From the broader scriptural perspective, such superior military might has typified Egypt since the time of Israel's exodus. Indeed Egypt was known from of old for this valuable and successful weapon. Homer, for example, sings the praises of the Egyptian city of Thebes as a city with a hundred gates, each of which opened to allow two hundred soldiers with their chariots and horses to go into battle in time of war (Ilias, I, 381-3). Although it is not stated, one can assume that Israel only had chariots and horses from the time of Solomon and never to any great extent (2 Sam. 8:4; 15:1; 1 Kgs 5:6; 10: 26-29; 18:5; 22:4; 2 Kgs 3:7; 7:13f.; 10:2; Ezek. 17:15; Amos 2:15; 6:12).

The words 'many' and 'strong' also have a role to play elsewhere in descriptions of military undertakings (8:7; 13:4; 16:14; 17:12f.; 30:25; 36:2) as well as of people or nations who appear in their own eyes or in the eyes of others to be 'mighty' with respect to God ('strong' [עצם]: Deut. 8:17; 9:1; Josh. 23:9; Isa. 47:9; Joel 1:6; Nah. 3:9; Zech. 8:22; Ps. 10:10; 38:20; 69:5; 'many' [רבים]: Deut. 7:1,17; Isa.

2:4; Jer. 25:14; 27:7; Ezek. 27:33; 32:10; Mic. 4:11; 5:7; Ps. 89:51; 135:10). Taken together, the terms represent the leading discourse which dominated that period in history. The prophetic discourse, however, which denounced such existential trust in a strong army instead of in YHWH, contradicted the given wisdom (Deut. 17:16; Jer. 17:5; Hos. 10:13f.; Ps. 20:8; 21:8f.; 33:16f.; 118:8; Prov. 21:31).

2 The description of YHWH's policy begins with the insistence that he is truly 'wise', thereby referring to a typically Isaianic point of discussion (חכם: 5:21; 19:11f.; 29:14; cf. 8:10; 28:29). The polemical tone reveals that the human quality of considered and dexterous acting is here applied to YHWH by way of exception (Jer. 10:6f.; Job 9:4; 12:13; Dan. 2:20ff.). The parallel term has its roots in common theological language: YHWH 'brings evil'. The term 'to let come' (בוא hiphil), with disaster or salvation as object, actualises the way in which God steers human history (Gen. 18:19; Deut. 26:19; Josh. 23:15; 2 Sam. 7:18; 17:14; 2 Kgs 19:25; Isa. 37:26; 43:5; 46:11; 48:15; 49:22; Jer. 25:13; 40:3; Ezek. 14:22; 20:10; 38:17; Ps. 66:11; 78:71; 105:40).[9] The parallel term also belongs to this topic. By bringing disaster ('evil', רע: 3:11), God has not taken back his former 'words' (דברים: Isa. 1:10; 2:1,3; 9:7; 16:13; 24:3; 28:13f.; 30:12,21; 37:22; 38:4,7; 39:5,8; 'to withdraw' [סור hiphil] with God as subject: Isa. 1:25; 3:1,18; 5:5; 18:5; 25:8; Exod. 23;25; 2 Sam. 7:15; 2Kgs 17:18,23; 23:27; 24:3; Jer. 32:31; Ps. 66:20). It is apparent, therefore, that YHWH's quarrel with Israel is nothing new.

The second line concretises YHWH's policy: he intends to undertake a hostile initiative (קום על, 'to rise against': Deut. 19:11; 22:26; 28:7; Judg. 9:18,43; 1 Sam. 17:35; 2 Sam. 14:7; 18:31; 2 Kgs 16:7; Ps. 3:2; 27:3; 54:5; 86:14; 92:12; 124;2; with God as subject: Isa. 14:22; Jer. 51:29; Amos 7:9). This term does not portray God so much as one of the parties in the conflict but rather as one who opposes evil, given the addition 'against (the house of) evildoers / those who work iniquity' (פעלי און / מרעים). Both expressions stem from the language of the psalms (Ps. 22:17; 26:5; 94:16 and Ps. 5:6; 28:3; 36:13; 59:3; 64:3; 94:4; 141:4; Hos. 6:8 respectively). The context usually points to threat and disaster engendering abuse of power, against which YHWH is obliged to intervene.[10] The imputation of such conduct to the 'clan' ('house') who were well disposed to Egypt marks it off as immoral and thus subject to God's judgement (cf. 'house of rebellion' in Ezek. 2:5ff.).

3 The polemic results in a consideration of the actual significance of Egypt and YHWH. Nominal clauses portray Egypt as static while a com-

---

[9] TWAT, I, 550f. (H.D. Preuß).
[10] און can be found in PI in 1:13; 10:1; 29:20; cf. TWAT, I, 152-6 (K.-H. Bernhardt).

pound nominal clause (with *yiqtol*) portrays YHWH as dynamic and thereby emphasises the superiority of the latter. The evaluative determinants 'men, not God' and 'flesh, not spirit' are not intended as a philosophical statement concerning the opposition between the spiritual and the material as essential to the distinction between God and human persons (cf. the survey of the discussion in Wildberger, 1231ff.). The purpose of the expression is related to its context. By placing its complete trust in Egypt, Judah's political class has turned its back on YHWH and made Egypt into its God (v. 1). In the wake of the relational reversal, the same individuals have forgotten the fact that the Egyptian horses are mere 'flesh', mere created things, both dependent and mortal (בשׂר: Gen. 6:3,12f.,17; 9:15ff.; Lev. 17:14; Num. 16:22; 18:15; 27:16; Deut. 5:26; Isa. 9:19; 10:18; 40:5f.; 49:26; 58:7; 66:16,23; Jer. 12:12; 17:5; Ps. 38:4; 56:4; 78:39; Job 10:11; 34:15; Prov. 5:11; Lam. 3:4). YHWH on the other hand is 'spirit' (רוח), the highest principle of life, which he bestows on human persons at creation (Gen. 6:3; 7:22; Num. 16:22; 27:16; Isa. 42:5; 57:16; Zech. 12:1; Job 27:3; 33:4; 34:14) and extends to them in support of their activities (Exod. 31:3; Num. 11:29; 24:2; Judg. 3:10; 6:34; 1 Sam. 10:10; 11: 6; Isa. 11:2; 40:13; 42:1; 44:3; 59:21; 63:14; Ezek. 36:27; 37:14; Joel 3:1f.; Ps. 51:13; 139:7; 143:10).

Having realised what Egypt and YHWH really represent, we are treated to an affirmation of God's vigorous intervention in human affairs: 'Yet YHWH stretches out his hand'. Elsewhere, this Isaianic expression is used to imply that YHWH has brought his judgement over Judah but that it did not result in the hoped for change of heart (הטה ידו: 5:25; 9:11,16,20; 10:4; 14:26f.). The same topic is present here also since it would appear from vv. 1-2 that God is already returning Israel's overtures to Egypt with disaster. The consequences of his intervention are presented in Isaianic metaphorical speech associated with military defeat ('to stumble' [כשׁל]: 3:8; 5:27; 8:15; 28:13; 35:3; 40:30; 59:10; 63:3; 'to fall' [נפל]: 3:8,25; 8:15; 10:4,34; 13:15; 22:25; 24:18,20; 31:8; 'to help' [עזר]: 10:3; 20:6; 30:5,7; 41:6,10,13f.; 44:2; 49:8; 50:7,9). In PI, the term 'to perish' (כלה) encompasses the fate of all those both within Israel and among the nations who have turned against YHWH (1:28; 10:18; 15:6; 16:4; 21:16; 24:13; 29:20; 32:10).

4-5 There is an animated discussion underway as to the tenor of the comparisons and their cohesion.

(1) With regard to their cohesion, according to some scholars, the second comparison (birds) announces salvation while the first (lion) does not. In the view of the majority, however, both comparisons must have the same intention,

for the following reasons. Firstly, both have 'YHWH of hosts' as subject. Secondly, the second comparison functions as a supplement to the first, linking up
as it does, not via the vehicle of the lion comparison but via the tenor: 'YHWH
comes down... Like birds hovering' (Duhm, 232). Thirdly, the second comparison is shorter, although it employs four verb forms ('to protect', 'to deliver', 'to
repel', 'to rescue') to describe what God is about to do (v. 5) while the first
leaves the result of 'he will come down to fight' open (v. 4). At the same time,
the word pair 'Zion / Jerusalem' is spread over both comparisons (v. 4b, v. 5a).

(2) With regard to the tenor of the comparisons, according to some scholars,
the lion who defends his prey cannot be employed as reference to salvation
since this animal clearly does not intend to allow his prey to live. Others suggest
the contrary, noting that the point of the comparison is quite focused: as the lion
refuses to be robbed of his prey YHWH refuses to allow Jerusalem to be taken
from him. Such an interpretation is supported by the explanation that while צבא
על might well mean 'to fight against', the preposition על belongs with ירד: 'He
will come down, in order to fight, upon mount Zion'.[11]

Based on the assumption that both comparisons have the same intention,
some authors even ascribe a negative significance to the bird comparison also.
Justifications for this position tend to vary. Some interpret the verb forms in v.
5b in a negative manner from the perspective of the flight patterns of birds of
prey: והציל as 'he snatches away' and והמליט as 'he escapes' (Sweeney, 406f.).
Others, on the assumption of a word-play, propose a second meaning for the
verb יגן in v. 5a, one based on West Semitic, namely 'to light upon', and, in
connection, consider v. 5b as a redactional addition which employs the customary meaning of יגן, namely 'to protect'. In this way, the originally negative intention of the second comparison is restructured into a positive one: 'he will light
upon Jerusalem' (v. 5a) becomes 'he will protect it' (v. 5b; Barré 1993).

Finally, there is also an explanation which accepts the negative intention of
the lion comparison side by side with the positive interpretation of the bird comparison but considers the latter as a whole to be a redactional elaboration of the
former. This position is based on the intrinsic ambiguity of the lion metaphor in
the Ancient Near East, clearly evident in the iconography, which allows a positive understanding thereof (Davis, Strawn 1996).

Of the explanations we have examined, the one which claims that salvation and doom need not be mutually exclusive as the intention of the
comparison appears to be the strongest. In the lion comparison, the topic
'prey' introduces an element of punishment, a fact which fits in particularly well with vv. 2-3, while at the same time YHWH lays claim to his
undivided authority over Jerusalem. Salvation and doom are subordinate
to this authority: YHWH will never hand his city over to 'a band of shep-
herds'.

In the Ancient Near East the term 'shepherd' is a royal title.[12] The
prophets likewise apply the concept to the princes of Israel and the kings

---

[11] Duhm (231) laid the foundation of this explanation of the comparison by asking the
methodically correct question as to the actual *punctum comparationis*; cf. Wildberger,
1240-3.
[12] *THAT*, II, 793 (J.A. Soggin); *TWAT*, VII, 570ff. (G. Wallis).

of the nations (רעה: 2 Sam. 5:2; 7:7; Isa. 44:28; Jer. 2:8; 3:15; 10:21; 12:10; 22:22; 23: 1f.,4; 25:34ff.; Ezekiel 34; Mic. 5:4; Nah. 3:18; Zech. 10:3; 11:4f.,8; 13:7). At first sight, this aspect of the metaphor does not apply here. Implicitly, however, while it clearly makes no reference to Egypt and only possibly to 'the evildoers' (v. 3) who desire to run things their own way without YHWH, it fits most appropriately to Assyria, the only power which had truly challenged YHWH's authority over Judah (Isa. 10:7-19; 36:7-10,14-20). As such, therefore, the lion comparison proclaims that Zion belongs to YHWH alone. Within this, punishment (v. 4a) and protection (v. 4b) are both possible, even at one and the same time.

The verb 'to come down' (ירד) used for YHWH's intervention characterises the text as a theophany (Isa. 63:19; Mic. 1:3; Ps. 18:10; 144:5; cf. Exod. 3:8; 19:11,18,20; 33:9; 34:5; Num. 11:17,25; 12:5; Isa. 34:5). The same term has been used in v. 1 for the initiative of the political classes: 'woe to those who go down to Egypt' (cf. 30:2; 34:5). This semantic agreement turns YHWH's intervention into a struggle against those who would rob him of Zion (v. 4) and at the same time, into a revelation of his power and his claims against those who have no interest in him (v. 1b). The fact that YHWH's struggle on Zion's behalf is against Assyria is evident from the word pair 'Mount Zion / its hill (of Jerusalem)' which only occurs elsewhere in PI in the context of the approach of the Assyrians against Jerusalem (10:32). Other terms from the lion comparison can also be found elsewhere in PI ('lion': 5:29; 15:9; 35:9; 'prey': 5:29; 'to terrify': 8:9; 20:5; 30:31; 31:9; 37:27; 'shouting' [קול in the threatening sense]: 10:30; 13:4; 15:4; 24:18; 33:3; 'noise': 22:2; 'to fight': 29:7f.). In addition, the word-play between 'YHWH of hosts' (צבאות) and the verb 'to fight' (צבא) is characteristic of Isaiah. It is apparent, therefore, that the comparison is firmly embedded in the immediate and broader context of PI.

In terms of form and language, the bird comparison – the only one in PI – is a particularisation of the lion comparison: in both YHWH constitutes the tenor.[13] The vehicle consists of only two words: 'Like birds hovering', literally 'flying' (כצפרים עפות), in contrast to the thirteen syntactic elements which make up the lion comparison. At the formal

---

[13] Exum (1981: 336ff.) strongly underlines this cohesive characteristic but does not conclude therefrom that the birds also protect the prey. In her opinion '...the birds hover over a young bird which has fallen out of the nest to defend it' (338). In contrast, Sweeney is correct in suggesting that, given the similarity between the two comparisons, we should characterise the birds as birds of prey who establish control over the remains of the prey left behind by the lions (407). One arrives at a quite different explanation if one considers the 'hovering birds' to be the object of YHWH's protection (Procksch, 406ff.).

level, one characteristic of the 'birds' in question, 'flying', is stated but
in fact, the combination of the two words merely indicates a generic
name (Gen. 7:14; Deut. 4:17; Prov. 26:2). Since the verb 'to fly' (עוּף)
expresses nothing more than a movement though air, one is thus obliged
to derive the nature and purpose of the flight from the context (Isa.
11:14; 60:8; Hab. 1:8; Ps. 55:7f.; 90:10). This means that the vehicle
of the comparison is intended to stimulate our curiosity while all the attention is focused on the tenor.

The tenor fills in the vehicle with one topic: 'to protect Jerusalem'.
The flight of the birds would appear to be a protective 'hovering' over
their prey (cf. 'hovering' over the young in Deut. 32:11; cf. Ps. 91:4).
The feminine gender of the words צפרים עפות supports the specific
significance of the comparison.[14] The second verse-half repeats the
word 'to protect' and elaborates this further with verbs which, strikingly enough, can be found in the narratives of chs. 36-38 concerning
Jerusalem's liberation from the might of the Assyrian army ('to protect,
to shield' [גנן]: 37:35; 38:6; 'to deliver' [נצל hiphil]: 5:29; 20:6;
36:14f.,18ff.; 37:11f.; 38:6; 'to rescue' [מלט hiphil]: 20:6; 37:38).
This discovery argues, in part, against those who would support a negative interpretation of the comparison's intention. Only the rare verb
פסח presents a problem in this regard. If it means 'to repel' (cf. 'Notes')
then it fits well with the vehicle of the comparison, i.e. the birds' efforts
to ward off other animals and keep their prey for themselves.

6 It has been suggested that the call to conversion must be a
redactional interpolation because it consists of prose. Moreover, Isaiah
ben Amoz would rarely use the term 'children of Israel' and then only
for the Northern kingdom (17:3,9; 27:12), and, perhaps most impor-
tantly, he would not preach conversion, only blame the people that they
did not change their ways (6:10; 9:12; 30:15) and expect a conversion
in the future which God himself was to inaugurate (1:27; 10:21f.;
19:22; 35:10).[15] While some of these arguments may be true, they cannot lead us to conclude that v. 6 does not fit well in the structure of the
woe cry after vv. 1-5. If a later redaction added v. 6, it was done on the
basis of a correct understanding of the preceding comparisons which
imply that YHWH does not and will not abandon his claim to Jerusalem.
This very sovereign choice is what constitutes the motif of conversion.
Within the rhetoric of this essentially paraenetic prophecy, such an appeal is hardly out of place (König, 280; Sweeney, 404, 407).

---

[14] Bullinger 1898: 105.
[15] Wildberger, 1239; for a survey of the texts concerned, cf. Holladay 1958: 124f.

The appeal itself is strikingly formulated: firstly as a monocolon, secondly because of the absence of the name YHWH (as the antecedent of the following relative clause; cf. the same construction in 28:12, in contrast to 31:9b). YHWH might not be named because of the revolt brought against him (סרה, 'apostasy': Isa. 1:5; 30:11; 59:13; Deut. 13:6; Jer. 28:16; 29:32), or because of the presence of idolatrous images (v. 7; cf. Exod. 20:3; Deut. 5:7). The phrase 'they have radically ('deeply', העמיקו) withdrawn' is reminiscent of the beginning of the third woe cry: 'Woe to those who, away from YHWH, hide deep their counsel' (29:15; cf. 7:11). Politics has driven YHWH away. The vocative 'children of Israel' sets up a contrastive background since it calls to mind the history of YHWH's solicitous presence in Israel. The expression itself implies more than just the political élite ('they have withdrawn') and as such it reveals an evident awareness that the abandonment of YHWH has touched the entire people (cf. 'Notes').

7 The temporal formula 'on that day' (ביום ההוא) does not refer to eschatological time but establishes rather a successive relationship in the immediate and near future between the return to YHWH (v. 6) and the removal of idols (v. 7) which in itself results in the defeat of the Assyrian army (vv. 8f.).[16] The expression as such makes these events more or less synchronous. The dogmatic question, therefore, as to whether the return to YHWH does not actually consist in the removal of idols and whether the removal of idols does not constitute the precondition for liberation from the yoke of Assyria, is not appropriate. The same holds true for the chronological period of these events. The future which dawns for Jerusalem given God's relationship with the city, holds a variety of events in store in which both YHWH and Israel take an active part but their initiatives are not presented as cause or condition and consequence. It is in this way that 'the ideological complexity of YHWH's decisive coming day' comes into focus.[17] This presents an alternative way of speaking about YHWH's sovereign intervention to that which the theology of grace has turned into Christian common property.

The expression 'on that day' may also have another function, particularly as a reference to what has already been said in PI with respect to the day of YHWH: 'On that day men will cast forth their idols of silver and their idols of gold which they made for themselves to worship...' (2:20).[18] The topic of idols is solidly present in ch.2 (vv. 8,18) which

---

[16] De Vries 1995: 42, 53f., 60.
[17] De Vries 1995: 125.
[18] De Vries 1995: 117, 258, 305.

lays the foundation for the repetition thereof it in the rest of PI (10:10f.; 19:1,3; 30:22). Thus, given the fact that v. 7 is intrinsic to PI, it makes no sense to suggest that it is a Deuteronomistic interpolation. The topic is interwoven in the present verses with a further topic intrinsic to PI, namely the charge that Israel has taken an active and arrogant stand against YHWH. The term employed here for 'sin', חטא, always appears in this same context (Isa.1:4,18,28; 3:9; 5:18; 27:9; 30:1; 33:14).[19] This stance is made concrete by the pagan idols which Israel has made with her own hands (the Hebrew term for 'idols', אלילים, could be a diminutive of אל to imply a degree of contempt or disdain: Ps. 96:5; 97:7; Lev. 19:4; 26:1; Jer. 14:14; Hab. 2:18f.; Zech. 11:17; Job 13:4; Sir. 11:3;[20] 'hands' [יד] in this sense: Isa. 1:12,15; 2:8; 3:11; 17:8; 37:19; for 'to make' [עשׂה] in the negative sense, cf. 29:16). 'To cast away (מאס) the idols' also constitutes the overturning of the fact that Israel has rejected YHWH's law (5:24; 30:12) and his guarantee of Shiloah's protection (8:6).

8-9a The defeat of the Assyrian army is essentially related to the rejection of idols (v. 7) and thus to the people's return to YHWH (v. 6). As with the preceding verses, the name of YHWH is not mentioned here. The first line makes it clear, nevertheless, that through God's agency Assyria, whose aggressive power extends far beyond human measure, will be subdued: 'by a sword, not of man' (v. 8a). We are thereby reminded of the delusions of the political élite who have forgotten that the Egyptians are merely 'men, and not God' (v. 3a). The defeat of Assyria exhibits further associations with v. 3: not only 'the helper' and 'he who is helped' shall fall but also those against whom help is sought (for 'to fall', cf. at v. 3b). Thus YHWH remains as the only trustworthy power.

The description of the defeat accentuates this fact even further. As such it does not intend to provide a military report concerning the course of the battle, given that the words do not constitute a logical sequence: 'to fall / to be devoured', 'to flee / to be put to forced labour', 'to pass away in terror / to desert in panic'. The initial verbs stand for defeat in general while the latter portray a reaction to a superior power, in the present context that of YHWH on Mount Zion (v. 9b).

The majority of terms in this passage are not foreign to PI:
- 'to be devoured by the sword' (חרב, אכל): Isa. 1:20; Deut. 32:42; 2 Sam. 2:26; 11:25; 18:8; Hos. 11:6; Jer. 2:30; 5:17; 12:12; Nah. 3:15

---

[19] TWAT, II, 864 (K. Koch). – The term recurs appropriately at the beginning of DI (40:2), summarising what has gone before.

[20] Commentators even accept that the term was created by Isaiah ben Amoz (TWAT, I, 306f. [H.D. Preuß]).

- 'sword' (חרב) as a weapon of war: 14:19; 21:15; on the day of YHWH: 3:25; 13:15; 22:2; as instrument of God: Isa. 27:1; 34:5f.; 37:7
- 'to flee' (נוס) before judgement: Isa. 10:3; 13:14; 17:13; 20:6; 24:18; 30:16f.
- 'to pass away' (עבר) as a response to judgement: Isa. 8:21; 23:6,12; 29:5
- 'to desert in panic' (חתת) in front of superior military force: Isa. 8:9; 20:5; 30:31; 37:27.

The enumeration of the casualties concentrates on the mainstays of the army: 'the elite troops' (בחרים, literally 'young men': 2 Kgs 8:12; Isa. 9:16; 40:30; Jer. 11:22; 18:21; 48:15; Ezek. 30:17; Amos 4:10; Ps. 78:31; Lam. 1:15[21]), 'the officers' (שרים for the military leaders of foreign armies: Num. 22:8; Judg. 7:25; 8:3; 1 Sam. 18:30; 29:3; 2 Sam. 10:3; Isa. 10:8; 19:11,13; Jer. 48:7; Amos 2:3[22]) and especially 'the rock' (סלע). This latter term is quite unusual – it clearly refers to the army chief since it is parallel to 'officers'[23] – and only makes sense as a term of ridicule for the king of Assyria. The one who was considered by his own people to be the solid ground of national power now flees before YHWH, as is elaborated in the next verse line, in the same way as rocks 'fall to pieces' before God (Nah. 1:6; cf. Job 14:8; 18:4) and clouds disappear (Ps. 18:13). Thus the king of Assyria is presented as the antithesis of YHWH who is rightly known as the 'rock' of the devout (Ps. 18:3; 31:4; 42: 10; 71:3),[24] and who rightly deserves the title 'the Rock of Israel' (Isa. 30:29). The context of these verbal allusions contains striking examples of word rhyme (in 31:8: חרב [three times] and בחור; in 31:8-9: נָס, מָס and נֵס; in 31:9: אור and תנור).

9b The subordinate clause associated with the divine name in the concluding oracular formula provides the basis upon which the prophecy supports itself: 'says YHWH, whose fire is in Zion, and whose furnace is in Jerusalem'. The fact that YHWH has associated himself with the city was already made explicit in the two comparisons (vv. 4-5). The metaphors for his presence in Jerusalem, 'fire / furnace' (תנור/אור), are, however, unique. Both terms appear frequently in technical and household contexts (אור: Isa. 44:16; 47:14; 50:11; Ezek. 5:2; תנור: Exod. 7:28;

---

[21] Weisman 1981; Ges.[18], 136; DCH, II, 134f.

[22] HALAT, 1259.

[23] This parallelism makes the idea that the term 'rock' is applied to the god Ashur, who is known in the annals of Sennacherib as 'the great mountain' (KB, II, 82), less likely (pace Feldmann, 377f.; Schoors, 190). For a survey of the different interpretations, cf. Dillmann-Kittel, 283; König, 281. An older explanation which considers 'his rock' to be an accusativus loci, no longer finds support since, given the parallelism, the word in question is better understood as subject (Ibn Ezra: 'He shall pass beyond his rock [stronghold] from fear'; Redaq: 'He will pass out of fear to his rock'; Rosenberg, 259; Duhm, 233).

[24] TWAT, V, 878f. (E. Haag).

Lev. 2:4; 7:9; 11:35; 26:26; Hos. 7:4,6f.; Lam. 5:10; Neh. 3:11). Because the term 'hearth' does not bear the same symbolic value in Mediterranean culture as it does further north, the expression signifies more than the mere fact that YHWH's dwelling place is in Jerusalem (Alexander, 492). The element of fire suggests a theophany on Zion (cf. 'furnace' with different words for 'fire' in the context of a theophany in Gen. 15:17; Mal. 3:19; Ps. 21:10, as well as the mention of 'fire' in the context of a theophany on Zion in Isa. 4:5; 10:17; 33:14; Jer. 4:4; Lam. 2:14; 4:11). An association with the temple and the fire on the altar, therefore, seems evident (cf. Isa. 29:1; Feldmann, 378; König, 281). The fall of the Assyrian army thus constitutes a manifestation of YHWH, who has established his dwelling on Mount Zion.[25]

2. 32:1-8: A Reign of Righteousness and Honesty

Introduction to the Exegesis: Form and Setting

This passage contains a description of an alternative society in which justice will constitute the guiding principle of governance and lying words will no longer poison social life. The sketch itself, however, describes more than some timeless ethical programme. It is first and foremost a promise formulated as a contrast to the kind of society which was portrayed in the accusations of the preceding woe cries. A significant number of semantic agreements clearly point in this direction. As such, the sketch is conscious that YHWH's judgement, as it is determined in the woe cries, is not his final judgement with regard to Israel. A time will follow in which the values which YHWH has introduced to his people will ultimately hold sway. The ethical challenge of the passage is thus subordinate to its promissory character. YHWH intends to inaugurate a time of salvation (Kaiser, 255). Furthermore, the announcement of a kingdom of justice constitutes the antithesis of the fall of the godless kingdom of Assyria announced in the preceding chapter (Oswalt, 578f.). The same contrast can be found in the transition from ch.10 to ch.11, between 'the haughty pride' of Assyria's king (10:12) and 'the fear of YHWH', bestowed on 'the shoot from the stump of Jesse' (11:1-3; Dillmann-Kittel, 284). Thus the redaction of BI is already familiar with what would later be referred to as the paradigm of the two kingdoms.

The model of a good society presented here is dependant on Ancient Near Eastern social and ethical paradigms. Such a society does not have

---

[25] *TWAT*, VIII, 713 (M. Oeming).

its roots in revolution but rather in the culture's own endeavour, its 'wisdom', to establish a community which functions in harmony with its interior order. It is in such a community, structured in accordance with the pattern of social classes, that the king, together with the other leading figures, promotes the interests of the people, especially of the needy. In the Ancient Near Eastern world view, the social order and the cosmic order were closely related. Social chaos and natural disaster went hand in hand as did justice and well-being.

Commentators often include this passage among those texts referred to as 'messianic'.[26] They are correct in doing so when they view this concept from its Old Testament perspective: the new era does not herald the end of history nor is the promised king a meta-historical figure. Both constitute a part of Israel's actual history. The king will be a son of Israel's royal house. Indeed, as before, the people he will rule will continue to need his protection and the provision of water for themselves and the land (v. 2).[27]

The passage is made up of two parts: the announcement of a king and just governance (vv. 1-5), and a description of the behaviour of the fool who, according to the wisdom tradition, is also an evildoer (vv. 6-8).[28] The first part is essentially prophetic in genre since it predicts what is going to happen. The second part, on the other hand, is chokmatic in genre, characteristically offering a description of the way human beings should behave in contrast to the way they actually behave. Such contrasts (Proverbs 10-16) and character sketches (Ps. 73:6-12; Prov. 31:10-31; Sir. 39:1-11) are typical of the literature emerging from the wisdom tradition.[29]

Based on the distinction between prophetic prediction and gnomic description, certain commentators have suggested that the second part is a later addition. Such a suggestion is difficult to substantiate, given that it is hard to restrict the language of the wisdom tradition to any particular time. While the temporal perspective between the two parts may differ, the terminology of the wisdom tradition tends to attune them to one another. It would appear that the second part presents itself as an expansion of the first, the terms 'fool', 'noble' and 'knave' of v. 5 receiving further systematic elaboration in v. 6, v. 8 and v. 7 respectively. Furthermore, vv. 6-8 exhibit semantic associations with the accusations of the

[26] With regard to this problem, cf. Wegner 1992: 290-8

[27] It is probably for this reason that RSV (annotation) refers to the passage as a non-messianic oracle.

[28] It is difficult to comprehend why Sweeney (410f.) associates v. 5 on syntactic grounds with vv. 6-8 instead of vv. 1-4.

[29] Gammie, Perdue 1990: esp. 295-306; Brown 1996: esp. 1-21.

preceding woe cries in precisely the same way as vv. 1-5. There are no particular indications to suggest, therefore, that the two parts have distinct literary roots.

The first part consists of four syntactically distinct pieces. The macrosyntactically ('behold', הֵן) introduced opening clause: 'for righteousness will reign a king' (v. 1: לְצֶדֶק יִמְלֹךְ)[30] is followed by three elements, linked in a series by verbal forms: 'each will be' (v. 2: וְהָיָה), 'the eyes of those who see will not be closed' (v. 3: וְלֹא תִשְׁעֶינָה) and 'the fool will no more be called' (v. 5: לֹא יִקָּרֵא). The second element is accompanied by a verse line with dependant compound nominal clauses (v. 4).

The second part is structured according to the three characters: 'the fool' (v. 6), 'the villain' (v. 7) and 'the noble' (v. 8). The first element is accompanied by two lines with infinitive constructs which describe the intentions of 'the fool' (v. 6b). The second element employs one single line with infinitive constructs to depict the intention and the method of working of 'the villain' (v. 7b).

We propose the following structure:

1-5   announcement of a society governed with righteousness
     1   announcement of righteous rulers
     2-5   their characteristics
         2   they will protect against natural disasters
         3-4   they will pay attention and speak genuinely
         5   they will not allow mendacity to govern social discourse
6-8   description of the contrast between the fool / the evildoer and the noble
     6   the fool
         6a   his behaviour
         6b   its impact with regard to YHWH and the destitute
     7   the villain
         7a-b′   his behaviour
         7b″-‴   its impact with regard to defenceless people
     8   the behaviour of the noble

Lack of any reference to a specific historical situation makes the passage extremely difficult to date. If one accepts that BI underwent a significant redaction during the reign of king Josiah with his reform of the cult and the revival of the Davidic ideology (from 620 BC onwards),

---

[30] The expression 'for righteousness' (לְצֶדֶק) is so clearly an inversion that it does not deprive v. 1 of its character as an introductory main clause.

then the passage appears to fit well therein.[31] If one is inclined to reject this theory, however, then one might be obliged to situate the text in the post-exilic period, especially if one is of the opinion that the single word 'king' (v. 1) is an insufficient basis for assuming the influence of Davidic ideology and one prefers to see it as an indication of a later re-orientation of Israel's expectations with regard to the house of David after the failure of Zerubbabel (Wildberger, 1235f.). The contrast, however, between the king and his 'princes' mentioned here and the king of Assyria and his 'princes' mentioned at the conclusion of the preceding passage is such an appropriate topic to the seventh century redaction that one is inclined to date the passage during this period.

Exegesis by Verse

1 Given the fact that the opening clause: 'Behold... a king will reign' introduces the literary form which draws attention to what the king has done or will do, the passage is immediately set against the background of the narratives concerning the kings, especially those about David and his successors (הנ[ה] with מלך and a verb: 1 Sam. 12:2,13; 18:22; 2 Sam. 19:2,9; 1 Kgs 1:18; 2 Kgs 7:6; Jer. 23:5; Zech. 9:19). The word 'righteousness' would appear to constitute the central concept of the passage, being placed in first position against the usual word order. Of course, the association of 'righteousness' (צדק[ה]) with 'to reign' (מלך) also constitutes a biblical topic in the context of narratives and expectations concerning Israel's kings (2 Sam. 8:15; 1 Kgs 10:9; Isa. 41:2; 62:2; Jer. 22:15; 23:5; Ps. 72:1; 99:4; Prov. 8:15; 16:12f.; 25:5; 29:14; 1 Chr. 18:14; 2 Chr. 9:8). Furthermore, 'righteousness' (צדק[ה]) and 'justice' (משפט) frequently appear as a word pair, in BI (cf. at 28:17) as well as in the Scriptures as a whole (Gen. 18:19; Deut. 16:18; Jer. 22:3,13; 33:15; Ezek. 45:9; Ps. 72:1f.). The unusual preposition 'for' (ל) preceding 'righteousness / justice' appropriately reveals that the establishment of these characteristics will be the ultimate intention of the new regime,[32] the same 'righteousness and justice' which YHWH had once announced that he expected of his vineyard Judah (5:7 is the only place in BI where the word pair in question is to be found with the same preposition).

Besides to 'a king', reference is also made to 'princes' (שרים) among those who will serve and promote a just society (the two terms are fre-

---

[31] Barth 1977: 213ff.; Sweeney, 415f.

[32] Olley 1983; לצדקה: Isa.5:7; Hos. 10:12; Joel 2:23; Ps. 106:31; למשפט: Isa. 5:7; 28:16; 34:5; 41:1; 54:17; 59:11 and 15 occurrences outside BI.

quently found together: 2 Kgs 11:14; Isa. 10:8; Jer. 1:18; 36:21; Ezek. 17:12; Hos. 3:4; 13:10; Amos 1:15; Prov. 8:15; Eccl. 10:16; Lam. 2:9; Ezr. 7:28). The 'princes' were the king's senior officials, with whose help he was able to exercise his authority across the various aspects of civil life: the court, the army, the judiciary, foreign policy and local administration. They constituted the upper level of society upon which the monarchy leaned for support.[33] In the prophetic literature, the princes are called to account along with the king (Jer. 2:26; 8:1; 32:32; 39:3; Hos. 7:3; 8:4; Zeph. 1:8). The strict parallelism between 'to rule' and 'to reign' provides the princes here with a degree of prominence (the roots שׂרר and מלך are rarely found together: Hos. 8:4; Esth. 1:22). This corresponds with the fact that where foreign policy and social order are concerned, Judah's leaders constitute the butt of the accusations of the woe cries (28:7,14; 29:10,14f.,20,24; 30:1-5,16,20; 31:1f.), just as 'the princes' in the remainder of PI are objects of accusation (1:23; 3:3f.,14; 43:28; foreign 'princes': 10:8; 19:11,13; 21:5; 23:8; 34:12; 49:7). In addition, the word pair 'king / princes' constitutes a counterpart to the 'rock / officers' (also שׂרים) in 31:9.[34] Thus the virtual equalisation of 'princes' and 'king' here (further emphasised in v. 2 by 'each will be...') fits well with the significant addressation of the preceding charges. It would appear then that v. 1 contains an actualisation of the traditional royal ideology for the sake of the immediate context.

2 The nature based comparisons are not chosen arbitrarily. They stem rather from the supposition that a fundamental harmony exists between the cosmic and the social order (cf. Isa. 4:6; 25:4f.), evil being seen as a disruption thereof (Isa. 29:17). Gods and good administrators work together to maintain that harmony. While such a worldview is rather alienating to our culture, it remains the common range of thought in the literature of the Ancient Near East and the Scriptures. Thus the maintenance of justice and the furtherance of life in all its aspects are indissolubly linked in the royal ideology.[35] Protection against natural disasters and abundance of water in arid territory are fruits of just governance (Ps. 72:6,16). As a matter of fact, the topic of the king as 'shade' and 'place of refuge' is widespread throughout Mesopotamia (cf. the texts mentioned by Wildberger, 1255f.; cf. Isa. 30:2; Lam. 4:20; Cant. 2:3).

---

[33] *TWAT*, VII, 861ff., 866-73 (H. Niehr).

[34] Of course the promised king is not referred to here as 'rock', a title which embodies the blasphemous arrogance of the king of Assyria!

[35] Keel (1972: 259-87) provides detailed documentation.

The two comparisons stand in contrast to one another in so far as the first portrays the superabundance of water and the second the absence of water as a situation of need.[36] Indeed, the parallelism between 'wind' and 'tempest' makes it clear that 'wind' here does not refer to a dry desert gale (cf. Exod. 10:13; 14:21; Isa. 27:8; 40:7; Jer. 18:17; Hos. 13:15; Jonah 4:8), but rather to a sea tempest (cf. 1 Kgs 18:45; 2 Kgs 3:17; Jer. 10:13; Ps. 104:3; 135:7; Job 30:15; Prov. 25:14). Together the comparisons reveal that righteous governance results in cosmic balance, since it offers protection against the destructive forces of water and against the deadly effects of drought.

The majority of terms in this passage are not alien to PI:
- 'hiding place' (מחבא) itself is a *hapax legomenon*; the root חבה is to be found in 26:20
- 'wind' (רוח) as a phenomenon of terror: 7:2; 11:15; 17:13; 25:4
- 'covert' (סתר): verb and noun occur often; cf. at 28:15
- 'tempest' (זרם): 4:6; 25:4; 28:2; 30:30
- 'streams of water' (פלגי מים): 30:25; 'water' in the context of fertility: 1:30; 15:6; 32:20; 35:6f.
- 'dry place' (ציון): 25:5 (nowhere else in MT)
- 'shade' (צל): 4:6; 16:3; 25:4f.; 30:2f.; 34:15; 38:8
- 'rock' (סלע): 2:21; 7:19; 16:1; 22:16; 31:9; 33:16
- the expression 'weary land' (ארץ עיפה) is only found elsewhere in Ps. 63:2; 143:6, but עיפה occurs in Isa. 5:27; 28:12; 29:8.

3-4 These verse lines belong together at the level of colometry (three times 4 + 4, once 4 + 5 accents),[37] syntax and semantics. V. 3 is chiastically structured.[38] The four cola of vv. 3-4 consist of one verbal clause (v. 3a), followed by three compound nominal clauses (vv. 3b-4a.b). The three run strictly parallel (human organ with a participle or adjective of the possessor in the plural with a verb, followed in v. 4a.b by an infinitive construct with ל.

The subject of each of the four clauses is a body part, representing a human function in the Semitic worldview, which takes first position in the three subordinate clauses: 'eyes, ears, heart (RSV: 'mind'), tongue'. The passage projects the ideal image of the human person taken from Ancient Near Eastern wisdom onto the promised righteous leaders of

---

[36] The words 'a covert from the tempest' in v. 2a lack the comparative prefix כ and thus constitute an appositional clause to 'like a hiding place from the wind' (זרם supplements רוח). The verse line in question, therefore, forms one single comparison and any text-critical reconstruction is unnecessary (Wildberger, 1250; *pace BHK, BHS*).

[37] The final word of v. 4, צחות, 'genuine words', disrupts the strict parallelism and forms a colometric plus. Therefore, it is often dropped by commentators. LXX (εἰρήνη) and 1QIs[a], however, were clearly familiar with it.

[38] The pattern is A-BC / BC-A (Watson 1994: 338).

v. 1. Careful oversight and an attentive ear together with steady under-standing and genuine speech are the fundamental characteristics of the wise. Almost all the terms in these verses are to be found in related verses in the book of Proverbs, sometimes in the more narrow context of governance and jurisprudence. For example:

V. 3 – 'eyes' (עינים) and/or 'to see' (ראה): 4:25; 6:6; 20:8,12f.; 22:3; 24:32; 27:12; 28:27; 29:16
- 'ears' (אזנים) and/or 'to hear' (שמע or קשׁב *hiphil*): 5:13; 12:15; 13:1; 15:31f.; 17:4; 18:13; 19:20; 21:13,28; 25:12; 29:12
V. 4 – 'heart' (לבב): 10:8;11:29; 14:30; 15:14,32; 16:1,21; 17:18; 18:12; 21:4; 22:11; 24:30f.
- 'rash' and 'eagerly' (root מהר): 1:16; 6:18; 7:23; 22:29; 25:8
- 'to have judgement' (בין): 14:6,15; 15:14; 16:21; 18:15; 19:25; 20:24; 29:7
- 'to know' (RSV: '*good* judgement') (ידע): 9:18; 10:32; 12:10; 14:7,10,33; 17:27; 24:14; 27:1,23; 28:2,22
- 'tongue' (לשׁון): 6:24; 10:20; 12:19; 15:2,4; 16:1; 17:4; 18:21; 25:15,23; 26:28; 28:23
- 'stammerer': 1:26; 17:5; 30:17 (עלג is a *hapax legomenon*; but it is possible that the word is a *metathesis* of the root לעג [Wildberger, 1250])
- 'to speak' (דבר): 16:13; 21:28; 23:9; 25:11.

Most commentators consider the announced transformation as the outcome of the exercise of just governance on *the people* but it seems more likely in the context that the transformation refers to the behaviour of *the leadership* themselves (Barth 1977: 213ff.). Firstly, it is evident that no new subject is introduced after v. 2. Secondly, after the accusa-tions of the woe cries which are primarily aimed at the leadership, the promise of a change from negative to positive behaviour – in respect of attentiveness, good judgement, genuine speech – would appear to have these individuals in mind. Wisdom will take hold of them. This shift is also more in line with v. 2 were it is promised that they will offer protec-tion.[39]

Closer examination, moreover, reveals an important distinction be-tween v. 3 and 4. V. 3 announces the end of the paradoxical situation in which those with eyes cannot see and those with ears cannot hear. V. 4, on the other hand, announces a transformation, a shift from foolishness to insight, from stammering to unambiguous speech. The promised changes are all constituent elements of a prophecy but v. 3 refers quite specifically to the end of the situation which the prophet Isaiah had been obliged to instigate: 'lest they see with their eyes, and hear with their ears...' (6:10). This topic from the call narrative resounds throughout PI

---

[39] This also explains the absence of an object in relation to 'to see', 'to hear', 'to have judgement' and 'to speak' (if one considers צחות to be an *accusativus modi*).

in the form of an announcement that the once condemned sinful condition would come to an end (29:18; 33:17-19; 35:5-6).[40]

In comparison to 6:10, the present text (32:4) exhibits two new elements. The promise: '...and the heart (ולבב) of the rash will have good judgement (יבין)' is partly new. While it echoes: '...and understand with their hearts (ולבבו יבין)' in 6:10[41] to a degree, the addition of 'of the rash' robs it of its paradoxical character. The expression 'the tongue of the stammerers will eagerly speak genuine words' is entirely new. It is not unusual as such that a sequence of body parts is broadened. In 35:6, for example, we find the topic of the renewed functioning of eyes and ears expanded to include 'the lame man' and 'the tongue of the dumb'. At the same time, however, the element of 'the tongue' raises the question as to whether 32:4 does not refer to a different text in PI after all. Given the fact that the stammering speech of the fool in 32:4 is explained in v. 6 as 'to speak error against YHWH', one is tempted to see a relationship with 3:8: 'For Jerusalem has stumbled, and Judah fallen; because their speech (literally 'tongue') and their deeds are against YHWH, defying his glorious presence'. There are more affinities between the two passages.[42]

As a consequence, it would appear that vv. 3-4 function on three distinct levels. They represent the ideals of human behaviour drawn from the broader wisdom tradition, they announce in the context of prophecy that these ideals will be realised in a transformed leadership, and they express this in terms drawn in part from Isa. 6:10 in order to make it clear that the hardening announced by Isaiah ben Amoz as judgement will come to an end.

5 The topic of genuine speech is continued in the promise that language will no longer serve to pervert the truth in civil life. Here too we recognise the triple linguistic level found in vv. 3-4. Firstly, we hear the concerns of the wisdom tradition. Since the natural order of the world is wisdom's goal, the actual naming of things is among her main priorities (Job 17:14; Prov. 16:21; 20:6; 24:8; Sir. 4:25-28). When people use language to misrepresent reality, the order of the world is disturbed precisely because it is the task of human persons to provide all that exists with a name (Gen. 2:19f.). Thus, it is possible to consider the book of

---

[40] The texts are classified and discussed in Aitken 1993. The group to which 32:3 belongs is discussed on pp. 34-9.

[41] The final word in 32:4a, לדעת, may have its roots in 6:9: ואל תדעו.

[42] The announcement of judgement in 3:1-12 has the absence of leaders as its primary theme (v. 4: 'princes'!) and also contains a description of the wise man and the fool (vv. 10-11).

Proverbs as one mighty attempt to name what is foolish and what is wise from the perspective of their contrastive manifestations. Against this background, it would appear that v. 5 is alluding to the end of a very threatening situation. If wickedness and folly influence the world under false title then they violate the right order of things. Indeed, they are all the more dangerous because they refuse to let themselves be exposed for what they really are.

As a promise of righteous leadership, v. 5 predicts the end of a process of degeneration in which injustice held sway by passing itself off as justice. In the complaints of the preceding woe cries it has become quite clear that the existing regime has introduced lies as principle and practice (28:15: 'We have made lies our refuge'; cf. 29:13,16,21; 30:10,12).

Finally, it is evident among the prophets, particularly in BI, that they allude to those who bear functional and vocational names rather than personal names as the visible embodiment of that which YHWH brings about, be it the initiation of judgement (14:20; 47:1,5; 48:8; Jer. 6:30; 19:6; 46:17; 30:17; Mal. 1:4), be it the dawning of salvation. Thus, the very restoration of Zion's judges will earn her the name of 'city of righteousness, faithful city' (1:26; cf. 35:8; 54:5; 56:7; 58:12; 60:14,18; 61:3,6; 62:2, 12; 65:15; Jer. 3:17; 33:16; Zech. 8:3).[43]

The word 'fool' (נבל) also has its place in the text's multi-functionality. The evident implication of the absence of wisdom is adeptly illustrated in the narrative of Nabal in 1 Samuel 25 (cf. Sir. 33:5). At the same time, however, the fool's contemptible behaviour (2 Sam. 13:12f.; Jer. 29:23; Job 30:8; Prov. 30:22; 17:21) and deceptive talk (Isa. 9:16; Job 2:10; Prov. 17:7; Sir. 4:27), even when addressing God (Deut. 32:6; Ps. 14:1; 74:18,22), together with his dependence on false certainties (Jer. 17:11-13; Ezek. 13:3; Ps. 32:9) has also earned him a dishonourable reputation.[44] The term 'noble' (נדיב), in contrast, refers primarily to those who belong to the leading classes (Ps. 47:10; 83:12; 118:9; 146:3; Job 30:15; Prov. 25:6f.; parallel to 'prince' [שׂר; cf. v. 1]: Num. 21:18; Job 34:18f.; Prov. 8:16) and who thereby enjoy a higher standing (Job 12:21; Prov. 25:7; Cant. 7:2). According to the chokmatic ideal, however, the concept of the noble also implies righteous and impeccable behaviour (Prov. 8:16; 17:7,26), even although this does not always square with reality (Job 21:28; 34:18).[45] – The sec-

---

[43] This topic is associated with *qal* and *niphal* forms of קרא; cf. *TWAT*, VII, 141f. (F.-L. Hossfeld, E.-M. Kindl).

[44] *TWAT*, V, 176-81 (J. Marböck).

[45] *TWAT*, V, 242-4 (J. Conrad).

ond half of the verse says the same thing in very rare terms which do not contribute to further nuancing.[46]

6 While the description of the 'fool' may appear a little static, according to present day norms, its well chosen terminology certainly testifies to the serious understanding of the problem of evil. From the syntactic perspective v. 6a constitutes a main clause followed by two lines with infinitive constructs in v. 6b. From the semantic perspective v. 6a and the first line of v. 6b are drawn together by the chiasm 'speaks / plots – to practice / to speak' (the roots דבר and עשׂה). The semantic pattern makes it clear that the fool in all his being – interior disposition, spoken language and active behaviour – is dedicated to the cause of evil. The syntactic structure also reveals that he sins with respect to both YHWH and the needy, not only by disregarding them but also by intentionally turning against them.

All of this is couched in a string of weighty terms: 'foolishness' (נבלה; cf. v. 5), 'iniquity' (און; cf. 29:20; 31:2), 'ungodliness' (חנף) and 'error' (תועה). In terms of content, the term 'ungodliness' implies threatening words and behaviour towards those with whom one is actually related in some fashion, suggesting further the notion of infidelity and maliciousness (Isa. 9:16; 10:6; 33:14; Jer. 23:11,15; Job 8:13; 20:5; Prov. 11:9).[47] The last term does not suggest that one has spoken amiss about God[48] but rather that one has spoken in such a way as to bring about alienation from him also in the community (cf. Isa. 3:12; 9:15; 29:24; 2 Kgs 21:9; Jer. 23:13; Ezek. 13:10; 44:10; 48:11; Amos 2:4; Hos. 4:12; Mic. 3:5; Ps. 119:176).[49]

The fact that the evildoer intentionally withholds food and drink from those who hunger and thirst has a particularly distressing sound to it if one considers it against the background of the Scriptures as a whole. The word pair 'hungry / thirsty' (צמא / רעב) is only to be found in one other admonition, namely in Prov. 25:21, where it is stated that one must even help one's enemy in such circumstances. Both texts represent the opposite extremes of human behaviour: perversity and generosity.[50]

---

[46] For כילי, 'villain', cf. 'Notes'. שׁוע, 'honourable', is also to be found in Job 34:20 (cf. HALAT, 1340).

[47] TWAT, III, 42-8 (K. Seybold).

[48] The fact that 'toward YHWH' is placed prior to 'error' makes it clear that in itself such speech is directed against the person of YHWH.

[49] TWAT, VIII, 724 (U. Berges).

[50] The word pair 'hungry / thirsty' can be found in other literary genres (Deut. 28:48; 2 Sam. 17:29; Isa. 5:13; 29:8; 49:10; 65:13; Amos 8:11; Ps. 107:5; Neh. 9:15; 2 Chr. 32:11).

7 The description of the 'villain' (כלי)⁵¹ follows that of the fool. The concept is a *hapax legomenon* and is supplemented by two further descriptive statements: 'his villainies are evil' and 'he devises wicked plans'. The first expression is partly tautologous and remains imprecise.⁵² The primary word of the second expression, 'to devise' (יעץ), however, has a dual function. It serves to root the description in the wisdom tradition in which the necessity, relativity and ethical ambivalence of deliberation prior to an action is a familiar topic (Prov. 1:25,30; 8:14; 11:14; 12:15,20; 13:10; 15:22; 16:30; 19:20f.; 20:5,18; 21:30; 24:6; 27:9). At the same time, it associates the description with a topic familiar to PI concerning YHWH's policy towards Israel throughout her history and the contrasting policy of those who oppose him (7:5; 14: 24-27; 19:11f.,17; 23:8f.; for the noun עצה, cf. 28:29). The object, 'wicked plans' (root זמם), is a chokmatic term (Prov. 10:23; 12:2; 14:17; 21:27; 24:8f.; 30:32; 31:16) to be found nowhere else in BI. Thus it appears once again that the wisdom tradition, with its ideal of the righteous person, has provided the images necessary to unmask the leaders whom Isaiah was called to denounce as persons who contravened and emasculated God's order.

Just as the behaviour of the fool is spelled out in his heartless attitude towards the needy (v. 6b, second line) so the behaviour of the 'villain' is portrayed as deception of the powerless in the administration of justice as a means to eliminate them. We have already discussed the terminology employed here ('poor / needy' in 29:19; 'lie' in 28:15; for the terms employed in v. 7b′′, cf. 'Notes'). The intention to maliciously harm one's helpless opponents in such a way as to definitively exclude them from society and the proper administration of justice is contained in the term 'to ruin' (חבל: Isa. 10:27; 13:5; 32:7; 54:16; Mic. 2:10; Job 17:1; 34:31; Eccl. 5:5; Neh. 1:7).⁵³

8 With the description of 'the noble' (נדיב), the passage returns to the promise of righteous leaders (v. 5). Via the figure of speech of *paranomasia* (different syntactical elements, here the subject and the object, are taken from the same root; the object, moreover, is repeated in the second half of the verse),⁵⁴ a pendant is established with 'the fool

⁵¹ The vocalisation differs from that of the term in v. 5. A number of commentators consider the present vocalisation to be artificial and intended to establish assonance with the following word (Wildberger, 1251).

⁵² 'His villainies' (כליו) says little more than 'his meannesses' (*TWAT*, IV, 182 [K.-M. Beyse]).

⁵³ *TWAT*, II, 713ff. (J. Gamberoni).

⁵⁴ The term *paranomasia* is used in a variety of ways. Some authors apply it only to words which immediately follow one another and at the same time enjoy a degree of as-

speaks foolishness' in v. 6. Via the term 'he devises' (יעץ), a pendant is
established with 'the villain devices wicked plans' in v. 7. The only new
element is the expression 'he stands (יקום) by noble things' which appears, once again, to have a chokmatic background. The wisdom tradition is familiar with the topic that the only life which stands a chance of
success is one which is in full agreement with its precepts. Any policy
which does not take account of YHWH is doomed to failure (קום in this
sense: Job 8:15; 22:28; Prov. 15:22; 19:21; 24:16; 28:12). This topic
runs parallel with that found in BI (and elsewhere in the prophets) which
insists that YHWH's plan for Israel and the nations will ultimately come
true (קום in this sense: Isa. 7:7; 8:10; 14:24; 28:18,21; 40:8; 33:10;
44:26; 46:10; cf. Num. 23:19; Jer. 23:20; 44:28f.; 30:24; 51:29).[55]
The verse takes up the primary theme of the woe cry against this background: in matters of foreign policy, thos who would not seek help from
Egypt against Assyria but are considerate of YHWH, will survive the confrontation with the world power.

sonance or consonance while they do not come from the same root and thus have a different meaning (Bullinger, 307, 314). Other authors do not consider a difference in meaning
to be necessary (Bühlmann-Scherer, 19; Watson 1984: 242).

[55] *TWAT*, VI, 1261ff. (J. Gamberoni).

CALL TO MOURN UNTIL THE SPIRIT COMES (32:9-20)

32:9   Rise up, you women who are at ease,
        hear my voice.
    You complacent daughters,
        listen to my speech.

10   In little more than a year
        you will shudder, you complacent ones.
    Truly, the vintage will fail,
        the harvest will not come.

11   Tremble, you women who are at ease,
        shudder, you complacent ones.
    Strip, and make yourselves bare,
        and put sackcloth on your loins.

12   Beat your breasts
        for the pleasant fields,
          for the fruitful vine,

13   for the soil of my people
        growing up in thorns and briers.
    Yes, for all the joyous houses,
        the jubilant town.

14   Truly, the citadel will be forsaken,
        the noisy city deserted.
    The hill and the watchtower will become
        bare places for ever,
    the joy of wild asses,
        a pasture for flocks.

15   Until is revealed over us
        the spirit from on high,
    and the wilderness becomes a fruitful field,
        and the fruitful field is regarded as a thicket.

16   Then justice will abide in the wilderness,
        and righteousness dwell in the fruitful field.

17   The effect of righteousness will be peace,
        and the result of justice trust for ever.

18   My people will dwell in a peaceful habitation,
           in trustworthy abodes,
                and in quiet resting places.
19   It will hail when the forest comes down,
           and the city will be utterly laid low.
20   Happy will you be who sow everywhere beside water,
           who let the feet of the ox and the ass range free.

NOTES

10 Given the general meaning of the verb אסף, 'to gather in', the noun of the same root must be understood as 'harvest' in the broad sense of the word and cannot be limited to 'fruit harvest' alone (Wildberger, 1268; *DCH*, I, 350).

11-12 The verb forms רגזה, פשטה, ערה and חגורה in v. 11 can be explained as Aramaising feminine imperatives (Barth 1902) but it is unnecessary to give the same form to the first masculine imperative, חרדו, and the masculine participle ספדים in v. 12 (GKC, §110 k; 145 p,t: 'dislike of using the feminine forms'; *pace* Wildberger, 1263). Moreover, the women do not continue to dominate the scene since 'my people' moves to the foreground from v. 13 onwards. Confusion between the feminine and masculine verb forms in vv. 11-12 is perhaps an indication that the accentuated female addressation of vv. 9-11 is no longer wanted after v. 12 and that the passage should basically be understood as a message for the entire population (Oswalt, 582, n. 2).

12 Irwin (1977: 129; likewise Watts, 415f.) considers ספדים to be an attribute of שדים: 'gird sackcloth on your loins, at your breasts that mourn' (with enjambment of v. 11b״ into v. 12a; cf. 2 Macc. 3:19; Apoc. 1:13). Although 'mourning breasts' is a somewhat unusual expression (but cf. 66:11: 'consoling breasts') this explanation seems to be supported by the fact that the parallel cola also consist of על with a noun and a modifier: 'for the pleasant fields' and 'for the fruitful vine'. It is more probable, nevertheless, that the inversion of על שדים gave rise to the form ספדים instead of ספדו.

The verb ספד, 'to wail', is uniquely connected here to על שדים 'upon the breasts' to the extent that the translation 'to beat the breasts' is inevitable (LXX: ἐπὶ τῶν μαστῶν κόπτεσθε). Since Gesenius, this unusual expression has led scholars to emend על שדים, 'upon the breasts', to read על שדים, 'on the fields' (still to be found in Wildberger, 1263, 1269). Since the plural of שדה is שדות, however, it would be better to maintain the poetic combination of ספד with על שדים, with which three other adjuncts with עַל are set in parallel (vv. 12b, 13a´; *TWAT*, V, 902 [J. Scharbert]), together with assonance of שָׁדַיִם and שָׁדַי. Oswalt (582, 586) considers עַל שָׁדַיִם to be elliptical and connects סֹפְדִים with the following adjuncts: 'Upon the breasts, moaning, for the pleasant fields'.

14 The difficult term בְּעַד is sometimes emended to read בָּעַד, 'forever' (Irwin 1977: 131). Besides the problematic fact that the resulting term can be found nowhere else, however, the colon in question is then left with a somewhat unusual word order. Emendation (Marti, 235: היה לבער, 'it will be devoured'; cf. 5:5) or scrapping (Wildberger, 1264) of this word is not advisable, given the pronounced assonance between this colon and the second colon of the following line. One would be better advised to maintain the text as היה בעד and consider it a variant of היה ל, meaning 'to serve as' (*DCH*, II, 235a). The preposition then functions as a negative qualification (G.R. Driver 1968: 52). This agrees with LXX which does not translate the word separately (καὶ ἔσονται αἱ κῶμαι σπήλαια ἕως τοῦ αἰῶνος). Cf. the explanation of Watts (416): 'עד defines the end result for the series of things governed by עַל in vv. 12-13 which are transformed' (translation: 'ultimately' or 'finally').

מְעָרוֹת is traditionally derived from the root ערר and translated 'dens'. The context suggests, however, that derivation from the root ערה should be considered more likely, leading to the translation 'bare places' (Duhm, 237; G.R. Driver 1968: 52; *HALAT*, 582).

15 The usual translation of יערה, 'is poured out', is open to discussion because in the act of pouring out, the verb ערה tends to have the vat as object while the verbs יצק and שפך tend to have the contents thereof as object (Barth 1977: 212f., n. 9). Furthermore, the *niphal* of ערה is found only here. It would seem more acceptable, therefore, to uphold the basic meaning of ערה as 'to unveil'. One can opt for this unique expression as an allusion to v. 11: 'make yourselves bare' (root ערר), as a means of strengthening the connection with the command to mourn.[1] In this way, the preposition עלינו is given an aspect of 'domination', 'lording over'.

Since vv. 15-17 exhibit a very regular metric pattern, it is striking that v. 17b appears to have one beat too many (v. 17: 4 + 5). The repetition of צדקה in v. 17b also draws our attention since, on the basis of the pattern of repetition and alternation of terms in vv. 15b-18 (cf. 'Introduction to the Exegesis'), one would expect the term משפט. Duhm (239) was already led to conclude in this regard that השקט was a copyists error for

---

[1] *TWAT*, VI, 371 (H. Niehr) explains this unique expression on the basis of the fact that an established term for the pouring out of the spirit did not exist at the time.

מִשְׁפָּט, prompted by 30:15: בהשקט ובבטח. It would then have become necessary to add a second צדקה taken from v. 17b′. Although the versions reflect the reading of the MT (including LXX; *pace* Wildberger, 1274), the argument based on the stylistic pattern of the significant words in the text is strong enough to follow Duhm's emendation (*pace* Irwin 1977: 133: 'The repetition of צדקה is an element of Hebrew style').

19 וברד of MT deserves preference over the much followed yet conjectural וירד: 'The forest will utterly go down' (*BHS*; RSV; Wildberger, 1273f.; Watts, 416). Firstly, the versions point unanimously to the noun 'hail'. Secondly, there is no need 'to restore' the paranomasia וירד ברדת (parallel with ובשפלה תשפל) since וברד ברדת also constitutes a paranomasia, albeit not from the same root ירד, just as היער and העיר constitute assonance (Barthélemy, 223f.; Kaiser, 263; Oswalt, 583). From the text critical perspective there is also no reason to vocalise ברד as a noun.[2] The option of the versions (LXX, Aq, Sym, Vg, Syr) to render the term as a noun can be explained by the fact that the verb form of MT is a *hapax legomenon* (Barthélemy, 223f.). For a completely different explanation, cf. Irwin (1977: 133f.): 'They will cut down the forest with an axe' (root ברד, 'to cut', normally פרד, from the Ugaritic root *brd*).

20 The translation of the RSV is corrected according to the REB. The customary translation 'beside all waters' accentuates the determination of the Hebrew word כל (without article!) too strongly (König, 285).

Essentials and Perspectives

The composite character of this passage is rooted in the fact that two different literary genres – a call to mourn in vv. 9-14 and a promise of salvation in vv. 15-20 – are bound together by the temporal indicator 'until' (v. 15). Some commentators consider this construction to be at odds with good logic and even good taste, but it seems more correct to note that both portions of the text do not only constitute a contrast with one another, they are also attuned to one another via a number of important catchwords: 'to trust / to be at ease' (בטח in vv. 9,10,11 ['complacent'], 17 ['trust'], 18 ['secure']; שאנן in vv. 9,11,18 ['quiet']), 'my people' (vv. 14,18) and 'forever' (vv. 14,17). The second portion is even related to 32:1-8 via the crucial word pair 'justice / righteousness' (in

---

[2] Rashi (Rosenberg, 265) and Ibn Ezra (151) were among the first to speak of the term as a verbal form.

v. 16 the terms of 32:1 are inverted). It remains a fact, nevertheless, that as the culmination of the five woe cries, the call to mourn establishes their ongoing operation while the promise of salvation connects their execution to a specific end, albeit a far off one. For this reason the suspicion must remain strong that these two textual portions came into existence at different moments.

For a long time, the first portion was held to be an authentic prophecy of Isaiah ben Amoz, partly because of its similarities with 22:1-14 and 3:16-24.[3] More recent authors have called this into doubt because, given the prophet's understanding of Zion as the city of YHWH, it would not have been possible that he expected the definitive end of Jerusalem.[4] Since the text does not mention concrete political issues, it remains difficult to anchor any particular dating thereof.[5] The temporal categories do oblige us, however, to situate the segment in its final form in a period when the ruin of city and land was expected but had not yet been realised. Sennacherib's military offensive against Jerusalem in 701 BC or the period prior to Nebuchadnezzar's destruction of the city in 587 BC would seem the most likely candidates. Authors who ascribe the segment to Isaiah ben Amoz opt for the first date[6] while those who consider it a redactional piece tend to go for the second.[7] Since we can establish, however, that the passage received its present form and function in combination with the woe cries and prior to the Josianic extension of 32:1-8, it must date from before the 7th century. This brings us close to the time of the prohet himself. Indeed, the very choice of words and imagery tends to give the impression of Isaiah ben Amoz.

The same cannot be said for vv. 15-20. Although up to and including the present day this segment has also been considered Isaianic,[8] two facts have led certain commentators to an exilic dating: the absence of the names Judah or Zion and the unusual function of 'the spirit from on high' as one who brings about new salvation.[9] Recently, however, a

---

[3] According to Duhm (236), the piece has its roots in the earliest period of Isaiah ben Amoz, when city and land still remained intact. According to Fohrer (128), it is Isaiah's final word, because he only expects the complete downfall of Jerusalem to take place at the end of his life (32:14; cf. 22:14). Vermeylen (425f.) places vv. 9-13 prior to the invasion of Sennacherib (701), but considers it possible that v. 13 stems from immediately after the destruction of Jerusalem in 587.

[4] Stade 1884: 269f.; Marti, 236f.; Kaiser, 259ff.; Wildberger, 1265ff.

[5] Duhm, 238; Sweeney, 415-8.

[6] Duhm, 236; Fohrer 1967: 129ff.; Barth 1977: 211; Sweeney, 417.

[7] Stade 1884: 267-71; Cheyne, 186ff.; Marti, 236f.; Wildberger, 1266f.; Kaiser, 259f.

[8] Duhm, 237f. It is characteristic of scholars of the older prophetic paradigm that they ascribe both vv. 9-14 and vv. 15-20 to Isaiah ben Amoz but only consider their combination via the temporal indicator 'until' as a banal redactional technique.

[9] Wildberger, 1277.

number of exegetes have recognised within the verses the specific conceptual universe of the Josianic redaction from which 32:1-8 also stem.[10] The expectation of a government of 'justice / righteousnes' is coupled therein with peace and prosperity for all time (cf. 32:1). The segment also exhibits similarities with 8:23b-9:6 and 11:1-10. Against this background, the topic of 'the spirit from on high' is also not strange (cf. v. 15 alongside 11:2).

From the semantic and thematic perspective, vv. 15-20 connect with both vv. 9-14 and vv. 1-8, but with the latter segment in such a way that they exhibit a partly different intention. They outline the reversal of the disaster announced in vv. 9-14 using terminology from the latter but they do not ascribe the new salvation to the government of the just monarch nor to the reconciliation of social injustice as we find in vv. 1-8. It is probable, therefore, that the redaction which added vv. 15-20 to vv. 9-14 already had vv. 1-8 before it from which it borrowed terminology but not the full intention.[11]

The literary genre of the call to mourn (32:9-14) fits well as a sort of epilogue to the five woe cries. Commentators have already argued that this textual segment should be viewed as the original conclusion to chs. 28-31.[12] A summons to mourn is clearly an appropriate way to express the fact that the judgement and its concomitant misfortune announced in the woe cry are about to become reality (cf. Isa. 23:1-14; Jer. 6:26; 9:1,16-21; 49:3; Ezek. 32:16; Joel 1:5-14; Jon. 3:6-8; Mic. 1:8-9; Ps. 69:11f.).[13] It would be mistaken to object here that the woe cries also announce salvation. Any remote prospect of salvation following after the judgement does little to dis-empower the woe cries' characteristic doom which maintains its full gravity via the emphatic nature of the summons to mourn in the phrase: 'Beat mourning upon your breasts' (32:12). In fact, it would appear from the descriptions of the situation of mourning that the actual cry 'woe' (הוֹי) is the object of 'to mourn' (ספד; 1 Kgs 13:30; Jer. 22:18; 34:5).[14] This semantic connection has thus found a literary application in the compilation of the five woe cries and the summons to mourn in as far as the latter command does not have the woe cries as its content but follows after them.

[10] Barth 1977: 211ff.; Sweeney, 415-20.

[11] Stansell 1983: 9f.

[12] Stansell 1983. Some exegetes are of the opinion that the text in question might even contain the 'last words of Isaiah' (Fohrer 1967: 129f.; Schoors, 192). A contrary vision of the genesis of ch.32 considers vv. 1-5,15-20 to be the conclusion of the Josian redaction of the collection of prophecies stemming from Isaiah ben Amoz and vv. 9-14 as an actualisation from the time after the fall of Jerusalem (Clements, 261f.).

[13] Sweeney, 516.

[14] Hardmeier 1979: 204-15.

It is striking, moreover, that the women are not only addressed in their professional capacity as mourners but they are also qualified negatively as 'women at ease / complacent daughters' (vv. 9-11; cf. Amos 6:1). Although these expressions primarily indicate that the women in question are not prepared for the coming disaster there is still an element of accusation therein. A similar accusation of superficial trust in one's own behaviour is directed in the woe cries at the leaders of the people (28:15; 29:1,15; 30:1-7,12,16; 31:1-3), sometimes with a similar term: 'to trust' (בטח: 30:12; 31:1). Thus, the accusation which is built-in to the summons to mourning is reminiscent of the complaint upon which the woe cries are based.

The announcement of disaster, i.e. the destruction of the harvest, follows upon the appeal to listen to the message and the recriminatory address of v. 9, with a temporal indicator: 'in a little more than a year' (v. 10; cf 29:1b). The period of doom and disaster has not yet commenced but it is expected imminently. This aspect does not sit well with the genre, of course, since in the original situation, deeds of mourning would have been the people's reaction to a disaster they had already been forced to confront.

A number of imperatives referring to the actual form of the mourning ritual follow in vv. 11-12a. At this point the reason for lamentation is introduced, namely the devastation of field and city (vv. 12b-13a, vv. 13b-14), but this is presented as an accomplished fact and even gives the impression of being a sort of retrospective glance at the initial advent of the disaster. The flora and fauna of devastation have already taken hold of what was once arable land. Thus a tension is established between the exhortation to listen and the command to mourn. Nevertheless, the difference in temporal perspective does not rob the passage of logical cohesion since it emerges from the combination of different literary genres. The exhortation to listen has a parenetic purpose and offers a last chance to the listener while the command to mourn anticipates the ultimate completion of the predicted catastrophe. Thus, we are not obliged to consider vv. 9-10 as an addition to vv. 11-14 for this particular reason.

The vocabulary of the actual summons to mourn (vv. 11-14) is closely related to the genre of lament in general. Thus the words employed barely exhibit any relationship whatever with chs. 28-31, in contrast to those used in vv. 1-8. The only words which are related in use are: 'soil' (אדמה) in v. 13 and 30:23f., 'people' (עם) in v. 13 and 28:5,11,14; 29:13f.; 30:9,19,26, and 'city' (קריה) in v. 13 and 29:1.

The summons to listen (v. 9-10), on the contrary, is closely connected to the introduction to the agricultural *mashal* concerning the wonderful counsel of YHWH, the four terms of the sentences 'hear my voice / give ear to my speech' also being present therein (28:23; cf. 1:2,10). The summons does not only call the listeners' attention to what they can observe with their senses, it also adjures an acceptance of the message (cf. Gen. 4:23; Mic. 6:1)[15] which in the present instance concerns the imminent arrival of disaster (v. 10), and next, the command to perform a ritual of mourning (vv. 11-12). Thus the appeal is evidently in harmony with the theme of '(not) listening to YHWH', which has a strong presence elsewhere in chs. 28-31 (28:12,14; 29:18; 30:9, 21,30). Furthermore, as we noted above, the accusation of 'being at ease' (vv. 9-11: בטח) which is applied to the women, constitutes a counterpoint to the deceptive faith of the leaders of Jerusalem in their allies (30:12; 31:1). Finally, the most important verb employed in the announcement of impending disaster, 'to come to an end' (v. 10: כלה), is a good sequel to what the woe cries have declared with respect to the oppressors and Egypt (29:20; 31:3).

Thus we conclude that a traditional summons to mourn, which in itself exhibits no relationship with chs. 28-31, has been placed under an appeal to listen in order to establish a connection with the primary complaint of chs. 28-31, namely the addressees' unwillingness to listen to YHWH. The appeal in question thus receives the following purport: since the addressees refuse to pay attention to the teaching offered therein, they will be forced to listen to an appeal to mourn over imminent judgement.

Why does this call to mourn direct itself so emphatically to women (Feldmann, 386)? It may be that the ritual of mourning is particularly at home among women (Jer. 6:26; 49:3) but exhortations to mourn are often directed towards the people as a whole and not just to the women (Isa. 14:31; 23:1-2,6; Jer. 4:5-8). Here, too, the women do not continue to dominate the scene since 'my people' moves to the foreground from v. 13 onwards. Apparently, the rest of the segment should be understood as a message for the entire population (Oswalt, 582, n. 2). The call to listen and the qualifications 'at ease / complacent', however, tend to reinforce the feminine addressation and place the women in a rather reprehensible position, similar to that of the leaders of the country who are the subjects of accusation in the woe cries. It is perhaps for this reason that they are not addressed as 'women of Jerusalem'. Given that the segment lacks any explicit mention of the name of the city, the women can be seen to represent the whole rebellious population of Judah.[16] Only the

---

[15] Arambarri 1990: 188.

[16] It was against this background that the Targum felt free to interpret 'women / daughters' as 'provinces / cities', an explanation which has been upheld by the Jewish tradition (Rashi, Redaq, Ibn Ezra).

terms 'my people' (v. 13) and 'Ophel' (v. 14) make it clear that we are, in fact, dealing here with the women of Jerusalem.

The emphatic appeal to the women also has a larger redactional function within PI. The segment has been compared with another passage in which Isaiah ben Amoz lashes out against the women of Zion, namely 3:16-4:1.[17] Commentators in question do not dispute the significant differences between both texts, they recognise, nevertheless, some of the prophet's style and realm of ideas in 32:9-14.[18] Questions of authenticity and dating aside, we are still confronted with the possibility that the redaction which created the literary construction of five woe cries with a call to mourn simultaneously intended to establish a compositional link between that call, directed to the women, and the prophecy against the daughters of Zion at the beginning of PI.

One does not then have to deny that both passages came into existence independently of one another, were built around different literary genres, exhibit a distinct style and have little in common at the semantic level. Indeed, semantic associations are limited to: 'to make bare' (3:17; 32:11: ערר), 'girdle' and 'to gird' (3:24; 32:11: root חגר), 'festal robes' and 'loins' (3:22: מחלצות; 32:11: חלצים). At the same time, however, this restricted semantic basis suggests that the passages may have a contrastive function. The women's obsessional concern for their clothing and make-up (3:16-4:1) was to result in an enforced neglect of their appearance at the dawn of the day of judgement (32:9-14).

A further and very significant connection exists between the passages in question: both are followed by a promise of salvation associated with the gift of the spirit (רוח; 4:4: 'a spirit of judgement and a spirit of burning'; 32:15: 'a spirit from on high'). While the choice of words and imagery are distinct in each text and thus a witness to their independent origins, the spirit appears to fulfil a comparable role in each: in 4:4 as a principle of purification and protection, in 32:15 of fertility and peace. There is also an evident verbal association between the two texts: the spirit brings protection and security (4:5-6; 32:17-18) and is accompanied by 'justice' (4:4; 32:16: משפט). On this basis, some level of connection between the two passages must be recognised.[19]

---

[17] Delitzsch, 346; Duhm, 326; Dillmann-Kittel, 286; König, 283; Procksch, 412; Schoors, 192; Oswalt, 585.

[18] Particularly Motyer, 259.

[19] Stansell (1983: 9f.) provides an adequate refutation of Barth's opinion (1977: 211ff.) that the spirit in v. 15 is promised to the king and not to the people. Barth's position is, of course, based on the fact that he ascribes both vv. 1-5 and vv. 15-18 to the Assyrian redaction.

The aforementioned accompanying term 'justice' is of particular importance since the beginning of the collection of woe cries contains a promise that YHWH himself will be 'a spirit of justice to him who sits in judgement' (28:6). The term 'spirit' itself, for that matter, has a distinct role to play in the woe cries, its use reflecting the way Israel must go: from blindness (29:10,24) to attentiveness to God's spirit in world events (30:1,28; 31:3). The opposition which the concept 'spirit' contains in chs. 28-31 is meaningfully resolved in 32:15 by the modifier 'from on high' (מרום: 22:16; 24:4,18,21: 26:5). It would appear, therefore, that the promise of 'the spirit from on high' is not a theological gimmick intended to revert the perspective of doom. While it offers a meaningful conclusion to chs. 28-31, it also establishes a relationship with the beginning of PI.

The *macarism* (v. 20) has its own specific role to play in the process by which chs. 28-32 became a literary construction. It seems evident that this particular literary form was appropriate to the task of supplying the collection of woe cries and an appeal to mourn with a salvific perspective: formally because 'happy' (אשרי) forms a contrast to 'woe' (הוי), and thematically because the promise of fertility and security reverts the announcement of the devastation of the land and the city. Moreover, it concerns a similar sort of ring composition as vv. 15-19, but this time involving the introduction to BI as a whole. The second half of the macarism: 'Happy will you be who... let the feet of the ox and the ass range free' alludes to the accusation with which BI opens: 'The ox knows its owner, and the ass its master's crib; but Israel does not know' (1:3). The inclusive ring formed by 'the ox and the ass' must be from a later date than that formed by 'the women' and 'the spirit' since ch. 1 presumes a later stage in the process by which BI came into existence.

SCHOLARLY EXPOSITION

Introduction to the Exegesis: Form and Setting

The literary genre of vv. 9-14 has been largely discussed above: a call to listen (v. 9) with an associated announcement of doom (v. 10) is followed by a call to mourn (vv. 11-12a) with an associated description of catastrophe (vv. 12b-14). The first call looks forward (v. 10: 'in a little more than a year') while the second describes the catastrophe in terms of its ongoing effects (vv. 13a, 14). Side by side with the same addressation (vv. 9a, 10a, 11a), however, the use of *perfecta prophetica* (vv. 10a, 14) guarantees the fundamental unity of the segment as prophetic announcement.

The call to mourn merges subtly with the description of doom, through the fact that v. 12, by means of the preposition על, places the object of the final act of the mourning ritual: '(beat) your breasts' (על שדים), on a syntactically equal footing with the motif: 'for the pleasant fields' (על שדי חמד), 'for the fruitful vine' (על גפן פריה). This is further reinforced by the fact that the preceding line (v. 11) ends with a similar adjunct: 'on your loins' (על חלצים), which is parallel with 'your breasts', while the following line (v. 13) opens with a similar adjunct: 'for the soil of my people' (על אדמת עמי), which is parallel with 'for the pleasant fields, for the fruitful vine'. Vv. 13b-14 contain a similar but nonetheless new motif for the mourning ritual: the depopulation of the city. The motif begins once again with an adjunct employing על but this is introduced with כי[20] and independantly elaborated in compound nominal clauses.

The promise of salvation (vv. 15-20) exhibits a regular syntactical structure: yiqtol (v. 15a: עד יערה) followed by five w^eqatals, each at the beginning of the line (v. 15b: והיה; v. 16: ושכן; v. 17: והיה; v. 18: וישב; v. 19: וברד). This series also exhibits a clear semantic pattern: it opens and closes with a verb of 'pouring out' (יערה and וברד) while the two verbs והיה are each followed by a verb of 'dwelling' (ושכן and וישב). We are then left with the following series: 'to be revealed, to be, to dwell, to be, to abide, to hail' (A, B, C, B´, C´, A´). In vv. 15b-18, the distribution of the significant words which embody the promise of salvation also follow a stylistic pattern, constituting a climax of repetition and alternation:

15b	wilderness / fruitful field	A / B
16	wilderness, justice / righteousness, fruitful field	A, C / D, B
17	righteousness, peace / justice, trust	D, E / C, F
18	habitation of peace / dwellings of trustworthiness	G, E / H, F

A macarism concludes the segment.

Based on the above we propose the following structure:

9-14   call for a mourning ritual
    9-10   call to listen
        9   call proper to listen with accusatory vocatives
        10   announcement of disaster
    11-14   call proper to mourn
        11-12a   call to various acts of mourning
        12b-14   the object of mourning

---

[20] Barthélemy (222f.) points to the fact that, as in 1 Chr. 29:11, כי functions here 'pour introduire avec emphase un nouveau substantif dans la même fonction que d'autres qui le précèdent'.

	12b-13a	the running wild of the land
	13b-14	the depopulation of the city
15-19	announcement of salvation	
	15a	the manifestation of the spirit
	15b-16	the recovery of the land
		15b fertility
		16 justice and righteousness
	17-18	the results
		17 peace and trust
		18 secure residence
	19	the decline of the hostile land and city
20	macarism	

Exegesis by Verse

9 The call to listen and the vocatives were discussed above (cf. 'Essentials and Perspectives'). At this point, the imperative 'rise up' demands our attention. The verb קוּם can render the beginning of an action, especially when it is associated with other verb forms (asyndetic imperatives: Gen. 28:2; 43:13; Mic. 6:1; syndetic: Judg. 18:9; Jer. 46:16; Hos. 6:1; further Ps. 102:14; Job 29:8).[21] At the same time, the transition to a different situation is thereby emphasised (Gen. 19:1; 24:54; 46:5; Exod. 12:30; 1 Sam. 20:25; 1 Kgs 3:20; Isa. 49:7), the speaker imposing the new situation via the imperative.[22] These aspects contribute to the present context also. The speaker draws to a close the hitherto complacent situation in which the women were at ease. Thus the word's function as a connective link with the preceding passage comes into its own. While 'the noble' stands firm through his noble deeds (v. 8: יקום), the women must stand up to receive their sentence.

10 Unusually for this genre, the announcement of disaster opens with a temporal indicator: 'in little more than a year'. The prophet thus achieves a rare degree of political concretisation, presenting the calamity to come as inescapable. The complacency of the women will give way to 'shuddering' (רגז). This verb indicates the physical expression of violent inner commotion brought about by God (Exod. 15:14; Jer. 33:9; Amos 8:8; Joel 2:10; Hab. 3:16; Ps. 77:19). In BI it refers to the reaction of human beings and the cosmos to YHWH's intervention (5:25; 13:13; 14:9, 16; 23:11; 37:28f.; 64:1).[23] Strangely enough, the reason for this

---

[21] *TWAT*, II, 638 (S. Amsler); *HALAT*, 1015b
[22] *TWAT*, VI, 1257 (J. Gamberoni).
[23] *TWAT*, VII, 327-30 (G. Vanoni).

consternation is not a foray of a hostile army but the loss of the harvest in the sense of the devastation of the arable land rather than a one-off crop failure (for 'to fail' [כלה], cf. 29:20; 31:3; in agricultural sense: 24:13; 27:10; for 'vintage' [בציר], cf. Lev. 26:5; Jer. 48:32; Mic. 7:1; for 'harvest' [אסף], cf. Gen. 6:21; Exod. 23:10; Lev. 23:39; Deut. 11:14; 28:38; Job 39:12).

11-12a The call to mourn demands first the expression of emotions of dismay and upset: 'tremble / shudder' (v. 11a). The first verb, חרד, is stronger than the second, רגז (which we already saw in the preceding verse), since it suggests the added connotation of panic (Isa. 19:16; 21:4; 41:5; Gen. 27:33; 42:28; Exod. 19:16; 1 Sam. 4:13; 14:15; 2 Sam. 17:2; 1 Kgs 1:49; Ezek. 26:16; 30:9).[24]

A summons to perform a number of acts of mourning follows: 'strip, make yourselves bare, put sackcloth on your loins, beat your breasts' (v. 11b). It is unlikely that this series of actions actually reflects the ritual process. The first two imperatives are hardly familiar to us from other texts (for 'to strip', פשט, cf. Ezek. 26:16). The use of unsightly clothing as a gesture of mourning, however, is well attested (for 'to gird', חגר, with שק [absent but implied in the present context], cf. 2 Sam. 3:31; 1 Kgs 20:32; Isa. 15:3; 22:12; Jer. 4:8; 6:26; 49:3; Ezek. 7:18; 27:31; Joel 1:8; Lam. 2:10). 'To beat (or rather 'to wail') the breasts' (ספד; cf. 'Notes') is the characteristic term for the performance of a mourning ritual which consisted of both gesturing and wailing. These were held primarily for the dead (Gen. 23:2; 1 Sam. 25:1; 2 Sam. 11:26; 1 Kgs 13:30; Zech. 12:10), but also on the occasion of some calamity which manifested the power of death (Jer. 4:8; 6:26; 49:3; Amos 5:16f.; Mic. 1:8; Joel 1:13; Zech. 7:5; Est. 4:1-3).[25]

12b-13a The first object of mourning is stated in triplicate over two verse lines: 'the pleasant fields / the fruitful vine / the soil of my people'. The first two terms refer in reverse order to the announcement of disaster: 'vintage / harvest' (v. 10; for 'vine', גפן, in the context of catastrophe, cf. Isa. 7:23; 16:8f.; 24:7; 34:4). The third term, 'soil' (אדמה), extends the catastrophe to the entire cultivated land which is frequently the scene of judgement and restoration in PI ('soil': 1:7; 6:11; 7:16; 14:1f.; 15:9; 19:17; 30:23f.; 'briers': 5:6; 7:23ff.; 9:17; 10:17; 27:4). The adjunct 'my people' constitutes a rather modest witness to the prophet's own involvement in the calamity which is about to overcome Israel (עמי with respect to the prophet: 3:12; 5:13; 10:2; 22:4; cf. 6:5,11; 8:16ff.; 24:16).

[24] TWAT, III, 177ff. (A. Baumann).
[25] TWAT, V, 904f. (J. Scharbert).

13b-14 The second object of mourning has to do with the city, presented here in four terms linked by external parallelism: 'houses' (v. 13b: בתים; cf. 6:11; 13:21; 22:10; 24:10), 'town', often with the connotation of 'fortified' and 'safe' in PI (v. 13b: קריה; cf. 1:21,26; 22:2; 24:10; 25:2f.; 26:5; 29:1; 33:20), 'citadel' (v. 14a: ארמון; cf. 23:13; 25:2; 34:13), and 'city' (v. 14a: עיר; cf. 1:7f.,26; 6:11; 14:17,31; 17:1f.,9; 22:2; 24:12; 25:2; 27:10; 33:8; 36:1; 37:26). The term 'joy' (משוש) forms an inclusion around the segment, indicating that what the people have lost (v. 13b: 'joyous houses'; cf. 24:8,11) the wild animals have gained (v. 14b: 'the joy of the wild asses'). The fall of the city is further illustrated via the contrastive word pairs 'jubilant / noisy' which often have connotations of self-satisfaction and affectation (v. 13b: עלז; cf. 22:2; 23:7; 24:8; v. 14a: המון; cf. 5:13; 13:4; 16:14; 17:12; 29:5,7f.), and 'forsaken / deserted' (v. 14: עזב; cf. 6:12; 7:16; 17:2,9; 27:10). A survey of this semantic field reveals that these terms frequently appear together in PI. They portray the city as a society which, on account of her self-importance and in spite of her fortifications, cannot fend off God's judgement.

The second half of v. 14 presents a vision of the city after she has undergone judgement. The city of Jerusalem emerges in the use of terms such as 'the hill' and 'the watchtower' but it is striking that we do not find direct mention of her name. 'The hill' (Ophel) was originally the name for the territory which connected the old city of the Jebusites with Solomon's palace and the temple and later came to refer to the temple quarter as a whole (Mic. 4:8; Neh. 3:27; 11: 21; 2 Chr. 27:3; 33:14; *HALAT*, 815). Nothing more is known with regard to 'the watchtower' (בחן; cf. the related term in 28:16: 'I myself have laid in Zion for a foundation a stone, a massive stone [אבן בחן]').

In v. 14b, the second colon of the first line and that of the second are attuned to one another via the assonance of a number of letters (ע, ר and ד), a feature which is further reinforced by the opening words of v. 15. Our attention is drawn, therefore, to the words 'bare places' (מערות) and 'pasture' (מרעה: Nah. 2:12; Job 39:8; 1 Chr. 4:39ff.) which call to mind the territory of animals in contrast to that of humans, namely the city. The temporal indicator establishes a further contrast between 'for ever' (עד עולם) and 'in little more than a year' (v. 10). In PI, 'for ever' is used in announcements of both judgement and salvation (עד עולם: 9:6; 30:8; 32:14,17; 34:17; לעולם: 14:20; 25:2; 26:4; 34:10). While the people's frivolous and shallow life will not continue much longer, the place where Jerusalem lies will remain deprived of human habitation for an unlimited time. Indeed, only 'wild asses' (פרא: Hos. 8:9; Job 24:5;

39:5) and 'flocks' (עדר: Isa. 17:2; Joel 1:18; Zeph. 2:14) will dwell there.

15a The announcement of salvation continues the temporal categories of this passage (v. 10,14) and limits the indefinite 'for ever' of v. 14 to an equally indefinite moment in the future when the spirit will manifest himself (cf. 'Notes'). It would be mistaken to read a degree of contradiction herein. The Semitic understanding of time allows for the possibility that an undetermined event in the remote and temporally unlimited future can be followed by another event, the arrival of which is likewise unspecified. This is particulary applicable where powers which surpass those of human beings are concerned. It is expressed here in the terms 'the spirit from on high', 'is revealed' and 'over us' with their implied meaning of 'to have at one's disposal'.

The precise range of the term רוח is difficult to determine here. On the one hand, the adjunct 'from on high' and not 'of YHWH' places the expression closer to the concept of 'wind' as YHWH's instrument (Gen. 1:2; 8:1; Exod. 10:13; Isa. 27:8; 30:28; Jer. 49:36; Amos 4:13; Jonah 1:4; Ps. 135:7) than to 'breath' or 'spirit' as anthropologically considered constituent part of YHWH (Gen. 6:3; Isa. 42:5; Zech. 12:1; Ps. 104:29f.; Job 33:4). One the other hand, 'from on high' (ממרום) means more than the place where the wind comes from, it is the place were YHWH dwells (2 Sam. 22:17; Isa. 24:21; 33:5; 38:14; 40:26; 57:15; 58:4; Ps. 102: 20; 144:7; Job 16:9). The text appears to side with those (post-)exilic expectations of salvation in which the spirit of YHWH is promised to the entire people (Isa. 44:3; 59:21; Ezek. 36:27; 37:14; 39:29; Joel 3:1f.; Hag. 2:5).[26] The present formulation might aim at expressing the dynamic and intangible character of YHWH's spirit without falling into the use of anthropomorphism as if something unique to YHWH's person, understood as a sort of rain, would bring about changes on earth beginning with the vegetation (v. 16b).

15b-16 The first effect of the revelation of the spirit is a transformation of the 'wilderness' (מדבר). The term need not necessarily imply a natural desert since it can also be used to refer to any devastated and desolate territory (Isa. 14:17; 27:10; 51:3; 64:9; Jer. 12:10; 22:6; Joel 3:19). In this sense it refers to the 'bare places' (v. 14) but it also prepares the way for the topic of the transformation of the natural desert in the time of restoration, a topic so characteristic of BI (35:1,6; 41:18f.; 43:20).

V. 15b sounds almost the same as 29:17 (for the nature of the comparison see the exegesis of 29:17) but differs significantly on two

---

[26] *THAT*, II, 728-53, esp. 743-53 (R. Albertz, C. Westermann).

points: the concept 'to turn back' (שוב) is absent here and instead of
'Lebanon' we have the broader concept 'wilderness'. Just as 29:17 contains a combined allusion to 10:25 and 34 whereby the referent entirely
changes (from Assyria to the godless oppressors within Israel), so
32:15b takes up the topic of transformation from 29:17, with the understanding that the arable land and city devastated by God's judgement
now constitute its subject. General prophetic language fills in the background (היה with ל in the context of judgement: Isa. 1:9; 6:13; 7:23;
34:9,13; Jer. 49:2,33; 51:43; Joel 3:19; Mic. 3:12; Zeph. 2:15; of salvation: Isa. 35:7; 40:4; 65:10; DCH, II, 530f.).

On the surface, v. 16 is the mirror image of v. 15b (both are chiastically constructed; מדבר occurs in the second place; end rhyme שֵּׁ-), although it clearly has a different purpose. In the first place, the second
colon is not climactic with respect to the first. Had this been so, the
verbs 'to abide' (שכן) and 'to dwell' (ישב) would have to have been in
reverse order[27] and the locatives would have to have taken up the positive terms of the preceding line, namely 'fruitful field' and 'thicket'
(כרמל and יער), and not the negative one, 'wilderness' (מדבר). Furthermore, the terms 'justice' (משפט) and 'righteousness' (צדקה) are not climactic but rather complementary concepts (cf. the exegesis of 28:17 and
32:1). Thus, behind the poetic similarity of v. 15b and v. 16 there are
evidently different conceptual movements at work. The first line is a
quotation from PI itself, the second belongs to the genre of aphoristic
blessings among which the term 'to abide' (שכן) is characteristically
present (Gen. 9:27; 16:12; 49:13; Deut. 33:20,28; 2 Sam. 7:10; Isa.
33:16; 65:9; Jer. 33:16; 46:26; Mic. 7:14; Ps. 16:9; 37:29; 78:55;
102:29).[28] The poetic agreements between v. 15b and v. 16, however,
uphold the message that the transformation of devastated territory into
fertile land and the establishment of justice and righteousness are both
the workings of the spirit.

17-18 The fertility and justice supplied by the spirit result in 'peace'
and 'trust' (v. 17). This is the climate in which 'my people' shall live
(v. 18 in contrast with v. 13). The question of 'the effect' (literally
'work', מעשה, also in 28:21 parallel with עבדה) of something is a characteristic topic of PI: shall YHWH's actions (5:12,19; 10:12; 19:25;
29:16,23) win out against the actions of human beings (2:8; 17:8;
19:14f.; 29:15; 37:19)? The question is answered programmatically in
26:12: 'YHWH, you will ordain peace for us, for indeed, all that we have

---

[27] TWAT, III, 1021f. (M. Görg): in Isa. 32:16 the verbs constitute synonyms.
[28] TWAT, VII, 1342ff. (M. Görg).

done, you have done for us'. This apart, 'peace' (שלום) is not a characteristic term for PI (9:5f.; 26:3,12; 27:5), although the parallel term
'trust' (בטח; cf. at 30:12) clearly is. This latter salvific gift undoes the
false trust of the women who are called to mourn (32:9ff.; cf. 12:2;
26:3: 'Those of steadfast mind you keep in peace – in peace because
they trust in you'). In fact, v. 18 refers to the said women's inappropriate
attitude: the terms 'trustworthy / quiet' (שאננות / מבטחים), applied here in
the positive sense to the people's future dwellings, served in v. 9 as
negative qualifications of the women (in reverse order: 'at ease / complacent'). Indeed, the salvific promise of secure dwelling is a response to
a common concern of PI (ישׁב: 5:3,8f.; 6:11; 8:14; 9:1; 10:13,24f.;
22:21; 23:18; 30:19; 33:24; שׁכן: 34:17; מנוחה: 28:12; cf. 14:1,3). The
promise 'for ever' makes the duration of salvation equal to that of the
devastation suffered (v. 14).

19 A secure dwelling for God's people implies the downfall of the
enemy (for 'hail' [ברד] as a punishment of the godless, cf. 28:2 ['Exegesis by Verse']). Since the enemy is not directly identified one is left
with the impression of a world power without equal.[29] For this reason,
the verse is sometimes considered to be an insertion with an apocalyptic
tone, related to the milieu of the Isaiah Apocalypse in which an unnamed
city is also subject to God's judgement (cf. 24:12; 25:1-5; 26:5f.;
27:10.[30] The verse is difficult to date. As a metaphor for a hostile force,
the term 'forest' (יער) is not unusual in PI (10:18,33f.). Since the beginning of the present segment, v. 15b, freely quotes from 29:17, which itself contains a combined reference to 10:25 and 34, one can accept that
v. 19, the concluding verse, also harks back to these verses. In this way,
the redaction of BI related the metaphor 'forest' from the exemplary woe
cry concerning Assyria (10:5-34) with that of 'city' from the Isaiah
Apocalypse (chs. 24-27). This is confirmed by the expression 'to be utterly laid down' (בשׁפלה תשׁפל) in v. 19 since the term שׁפל, which is
characteristic of the vocabulary of Isaiah (2:9,11f.,17; 5:15; 13:11;
29:4), can be found in both source texts (10:33 and 25:11f.; 26:5). Thus
'forest' and 'city' embody that particular enemy which refuses to be less

---

[29] König, 284f.; Procksch, 416. According to a different exegetical trend, the mention
of Assyria in this context would have no meaning. As such, the verse would constitute an
announcement of the fall of Jerusalem which preceded the salvific intervention of YHWH
which was still to come (Hitzig, 384; Alexander, 5; Dillmann-Kittel, 290f.; Feldmann,
384f.; Penna, 298; Oswalt, 588). Others still are of the opinion that 'the forest' in the first
half of the verse refers to Assyria, 'the city' in the second to Jerusalem (Delitzsch, 348;
Motyer, 261).

[30] Kaiser, 266; Kilian, 189.

than a tool in YHWH's punishment of his people but, in turning against them, desires only their complete downfall.

20 The form of this macarism does not constitute an exception among the macarisms in the Old Testament (Jesus Sirach included) even although it is not directed to God as an act of praise (Ps. 84:5f.) nor does it mention God as the source of promised happiness (Ps. 32:2). It is directed rather to the fortunate recipients of the macarism themselves and it limits itself to a description of their future prosperity (Ps. 127:5; Eccl. 10:17; Sir. 25:7-9; 26:1; Käser 1970).

Our explanation of the verse must deal with two difficulties:

(1) Is v. 20a a prerequisite with a chokmatic-ethical connotation, i.e. people who sow with forethought in places where water is present can allow their livestock to graze freely or will need them as beasts of burden to treat the harvest? Or does 'everywhere beside water' constitute an independent promise, i.e. water will be present wherever one sows and thus the abundance of the crop will be enormous?

(2) Does v. 20b mean that with the arrival of the expected fruitful harvest, the ox and the ass will be allowed to freely graze in the fields and thus share in the overall blessing (cf. Isa. 30:23f.),[31] or that they will be absolutely necessary for bringing in the harvest and for threshing? The latter interpretation is that of Tg which, in line with Deut. 22:10 ('You shall not plough with an ox and an ass harnessed together'), ascribes different tasks to each of the animals: 'Happy are you, the righteous... you who resemble those who sow beside irrigation, who send the oxen to thresh and the asses to gather'.[32]

With regard to the first question, the syntactic form of the two participles in 32:20 ('sowing / letting free') does not permit us to treat the first clause as a situational sketch or precondition of the second. Both clauses are to be treated as completely equal: sequentially parallel (cf. Ps. 65:5) without, of course, being synonymously parallel (cf. Prov. 3:13). Two forms of happiness are summarised: the first related to the agricultural situation and the second to animal husbandry.

The first form of prosperity, 'sowing everywhere beside water', evidently implies the presence of water wherever the farmer sows (Wildberger, 1202f.). This topic connects the macarism with texts found in the two collections of the prophecies of Isaiah ben Amoz (8:6f. and 30:24f.) as well as with the final song of the first collection (12:3) and the introduction to the whole of BI (1:30). Water functions in these contexts as a

---

[31] Redaq (Rosenberg, 266); Dillmann-Kittel, 291; Nielsen 1953: 265.
[32] Chilton, 65.

metaphor for salvation and judgement and as such constitutes an important theme in the actualisation of Isaiah's prophecies.

With regard to the second question, another explanation of the possibility of letting one's ox and ass roam freely than the two mentioned above might be that there will be no need to keep an eye on them as they will not be attacked by wild animals nor stolen nor wander off and that they will return to the fold by themselves (Duhm, 239). The context of 32:15-19 offers firm support to this interpretation since the 'spirit from on high' is not only to bring about fertility (v. 15) but also security (vv. 17f.). Under the new order the human environment is to change dramatically: wherever people sow, there they will find water, while the care and protection of their costly beasts of burden will no longer be a matter of concern.

Understood thus, the text in question fits well into PI itself, since it agrees in terms of imagery with 1:3, the only other text in BI where 'the ox and the ass' appear[33] The latter text portrays 'the ox and the ass' as knowing their master and the way to his crib. In 32:20, however, it is not a question of the master's concern for feeding his animals: he lets them roam freely without fear that he might lose them. There is a subtle contrast evident at the level of the application. In 1:3, the prophet accuses Israel of not even having the insight of 'the ox and the ass' because they do not know their way to YHWH. In 32:20, however, there is no clear statement that the shortcoming in question has been discontinued, only that restoration is guaranteed by the outpouring of the spirit. In other words, new salvation is not expected as a result of Israel's conversion but from 'the spirit from on high' (Kilian, 188).

---

[33] The same animals are mentioned in 30:24 but with different terms and in the plural. This text constitutes a thematic climax with respect to 1:3, in so far as the animals are allowed to graze here on fertile pastures (Kaiser, 266).

THE SIXTH WOE CRY: 'WOE TO YOU, DESTROYER' (33:1-24)

TRANSLATION

1   Woe to you, destroyer, who yourself have not been destroyed!
      You treacherous one, with whom no one has dealt treacher-
                                        ously!
      When you have ceased to destroy, you will be destroyed.
        When you have made an end of dealing treacherously,
        you will be dealt with treacherously.

2   YHWH, be gracious to us;
        we hope in you.
      Be their arm every morning,
        our salvation in the time of trouble.

3   At the thunderous noise peoples flee.
      Before your raising yourself high, nations are scattered.

4   Your spoil is gathered the way the grasshopper gathers;
      as locusts rush, so one rushes upon it.

5   YHWH is exalted, truly, he abides on high,
      he will fill Zion with justice and righteousness.

6   He will be the steadfastness of your times,
      abundance of salvation, wisdom, and knowledge;
   the fear of YHWH is her treasure.

7   Behold, I see them! They cry in the streets,
      the envoys of peace weep bitterly.

8   The highways lie waste,
      the wayfaring man ceases.
   The treaty is broken,
      witnesses are despised,
        human beings are not taken into account.

9   The land mourns and languishes;
      Lebanon is confounded and withers away;
   Sharon is like a desert,
      and Bashan and Carmel shake off their leaves.

10   'Now I will stand up', says YHWH,
      'now I will raise myself high; now I will lift myself up.

11   You conceive chaff, you bring forth stubble;

your breath is a fire that will consume you.

12 The peoples will be as if burned to lime,
   like thorns cut down, that are burned in the fire.

13 Hear, you who are far-off, what I do;
   and you who are near, acknowledge my might'.

14 Afraid in Zion are the sinners;
   trembling has seized the impious:
   'Who among us can sojourn with the devouring fire?
   Who among us can sojourn with the ever burning flames?'

15 One who walks righteously and speaks uprightly,
   who despises the gain of oppressions,
   who shakes his hands, lest they hold a bribe,
   who stops his ears from hearing of bloodshed
   and shuts his eyes from looking upon evil,

16 he will abide on the heights,
   rock fortresses will be his place of defence.
   His bread will be given him,
   his water will be sure.

17 Your eyes will see the king in his beauty;
   they will behold a land that stretches afar.

18 Your heart will muse on the terror:
   'Where is the one who counted?
   Where is the one who weighed the tribute?
   Where is the one who counted the towers?'

19 You will see no more the insolent people,
   the people of an obscure speech that you cannot comprehend,
   stammering in a language that you cannot understand.

20 Look upon Zion, the city of our appointed festivals!
   Your eyes will see Jerusalem, a quiet habitation,
   an immovable tent,
   whose stakes will never be plucked up,
   nor will any of its cords be broken.

21 There, rather, YHWH will be mighty for us;
   it is a place of rivers, broad streams,
   where no galley with oars goes,
   nor mighty ship passes.

22 Truly, YHWH is our judge,
   YHWH is our ruler,
   YHWH is our king;
   he will save us.

23 Your cords shall hang loose,

they cannot secure the pedestal of their flag staff,
    they cannot spread the signal.
Then booty and spoil in abundance will be divided;
    even the lame will fall to plundering.
24   And no one abiding (there) will say: 'I am ill'.
    The people who dwell there will be forgiven their iniquity.

NOTES

2 There is insufficient reason to emend 'their arm' to read 'our arm' in parallel with 'our salvation' (Barthélemy, 226f.).

3 The word מרוממתך is found in 1QIsᵃ as מדממתך, 'at your roar' (REB) or 'at your rustling' (Ges.¹⁸, 255). LXX (ἀπὸ τοῦ φόβου σου) apparently read the same, deriving the term from the root דמם, 'to be scared stiff'.[1] Kutscher (228) considers the reading of 1QIsᵃ to be preferable because the word דממה can be found three times in the MT (together with קול in 1 Kgs 19:12 and Job 4:16; further in Ps. 107:29), while רוממות is a *hapax legomenon*. Aq, Theod, Sym, Tg and Syr agree, nevertheless, with MT. LXX and 1QIsᵃ, moreover, constitute a *lectio facilior*. 1QIsᵃ embraces two different sorts of uproar, that of the people in v. 3a and that of YHWH in v. 3b, thus avoiding having YHWH as subject of the word המון in v. 3a. LXX interprets the suffix of מדממתך as a *genitivus obiectivus* ('for fear of you') thus achieving the same as 1QIsᵃ. Therefore, we maintain the reading of MT and interpret the word מרוממתך as a *nomen actionis* (Barthélemy, 228; *HALAT*, 1125).

4 The comparison presents us with a number of difficulties:
(a) The usual translation of the word חסיל as 'caterpillar' is not convincing. One would prefer a synonym of 'locust', perhaps one designating a certain phase in the locust's development (*HALAT*, 324; *DCH*, III, 283).
(b) The absence of a comparative particle in v. 4a has resulted in the division of שללכם into שלל כמו: 'spoil (is gathered) as' (many translations from Duhm, 240, onwards). MT, however, represents genuine Hebrew idiom: the finite verb form is connected with a noun of the same root in order to make the action more precise (König, 286; Barthélemy, 229; *pace* Sweeney, 422). Therefore, the 2nd person address should be maintained: 'Your spoil'.

---

[1] P. Wernberg-Møller, "Ugaritic and Phoenician or Qumran and the Versions"; in: *Orient and Occident: Essays Presented to Cyrus H. Gordon* (ed. H.A. Hoffner Jr), Neukirchen 1973, 53f.

(c) The noun phrase אסף החסיל can be understood as a *genitivus subiec-tivus* or a *genitivus obiectivus* (החסיל is a collective noun): 'as grass-hoppers gather', namely their food, or 'as grasshoppers are gathered', namely for the purpose of their destruction (older commentators, also Calvin) or for human food (*Ges.[18]*, 85; NJV with the note: 'cf. Lev. 11:22'). The parallel noun phrase כמשק גבים, however, can only be un-derstood as a *genitivus subiectivus*: 'as the rushing of locusts' (unless one reads the verb קשש, 'to amass', instead of שקק, 'to rush at' [Gins-burg 1950]). A *genitivus subiectivus* in v. 4a is thus more likely (Schoors, 196).

7 The word אראלם (RSV: 'the valiant ones') is a *crux interpretum*. The tradition of MT has been partly determined in this case by the his-tory of interpretation. Almost all of the versions (1QIs[a], Aq, Sym, Th, Syr, Tg) read two distinct words at this point: a form of the verb ראה, 'to see', and the preposition ל with a 3rd pers. masc. plur. suffix: ל(ה)ם. While LXX also reads two words, it appears to have derived the first from the verb ירא, 'to fear'. Vg reads one word, namely the verb form *videntes*. In the MT tradition, one always finds the consonants in ques-tion as a single word, while a small number of manuscripts adopt a plu-ral nominal form, ending in -ים, based probably on the parallel express-ion מלאכי שלום in v. 7b. This textual form has resulted in a variety of interpretations (Alexander, 9), and ultimately in that which has tended to dominate modern exegesis (the final ם as a 3rd person plural possessive suffix; so M. Luther: 'Jre Boten'; AV: 'their valiant ones'). The medi-eval vocalisation continues, however, to reflect a textual form of two words, side by side with a textual form of one word. Given these facts, a return to the majority interpretation of the versions is advised: ארא ל(ה)ם. In this case, the interpretation of the verbal root remains a ques-tion. The *niphal* and the *hiphil* conjugations fashion the clause into the announcement of a theophany and fit appropriately in the medieval in-terpretation, the *qal* conjugation constitutes a *lectio difficilior* and ap-pears to belong to the *textus receptus* (cf. Ps. 64:6: מי יראה למו; Weis 1991; *pace* Barthélemy, 231ff.). This leads to the translation: 'Behold, I see them!'. The context also leaves one with the impression that the prophet is speaking at this point and not God.

8 The suggestion that the MT reading ערים, 'cities' (likewise Sym, Vg, Syr and Tg), be replaced with עדים, 'witnesses', based on the paral-lel term 'treaty', now has the support of 1QIs[a] (perhaps also that of LXX). The graphic interchange of ד and ר does indeed appear to be a possibility here (Barthélemy, 233f.). Such an explanation seems more plausible than that which would understand the term as a *hapax*

legomenon cognate with the Akkadian and Old Aramaic words for a treaty (*pace* Cohen 1975: 42ff., 78-81). One arrives at a similar conclusion if one reads the term עֵרִים on the basis of the Aramaic word עִיר, 'watcher, guardian deity' (Murray 1984). Finally, the explanation of אֱנוֹשׁ as 'land-tax', based on texts from Alalakh and Ugarit (Hillers 1971), has not been taken up by recent lexica (*HALAT, DCH, Ges.[18]*).

23 Difficulties with the first half of this verse have led to some quite distinct interpretations. The oldest and most predominant understanding suggests that the text is descriptive of a ship, three substantives being translated as maritime terminology: חֲבָלִים as 'tackle', כֵּן תֹּרֶן as 'mast', נֵס as 'sail', the verb נטשׁ as 'to hang loose'. While LXX and Tg follow this line of interpretation, Vg and Syr translate the words in question in such a vague fashion that they allow the description to refer to something other than a ship. We can summarise the difficulties as follows:

(a) While the word נֵס cannot be found elsewhere with the meaning 'sail' (Ezek. 27:7?), the word pair נֵס / תֹּרֶן can be found in reference to a military signal (cf. Isa. 30:17; cf. 5:26; 13:2).

(b) Who or what is the addressee (2nd pers. fem. sing.) of חֲבָלַיִךְ ('your cords')? In light of the topic 'booty / spoil' in v. 23b, the most frequently adopted explanation tends to understand the addressee to be an enemy ship. If this were correct, however, the suffix of 'your cords' would have to refer back to 'galley with oars' (אֳנִי שַׁיִט is feminine) in v. 21, while this is followed by a masculine word for ship, צִי אַדִּיר, meaning 'stately ship'. Furthermore, v. 21 states that no hostile ship will be given the chance to sail into Zion. For these reasons, other commentators have understood the ship of v. 23 as a reference to Zion or Judah, saying that although this ship (these localities) is in disarray, 'booty' is within reach (Delitzsch [357] and some older commentators mentioned there; Feldmann, 395; König, 289; Oswalt, 605; Motyer, 268). This explanation relies on the temporal contrast expressed by 'then' (אָז) at the beginning of v. 23b but it continues to leave a number of problems unexplained (Holmyard III 1995).

(c) Following v. 22 and prior to vv. 23b-24, v. 23a appears somewhat isolated within the interpretation of an unrigged ship, a fact which has led some commentators to view it as a gloss, sometimes in combination with v. 21a''.b (Duhm, 247; Wildberger, 1313), while others place it after v. 21 (Dillmann-Kittel, 298; Penna, 309f.).

Since existing explanations have failed to solve all of the problems associated with the text in question, a number of authors have abandoned the idea that v. 23a refers to a ship. Kissane (378f.), for example, considers the three technical terms: חֲבָלִים, 'cords', כֵּן תֹּרֶן, 'mast', נֵס,

'signal', as referring to the parts of a military signal (cf. Isa. 30:17; 5:26; 13:2) and explains the expression as follows: 'Sion will be so se- cure that she will not need to set up the signal to summon her warriors, and even the blind and the lame will suffice for her defence'. Given that such an explanation fits well in the context of Zion's inviolability, obvi- ates the need to apply uncommon interpretations to certain terms and explains the 2nd and 3rd person feminine singular suffixes (v. 23a: חבליך; v. 24b: בה), we adopt it here.[2]

ESSENTIALS AND PERSPECTIVES

Ch.33 constitutes the last of the woe cries in chs. 28-39. It is directed in this instance against a foreign enemy (v. 1). Given the fact that it is placed after the call to mourn (32:9-20) and does not follow upon the five woe cries directed against Israel's leaders (28:1-32:8) the present woe cry is probably a later addition. From the perspective of literary genre and patterns of addressation, these verses contain a colourful col- lection of textual types. In light of the quantity of cultic material found herein, commentators have styled the chapter a 'prophetic liturgy',[3] a designation which says little, however, concerning the material's unique literary shape and function.

For more than a century (since Stade 1884), the majority of exegetes have been of the opinion that no part of ch.33 can be traced back to Isaiah ben Amoz. As a consequence there has been a tendency to date the origin of these verses somewhat late: in the Persian period (vv. 1-6; Wildberger, 1288) or the Hellenistic period (Kaiser, 271) or an un- datable 'proto-apocalyptic' (vv. 7-24; Wildberger, 1298, 1314). Dissi- dent voices have pointed out, however, that v. 1 can be traced back with good reason to the prophet himself (during Sennacherib's siege of Jeru- salem in 701 BC), while the cultic material (in vv. 2, 5-6,7-9,22), the so- called 'entrance liturgy' (vv. 13-16) and the Zion psalm (vv. 17-24) con- tain topics and forms which can be situated either before,[4] during[5] or af-

---

[2] The same interpretation can be found in substance with Watts (425-8), with the ex- ception that he interprets חבלי as 'apportionments' and considers only v. 23a′ as ad- dressed to Zion, while he understands the remainder of v. 23a as a description of the Assyrian army. Cf. also Sweeney (425f.), except that he interprets the word חבליך as 'your pains'.

[3] Gunkel 1924. Childs (1967: 112-7) also considers the chapter to be a liturgical (post-exilic) text, although he believes that it has integrated the Assyrian crisis of 701 BC.

[4] Roberts 1983.

[5] Barth 1977: 46f., 287f.

ter[6] the exile. Given the lack of any historical reference side by side with the evidence of thematic and literary conventions which extend over a lengthy time period, the discussion concerning date of origin and the identification of source and redaction tends for the most part to be unproductive.

An alternative vision of ch.33 emerged when it turned out that it did not have to be understood as a disparate collection of literary fragments but could be viewed as a single, albeit ancient, coherent ritual intended to contain hostile supernatural and political forces which violated the cosmic order (v. 8: treaty').[7] It seems clear, however, that the chapter contains too many prophetic elements and is too much of a visionary narrative to lead one to suspect a cultic *Sitz im Leben*.

Redaction-historical research has taken a different approach and has revealed that the chapter has a role to play in the association of PI with DI. Firstly, the chapter draws attention to itself by way of the large number of explicit textual references to other chapters in BI. This is especially so with respect to chapters in PI but also, to a lesser extent, with respect to chapters in DI. On the one hand, the phenomenon can be explained by the literary genre of a mirror text.[8] This artistic device, which is found in the literature of every age, serves as an interpretative key to the intrigue of a story. Ch.33 has the same function. Here the redaction looks upon the bulk of Isaiah 1-55 (without later additions) as a narrative whole, as the epic of God's dealings with Israel which lead from punishment to delivery. On the other hand, this redaction may have to be identified with DI himself.[9] The fundamental shape of the chapter as a progression from judgement to salvation is most appropriate to prefigure the transition from PI to DI. Moreover, textual details in a series of places in ch.33 establish a basis for what will be treated in chs. 40-55 (e.g.: 'iniquity' in 33:24 and 40:2; God's kingship in 33:17 and 41:21; 43:15; 44:6; 52:7; the lament phraseology of 33:2 returns in many places of DI; the tent metaphor in 33:7 and 54:2-3; the summons to recognise what God is doing in 33:13 and 40:21,28). From this redaction-historical perspective, the 'colourful' character of the material and the intermingling of literary genres does not constitute a negative quality. On the

---

[6] Vermeylen 1977: 429-38.

[7] Murray 1982; 1992: 22f.

[8] Beuken 1991. This study has rightly been corrected by Williamson (1994) in the sense that references to TI are too meager to be taken into account. Likewise, the additions proposed by Sweeney (430) with respect to the connections between ch.33 and ch.1 are to be welcomed.

[9] Williamson 1994: 221-39.

contrary, they tend rather to support the chapter's compositional function in BI as a whole.

The structure of ch.33 also serves its compositional function in BI. For the last time in PI, the speech of both YHWH and the prophet are clearly demarcated.[10] The divine oracle (vv. 10-13), however, is imbedded within the prophet's argumentation (vv. 1-9 and vv. 14-24) in such a way that it functions as both its climax and its confirmation. Via the interchange of patterns of address and topics, a kaleidoscopic synopsis emerges of the prophet's preaching – its primary genres being the announcement of judgement, exhortation and the promise of salvation – and his functions with respect to YHWH and his own people as well as with respect to the nations.

The sinners, confronted in the exhortatory section (vv. 14-16) with YHWH's determination to take action against those who do evil, are now witness to the fact that only a life lived in righteousness can entitle one to participate in the salvation which YHWH has set aside for Zion. A quite remarkable attitude to God's judgement emerges at this point. The downfall of the godless is not presented as a compensation for their victims but rather as a pointer to the latter towards the righteous life which ultimately brings happiness. Since the literary form of this paraenesis reflects the ritual which confers access to the temple ('entrance liturgy'), attention is not only drawn to the indissoluble alliance between ethical behaviour and liturgy but also to the ancient conviction that Zion is the place where YHWH obliges his people to 'justice and righteousness' (v. 5, cf. vv. 15,22a).

Exegetes commonly refer to the final section (vv. 17-24) as the vision of God's salvific dominion (esp. Sweeney, 424f., 428-32). Such a designation relies on the confession 'YHWH is our king' in v. 22 and on the interpretation of the introductory expression 'the king in his beauty' as a reference to YHWH.[11] Counter to this latter interpretation, however, one might object that mention of the name YHWH ought to be expected and that the term 'glory' (כבוד) would be more appropriate than 'beauty' (יפי). It seems more obvious that the expression 'the king in his beauty' refers to a king from the house of David. Several commentators read

---

[10] In 34:5 the subject YHWH is briefly 'condensed' to a single person. Prose chs. 36-39 constitute a case apart.

[11] According to Rosenberg, 273, as early as Rashi; Vitringa, 299; Procksch, 422; Kaiser, 75: 'kultische Gottesschau'; Wildberger, 1312-6; Roberts 1983: 22: 'the true king even as Isaiah saw him in the temple'; Kilian, 193. Brettler (1989: 173) summarises the arguments in favour of this interpretation but the semantic parallels, especially with Psalm 48, are far from definite. – Gunkel (1924: 179, 205) alters the text to read: 'eine Vollendung von Schönheit'.

Isaiah ben Amoz' contemporary Hezekiah here[12] while others suggest the Messiah.[13] It seems to the present author, however, that contextually speaking the good Davidic king promised in 32:1-8 would be more appropriate.[14] His appearance will engender the same delight as the expansion of the land will engender, probably in contrast to his humiliated appearance under a failing foreign policy and the diminishment of the land under Assyrian domination. Understood thus, the passage summarises a number of parameters from which the prophets frequently have read the dawning of the time of judgement but from which they now read evident salvation: a king with charisma and a land that stretches afar (v. 17), no more extortion and no more obscure speech (vv. 18-19).

The vision of a new Zion follows, a vision in which the city is seen as a place of safety and festival gathering (v. 20), a city which, in the presence of YHWH, takes on the geographical configuration of an open yet unintimidated river landscape (v. 21). The reader is reminded here of Egypt to which Jerusalem's leaders turned for help (30:1-7; 31:1-3), but which turned out to be far less invincible than they thought as it too was forced to succumb to the judgement of YHWH (19:1-17). Conversely, in confessing YHWH's salvific kingship (v. 22), Zion will enjoy the spoils without having to go to war (v. 23). The promise that no inhabitant of the city will be heard to complain about sickness (v. 24a), refers back to the lament concerning Israel at the beginning of the book (1:5) and forward, at the same time, to king Hezekiah (38:1,9; 39:1) whose illness would become so paradigmatic for the fate of Jerusalem (the root חלה is only found here in PI). Likewise, the promise: 'The people who dwell there will be forgiven their iniquity' provides a gradual introduction to the promise that Jerusalem will be comforted, a promise with which the second half of BI begins (40:1-2).

Although redaction critics tend to date the entire chapter late, the chapter itself is surprisingly attuned to the core of Isaiah's preaching: YHWH exercises his kingly dominion on Zion as an *exclusive* privilege (6:1,5) and thereby transforms the mountain into an inviolable place of safety for his people (28:16). In his unwillingness to endure other conquerors, God offers security on Zion. This has two distinct aspects: con-

---

[12] Ibn Ezra, 154; further Hitzig, 334; Alexander, 13; Delitzsch, 354; Dillmann-Kittel, 297; Feldmann, 394; König, 288; Watts, 428; Hayes, Irvine 1990: 369. The 'beauty' of the king is thereby understood as a contrast to his mourning apparel (Isa. 37:1) or his sickness (Isa. 38:1).

[13] Duhm, 245; Penna, 307; Oswalt, 602f.; Motyer, 267.

[14] Murray 1982: 211; Seitz, 234; *pace* Beuken 1991: 23ff.; Williamson 1994: 226f., 237.

quer by external force ultimately no longer stands a chance of success (10:12; 31:4f.,9; 37:22) while unjust treatment of one's own people is inevitably revenged (14:32; 28:14). The relationship between these two aspects is not artificial but has its roots, rather, in the peculiar understanding of YHWH's kingship as exclusive. Thus, ch.33 is in a position to announce both the end of 'the destroyer' and the end of 'the sinners in Zion' and their respective abuses of power.

The suggestion that YHWH as Israel's guard has his throne in Zion (8:18; 18: 7), is based on Jerusalem's cultic traditions (Ps. 46; 48; 76).[15] While it is possible that such traditions stretch back as far as the liturgy of the Ark in Shiloh, it is evident that they have provided the redaction of BI with an appropriate paradigm in order to give form to the expectation of Zion's future after the time of the judgement which Isaiah had announced (2:3; 4:5; 24:23; 33:5).

SCHOLARLY EXPOSITION

Introduction to the Exegesis: Form and Setting

In the first part of his argument (vv. 1-9), the prophet addresses himself first to the enemy (v. 1), then to YHWH (vv. 2-3) – partly in association with his audience (v. 2: 'we'), partly as their spokesperson (v. 2: 'their arm'[16]) –, then in a sort of aside to the nations (v. 4: 'your spoil'[17]) and then to his audience as such (vv. 5-6: 'your times'). He concludes in descriptive style with a portrayal of the social, moral and geophysical decay around him (vv. 7-8a, 8b, 9-10). From the perspective of literary genre, the prophet's words constitute a woe cry against the nations (v. 1), an appeal for salvation to YHWH on behalf of the people (vv. 2-3), a warning threat to the nations (v. 4), a praise of YHWH (vv. 5-6) and a descriptive complaint (vv. 7-9) which forms his argument for YHWH's intervention (v. 10).

The divine oracle (vv. 10-13) does not begin with a messenger formula but, unusually, with an emphatic 'now' (ועתה). This transforms the

---

[15] The study of Ollenburger (1987) does not discuss Isaiah 33 because he focuses his attention exclusively on those texts which hark back to Isaiah ben Amoz himself (107-29). Nevertheless, this study clarifies the general tendency of the chapter.

[16] The suffix attached to זרעם cannot be seen to refer proleptically to 'peoples' in v. 3, partly because one would then expect the parallel word pair 'their arm / our salvation' to appear in reverse order (cf. Ezek. 22:6, where the prefix ב indicates the one against whom the arm is raised; *pace* Sweeney, 423).

[17] The suffix attached to 'your spoil' does not exclusively refer to those who acquire spoil (Judg. 8:24f.; Isa. 10:2; 2 Chr. 20:25; 24:23), but can also refer to those who must surrender it (Deut. 13:17; 20:14; Josh. 8:2; Ezek. 29:19; Zech. 14:1; Esth. 3:13; 8:11).

oracle into a reaction to the preceding verses in which the prophet has acted as intermediary, lamenting the appalling state of the land (vv. 7-9). This is also apparent from the content of the oracle. God's intervention concerns two distinct groups: 'you' (v. 11) and 'the peoples' (v. 12), both having been addressed by the prophet and discussed by him. V. 11 corresponds to v. 1 ('you'), v. 12 to v. 3 ('peoples') and v. 10b to v. 3b ('your raising yourself high'). It would appear that the addressees of the direct (v. 11) and indirect (v. 12) speech respectively return in v. 13, both to be addressed directly in geographical terms and in reverse order: 'you who are far-off' and 'you who are near'. In this way, a sort of articulation is established within the chapter's headline figure, 'the destroyer' (v. 1). The close harmonisation of the divine oracle and the prophetic utterance makes it clear that YHWH intends to bring about what the prophet has announced and that he stands as guarantor thereof. In this way, the woe cry concerning the foreign enemy does not constitute an independent chastisement but is taken up rather within the body of God's intervention which creates 'justice and righteousness' in Zion (v. 5). This intervention has the punishment of the alien oppressors as well as the removal of the godless among YHWH's own people as its consequence.

From a genre-critical perspective, vv. 10-12 do not appear to constitute true literary forms: v. 10 contains YHWH's decision to exert authority while vv. 11-12 contain two similes for the result of his punitive action. Only the call to listen (v. 13) can be found in prophetic and chokmatic literature with any frequency. Nevertheless, its rather unusual location here, at the end of the divine oracle, brings about a change in its function, situating the preceding announcement of judgement within the recognition of God's actions and leading over to what the prophet is about to say (Sweeney, 427f.).

The second part of the prophetic address contains specimens of familiar literary genres: an entrance liturgy (vv. 14-16) and a Zion psalm (vv. 17-24). The entrance liturgy genre has its *Sitz im Leben* in the temple cult. A ritual of questions (cf. v. 14) and answers (cf. v. 15) guarantees the visitors' correct ethical and cultic status and concludes with a promise that they will attain salvation in the place where God has chosen to dwell (cf. v. 16; Psalms 15 and 24 are considered prototypes of the genre).[18] In Isaiah 33, however, the genre has undergone a literary adaptation. While the interrogation was normally performed by the cultic officials, here the questions are to be found on the lips of the sinners them-

---

[18] Steingrimsson (1984) offers the most recent study of this genre.

selves, giving expression to their fear that the judgement, portrayed in terms of the sacrificial fire found on the temple mountain, will devour them (v. 14). Their words constitute the witness of those whose correct insight comes too late. The response, likewise, constitutes a sort of guideline for those who would hope to avoid judgement (v. 15). Thus the sinners implicitly draw attention to the prophet's ethical admonition as a means to survival. The behaviour proposed here does not refer to common people, however, but rather to those in authority.[19] The sinners thus take on the form of the leading classes against whom many of the complaints of chs. 28-32 were raised. While the promise of salvation, true to the genre, is formulated as a promise of dwelling in the presence of God (v. 16a takes up v. 5a), it is expressed simultaneously in terms of secure occupation of the land and the provision of the necessities of life (v. 16b).

From a syntactical perspective, the final part of the prophet's address, a description of the beneficial consequences of God's intervention on Zion's behalf (vv. 17-24), is not sharply distinguished from the verses preceding it. The five verse lines of v. 16b and vv. 17-19 contain sentences of the same clause type (compound nominal). They describe the blessings which flow from a dwelling under God's protective care. Indeed, if it were the case that v. 17a served to introduce a new segment with a new topic then one would have expected an independent verbal clause at this point. The only distinction between v. 16 and vv. 17-19 is the transition from 3rd person to 2nd pers. sing. (v. 16b: 'his bread / his water'; vv. 17-19: 'your' and 'you').

The smooth transition enables the imperative 'Look upon Zion' (v. 20) to shed full light upon the theme of the city, to the extent that it will dominate the verses which follow (vv. 20-24). This portion of ch.33 exhibits a somewhat ill-defined structure. Three deictic elements expose the text's points of articulation: the imperative 'Look upon' (חזה) in v. 20, the emphatic-adversatory locative 'There, rather' (כי אם שם) in v. 21 and the emphatic opening of the confession 'Truly' (כי) in v. 22. Each of the three segments established by this articulation, v. 20, v. 21 and vv. 22-24, concludes with a pointed negation (בל): the contrary of the preceding promise is negated in v. 20b and v. 21b while v. 24 negates further examples of affliction, namely sickness and guilt.

The first two verses of the last segment exhibit a thematic relationship (vv. 22-23 within vv. 22-24). The confession 'he will save us' (v. 22) is

---

[19] While Sweeney (424, 428) has correctly distinguished this 'class ethics', he considers it to be a programme intended for the monarch himself.

illustrated by a portrayal of the pinnacle of secure existence: copious booty without having to go to war, even for the lame who do not usually benefit from such spoils (v. 23). Yet, v. 24 does not take up this theme. While it conforms with the stylistic pattern of the segment by means of the emphatic negation at the end, it makes use of topics which are determined by the overall redaction of PI.

The structure of ch.33 can be presented schematically as follows:

1-9   first prophetic announcement: the fall of the oppressor, the rescue of Zion
      1   woe cry against the oppressor
      2-3   supplication to YHWH
            2a   prayer for favour
            2b   prayer for intervention
            3   act of confidence in YHWH's subjection of the peoples
      4   announcement to the nations of their defeat
      5-6   praise of YHWH / announcement of salvation to Zion
      7-9   lament: sketch of the present disaster
            7   wailing in the city
            8a   cessation of commerce
            8b   disruption of public morality
            9   devastation of the land
10-13   judgement speech of YHWH against the oppressors
      10   decision to intervene
      11   punishment of the oppressors directly addressed
      12   punishment of the peoples in general
      13   call to all the world to be attentive
14-24   second prophetic announcement:
      criteria for staying close to YHWH's abode and prophecy concerning Zion
      14-16   entrance liturgy
            14   entrance questions by the sinners in Zion
            15   entrance responses
            16   promise of secure dwelling
      17-24   prophecy of Zion's bliss
            17-19   sketch of Zion's political situation
                  17a   the king respected
                  17b   the land extended
                  18-19   absence of oppressors:
                        18   extortioners
                        19   arrogant foreigners

20-24	sketch of Zion's inviolability
20	guarantee of everlasting security
21	YHWH's presence creates safe rivers
22	confession of YHWH's kingship
23	no military mobilisation needed
24	no illness; iniquity forgiven

A variety of factors determine the time in which ch.33 came into existence. It is certainly later than chs. 28-32 which more clearly exhibit
characteristics of the sixth century Josianic redaction of the oracles of
Isaiah ben Amoz during the time of Sennacherib's campaign (705-701
BC). The chapter appears, in principle, to belong to the period which
witnessed the redaction of BI as a whole. Evident thematic associations
with ch.1, the multiplicity of quotation-like, overarching references to PI
and DI (perhaps even to TI, in particular ch.66)[20] tend to point in this
direction. The anonymity of the foreign tyrant (v. 1) appears to be an example of 'the blurring of the actants', a phenomenon which makes texts
applicable to a variety of situations (cf. ch.28). In this case, it permits the
woe cry of v. 1 to apply to Assyria (plausible in light of chs. 28-32 and
chs. 36-37),[21] Babylon (plausible in light of ch.39 and chs. 40-48)[22] and
Persia (plausible in light of vv. 18-19). Since the first two names exhibit
unequivocally negative associations in BI while the third does not (cf.
44:28; 45:1; furthermore, an oracle against Persia is lacking in chs. 13-
23), it would seem more appropriate to locate this chapter within the
emerging unity of BI, during the period of Persian domination.[23]

Exegesis by Verse

1 In every respect, the woe cry possesses the character of a literary
form which does not have its roots in a ritual context (cf. 'Introduction
to Isaiah chs. 28-39').[24] It differs from the preceding five woe cries in a
variety of ways, but particularly in the direct address 'you' (personal
pronoun, suffixes and prefix of the 2nd pers. sing.). In the two parts of
ch.33 in which the prophet himself speaks, the direct address of the adversary can be found in only one other place, namely 'your spoil' in v. 4.
This literary device abruptly introduces the enemy, allowing him to disappear with equal alacrity. While he returns in the divine oracle itself, he

[20] Sweeney, 431.
[21] Vermeylen 1977: 429.
[22] Williamson 1994: 222.
[23] Sweeney, 430ff.
[24] Hardmeier 1978: 243-55.

does so with similar abruptness (vv. 11-13). As a result, the downfall of the adversary does become reality within the literary fiction of the text while it is forced to make way for the chapter's primary point of interest: Zion's renewed well-being.

The verse clearly makes reference to Isa. 21:2b: 'The betrayer betrays, the destroyer destroys. Go up, O Elam, lay siege, O Media. All the sighing I bring to an end' (RSV).[25] No further examples of the word pair 'to betray (to deal treacherously) / to destroy' (בגד / שדד) can be found in the Scriptures. The recurrence of these terms in reverse order in 33:1 also suggests a 'quotation'.[26]

It is not clear from the wording of 21:2 whether the terms 'betrayer / destroyer' refer to 'Elam / Media' which is summoned to overpower Babylon (v. 9),[27] or to Babylon itself which has acted against Judah and the nations with brutal violence and must now, therefore, face punishment by Persia (Elam and Media).[28] The latter problem goes hand in hand with the question as to the meaning of the root בגד in this context: 'to betray, to deal treacherously' as elsewhere in the Scriptures,[29] or 'to plunder' as in the two other references in PI (24:6; 33:1).[30] Where the first meaning is concerned ('the betrayer betrays'), the sentence sounds like an accusation providing the basis for an announcement of judgement in which case it would be more likely to point to Babylon (Wildberger, 776). As for the second meaning ('the plunderer plunders'), which is more a synonym of 'the destroyer destroys' (שדד), the sentence sounds like the description of a punitive expedition in which case it would be more likely, therefore, to point to 'Elam / Media'.

Such lack of clarity does not detract from the fact that 33:1 formulates the reference to 21:2 as a motivation for the woe cry and thus as an accusation. Since the 'destroyer / treacherous one' himself appears to be immune to the havoc he has wrought ('who yourself have not been destroyed,...with whom no one has dealt treacherously') his deeds must

---

[25] Beuken 1991: 12f., 28f.; Williamson 1994: 230, 232.

[26] Beentjes 1982. Another text, 24:16, also points to 21:2.

[27] Alexander, 372; Dillmann-Kittel, 187; Gray, 352; Feldmann, 247; Procksch, 261; Fischer, 149; Penna, 197; Schoors, 126, with an appeal to Galling 1963 (esp. 56): '... eine Maxime für die Angesprochenen (das Participium als Berufsbezeichnung): Aufgabe des Räubers ist es, zu rauben, Aufgabe des Verwüsters, zu verwüsten! Und das ist jetzt eure gegen Babylon durchzuführende Aufgabe!'.

[28] Duhm, 150; König, 211f.; Kaiser, 101; Wildberger, 770, 776; Williamson 1994: 222. Some commentators are of the opinion that war and violence constitute the vision as a whole (Delitzsch, 258; Oswalt, 392). According to Macintosh (1980: 11ff., 118f.), Isaiah 21 refers back to an authentic prophecy from the eighth century in which v. 2b ('betrayer / destroyer') originally referred to the Assyrian conqueror. It was only at a later date that the terms came to refer to Babylon.

[29] Often with an appeal to 24:5 (BDB, 93; HALAT, 104; TWAT, I, 510f. [S. Erlandsson]; DCH, II, 90f.).

[30] From GesB via authors such as Rudolph 1933: 31f. and now including Ges.[18], 123.

therefore be considered unjust. At the same time, however, his actions are presented as if he were implementing some sort of plan: 'when you have ceased to destroy,…when you have made an end of dealing treacherously'. This often military idiom (תמם and כלה together: Josh. 8:24; 10:20; Jer. 44:27) expresses the conviction that the punishment being endured will eventually come to an end, no matter how grievous it has been (the same terms are to be found in Lam. 3:22 and maybe Dan. 9:24). The Isaianic redaction relies hereby on the prophecy of Isaiah ben Amoz himself (10:18,25: כלה). In addition, the almost word for word parallel with Isa. 16:4-5[31] reveals that the expectation of an end to the judgement goes hand in hand with the question as to the form YHWH's salvation will take once his judgement is complete (Wildberger, 622f.). In this sense, the expression 'woe to you, destroyer' constitutes no more than the beginning of a vision of salvation (cf. 29:17-24).

Against such an intertextual background, the identity of the 'destroyer / treacherous one' in 33:1 must remain indefinite. The source text (22:1) can apply to both Babylon and Persia. The collection of woe cries in chs. 28-32 focused on Assyria as the arch-enemy and these chapters, together with the announcement of the downfall of this formidable worldpower in ch.10, may have influenced the reference of 33:1. All three world-powers melt into one hostile force who in the present chapter will be forced to go to ground in the face of the imminent arrival of YHWH's dominion.

2 The split between v. 1 and v. 2 is not absolute. Although the literary genre changes from a woe cry against the enemy to a prayer to YHWH, the speaker remains the same as in v. 1: the prophetic figure who both identifies himself with his people ('we') and distinguishes himself therefrom ('their arm'). In addition, the notion of a 'time of trouble' corresponds with the announcement of the end of oppression in v. 1. In this way, v. 1 and v. 2 together portray the situation of a people who yearn for salvation in the midst of their misfortune, the prophet himself being their spokesperson in prayer.

The first part, v. 2a, constitutes both a prayer for favour and a confession. The verb in which the prayer is made, 'be gracious to us' (חנן), expresses freely extended goodwill between human persons, with the associated dimensions of mercy and forgiveness in the case of God's benevolence towards Israel (Exod. 3:14; 34:6; Num. 6:25f.; 2 Kgs 13:23; Ps. 67:2; 84:12; 123:2f.; Isa. 26:10; 27:11; 30:18f.; Jer. 31:2; Amos

---

[31] Not only do we find the terms שדד, תמם and כלה applied similarly in both 16:4 and 33:1 but also the prayers: 'Be a refuge to them' (16:4: הוי) and 'Be their arm' (33:2: היה) are similar. Cf. further 21:16.

5:15; Joel 2:13; Jonah 4:2; Mal. 1:9; Dan. 9:2ff.; Ezr. 9:8).[32] The temporal aspect of the verb employed in the confession, 'to wait for' (קוה),
takes, when God is the object, a background position to that of personal
relationship with him: 'to hope in' (particularly in the psalms; cf. Ps.
25:3,5,21; 27:14; 37:34; 39:8; 40:2; 71:5; 130: 5; Isa. 26:8; 40:31;
49:23; 51:5; Jer. 14:22; cf. 'the hope of Israel': Jer. 14:8; 17:13).[33]

The second part, the prayer for intervention in v. 2b, employs general
biblical concepts. 'The arm of YHWH' (זרוע) is a metaphor for the power
with which God intervenes in creation (Isa. 51:19; Jer. 32:17; Ps.
89:11,14) and in history as both saviour and judge (in as far as these two
dimensions are distinct from one another; cf. Exod. 15:16; Deut. 7:19;
1 Kgs 8:42; Isa. 51:5,9; 59:16; Ezek. 20:33f. and 2 Kgs. 17:36; Isa.
40:11; Hos. 11:3; Ps. 44:4; 71:18; 77:16; 79:11; 89:22; 98:1).[34] The
expressions 'every morning / in the time of trouble' are not intended to
denote specific moments in time, as if God's assistance were restricted
to these alone. 'Morning', in the present context, does not stand in contrast to 'day'.[35] The distributive significance of 'every (morning)' is parallel to 'trouble', just as 'morning' is to 'time' (לבקרים: Ps. 73:14;
101:8; Job 7:18; Lam. 3:23). Taken together these terms express the
fact that misfortune and continued need of YHWH's assistance always determine Israel's existence. While it is possible that the religious-histori-
cal antithesis between night and day, and darkness and light plays a
background role here, the conviction that Israel's historical experience
had given rise to the belief that 'morning' (Exod. 14:27; Isa. 37:36) was
the appropriate moment for God's salvific intervention (Ps. 46:6),
should stand aside in favour of the metaphorical explanation of 'morning' as a moment of longed for newness, even from the perspective of
YHWH (Ps. 5:4; 30:6; 59:17; 88:14; 90:14; 143:8; Zeph. 3:5).[36]

The noun 'salvation' (ישועה) appears here for the first time in chs. 28-
39, whereas it plays a central role together with the verb 'to save' (root
ישע) in chs. 40-66 and is established as a programmatic term for BI as a
whole in ch.12, the concluding song of the first collection of the prophecies of Isaiah ben Amoz. In the collection of woe cries the verb ישע is
employed only once in 30:15 (see *in loco*). The contrast between the

---

[32] *TWAT*, III, 32-40 (D.N. Freedman, J. Lundbom).

[33] *TWAT*, VI, 128-33 (G. Waschke).

[34] *TWAT*, II, 653-7 (F.J. Helfmeyer).

[35] L. Delekat, "Zum hebräischen Wörterbuch", *VT* 14 (1964) 7-9.

[36] Cf. *TWAT*, I, 751-4 (Ch. Barth) for the discussion set in motion by J. Ziegler, "Die
Hilfe Gottes 'am Morgen'"; in: *Alttestamentliche Studien F. Nötscher gewidmet* (eds H.
Junker, J. Botterweck), (BBB, 1), Bonn 1950, 281-8. Cf. also J. Renkema, *Klaagliederen*
(COT), Kampen 1993, 279f.

accusation in 30:15 and the present prayer typifies the direction taken by Israel under the prophet's leadership: Israel recognises the fact that only her God can bring salvation.

The prayer gains further significance against the background of PI as a whole, more specifically from the fact that the thanksgiving song of the redeemed in ch.12, in anticipation of the day in which Isaiah's prophecy will be fulfilled, is reformulated in ch.25 in anticipation of the day of festival banquet which will be set for all peoples on Mount Zion (cf. 12:1,4 and 25:9: 'You (one) will say on that day').[37] In the latter text, the song of thanksgiving is augmented with the expression 'to hope in' (קוה), a notion which the prophet had already employed to express how he had come to terms with the people's rejection and bridged the gap between the announcement of his message and its fulfilment (cf. 8:17: 'I will wait for YHWH, who is hiding his face from the house of Jacob, and I will hope in him'; 25:9: 'Lo, this is our God; we have hoped in him, that he might save us. This is YHWH; we have hoped in him; let us be glad and rejoice in his salvation').[38] Now, the text of 33:2 shares the form of a confession as well as a number of semantic elements with 25:9. It seems reasonable, therefore, to suggest that the redaction of PI provided the future song, announced in chs. 12 and 25, with a forerunner in 33:2: the prayer for 'grace' in the present 'time of trouble'.

Other terminological correspondences confirm this redactional red line. With regard to the concept 'grace' (חנן), it seemed apparent that it had an important role to play in 30:18f., in which the tradition offered a perspective of salvation after the judgement announced by Isaiah ben Amoz (see there; cf. also 26:10; 27:11). Likewise, the 'arm of YHWH' concept is only to be found elsewhere in PI in a similar context (30:30: 'YHWH will cause his majestic voice to be heard and the descending blow of his arm to be seen'[39]). In addition, the words of the expression 'time of trouble' (עת צרה) also occur in the passage in which the prophet reflects on the success or failure of his mission (8:22f.).

3 The act of confidence expects God's intervention to result in the flight of the 'peoples / nations' (גוים / עמים). In PI, this word pair is only found in passages which commentators ascribe to the redaction (in this word sequence: 11:10; 14:6; 25:7; in the other word sequence: 2:2-3;

---

[37] Beuken 1991: 13ff.; discussed by Williamson 1994: 230f.

[38] The root קוה, with human persons as subjects, is only found prior to 25:9 in 8:17 and after 25:9 in 26:8 in a similar context (with God as subject in 5:2,4,7).

[39] If the word 'voice' in 33:3 refers to YHWH, the allusion of 33:2-3 to 30:30 becomes even stronger.

30:28). BI took shape in a milieu which was preoccupied with questions concerning the future status of the nations in the context of Israel's anticipated restoration. The texts reveal that they will participate in YHWH's salvation in so far as they themselves have been the victims of deception and violence (2:2f.; 11:10; 25:7), but in so far as they had resisted YHWH's might they would taste defeat (30:28; 33:3). In this respect, the Isaiah tradition builds upon texts from Isaiah ben Amoz which share similar topics associated with the words עמים and גוים individually, as will be apparent from the following survey (which does not distinguish between original and redactional texts):

- the nations as victims of violence: 10:7,13f.; 14:9,12,18; 36:18; 37:12
- the nations as perpetrators of violence: 8:9; 17:12; 25:3; 29:7f.
- the nations in submission to YHWH: 2:4; 3:13; 5:26; 8:9; 11:12; 12:4; 13:4; 14:2, 26; 24:13; 25:3; 33:12.

The verb 'to flee', נדד, is characterised by the fact that the destination of the subject's flight is rarely if ever mentioned. As such, it only signifies a panic driven, purposeless flight, and never a flight to a place of safety (Isa. 10:31; 16:2f.; 21:14f.; 22:3; Jer. 4:25; 9:9; 49:5; Hos. 7:13; 9:17; Nah. 3:16f.; Ps. 31:12; 55:7f.; 68:13; Job 15:23; 18:18; 20:8f.; Prov. 27:8).[40] The parallel term 'to be scattered' (נפץ) underlines this associated aspect of annihilation (Isa. 11:12; 27:9; Jer. 13:14; 22:28; 51:20-23; Ps. 2:9; 137:9; Dan. 12:7).

Against this background, the interpretation of the expression 'at the thunderous noise' (מקול המון) as either enemy sabre rattling or divine theophany can be resolved.[41] The absence of a 2nd person suffix together with the topics of vv. 1,4 tend to support the first interpretation while the parallel expression 'before your raising yourself high' (מרוממתך) tends towards the second. Even with the explanation of 'at the thunderous noise' as the clamour of war, however, the parallelism still implies that it is YHWH who brings this about since the suffix of 'before your raising yourself high' also exercises some influence on the first half of the verse (double duty suffix).[42] God, nonetheless, is never the direct subject of המון. Where this term and the root המה appear in association with YHWH, they always imply some sort of natural force (Jer. 5:22; 10:13; 31:35; 51:16; Ps. 46:4; 65:8) or human adversary (1 Kgs 20:13,18; Isa. 5:14; 13:4; 16:14; 17:12; 29:5-8; Ezek. 31:2,8;

[40] *TWAT*, V, 247f. (W. Groß).

[41] From Rashi onwards (Rosenberg, 267), most commentators have accepted that the noise refers to the thunder of YHWH (Hitzig, Alexander, Delitzsch, Dillmann-Kittel, Feldmann, Procksch, Kaiser). Ibn Ezra (154) ascribed it to the Assyrian army.

[42] Schoors, 196; Wildberger, 1289.

Ps. 83:3), who at first endeavour to resist YHWH but are ultimately forced
to submit to his rule.[43] Therefore, the verse appears to say the following:
the clamour unleashed by the nations puts them also to flight because
YHWH himself rises up in the midst of it.[44] The redaction employs the
term 'to raise yourself high' (root רום) to hark back via 30:18 (see there)
to the call vision of Isaiah ben Amoz himself (6:1).

4 The preceding act of confidence results in the announcement to the
nations that their possessions will become spoil ('your spoil' [2nd pers.
plur. suffix]). According to some, this includes a reference to v. 1: the
nations will have their unjustly gained riches taken from them (Rashi
[Rosenberg, 267]). The imagery of the 'grasshoppers / locusts' creates a
picture of almost instantaneous and complete despoliation since such a
plague ranks high among biblical disasters (Deut. 28:38; Judg. 6:5; 1
Kgs 8:37; Amos 7:1f.; Joel 1:4; 2:25; Nah. 3:17). No mention is made
of the recipients of the booty. The verses focuses its attention on the
complete destruction of YHWH's adversaries and not on retribution.

5-6 A hymn of praise to YHWH as guardian of Zion, akin to the literary
genre of descriptive praise, concludes the prophecy concerning the
downfall of the enemy. Our attention is not drawn to a single act of salvation on YHWH's part but to YHWH's abiding attributes and their ultimate
significance for Zion. The inspecific character of the hymn of praise
concurs with the prayer for help in time of trouble (cf. the temporal indicators in v. 2b and in v. 6a). In addition, the hymn takes on a prophetic
character since it is addressed to Zion (v. 6a') and not to YHWH. Indeed,
in speaking of Zion, the hymn even advances a proposition: 'The fear of
YHWH is her treasure' (v. 6b).

The two verses exhibit an ingenious structure by way of the colometric figure
of 'paired tricola', the two bicola of v. 5 and v. 6a''.b sharing the single colon v.
6a' (cf. the layout of the translation). V. 6a' concurs to a certain degree with
each of the four surrounding cola.[45] The structure also exhibits a supportive metrical pattern: 4+4/3/4+4. The name of YHWH occurs in the first and the final colon. While the central colon, v. 6a', continues the subject of v. 5, namely YHWH,
and the verb forms of v. 5b (והיה ....מלא), the verb of v. 6a' (והיה) also governs
v. 6a''. In its turn, the nominal clause of v. 6b continues the והיה-clause with the
long subject complement of v. 6a'-a''. The three cola of v. 6 conform with one
another at a primarily semantic level. Firstly, the word groups אמונת עתיך and

---

[43] TWAT, II, 447 (A. Baumann).

[44] Watts, 421: 'The roaring sound combines the possibilities of battle with indications
of Yahweh's approach. They are in some sense identical'; cf. J. Lust, "A Gentle Breeze
or a Roaring Thunderous Sound?", VT 25 (1975), 111f. Therefore, it attests to literary
skill that in the first half of the verse, the one who causes the noise is not called by name
whereas in the second half, a suffix refers to YHWH (König, 286).

[45] Van Grol 1983 (without mentioning Isa. 33:5-6).

חסן ישועת exhibit 'gender-matched parallelism' (feminine noun singular with masculine noun plural and masculine noun singular with feminine noun plural).[46] Secondly, the parallel terms חסן and אוצרו, both masculine nouns, chiastically encircle four feminine nouns ending in ‑ ת and ‑ ת. Thirdly, the suffix of אוצרו harks back to עתיך which itself harks back to ציון.

Far from being a random hotch-potch of praiseworthy divine characteristics, the verses in question provide an answer to the ongoing and centuries old question of YHWH's disposition towards Zion. The spatial order (v. 5) has a primary role to play herein. The fact that YHWH dwells 'in the height' implies, in the language of PI, that he is not bound to the earth and to earthly proportions. Indeed, his superior power will be made manifest to all those who turn against him ('exalted' [root שגב]: 2:11,17; 12:4; 'on high' [root רום]: of the pretensions of the adversary: 2:12ff.; 10:33; 14:13; 37:23; of YHWH: 6:1; 26:11; 30:18; 32:15). The fact that his dwelling is not restricted to Zion does not simply imply that he has dominion over the place and that he 'fills' (מלא) her with one or other form of his presence (Exod. 40:34f.; 1 Kgs 8:11; Isa. 6:1; Ezek. 10:4; 43:5; 44:4; Hab. 2:14; 3:3; Hag. 2:7; Ps. 33:5; 119:64; 2 Chr. 5:13). Zion, rather, is to be filled with that which ought to be her essential characteristic: 'justice and righteousness' (משפט וצדקה). A distinguishing topic of PI, at the level of the prophecies of Isaiah ben Amoz as well as that of the redaction, is hereby given due expression (1:21,27; 5:7; 9:6; 16:5; 28:17; 32:1,16).

The text then turns to a second topic, the temporal aspect of YHWH's disposition towards Zion (v. 6a'). The promise that YHWH himself will be 'the steadfastness of your times' (אמונת עתיך) constitutes a response to the prayer in 'time of trouble' (v. 2) and to the lament over the treachery of the treacherous (v. 1). In line with Isaiah ben Amoz' conception of Zion's well-being (28:11ff.; 30:1-5, 12-17), these times of safety are presented as a consequence of 'justice and righteousness' (cf. 11:5: 'righteousness / faithfulness' [צדק / אמונה]). 'Faithfulness', for that matter, is a characteristic of YHWH himself (11:5; 25:1). Having founded Zion on faithfulness, however, he has found it painfully absent therein (1:21; 7:9). Nevertheless, YHWH's purpose continues to be that Zion will ultimately be called 'town of righteousness / faithful city' (1:26).

In the third place, YHWH's guarantee of Zion's salvation is dealt with in more detail (v. 6a''.b). While the term 'salvation' continues to be a response to the prayer for intervention (v. 2b), 'wisdom and knowledge' and 'the fear of YHWH' appear to be further elaborations which are alien

---

[46] Watson 1994: 216, 224.

to the context. Nevertheless, this is only how it appears. YHWH's adversaries, both within Israel and outside her, have tendered their arrogant conduct as 'wisdom' (חכמה; root חכם: 5:21; 10:13; 19:11f.; 29:14). The prophet, in contrast, has claimed genuine wisdom for YHWH alone (11:2; 31:2). The term 'knowledge' carries similar implications (דעת: 5:13; 11:2; 32:4; root ידע: 1:3; 5:19; 6:9; 19:12,21; 29:15,24; 33:13; 37:20; for the same theme employing the term עצה see 28:29). The historical background of this topic frames the opposition between Isaiah ben Amoz and the policy makers at the court who originated from cultivated wisdom circles.[47]

The topic 'to fear' (ירא) belongs to the same public discourse. The prophet and his adversaries were divided on this question: should one fear YHWH or the enemy at the door (7:4; 8:12; 10:24; 18:2; 25:3; 29:13; 35:4; 37:6)? For this reason, the promise of sincere 'fear of YHWH' fits well in the perspective of Isaiah's preaching (11:2f.). Zion's 'treasure' is to be found therein, not in material wealth or military armaments (אוצר: 2:7; 30:6; 39:2,4).

7-9 The prophet returns here to the actual situation which gave rise to the woe cry. With an introductory 'behold' (הן; cf 23:13; 32:1) he draws attention to his own vision of reality: the decline of civil life and of the common land. The interpretation of the first word (אראלם; cf. Notes) as 'I see them!' has its appropriate place within the theme of the prophet's call 'to see' on behalf of the people (ראה with the prophet as subject: 6:1,5; 21:3; 30:10). The proleptic use of the object 'them', focuses attention on the effects of YHWH's judgement on human persons. The introductory clause thus transforms the situation of need into a personal experience on the part of the prophet as well as a confirmation of his preaching. As we shall see, this will also be apparent from the word usage.

The portrayal of the ruination of land and civil life is not consistent with the topics of war and the violence associated therewith but with the desolation, both moral and physical, which follows upon some form of disaster. The terminology partly belongs to the verbal idiom of the lament genre and partly to that of PI. The impression that the prophet Isaiah is bewailing the fact that the judgement he was forced to announce has now become a reality is thus reinforced.

---

[47] W. McKane, *Prophets and Wise Men* (SBT, 44), London 1965; H.-J. Hermisson, "Weisheit und Geschichte"; in: *Probleme biblischer Theologie Gerhard von Rad zum 70. Geburtstag* (ed. H.W. Wolff), München 1971, 136-54; J.W. Whedbee, *Isaiah and Wisdom,* Nashville 1971; J. Vermeylen, "Le Proto-Isaïe et la sagesse d'Israel"; in: *La Sagesse de l'Ancien Testament* (ed. M. Gilbert), (BETL, 51), Leuven 1990[2], 39-58.

After Zion has been the focus of attention in vv. 5-6, the locative of v. 7, 'in the streets', brings the city to mind once again (cf. 5:25; 24:11), even although the term 'streets' can be considered a natural part of almost any description of urban disaster (Isa. 15:3; 51:20,23; Jer. 9:20; 51:4; Ezek. 11:6; 28:23; Lam. 2:19; 4:1). Similarly, while the verbs 'to cry' and 'to weep' are to be found in PI (and elsewhere) in connection with Jerusalem, they are also associated with other places (צעק: Isa. 5:7; Zeph. 1:10; Lam. 2:18 and Isa. 19:20; Jer. 22:20; 49:3; בכה: Isa. 22:4,12; 30:19; Lam. 1:16; 3:51 and Isa. 15:2-5; 16:9; Ezek. 27:31). Finally, 'the envoys of peace' are reminiscent of the diplomatic intrigues which the prophet has frequently berated (מלאכים: 14:32; 18:2; 30:4; [31:1]; 37:9,14; שלום: 9:5f.; 26:3,12; 32:17f.).

While land itself becomes the focus of attention in v. 8a, it is not spoken of in terms of depopulation but rather in terms of broken lines of communication ('highway' [מסלה]: Num. 20:19; Judg. 5:6; 20:31f.,45; 21:19; 2 Sam. 20:12f.; Ps. 84:6). Thematic and semantic associations with PI are somewhat scarce at this point ('to lay waste' [שמם]: 1:7; 6:11; 17:9; 'to wayfare' [עבר]: 8:21; 34:10; 35:8). At the same time, the topic 'highway' has a different function therein (Isa. 7:3; 11:16; 19:23; 36:2; cf. 49:11; 62:10).[48] In line with the theme of Zion, it is possible that the verse is implying that the city is no longer being visited (the contrast of 2:2-5?).

Echoes of PI are a little more evident in vv. 8b-9, especially in relation to 24:4f.,7. While it is possible, from the diachronic perspective, that the Isaiah Apocalypse appropriated or 'quoted' terms and images from ch.33,[49] from the synchronic perspective, the prophet is clearly referring to former oracles.

The portrayal of moral decline in v. 8b harks back to former indictments in PI. While the expression 'the treaty is broken' alludes synchronically to 24:5, the latter text speaks of the 'eternal' treaty being broken[50] (cf. the verb 'to break' [פרר hiphil] in comparable contexts: 8:10; 14:27). Several additional terms are also reminiscent of the accusations of PI ('to despise' [מאס]: 5:24; 8:6; 30:12; 31:7; 33:15; 'witnesses' [עד]: 8:2; 19:20; 30:8 corr.; 'to take into account' [חשב]: 2:22; 10:7; 29:16; 'human beings' [אנוש]: 2:22; 13:7,12; 24:6; 29:13).

The precise meaning of the term 'treaty' (ברית) is difficult to establish. Given the fact that the term is rare among the older pre-exilic

---

[48] According to Williamson (1994: 234), the redaction of BI is anticipating the opening of DI (40:3) at this point.

[49] Williamson 1994: 234f.

[50] This fact might suggest that 24:5 is diachronically dependent on 33:9.

prophets (Hos. 6:7; 8:1)[51] and, with the exception of 24:5 and 33:8, is only found elsewhere in PI in 28:15,18, in a completely different context, it would be wrong, at this point, to ascribe to it the theological significance which the concept enjoys in Genesis – 2 Kings. Since the present text lacks the term 'eternal' some exegetes have set the textual association with 24:5 to one side and endeavoured to explain 33:9 against the background of vv. 1,7 as a reference to a political treaty of some sort. Those commentators who are convinced that this passage stems from Isaiah ben Amoz himself are particularly inclined to read the text as an allusion to Sennacherib's breach of promise at Lachish (2 Kgs 18:13-17).[52] Even in the absence of such a point of departure, other exegetes tend to understand the term as a reference to some sort of business or political agreement.[53] If one is more inclined to attach significance to the terminological similarity with 24:5, then one might read the term as a reference to the Noachic[54] or Mosaic covenants[55] or even to the cosmic covenant which embraces God and human beings in history and creation.[56] An alternative interpretation, however, reads the 'treaty' in 24:5 as establishing an inter-textual construction in which the various traditional applications flow together.[57] The latter explanation seems preferable since it does justice to the semantic cross-referential plurality of the text.[58] A similar explanation would hold true for Isa. 33:8, since this verse also belongs to a late redactional complex. In the context of ch.33 as a whole, and against the background of chs. 28-32, the political interpretation clearly lies at the basis of the term. In the context of the lament genre with its focus on nature's decline, however, it seems equally reasonable to explain the text as a reference to the cosmic covenant and thereby to a violation of YHWH's world order. The redactional context of PI further supports such an explanation.

V. 9a´: 'The land mourns and languishes' (אבל אמללה ארץ) describes nature's decline in terms used in 24:4a ('The earth / land mourns and

[51] The term is not found in Amos, Micah Nahum, Habakuk and Zephaniah.

[52] Alexander, Delitzsch, Feldmann, Procksch, Oswalt. Likewise Kaiser, 273. Penna (303f.) offers a detailed reflection on the possible accuracy of this explanation.

[53] Kutsch 1973: 93, although he considers the term in 24:5 to be an 'obligation imposed by YHWH' (135). Kilian, 191.

[54] Seitz, 179.

[55] Wildberger, 1299; Johnson 1988: 27.

[56] Murray 1992: 22-5.

[57] Polaski 1998: 69: 'The ברית עולם in Isa. 24.5 redeploys the Mosaic covenant by rendering it perpetual – violation is a matter for the future – and by yoking it to cosmic catastrophe'.

[58] König (290ff.) has already made an attempt at combining the various literary-historical interpretations.

withers, the world languishes and withers' [אבלה נבלה הארץ אמללה
נבלה תבל]). The locative 'land (earth)' upholds a frequently occurring
theme in PI, namely what will happen to the land under YHWH's judgement (1:7; 2:21; 5:30; 6:12; 7:24; 10:23; 13:5,9; 16:4; 24 *passim*).
The four locatives 'Lebanon', 'Sharon', 'Bashan' and 'Carmel' cover
the north and the centre of Israel, from west to east, information which
might lead one to surmise that the situation of need was brought about
by an invasion from the north (cf. 7:2; 8:23; 14:26 and other 'realistic'
geographical descriptions in 10:28-32 and chs. 15-16). Each region in
itself is well known for its fertility: Lebanon for its cedars (2:13; 10:34;
14:8; 35:2; Judg. 9:15; 1 Kgs 5 *passim*; Jer. 22:23; Ezek. 31:3; Hos.
14:6; Ps. 29:5), Sharon for its fertility and flowers (35:2; 65:10; Cant.
2:1), Bashan for its oaks (2:13; Jer. 50:19; Ezek. 27:6; Zech. 11:2) and
Carmel for its forestry (35:2; Amos 1:2; 9:3; Cant. 7:5).

The configuration of these place names in PI, however, carries a further significance. 'Lebanon', 'Sharon' and 'Carmel' are to be found together in only one other place, namely 35:2. While it is true that
'Bashan' is lacking there, 35:1(6), besides mentioning 'wilderness' and
'dry land', also speaks of the 'desert' (ערבה), a word which is found for
the first time in PI in 33:9 and then once again in 40:3 (parallel with
'desert'). While the vegetation motif in 33:9 functions at the level of
genre, the verbal configurations legitimate the suggestion that the specific place names imply a secondary function, namely the establishment
of a link between ch.24 and ch.40.[59] This dual function contributes to the
redactional function of ch.33, taking up elements from PI and aligning
them with corresponding elements in DI. Ch.35 serves thereby as a second coupling.

In addition, the context of PI as a whole provides the verse with a
third function. The place name 'Bashan' can only be found elsewhere in
2:13. As with 33:9, the term appears here together with 'Lebanon' and
both place names function as metaphors for powers which rise up
against YHWH. 'Lebanon' returns with the same significance in 29:17
and 37:24. Given such a background, the notion of earthly powers
which lack respect for YHWH also has an echo in v. 9, powers which ultimately must lose ground because of their own complacency.[60]

10 By way of the triple 'now' (עתה [not ועתה]: 29:22 twice; 30:8;
36:5; 37:26) and the embedded quotation formula 'says YHWH' (*yiqtol*,

---

[59] Beuken 1991: 19f.; Williamson 1994: 234f.

[60] Texts in which כרמל can be found as a common noun have been left out of consideration (10:18; 16:10; 29:17; 32:15f.; 37:24).

not *qatal*), the divine utterance of vv. 10-13 serves as an emphatic reaction to the preceding lament. V. 10 contains three verbs in the 1st person singular with YHWH as subject, without a single syntactical complement. YHWH's initiative is thus the primary and exclusive focus of the verse. In PI, the first verb, 'to stand up', embodies the rivalry which exists between YHWH and his adversaries, a rivalry in which YHWH ultimately has the upper hand (קום: with YHWH as subject in 2:19,21; 14:22; 28:21; 29:3; 31:2; with the enemy as subject in 7:7; 14:21; 23:13; 24:20; 27:9; 28:18). With the second verb, 'I will raise myself high', YHWH responds affirmatively to the prayer for intervention in v. 3 (for רום,[61] see *in loco*; for the third verb, 'I will lift myself up' [נשא], cf. 6:1 and 2:12ff.; 37:23).

The three verbs call 2:6-22 to mind, a passage dominated by the theme of YHWH's exclusive exaltedness above all those who raise themselves above the condition of human beings (cf. the terms קום in vv. 19,21, גאון in vv. 10,19,21 and נשגב in vv. 11,17, all used with regard to YHWH). That passage is, moreover, interlarded by the temporal indicator 'on that day' (vv. 11f.,17,20; cf. the temporal clause: 'when he rises' in vv. 19,21). Thus the events predicted in ch.2 seem now to be taking place (33:10: triple 'now'). Thus, ch.2 and ch.33 are clearly interrelated, and v. 10 contributes to the concluding function of ch.33 within PI.[62]

11-12 While YHWH's addressee's are not immediately evident, the preceding verses allow us to assume that they follow the line of the 'destroyer / treacherous one' in v. 1, the 'peoples / nations' in v. 3 and those who have destroyed the land in vv. 8-9. By adding the vocative, 'you, nations' in v. 11, the Targum explains things in similar fashion.[63] Judgement is not presented, however, as a personal act of YHWH but rather as a process of mundane causality which links up with the astonishment expressed by the woe cry: to the enemy himself has not yet happened what he has done to others (v. 1).

The imagery of v. 11a elaborates this employing two conventional metaphors: 'to conceive / to bring forth' (Isa. 26:17f.; 59:4; Ps. 7:15; Job 15:35) and 'chaff / stubble'.[64] While 'stubble' (קש) functions broadly as a metaphor for everything that is worthless (Isa. 40:24; 41:2; Job 13:25; 41:20f.), it is also employed as a metaphor in prophetic judgement preaching because it is destined for the fire (Exod. 15:7; Isa. 5:24; 47:14; Joel 2:5; Ob 18; Nah. 1:10; Mal. 3:19; cf. 'thorns' and

---

[61] ארוממ is an abbreviated form of the *hithpalel*, cf. 1QIs[a] (*HALAT*, 1124).

[62] Beuken 1991: 20; Williamson 1994: 235.

[63] *pace* Wildberger, 1296, 1301: v. 11 is addressed to Israel.

[64] 'Chaff' (חשש) can only be found elsewhere in 5:24.

similar materials: 2 Sam. 23:6f.; Isa. 1:31; 9:17; 10:16f.; 64:1; Ps. 80:17; 118:12).[65] Taken together, this suggests that for what they have planned and carried out the addressees of v. 11 can expect nothing more than the fate of worthless things.

V. 11b further elaborates upon the association between 'stubble' and 'fire'. While the imagery is conventional, the verse takes things a step or two further. In the first place, the addressees themselves are now considered to be 'stubble' destined for the fire. Secondly, the fact that the fire in question is put on a par with the addressees' own vitality ('your breath') is quite unique (רוח in this anthropological sense: Gen. 45:27; Judg. 15:19; 1 Sam. 30:12; 1 Kgs 21:5; Isa. 19:3; 25:4; 26:9; 38:16).

V. 12 appears to enlarge upon v. 11 as a whole. The addressees of v. 12 are now named directly: 'peoples / nations'. Associations with the prayer for intervention are thus fortified (cf. v. 3). In addition, the activity of the fire is characterised as both all consuming (v. 12a: 'to lime'; cf. Amos 2:1) and fast (v. 12b: 'like thorns'; cf. 2 Sam. 23:6f.).

13 A call 'to hear / to acknowledge' (ידע / שמע) is found appropriately where YHWH speaks by means of his prophets (Num. 24:16; Jer. 6:48; Ezek. 2:5; Neh. 6:16) or inspires the wise (Ps. 78:3; 143:8; Job 5:27; 42:4; Prov. 4:1). In the present verse, the call in question does not appear to exhibit the form of a call to attention as such (as in 32:9), but focuses the addressee immediately on the object of attention as a general truth and not as a new and unique fact: 'what I do / my might' (שמע [את] אשר: Exod. 18:1; Josh. 2:10; 5:1; 9:3f.,9f., 16; 1 Sam. 31: 11; 1 Kgs 5:22; 11:38; 2 Kgs 22:19; Isa. 37:11; Jer. 23:25; 33:9; 36:6; Ezek. 44:5; Mic. 6:1).[66] A topic of PI is touched upon once again, namely the contrast between what YHWH brings about and what his adversaries bring about (for עשה, cf. 29:16; for גבורה, cf. 28:6). The position of v. 13 at the end of the divine oracle further nuances the judgement declared by YHWH as an event which will not end with the enemy being cast into the fire (vv. 11f.), but rather as one which will ultimately lead to the recognition of His mighty deeds.[67]

How are we to identify the addressees: 'you who are far-off / you who are near'?[68] After v. 12, the identification of the first category, at

[65] TWAT, VII, 196f. (K.-M. Beyse).

[66] Arambarri 1990: 252-5.

[67] A number of older commentators assume a caesura after v. 12 and consider v. 13 to be an authoritative summons on the part of YHWH introducing the prophetic speech of vv. 14-24 (Dillmann-Kittel, 295; Feldmann, 393; König, 287; Penna, 305f.). Such an approach is often influenced by the paradigmatic conviction that the prophet preached God's judgement as the absolute end. LXX and 1QIs[a], both of which read future tenses in v. 13 instead of imperatives, would also appear to associate the latter with v. 14.

[68] Commentators are divided. The Jewish tradition tends for the most part to follow the explanations of the Targum and Rashi who understand 'you who are far-off' to be the

least, as 'the peoples' seems inevitable. Given the fact that the word pair 'far-off / near' frequently refers to a division within the same single entity, one might be tempted to identify both categories as the nations (Deut. 13:8; 1 Kgs 8:46; Isa. 57:19; Jer. 25:26; 48:24; Ezek. 6:12; 22:5; Esth. 9:20; Dan. 9:7; 2 Chr. 6:36). Within the context, however, it is possible that the expression 'you who are near' anticipates 'the sinners in Zion' of v. 14, since the object of the imperative 'acknowledge' (דעו), namely 'my might', is something which Israel must also accept, certainly now that the latter term is in parallel with 'what I do' (cf. the texts mentioned above). Moreover, v. 4 announces that YHWH intends to realise 'justice,righteousness and knowledge (דעת)' in Zion.

On the basis of these facts, we suggest that the word pair 'far-off / near' constitutes a merism, a style-figure which associates opposite extremes in order to express totality.[69] The expression offers a reverse order geographical rendering of the direct ('near') and indirect ('far-off') addressation of v. 11 and v. 12. The entire world is invited to 'acknowledge' YHWH's deeds (cf. Ps. 47:1; 66:1f.; 96:1; 98:4; 100:1-3; 117:1). This would match the role of the peoples as the primary instigators of doom and misfortune from v. 1 onwards and in v. 3 in particular, conditions which have led to this present lament (vv. 7-9) and ultimately to YHWH's response (vv. 10-13). This appeal to nations far-off and peoples close-by does not, however, exclude Israel herself, especially since the latter is supposed to fully recognise YHWH's works. It is understandable, therefore, that the following verse offers some explanation of this fact. Both groups, the oppressors of Israel and 'the sinners in Zion' (v. 14), have still to recognise YHWH's powerful deeds.

14 While, from a genre-critical perspective, the 'entrance liturgy' might appear unrelated to the divine oracle, intertextual associations are evident if one calls to mind the fact that v. 10 harks back to ch.2. Indeed, the very first word of v. 14, 'to be afraid' (פחד), embodies YHWH's personal intervention against the godless (2:10,19,21: 'from before the terror of YHWH, and from the glory of his majesty'). The notion enjoys isotopic consistency in PI (Israel need not 'be afraid': 12:2; Egypt, the dwellers upon the earth and those who serve idols should 'be afraid': 19:16f.; 24:17f.).[70] The concept as such pertains to the reaction of peo-

repentent sinners and 'you who are near' to be the righteous (according to Delitzsch [353] also, both categories refer to Zion). Following Duhm (243), other exegetes interpret 'far-off' and 'near' as the totality of humankind (Procksch, Kissane, Penna, Kaiser). Others still are of the opinion that the first category implies the nations and the second the 'sinners in Zion' (cf. Ibn Ezra, 154; Dillmann-Kittel, Wildberger, Kilian).

[69] Krašovec 1977: 144; Motyer, 266.
[70] Beuken 1991: 21ff.; Williamson 1994: 235f.

ple whose very existence is under threat (Isa. 12:2; 44:8; 51:13; Jer. 30:5; 36:16; Hos. 3:5; Ps. 14:5; 27:1; 78:53; Job 3:25; 15:21; 21:9; Prov. 3:24; Sir. 9:13).[71] Similarly, the parallel term has a religious and existential significance ([ה]רעד: Exod. 15:15; Ps. 2:11; 48:7; 55:6; Job 4:14).

The word order in v. 14a draws our attention to the locative 'in Zion', the place in which the action of the remainder of the chapter will take place (cf. vv. 16, 18,20f.,24). The immediate context announces thereby that YHWH's judgement will not only fall upon the nations (vv. 12f.), but also upon people in Zion herself, a group who can expect judgement ('Who among us?').[72] This turn of events contains important implications for the chapter as a whole. The new Zion portrayed here will not only be free of foreign domination (vv. 18f.,21b), she will also witness the end of internal oppression. The fact that these people themselves are responsible for the questions[73] and that they expect a negative response from their partisans ('Who among us?'), makes them witnesses of their own removal from the protected dwelling offered by YHWH on Mount Zion ('to sojourn', i.e. as resident alien [גור]: Gen. 12:10; 20:1; 35:27; Exod. 6:4; 12:48f.; Lev. 16:29; Judg. 5:17; 2 Sam. 1:13; Isa. 16:4; 23:7; 52:4; Jer. 35:7; 42:15; Ps. 5:5; 120:5; Ruth 1:1; Lam. 4:15; Sir. 41:19; 42:11; with respect to God: Lev. 25:23; Ps. 39:13; 1 Chr. 29:15).

The fact that 'the sinners in Zion' are the focus of attention is in harmony with the reference to ch.2 (cf. v. 6: 'the house of Jacob'). At the same time, however, reference is clearly made to ch.1 (v. 28: חטאים; cf. vv. 4,18). Similarly, the parallel expression, 'the impious' (חנפים), with its associated implication of deceit and its damaging social and religious consequences (Jer. 23:11,15; Mic. 4:11; Job 8:13; 13:16; 15:35; 17:8; 27:8; 34:30; 36:13; Prov. 11:9; Dan. 11:32; Sir. 16:6; 40:15; 41:10),[74] is applied in PI to the people in Zion themselves (9:16; 10:6; 32:6). As such, the 'entrance liturgy' offers a sort of narrative dénouement. What was predicted at the beginning and in subsequent chapters of PI is now becoming a reality.

God's presence in Zion establishes her as the place of protection. In contrast to the genre of the entrance liturgy proper (Ps. 15:1: 'thy tent /

[71] *TWAT*, VI, 555f. (H.-P. Müller).

[72] Sweeney (432) concludes from the fact that the locative 'in Zion' is found prior to 'the sinners' that the latter are foreign oppressors. Such a position, however, is difficult to reconcile with the theme of dwelling in God's presence.

[73] In the original genre, one among the circle of the devout was certainly responsible for these questions (Ps.15:1; 24:3).

[74] *TWAT*, III, 42, 46f. (K. Seybold).

thy holy mountain'; Ps. 24:3: 'the mountain of YHWH / his holy place'),
Zion is rendered functionally here as the place in which YHWH effects his
judgement. This is accomplished on the basis of two metaphors. The
first stems from the topic of judgement: 'devouring fire' (with respect to
God: Exod. 24:7; Num. 16:35; Deut. 4:24; 9:3; 32:22; 1 Kgs 18:38; 2
Kgs 22:17; Isa. 30:27; Ezek. 15:7; Ps. 18:9; 21:10; 50:3; Lam. 2:3).
The second metaphor employs a place name: 'the everlasting burning
flames' (מוקדי עולם),[75] which refers to the hearth of the altar of the burnt
offerings (Lev. 6:2: 'The burnt offering shall be on the hearth upon the
altar all night until the morning, and the fire of the altar shall be kept
burning on it'; cf. vv. 12f.). The term עולם is never used otherwise to
designate the fact that fire remains burning. As such, it supports the
metaphorical function of the term 'hearth' as a reference to YHWH (cf.
Isa. 9:6; 24:5; 32:14,17; 34:10,17; 35:10).[76]

15 The response to the sinners' questions originates in principle from
the prophet himself who, as narrator, has taken the floor once again in v.
14. Given the fact, however, that the prophet is not introduced as an
actant, as the sinners' dialogue partner, we are left with the impression
that they answer their own question, as a belated witness to the salvation
they might have enjoyed. Their response constitutes a digest of six concrete codes of ethical behaviour. The grammatical form of singular participles corresponds to the question: 'Who among us?' and is characteristic of the genre (cf. Ps. 15:2,5; 24:3-5).

The series of codes is carefully structured, the first two being formulated positively ('to walk righteously / to speak uprightly'), the following four being formulated negatively as behaviour to be avoided. The
first of the negative group ('to despise the gain of oppressions') partly
follows the structure of the first two positive codes with which it forms a
single verse line. The final three negative codes possess the same structure: three times an expression with מן ('from holding a bribe / from
hearing of bloodshed / from looking upon evil') and three times a mention of a specific body part as an instrument of negative conduct ('hands
/ ears / eyes').

The wicked behaviour accused of here is clearly that of the rulers.[77]
While the first code, 'to walk righteously' (הלך צדקות), is general in nature (cf. this verb with a noun of quality as object: Isa. 50:10; 57:2;

---

[75] The plural is not a plural of distinct beings but of composition or extension (J-M,
§136 a-c).

[76] עולם expresses both duration and quality (Dillmann-Kittel, 296; Oswalt, 599).

[77] Sweeney (424, 428, 431f.) narrows the aim of this ethical catalogue by designating
it as the ideal programme for the 'righteous monarch'.

Ezek. 3:14; Mic. 2:7; Job 29:3; Prov. 2:7; 6:12; 10:9), the remaining codes presume a situation in which differences in social standing and well-being allow for the exploitation of the less fortunate.

- 'to speak uprightly' (דבר מישרים). For examples of the use of this verb with an object from the judicial arena, cf. Isa. 32:7; 59:3,13; Jer. 9:4,7; 12:1; 29:13; Mic. 6:12; Zech. 8:16; 13:3; Ps. 34:14; 37:30; 38:13; 52:5; 58:2; 73:8; Job 13:7; 27:4.
- 'the gain of oppressions' (בצע מעשקות). For references to the phenomenon of the unjust pursuit of gain (בצע) and the struggle against it, cf. Exod. 18:21; 1 Sam. 8:3; Isa. 56:11; 57:17; Jer. 6:13; 22:17; 51:13; Ezek. 22:27; Hab. 2:9; Ps. 119:36; Prov. 1:19; 15:27; 28:16. In addition, the verb 'to oppress' (עשק) bears connotations of the economically powerful maintaining a policy which threatens the very existence of the less well-off (Lev. 19:13; 1 Sam. 12:3f.; Isa. 30:12; 52:4; 54:14; 59:13; Jer. 21:12; 22:3; Ezek. 22:29; Amos 4:1; Mic. 2:2; Ps. 62:11; 72:4; Prov. 14:31; 22:16; Eccl. 4:1; 5:7).
- 'bribe' (שחד): Exod. 23:8; Deut. 16:19; 27:25; 1 Sam. 8:3; Isa. 1:23; 5:23; Ezek. 16:33; 22:12; Mic. 3:11; Ps. 15:5; Job 6:22; Prov. 17:23. It is significant in this context that YHWH himself is immune to such bribes (Deut. 10:17; 45:13).
- 'bloodshed' (דם): the term 'blood', in association with violent attack on mostly innocent human persons, is frequently found as the object of verbs of concrete action (Mic. 7:2; Prov. 1:18: 'to lie in wait for'; Ps. 94:21: 'to band against'; Lev. 19:16: 'to stand forth against'; Ezek. 22:3: 'to shed'; Gen. 9:5; Ezek. 33:6: 'to require a reckoning for'; Gen. 37:26: 'to conceal'; Deut. 22:8; Jer. 26:15: 'to bring upon').
- 'not looking upon evil' (ראה ברע) does not imply 'ignoring social evil, but refusing to be a part of such conspiracies' (Oswalt, 600). Together with the preposition ב, the verb implies consensual involvement in what one sees, frequently the downfall of one's enemies (Judg. 16:27; Ezek. 28:17; Mic. 7:9f.; Ob 12; Ps. 22:18; 37:34; 54:9; 112:8; 118:7).

16 The second part of the response to the question who can reside in YHWH's presence (v. 14b), does not make reference to the terms of the question as such, the words 'to abide / place of defence' (מִשְׂגָּב / שָׁכַן) taking the place here of the double use of 'to sojourn' (גור) in v. 14. Terminological variation between question and answer is typical of the genre (cf. Ps. 15:1 and 5: 'to sojourn / to abide' and 'not to be moved'; Ps. 24:3 and 5: 'to ascend / to stand' and 'to carry away a blessing'). The difference between v. 16 and v. 14 lies primarily in the fact that the terms expressing YHWH's presence in the temple, 'devouring fire / ever burning flames', are replaced by purely locative terms 'heights / rock fortresses'. Attention is thus shifted from the temple to the elevated city.

At the same time, v. 16 borrows three terms for God's dwelling from v. 5a: 'to abide' (שכן), 'heights' (v. 16: מרומים; v. 5: מרום) and 'his place of defence' (משגבו), comparable to 'he is exalted' (v. 5: נשגב). The connection is strong enough to have one conclude that the promise of dwelling in YHWH's presence on Mount Zion is presented here as a way of living which shares in the inviolability of the divine domain. Equalling God's dwelling and that of the just person, however, is avoided by the surprising additional guarantee of elementary essentials of life: bread and secure water (Gen. 21:14; Exod. 23:25; 34:28; Num. 21:5; Deut. 23:5; 1 Sam. 25:11; 30:11; 1 Kgs 13:8; 18:4; 22:27; 2 Kgs 6:22; Isa. 3:1; 30:20; Ezek. 4:16; 12:18; Hos. 2:7; Amos 8:11; Ps. 78:20; Job 3:24; 22:7; Prov. 25:21; Ezr. 10:6; Neh. 9:15). Even the expression 'sure (נאמנים) water' contains an echo of the praise of YHWH with his promise of 'steadfastness (אמונה) of times' (v. 6).

17 The list of blessings which will be the result of the ethical conduct of the leadership continues. (The compound nominal clauses in the first colon of all the verse lines of vv. 16-19 establish this segment as a unity.) Following upon the guarantee of a secure dwelling and the provision of the necessities of life (v. 16), the text promises a king who will fulfil his task as a king ought, and in so doing will bring prosperity to the land and the city.

The continuation of the list of blessings is coupled with a new, direct, singular addressation: 'your eyes', 'your heart' and 'you' (vv. 17-19). While the addressee may ultimately be the implied reader of BI, in the first instance, the he-figure who abides by the norms of v. 15 and for whom the blessings of v. 16 are set aside, emerges as such. At the same time, 'the sinners' of v. 14 disappear as actants from the scene for the remainder of the chapter.

The addressee is promised that he will see this new salvation 'with his own eyes' (cf. v. 20). This idiomatic phrase expresses both the objective presence of what is observed and the personal involvement of the observer (a verb for 'to see' with עינים: Gen. 45:12; Lev. 13:12; Num. 11:6; Deut. 3:21,27; Josh. 24:7; 1 Sam. 14:7; 1 Kgs 1:48; Isa. 6:5; 11:3; 17:7; 29:18; 30:20; 32:3; 52:8; 64:3; Jer. 20:4; Ezek. 12:2; Mic. 7:10; Zech. 9:8; Ps. 35:21; 91:18; 139:16; Job 7:7; 19:27; Eccl. 5:10; 6:9).[78]

The prophecy of 32:1-2 is brought to fulfilment with the promise that the addressee will see 'the king in his beauty'. The reference in v. 17 is probably not to YHWH as king but to the king in Jerusalem since the king is only one item in the list of blessings in vv. 17-20 (cf. 'Essentials and Perspectives'). The expression '(in his) beauty' (יפי) refers for the most part to the external appearance of human persons (Gen. 12:11; 39:6; 1

---

[78] Cf. TWAT, VII 231ff. (H.-F. Fuhs) for the complete list.

Sam. 16:12; 25:3; 2 Sam. 14:25,27; 1 Kgs 1:3f.; Job 42:15; Prov.
6:25; Esth. 1:11). It is possible that where the king is concerned, reference is being made to 'the official royal regalia' (Watts, 428). Sometimes, however, precisely where the king is concerned, the term is paral-
leled with moral qualities (Ps. 43:3: 'fairest of the sons of men / grace is
poured upon your lips'; Ezek. 28:12: 'full of wisdom and perfect in
beauty'; cf. v. 17; Eccl. 3:11; 5:17; Sir. 14: 16).[79] In that case, the term
'beauty' also includes the following: successful policies with respect to
the maintenance of a land 'that stretches afar' as well as the repulsion of
foreign adversaries and oppressors.

The king's good governance implies the prospect of beholding 'a land
that stretches afar'. The promise which instigated Abraham's journey,
gave birth to Israel and was made good to Moses at the end of his life is
thus fulfilled ('to see the land': Gen. 12:1; 13:15; 49:15; Num. 13:18;
14:23; 27:12; 32:1,8f.; Deut. 1:8,35f.; 2:31; 3;25,28; 32:49,52;
34:1,4; Josh. 2:1; 5:6). The fact that this land will be extensive[80] implies the realisation of Israel's most daring dreams (Gen. 15:18-21;
Deut. 11:24; Josh. 1:4; Isa. 27:12), associated as they were especially
with a king from the house of David (1 Kgs 5:1-5; Ps. 72:8-11).

18-19 The digest of blessings stands in stark contrast to the reflection
on the 'terror' already endured (אימה of people, sometimes sent by God:
Exod. 15:16; 23:27; Josh. 2:9; Deut. 32:25; Hab. 1:7; Ps. 88:16; Job
9:34; 13:21; 33:7; Prov. 20:2). It is not only a question here of amaze-
ment that the time of oppression has passed by, but also of the lesson
which the wise are inclined to draw from their experience ('to muse on'
[הגה]: Josh. 1:8; Ps. 1:2; 63:7; 77:13; 143:5; Prov. 15:28; Sir. 6:37;
14:20; 50:28; 'heart' [לב] as the seat of terrifying experiences: Isa.
7:2,4; 13:7; 15:5; 19:1; 21:4; 24:7; 35:4). In addition, questions relating to a person's place in this world are often an expression of the conviction that power has its limits ('Where is [איה]..?': Deut. 32:37; 2 Kgs
18:34; Isa. 36:19; 37:13; 51:13; Jer. 2:28; Ps. 42:4,11; 79:10; 115:2;
cf. in the lament: Isa. 63:11,15; Joel 2:17; Mal. 2:17). The questions of
the addressees constitute a pendant to those of 'the impious' in v. 14.
The implied answer is the same: the oppressors cannot stand firm in
God's presence, therefore they have disappeared.

---

[79] *Ges.[18]*, 479. An alternative interpretation also deserves consideration. The emphatic
position of 'in his beauty' (cf. v14: 'in Zion') gives the impression that the term 'beauty'
refers to Zion since Zion is so titled in the related Psalm 48 (cf. Ps. 50:2; Lam. 2:15). In
addition, the parallel member contains the locative 'land'.

[80] The plural ארץ מרחקים, 'land of distances', has developed the meaning 'wide' together with 'far' (cf. Isa. 8:9; Jer. 8:19; Zech. 10:9). Emendation to read מחמדים is arbi-
trary and has no support among the versions (BDB, 935; König, 288; *TWAT*, VII, 493 [L.
Wächter]; *pace* H. Gunkel 1924: 179: 'ein köstliches Land').

The three types of people whom the addressees need no longer fear (v. 18) are apparently the perpetrators of economic oppression.[81] The first two represent different types of money gathering: the 'counting' of coins and the 'weighing' of precious metals (cf. 2 Kgs 18:14ff.). The third category is less evident. The counting of towers may have had to do with some aspect of military reconnaissance in which towers were counted by the conqueror with a view to their demolition (cf. Isa 22:10) or the preservation of a limited number (cf. Ps. 48:13). It has also been suggested that towers were subject to taxation (Ibn Ezra, 155).

In contrast to the person whom the addressee will see, 'the king in his beauty' (v. 17), are those he will no longer see: brutal, insolent people who are responsible for the organisation of economic oppression. Their stammering, unintelligible speech is a symbol of their arrogance and the instrument of their oppression (cf. Isa. 28:11; 36:11; Ezek. 3:5).

20 The sketch of the liberated city stems from a different perspective: 'we' ('our festivals'; cf. vv. 21f.). Now that 'the insolent people' are gone, the true inhabitants of Zion can make their appearance. The city is referred to as 'Zion / Jerusalem', a double designation which is only found in PI in the context of salvation (2:3; 4:3f.; 10:12,32; 24:23; 30: 19; 31:9; 37:22,32). The sketch opens with the imperative 'look upon' which invites the just one of v. 17 to participate in the new reality which is brought a bit closer by this imperative than by the assurance 'you will see' in v. 19 (cf. the imperative of חזה or ראה: Gen. 13:14; 37:14; Exod. 14:13; Num. 27:12; Deut. 32:49; Josh. 2:1; 22:28; 1 Sam. 24:12; 2 Sam. 7:2; 14:30; 2 Kgs 10:16; Isa. 37:17; 48:6; 63:15; Jer. 40:4; Ezek. 8:9; Ps. 9:14; 46:9; 80:15; 84:10; Job 22:12; 40:12; Prov. 6:6; Eccl. 1:10; 7:13; 9:9; Lam. 1:11). The verb חזה thus implies 'to inspect, to make certain of...' (Exod. 18:21; Isa. 47:13; Ps. 11:7; 17:2; Job 15:17; Prov. 22:29; 24:32; 29:20; Cant. 7:1).

The city's new appearance invalidates former accusations concerning injustice, faithless religious gatherings and foolhardy dependence and brings former prophecies to fulfilment (cf. the context of the terms employed here elsewhere in PI: 'city' [קריה] in 1:21,26; 22:2; 24:10; 29:1; 32:13; 'festival' [מועד] in 1:14; 'quiet' [שאנן] in 32:9,11,18). The fact that this 'city' stems from a different reality is evident from the course of the imagery: from 'city' through the more rural 'habitation' to 'tent' ('habitation' [נוה] means 'abode of animals' [2 Sam. 7:8; Isa. 32:18; 34:13; 35:7; Jer. 25:30; 33:12; Amos 1:2; Zeph. 2:6] or 'habi-

---

[81] Wildberger (1317) does not interpret 'the one who weighed the tribute' as a tax collector but rather as a tax payer (cf. שקל in Exod. 22:16; 1 Kgs 20:39; Isa. 55:2; Esth. 3:9; 4:7). Given the context of the summary as a whole this seems unlikely.

tation in the country' [Isa. 27:10; 32:18; Jer. 10:25; 25:30; 31:23; Ps. 79:7; Job 5:3,24; 8:6; 18:15; Prov. 3:33; 24:15]). Thus 'Zion / Jerusalem' absorbs the ancient *Chiffre* of 'the land' and the promises associated therewith into herself. At the same time, the insistence that this 'tent' will never be 'plucked up' contradicts the very notion of 'tent' as a temporary dwelling (cf. Isa. 54:2; Jer. 10:20). In this sense one can assume that the tent of YHWH is being alluded to at this point (2 Sam. 6:17; 1 Kgs 1:39; 2:28ff.; 8:4; Ezek. 41:1; Ps. 15:1; 27:5; 61:5), especially given the background of certain texts in BI which speak of God's dwelling in Zion (v. 14; cf. also 4:5f.; 6:1; 8:18).

21 The meaning of this verse is the subject of some dispute. The first clause: 'There, rather, YHWH will be mighty for us' follows naturally upon v. 20 in which the 'the immovable tent' already makes allusion to YHWH's presence, and connects without complication with v. 22. The metaphor of YHWH's presence providing Jerusalem with rivers is not unusual (Ps. 46:5; Ezekiel 47; Joel 4:18; Zech. 14:8) and probably belongs to Zion's ancient cultic traditions.[82] A problem, however, is created by the traditional interpretation of the second colon as an apposition to 'YHWH' in the first colon: 'There YHWH in majesty will be for us a place of broad rivers and streams' (RSV). Such a geographically concrete presentation of YHWH as a river course for sailing ships runs counter to every biblical image of God, even those set in poetical contexts.

One solution to this problem would be to consider 'place' (מקום) in apposition to 'there' rather than to 'YHWH', especially since the word stands in an emphatic first position.[83] In this way, the imagery presents Jerusalem as surrounded by water but protected from attack from any hostile fleet (cf. Nah. 3:8; Ibn Ezra [155] refers hereby to the 'terror' in v. 18).

Other commentators consider any association of the mythical theme of Jerusalem being bathed by a mighty river with the military theme of a battle at sea rather absurd (Procksch, 423). Basing themselves on the fact that the word streams', יארים, usually refers to the Nile and its tributaries, they insist that v. 21a''-b should be understood as an independent clause, a declaration concerning Egypt: 'On the place of rivers and broad streams will no galley with oars go nor stately ship pass' (cf. the topic Egypt in Isa. 18:1; 19:5-10; Ezekiel 30 and the lament / dirge over Tyre in Ezekiel 27; Wildberger, 1320f.). In short, while Zion now finds

---

[82] Ollenburger 1987.

[83] Alexander, 17; Delitzsch, 356; Schoors, 199. The interpretation of מקום as 'instead of' (cf. 1 Kgs 21:19; Hos. 2:1) ought to be avoided since the negations of v. 21b would then be left with no meaning (*pace HALAT*, 592; Dillmann-Kittel, 298).

itself miraculously surrounded by rivers, the rich trade which once characterised the Nile delta is now at an end. One argument against such an
explanation is the fact that, prior to the words 'a place of rivers', the text
lacks an adversative element (even a simple *waw*).

For this reason we prefer to opt for the first explanation: 'There,
rather, YHWH will be mighty for us; it is a place of rivers, broad
streams...' ('a place' as apposition to 'there'). Nevertheless, given the
fact that the words 'broad streams (of the Nile)' stand in apposition to
'rivers', they may constitute a gloss allowing potential reference to
Egypt. In the same way, the word 'mighty' as a description of 'ship' in
the next verse line evidently introduces a note of irony following the
mention of the only one to whom such a title can genuinely be ascribed:
YHWH (cf. Duhm, 246).

The imagery of v. 21 is not so unusual when read side by side with
v. 20b. Just as Zion in v. 20b dissolves the division between the city and
the land and her security is no longer dependent on the vagaries of history so here she dissolves the boundaries between water and land. That
Zion is now surrounded by water has nothing to do with her geographical location but is due rather to the fact that YHWH, who has proved himself 'mighty' (אדיר) in the waters of creation (Ps. 93:4) and liberation
(Exod. 15:6,11; 1 Sam. 4:8) as well as on the land (Isa. 10:34; Ps.
8:2,10; 76:5), has now taken her side. Thus, if one does not overesti-
mate the function of v. 21b, v. 21a makes perfect sense. While employing terms for election which may be somewhat unusual, the text is stating, nevertheless, that YHWH has joined himself to this city ('there') and
her inhabitants ('for us'). This is also evident in the way the divine name
is spread throughout the text. After the introduction to the divine utterance in v. 10, the word 'YHWH' appears here again for the first time.
While the prophet was addressing the negative conclusions emerging
from this divine oracle (vv. 14-19), the absence of the name of YHWH
had some meaning. Now that he has turned to the positive aspects of
YHWH's utterance the divine name returns to its rightful place. The name
of YHWH belongs in his city alongside its inhabitants.

22 The portrayal of Zion's inviolability arrives at its roots in the confession of YHWH's kingship (מלך). The divine name itself is mentioned
three times in this verse, together with a single reference thereto ('he'
[הוא]). On all these four occasions, he is the subject of action with respect to the we-figure. Thus, in harmony with the unique dynamic of
ch.33, YHWH's exclusive kingship is here proclaimed over Zion. The
confession also has a function within the structure of PI as a whole. The
prophet himself has already proclaimed the kingship of 'YHWH of hosts'

in the narrative of his mission (6:1) and thereafter on one further occasion as an expectation for 'Mount Zion and Jerusalem' (24:23). In the
present verse, YHWH's kingship becomes the object of the people's confession. Preparation is hereby made for chs. 36-39 in which the term
'(great) king' is employed with frequency for the monarchs of Assyria
and Babylon in narratives which ultimately show that their kingship is
without substance before that of YHWH.[84]

The core word 'king' is prepared for by the terms 'judge' and 'ruler',
and elaborated in the expression 'he will save us'. The Scriptures frequently employ the verb 'to judge' (שׁפט) of YHWH, implying thereby that
God establishes justice in the broadest sense of the word: he promotes
the interests of the weak and helpless, punishes evil-doers and ordains an
objective order in which peace and prosperity flourish (Gen. 16:5;
18:25; Exod. 5:21; Judg. 11:27; 1 Sam. 3:13; 24:13; 1 Kgs 8:32; Isa.
42:26; 51:5; 66:16; Ezek. 7:3,8; 11:10f.; 21:35; 24:18; 36:19; Joel
2:4; Ps. 7:9; 9:9; 26:1; 35:24; 75:8; 82:8; 94:2).[85] The same theme is
also represented in PI: Jerusalem has sinned by her corrupt administration of justice (1:17,23,26; 3:2; 5:3), but YHWH will establish justice
once again through the house of David (11:3f.; 16:5) and judge in Jerusalem between the nations (2:4; for the important term מִשְׁפָּט in PI, cf.
28:6).

In itself, the second term, 'ruler' (מְחֹקֵק), bears the military significance of 'commander' (Deut. 33:21; Judg. 5:14). While this fits to a
degree in the context of the chapter (vv. 18,21b,23), the term is more
likely to be a variant of 'to judge' (cf. the fact that חקק[ה] and מִשְׁפָּט frequently occur together, especially in the plural, in Deuteronomy, Kings,
Ezekiel and Chronicles). The term is not used with any special significance elsewhere in PI (10:1; 24:5; 30:8).

The verb 'to save' (ישע hiphil) connects this confession with the
prayer for intervention in v. 2 and the announcement of rescue in v. 6.
At the same time, it reflects the central theme of BI as a whole, a theme
vouched for by the prophet's own name (see 30:15).

23 According to a less-common interpretation of this verse, the imagery employed here is military in nature and not maritime (cf. 'Notes').
Technically speaking, however, the presentation of the instrument remains the same in both cases. While the 'mast' or 'flag staff' (תֹרֶן) rests
on a 'pedestal' (כֵּן), it is attached to it, at the same time, with 'cords'
(חֲבָלִים) in order to prevent it from swaying. An additional set of 'cords'

---

[84] V. 22 also prepares for and anticipates the topic of YHWH's kingship in the second
half of BI (מֶלֶךְ: 44:21; 43:15; 44:6; 52:7; מָשַׁל: 40:10; 63:19).

[85] TWAT, VIII, 425ff. (H. Niehr).

ensures that the piece of cloth which serves as a signal (or 'sail'; נס) is sufficiently spread out.[86] The imagery contradicts the need for military armament, both offensive and defensive: there will be no banner to signal the place where the troops should establish their operations and place of withdrawal. This verse thus forms the counterpart of 30:17, in which the abandoned banner visually represents the entire flight. Within ch.33, the use of the same term 'cords' (חבלים) in 'the tent... whose cords will not be broken' (v. 20) and the signal 'whose cords hang loose' (v. 23) creates a contrast of imagery. Taken according to their tenor, however, v. 17 and v. 23 offer the promise of unrivalled security for Zion.

The temporal indicator 'then' (אז) in v. 23b calls attention to a specific event in the future (Ps. 56:10; 69:5)[87] rather than implying temporal succession: even without military engagement there will be copious amounts of booty to share out (cf. Isa. 9:2). It is possible that the three words 'booty', 'spoil' and 'to plunder' reflect military practice after a victory in battle. The rare term 'booty' (עד: Gen. 49:27; Zeph. 3:8) may refer to the 'booty' determined by a superior instance which is then shared out as 'spoil' (שלל) according to military rank. Such 'booty' includes prisoners of war (Judg. 5:30), flocks (1 Sam. 14:32; 15:19) and the goods and chattels of conquered cities (Deut. 2:3; Josh. 8:2,27; 2 Sam. 12:30). The term 'to plunder' (בזז) refers to the violent acquisition of persons and goods by the ordinary troops where this is permitted by the military leadership (people: Deut. 20;14; Isa. 10:2; 11:14; 17:14; 42:24; Jer. 30:16; Ezek. 39:10; animals: Num. 31:9; Deut. 2:35; Josh. 8:2,27; precious things: Num. 31:9; Jer. 20:5; Nah. 2:10; merchandise: Ezek. 26:12; Ps. 109:11).[88]

This distinction in meaning may be intended to illustrate the very abundance of the booty: even for the lame, who are normally excluded from acquiring booty and are unable to engage in plundering on account of their disability, there are spoils a plenty (cf. Deut. 15:21; Isa. 35:5f.; Jer. 31:8). It is possible that reference is being made here to the story of the defence of Jebusite Jerusalem in which the blind and the lame took part (2 Sam. 5:6ff.).[89] In this event, the imagery of this segment once again exhibits a surrealistic trait: the inhabitants of the city protected by God from every form of military threat are themselves given the chance to acquire booty.

---

[86] For details, cf. Delitzsch, 357; Dalman, *AuS* VI, 365.

[87] *Ges.[18]*, 29.

[88] The terms שלל and בזז are also frequently synonymous (*TWAT*, I, 586 [H. Ringgren]; *HALAT*, 1417).

[89] Procksch, 424; Kissane, 379; Kaiser 277.

24 In contrast to the rather specific imagery of vv. 20f.,23, the final verse broadens and deepens the picture of the new Zion, establishing redactional connections within BI at the same time.

The connection with the preceding verse is to be found in the verb 'to be ill' (חלה), understood in its general sense of physical and spiritual weakness, as the twilight zone between life and death (cf. Isa. 14:10; 38:1 and 9; 2 Kgs 1:2; 8:7f.,20). Just as the lame are no longer outcast, the population as a whole will no longer have to complain about their needs ('to say' [אמר] in this sense: Isa. 3:7; 4:1; 6:5; 20:6; 22:4; 23:4; 24:16; as an expression of pride: Isa. 9:8; 10:13; 14:13; 19:11; 28:15; 29:15).

This blessing awaits the one who 'abides (there)' (v. 24a). The verb שכן harks back to v. 16: 'he will abide on the heights', thereby applying the blessing to the one who respects the ethical norms of vv. 14f. The parallel element 'the people who dwell there' (העם הישב בה) extends the promise over the entire population of Jerusalem, since the locative 'there', literally 'in her', points beyond v. 21 ('there') to 'Zion / Jerusalem' (v. 20). In the course of ch.33 this implies that 'the insolent people' have made room for a people which has been liberated from sickness and guilt. At the same time, within the broader composition of chs. 28-33, reference is made here to 30:19: 'Truly, a people shall dwell in Zion (כי עם בציון ישב), in Jerusalem you shall weep no more' (cf. 32:18). V. 24 ultimately refers back to the opening of BI as a whole: 'Woe, sinful nation, a people (עם) laden with iniquity (עון)' (1:4), all the more so in light of the fact that 'iniquity' is portrayed as an illness in 1:5f. (חלי).[90]

The term 'iniquity' (עון) brings an important theme of PI to completion. YHWH, the Holy One, has gone to war with sinfulness of every kind, both in Israel (1:4; 5:18; 6:7; 22:14; 27:9; 30:13; cf. the name 'Holy' in these contexts: 1:4; 5:19; 6:3; 30:12) and among the nations (13:11; 14:21). The formulation of v. 24 presents forgiveness as something which is bestowed on the people (passive participle of נשא; cf. Ps. 32:1), not as a process of carrying and expiating sins (נשא עון in active verb forms: Gen. 4:13; Lev. 5:17; 24:15; Num. 9:13; 2 Kgs 18:14; Ezek. 16:58; 44:9-14; Mic. 7:9). Strikingly enough, this isotope returns at the opening of DI: 'Comfort my people... / speak to the heart of Jerusalem... that her iniquity is pardoned' (40:1-2; here also in a passive verb form). Thus v. 24 exhibits both a retrospective and a prospective construction (Williamson 1994: 225f.).

The various references incorporated within v. 24 serve to reinforce the character of ch.33 as a provisional apotheosis of PI.

---

[90] This reference to the beginning of BI strongly resembles the procedure whereby the word pair 'the ox and the ass' in 32:20 harks back to 1:3 (cf. the exegesis of 32:20).

CALL TO THE NATIONS TO WITNESS
THE PUNISHMENT OF EDOM (34:1-17)

1   Draw near, O nations, to hear,
      and hearken, O peoples!
   Let the earth listen, and all that fills it;
      the world, and all that comes from it.

2   Truly, YHWH is enraged against all the nations,
      and furious against all their host.
         He has doomed them, has given them over for slaughter.

3   Their slain shall be cast out,
      and the stench of their corpses shall rise.
         The mountains shall flow with their blood.

4   (All the host of heaven shall rot away.)
   The heavens roll up like a scroll.
      all their host shall fall,
   as leaves fall from the vine,
      like leaves falling from the fig tree.

5   Truly, my sword has appeared in the heavens.
      Behold, it descends upon Edom,
         upon the people I have doomed – for judgement.

6   YHWH has a sword; it is sated with blood.
      It is gorged with fat,
   with the blood of lambs and goats,
      with the fat of the kidneys of rams.
   Truly, YHWH has a sacrifice in Bozrah,
      a great slaughter in the land of Edom.

7   Wild oxen shall go down with them,
      and young steers with the mighty bulls.
   Their land shall be soaked with blood,
      and their soil made rich with fat.

8   Truly, YHWH has a day of vengeance,
      a year of recompense for the cause of Zion.

9   Her streams shall be turned into pitch,
      and her soil into brimstone.

Her land shall become
   burning pitch.
10 Night and day it shall not be quenched;
     its smoke shall go up for ever.
  From generation to generation it shall lie waste;
     none shall pass through it for ever and ever.
11 But the hawk and the porcupine shall possess it,
     the owl and the raven shall dwell in it.
  He shall stretch the line of confusion over it,
     and the plummet of chaos.
12 For its nobles – they shall proclaim no kingship,
     and all its princes shall be nothing.
13 Thorns shall grow over its strongholds,
     nettles and thistles in its fortresses.
  It shall be the haunt of jackals,
     an abode for ostriches.
14 Wild beasts shall meet with hyenas,
     the satyr shall cry to his fellow.
  Yea, there shall the night hag alight,
     and find for herself a resting-place.
15 There shall the arrow-snake nest and lay
     and hatch and foster her young in her shadow.
  Yea, there shall the kites be gathered,
     each one with her mate.
16 Seek and read from the book of YHWH.
  Not one of these shall be missing;
     none shall be without her mate.
  Truly, by my mouth he has ordered it,
     and by his spirit he has brought them together.
17 He has cast the lot for them,
     his hand has portioned it out to them with the line.
  They shall possess it for ever,
     from generation to generation they shall dwell in it.

NOTES

3-4 These verses have preoccupied exegetes because the assonant verb forms ונמסו (v. 3b) and ונמקו (v. 4a) do not appear in a parallel verse line and 'all the host of heaven' is mentioned too early and twice: before 'the heavens' (v. 4a´) as well as after it (v. 4b´). A traditional conjecture

which reads 'hills' instead of the first 'the host of heaven' (הגבעות instead of צבא השמים; vv. 3b-4a: 'The mountains shall flow with their
blood, and all *the hills* shall rot away'), seems to offer a solution to both
problems but it receives no support from the versions (Bickel 1882;
Duhm, 249; *BHS*). The earlier versions confirm the existence of the two
problems. V. 4a′ is missing in LXX. Instead of the first word of v. 4a
(ונמקו), 1QIsᵃ reads the following clause: והעמקים יתבקעו ('The valleys
shall be split'), apparently borrowed from Mic. 1:4 (Kutscher, 273), and
adds יבולו, evidently taken from v. 4b′, to the remainder of v. 4a′ (כל
צבא השמים), with the result that the clause 'all their host shall fall' (v.
4b′) is anticipated by the clause 'all the host of heaven shall fall'. In
other words, one of the problems of MT remains. The reading of the
original text is hard to find. The plus of 1QIsᵃ ('valleys') seems to be inspired by the want of a parallel to 'mountains' in the text of MT. V. 4a′
of the latter might stem from a desire to have the host of heaven suffering from the slaughter on earth (cf. the problem of the next verse). Consequently, there is a possibility that LXX in which v. 4a' is missing offers the original reading.

5 1QIsᵃ reads 'has appeared' (תראה) instead of 'has drunk its fill'
(רותה), in conformity with Tg (תתגלי; cf. Josephus, *BJ*, VI, 289). The
same reading was proposed even prior to the discovery of 1QIsᵃ because
it appears more logical that the sword would not quench its thirst for
blood in the heavens but rather on the earth (cf. v. 7b; Deut. 32:42; Jer.
46:10). It is probable that the transmission of the text is closely connected to problems which arose in the history of its interpretation with
respect to the role of celestial bodies. Given that Isa. 24:21 is conscious
of a punishment in the heavens prior to that on earth, it seems reasonable
to maintain the MT (likewise LXX, Vg and Syr; Barthélemy, 236ff.;
Kutscher, 285). The parallel 'behold', however, supports the Qumran
reading which we prefer to follow here.

12 There does not appear to be sufficient reason to read the difficult
first word of this verse חריה ('nobles') as part of v. 11 (RSV) or to
emend it to read חדיה (REB: 'frontiers' [following Driver 1937: 46,
who bases himself on an Akkadian word]). All of the versions have rendered the term with a word referring to the leading classes. The interpretation 'caves' as a metonym for the people who live therein (cf. 1 Sam.
14:11; Nah. 2:13; Job 30:6), is also far-fetched (*pace* Alexander, 27;
cf. his survey of interpretations). Parallelism with 'princes' supports the
traditional explanation 'nobles'. We are left with the question whether
the proleptic term 'nobles' is subject or object of the verb יקראו. If, on
the basis of Gen. 36:31-39, one can assume that the kings in Edom were

elected, one might then propose that the 'nobles' should be understood as the electoral college and the 'princes' in v. 12b as the candidates for the throne (Delitzsch, 361; Procksch, 431; Barthélemy, 240f.). We follow this explanation here. The term 'kingship' is perhaps an *abstractum pro concreto* for 'king' (Oswalt, 615f.).

13 For the most part, commentators read חצר, 'abode', instead of חציר, 'grass', in conformity with 1QIsᵃ, LXX, Syr and Tg (one encounters the same situation in 35:7).

15 The word קפוז is rendered by the RSV as 'owl' (likewise ינשוף in v. 11b). Although many commentators are of the opinion that the term refers to a bird, because there is mention of a 'nest' and 'to lay eggs' (REB: 'sand-partridge'; Torrey, 292f.), *HALAT* (1044; already Ges-B) interprets the word as 'arrow-snake'. Snakes are also considered to be impure animals (Lev. 11:10; Deut. 14:10).

16a Some data give credence to the suggestion that v. 16a' (דרשו מעל ספר יהוה וקראו) is a gloss (Lauterjung 1979). From the standpoint of colometry, the phrase either forms a monocolon or it is prose (Wildberger, 1334). The LXX's translation, using only one verb (ἀριθμῷ παρῆλθον), leads one to suspect that one of the two verb forms in v. 16a MT, דרשו or וקראו, is itself an addition (*BHS*). The unfamiliar preposition could point to an attempt to reduce the two verb forms to a common denominator, since the second of the two has no object.

It is consequently strange that we hear on two occasions that the animals appear in pairs (vv. 15b,16a [2nd and 3d colon]). From a textual point of view, these clauses are similarly fraught with problems. In v. 15b MT ('each one *with* her mate'), the preposition is sorely missed. V. 16a‴ ('none shall be without her mate') partly repeats v. 15b. While the words אשה רעותה form a better sentence with לא פקדו in v. 16a‴ than with נקבצו in v. 15b, the former verb form is absent from 1QIsᵃ. Perhaps v. 16a‴ is intended to ensure that v. 16a″ ('not one of these shall be missing') refers to the list of animals.

16b The translation of the RSV ('For the mouth of YHWH has commanded, and his Spirit has gathered them') is based on frequently chosen solutions for two difficulties in MT: (1) פי stands for פי יהוה (likewise LXX; 1QIsᵃ [פיהו הוא], Syr and Tg follow the same interpretation: 'his mouth'); (2) the suffix attached to רוחו refers to the presumed divine name in the preceding colon. Where the first problem is concerned, Vg and Luther maintain MT: 'quia quod ex ore meo procedit ille mandavit' and 'Denn er ists der durch meinen Mund gebeut' respectively. Given that it is part of the biblical idiom that God speaks through the mouth of a prophet, one is left with insufficient reason to mistrust the MT. In a context which refers to 'the book of YHWH', moreover, an allusion on the part of the 'implied prophet' to his own role is not unusual. For this reason we translate: 'By my mouth he has ordered it' (*pace* Orlinsky 1954: 88ff.: The Hebrew *Vorlage* of LXX was original with regard to MT). With respect to the second colon, the personal pronoun הוא is usually considered to be a reference to the preceding word רוחו. If this were correct one would be obliged to understand רוח as masculine here – a possibility indeed, albeit quite rare (*HALAT*, 1117: 14x from a total of 378x) and never where it concerns the spirit of YHWH himself. The problem vanishes if one considers רוחו, parallel to פי, as an *accusativus modi*: 'by his spirit he has brought them together' (Barthélemy, 242f.; REB). The contrast between 'my mouth' and 'his spirit' then functions in the distinction between the way in which God announces something and the way in which he brings it about.

ESSENTIALS AND PERSPECTIVES

In the final form of BI one can only view ch.34 and ch.35 side by side, wedged as they are between the two substantially autonomous blocks of chs. 28-33 (six woe cries and a call to mourn) and chs. 36-39 (narratives in prose). Broadly speaking, they stand in contrast to one another as salvation and judgement. In addition, they have a number of terms in common, some of which are quite significant and clearly reveal that the chapters are attuned to one another (34:8: 'YHWH has a day of vengeance', and 35:4: 'Behold, your God will come with vengeance'; 'streams' in 34:9 and 35:6; 'shall not pass' in 34:10 and 35:8; 'haunt of jackals' in 34:13 and 35:7; 'abode' in 34:13 and 35:7 [corr.]; a threefold 'there' in 34:14f. and 35:8f.). It is for these reasons that commentators often refer to the diptych as the 'Minor Apocalypse' of BI, simultaneously underlining the connection between the two chapters.[1] It remains improbable, however, that the chapters constitute a single draft, especially since ch.35 clearly does not advance the judgement on the nations in ch.34 as the basis for Zion's salvation (Wildberger, 1355f.). From the redactional perspective, moreover, significant terminological agreement establishes the important role of ch.35 in the association of PI with DI and TI (Steck 1985), while ch.34 is less remarkable as such (Graetz 1891) and exhibits a greater tendency to look back to PI,[2] espe-

---

[1] Vermeylen 1977, 439; Peels 1995: 148ff.
[2] Beuken 1992; Williamson 1994: 215-21.

cially since it is semantically and structurally very similar to the prophecy against Babylon in ch.13.[3] Thus the relationship between ch.34 and ch.35 is not so much a question of authorship but rather of the final redaction of BI.[4] In this respect, the fact that this prophecy concerning Edom is not included among the oracles against the foreign nations (chs. 13-23) says a great deal.[5] There would seem to be a stronger argument in favour of viewing ch.34 rather than ch.35 as the interpolated conclusion to PI, whereby the identity of the enemy of God's people underwent a typological shift from Babylon, which is characterised as such in ch.13, to Edom. This would have happened partly because of the fact that Babylon has a further role to play in chs. 40-48. As a consequence of the interpolation of ch.34, it appeared to be necessary to insert ch.35, bearing in mind the specific promise of return through the desert in ch.40.[6]

The redactional purport of ch.34 is closely linked with the relationship between the nations (vv. 1-4) and Edom (vv. 5-15) portrayed therein. From a literary-historical perspective, scholars have explained the opening verses as an expansion of an announcement of judgement, possibly at the hand of the redactor of ch.35,[7] which was originally limited to Edom. The chapter is also depicted as a combination of three prophecies – against the nations (vv. 2-3[4],7), against Edom (vv. 5f.) and against Zion (vv. 8-15) –, whereby the redaction of PI introduced a coordinative relationship with ch.13 and ch.1. Thus the redaction Edom, Babylon and Zion to be the embodiment of corrupt humanity.[8] The redactional perspective does indeed point the way. It is significant that the overall literary genre of ch.34 constitutes a 'prophetic instruction' rather than an announcement of judgement (vv. 1,16f.).[9] The judgement whereby YHWH equates Edom with Sodom and Gomorrah was intended as a lesson for the nations (vv. 2-4). While it is clear that 'YHWH is enraged against all the nations' (v. 2) and has already pronounced his judgement against them (vv. 3f.), the implementation of the sentence is limited to Edom and serves as a warning to all the nations that YHWH exercises power over them.[10]

---

[3] Vermeylen 440f.; Gosse 1988: 159ff.; *id.*, 1990; Zapff 1995: 240-57.

[4] A survey of the interpretations of chs. 34-35 can be found in Mathews 1995: 9-33; Zapff 1995: 240-8; Sweeney 1996: 435, 441-4.

[5] Mathews 1955: 157.

[6] Williamson 1994: 213-21.

[7] According to Steck (1985: 49-59), 34:1,5-15 even constitute the original continuation of ch. 33*. Williamson (1994: 217-20), however, has raised a number of objections to this.

[8] Lust 1989; cf. the discussion with Mathews 1995: 19f.

[9] Sweeney 1996: 435-41.

[10] Steck 1985: 53f.; Mathews 1995: 35-42; Peels 1995: 151f.; Sweeney 1996: 444ff.

In this way, ch.34 conforms to the broader intention of BI. The execution of judgement against Edom is not conceived from the perspective of ethnic contrast (Israel versus Edom) but from the theological perspective of the composition of the book as a whole. It is not Israel which is summoned to hear the decision of judgement, but the nations. It is the nations with whom YHWH enters into discussion further down the line (41:1), in the same way as will his Servant (49:1). The semantic affinity between these texts compels us to recognise the continuing course of BI as a principle of meaning, and to account for the relationship of the nations with Edom in such a way that they are not immediately to share the latter's ruin. Before the story of the salvation of Jerusalem (chs. 36-39) and the effective consolation of the city in DI (chs. 40-55), the redaction wanted to show in the course of BI that the judgement of the nations, announced with vigour in chs. 13-33, was not an idle threat but would somehow be realised, if only against Edom. This would have seemed necessary since the lawsuit against the nations is fully unfolded in DI. The redaction was obliged, on the one hand, to allow the judgement against the nations, announced by PI, to take place somehow before the consolation of Jerusalem. On the other hand, it had to recognise the respite that the nations enjoy in DI. It has given form to this tension by connecting the decision of the judgement of the nations with the execution of the destruction of Edom at the point of the transition from PI to DI. The nations are now witnesses to the decision and the execution, not because they deserved better, but because for them, within the same BI, the possibility exists of recognising YHWH as the only ruler of the earth (45:22-25).

Given the position of the chapter in BI, the role of Edom is both symbolic and concrete. Just as Assyria (ch.10), Babylon (chs. 13-14) and many other nations (chs. 14-23) were to experience YHWH's supremacy in his judgement, the same was to be the case for the neighbouring nation Edom, located to the southeast of the Dead Sea. Edom had been Israel's enemy throughout the centuries.[11] From a geographical perspective, both nations found themselves in a natural dispute concerning the possession of the Negev and access to the Red Sea (Num. 34:3; Josh. 15:1; 1 Sam. 14:47; 2 Sam. 8:13; 1 Kgs 9:26; 11:14-22; 22:48; 2 Kgs 8:20ff.; 14:7; 24:2).[12] This situation gave birth to the genre of an-

---

[11] Cf. Bartlett 1989: 83-102: 'Ch. 5. Edom in the Late Second Millennium BCE: The Biblical Evidence'.

[12] It would appear from numerous Ancient Near Eastern texts that during Assyrian rule, the pressure on Edom was just as intense as that on Judah. There was nothing to be gained, therefore, from engaging in a war and in fact everything to be gained from political co-operation between the two nations (Jer. 27:3). In contrast, the Babylonians were

nouncements of judgement against Edom (Num. 24:18; Isa. 11:14; Jer. 9:25; 25:15-25; 49:7-22; Ezek. 25:12-14; 35; 36:5; Joel 4:19; Amos 1:11f.; Ob. 8-15; Mal. 1:4; Lam. 4:21f.). In the exilic period, however, Edom was transformed from 'an' enemy to 'the' enemy, probably because it had taken possession of southern Judah.[13] Thus the fact that Edom embodies the judgement now being carried through leans on both the traditional content of this name and the exilic situation in particular. In ch.34, however, this reference is not limited to the identity of Israel's rival. In the context of world judgement, Edom no longer represents herself alone, but stands as an example for all nations, both now and in the future, who would dare to rise up against YHWH. The new model combines the old image of Edom with that of Sodom and Gomorrah (cf. Jer. 49:18). Indeed, the description of the land overtaken by YHWH's judgement is reminiscent of the story of the destruction of these cities (cf. Isa. 34:9f. with Gen. 19:24f.,28). Edom thereby becomes a *Chiffre* for tyrannical powers wherever they might be who would resist YHWH's dominion in Zion.[14]

In the same way as 'Edom' derives its content from the literary-theological construction of ch.34, so do 'the nations'. In as far as 'the rage' of YHWH hangs over them (v. 2), the idea of 'the nations' retains the traditional meaning which it derives from the oracles against the nations. In as far as the nations learn that the judgement is resolute but must first descend on Edom (vv. 1-7), however, they find themselves rather on Israel's side, the land which traditionally fulfils the role of spectator at the downfall of Edom (Ezekiel 35; Psalm 137). Now that these roles merge, the nations – both invited to hear the judgement (v. 1) and placed under the wrath (v. 2) – are turned into a *Chiffre* with a unique content. They now embody those who can still learn something from the pronouncement of judgement.

Consequently, as far as the final form of the chapter is concerned, it has to be said that the nations and Edom do not coincide.[15] The differentiation between the four attributes of God, which bring about his judgement, has a function. YHWH's 'rage' hangs over the nations (vv. 2-3). A

known to exploit the rivalry between the smaller states along the edge of the Arabian desert (2 Kgs 24:2; cf. Wildberger, 1335-9).

[13] Bartlett 1989: 186; Glazier-McDonald 1995: 31.

[14] Mathews 1995: 171-8

[15] In the explanation of some authors, the symbolic interpretation blurs the functional difference between the nations and Edom. In this case, the general judgement over the nations is particularised into that over Edom (Alexander, 19; Duhm, 248; Penna 312; Snijders, 329f.; Oswalt, 608). This interpretation generally goes hand in hand with explanations that fail to understand v. 1 as a summons to instruction.

destruction awaits them in which both heaven and earth will be involved
(v. 4). The wording points more to a divine decision concerning the destiny of the nations and the world than to its realisation. Conversely, the
'sword' has prepared itself in the heavens for its task and now it advances in all reality against Edom (vv. 5-6a). Thus we see the judgement
of the world descending from heaven and beginning to be carried out
upon this particular people. In this way, the nations can learn from what
happens to Edom. It is implied, therefore, that they enjoy a respite although YHWH's 'rage' has already turned against them.

The end of the chapter (vv. 16-17) functions as a *metatext* next to the
preceding 'instruction for the nations' because it invites its audience to
place the outcome of the prophecy against the background of the 'the
book of YHWH'. The speaker is not actively engaged within the instruction, he reveals rather how one is to verify its reliability. It is likely that
this segment was originally limited to the assurance that the animals
mentioned in vv. 11-15 would indeed inhabit the land of Edom because
YHWH had commanded it and his spirit had brought it about (v. 16b). The
probable interpolation 'seek and read from the book of YHWH' (v. 16a)
bases the realisation of the prophecy in question, i.e. the gathering of the
aforementioned animals, on the fact that they are announced in the
Scriptures. Thus the guarantee of reliability becomes a guideline for
reading.

The addition seems to be inspired by the fact that ch.34, as we shall
see, reveals several analogies with BI and other texts which would have
a place in 'the book of YHWH' (cf. 'Exegesis by Verse'). The author of
the exhortation in v. 16 may have been aware of these analogies but he
was particularly interested in the animals, most of all in their appearance
in Isaiah 13, Leviticus 11, Deuteronomy 14 and Zephaniah 2, and in
their qualification as unclean in the Torah texts mentioned. The original
author of ch. 34 used allusive language in order to convey the Isaianic
foundation of his prophecy to his readers. The interpolator of v. 16a,
however, presents himself as a scribe next to the prophet and points to
the similarity of this passage with preceding oracles of Isaiah and other
biblical writings.

In this way, the reading guideline brings about an 'over-interpreta-
tion'. While the allusive style of the entire chapter tries to induce the
readers themselves to make the many semantic connections between
ch.34 and the first and the second halves of BI, and thereby lay down
conceptual links between the two parts of the book, the guideline directs
them to limit themselves to the list of animals and to further explore the
fact that these appear elsewhere in Scripture. The interpolator has partly

understood what the author of ch.34 wanted to achieve but he has over-publicised that intention. At the same time he re-orders the latter's concern for the semantic coherence of the ch.34 with BI into scribal preoccupation for the objective concordance of animal names throughout the Old Testament.

Moreover, the interpolator has changed the intended audience of the chapter. It can hardly be his purpose to invite the nations, the addressees of the beginning of the chapter (v. 1), to 'seek and read in the book of YHWH'.[16] This summons must have Israel itself in mind. The change of addressee, however, is not lost. What was intended to be a lesson for the nations – i.e. the fate of Edom, the progeny of Esau – ought to be taken into account by Israel, the progeny of Jacob.

SCHOLARLY EXPOSITION

Introduction to the Exegesis: Form and Setting

The chapter includes two direct addresses: an appeal to the 'nations / peoples' to listen (v. 1) and an invitation to study the Scriptures directed to a group which is not further identified but one which is familiar with the Scriptures nonetheless (v. 16a). An account of the judgement in purely descriptive language follows the first direct address (vv. 2-15) while the second is followed by a guarantee of YHWH's reliability (vv. 16b-17). The chapter's two primary parts are thus evident (vv. 1-15 and vv. 16-17).

The first part appeals to the nations to acquaint themselves with YHWH's judgement upon them and its realisation upon Edom which now takes effect (vv. 2-8), and follows this with a description of the land which has experienced judgement employing language from the lament genres (vv. 9-15).

The structure of the first segment, vv. 2-8, is defined by four themes: 'the rage of YHWH' (vv. 2-4), 'the sword of YHWH' (vv. 5-6a), 'the sacrifice of YHWH' (vv. 6b-7) and 'the day of YHWH' (v. 8; Muilenburg 1940: 342f.). These words occur in the same phrasing: the respective noun – קצף, חרב, זבח and יום נקם - with ליהוה. In three cases the noun is immediately preceded by the particle כי (vv. 2,6b,8). In the second section, the particle introduces the topic, 'the sword of YHWH', in a different way (v. 5: כי רותה בשמים חרבי) and follows the characteristic phrasing, חרב ליהוה, one line later (v. 6). This deviation from the pattern may be due to

[16] *Pace* Sweeney, 438-41.

the fact that only here in the chapter does the announcement of judgement proceed from the mouth of YHWH (v. 5: 'My sword... the people I have doomed') and not from the mouth of the prophet.

The second segment, vv. 9-15, does not appear to have a fixed structure. It describes the announced devastation at first in terms of Sodom and Gomorrah (vv. 9-10) and then in terms of the animals which will occupy the once cultivated land (vv. 11,14-15). The descriptions are interrupted by two different topics: there will no longer be an authoritative structure (v. 12) and the flora associated with abandoned places will overrun the strongholds and fortresses (v. 13).

The second part of the chapter, vv. 16-17, urges the reader to verify the fulfilment of the foregoing prophecy 'in the book of YHWH'. It is also deeply involved with the chapter's central subject: 'the land of Edom' (v. 6b; cf.v. 5). This is apparent from v. 17. On three occasions here there is talk of an object which is expressed by a feminine suffix: 'His hand has portioned *it* out... They shall possess *it*... they shall dwell in *it*' (חלקתה / ירשוה / ישכנו בה). The antecedent of this objectival suffix is missing from the immediate context (גורל, metonymically used for 'the allotted land', in v. 17a cannot be the antecedent since this word is masculine). The reference runs back via the triple 'there' in vv. 14b-15 to the same verbs with feminine suffixes in v. 11: 'The hawk and the porcupine shall possess *it*, the owl and the raven shall dwell in *it*'. Here, the question of antecedent arises once again. The reference goes back via the feminine suffixes and prefixes of vv. 9-10 ('*Her* streams... *her* soil... *her* land... *it* shall lay waste... none shall pass through *it*...) and the terms 'their land / their soil' in v. 7b to 'Bozrah / the land of Edom' in v. 6b.[17] We encounter here an uncommonly long tension curve concerning an object of interest assumed in the entire text but not restated.

The predominant interest in the land of Edom is decisive for the first question with which we are occupied in v. 16. Does the statement: 'Not one of these shall be missing; none shall be without her mate' refer to the events announced in vv. 2-15 or to the animals mentioned in vv. 11-15?[18] Both explanations are philologically possible (Donner 1990: 285), but the central topic of the land of Edom favours the latter explanation.

[17] Only a few commentators suggest that the suffixes in v. 17 refer to the land of Edom: Alexander, 33; Delitzsch, 363; Dillmann-Kittel, 305.

[18] Tanghe (1991) defends a third possibility. In his opinion, 'not one of these is missing, none shall be without her mate' (v. 16a) refers to the lands of the nations. Vv. 16-17 then contains a refutation of vv. 1-15: no land shall disappear because God himself assigned the lands to the nations. It remains difficult to grasp, however, how a land could be 'missing' or how lands 'miss' one another (פקד).

Interest lies with the land that these animals are going to inhabit. The devastation of Edom will indeed be so terrifying that all twelve of these creatures which inhabit ruins will be encountered there. For YHWH has so ordered it (v. 16b). In vv. 16b-17a the plural suffixes refer to these animals in the same way as the singular feminine suffixes refer to the land ('By his spirit he has brought them together. He has cast the lot for *them*, his hand has apportioned it out to *them* with the line'). In v. 17b they form the subject ('*They* shall possess it forever... *they* shall dwell in it').

A second question arises at this point. An invitation to verify that all the animals mentioned do indeed inhabit the land which has been struck by God's judgement is imaginable in a prophetic context but why and how must the readers verify this 'in the book of YHWH'? The assumption presents itself that the exhortation of v. 16a´ ('Seek and read from the book of YHWH') restructures the original purpose of the passage, i.e. to check the presence of these animals in the land of Edom, by inviting the readers to verify that all these animals are mentioned *in the Scriptures*. This incitement to perform a scribal investigation is likely to stem from a later date, as does the concept of 'the book of YHWH' (the text-critical situation seems to confirm this; cf. 'Notes'). The assertion that all these animals can be found in the Scriptures, however, does not tally with the facts. The 'night hag' and 'the arrow-snake' (vv. 14-15) appear nowhere else in the Bible and the 'porcupine' (v. 12), 'the hyena' and the 'wild beast' (v. 14) do not appear in the Pentateuch. In order to prove the assertion we would have to understand 'the book of YHWH' to be the Pentateuch with the Prophets. Nonetheless, even in that case two animals are missing.

The chapter thus reveals the following structure:[19]

1-15   instruction for the nations: judgement
    1   summons to listen
    2-15   the realisation of judgement
            2-8   YHWH's punitive action under four metaphors
                    2-4   'the rage of YHWH' against the nations
                    4-6a   'the sword of YHWH' upon Edom
                    6b-7   'the sacrifice of YHWH' in Bozrah
                    8   'the day of vengeance of YHWH' for Zion
            9-15   a description of the devastated land
                   9-10   everlasting desolation

---

[19] This schema is partly based on the genre-critical structure provided by Sweeney, 437f.

11a	the entry of unclean birds
11b	the entry of chaos
12	the breakdown of social order
13a	the entry of waste vegetation
13b-15	the entry of desert animals

16-17 confirmation of YHWH's power to bring about judgement
    16a´   summons to investigate 'the book of YHWH'
    16a´´   the foreseeable result: none shall be missing
    16b-17 confession of YHWH's power
        16b-17a YHWH's action
        17b   consequences: everlasting presence of the animals

With respect to the dating of the chapter as a whole – apart from the interpolation in v. 16a´ which presumes an early form of a biblical canon – recent redaction-historical research no longer seems interested in the period immediately after the destruction of Jerusalem during which Edom was perhaps more at liberty to assault defenceless Judah (cf. 2 Kgs 24:2; Ezek. 25:12; 35:5; Amos 1:11; Joel 4:19; Ob 11; Mal. 1:2-5; Ps. 137:7; Lam. 4:21f.), but concerning which little historical data is available to us.[20] The chapter would appear to stem from a more advanced phase in the genesis of BI. Depending on the weight commentators are inclined to ascribe to resonances with PI or to the relationship between ch.34 and 63:1-6, they consider the chapter to have been designed as a conclusion to PI and/or a bridge to DI and TI. The chapter would then date from just before or at the same time as the final redaction of BI as a whole. In this context the question as to whether the redaction of PI constituted a more or less independent process plays a significant role. It remains a further point of dispute whether the chapter precedes the interpolation of chs. 36-39 or whether it came into exist with the said interpolation in view. It would seem impossible to provide anything more than a relative date for the chapter at some point during the fifth century.

Exegesis by Verse

1 The present chapter opens with a 'summons to listen' to a teaching concerning the particular situation of the addressees (cf. Joel 4:9-12; Mic. 1:2),[21] and not with the 'summons to witness' addressed to a third party, which one would expect in the context of a lawsuit, given, moreo-

---

[20] Bartlett 1982:13-24; *AncBD*, II, 292f.
[21] Mathews 1995: 35-41.

ver, the parallels of this genre-critical form in BI as a whole (Deut. 32:1; Isa. 1:2; 41:1; 43:9; 45:20; 49:1; Jer. 6:18; 31:10).[22] The 'nations' are not invited in the first instance to observe YHWH's judgement upon Edom but rather his judgement against themselves (vv. 2-4). This is evident from the fact that the 'nations' themselves are both addressee (v. 1) and object (v. 2) of the announcement.

By way of verbal agreements with other texts in BI, the summons in question establishes connections with both DI and PI. In v. 1a, the vocatives 'nations / peoples' point to 43:9 and the verbs 'to hear / to hearken' to 49:1. The word pair 'earth / world' in v. 1b is reminiscent of 18:3; 24:4; 26:9,18, the expression 'the earth and all that fills it' of 6:3; 8:8 and 'all that comes from it' of 42:5; 44:3; 48:9; 61:9; 65:23. (The two latter terms do not refer here to the plant world but to the inhabitants of the earth; cf. LXX.) In other words, the verbal affinity of 34:1 is concentrated on specific reference points in BI. The summons does not simply announce once again the judgement against the nations, but situates their verdict between the vision of YHWH of hosts which inaugurates the judgement of Israel (ch.6) and the mission of the Servant, which is also to the nations (42:5f.; 49:1-6). This allusive style prepares the particular construction of the relationship between the nations and Edom in this chapter.[23]

2-4 The segment 'the rage of YHWH' describes God's action (v. 2) as well as the consequences thereof: death's omnipresence (v. 3) and the decline of the heavenly bodies (v. 4). The expression 'all their host' (vv. 2,4: כל צבאם; cf. 24:21; 40:26; 45:12) connects both domains, makes the extent of the destruction explicit and hints at the emptiness of earth and heaven in the aftermath of the disaster.

The terms of the word pair 'rage / fury' (חמה / קצף) are almost absent in PI ('fury' further in 27:4), although they are to be found separately in DI and TI (the root קצף in 47:6; 54:9; 57:16f.; 58:8; 60:10; 64:4,8; חמה in 42:25; 51:17,20,22; 59:18; 63:3,5f.; 66:15). While Gods 'rage' (likewise his 'fury' in DI) always has to do with Israel in PI, in TI it has to do with the nations. It is evident, therefore, that at the level of both terminology and content ch.34 anticipates the theme of 'judgement on the nations' found in the second half of BI. At the same time, however, ch.34 builds upon developments in PI in which the theme of 'the reversal of YHWH's anger' – from Israel to her oppressors – plays an important role, albeit in different terminology (cf. 10:25 to 5:25; 9:11, 16,20; 10:4). The enemy whose downfall is announced in 10:25 is

---

[22] *pace* Wildberger, 1330f.
[23] Beuken 1992: 79f.

Assyria, which at the same time is compared to Egypt and Midian (v. 26). In a word, Assyria is exemplary for the nations. In PI, from 10:25 onwards, the theme of God's wrath against the nations is continued by a variety of terms (אף: 13:3,9,13; 30:27,30; זעם: 13:5; 26:20; 30:27; חרון and עברה: 13:9,13; זעף: 30:30). It would appear, therefore, that the word pair קצף / חמה, characteristic terms in the second half of BI, pursues a typical theme from PI, the judgement of the nations, into 34:2 and connects it with TI. The fact that we only have a description of the actualisation of the judgement, and not the motivation behind it, makes it evident that it was assumed to be something real.

Viewed from a contemporary perspective, the terms 'rage' and 'fury', as descriptive of YHWH, might easily be misunderstood as an unseemly emotion or utterance of aggression which admits of no excuse on the part of God. In such a case the terms would constitute a further example of the erroneous belief that the Old Testament represents an impure image of YHWH. The semantic field surrounding these concepts, however, makes it clear that they stand for God's reaction to Israel's sin (Deut. 9:22; Isa. 64:4; Ps. 38:4 and 2 Kgs 22:13; Jer. 4:4; Ps. 89: 47) and that of the nations (Jer. 10:10; 50:13 and Isa. 63:3,6; Ezek. 30:15; Mic. 5:14) as well as for YHWH's determination to restore social order and his bond with humanity (Isa. 54:9; Zech. 1:2f.; Lam. 5:22; and Deut. 29:26f.; Ezek. 20:13,21). The Scriptures themselves evaluate God's anger positively as a means to establish his just dominion (Ps. 59:14; 79:6).

Moreover, the form of the expression employed here, literally: 'There is rage (fury) for YHWH' (קצף ליהוה), shows signs of an endeavour to set YHWH apart from his anger and to view it as an almost autonomous function (with regard to 'rage', cf. Num. 17:11 [RSV: 16:46]; Zech. 7:12; 2 Chr. 19:2 with Jer. 50:13; 2 Chr. 29:8; 32:26; with regard to 'fury', cf. Deut. 9:19; Isa. 51:20; Jer. 6:11; Ezek. 5:13; 21:22 [17]; 25:14; 2 Chr. 36:16 with 2 Kgs 22:13; 2 Chr. 28:9). Although the third colon ('He has doomed them, has given them over for slaughter') seems to regard the act of punishment as something stemming from YHWH himself, the verbs in question assume at the same time that the execution of the judgement will be carried out by others. The verb 'to doom' (חרם), on the other hand, typifies the act of punishment as something sacred (God as initiative subject of 'to doom' [חרם]: Josh. 11:20; Isa. 11:15; 43:28; Jer. 25:9; 50:21; Zech. 14:11; Mal. 3:24). One can only conclude, therefore, that the language of poetry, while not familiar with the principle of correct theological terminology, reveals signs nevertheless of its discomfort with overly human representations of YHWH.

The lines which follow portray the horrors of the slaughter employing topics from war reports and traditional imagery. The extent of the slaughter constitutes the background of v. 3. The dead are so numerous that their corpses must be left unburied (cf. Isa. 14:19f.; Jer. 36:30; Ezek. 16:5; Amos 4:10; Joel 2:20; Nah. 3:3; Lam. 2:21), a situation which would have been considered contemptible (Deut. 28:26; 2 Sam. 21:10ff.; Jer. 7:33; Ezek. 32:5; Tob. 2:3f.). A surrealistic digression depicts the superabundance of blood as causing the mountains to melt ('mountains' as theatre of war: Isa. 5;25; 13:4; 14:25; 18:3,6; 30:17; contrast: 25:6f.).

In conjunction with the moderately cosmic motif of 'the mountains', v. 4 further extends the judgement to include the total collapse of the heavens (cf. Isa. 13:10,13; 51:6; 65:17; 66:22; Joel 2:10,30f.; Ps. 102:27). If one takes into account the fact that the religious culture of the time considered the celestial bodies to be gods and protectors of the nations (cf. Deut. 4:19; 17:3; 2Kgs 17:16; 21:3,5; 23:4f.; Isa. 14:12ff.; 24:21; Jer. 8:2; 19:13; Zeph. 1:5), then the present punishment serves to reveal the supremacy of Israel's God over them (Gen. 1:14-19; 2:1; Ps. 148:2-6). The triple occurrence of the term 'to wither and fall' (נבל) in v. 4 is striking. It may be assumed to have both a retrospective and a prospective function (1:30; 28:1,4 and 40:7; 64:5) and to assist the chapter in connecting the two major parts of BI.

5-6a The second metaphor for the judgement, 'the sword of YHWH' (חרב), also belongs to the redactional fabric of BI. It appears in BI in the hand of God (27:1; 49:2; 65:12; 66:16) or of others commissioned by God (1:20; 31:8; 37:7; cf. also Gen. 3:24; Josh. 5:13-22; Jer. 12:12; Ezek. 21:1-10). It represents God's answer to the rebellious in Israel (1:20; 65:12) and to his enemies all over the world (66:16). In the present segment, the text concentrates briefly on God himself in a first person address (v. 5)[24] which does not recur throughout the chapter. This literary fact underlines the function of the segment: what 'the sword' is to accomplish will be a consequence of the preceding 'rage'. The phraseology is quite carefully put together: the sword descends 'upon the people I have doomed' (v. 5b; cf. v. 2: 'He has doomed them').[25] In a minor fashion, the previous announcement that the heavens will collapse (v. 4) serves to interpret the descent of the sword as a narrative sequel to the rage scene since it is in the heavens that YHWH's sword has appeared (although 'the heavens' in v. 4 constitute the horizon of the earthly event and in v. 5 the dwelling place of YHWH). The reference 'for judgement'

---

[24] Objections to the first person suffix are text-critically unfounded (Barthélemy, 238f.).

[25] The expression 'the sword descends' is to be found nowhere else in MT.

(למשפט) places the otherwise violent scene within the broader perspective of chs. 28-33: YHWH applies this measure to both Israel and the nations alike (28:17; 30:18; 32:1,7,16; 33:5).

The scene continues in v. 6 which maintains cultic language in poetic style. The word pair 'blood / fat' is found in both verse lines: in the first spread over the end of each colon, in the second over the beginning thereof. Both words are assonant with the focal words of the context: 'blood', דם, with 'Edom', אדם; 'fat', חלב, with 'sword', חרב. 'Blood' and 'fat of kidneys', however, also play an important role in the terminology of sacrifice (Exod. 23:18; Lev. 3:17; 7:33; 17:6; Isa. 1:11; Ezek. 39:19; 44:7,15).[26] At the same time, 'lambs',[27] 'goats' and 'rams', do not only constitute a symbol of abundance (Deut. 42:14; Ezek. 27:21; 39:18), they are also animals suitable for sacrificial offering (Num. 7:17; Jer. 51:40).

6b-7 The third metaphor for judgement, 'the sacrifice of YHWH' (זבח) – not in the usual sense of sacrificial victim but rather of sacrificial celebration (1 Sam. 9:12; 16:3; 20:29; Jer. 46:10)[28] – builds upon the preceding metaphor, 'the sword of YHWH'. While the ritual content of this sacrifice is unclear and evidently dependant on its temporal situation, the core thereof was probably the pouring of blood.[29] The context appears to suggest that this is also the case here ('slaughter', 'blood'). Elsewhere in Scripture we also find images of war and ritual slaughter in combination, representing God's punishing activity (Ezek. 39:17,19; Zeph. 1:7).[30] In BI, 'to sacrifice' and 'sword' belong to the terms which enclose the opening and closing chapters in the framework of the accusation of false cultic practices (1:11; 65:3; 66:3; cf. 44:23f.; 57:7; 65:12: 'sword / slaughter'). Thus the term 'sacrifice' owes its place both to the semantic field in use here and to the over-all redaction of BI.

After the mention in v. 6a of small livestock, the most common animals used for sacrifice, the mention of larger livestock in v. 7 is quite striking[31] and creates the impression of a climax in this overwhelming sacrificial feast ('great slaughter'). Solomon also included both sorts of

[26] Watson 1994: 275f.

[27] According to Péter-Contesse (1992: 70), כר means 'young ram' and not 'lamb' (cf. Ezek. 4:2; 21:27).

[28] According to Péter-Contesse (1992: 70), the dominant metaphor is 'ban' and not 'sacrifice' and the term זבח refers to 'meal' rather than 'offering'. It is difficult to comprehend, however, how 'ban' and 'meal' go hand in hand.

[29] TWAT, II, 522f. (B. Lang).

[30] ibid., 531.

[31] The expression 'with them' in v. 7a may refer to the animals in v. 6, but it is also possible that it refers back to 'Edom', understood as a 'people' (the last word of v. 6), as the suffixes in 'their land / their soil' in v. 7b clearly do (Barthélemy, 239f.).

livestock in the dedication of the temple (1 Kgs 8:63). 'Young steers' and 'bulls' are mentioned elsewhere as sacrificial animals (פרים: Exod. 24:5; Lev. 23:18; Num. 7 *passim*; Judg. 6:25; 1 Sam. 1:24; Ps. 50:9; 51:21; אבירים: Ps. 50:13). While the first sort, 'wild oxen' (ראמים), is used nowhere else as a sacrificial animal, it is frequently employed as a symbol of power and strength (Num. 23:22; Deut. 33:17; Ps. 22:22; 92:11; Job 39:9ff.).[32] Since the word for 'bulls' also means 'mighty men' (Isa. 10:13; 46:12; Ps. 22:13; 68:31; 76:6; Job 24:22; 34:20; Lam. 1:15) and 'young steers' can stand for 'leaders' (Jer. 50:27; Ezek. 39:18), commentators have long assumed that these three types of powerful animal symbolise the political élite of Edom (Tg, Rashi).

The location of the sacrifice in 'Bozrah' is meaningful in this regard. Bozrah was the elevated capital of Edom (cf. Isa. 63:1; Jer. 49:13,22; Amos 1:12), whose name had become associated with the word 'fortification' (מבצר).[33] The final line (v. 7b) returns the entire territory of Edom once again to the sacrificial feast via the word pair 'land / soil' (עפר in this sense: Ezek. 26:4,12; Hab. 1:10; Zech. 9:3; Job 14:8; 41:25). Repetition of terminology from the sword segment is also evident (v. 6a: 'blood / fat', 'made rich'), underlining the association of 'sword' and 'sacrifice'.

8 The fourth metaphor, 'the day of vengeance for YHWH / a year of recompense' (שנת שלומים / יום נקם), is limited to a single line (cf. vv. 9-10). The language is distinct from that which precedes it. The verse promises God's punishing intervention against Edom for an undetermined point of time ('day / year') and provides his actions with a theological qualification: 'vengeance' (נקם; the infrequent 'recompense' provides no essential nuancing; cf. Deut. 32:41; Hos. 9:7). Given both the fact that 'vengeance' is also to be found in the following chapter (35:4) and the affinity of other texts with the word 'day' (namely the opening oracles of PI and TI), some of which are also allied to the term 'vengeance', it is evident that this concept is closely associated with the redaction of BI:

- 'YHWH of hosts has a day against all that is proud and lofty' (2:12; cf. vv. 11,17, 20)
- 'The Lord YHWH of hosts has a day of tumult... in the valley of vision' (22:5)

---

[32] Lust (1989: 279) points out that the term ירד does not belong to the vocabulary of sacrifice. In his opinion it implies nothing more than the movement of livestock from one place to another, in this case the place of slaughter (Jer. 48:15; 50:27). No clear parallels exist for the translation 'to fall' (RSV; cf. *Ges.[18]*, 492f.).

[33] The place was located in Edom's northern territory near an important copper mine and close to a cross-roads at which the King's Highway, among others, intersected with other major routes (*AncBD*, I, 774; Bartlett 1989: 45f.).

- 'to proclaim the year of YHWH's favour, the day of vengeance of our God' (61:2)

- 'A day of vengeance is in my heart, my year of redemption has come' (63:4).

The word 'vengeance' (נקם) may be absent from 2:12 but a similar qualification of 'the day' is clearly intended by the context of vv. 6-22. Isa. 34:8 seems to function, therefore, in a very specific double way. Firstly, it encloses PI (chs. 2-34) since the expression 'YHWH has a day...' does not occur elsewhere in PI but in 2:12; 22:5 and 34:8. Secondly, it connects PI and TI since the term 'day of vengeance' occurs only in 34:8 and 61:2; 63:4, each time parallel with the term 'year' which, again each time, is determined by a noun which qualifies God's action: 'recompense' (שלומים), 'favour' (רצון) and 'redemption' (גאולה) respectively. In other words, it becomes clear in the course of BI that the day fixed for YHWH on which he will rear up against all the arrogant in the world (2:12), will decide the fate of sinners, both in Zion (22:5) and in Edom, with the nations in the background (34:8; 63:4), but will bring, above all, comfort for those in Zion who mourn (61:2), and ransom from bondage for them (63:4). If we account for the fact that in chs. 28-33 'Zion' is only the beneficiary of God's salvation (28:16; 29:8; 30:19; 31:4,9; 33:5,14,20), then 34:8 brings this major textual complex to an appropriate conclusion by envisioning Edom's judgement from the perspective of 'the cause (ריב) of Zion'. Indeed within BI this last notion anticipates an important theme which will emerge in DI: YHWH advocates Israel's lawsuit (3:13; 41:21; 49:25; 50:8; 51:22).[34]

The concept 'vengeance of YHWH' has encountered a degree of resistance in recent years because it seems to portray God as violent. Difficulties are multiplied by the apparent fact that in BI the term 'vengeance' is exclusively used with regard to God (1:24; 35:4; 47:3; 59:7)! In principle, however, the same applies here as did with respect to 'the rage of YHWH' (cf. v. 4). The notion 'vengeance' has its origins in the juridical world of ancient Israel and must be viewed differently, no doubt, from our contemporary understanding of law and justice. 'Vengeance' is an act intended to redress serious injustice, a punitive measure for a crime committed by a person (or persons) who do(es) not form part of the juridical or actual community of the injured party. Thus 'vengeance' is primarily sought between groups of people who do not (yet) have a mutual legal instance which governs both and to which both can appeal. The Scriptures speak, therefore, of both the duty to exact vengeance

---

[34] Peels 1995: 152f., 270.

(Num. 31:2; Josh. 10:13; 1 Sam. 14:24; 18:25; Jer. 50:15; Esth. 8: 13) as well as its limitation and even prohibition (Exod. 21:20f.; Lev. 19:18; Josh. 20:1-9; 1 Sam. 24:13; 2 Sam. 4:8-12; Prov. 6:34). Against such a background, the topic of YHWH's 'vengeance' against Israel's enemies is understandable. It implies a sovereign intervention by YHWH, rooted in his concern for justice and his engagement on behalf of his people, whereby he restores the damaged legal order between nations (Num. 31:2; Deut. 32:35,43; Judg. 11:36; 2 Kgs 9:7; Isa. 35:4; 47:3; Jer. 15:15; 50:28; 51:36; Ezek. 25:12-17; Ps. 79:10; 149:7). That the concept is theologically 'purged' is evident from the fact that YHWH also exacts vengeance for injustices committed in Israel itself (Lev. 26:25; Isa. 1:24; Jer. 11:20; 20:12; Ezek. 24:8; Ps. 18:48).[35]

Besides, the composite notion 'a day of vengeance' (cf. combinations of 'day' and similar words: Isa. 22:5; Ezek. 7:19; Zeph. 1:1,8; 2:2f.; Lam. 2:22) constitutes a more explicit interpretation of the more frequent expression 'the day of YHWH' (cf. Isa. 13:6,9; Ezek. 13:5; 30:3; Joel 1:15; 2:1,11; 3:4; 4:14; Amos 5:18,20; Ob 15; Zeph. 1:7,14; Zech. 14:1; Mal. 3:23). This temporal indicator implies the expectation of God's intervention *in history*, in pre-exilic texts primarily with a view to the punishment of his people and in post-exilic texts primarily with a view to saving them.

9-10 Several commentators connect these verses with v. 8 because of the syntactic conjunction (*weqatal*). It would appear from the possessive suffix attached to 'her streams / her soil' (v. 9), which in the final form of the text cannot possibly refer to Zion, that the theme 'Edom' from v. 7 is being continued here in v. 9. The segment constitutes a unit consisting of a verbal clause, v. 9, three compound nominal clauses and one simple nominal clause, v. 10. By way of the *weqatal*, the verbal clause connects with the same verb forms in v. 7 over the top of v. 8. The piece describes the actualisation of judgement upon Edom in terms of what happened to Sodom en Gomorrah (Gen. 19:24-29). While the first word, 'to be turned' (הפך), sets the trend for the reference (cf. Gen. 19:21,25,29), the term 'brimstone' (Gen. 19:24: גפרית) and the phrase: 'its smoke shall go up' (עלה), to be understood as from 'the land' (Gen. 19:28), further establish the allusion.[36] Since the prophet Hosea, the

---

[35] *THAT*, II, 106-9 (G. Sauer); *TWAT*, V, 605-12 (E. Lipiński). Peels (1995) describes the semantic field of the concept 'vengeance' on the basis of which he offers the following definition: 'The punishing retribution of God, who in kingly sovereignty – faithful to his covenant – judging and fighting arises to defend the honour of his name, insures the maintenance of his justice and works for the liberation of his people' (277).

[36] The words for 'smoke' differ, but the term used in Isa. 34:10, עשן, is also to be found in the context of judgement in Isa. 9:17; 14:31. For 'to lie waste', חרב, in BI, cf.

topic of Sodom and Gomorrah (11:8) has become biblical in the broad-est sense of the word (Deut. 29:22; Isa. 1:7,9; 13:19; Jer. 20:16; 49:18; 50:40; Amos 4:11; Jon. 3:4; Lam. 4:6). The judgement of these corrupt cities constitutes the paradigm par excellence for the total and irrevocable judgement of God over a sinful people.[37] It would appear that v. 10 functions solely to express this fact, the phrase 'it shall not be quenched' (לא תכבה) establishing a redactional connection with both the beginning and the end of BI (1:31; 66:24). The temporal indicators 'night and day[38] / for ever' and 'from generation to generation / for ever and ever' refer to the execution of the judgement against Babylon and against the 'hill / watchtower' of Jerusalem (cf. Isa. 13:20; 14:20; 32:14). The final expression, 'for ever and ever' (לנצח נצחים), is a *hapax legomenon*, and establishes a climax with respect to the destruction of Babylon (13:20).[39]

11-15 This passage is dominated by a list of twelve animals or de-mons, the majority of which are real and impure while some are ima-ginary and constitute embodiments of chaos (cf. 30:6)[40]. The animals in question will occupy Edom after her destruction (v. 11a and vv. 13b-15). It is evident that the segment exhibits a composite character. Firstly, one would not expect the list to be interrupted by vv. 11b-13a if it were an original unity. Secondly, the subject of v. 11b ('He shall stretch') harks back over vv. 9-11a to 'YHWH' in v. 8. Finally, by way of the unique word pair 'to possess / to dwell' (שכן / ירש), the redaction has created a framework out of v. 11a and v. 17b surrounding the verses which lie in between.[41] The framework thus transforms the occupation of Edom by impure animals into the primary and inclusive theme of vv. 11-17.

19:5f.; 37:18,25; 42:15; 44:27; 50:2; 60:12; for 'to be quenched', כבה, in a compara-ble context, cf. 2 Kgs 21:3f.; Isa. 1:31; Jer. 4:4; 21:12; 17:27; Ezek. 21:3f. [RSV 20:47f.]; Amos 5:8; for 'none shall pass', אין עבר, cf. Isa. 60:15; Ezek. 33:28.

[37] *TWAT*, II, 458 (K. Seybold).

[38] The sequence of 'night and day' is a post-exilic idiom borrowed from the Mesopo-tamian custom of counting a day as running from evening to evening (cf. 1Kgs 8:29; Isa. 27:3; Ps. 55:18; Est. 4:16; Dan. 8:14; Jud. 11:17; Sir. 38:27; *TWAT*, IV, 554 [A. Stiglmair]).

[39] Zapff 1995: 250-2.

[40] Zapff 1995: 251. Zoological determination is particularly difficult in v. 14 where two demonic beings are mentioned: the 'satyr' (שעיר; cf. Lev. 17:7; Isa. 13:21; 2 Chr. 11:15) and the 'night hag' (לילית; only here and perhaps Job 18:15), creatures with mythological roots. The latter, 'Lilith', was well-known in Mesopotamia as a female de-mon associated in Sumerian with the storm (*líl*), in Akkadian (for etymological reasons) with the night (*lilîtu*; in Hebrew *laylah*). It was said that she caused human beings, and especially men, all sorts of misery. Later traditions, both Jewish and Christian, developed a pictorial image of 'Lilith' although little can be said about it from the perspective of the Old Testament (in detail: *DDD*, 520f.; Wildberger, 1347ff.; Watts, 13f.).

11a. 13b-15 The series of animals begins with 'hawk / porcupine' (v. 11a). This word pair only appears elsewhere in Zeph. 2:14, a prophecy against Nineveh which seems to stem from before the fall of that city (612 BC).[42] Perhaps the redactors saw the sin and destiny of 'Bozrah / Edom' (v. 6) as a continuation of the sin and destiny of the Assyrian capital. By being borrowed these two animal names entered into a different tradition-historical context of meaning.[43]

Firstly, by taking the 'hawk' and adding the 'owl' and the 'raven' in parallelism, the redactors created an association with the list of unclean animals in Deuteronomy 14, where not only these animals occur (respectively vv. 17,16,14) but also two animals mentioned in Isa. 34:13 and 15, i.e. the 'ostrich' and the 'kite' (vv. 15,13 respectively). With this the total number of animals in ch. 34 reaches twelve (four in v. 11 and eight in vv. 13-15), an idealised number.[44]

Secondly, the 'porcupine' only appears elsewhere in Isa. 14:23 ('I will make it a possession of the porcupine'), here too in connection with the root 'to possess' (ירשׁ). Isa. 14:23 is the concluding verse of the prophecy against Babylon (13:1-14:23). This passage includes a list of animals, 13:21f., which is very similar to the list in 34:13-15,[45] only differing from it with respect to sequence. Moreover, the names of two desert creatures in 34:14-15, 'night hag' and 'arrow-snake', are absent from 13:21f., while the 'owl' of 13:21 is lacking in 34:13-15. This indicates the mutual independence of these lists. The redaction has harmonised them by taking over the 'owl' from Deut. 14:16 into Isa. 34:11, employing, nevertheless, the term used there (ינשׁוף) and not that of 13:21 (אחים). Thus the final redaction of 34:11-15 contains the complete list of animal names from Isa. 13:21f., albeit it in a different sequence and with one alternative term for the same animal, the 'owl'.

In short, by this set of references to Zeph. 2:14, Isa. 13:21f. and Deut. 14:13-17 the redaction has been able to achieve an equation of Edom with Nineveh and Babylon and to portray the desolate land after the judgement as the most abominable place because all the unclean and ominous animals which are forbidden by the relevant canon in the Law

---

[41] This *inclusio* is supported by the theme of measuring out with 'the line' (קו) in v. 11b in v. 17a.

[42] A.S. van der Woude, *Habakuk Zefanja* (POT), Nijkerk 1978, 122f.

[43] For the following, cf. Beuken 1992.

[44] Donner 1990: 292.

[45] Cf. also the corresponding term 'to dwell' (שׁכן) in 13:20f. and 34:11, which creates, in BI, a contrast between the animals that dwell in Babylon and Edom, on the one hand, and, on the other hand, the dwelling of 'justice / righteousness' in Israel (32:16) and of YHWH in Zion (8:18).

will dwell there. In addition to this, a contrast with Zion is created by several words for dwelling place which are used elsewhere in PI for that city (cf. 'haunt' [נוה] in v. 13b with 32:18; 33:20; 35:7; 'resting-place' [מנוח] in v. 14b with 28:12; 32:18; 'shadow' [צל] in v. 15a with 4:6; 25:4f.; 32:2).

11b-13a YHWH appears as subject once again in v. 11b via an implied association with v. 8. In this way, the author was able to further elaborate on the abandoned state of the land with the help of two themes which are, in fact, divine titles.

Firstly, YHWH is spoken of as the one who measures out the land of the nations (Deut. 32:8; Mic. 2:4), in this case the inhospitable land of Edom. While the expression 'to stretch the line' has its roots in the construction trade (1 Kgs 7:23; Job 38:5; Ps. 19:5 [?] and Isa. 44:13) and is employed figuratively by the prophets in their announcements of judgement (2 Kgs 21:13; Isa. 28:17; Lam. 2:8; cf. Amos 7:7-9), it is similarly at home in announcements of salvation when they speak of the division and allocation of land (Jer. 31:39; Ezek. 47:3; Zech. 1:16). The 'plummet' (literally 'stones [of chaos]') is likewise an instrument from the building world (Zech. 4:10) but it can refer, in association with the distribution of land, to the boundary stones which were employed to mark off territory (Schoors, 204). Allusions to the construction trade introduce an element of irony into this context of destruction and ruin (Oswalt, 615).

Secondly, YHWH alone has power over 'confusion / chaos' (בהו / תהו). Since this word pair is only found in the context of creation (Gen. 1:2: 'The earth was without form and void'; cf. Jer. 4:23), v. 11b implies that YHWH intends to return Edom to the state of disorder and hostility which existed on earth prior to his creative intervention.[46] Thus v. 11b makes explicit what lies hidden in the Sodom and Gomorrah motif of vv. 9-10.

Vv. 12-13a portray the consequences of the chaos. V. 12 speaks of the collapse of the social order – embodied and guaranteed in the Ancient Near East by the monarchy (cf. Isa. 8:21; 9:6; 17:2f.; 32:1; 33:22; Psalm 72) –, there being no leaders left to choose a king or to be chosen as king (cf. 'Notes'). Following on v. 12, v. 13 announces the intrusion of plants belonging to the prairie, associating 'kingship' with 'fortresses' (מבצר; cf. 17:3), and ruined 'strongholds' (ארמון) with the flora and

---

[46] This reference to the creation narrative has been accepted down through the history of research. Recent doubts in this regard have been refuted in *TWAT*, VIII, 560f. (M. Görg).

fauna common to such abandoned regions (cf. 23:13; 32:13-14). The word 'fortresses' is probably an allusion to 'Bozrah' in v. 6, setting the scene for the list of unclean animals in vv. 13b-15.

16-17 The concluding verses of the chapter consist of a commentary on the preceding verses. The addressees are no longer the 'nations / peoples' of v. 1, but those people who are familiar with reading 'the book of YHWH'. It is difficult to determine what the redaction considered 'the book of YHWH' to be but it would certainly have included the (books with) texts which mention the animals to which allusion has been made, namely the Pentateuch and a rudimentary form of the Prophets (v. 16a).[47] It is evident in fact that these addressees have been part of the audience from v. 1 on,[48] since they too have a vested interest in what YHWH has in store for the nations in vv. 2-15: Edom's fate is an example for the world just prior to its meeting a similar fate. It is not only the new audience, or rather readership, of the prophecy which emerges here, however. The prophet himself (v. 16b: 'by my mouth') also explicitly appears, in line with the biblical conviction that YHWH speaks through the mouth of his prophets ('mouth', פה, in this sense: Isa. 6:7; 49:2; 51:16; 53:7,9; 59:21; Exod. 4:15; Num. 22:38; 23:5,12; Deut. 18:18; 2 Sam. 14:3,18f.; Jer. 1:9; 5:14; 9:7; 15:19; 23:16,29; Ezek. 3:27; Ezr. 8:17). The entire 'production process' of BI is thus thematised: from the moment that YHWH speaks to Israel through the prophet to the moment that the readers discover these words in book form.

It is probable that the redaction, which intended ch.34 together with ch.35 to constitute one of the pillars upon which the entire structure of BI would rest, had its own influence on the formulation of v. 16. An appeal to the readers to see for themselves that it was possible to lean on 'the book of YHWH' was quite appropriate at the point where PI, in rudimentary form, came to an end and DI, also in rudimentary form, started. This opportunity to verify matters has its roots in the prophecy itself, considered here as announcement *and* realisation. YHWH ordered the occupation of Edom by impure animals through the mouth his prophet and realised that occupation by the power of his own spirit (v. 16b).

It would appear that as the Scriptures underwent the process of becoming a book, the commission 'to seek from the book of YHWH' took the place of the more traditional ideal 'to seek (דרש) YHWH' (or 'to seek what belongs to the domain of YHWH'; cf. Deut. 4:29; 12:5; 1 Sam.

---

[47] It is interesting to note that by 'the book of YHWH' Redaq primarily understands the book of Isaiah, although he notes thereby that his father thought the reference was to Leviticus because of the mention of the unclean animals (Rosenberg, 281).

[48] Lutz 1968: 87.

9:9; 1 Kgs 14:5; 22:5; 2 Kgs 3:11; 8:8; Isa. 9:12; 58: 2; 65:1,10; Jer. 21:2; 29:12ff.; Hos. 10:12; Amos 5:4ff.; Zeph. 1:6; Ps. 9:11; 22:27; 24:6; 111:2; 119:45,94; 1 Chr. 13:3; 28:8; 2 Chr. 1:5; 19:3; 26:5; Ezr. 7:10).[49] 'The book of YHWH' is now the place in which its readers can find salvation by familiarising themselves with YHWH's initiatives. The reversed sequence 'Seek and read' (v. 16a; *hysteron proteron*) makes it clear that the reading of this prophecy is not recommended for its own sake but that it has a purpose (cf. Jer. 36:6f.: 'You shall read... It may be that their supplication will come before YHWH'; not in this way: Isa. 29:11f.), in the present case the experience that 'Not one of these shall be missing; none shall be without her mate'. While the first clause allows one to imagine that 'these' refers to the 'events' prophesied in vv. 5-15, the second clause makes it clear that the allusion is to the animal pairs listed in vv. 11-15. The animals in question are to be found in 'the book of YHWH'.

The appeal would appear to be based on the double use of the term 'to gather' (קבץ). In the 'animals section' of the text, the verb (*niphal*) refers to the behaviour of the 'kites', who gather together over their prey (v. 15; cf. Ezek. 39:17; comparable Isa. 60:7; Ezek. 29:5). In the words of assurance that the prophecy would be actualised, the same verb (*piel*) refers to YHWH's initiative to assemble the animals (v. 16b).[50] The command 'Seek...' adds to this – looking back to v. 15 and forward to v. 16 – that all the animals can be found 'in the book of YHWH', as a means to confirm the prophecy concerning Edom.

While v. 17 continues the assurance that YHWH has determined to populate Edom with impure and dangerous animals, it returns thereby to the word usage of v. 11 with respect to the occupation of the land (cf. above for the terms 'to possess / to dwell'). The verbs of vv. 16b,17a constitute a logical series with the same subject, YHWH: 'to order', 'to bring together', 'to cast the lot' (three times an emphatic 'he' as subject) and 'to portion out' (subject: 'his hand'[51]). The two latter verbs have to do with the division of the land, a topic not mentioned in v. 11. Thus the conclusion of the chapter appropriately portrays YHWH as the owner of all land which he gives into the possession of others (Deut. 4:19; 29:25;

---

[49] Literary-historical and institutional differences between the texts mentioned aside. For this purpose, cf. *TWAT*, II, 318-26 (S. Wagner).

[50] Likewise, 'each one with her mate' in v. 15 has to do with each individual 'kite' (Rashi notes the parallel with Gen. 6:19-22; Rosenberg, 281), while 'none shall be without her mate' in v. 16 refers to the animals mentioned in pairs in vv. 11-15 (Alexander, 32).

[51] The 'hand' of YHWH occurs often in BI in the context of judgement (5:25; 9:11,16,20; 10:4,10; 11:15; 14:26; 23:11; 31:3).

32:8; Ps. 60:18; Mic. 2:4). In this way the text harks back to an aspect of Israel's earliest experience: through Joshua's mediation YHWH ascribed a portion of land to each of the twelve tribes ('[to cast] the lot [גורל]' in this context: Num. 33:54; 36:2f.; Josh. 14:2; 15:1; 17:1; 18:6-11; 19:10; 21:4,8; Judg. 1:3; Jer. 13:25; Mic. 2:5; Ps. 125:3; Neh. 11:1; 'to portion out territory', 'portion' [root חלק]: Num. 18:20; 26:53; Deut. 10:9; 12:12; Josh. 11:23; 14:5; 18:2; 19:51). In logical fashion, the final words declare the apportioning of the land to such repugnant animals as having the same ongoing validity as the devastation of the land (vv. 10,17b: 'for ever / from generation to generation').

CALL TO THE NEEDY TO REJOICE OVER THE RETURN TO ZION (35:1-10)

1   Let the wilderness and the dry land be glad,
        let the desert rejoice,
             and blossom like the crocus.
2   It shall blossom abundantly, and rejoice
        with joy and shouting.
      The glory of Lebanon shall be given to it,
        the majesty of Carmel and Sharon.
      They shall see the glory of YHWH,
        the majesty of our God.
3   Strengthen the weak hands,
        and make firm the feeble knees.
4   Say to those who are of a fearful heart:
        'Be strong, fear not!
           Behold, your God!
      Vengeance shall come,
        the recompense of God.
             He himself shall come that he might save you.
5   Then the eyes of the blind shall be opened,
        and the ears of the deaf unstopped.
6   Then shall the lame leap like a deer,
        and the tongue of the dumb shout for joy'.
      Truly, waters shall break forth in the wilderness,
        and streams in the desert.
7   The burning sand shall become a pool,
        and the thirsty ground springs of water.
      In the haunt of jackals, their resting-place,
        the grass shall become reeds and rushes.
8   There shall be a highroad, a way,
        and it shall be called 'the holy way'.
      The unclean shall not pass over it,
           but it shall be for the one who goes the way.
                Yet fools shall not err (therein).

9   No lion shall be there,
         nor shall any ravenous beast come upon it;
             they shall not be found there.
     But the redeemed shall go,
10   and the ransomed of YHWH shall return.
     They shall come to Zion with shouting,
         everlasting joy shall be at their head.
     Joy and gladness shall overtake (them),
         sorrow and sighing shall flee away.

NOTES

1 It is not clear whether the term חבצלת refers to a sort of lily, or to a crocus or a narcissus (cf. Cant. 2:1; Wildberger, 1353; *DCH*, III, 153; *Ges.*[18], 320). The translation 'crocus' found in RSV is maintained here.

1-2a In light of the fact that the verbal form תגל is a jussive, many translators interpret the other *yiqtol*-forms, ישׂשׂום and תפרח, as such (Feldmann, 400; König, 297; Procksch, 433; Schoors, 206; Wildberger, 1353f.; M. Buber). LXX has imperatives in v. 1 and indicatives of the future in v. 2; Tg has *yiqtols* throughout. This goes hand in hand with the fact that several scholars (already Ibn Ezra and Qimchi) explain the suffix of the first verb, ישׂשׂום, as stemming from a *nun paragogicum* assimilated to the following word מדבר (cf. Num. 3:19). (Other exegetes see it as a dittography or a reference back to the announcement of ch. 34 but this is somewhat forced since a preposition would then be necessary.) The indicative is clearly present at the beginning of v. 2a (פרח תפרח) in light of the affirmative prepositive infinitive, further in the second line of v. 2a (נתן) and v. 2b (יראו). Translation is made all the more difficult by the fact that jussive and indicative tenses are closer to one another in Hebrew than they are in modern languages. Our translation, therefore, reflects the interpretation of LXX: jussives in v. 1, indicatives in v. 2. V. 4b also exhibits the association of a *yiqtol* (יבוא) with a jussive (ישׁעכם).

The unusual verb form גילת in v. 2a″ is explained as 'an intentional reversion to the feminine ending *ath*, in order to avoid the hiatus *-ah w*[e]' (GKC, §130 b) or as an infinitive construct in a *hendyadys* (Procksch, 434).

4 This verse consists of two tricola: v. 4a-b′ and v. 4b″-″″′. The syntactical subdivision of v. 4b corresponds to the interpretation that the presence of YHWH, with a view to 40:9-11, is explained here first as the

arrival of his 'vengeance / recompense'. According to this approach, נקם is the subject of the first יבוא and גמול אלהים stands in apposition thereto (Vitringa, 346f.; Hitzig, 406; Alexander, 36f.; König, 297; Kaiser, 285; Wildberger, 1352ff.; Watts, 5ff.). The traditional interpretation does not satisfy. It is difficult to see how these words could constitute an indirect accusative of specification, with אלהיכם as subject of the verb, since one would then be left with an unusual word order (*pace* RSV: 'your God will come with vengeance, with terrible recompense'; Delitzsch, 365; Clements, 276; Oswalt, 619). Furthermore, it is improbable that הוא in v. 4b refers back to גמול and not to אלהים (Dillmann-Kittel, 306; Kiesow 1979: 147; *pace* Steck 1985: Synopse). The emphatic personal pronoun only has meaning if it indicates a *new* subject of the actions 'to come' and 'to save' (BrSyn, §67 b). Commentators offer a variety of solutions: Duhm (255) vocalises נקם as a participle; Schoors (207), following Jerome, vocalises יבוא as a *hiphil*; according to Wernberg-Møller (1957: 73), אלהיכם stems from the preposition אל and ישעכם is a noun, which results in the translation: 'Behold, to you vengeance will come, the recompense of God will come, and (so will) your salvation'.

7 The feminine suffix of רבצה is too clearly evident in the Tiberian manuscripts to be dismissed (Barthélemy, 244f.). The versions avoided the difficult question of the suffix's referent either by dropping it altogether (1QIsᵃ) or by translating it somewhat freely (LXX, Vg, Syr, Tg). Throughout the history of exegesis, a variety of solutions for this verse line have been proposed (cf. the extensive survey of Alexander, 39f.). RSV, for example, emends רבצה to read בצה: 'The haunt of jackals shall become a swamp'. Wildberger's emendation (1354) is clearly the simplest: 'An der Stätte, wo Schakale lagerten' (read the verb form רבצו). The feminine suffix, however, should be maintained. It can refer to the plural of things or animals (König, *Lehrgebäude*, II.2, §348 g, h: cf. Deut. 29:21b; Jer. 36:23; Ezra 11:5; GKC, §135 p). As such, the word רבצה can be considered to stand in apposition to the preceding clause: 'In the haunt of jackals, their resting-place...' (Hitzig, 407f.; Oswalt, 619). Although this pleonasm is not very satisfactory, colometrically speaking a third word in the first colon is probable, and the term רבץ is found elsewhere in parallel to נוה (Isa. 65:10).

This explanation makes it unnecessary to read חצר, 'enclosure' in v. 7b'' instead of חציר, 'grass' (cf. LXX: ἔπαυλις). Such emendation is frequently resorted to, partly based on the literary-historical argument that the word חצר also appears in Isa. 34:13 (written חציר) parallel to נוה תנים, 'the haunt of jackals' (Wildberger, 1354; Watts, 7).

8 It is unlikely that the first occurrence of the word ודרך is due to dittography, although it is not found in 1QIsᵃ and Syr. LXX translates מסלול ודרך as a *hendiadys* (ὁδὸς καθαρά) while Vg and Tg also provide a translation of both terms. Furthermore, the term fits well as an antecedent of לה in the chiastic structure of the verse line (Barthélemy, 245f.). More likely, however, ודרך is an apposition to מסלול (with explicative *waw*). The 'highroad' is thus explained as a 'public way'.

V. 8a‴-b, without the words והוא לָמו הלך דרך, provides a strictly chiastic line, reason enough for RSV and a number of other translations, to drop them (cf. Duhm, 257). The evidently complicated syntax suggests a later expansion. Among those who would maintain these words, some ignore the *atnach* and interpret the clause as parenthetic with God as the antecedent of הוא: 'He himself shall be going in the way for them' (J. Calvin, M. Buber, BJ, TOB). While the versions offer a variety of different translations, they do not allow us to correct or explain MT (Barthélemy, 247). If one takes the *atnach* into account, the first two words then constitute the antithesis of the preceding line: 'The unclean shall not pass over it, but it shall be for him (them)'.[1] The words following the *atnach* then introduce the second clause: 'The traveller – even fools shall not err therein' (Vitringa, 354f.; Hitzig, 408; Alexander, 40f.; Delitzsch, 365f.; König, 298; Motyer, 275). Such a construction remains unusual, however, especially with respect to the sequence of singular followed by plural. The term 'fools', moreover, has ethically unfavourable connotations and runs parallel with 'the unclean'. Therefore, other exegetes take the four words surrounding the *atnach* as a single clause: 'It is for the one who goes the way'. In this case, the nominal clause והוא למו הלך דרך anticipates v. 9: 'The redeemed shall go' (Watts, 5,7; Oswalt, 620). This interpretation is followed here. Basically the same explanation, except for the emendation of למו into לעמו, runs: 'wird sie doch für sein Volk sein, wenn es den Weg betritt' (Duhm [256]; followed, among others, by Wildberger [1352, 1355]).

9 There is evidence that v. 9a has been the subject of expansion, either the verb בל יעלנה or the verb לא תמצא being redundant. The latter feminine verb form is particularly out of place since it does not reflect the masculine noun פריץ (Duhm, 257). In the first instance, the adverb שם would appear to be better placed with v. 9b: 'There will the redeemed walk' והלכו [*qal*] having originated from יהלכו [*piel*] via confusion of י and ו; Emerton 1977; cf. BHS). The disadvantage of such a reconstruc-

---

[1] As the preceding term טמא and the following term הלך, למו is more likely to be a singular than a plural.

tion lies in the fact that the sequence of verbs which depend on v. 6b is thus lost (cf. 'Introduction to the Exegesis').

10 The accepted translation of v. 10: 'Everlasting joy shall be upon their heads' appears to suggest that the returning exiles will wear joy as an ornament upon their heads. It is also possible, however, that the expression is referring to a caravan: 'Everlasting joy shall be at their head'; in other words 'joy' will form the advance guard while 'joy and gladness' will bring up the rear (ראש in this sense: 1 Kgs 21:9,12; Amos 6:7; Mic. 2:13; 1 Chr. 4:42; 2 Chr. 20:27; cf. the concept of a caravan in: Isa. 52:12; 58:8; Joel 2:3,20; Hab. 3:5; Ps. 23:6; 43:3; 68:26; 85:11; נשׂא hiphil metaphorically: Isa. 59:9; Jer. 42:16; Zech. 1:6).[2] A strong argument in favour of this interpretation – which is followed here – lies in the fact that 'joy and gladness' then become the subject of the verb ישׂיגו (LXX: εὐφροσύνη καταλήμψεται αὐτοὺς;[3] cf. Deut. 28:2), just as 'sorrow and sighing' are the subjects of ונסו.

ESSENTIALS AND PERSPECTIVES

Since ch.35 exhibits strong associations with chs. 40-55, the history of its exegesis has been dominated for a long time by the question of authorship: do ch.35 and chs. 40-55 stem from the same author?[4] Indeed, it has been conjectured that, together with ch.34, the present chapter constitutes the beginning of DI.[5] Other commentators have drawn attention to the differences between ch.35 and DI at the thematic and terminological levels,[6] giving rise to questions concerning the function of the chapter in the overall structure of BI.[7] A consensus has been steadily emerging which treats ch.35 as a later addition than ch.34, intended to smooth out the connection between 40:1-11 and chs. 32-34. Ch.35 is, however, clearly attuned to ch.34 both in its use of topics and terminology.[8]

---

[2] According to Alexander (43) as early as Clericus. Alonso Schökel and Carniti (1986) follow a similar line of thought, pointing to the fact that the prepositions על and ב are interchangeable in relation to ראשׁ; cf. Judg. 9:7; and 1 Sam. 26:13f.; 2 Sam. 2:25; likewise Exod. 17:9; 34:4 and Prov. 8:2.

[3] LXX assumes the returnees to be the object of the verb ישׂיגו. In the caravan interpretation, the 'advance guard' (ראשׁם) is the implicit object of the verb.

[4] Graetz 1891; Scott 1935; Pope 1952.

[5] Torrey 1928: 295-301; McKenzie 1968: 9-12.

[6] Caspari 1931; Elliger 1933: 272-8; Wildberger, 1358f.

[7] Steck's research into this question (1985) has been pioneering. Cf. also Williamson 1994: 211-5, 220; Sweeney 1996: 450ff.

[8] Mailland 1956; Peels 1995: 148ff.

The most important theme of the chapter is the transformation of the 'wilderness / desert', eternally cursed according to ch.34, into a fertile landscape through which the exiles (vv. 9-10), and later YHWH, will be free to return to Zion (40:9-11). The word 'vengeance' constitutes the hinge term here (Peels 1995: 150). In harmony with 34:8 ('Truly, YHWH has a day of vengeance, a year of recompense for the cause of Zion'), YHWH's appearance in 35:4 is focused on the salvation brought by his 'vengeance / recompense', in anticipation of his ultimate arrival as saviour. Thus, the full disclosure hereof is reserved for 40:3-5 which speaks of the revelation of his glory to all the living. Moreover, in light of 33:5,20,22, in which YHWH is said to reign over his people in Zion once more, it was necessary to speak of the return of the exiles thereto (35:8-10). The motif of the return of the exiles, however, has a broader function than the association with ch.40 alone. It belongs to a redactional layer which runs from 2:5 to 62:10-12, a redaction which is evident in PI in 11:11-16 and 27:12-13 and which integrates the theme of the new exodus of DI (41:17-20; 4:14-16; 43:1-8,16-21; 48:20-22; 49:9-12; 51:10-11; 55:12-13).

Given the fact that a commentary is primarily obliged to treat an individual chapter 'in its own right' and not as a preparation for subsequent texts, our discussion of the redaction of ch.35 must of necessity remain limited. Such a discussion can help us, however, in distinguishing the characteristic form exhibited by certain topics as well in the discernement of certain 'omissions'. For example, since there is mention here of the return of the exiles and not of YHWH, the summons to 'make a highway for God' in 40:3 is replaced by an appeal to the wilderness to rejoice (vv. 1-2). After the announcement of YHWH's judgement against the nations and the realisation thereof in Edom and surroundings in ch.34, it is quite understandable that the transformed landscape should be graced with a vision of 'the glory of YHWH' (v. 2), and not 'all flesh' as in 40:5. Similarly, the theme of the forgiveness of Israel's sins in 40:1-2 is redundant here since accounts have already been settled with 'the sinners in Zion' in 33:14 and the present text promises salvation to those who have endured the exile (vv. 3-10). Finally, it is possible that the leveling of the mountains in 40:4 was not taken up in the present text because 34:3 had already mentioned their dissolution in the context of YHWH's judgement of the nations. On the other hand, in contrast to the impassability of the land in ch.34, the theme of 'the highroad' called for further elaboration while it would have been premature to burden Zion with a proclamatory role, as in 40:9, since this is prepared for there in the commissioning scene of vv. 6-8.

The chapter as a whole consists of a prophetic announcement of deliverance, the core of which exhibits the characteristic form of a priestly oracle of salvation (vv. 4-6a; Sweeney, 499f.). This announces salvation as present here and now. Therefore, the text tends to emphasise the actual experience thereof, expressed in terms of encouragements (vv. 3f.) and the topic 'joy'. The term 'to be glad' even constitutes an inclusion, the root שׂושׂ being found at the beginning of v. 1 and v. 10b. The abrupt transition from ch.34 to ch.35 marks the contrast between judgement and salvation. Although significant reference is made to former misfortune (vv. 3-4: 'weak, feeble, fearful'; vv. 5-6a: 'blind, deaf, lame, dumb'; vv. 8-9: 'unclean, fools, lion, ravenous beast'; v. 10: 'sorrow and sighing'), these references do not allude to the curse which has descended upon the land of Edom in ch.34 but rather to the punishment of the exile. This background, which dominates the entire chapter, is clearly borrowed from DI since in PI YHWH's judgement consists primarily of the devastation of the land and there is little talk of deportation of its population. It is evident, therefore, that ch.35 has been composed for later readers who are familiar with BI as a whole. For such readers, in their distressful sojourn in foreign territory, the prophecies of Isaiah ben Amoz have become a reality.

The return to Zion thus constitutes the primary theme of ch.35. While it could not have played a role in the preaching of the historical prophet himself, its role in the actualisation thereof for the exiles is all the more appropriate. This primary theme relativises the beginning of the chapter, namely the transformation of desert into garden, since this transformation does not take place in Zion as one might expect, and the fertile and rejoicing landscape is not presented as a new destination for God's people, a sort of 'garden of Eden'. Therefore, the miracle announced must be considered subordinate to the return. In other words, the real Zion enjoys preference to the transformed desert. It is evident, therefore, that nature's metamorphosis does not precede the return to Zion but constitutes rather an imaginative representation thereof. The return has its beginning wherever people are prepared to accept the desert as a place of divine revelation (v. 2), a place where the weak find encouragement (v. 3), where fear makes way for strength (v. 4) and every form of impediment to the way is remedied (vv. 5-6). When this happens, the road to Zion serves as a holy and secure highroad (vv. 8-9) a highroad which terminates joyfully in Zion (vv. 9-10). The miracle which takes place among those who accept the return to Zion has its origins, therefore, in the desert, the ultimate starting point of the journey.

Scholarly Exposition

Introduction to the Exegesis: Form and Setting

Given that the speaker of this prophetic announcement of salvation nowhere materialises as God (first person), we must assume him to be the prophet himself by virtue of the superscription of BI. Strictly speaking, the addressees are those who are given the task of bringing a message of encouragement to the weak but they remain anonymous as such (vv. 3-4). In fact, the prophecy is thus addressed to those whom the message concerns, namely the people who dwell in the wilderness, the very ones who want to return to Zion. The prophet appears as one sent by God (v. 4: 'Your God'), yet he shares the fate of his people (v. 2: 'our God').

Although a prophetic announcement of salvation cannot be identified here on the basis of characteristic formal elements, the core thereof can be distinguished in an adapted form of the so-called priestly oracle in vv. 3-6a, a genre which is also found in DI and likewise in frequent association with a prophetic announcement of salvation (41:8-13, 14-16; 43:1-4, 5-7; 44:1-5; 54:4-6).[9] The oracle in question lies embedded between two segments, each of which begins with the word pair 'wilderness / desert' (v. 1a and v. 6b) and portrays the salvation to come in terms of a metamorphosis of the landscape which will allow the exiles to make their return (vv. 1-2 and vv. 6b-10).

A narrative line runs through the entire chapter. The first segment appears to be a theophany report in which nature's unusual reaction (vv. 1-2a) is explained by the appearance of YHWH (v. 2b). Words of encouragement (v. 3-4a'), the actual oracle of salvation in the form of an announcement of the theophany (v. 4a''-b) and the healing of the disabled (vv. 5-6a) follow in the second segment. Just as the desert trades its barrenness for fertility, so the weak abandon their fear and the disabled are healed, allowing them to imitate nature in their rejoicing (vv. 2a,6a: 'to shout' [רנן]). Ultimately, their healing allows them to undertake the return journey through the wilderness. The third segment describes how this process is to take place (vv. 6b-10). The desert brings forth water in abundance (vv. 6b-7), together with a passable and secure highway which terminates in Zion (vv. 8-10). Rejoicing already on account of

---

[9] J. Begrich, "Das priesterliche Heilsorakel", *ZAW* 52 (1934) 81-92; C. Westermann, *Grundformen prophetischer Rede* (BEvTh, 31), München 1960[1], 1978[5]; transl. *Basic Forms of Prophetic Speech,* Philadelphia 1967; A. Schoors, *I Am God Your Saviour. A Form-Critical Study of the Main Genres in Is. XL-LV* (VT.S, XXIV), Leiden 1973.

their renewed vigour (v. 6a), the disabled are now called 'the ransomed of YHWH' who rejoice at the return to Zion (vv. 6a,10: 'to shout' [רנן]). Nature's response, in this narrative presentation of the return to Zion, is divided into a reaction to 'the glory of YHWH' (vv. 1-2) and support for the returning exiles (vv. 6b-9a).

Each of the three segments exhibits its own unique structure. In the first segment (vv. 1-2), the new subject in 'they shall see' (emphatic המה) establishes a point of articulation between vv. 1-2a and v. 2b, while the word pair 'glory / majesty' functions therein as a semantic hinge.

The second segment (vv. 3-6a) is chiastic in structure: the encouragement of the fearful (vv. 3-4a´) and the healing of the disabled (vv. 5-6a) enclose the actual oracle of salvation (v. 4a´´-b). The two imperatives 'strengthen' and 'say' provide the first piece with a point of articulation (v. 3 and v. 4a´), the twofold consequence of God's salvation the third (vv. 5-6a: twice 'then' [אז]).

The third segment (vv. 6b-10) announces the primary event: the appearance of sources of water in the wilderness (v. 6b) which make the return journey possible (vv. 7-10). This primary event is introduced by the term 'Truly' (כי), a particle which is not found elsewhere in ch. 35. The remaining verses consist of a syntactic sequence of four *weqatals:* twice והיה (vv. 7,8) and twice a term for the notion 'to go' (v. 9b: והלכו; v. 10a´´: ובאו). The overall structure can be arranged schematically as follows:

1-2   announcement of theophany
     1-2a   the transformation of the wilderness: blossom and joy
     2b   the vision of YHWH
3-6a   announcement of salvation
     3-4a´   encouragement
         3   command to strengthen the weak
         4a´   command to speak to the fainthearted
     4a´´-b   oracle of salvation
         4a´´   'fear not'
         4b´   proclamation of God's presence
         4b´´-´´´   the coming of vengeance
         4b´´´´   YHWH shall come for salvation
     5-6a   the healing of the disabled
         5   the blind and the deaf
         6a   the lame and the dumb
6b-10   announcement of the return to Zion
         6b-7   the transformation of the wilderness and its consequences

6b	the desert abounding in water
7	dry places become wet
8-9a	a passable highroad is opened
8a´-´´	the character of the highroad
8a´´´-9a	categories excluded from travelling the highroad
9b-10	the return voyage
9b-10a´	the redeemed undertake the journey
10a´´-b	they arrive in Zion with joy at their head

The colometry accentuates the beginning of the chapter in v. 1 as well as the actual salvation oracle in v. 4 with tricola. V. 8a´´´-b and v. 9a are also tricola but they appear to be the result of some form of expansion (cf. 'Notes'). It should also be noted that several verse lines, especially in the third segment, exhibit a chiastic structure (vv. 3, 5, 6b, 8a´-´´, 8a´´´-b, 9a´-´´, 9b-10a´, 10a´´-´´´,10b).

The genesis of ch.35 should be dated, in light of its connections with DI and TI, in a late phase of the redaction of BI. Given the fact that ch. 33 and ch.34 appear to be older than ch.35 which makes reference thereto, the latter chapter is clearly not the first redactional connection between PI and chs. 40-66 (Becker 1997: 270). If one can agree that the macro-redaction of BI was completed around 400 BC, this appears to be the approximate point in time when ch.35 received its present form. It is alleged to have functioned in the Succoth celebration of the Second Temple (Sweeney, 452ff.).

Exegesis by Verse

1-2 The theme of the transformation of the devastated land is governed by the word pair 'wilderness / desert' (מדבר / ערבה), which typifies both the opening and further development of DI (40:3; 41:19; 51:3; 'wilderness' alone: 41:18; 42:11, 19; 43:19f.; 64:9).[10] Since the word pair in question is found nowhere else in PI outside ch.35 (v. 1 and v. 6) it tends to draw the experienced reader's attention to the second part of BI from the outset.

The term 'wilderness' itself, however, is reminiscent of the promise which brought chs. 28-32 to a conclusion: 'the spirit from on high' shall make 'the wilderness' fertile and establish 'righteousness' therein (32:15f.). At the same time, the term 'desert', in association with 'Leba-

[10] The third word 'dry land' (ציה) is also to be found in 41:18, together with 'wilderness'.

non', 'Carmel' and 'Sharon', seems to make reference to 33:9: 'The land mourns and languishes; Lebanon is confounded and withers away; Sharon is like a desert, and Bashan and Carmel shake off their leaves' (for the metaphorical significance of these placenames, cf. 'Exegesis by Verse' of 33:9). From the geographical perspective, the common noun 'desert' (*arabah*) in v. 4 points to YHWH's judgement on Edom, compared in ch. 34 with that of Sodom and Gomorrah, because it coincides with the name (*Arabah*) of the plain in which these cities were situated. This might perhaps explain why the desert is singled out, strictly speaking, as the subject of renewed fertility. (The feminine forms of vv. 1b-2a refer to 'the desert' [ערבה].) In any event, the judgement over these regions, which appears to have reached completion in 33:9, is here reversed. Thus, within BI, the opening of ch. 35 clearly points both forwards and backwards, establishing the chapter's bridging function between the two primary parts of BI.

The transformation in question consists of joy and fertility. It is striking that the chiastic arrangement of the verb forms concerned places greater emphasis on the rejoicing: 'to be glad... to rejoice... to blossom... to blossom... to rejoice... to shout'. The metaphorical significance of the transformation is thus brought to the fore: nature's joy anticipates the joy of those who return to Zion (v. 10). While the theme of joy in response to salvation is primarily evident in the second half of BI ('to be glad' [root שׂושׂ]: 51:3,11; 60:15; 61:3,10; 62:5; 64:4; 65:18f.; 66:10,14; 'to rejoice' [root גיל]: 9:2; 25:9; 29:19; 41:16; 49:13; 61:10; 65:18f.; 66:10; 'to shout' [רנן]: 42:11; 44:23; 48:20; 49:13; 51:11; 52:8f.; 54:1; 55:12)61:7; 65:14), it is also to be found in the song of praise which concludes the first collection of the prophecies of Isaiah ben Amoz (12: 3,6). In contrast, the topic 'to blossom' is less frequent in BI (root פרח: 27:6; 66:14; negatively: 5:24; 17:11; 18:5).

The second line of v. 2a elaborates the joy and fertility of the 'desert' (compound nominal clause, feminine subject). The fertile growth for which 'Lebanon / Carmel and Sharon' are celebrated is now ascribed to the desert also. The terms, however, are more theological than botanical. Bereft of vegetal associations, the word pair 'glory / majesty' (הדר / כבוד) expresses the magnificence which is peculiar to YHWH (Ps. 29:2; 96:8f.; 145:5,12). YHWH graces the king (Ps.21:6), humanity as ruler of the earth (Ps.8:6; cf. Isa. 53:2) and even Zion herself with such magnificence (Ezek. 16:14: הדר only), although the latter also loses her claim thereto (Isa. 5:14; Lam. 1:6). The terms are quite unusual in relation to vegetation ('glory' figurative for might: Isa. 10:18; Isa. 60:13 [an allusion to 35:2]; Ezek. 31:18; 'majesty': Lev. 23:40). This exceptional qualification of the landscape goes hand in hand with the remarkable expression 'shall be given' (נתן *niphal* is never used in association with vegetative processes). The passive form anticipates the mention of the One who can restore magnificence to this barren landscape, since magnificence is his essential characteristic and he disposes thereof (cf. Isa.9:5).

V. 2b unfolds that God's glory will be made visible in the transformation of the wilderness. Attention is drawn by the phrase: 'They shall see (the glory of YHWH)'. Grammatically speaking, the emphatic 'they' (המה) has to refer to 'wilderness and dry land / desert' in v. 1.[11] There is nothing strange in the fact that these regions recognise what they are experiencing as stemming from God himself (for 'to see' God in the sense of 'to recognise' him or his work: Gen. 16:13; Exod. 14:13; 34:10; Num. 14:22; Josh. 24:7; 1 Kgs 18:39; Isa. 5:19; 6:9; 26:10; 52:8,10; 66:19; Ezek. 21:4; Mal. 1:5).[12] What is surprising, however, is the fact that the landscape 'sees' God's 'glory / majesty' since the vision of his magnificence is elsewhere restricted to human beings (in the non-cultic sense: Exod. 16:7; 24:10f.; 33:18; Num. 14:10; Deut. 5:24; Judg. 6:25; Isa. 6:5; 17:7; 33:17; 38:11; 40:5; 60:1f.; Ezek. 1:28; Job 19:27; 42:5). Nature, in contrast, reacts to his appearance (Hab. 3:10; Ps. 77:17; 97:4; 104:3). It is probably for this reason that LXX replaced 'they' with 'my people' and Tg with 'the house of Israel'.

Commentators have consistently defended the hypothesis that 'they' alludes to the disabled of vv. 3-4 or to Israel (or rather Zion) as Edom's adversary in the preceding chapter.[13] The proleptic function of the personal pronoun has, indeed, been recognised by the grammars.[14] Furthermore, the personal pronoun is never pleonastic where finite verbs are concerned. It always functions to focus attention.[15] Something similar may be at work here. The retrospective function of 'they' appears to

---

[11] Since Vitringa most commentators agree to this. After the singular (feminine) forms of vv. 1-2a which allude to 'desert', the plural (masculine) personal pronoun is a necessary reference to the three territories which will witness YHWH's glory.

[12] *TWAT*, VII, 253-f. (H.-F. Fuhs); *HALAT*, 1079f.

[13] As early as Ibn Ezra; further Duhm, König, Kaiser, Fohrer, Clements, Oswalt; Mathews 1995: 129. Surveys of the older opinions can be found in Alexander, 34f.

[14] König, *Lehrgebäude* II.2, §3, refers to Num. 24:23; Isa. 13:2; 21:2; Nah. 2:2,6; Ps. 87:1; GKC, §135 d (without mentioning of texts). המה is only rarely a non-personal referent (Exod. 32:16; Num. 20:13; 1 Sam. 12:21; Jer. 7:4; 10:15; 51:18; Hos. 2:14; Ps. 94:11; Eccl. 3:18).

[15] Where 1st and 2nd person pronouns are concerned, attention is primarily drawn to the emotional interaction between dialogue partners whereas 3rd person pronouns tend to highlight a contrast with regard to the information; cf. T. Muraoka, *Emphatic Words and Structures in Biblical Hebrew*, Jerusalem-Leiden 1985, Ch. 2, 47-59.

dominate, thus emphasising the fact that the devastated territories will
see, i.e. recognise, 'the glory of YHWH'. At the same time, however, the
emphatic 'they' raises the possibility that there are other beings who do
not (yet) share this appreciative vision of YHWH.[16] The wilderness thus
constitutes a contrastive example for those in need of YHWH's assistance,
the people to whom the message of God's imminent manifestation is ultimately addressed (v. 4: 'Behold, your God'). The formulation 'our
God' (v. 2) versus 'your God' (v. 4) also enjoys a function in this implied contrast. The prophetic speaker identifies himself with those who
experience God.

3-4 Following the complete absence of human persons in the expected
transformation of nature, a situation which reaches its paradoxical climax in the fact that the landscape, and not human beings, will be graced
with a vision of YHWH, the present segment introduces the readers into
Israelite society ('your God') with words of encouragement for the
weak. The task of reassuring the feeble of heart is not addressed to the
speaker, the implied prophet, but rather to a plural audience which is not
further defined. While all attention is thus drawn to those for whom this
message of encouragement is intended: 'the weak hands... the feeble
knees... those who are of a fearful heart',[17] they too are left undefined
by any extratextual reference (Peels 1995: 149,156). It would seem that
this intriguing dialogical situation, together with a significant number of
actual terms, is borrowed from 40:1-11 (Steck 1985). The verses thus
portray how prophecy again becomes operative in a milieu in which God
is experienced as absent. The message 'Behold, your God!' (with the
emphasis on 'your') is intended to bring about a fundamental change
which will take away weakness and anxiety. V. 3 speaks of physical re-
assurance, while v. 4 provides the argument: the message of salvation.
The connection is to be found in the commands 'strengthen' and 'be
strong' (חזק piel and qal).

V. 3 exhibits a simple chiastic structure with rhyming internal elements: 'weak hands / feeble knees' (ברכים כשלות / ידים רפות). The imperatives 'strengthen / make firm' (אמצו / חזקו) are characteristic ele-

---

[16] Cf. J-M, §146 a 1): 'The pronoun is added to bring out antithetical contrast: one
member of a set is highlighted to the exclusion of others'. The uniqueness of Isa. 35:2 lies
in the fact that the 'others' are still implied.

[17] The expression 'those who are of a fearful heart' (נמהרי לב) has a parallel in 'the
heart of the rash' (לבב נמהרים) in 32:4. While the meaning in each text is not exactly the
same (cf. BDB and HALAT; TWAT, IV, 716f [H. Ringgren]), the strongly intertextual
character of ch. 35, together with the fact that the niphal participle of the verb מהר is not
found beyond these texts, allows us to make a connection here (Aitken 1993: 35). The
leading classes constitute the subject of expected salvation in 32:4, the disabled in the
present text.

ments of the narratives concerning the transfer of leadership from Moses to Joshua, underlining the topic that courage and strength are necessary to enter the promised land (Deut. 3:28; 31:6f.,23; Josh. 1:6-9,18; 10:25). Also outside this context, the word pair frequently occurs against a background of war or violence (Amos 2:14; Nah. 2:2; Ps. 27:14; 31:25; 2 Chr. 32:7) while the transfer of leadership has found further application in the narratives concerning the house of David (1 Chr. 22:13; 28:20; 2 Chr. 11:17; 13:7). Similarly, the expression 'weak hands' occurs almost exclusively in a context of struggle (Josh. 10:6; 2 Sam. 4:1; 17:2; Isa. 13:7; Jer. 6:24; 38:4; 50:43; Ezek. 7:17; 21:12; Zeph. 3:16; Ezra 4:4; Neh. 6:9; 2 Chr. 15:7).[18] This tradition-historical background finds its rightful place in the present words of encouragement prior to the return to Zion, suggesting that a new era has dawned for God's people and that strength and courage will be demanded of those who would participate in it.

The command to encourage is substantiated in v. 4a in the promise of salvation brought about by the gracious presence of YHWH. The expectation of this has already been raised by the exhortation 'be strong' in combination with 'fear not!' (Deut. 31:6; Josh. 10:25; Zech. 8:13; 1 Chr. 32:7). The verse is primarily characterised as an oracle of salvation, however, via the association of the exhortation 'fear not!' with a statement concerning God's beneficial presence among the needy: 'Behold, your God!'.[19] Borrowed from the cult and featuring regularly in DI, the latter statement evidently here exhibits the form of a 'Selbstprädikation' ('I am...'; both elements occur together in Isa. 41:10,13f.,17; 43:1,5; 44:2,8; 51:12; further in Gen. 15:1; 21:17; 26:24; 46:3; 2 Kgs 19:6f.; Jer. 30:10f.; Lam. 3:57).[20] The fact that YHWH does not (yet) present himself here in the first person as the bearer of salvation fits the anticipatory character of ch.35. Within the progression of events which the redaction of BI has introduced, chs. 40-55 are the most appropriate location for YHWH's first person presentation. The prophetic oracle of salvation found here points those who live in weakness and fear to the renewed presence of the God whom they have known for so long.

V. 4b specifies the effects of God's presence (cf. 'Notes'). In the first colon, the term 'to come' (בוא) remains limited to the 'vengeance / recompense of God' (גמול/נקם), while in the final colon it is also stated that

---

[18] The other expressions are much less frequent (for 'feeble knees', cf. Ps. 109:24; Job 4:4; for 'fearful heart', cf. Isa. 32:4; Prov. 6:18; Eccl. 5:1).

[19] Peels 1995: 159: 'The pronominal suffix is possessive here in the sense of the covenant and election'.

[20] TWAT, III, 884f. (H.-F. Fuhs).

YHWH 'shall come'. This usage stands in contrast to 40:10, the source text of our verse, in which the same appeal: 'Behold, your God!' (v. 9)[21] is at first elaborated as 'Behold, the Lord YHWH comes with might' and then as 'His reward is with him, and his work before him' (פעלה / שכר). It would seem that the redaction of BI wanted to mention only the beneficial effects of YHWH's arrival in 40:10 while it focused here in the first instance on the retributory effects thereof. The first term, 'vengeance', harks back to 34:8: 'Truly, YHWH has a day of vengeance (נקם), a year of recompense (שלומים) for the cause of Zion' (see there). Consequently, the initial effect of YHWH's presence is the actual advent of his 'vengeance' over Edom, understood, of course, in a salutary sense with respect to the unfortunate disabled. It is appropriate, therefore, that the verb 'to come' makes its first appearance here and not in 34:8. In addition, the terms of v. 4b shift from negative to positive: from 'vengeance', i.e. over Edom, to 'that he might save you'. The expression 'recompense of God' can thus serve as neutral and intermediary,[22] since גמול is found both in the negative (Isa. 3:9,11; 59:18; 66:6; Jer. 51:6; Joel 4:4; Ps. 137:8; Sir. 32:24) and the positive sense (Judg. 9:16; 2 Sam. 19:37; Isa. 63:7; Ps. 103:2; Prov. 19:17; 2 Chr. 32:25).[23] Without 'your' or 'our', the word 'God' (v. 2) substantiates the ambiguous tone of 'recompense'.

The final colon ('He himself shall come that he might save you') explains the fact that 'vengeance / recompense' are not simply anonymous forces in world history. Rather, they are modalities of God's arrival which has no other purpose than 'to save you'. This important topic (root ישע) has been notably low-key in chs. 28-32 (it occurs only in 30:15) but after being taken up in 33:2,6, in a supplication and an announcement of a new era, it now brings the promise of 12:2f. closer to fulfilment.

5-6a This segment further elaborates the concluding promise of the oracle of salvation: 'that he might save you' (v. 4b). From the perspective of form and theme these verses constitute a pendant of vv. 3-4a'. The double temporal indicator 'then' of vv. 5-6a echoes the two imperatives which introduce vv. 3-4. As with v. 3, v. 5 is chiastically structured and exhibits rhyme, here of verb forms (תפקחנה / תפתחנה). V. 6a matches v. 4a in parallel verse structure, the fearful there corresponding

---

[21] The sentence 'Behold, your God!' (with this possessive pronoun) occurs only here in the Scriptures.

[22] Peels 1995: 153,159.

[23] The verb גמל also occurs in both a positive and negative sense; cf. the dictionaries. K. Seybold favours the positive interpretation for v. 4; cf. VT 22 (1972) 116; TWAT, II, 31-5, esp. 34; likewise Kiesow 1979: 152.

with the disabled in here. The double temporal indicator of the present segment (twice 'then', אז), however, appears to place the salvific turn of events more in the future than v. 4, perhaps even after the coming of 'vengeance' (cf. Isa. 33:23; 60:5). Given the fact that ch.35 anticipates chs. 40-55 in many respects, this future moment would appear to coincide with the time of salvation as it is announced in these latter chapters of BI. The text provides no evidence, however, for the dating of the future expectation.

The description of those who stand to benefit from YHWH's salvific intervention corresponds with those mentioned in vv. 3-4a, the anthropological terms 'eyes, ears, tongue' in the present text paralleling 'hands, knees, heart' in vv. 3-4a. A thematic connection is also evident between 'feeble knees' and 'lame'. Both passages, vv. 3-4a and vv. 5-6a, thus surround and enclose the oracle of salvation.

The series of terms 'eyes, ears, tongue' in v. 5 would appear to have an intertextual background. First of all, it has a parallel in the context of a similar description of future salvation in 32:3-4 (cf. also 'the heart of the rash' found there with 'the fearful of heart' found here in v. 4). While it may not be correct to speak of a direct cross-reference, the connection is relevant nevertheless. When salvation dawns, the healing of the human capacity to see, hear and speak will not only be for the benefit of Israel's leaders, it will also advantage her disabled inhabitants.

Even more important is the following. The promise that the 'blind' shall see and the 'deaf' hear evidently refers to the restoration of bodily disabilities such as those mentioned in vv. 3-4. At the same time, however, just as the terms 'weak', 'feeble' and 'fearful' in vv. 3-4 extend beyond the physical to embody Israel's powerlessness as a nation, likewise the 'blind / deaf' here represent the people to whom the prophet has been sent. Israel's refusal to see, hear and understand had ultimately become grounds for a verdict (Isa. 6:9-10). When YHWH puts an end to every form of resistance, however, 'the deaf shall hear the words of the writing, and out of gloom and darkness the eyes of the blind shall see' (cf. at 29:18). There, the reversal of YHWH's judgement is promised to those who suffer under the lack of belief in Israel, in 35:5 to those who are about to undertake the return to Zion. Furthermore, just as 'the blind and the deaf' serve to round off an important theme in PI, they simultaneously serve to anticipate the function thereof in DI (42:18f.; 43:8).

If the first and second term of the series 'the blind, deaf, lame and dumb' exhibit an intertextual background, there would appear to be solid grounds for making a similar assertion with respect to 'the lame' (פסח). While the combination 'the lame and the dumb' is not found elsewhere in the Scriptures, the combination 'the blind and the lame' does occur: firstly, as a category of those disqualified from the cult (Lev. 21:18; Deut. 15:21; Mal. 1:8; Job 29;15); next, as a group who played a nega-tive role in the capture of Jerusalem (2 Sam. 5:6-8), and finally, as indi-gent people, side by side with pregnant women and women in childbirth over whom YHWH extends his merciful help when he brings his people back to the land (Jer. 31:8; the context of this verse shares a number of terms and topics with Isa. 35:4-10[24]). Within the overarching theme of the return to Zion, 'the blind and the lame' would appear to function as the prototype of those for whom the journey back will be far from easy.[25] It is probable that in Isa. 35:5-6 the term 'blind' in the typically Isaianic word pair 'blind / deaf' has become associated with the term 'lame' under the influence of the theme of return to Zion, in the same way as in Isa. 33:23 Tg added 'the blind' to 'the lame': 'Although there are blind and lame among them, even they will divide booty and spoil in abundance'.[26]

The healing of his handicap provides 'the lame' with something of an edge, the capacity 'to leap like a deer' signifying a more than human dynamism (2 Sam. 22:30,34; Cant. 2:8; Sir. 36:31). The healing of 'the dumb' (אלם: cf. Ps. 39:3, 10) likewise sets him at an advantage. When 'he shall shout for joy', he will occupy a primary place in responding, together with nature itself, to the vision of 'the glory of YHWH' (cf. v. 2: root רנן). Both disabled groups are thus placed in a privileged position, strengthened for the return journey.

6b The first line of the third segment resumes the central topic of the first segment by means of the word pair 'wilderness / desert' (v. 1). The promise of water is supplementary to the announcement that the desert will blossom and rejoice. As with the opening lines of vv. 3-4 and vv. 5-6a, v. 6b is also chiastic in structure.[27] An emphatic 'Truly' (כי) and a *perfectum propheticum* at the beginning of the clause characterise this verse more than any other in ch.35 as a prophecy. (This is the only

---

[24] 'To shout with gladness' in Jer. 31:7 and Isa. 35:10; 'to save' in Jer. 31:7 and Isa. 35:4; 'to return' in Jer. 31:8 and Isa. 35:9; 'to come' in Jer. 31:9 and Isa. 35:10; 'an even way' in Jer. 31:9 and 'a holy way' in Isa. 35:8; 'streams of water' in Jer. 31:9 and Isa. 35:6; 'weeping and supplications' in Jer. 31:9 and 'sorrow and sighing' in Isa. 35:10; 'to shout with gladness' in Jer. 31:7 and Isa. 35:10.

[25] In Jer. 31:9, God's concern for the state of the territory refers precisely to 'the blind and the lame' of v. 8; cf. W. McKane, *A Critical and Exegetical Commentary on Jer-emiah II* (ICC), Edinburgh 1996, 790.

[26] Chilton, 67; *TWAT*, VI, 686f. (R.E. Clements).

[27] 1QIs^a's supplementary ילכו, at the end of v. 6b, is lacking in all the versions and can easily be explained by a desire for completeness (Barthélemy, 243f.).

clause to open with a *qatal*.) From the perspective of syntax, the following verses are dependent on v. 6b (cf. 'Introduction to the Exegesis').

'Water' in PI is mainly an instrument of God's judgement (1:30; 8:6f.; 14:23; 15:6; 17:12f.; 19:5,8; 28:2,17; 30:14; 32:2), and is less frequently seen as a result of YHWH's grace (12:3; 30:25; 32:20). In DI, however, it constitutes an important metaphor for God's benevolent intervention in the metamorphosis of nature (41:17f.; 43:20; 44:3f.; 48:21; 49:10). The parallel term 'streams' (נחלים) underlines this aspect (30:28,33; 66:12), establishing a contrast with the fate of Edom: 'Her streams shall be turned into pitch' (34:9). The verb 'to break forth' indicates that power beyond human reach makes the water emerge from unknown storerooms (בקע *qal* and *niphal*: Gen. 7:11; Exod. 14:21; Isa. 48:21; 63:12; Ps. 74:15; Prov. 3:20). These passages indicate that, far from being uniform, the theme of the transformation of nature is elaborated in a variety of topics. Where the wilderness in vv. 1-2 primarily embodies Israel's poor and withered condition, in combination with the theme of return in vv. 6b-10 it has more the character of a '*terra intermedia* between Babylon and Palestine' (Mathews 1995: 124-9).

7 When water surges through the wilderness (v. 6b), both the earth's surface itself (v. 7a) and its produce (v. 7b) undergo a transformation. The association between the soil and its produce comes to the fore in the verbal expression היה ל, 'to become', which governs both verse lines. The first attests that the soil will retain its water, the second that it will offer ever fresh water. The formulation is quite similar to that of 49:10: 'Neither burning heat nor sun shall smite them, for he who has pity on them will lead them, and by springs of water will guide them'. The word שרב – 'burning sand' in 35:7, 'burning heat' in 49:10 – and the term מבועי מים, 'springs of water', are not found elsewhere. The word 'pool' (אגם) should similarly be included among the terms which make forward reference to DI (41:18; 42:15). The main difference between the present verse and related passages in DI lies in the absence of the topic that YHWH will accompany the returnees, a fact which fits the obvious plan of the redaction not to mention YHWH's return to Zion prior to ch.40.

Transformation of the soil brings with it a similar transformation of its produce: 'steppe-grass', the characteristic lair of the jackal, becomes 'reeds and rushes', vegetation characteristic of well-watered regions such as the Nile delta ('reeds': 1 Kgs 14:15; Isa. 19:6; Ps. 68:31; Job 40:21; 'rushes': Isa. 18:2; Job 8:11). The wilderness also serves elsewhere as a home for the jackal (Jer. 9:10; 10:22; 49:33; 51:17; Mal. 1:3; Ps. 44:20. In connection with Isa. 34:13 ('Thorns shall grow over its strongholds, nettles and thistles in its fortresses. It shall be the haunt of jackals...'), which employs the same terminology in the last words (נוה תנים), mention of the 'jackals' here is signficant. With the disappearance of both the flora and the fauna of the desert which arrived in the aftermath of the judgement, the implication is made that other living beings will take their place. V. 7 thus prepares the way for v. 8.

8-9a Besides abundant water, the transformed landscape, indicated by the triple 'there', will also enjoy the presence of a 'highroad' (מסלול).[28] More than a simple pathway, this technical term implies a substantial road with a raised groundwork made of rubble and stone (Isa. 40:3; 57:14; 62:10; Jer. 18:15). Such roads were built by the state authorities for controled economic as well as political and military purposes.[29] The term 'way' (דרך), in contrast, has a much broader range of significance, extending from simple 'path' to 'public road'. As an apposition to 'highroad', 'way' thus serves to widen the possible usage thereof. At the same time, it anticipates the 'holy way', a qualification which does not naturally apply to a 'high road'.

The concept 'highroad' (מסלה   and the root סלל) is related to an elaborate motif which binds the three parts of BI together (Mathews 1995: 131-5): the return of the exiles from Assyria, which is compared to the exodus from Egypt (11:16), the return from exile in general and from Babylon in particular (49:11), but also the return of YHWH as leader of his people (40:1-11, esp. v. 3) and the return of the people to YHWH (57:14) and to Zion (62:10). The latter text appears to exhibit the strongest associations with 35:8.

The expression 'holy way' is unique to the present verse, its meaning being determined primarily by the context. In PI the qualification 'holy' (קדש) applies in the first place to YHWH himself (5:16; 8:13; 29:23) but it is also used of his dwelling ('mountain': 11:9; 27:13) and of the remnant which will grow, after the judgement, into a new people (6:13). In the immediate context, the significance of the 'holy way' is determined by the references to those who will not be found to travel it (four times לא, once בל). This fits the character of a 'highroad' whose usage is determined by the authorities.

---

[28] The noun מסלול is found only here, מסלה being the more usual form. The suggestion that מסלול, together with the following דרך, refers to a territory rather than a 'way', is inspired by particular literary-historical opinions (*pace* Hubmann 1977: 35-8).

[29] K.J.H. Vriezen, "Wegen en wegaanleg. Opmerkingen naar aanleiding van het vocabulaire in de Profeten en de Geschriften"; in: *Door het oog van de profeten* (FS C. van Leeuwen) (eds B. Becking, J. van Dorp, A. van der Kooij), (Utrechtse Theologische Reeks, 8), Utrecht 1989, 129-32; D.A. Dorsey, *The Roads and Highways of Ancient Israel* (The ASOR Library of Biblical and Near Eastern Archaeology), Baltimore, London 1991, 233f.

The 'unclean / fools' and the 'lion / ravenous beast' are excluded from travelling along this 'holy way'.[30] The exclusion of 'the unclean' (טמא) can be explained in terms of what is to be left behind: in PI the worship of idols (30:22) and the sinful people (6:5; cf. 64:5), in DI the impurity of the place of exile (52:11) in contrast to 'the holy city Jerusalem' (48:2; 52:1). The exclusion of 'fools' (אוילים) is based on the sinful, godless tendencies which characterise such individuals (Jer. 22:16; Hos. 9:7; 13:13; Zech. 11:15; Ps. 38:6; 69:6; 107:17; Job 5:2f.; Prov. 24:9).[31] The exclusion of dangerous animals corresponds with a motif from the theme of impending salvation (Lev. 26:6; Ezek. 34:25,28) and can be explained in terms of the raised foundations of the 'highroad' (v. 9a: 'shall not come up on it').

The mention of 'fools' here clearly has further implications. Because ch.35 appears in a number of ways, terminology included, to bring closure to PI, the term 'fools' thus reminds us of Isa. 19:11-15, which speaks of the 'foolish' (v. 11) princes of Egypt who have led their land astray (the verb 'to err' [תעה] is found twice in this passage [vv. 13f.]). The term 'fools' can therefore be interpreted as a reference to the Judean ambassadors who sought political assistance in Egypt (30:1-7; 31:1-3).[32] For those whose ultimate destination is Egypt, the road to Zion is clearly the wrong road. It is for this reason that such individuals are not found thereon.[33]

In the middle of this segment which speaks of those who will *not* be allowed to travel the 'holy way', we find a colon with a positive message: 'It shall be for the one (those) who go(es) the way' (v. 8: והוא למו הלך דרך; cf. 'Notes'). While the imprecise syntactic structure together with the interruption of the chiastic verse line leads one to suspect an interpolation, the intention of the colon remains pure guess work. Should one understand למו as a plural then the clause might refer to the disabled whose salvation is at hand (vv. 5-6a). In this event, the clause would constitute a remark introduced into the main text (without adequate integration) by an author who wanted to identify the disabled with those who undertake the journey to Zion (vv. 9b-10). On further investigation, however, it seems impossible to construct a sentence with למו as a plural

---

[30] Dorsey 1991: 215: 'The phrase עבר דרך designates "to travel along, not across, a road" (cf. Deut. 2:8; Isa. 35:8)'.

[31] *TWAT*, I, 150f. (H. Cazelles).

[32] Reference to these texts as well as to Isa. 19:11 might explain the fact that the plural 'fools' is found here, surrounded by other categories referred to in the singular.

[33] Since the segment in its entirety clearly excludes certain categories from using the way, it cannot imply that the 'fools' will lose their way and not reach their destination. They are simply not to be found on the way (*pace* Delitzsch, 366).

in combination with the singular הלך דרך. Therefore, if we understand למו as a singular, then it seems possible that the clause makes reference to a promise found frequently in DI, namely that YHWH will protect the 'way' of those among the people who have the courage to return (40:29-31; 42:16; 43:2-8,19-21; 48:17-21; 49:9-12; cf. 30:21). In that case, the collective perspective changes into an individual one.

9b-10 It is generally accepted that these verses were borrowed from 51:10-11 by the final redaction in order to create an overarching frame-work for BI. Three *verba movendi* are employed to render the return journey to Zion: 'to go' (הלך) for the initiative to begin the journey, 'to return' (שוב) for the chosen destination and 'to come in' (בוא ב) for the arrival in Zion. The first and third verbs, 'they shall go' and 'they shall come in', are *w^eqatals* in first position which follow upon the clause: 'There shall be a highroad' in v. 8. As such they structure the passage.

The first verse line (v. 9b-10a') serves further to designate those for whom the 'highroad' is intended: 'the redeemed / the ransomed of YHWH'. The term 'to redeem' (גאל) appears here for the first time in BI, giving prior announcement of its important role in DI and TI as a divine title and in the context of liberation from exile (41:14; 43:1,14; 44:6,22-24; 47:4; 48:17,20; 49:7,26; 52:3,9; 54:5,8; 59:20; 60:16; 62:12; 63:9,16). It is characteristic of the term that it assumes a blood relationship between the redeemer and the one redeemed.[34] Since this is a new topic for PI, the question arises as to the identity of 'the redeemer' of the returnees. The parallel term provides the answer: 'the ransomed of YHWH'. The term 'to ransom' (פדה) has its roots in trade law where it refers to the appropriation of persons or goods in exchange for a deter-mined price. In theological context, however, the latter element disap-pears to be replaced by God's liberation of Israel from the oppression of a more powerful adversary (Isa. 1:27; 29:22 [see there]; 50:2; 51:11; Deut. 7:8; 9:26; 15:15; 24:18; 2 Sam. 7:23; Mic. 6:4; Ps. 78:42; 111:9; Neh. 1:10). In contrast to the source text (51:9-14), the context of ch.35 does not provide a clear image of the oppressor in question. Only the fear (v. 4) and the lamentation (v. 10b) suggest some kind of hostile power. Taken together, however, both terms, 'to redeem' and 'to ransom', situate the returnees between two parties: YHWH, who can claim special rights over Israel, and an occupier who does so but cannot. These relationships are reflected in the return to Zion, the ground in which YHWH's association with Israel has its very roots.

---

[34] *TWAT*, I, 886-90 (H. Ringgren); *DCH*, II, 294.

The return journey takes place under the accompaniment of 'joy and gladness'. The first term (root רנן) guarantees that the transformed land-scape (v. 2) will be engrossed witnessing the new events and that the now healed disabled (v. 6) will join the caravan which is making its way to Zion. While this stands in stark contrast to nature's bursts of joy as the king of Babylon enters the realm of the dead (14:7-9), it firmly ac-cords with the expectations expressed in the song of praise which brings the first collection of the prophecies of Isaiah ben Amoz to a conclusion (12:6; cf. 24:14; 26:19). In PI, the second term (root שׂמח) connotes the end of oppression (9:2; 25:9; 29:19; 30:29), a notion unfolded here in the final clause: 'Sorrow and sighing shall flee away', in contrast to Is-rael's experience of the need to flee and sigh ('to flee' [נוס]: Isa. 10:3; 30:16f.; 'sorrow' [root יגה]: Isa. 51:23; Jer. 8:18; 31:13; Lam. 1:5,12; 'sighing' [root אנח]: Isa. 24:7; Ezek. 21:11; Lam. 1:4,8,22).

The theme of the return (שׁוב) to Zion is not found in BI prior to this point (that of the return to YHWH occurs in 1:27; 6:10; 10:21f.; 19:22; 31:6, that of entry into Zion [בוא] also in late texts: 27:13; 30:29). The only parallel to set off for the journey (הלך) to Zion is to be found in the summons to the nations at the beginning of BI (2:2-4), a text which also functions in its overarching structure. One is forced to conclude that the redaction of the book not only presents the prophecies of Isaiah ben Amoz to a later audience as an explanation for their compulsory stay in exile but also responds to their 'sorrow and sighing' by the promise of a return to Zion.

THE FIRST STORY: THE DEFEAT OF THE KING OF ASSYRIA AGAINST THE GOD OF ISRAEL (36:1-37:38)

36:1 It happened in the fourteenth year of king Hezekiah
   that Sennacherib, the king of Assyria, went up
   against all the fortified cities of Judah and took them.

2 Then the king of Assyria sent the Rabshakeh from Lachish
   to king Hezekiah at Jerusalem, with a great army.
   He took his stand by the conduit of the Upper Pool
   on the highway to the Fuller's Field.

3 There came out to him Eliakim, the son of Hilkiah, who was over
   the house-hold, and Shebna, the secretary, and Joah, the son of
   Asaph, the recorder.

4 The Rabshakeh said to them:
   Say to Hezekiah:
   Thus says the Great King, the king of Assyria:
    What is this trust by which you have trusted?

5   I say: mere words of lips are counsel and strength for war!
    Now, in whom have you put your trust
    that you have rebelled against me?

6   Behold, you have put your trust in Egypt,
    that staff of a broken reed,
    which if one lean on it
    it will go into one's hand and pierce it.
    Such is Pharaoh, the king of Egypt, to all who trust in him.

7   But if you say to me:
     'We have put our trust in YHWH, our God',
    is it not he
    whose high places and altars Hezekiah has removed,
    saying to Judah and to Jerusalem:
     'Before this altar you shall worship'?

8   Now, please negotiate with my lord, the king of Assyria.
    I will give you two thousand horses,
    if you are able on your part to set riders upon them.

9   How then can you turn aside the face of an officer,
    one of the least of my lord's servants,

so that you have put your trust in Egypt
for chariots and for horsemen?

10   Now, is it without YHWH
that I have gone up against this land to destroy it?
YHWH said to me:
    'Go up against this land, and destroy it'.

11   Then Eliakim, Shebna, and Joah said to the Rabshakeh:
Please, speak to your servants in Aramaic,
for we understand it.
Do not speak to us in Judean
within the hearing of the people who are on the wall.

12   But the Rabshakeh said:
Is it to your lord and to you
that my lord has sent me to speak these words?
Does it not concern the men sitting on the wall
in that they will eat their dung and drink their urine with you?

13   Then the Rabshakeh stood
and called out in a loud voice in Judean:
Listen to the words of the Great King, the king of Assyria!

14   Thus says the king:
Do not let Hezekiah deceive you,
for he will not be able to deliver you.

15   Do not let Hezekiah make you trust in YHWH by saying:
'YHWH will surely deliver us.
This city will not be given
into the hand of the king of Assyria'.

16   Do not listen to Hezekiah.
For thus says the king of Assyria:
Make a blessing agreement with myself
and go out to me.
Then every one of you will eat of his own vine,
and every one of his own fig tree,
and every one of you will drink the water of his own cistern,

17   until I come
and take you away to a land like your own land,
a land of grain and wine, a land of bread and vineyards.

18   Beware lest Hezekiah mislead you by saying:
    'YHWH will deliver us'.
Has any of the gods of the nations delivered his land
out of the hand of the king of Assyria?

19   Where are the gods of Hamath and Arpad?
Where are the gods of Sepharvaim?

Have they delivered Samaria out of my hand?
20 Who among all the gods of these lands
have delivered their land out of my hand,
that YHWH should deliver Jerusalem out of my hand?
21 But they were silent
and answered him not a word.
For the king's command was:
'Do not answer him'.
22 Then Eliakim, the son of Hilkiah, who was over the household,
and Shebna, the secretary, and Joah, the son of Asaph, the recorder,
came to Hezekiah with their clothes rent,
and reported to him the words of the Rabshakeh.

37:1 It happened when king Hezekiah heard (these),
that he rent his clothes,
covered himself with sackcloth
and came into the house of YHWH.
2 He sent Eliakim, who was over the household, and Shebna, the
secretary, and the senior priests, covered with sackcloth,
to the prophet Isaiah, the son of Amoz.
3 They said to him:
Thus says Hezekiah:
This day is a day of distress, of chastisement and rejection.
For children have come to the birth,
and there is no strength to bring them forth.
4 Perhaps YHWH, your God, will hear the words of the
Rabshakeh,
whom his lord, the king of Assyria, has sent
to mock the living God,
and will chastise (him)
for the words which YHWH, your God, has heard.
Therefore, lift up a prayer for the remnant to be found
(here).
5 So the servants of king Hezekiah came to Isaiah.
6 Isaiah said to them:
Thus you shall say to your lord:
Thus says YHWH:
Do not be afraid because of the words that you have heard,
with which the lackeys of the king of Assyria have reviled
me.
7 Behold, I will put a spirit in him,
so that he shall hear a rumour,

and return to his own land.
And I will make him fall by the sword in his own land.

8   The Rabshakeh returned,
and found the king of Assyria fighting against Libnah,
For he had heard that (the king) had left Lachish.

9   (The king) had heard concerning Tirhakah, the king of Ethiopia:
'He has gone out to fight against you'.
When he heard it,
he sent messengers to Hezekiah, saying:

10   Thus shall you say to Hezekiah, the king of Judah:
Do not let your God in whom you trust deceive you by saying:
'Jerusalem will not be given
into the hand of the king of Assyria'.

11   Behold, you have heard
what the kings of Assyria have done to all lands,
destroying them utterly.
And shall you be delivered?

12   Have the gods of the nations delivered them,
the nations which my fathers destroyed,
Gozan, Haran, Rezeph,
and the people of Eden, who were in Telassar?

13   Where is the king of Hamath, the king of Arpad,
the king of the city of Sepharvaim, the king of Hena,
or the king of Ivvah?

14   Hezekiah received the letter from the hand of the messengers,
and read it.
Hezekiah went up to the house of YHWH,
and spread it before YHWH.

15   Hezekiah prayed to YHWH:

16   O YHWH of hosts, God of Israel,
who are enthroned above the cherubim,
you are the God, you alone, of all the kingdoms of the earth.
You have made heaven and earth.

17   Incline your ear, O YHWH, and hear;
open your eyes, O YHWH, and see,
and hear all the words of Sennacherib,
which he has sent to mock the living God.

18   Of a truth, O YHWH,
the kings of Assyria have laid waste all the lands,

19   have cast their gods into the fire

- for they were no gods, but the work of human hands, wood
and stone -
and have destroyed them.

20   So now, O YHWH, our God,
save us from his hand,
that all the kingdoms of the earth may know
that you alone are YHWH.

21   Then Isaiah, the son of Amoz, sent to Hezekiah, saying:
Thus says YHWH, the God of Israel:
Because you have prayed to me
concerning Sennacherib, the king of Assyria,

22   this is the word that YHWH has spoken concerning him:
'She despises you, she scorns you
- the virgin daughter of Zion.
Behind you, she wags her head
- the daughter of Jerusalem.

23   Whom have you mocked and reviled?
Against whom have you raised your voice
and lifted your eyes on high?
Against the Holy One of Israel!

24   By your servants you have mocked the Lord,
and you have said:
'With my many chariots I myself have gone up
the heights of the mountains,
to the far recesses of Lebanon.
I felled its tallest cedars, its choicest cypresses.
I came to its remotest height, its densest forest.

25   I myself dug wells and drank waters,
dried up with the sole of my feet
all the streams of Egypt'.

26   Have you not heard?
From long ago I have determined it,
from days of old I have planned it.
Now I bring it to pass,
that you should make crash into heaps of ruins
fortified cities,

27   while their inhabitants, short of hand,
are dismayed and confounded,
and have become like plants of the field and like tender grass,
like grass on the housetops, blighted before the eastwind.

28   But your rising up and sitting down,

your going out and coming in,
    I know, and your raging against me.

29   Because you have raged against me
    and your arrogance has gone up to my ears,
I will put my hook in your nose and my bit in your lips,
    and I will turn you back on the way
    by which you came''.

30   But for you, this shall be the sign:
this year eat what grows of itself,
    and in the second year what springs from that.
Then in the third year sow and reap,
    and plant vineyards, and eat their fruit.

31   Those who survive from the house of Judah, the remnant,
shall again take root downward,
    and bear fruit upward.

32   Truly, out of Jerusalem shall go forth a remnant,
    and out of Mount Zion a band of survivors.
The zeal of YHWH of hosts will accomplish this.

33   Therefore thus says YHWH concerning the king of Assyria:
He shall not come into this city,
    or shoot an arrow there,
or bring a shield before it,
    or cast up a siege mound against it.

34   By the way on which he came, he shall return,
    and he shall not come into this city, says YHWH.

35   For I will shield this city to save it,
    for my own sake and for the sake of my servant David.

36   The messenger of YHWH went out
and slew a hundred and eighty-five thousand in the camp of the
Assyrians.
When they arose early in the morning,
behold, these were all dead bodies.

37   Then Sennacherib, the king of Assyria, broke camp,
went home
and returned.
He remained at Nineveh.

38   It happened,
while he was worshipping in the house of Nisroch, his god,
that Adrammelech and Sharezer, his sons, slew him with the sword.
They escaped into the land of Ararat.
And Esarhaddon, his son, reigned in his stead.

NOTES

36:5 There would appear to be no text-critical justification for changing the 1st person verb form אמרתי into a 2nd person form as one finds in 1Kgs 18:20 (Barthélemy, 248). Those who opt for emendation do so on the presumption that the text of the narrative in 1 Kings is older. The text-critical independence of chs. 36-39, however, will be maintained throughout.

8 Although התערב is traditionally translated 'make a wager', the translation 'to consort, associate' comes closer to the meaning of the root (W. von Soden, "Hebräische Problemwörter", *UF* 18 [1986] 341-4).

9 The construct state of the word פחה ('officer') is better explained as an assimilation to its apposition אחד than as a gloss since it is to be found in all of the versions (Barthélemy, 249).

19 It is a source of some surprise that gods foreign to Samaria should have to deliver the city. Translators tend for this reason to insert the plus found in the parallel text of 2 Kgs 18:34 of LXX and VL: 'Where are the gods of the land of Samaria?'. The versions of Isa. 36:19, however, do not support such an emendation. The historical situation might provide some explanation of the MT text (Barthélemy, 251f.). One year after the fall of Samaria to Salmanassar V (722 BC), a coalition against his successor Sargon II, the father of Sennacherib, under the leadership of Hamath was hardly even able to offer any resistance to the Assyrian army let alone reverse its recent victories (cf. the inscription mentioned in *ANET*, 284).

37:4 1QIs[a] adds בעיר הזאת to the end of the verse in an evident attempt to avoid the last word of MT, הנמצאה, being interpreted in its late, post-exilic significance of 'one in captivity'. MT, however, deserves preference (Iwry 1966).

9 Instead of the second וישמע, the parallel version of 2 Kgs 19:9 reads וישב. 1QIs[a] provides both words (1QIs[b] does not) and LXX translates both words. The double version would appear to be a conflation of the two words. As will be the case elsewhere with the narratives of chs. 36-39, the version of 2 Kgs does not enjoy any degree of precedence (Barthélemy, 251).

18 The last words of v. 18, ואת ארצם, are lacking in 1QIs[a] which might offer the original reading. Probably because of the fact that these words repeat those which precede them (את כל הארצות), LXX, Vg, Tg and modern translations (e.g. RSV) render here with two different nouns. The repetition can be explained as an unsuccessful attempt to

adapt the text to 2 Kgs 19:17 (הגוים). In the present commentary, therefore, it is left untranslated.

20 After the tetragrammaton, the parallel text of 2 Kgs 19:20 reads an additional word אלהים, thereby harmonising the conclusion of the prayer with the opening thereof: 'You are the God, you alone, of all the kingdoms'. The versions were apparently aware of the difference between v. 16 and v. 20 of ch. 37: 1QIs[a] adds אלהים after the tetragrammaton in v. 20, LXX and Syr replace the tetragrammaton with אלהים. Vg and Tg, on the other hand, follow MT. The latter clearly offers the *lectio difficilior*, which, in light of Neh. 9:6, would appear to be within the bounds of possibility (Barthélemy, 253f.).

22-35 This speech of YHWH has the form of poetry, the colometry of which is reflected in the translation.

26 Counter to the accents of MT, the parallelism inclines us to connect the temporal indicator 'from long ago' to the following verb 'I have determined it' (Delitzsch, 380; Alexander, 68; König, 309; Wildberger, 1415, 1433; Watts, 39,45).

27-28 Instead of ושדמה לפני קמה (v. 27: '[like grass of the housetops and] the field before the standing corn')[1], the parallel text of 2 Kgs 19:26 has the term שדפה ('a blasted thing before the standing corn, i.e. before maturity'). While 1QIs[a] (cf. Vg, Tg) also reads the root of שדף (*niphal*) in v. 27 ('to scorch, to blight': Gen. 41:6,27; Deut. 28:22; 1 Kgs 8:37; Amos 4:9; Hag. 2:17), it offers, moreover, the term 'eastwind' (קדים), prior to 'the standing corn' of MT (קמה), which it renders as קומכה ('your rising'). In this way, according to 1QIs[a], the end of v. 26 and the beginning of v. 27 thus reads: 'like grass on the housetops, blighted before the eastwind. But your rising up and sitting down, your going out and coming in, I know'. Given the consistency of the topic of grass being scorched by an eastwind (Isa. 15:6; 40:6ff.; Ezek. 17:10; 19:12; Ps. 90:6; Job 8:12), and the possibility of a sort of haplography between קדים ('eastwind') and קומך ('your rising') the reading of 1QIs[a] deserves preference (Barthélemy, 257ff.; Wildberger, 1419; Watts, 41; Oswalt, 657).

31 The reading of 1QIs[a], והנמצא, is not original with respect to MT הנשארה but stems rather from the late post-exilic period when the word meant 'one in captivity' (Chron., Ezra and probably Dan., Esth.; cf. the note at 37:4). This alteration affords deliverance not only to 'those who survive from the house of Judah', i.e. in Jerusalem, but to all of the exiles (cf. in this verse the emendation of MT ויספה in 1QIs[a] ואספה [from 24:22?] and 37:4; Iwry 1966).

---

[1] For 'fields', cf. Deut. 32:32; Isa. 16:8; Job 3:17.

Essentials and Perspectives

It is generally accepted among contemporary exegetes that from the theological and literary perspectives, chs. 36-39 do not constitute an unusual or alien element in BI. On the contrary, the chapters in question are quite at home in the book, given that they exhibit strong associations with PI and prepare the way for DI by way of a number of evident allusions.[2] Many commentators have been inclined, therefore, to abandon the classical theory that the chapters were borrowed from 2 Kgs 18:13-20:19.[3] Scholars now consider the chapters either to have been devised in view of the final form of BI[4] or to have been older independent texts which were adapted in a far-reaching redaction.[5] Since then we have been able to achieve a greater degree of insight into the perspective of these three narratives. They are intended, in fact, to show that the events of history have proved the prophecies of Isaiah in chs. 1-35 to have been correct. YHWH was firmly determined and he had the power to protect Jerusalem from foreign domination, should the king of the city place his trust in God in line with the prophet's preaching. Indeed, YHWH demonstrated this will in the face of the tyrant Assyria during the life of Hezekiah (chs. 36-38). At the same time, with the entrance of the king of Babylon (ch.39) the foundations were laid for the second part of BI, in which the downfall of the latter's world empire is presented as God's response to the destruction of Jerusalem. These chapters thus establish a powerful bond between PI and DI[6], a fact which is confirmed by studies which show a variety of agreements between chs. 36-39 and both PI and DI.[7]

[2] Seitz 1991: 47-118; Vermeylen 1997: 101ff.

[3] The older perspective was first proposed by Gesenius (932-6) and more recently revived and thoroughly revised by Gonçalves (1986: 331-487) and Camps (1990: 53-61). Traces thereof are also to be found in Becker's explanation (1997: 230-2). In the latter's opinion, chs. 36-37 were borrowed from 2 Kings and supplemented in the context of BI with chs. 38-39, chapters which after much emendation were taken up in the final redaction of 2 Kings. This entire process, according to Becker, would have taken place for the most part in the post-exilic or indeed proto-Chronistic period.

[4] While a relatively large number of authors proposed this theory more or less simultaneously, its first systematic elaboration stems from Smelik (1986); cf. the surveys of Williamson 1994: 189-93; Vermeylen 1997: 95-108.

[5] Although Williamson (1994: 209-11), for example, recognises the strongly Isaianic character of the chapters, he maintains, nevertheless, that they owe their existence to the circles which 'administered' the prophet's patrimony. In his opinion, they were first taken up in the Deuteronomic History and later borrowed from 2 Kings by the redaction of BI, albeit with greater probability during the period in which TI came into existence than the period in which PI and DI were combined.

[6] Seitz 1991: 37-46, 193-208.

[7] With regard to PI, cf. the studies of Ackroyd, Smelik, Groves and Conrad; with regard to DI, cf. especially Groves. For a discussion of these data, cf. Williamson 1994: 188-212.

Given that chs. 36-39 play a major role in the final form of BI, which came to completion over a long period of time stretching from before the exile up to the Persian period, it is of some importance that we provide ourselves with a clear perspective on the redaction history of the chapters in question. Literary-historical research traditionally distinguishes three sources in chs. 36-37: 36:1, which should be understood as a summary of 2 Kgs 18:13-17, the oldest 'historical report' (source A); 36:1-37:9a,37-38 (source B^1) and 37:9b-36 (source B^2).[8] The distinction between the latter two sources is based on apparent repetitions (two diplomatic missions from the Assyrian king: 36:1-2 and 37:9b; two visits by Hezekiah to the temple: 37:1 and 14; two messages from Isaiah: 37:6 and 21) and contradictions (the Assyrian conception of YHWH: 36:10 and 37:10-12; Isaiah's prophecy and the outcome thereof: 37:7 and 36). Given the ambiguous order of events in 37:8-9, the seam between the two sources would appear to be located in these verses (between v. 9a and v. 9b).

The insight has gradually emerged that we are not dealing with two *independent* sources here but rather of two *interdependent* sources. At the same time, however, given that the defamation of YHWH, the sinful climax of events, is found in both sources (36:15, 18-20 and 37:10-12), one cannot place them side by side as historical report and theological drama. Since B^1 contains a greater degree of historical information, scholars have long considered B^2 to be a post-exilic creation inspired by B^1, which is said to stem from the middle of the 7th century.[9] Recent research, however, tends to permit the opposite view, associating the second source with the pre-exilic literary layer of BI which proclaims the inviolability of Zion (cf. the verb 'to shield' in 37:35 and 31:5; the verb 'to trust' in 37:10 and 31:1; 32:9-11; the topic of YHWH's sovereignty over the nations in 37:16-20 and 8:9; 14:26; 17:12; 29:7; the 'mythical' character of the fall of the Assyrian army in 37:36 and 8:8-10). The first source is then said to be a Deuteronomistic reworking. This explanation would appear to be in conformity with the redactional history of BI.[10]

An essentially different approach to the explanation of chs. 36-39 lays greater emphasis on their original independence and on the role of the 7th century redaction of BI.[11] Given that 39:6-7 do not announce the destruction of Jerusalem in 587 BC, but rather her plundering and the first deportations in 597 BC,[12] commentators tend to locate ch.39 in the final decade of the kingdom of Judah. Furthermore, since this chapter

[8] Beginning with Stade 1886.
[9] Dion (1989) rejects the historical reliability of B^2 out of hand while ascribing it, to a limited degree, to B^1.
[10] Vermeylen 1997: esp. 112-8.
[11] Sweeney, 476-87.
[12] Clements 1983.

brings criticism to bear upon the policy of Hezekiah (726-697 BC) with respect to Babylon, while chs. 36-37(38) portray him as the ideal ruler, scholars tend to view ch.39 as a corrective of chs. 36-37(38), situating the latter chapters prior thereto. It is possible that the chapters in question stem from opposition during the time of Hezekiah's son Manasseh (697-642 BC), who was the antithesis of his father in almost every respect and whose politics with respect to Assyria came to such a disastrous conclusion (2 Kings 21; 2 Chronicles 33).[13] At the same time, however, the reign of Manasseh's grandson Josiah (640-609 BC) might also form the background of the chapters in question, the Deuteronomistic movement confronting the court with Hezekiah's rule as the ideal.[14] This exegetical approach does not consider chs. 36-39 so much to have been *designed* to establish a bridge between the two major segments of BI but rather as composition made up of narratives which once functioned in a different context and were later combined and *reworked* for their incorporation in BI, firstly as a conclusion to PI and then as a preparation for the theme of the return from Babylonian exile in DI. A number of important points in which PI and chs. 36-39 do not agree, confirm the impression that these chapters originally existed independently.[15] This view of chs. 36-39 will also constitute the point of departure of the present commentary in which we have already situated a significant amount of prophetic material in chs. 28-32 together with the redactional blue print thereof in the period prior to the exile.

Should these chapters stem in essence from the period of the Assyrian hegemony, the question of the extent of their historical reliability must be faced.[16] The fact of Sennacherib's campaign against Jerusalem is beyond question since it is also mentioned in the 'Annals of Sennacherib'.[17] With respect to the outcome of the campaign, the Annals make no mention of a massacre among the Assyrian troops and portray the tribute Sennacherib exacted from Hezekiah (mentioned only in 2 Kgs 18:14-16 as a victory:

'Hezekiah himself, whom the terror-inspiring splendour of my lordship had overwhelmed and whose irregular and elite troops which he had brought into Jerusalem, his royal residence, in order to strengthen it, had deserted him, did send me later, to Nineveh, my lordly city, together

---

[13] Seitz 1991: 96-116.

[14] Sweeney, 484f.

[15] 10:9-11 and 36:19; 37:13; likewise 22:15 and 36:3; 37:2. Further the unique term 'the remnant of the house of Judah that remains' in 37:31 (Sweeney, 480f.).

[16] The most detailed comparison of the biblical texts and other Ancient Near Eastern material has been provided by Gonçalves 1986; cf. also Dion 1989.

[17] The relevant stock of texts is discussed in great detail by Stohlmann 1983: 149-61.

with 30 talents of gold, 800 talents of silver, precious stones... and all kinds of valuable treasures, his (own) daughters, concubines, male and female musicians. In order to deliver the tribute and to do obeisance as a slave he sent his (personal) messenger' (*ANET*, 288).

It may have been the Assyrian king's policy not to conquer and destroy Jerusalem but rather to reduce Judah to a city state and to make her king a vassal. It is also possible that some sort of epidemic ultimately led to the retreat of the Assyrian army for a number of such instances are know to us.[18] Whatever the case, it is clear that the Annals of Sennacherib are less intertwined with myth than has been hitherto assumed. Chs. 36-37 would appear to have some historical basis, perhaps more than one might spontaneously ascribe. The speeches of the Rabshakeh which endeavour to further the surrender of the city have parallels, for example, in the Assyrian and Babylonian sources. They contain topics and expressions which were employed in the diplomatic service of the empires in question.[19] On the whole, however, the facts appear to be attuned to the theological framework in which the narrative functions.[20] This is also evident, for example, from the fact that Sennacherib's death, which took place 20 years later (681 BC), is presented as an immediate consequence of his 'defeat'. The intervention of Pharaoh Tirhakah and the use of the title 'king' in his regard (37:9) are likewise anachronistic for the year 701 BC, given the fact that his reign did not commence until 690 BC. It is probable that Sennacherib's second campaign into Palestine between 688 and 686 BC, during which he did battle with this Pharaoh, and that of 701 BC have been woven together into one single event.[21] In other words, 'the present narrative telescopes historical events ranging over several decades into a single account of Sennacherib's invasion of 701' (Sweeney, 478).

The evident variety of historical-critical opinions concerning chs. 36-37 is partly due to the strong literary cohesion of this first narrative which is difficult to dissect into constitutive parts (Smelik (1986). The explanation is bound to this fact. Chs. 36-37 constitute a narrative unity

---

[18] Von Soden 1985: 155.

[19] Cohen 1979; Von Soden 1985: 152-4.

[20] Groves 1987; Kruger 1996.

[21] The old theory that Sennacherib engaged in two campaigns around 701 BC was developed to explain the problem of 2 Kgs 18:13-16 side by side with 18:17-19:36 but has enjoyed little support for some time. After Na'aman (1979) combined two fragments from the British Museum and associated them with Sennacherib, Shea (1985 and 1997) concluded on the basis of this 'new text' and two other Egyptian texts that Sennacherib had engaged in a campaign later than 701. Since 2 Kgs 18:14-16 is lacking in Isaiah 36, this theory is much less compelling for the Isaiah-recension.

surrounded by the arrival and withdrawal of the Assyrian army. The most imposing actant in this first narrative is Sennacherib, the king of Assyria, since he has two opponents. His natural opponent is Hezekiah, the king of Judah. At the same time, however, since Sennacherib imagines himself to be a god greater than the God of Israel, YHWH constitutes his other opponent. Sennacherib is possessed with the idea that he can enter Lebanon, the dwelling of the gods, as his own territory and, as a creator god, place the waters of the Nile at his disposal (37:24-25). While he challenges YHWH to prove his might over Israel he does not do so directly. Instead he endeavours to undermine the faith which Hezekiah, the king of Judah, so clearly exhibits in YHWH (36:7,15,18-20; 37:10-11).

In this context the second level actants come to the fore: primarily the strategist general, the 'Rabshakeh', who speaks on behalf of the king of Assyria, and the prophet Isaiah, the messenger of YHWH, together with the servants of Hezekiah. The central figure on this level is also king Hezekiah of Judah who is in direct contact with Isaiah and YHWH and indirect contact with the Assyrian general and his king through the mediation of his servants. Far from being a mere plaything in the hands of the invader, Hezekiah opts for YHWH and his prophet. His servants endeavour to protect the people from the blasphemous language of the Assyrian leadership (36:11) and he himself refuses to enter into negotiations (36:21). Instead he goes to the temple of YHWH (37:1), asks the prophet to intercede on his behalf (37:3-4) and prays to his God (37:15-20). In this sense Hezekiah is the ideal example of a faithful king and the opposite of his father Ahaz in ch. 7 (cf. the similar locatives in 7:3 and 36:2 as well as the rejection and silent acceptance of a sign in 7:12 and 37:30).

The outcome of the narrative is that the Assyrian king goes to the wall. Sennacherib loses his army because of the intervention of God's angel (37:36), is unable to take Jerusalem and is forced to accept a withdrawal (v. 37). He ultimately tastes a humiliating death at the hands of his sons. His own god Nisroch looks on in silence (v. 38), in stark contrast to YHWH, who answers Hezekiah's prayer (37: 21,30-32).

The narrative framework is rather sober. It opens with a description of military emergency: all the cities of Judah have fallen, the enemy army has taken position outside Jerusalem (36:1-2). The end of the narrative consists of an abbreviated report of the defeat (37:36-37). The central part of the narrative intimates that the Assyrian king's military supremacy is not universally accepted (37:8-9).

The struggle between the king of Assyria and YHWH finds expression within the narrative framework, especially in the bragging declarations of the king. The three speeches which originate from the Assyrian camp exhibit an increasing degree of arrogance (36:4-10, 12-20; 37:10-13). Hezekiah's initiatives, on the other hand, exhibit an increasing degree of piety, ascending from an appeal for prophetic intervention (37:3-7) to a direct appeal to YHWH (37:14-20). In the second divine speech, directed to Hezekiah (37:21-35), YHWH responds to both Sennacherib (vv. 22-29, 33-35) and Hezekiah (vv. 30-32), albeit in a complex and indirect manner: while he does not condescend to send a message to the Assyrian king in person, he formulates his response to Sennacherib as a word of encouragement for Hezekiah.

The motif-word which opens chs. 36-37 and connects them with chs. 28-32, is 'to trust' (בטח).[22] In the series of 'woe cries' (chs. 28-32), Isaiah already denounced Judah's trust in Egypt as an affront to YHWH's promise of assistance (30:12,15; 31:1). Now, however, it is the Great King himself who, not without sarcasm from the side of the narrator, draws Judah's attention to the illusory character of that trust (36:4 [bis], 5, 6 [bis], 9). In this regard, he could be considered an ally of the prophet.

Sennacherib goes beyond all limits, however, when he attempts to undermine Judah's trust in YHWH. Initially it would appear that he only intends to bring Hezekiah's trust in YHWH into disrepute (v. 7) and to present himself as carrying out YHWH's policy in history (v. 10), but later on he refers to Hezekiah's trust in YHWH as nothing more than fantasy and self-deceit (v. 15), contending that YHWH is powerless to save anyone from his hand (v. 20). All this reaches a climax in his assertion that YHWH's very claim upon his people's trust is itself a delusion, since he is no greater than any of the other gods of the nations, whom he, the Great King, has subjected to his rule (37:10).

We already noted that besides 'to trust' the topic 'to deliver' (נצל hiphil) and 'to save' (ישע hiphil) also governs the narrative. In the second address of the Rabshakeh, the latter topic constitutes the opening line of the dispute: who can save Hezekiah and Jerusalem (36:14f., 18-20: 'to deliver' [נצל hiphil])? The Great King takes up this term, transforming the ability 'to deliver' into the actual proof of divinity (37:11f.). Hezekiah and YHWH likewise consider the capacity to deliver nations to be proof of divinity (ישע hiphil: 37:20,35; cf. 38:20). Does their use of a different term for deliverance contain some acknowledgement of the name Isaiah ('YHWH saves')?

---

[22] The following description of the most important motif-words is based on the study of De Jong 1989.

The appearance of Hezekiah's opponent, Sennacherib, is also characterised by a number of significant terms. He is not simply a foreign king
who knows nothing of the God of Israel. On the contrary, he maintains
that he knows YHWH and that he has reason to hold him in contempt ('to
mock' [חרף]: 37:23f.; 'to revile' [גדף]: 37:6,23). It is typical of the figure of Hezekiah that he makes the defamation of his God good with the
title 'the living God' (37:4,17), a name which YHWH will ultimately jus-
tify (37:35).

The motif-words examined above illustrate, therefore, that these stories offer a narrative key to the readers of BI, allowing them to apply the
prophecies of Isaiah ben Amoz to situations in which it would appear
that the puffed-up arrogance of those in power is able to reduce the saving presence of YHWH for those who trust in him to farcical proportions.

SCHOLARLY EXPOSITION

Introduction to the Exegesis: Form and Setting

The new vision of the contextual significance of chs. 36-37 and the
manifest difficulty involved in isolating and dating the sources at their
foundation make it advisable that we explain the narrative as an independent literary unit (without referring to 2 Kgs 18:13-19:37 or 2 Chr.
32:27-31). At first sight, we would seem to be dealing with a number of
speeches with a great deal of repetition in an apparently insubstantial
narrative framework. On closer inspection, however, one can discern a
chain of events leading from the arrival of the Assyrian army to its ultimate downfall. The differences in content and addressation of the
speeches serve to provide this development with a degree of dynamism.
While the final outcome, the relief of the city, is not unexpected, the
manner in which it happens is rather surprising: 'the messenger of
YHWH' himself sows death and destruction among the Assyrian troops
(37:36). The dramatic progress of the chapters would thus appear to be
strong enough to provide their narrative pattern.[23]

The opening scene (vv. 1-3) does not only describe the military threat,
it also introduces the actants: the king of Assyria and the king of Jerusalem in the background, the Assyrian general, the Rabshakeh, and three
courtiers from Jerusalem, 'by the conduit of the Upper Pool on the high-

---

[23] Sweeney (460-5, 471-5) explains the structure of the narrative from the perspective
of the literary genres used. Although these are narrative, their form does not appear to be
established enough to determine the pattern of the text. This would appear to depend
more on the sequence of scenes with their varying actants.

way to the Fuller's Field', in the foreground. YHWH is not mentioned at this point.

In the first dialogue scene (vv. 4-10), the Rabshakeh addresses himself to Hezekiah's courtiers. Instead of demanding surrender, however, he challenges the king to make an honest assessment of his military chances. While the king, on the one hand, cannot rely on Egypt (vv. 4-6), he is likewise unable to turn to YHWH because he has placed restrictions on divine worship (v. 7). Indeed, even if the Assyrians were to supply him with horses, he would be unable to provide the necessary horsemen to ride them. While this latter assumption might seem somewhat bizarre, the expectation of a cavalry from Egypt is equally outlandish (v. 8-9). The Rabshakeh concludes with the assertion that the course of the campaign thus far would suggest that YHWH himself has empowered the Assyrian king to destroy Judah (v. 10).

In the second dialogue scene (vv. 11-21) the Rabshakeh addresses himself primarily to the people in a speech prepared for by an inconspicuous aside to Hezekiah's entourage (v. 7: 'If you say: *We* have put our trust in YHWH') and consisting of two sub-scenes. The first contains a discussion between the courtiers of Hezekiah and the Rabshakeh as to whether diplomatic negotiations should remain secret (vv. 11-12). The general insists on open negotiations, thereby addressing himself to the courtiers as the representatives of the people ('...in that they will eat their dung and drink their urine with you')[24] and making the question of who can be trusted a matter for the entire population. The narrator's sarcasm surfaces here once again as he transforms the enemy into the spokesperson for the responsibility of the people as a whole. In the second sub-scene, the general addresses himself directly to Hezekiah's subjects, speaking in the name of the Great King (vv. 13-20). He endeavours to drive a wedge between the king and YHWH on the one hand and the people on the other (vv. 15f.,18). By presenting himself as the bearer of prosperity (vv. 16-17) and YHWH as no more powerful than the gods of the nations (vv. 18-20), Sennacherib lays personal claim to divine characteristics. Indeed, by way of the exhortation 'go out to me', in association with the promise of a contented existence on their own land and a journey to his own equally fertile land (vv. 16-17), Sennacherib pretends to be equal to YHWH, who led Israel to the land which he had promised. In so doing, however, Sennacherib unmasks himself, in line with the narrator's sarcastic intentions, as a mere braggart. Once again the theological design of the narrative comes to the fore.

---

[24] De Regt (1999: 45f.) points to the fact that the address switches from the singular ('to your lord and to you') to the plural ('with you').

The third dialogue scene (36:22-37:7) increases the tension as king Hezekiah now takes the initiative and the prophet Isaiah begins to speak. Once Hezekiah hears the Assyrian message (36:22), he and his courtiers go into mourning, probably on account of Sennacherib's blasphemy (36:18-20), ascend to the temple (vv. 1-2) and make contact with Isaiah (vv. 2-4). By his appeal to the prophet to intercede with YHWH Hezekiah appears to be an exemplary king. Isaiah is no more than God's messenger and he communicates nothing more than YHWH's response – the downfall of the Assyria king (vv. 6-7). Thus, behind these two dialogue partners, 'the living God' enters the scene.

The fourth dialogue scene (37:8-13) introduces a further degree of tension. The Assyrian king has the floor, speaking albeit through messengers who nevertheless do not speak in their own name as the Rabshakeh had done. As a matter of fact, the Rabshakeh disappears from the scene as an actant at this point. The change in the strategic situation is appropriately exploited against the background of Sennacherib's hubris (vv. 8-9). While his military supremacy is being contested by the king of Ethiopia, he nevertheless has the gall to scoff at Hezekiah's God even more than he had allowed the Rabshakeh to do. While the latter had warned against Hezekiah's deceptive trust in YHWH (36:14,20), Sennacherib now warns against the deceptiveness of YHWH himself (37:10-13). His underestimation of his political opponent, the king of Ethiopia, is symptomatic of his underestimation of YHWH and his overestimation of himself. The fact that Hezekiah does not answer him is in line with his policy with respect to the Rabshakeh (36:21) and serves to illustrate Sennacherib's monomaniacal loneliness.

The fifth dialogue scene (37:14-35), as with the third, brings Hezekiah and YHWH together. In this case, however, the king himself turns to YHWH in prayer (vv. 15-20). YHWH's response, mediated once again by the prophet (v. 21), comes in the form of a lengthy 'taunt-song' against Sennacherib (vv. 22-29) and the promise of a 'sign' for Hezekiah (vv. 30-35). The literary construction of a taunt-song against the Assyrian king (2nd person), which is addressed nonetheless to the king of Judah without the command to convey it to its intended addressee, has a remarkable effect. It ultimately anticipates the disappearance of Sennacherib and serves even more effectively as a sign of YHWH's support for Hezekiah.

The concluding scene (37:36-38) narrates the fall of the Assyrian army and the liberation of Jerusalem. Strikingly enough no words are spoken. The facts speak for themselves: YHWH alone would appear to have control of the battlefield, the king of Assyria is forced to fall back.

After all the high-handed bragging, the silence of death dominates the scene. The remarkably undefined 'they' (v. 36: 'When they arose early in the morning, behold, these were all dead bodies') and the clause 'the king broke camp' (v. 37) suggest that there were survivors enough to observe the slaughter and to beat the retreat. Without an army, Sennacherib returns to Nineveh, his own city (v. 37b). Here too, however, even under the protection of his own God and in the midst of his own family, his safety is far from guaranteed. While his fate is ultimately the same as that of his army (vv. 36,38: 'to slay'), he does not perish at the hand of 'the messenger of YHWH'. To the very end, the God of Israel does not consider a direct encounter with the king of Assyria worth his while.

The dramatic progression of the narrative can be seen in the following structural schema (H = Hezekiah; R = Rabshakeh; S = Sennacherib):

36:1-3 opening scene: S's campaign against Judah and Jerusalem
       1   Judah's cities conquered
       2   the Rabshakeh sent to Hezekiah
       3   meeting of the Rabshakeh with Hezekiah's courtiers
4-10   first dialogue scene: R's address to H's courtiers
       4-7   the Rabshakeh on behalf of Sennacherib
             4-6   trust in Egypt's power is profitless
             7   trust in YHWH's benevolence is groundless
       8-10 the Rabshakeh on his own behalf
             8-9   challenge of military confrontation
             10   appeal to YHWH's command
11-21   second dialogue scene: R's address to the people on the wall
       11   request of H's courtiers to R to negotiate in Aramaic
       12   request refused
       13-20 R's address: attempt to gain popular support
             13a   the Rabshakeh takes his stand
             13b-16a first message: warning against Hezekiah's trust in YHWH
             16b-20 second message: agreement of surrender offered
                   16b-17 favourable conditions
                   18-20 YHWH's impotence to rescue argued
       21   no answer of the courtiers
22-37:7 third dialogue scene: Hezekiah and Isaiah
       22   report by courtiers to Hezekiah
       1   Hezekiah's mourning

    30   vehicle: food supply
    31-32a tenor:
          31   new growth for Judah
          32a   a remnant will sprout from Zion
          32b   confirmation: YHWH's zeal will do it
    33-34   judgement speech concerning S
          33a´   messenger formula
          33a´´-34 verdict:
          33a´´-b   no conquering of Jerusalem
          34   return home
    35   announcement of salvation for Jerusalem
36-38   concluding scene: defeat of the Assyrian army; death of S
    36   slaughter of the Assyrian army
    37   return of Sennacherib to Nineveh
    38   assassination of Sennacherib

Exegesis by Verse

36:1-3 One can establish from the 'Annals of Sennacherib' that the Assyrian king's campaign took place in 701 BC although this was not the 14th year but rather the 24th (or 25th) year of Hezekiah's reign if we are to take the chronology found in 2 Kgs 18:1,9f. seriously. A common solution for this problem is to maintain that the datum of the 14th year originally belonged to ch.39 and that the redaction has situated the illness of Hezekiah and the siege of Jerusalem according to its own chronology (cf. 38:5-6) under one date.[25] Such a solution, however, cannot be substantiated. The simplest explanation remains a scribal error, the difference between the two numerals consisting of only two letters (םי- for ה-).[26]

After the death of his father Sargon II, Sennacherib (705-681 BC) first had to deal with uprisings in Mesopotamia before he was able to turn his attention to the smaller western states which had thrown off the yoke of Assyria with the help of Egypt. According to his annals, Sennacherib first brought the coastal region, from Sidon in the north to Ashkalon in the south, under control, defeating an Egyptian army at Eltekeh (20 miles west of Jerusalem) in the process. Thereafter he set about a more difficult

---

[25] Delitzsch, 369; Duhm, 259; Rowley 1963: 98ff.
[26] More complicated explanations which uphold 'the fourteenth year' include Watts, *Isaiah 1-33*, 4-8; Motyer, 277: the fourteenth year of sole reign, which was preceded by ten years of co-regency with Ahaz.

campaign in the mountainous regions of Judah, laying siege at first to Lachish in the Shephelah, the most important city in Judah outside Jerusalem.[27] The narrative of chs. 36-37 begins at this point (cf. 37:8).

The narrator gives the impression that Sennacherib had already conquered 'all the fortified cities of Judah' when he sent the Rabshakeh with military support to demand Hezekiah's surrender. By doing so, he positions the latter in a situation of extreme distress, making him into a king almost bereft of his land. Sennacherib describes the situation in his annals as follows:

'As to Hezekiah of Judah, he did not submit to my yoke, I laid siege to 46 of his strong cities, walled forts and to the countless small villages in their vicinity, and conquered (them) by means of well-stamped (earth-) ramps, and battering-rams brought (thus) near (to the walls) (combined with) the attack by foot soldiers, (using) mines, breeches as well as sapper work... Himself I made a prisoner in Jerusalem, his royal residence, like a bird in a cage. I surrounded him with earthwork in order to molest those who were leaving his city's gate. His towns which I had plundered, I took away from his country and gave them (over) to Mitinti, king of Ashdod, Padi, king of Ekron, and Sillibel, king of Gaza' (*ANET*, 288).

It is striking that the narrator does not refer to Hezekiah as the 'king of Judah', but only as 'king at Jerusalem', although Hezekiah has not been mentioned up to this point in BI. In the narrative as a whole, the fate of Judah is of secondary importance. Everything turns around the preservation of Jerusalem. Indeed, the royal title as such is often conspicuously absent in the narrative where Hezekiah is concerned. The fact that the Assyrians never refer to him as king might be understood as contempt (36:4,7,14ff.,18). Sennacherib uses the title on only one occasion, in a messenger formula intended for his own servants (37:10).[28] The title is sometimes found on the lips of the narrator (36:1f.,21; 37:1,5), sometimes not, its pointed absence seeming to be intended to underline the seriousness of the situation (36:22; 37:3,9,14f.,21). The term 'king', in contrast, is always used with respect to Sennacherib (36:1f.,4,8, 13f.,16,18; 37:4,6,8-11,18,21,33,37), the one exception being in Hezekiah's prayer to YHWH (37:17).[29] The presence or absence of

[27] For a survey of Sennacherib's campaign, cf. Hayes and Miller 1977: 446-51.

[28] Revell 1996: 130f.

[29] Revell 1996: 151: 'This contrast with the narrator's practice presumably represents Sennacherib as a person under the control of God'.

the title 'king' would thus appear to have something to say about the actual balance of power.

Sennacherib's envoy bears the title 'Rabshakeh', literally and originally 'chief cup–bearer', but it is not clear whether the title implies a civilian or a military function (Wildberger, 1396). The three officials in Hezekiah's employ would appear to exercise civilian functions. Although the precise content and development thereof is unknown to us, the titles are probably borrowed from the Egyptian constitutions where the same titles can be found. The individual who held sway 'over the household' was the most important person in the court (Gen. 41:40; 1 Kgs 4:6; 16:9; 18:3; Isa. 22:15). While the 'secretary' (ספר) may have had an executive task in the royal chancellery, he also functioned as a counsellor (2 Kgs 12:11; 22:3,8ff.; Jer. 36:12,20; 37:15,20). Although a significant amount of literature exists with respect to the 'recorder' (מזכיר cf. 2 Sam. 8:16; 20:24; 1 Kgs 4:3; 1 Chr. 18:15; 2 Chr. 34:8), the precise function thereof remains unclear.[30] Of the three individuals mentioned, only one, Eliakim, is known to us (Isa. 22:20). As successor to the Shebna mentioned there he embodies the fact that the prophecies of Isaiah prove to be genuine. Whether the Shebna mentioned in the present verse is the same person, albeit now in a different, less important function, is impossible to determine. The fact that the name is found with relative frequency in Palestinian inscriptions makes the identification of the two unnecessary (Wildberger, 837).

The place where the Assyrian general and the envoys of Hezekiah meet, 'by the conduit of the Upper Pool on the highway to the Fuller's Field', constitutes the final element of the setting of the scene and one which is simultaneously practical and programmatic. It is in fact the same place where Hezekiah's father, king Ahaz, and the prophet Isaiah met face to face during an earlier threat to Jerusalem's security, at that time from Aram and Israel (7:3). The redaction thus establishes a contrast between the two kings, at the level of their trust in YHWH.

4-10 The Rabshakeh's speech is characterised by its vigour (questions [vv. 4,5b,7b,9,10], exclamations and an imperative [vv. 5a,6a,8], discourse particles [vv. 5b,6a, 8a,10a]), as well as its extreme brutality. The tone is set by his use of the title 'king' (twice) for his own sovereign and the absence thereof with reference to Hezekiah (v. 4). The questions are hardly intended as such, given that the Rabshakeh provides his own answers (vv. 4b-5a ['I say'], 5b-6a,9a) and on two occasions even provides his own retort to an assumed response on the part of Hezekiah (vv. 7, 8-

---

[30] Cf. the extensive discussion in Wildberger, 1397.

9 [v. 9a presumes a negative answer to v. 8b])! Not the siege of Jerusalem but the campaign against Judah must of necessity constitute the background to the speech, a cavalry being of little use in the siege of any city (vv. 8-10). The Rabshakeh speaks in front of the gates of Jerusalem, adopting the perspective of his king Sennacherib who is planning the next step in his campaign from Lachish. Sennacherib's initial plan, however, is to attempt to achieve his goal, the surrender of Jerusalem, via the Rabshakeh's diplomatic mission.

The speech itself is an authentic sample of biblical literature and not a translation or adaptation of an originally Assyrian address. While it is true that certain expressions and topics can also be found in Assyrian texts – such as the theme of rebellious vassals who depend on the support of their allies while the Assyrian king relies only on the help of his god –, the speech as a whole is more closely related to the thought patterns present in BI. In this context, it is extremely difficult to distinguish between associations with the words of Isaiah ben Amoz himself and associations with later redactions (such as the Josianic or later Deuteronomistic redactions). On the whole, however, the speech reflects 'the rules of thinking of at least one group in Judean society (the one to which the writer[s] and readers /hearers belonged)'.[31] The intention of the speech is to illustrate how absolute political power goes about its business. Whenever it is in a position to deal out uncontested destruction, it not only pretends to have God on its side (v. 10), it also assumes that it has the right to determine whether one can rely on someone or not (vv. 4-7). Genuine trust in God, however, possesses a different kind of rationale.

4-7 The purpose of the first part of the speech, spoken in the name of Sennacherib, is to undermine Hezekiah's 'trust' (בטח) both in Egypt (vv. 5-6) and in YHWH (v. 7; cf. 'Essentials and Perspectives'). The first segment is political in character. The heart of the matter is that Hezekiah has endeavoured to sever his political dependence on Assyria (cf. 1 Kgs 18:7: 'He rebelled against the king of Assyria and would not serve him'). The term 'to rebel' presumes some kind of agreement – either enforced or voluntary – entered into for economic or strategic reasons. In terms of Ancient Near Eastern political relationships, therefore, it implies a breach of faith (מרד: Gen. 14:4; 2 Kgs 24:1,20; Ezek. 17:15; Neh. 2:19; 6:6; 2 Chr. 13:6; 36:13).

The same initial segment has a hidden significance, however, at least with respect to the readers of BI, since Sennacherib is implied repeating

---

[31] Ben Zvi 1990: 92.

an observation which the prophet himself has always maintained. By making a mockery of the 'counsel' and 'strength' of Hezekiah (v. 5) he manipulates a theme of Isaiah who has consistently proclaimed the superiority of YHWH's 'counsel' and 'strength' in contrast to that of human persons, both in Israel and Egypt (עצה: 5:19; 8:10; 11:2; 14:26; 19:3,11,17; 25:1; 28:29; 29:15; 30:1; גבורה: especially 30:15; further 3:25; 11:2; 28:6; 33:13). One of the primary theme's of Isaiah's theopolitical message, moreover, is that Egypt does not deserve to be trusted (19:1-17; 20:1-6; 30:1-7; 31:1-3). Even the sort of comparison employed by the Assyrian has Isaianic qualities (cf. v. 6 with 28:4; 29:8,11f.; 30:13; 31:4f.). Finally, Isaiah is also of the conviction that what his people are inclined to assert is much at odds with reality (cf. 'lips' in v. 5 and 29:13).

In the second segment, v. 7, Sennacherib involves the people in his argument by quoting Hezekiah in the plural: 'If you say (singular): We have put our trust in YHWH'. In so doing he provides himself with the opportunity to present Hezekiah's religious policy – the centralisation of the cult in Jerusalem – to his subjects as a deed hostile to YHWH (v. 7b). Far reaching historical considerations have been attached to this verse. Does it reflect the Assyrian perception of Hezekiah's reforms (Childs 1967: 82) or is it an addition from the time of king Josiah (Wildberger, 1386f., 1400f.)? While Hezekiah only took action against the sacrificial high places in the land (2 Kgs 18:1-6), which was already a demand of the prophetic movement (Hos. 10:8; Amos 7:9; Jer. 19:3-5; cf. the criterion in 1-2 Kings for judging kings from 1 Kgs 14:22f. onwards), Josiah (640-609) pushed through the centralisation of worship in Deuteronomistic fashion (2 Kgs 23:8f.). Whether the verse in question can decide matters, however, remains unclear. From the perspective of the post-exilic redaction of BI, the reforms of Hezekiah and Josiah may have converged. It would have been important for the narrator to establish that the Assyrian wanted to drive a wedge between the king and his people with respect to their shared trust in YHWH. This fits well within the idealised image of Hezekiah while at the same time anticipating the Assyrian's refusal to engage in secret diplomacy (vv. 11-12).

8-10 In the second part of the speech, the Rabshakeh speaks at first under his own authority (v. 8: 'my lord, the king of Assyria'; v. 9: 'one of the least of my lord's servants'), although he appears to return to speaking in his master's name by the end of the speech v. 10: 'I have gone up'; cf. v. 1).

The suggestion that the parties enter into negotiations is intended to be sarcastic, and to illustrate that Hezekiah and his army are no match for the cavalry of the Assyrian king. Indeed, even if the Rabshakeh were to provide the horses so coveted by Judah (2:7; 30:16; 31:1-3), Hezekiah would not be able to muster the necessary cavalrymen to put them to any effective use. The Rabshakeh's personal as well as national-istic arrogance comes to the fore once again. Whether he himself is the referent of 'one of the least of my lord's servants' or whether merely a minor commander in one of the army battalions is intended,[32] both come under the king of Assyria whose horses make him and his people more powerful than the Egyptians. Strategically speaking, to reject him would be simply illogical ('to turn aside the face of' [השיב את פני]: 1 Kgs 2:16f.,20; Ps. 132:10; 2 Chr. 6:42).[33]

As in v. 7, the Assyrian introduces a religious dimension into his po-litical assertions. In view of the success of his campaign against Judah, there can be no other assumption than that YHWH has sent him to destroy this land. Why Hezekiah's God should desire such a thing he does not say. Given his assertions in v. 7, however, this may have to do with the abolition of the sacrificial high places.

11-12 The second dialogue scene opens with a dispute between the courtiers of Hezekiah and the Rabshakeh concerning the public nature of the negotiations. This intermezzo is partly responsible for the shift in strategic attention from the land of Judah to the city of Jerusalem and her inhabitants. If they continue to support Hezekiah's politics, the threat of a siege and a dehumanising lack of food and water awaits them (v. 12).

According to one's option in dating it, v. 11 has a role to play in the history of the Hebrew and Aramaic languages. It is more or less estab-lished that the term 'Judean' refers to the Hebrew language (cf. Neh. 13:24). The term 'Hebrew' in the Old Testament is never used for the language of Israel or Judah (Burney 1912). Given, however, that at-tempts to ascribe a pre- or post-exilic date to v. 11 have been unsuccess-ful, considerations based on this verse with reference to the socio-his-torical development of these languages remain uncertain.

The scene fulfils an important function in the progress of the narrative itself, placing the Rabshakeh's intention to undermine the people's faith in Hezekiah's political stance in the spotlight while simultaneously high-lighting the courtiers' efforts to protect the people from the Assyrian's

[32] According to Wildberger (1402), the gloss 'officer' (פחה) is intended to associate the expression 'one of the least of my lord's servants' with the Rabshakeh.

[33] Most commentators assume that the expression 'to turn aside the face of' means 'to offer military resistance', but the relevant parallel texts show that the expression has more to do with 'the rejection of an offer'. In the present context, this refers to the Rabshakeh's offer to provide horses.

demoralising words. The Rabshakeh has clearly belittled the king and pointed blasphemously to YHWH as the one who had ordered him to wreak havoc in the land. Sure of what he is doing, the Rabshakeh insists on public debate as part of his tactic of psychological warfare. There is one thing, however, that he did not reckon with. Later in the narrative, YHWH himself will join in the debate to unmask (37:22-29) and confound (37:36) Sennacherib's divine pretensions. At the same time, however, the courtiers are also guilty of underestimating the situation. Their angst for a public debate with the military conqueror – a debate about their own God and his power to deliver – betrays the weakness of their own faith in YHWH (37:6-7). Here also YHWH will actively intervene to strengthen and restore trust (37:16-20), at least that of Hezekiah, and respond to it through the intervention of his messenger (37:30-38). The intermezzo thus constitutes an appeal to avoid reducing the supposedly dangerous discussion of God as guarantor of the people's well-being to a matter of political responsibilities. Such a matter should be handled within the faith community itself. YHWH will ultimately prove himself true.[34]

13-20 The second of the Rabshakeh's speeches opens with a solemn petition addressed to the people, calling upon them to give ear to the message of the Great King (v. 13). The remainder of the speech consists of two panels, each introduced by a message formula (vv. 14-16a and vv. 16b-20). The two parts of the first panel correspond with the two parts of the second panel (v. 14 / vv. 16b-17 [A/A´]; vv. 15-16a / vv. 18-20 [B/B´]). The first segments (A/A´) oppose Hezekiah and Sennacherib while the second segments (B/B´) contrast what the two kings contend with respect to YHWH. Hezekiah is a deceiver who is unable to liberate his people (v. 14), but the Great King is a trustworthy treaty partner who promises general well-being and can deliver on his promises (vv. 16-17). Hezekiah disseminates a deceptive faith in YHWH (v. 15) but given the fact that no god has been able to deliver his people from the might of the Assyrian king, is it likely that YHWH will be able to do much better (vv. 18-20)? By placing YHWH and the other gods on the same footing, in this way, the Rabshakeh's second speech reaches its brazen climax.

14-16a The two parts of the first panel exhibit a similar structure. Each of the two prohibitives, 'Do not let Hezekiah deceive you' (v. 14a) and 'Do not let Hezekiah make you trust in YHWH' (v. 15), is given further elaboration in the question whether Jerusalem can expect 'deliverance' (נצל hiphil). A characteristic theme of Isaiah himself is thus taken

[34] Brueggemann 1988.

up (31:5). The king of Judah is in no condition to provide deliverance
(v. 14b), yet he still maintains that YHWH can be trusted to do so (v.
15a´´-b). The rhetoric of the second prohibitive is subtle because it is incomplete (v. 15a´). While the Rabshakeh does not explicitly argue that
YHWH is unable or unwilling to bring deliverance, the idea is implied
nonetheless in his assertions that Hezekiah is deceiving the people by
exhorting them to have faith in YHWH ('to deceive' [נשׁא] in political
sense: Isa. 19:13; Jer. 4:10; 29:8; 37:9; 49:16; Ob. 3,7). Of necessity,
therefore, these verses require a degree of supplementation: what is the
status of YHWH's relationship with Jerusalem? The answer to this implicit question is found in vv. 18-20: YHWH cannot deliver.

16b-17 The first part of the second panel consists of a series of imperatives: 'Make a blessing agreement... go out... eat... drink', the latter two, in terms of meaning, being a consequence of the first (cf. the
translation). The first clause is formulated in an unusual way, literally:
'Make with me a blessing (ברכה)'. While there are no parallels for this
usage of 'blessing', the context points to a peaceful agreement, leading
many to translate with 'treaty' or 'peace' (cf. Tg).[35] The deliberate posi-
tioning of the adjunct 'with me' prior to the object ('blessing') creates a
contrast with the reference to Hezekiah at the end of the preceding
verse: 'Do not listen to Hezekiah', but 'make a blessing with me'. The
imperative then invites the recognition of the king of Assyria which will
function as a 'blessing' (cf. 'to bless' with the king as object: Gen.
47:7,10; 2 Sam. 8:10; 14:22; 1 Kgs 1:47; 8:66; 21:10,13; Ps. 45:3;
72:15; 145:2).

The second precondition is departure from the city and surrender to
the Assyrian king: 'Go out to me' (יצא; cf. 1 Sam. 11:3). Surrender will
not lead to captivity or destitution, in contrast to the terrible living conditions which can be expected in a city under siege (v. 12). The people
can look forward to a peaceful and prosperous existence in the land, a
prospect which the Rabshakeh expresses in traditional metaphors for the
free availability of the food and drink necessary for everyday survival
(v. 16b; cf. 1 Kgs 5:5; Mic. 4:4; further Deut. 6:11; Jer. 5:17; Neh.
9:25).

V. 17 is unmistakably a later addition: 'until I come and take you
away to a land like your own land'. If one reads vv. 16-17 as a single

---

[35] Murtonen 1959: 173f.: 'mutual blessing'; Watts, 19: 'mutually advantageous agreement'. Some commentators reduce ברכה to the root 'to kneel' rather than 'to bless' and
translate with 'submission' or 'surrender' (Alexander, 50; BDB, 139; HALAT, 154: 'Ka-
pitulation'; Ges.[18], 180b: 'Ergebung'). In the present context, however, one would expect
the reverse order: 'Go out and make an act of submission'. For a survey of opinions cf.
Wildberger, 1382; Watts, 21.

proposal of conditions for surrender, then the promise of a peaceful existence in the land would appear to be nothing more than a temporary arrangement. One is then faced with the inevitable question as to the Assyrian king's immediate military plans (a campaign against Egypt?) prior to the deportation of the population of Jerusalem to his own land. V. 16, however, would appear to portray a definitive way of life. It is possible that the redaction of v. 17 wanted, nevertheless, to state what actually happened and introduced a reference to the exile, describing it in the naive or perhaps malevolent terms used by the king of Assyria – 'a land of grain and wine, a land of bread and vineyards' – and not in terms of what really took place. While the addition serves a need for actualisation, it also provides the opportunity to present the Great King as someone who was not aware of the true significance of the land for the people of Israel, as if the land given them by YHWH could be exchanged without further ado for any other fertile land ('grain and wine' in this context: Gen. 27:28; Num. 18:12; Deut. 7:13; 11:14; 12:17; 14:23; 18:4; 28:51; 33:28; Isa. 62:8; Jer. 31:12; Hos. 2:10; 7:14; Joel 1:10; 2:19; Hag. 1:11; Zech. 9:17; Ps. 4:8; Neh. 5:11; 13:12).

18-20 The second part of the second panel takes the argument a step further, moving from a comparison of Israel with the land of the exile in v. 17 to a comparison of YHWH with the gods of the nations. At the same time, it further develops the warning against Hezekiah's faith in YHWH from the first message in vv. 15-16a. The warning is now presented as if it were the result of genuine concern for the well-being of the addressees ('Beware lest': cf. Gen. 44:34; Exod. 34:15; Num. 20:18; Jer. 51:46; Job 32:13; Prov. 24:18).[36] They ought not to be the victims of Hezekiah's deceitful endeavour to convince his people to support a policy which will lead to disaster (סות hiphil in this sense: Deut. 13:7; Josh. 15:18; 1 Sam. 26:19; 2 Sam. 24:1; 1 Kgs 21:25; Jer. 38:22; 43:3; Job 2:3; 36:16; 1 Chr. 21:1; 2 Chr. 18:21).[37]

The rhetorical dynamic of the speech is supported by the expression 'to deliver from the hand of' (צנל hiphil with מיד). Three questions with 'gods' as subject each employing a verb in the past tense (vv. 18b,19b,20a) which expects a negative answer, serve as the basis for the central question using the same verb in the future tense: 'Should YHWH deliver Jerusalem?' (v. 20). The questions aim first at the denial of the deliverance (v. 18: 'Has any of the gods delivered?'), then at the denial of presence (v. 19: twofold 'Where?') and finally at that of uniqueness

---

[36] פן at the beginning of a clause expresses a sense of fear or precaution (GKC, §152 w; J-M, §168 g).

[37] TWAT, V, 812ff. (G. Wallis).

(v. 20: 'Who among all the gods?'). It is precisely this last question which attempts to make YHWH into a god among many other gods.

With respect to v. 15, the perspective of inevitable ruin constitutes the new element introduced via a comparison with the impotent gods of the defeated nations. In the first instance, Sennacherib compares these gods, not with the gods of Assyria, but with himself (v. 18b). In so doing he lays personal claim to divine power. These gods have been forced to taste defeat at the hands of the king of Assyria. The city states mentioned in v. 19, Hamath, Arpad and Samaria, belong to a coalition from the region defeated and annexed by Sargon II between 722 and 717 (cf. Isa. 10:9).[38] The choice of these particular city states from the countless states defeated by the Assyrians draws attention to the fall of Samaria, Jerusalem's northern counterpart. If these regional gods were powerless to protect their cities, how can YHWH, the God of Jerusalem, be expected to do any better (cf. 10:10f.)? The question: 'Where are the gods?' or 'Where is God?' also functions elsewhere in the Scriptures in the discussion between believers on non-believers both inside and outside Israel (איה with 'god': Jer. 2:28; Joel 2:17; Mal. 2:17; Ps. 42:4,11; 79:10; 115:2; Job 35:10).

Remarkably enough, Sennacherib presents the situation in such a way that the gods of the surrounding nations should have protected Samaria (cf. 'Notes'). He would seem not to have considered YHWH as the god of the northern Kingdom. Questions concerning the intention of the narrator, however, are more appropriate here than questions concerning Assyrian knowledge of the pantheon of the defeated nations. It is possible that the author wanted to highlight Assyrian ignorance of religious matters. It is likewise possible that he did not want the Assyrian to use the fall of Samaria, which had also been a painful event for Judah, as a further argument against YHWH. He may even have considered YHWH no longer to be the god of Samaria which was now in ruins and populated by other peoples (cf. the historical note in 2 Kgs 17:24-25: 'The king of Assyria brought people from Babylon, Cuthah, Avva, Hamath and Sepharvaim, and placed them in the cities of Samaria instead of the people of Israel... At the beginning of their dwelling there, they did not fear YHWH').

The scene concludes with the silence of the courtiers in obedience to the command of the king. The root of the verb 'to be silent', חרשׁ, connotes the idea of 'not listening' (Lev. 19:14; Isa. 29:18; 35:5; 42:18f.; 43:8; Ps. 38:14) and of intentional refusal to speak (Gen. 24:21; Exod.

[38] Likewise Hena and Ivvah, which are mentioned in the parallel text of 2 Kgs 18:34. Little is known with any certainty concerning Sepharvaim.

14:14; Judg. 18:19; Jer. 4:19; Ps. 32:3; 58:5; Job 13:5; Prov. 11:12; 17:28). The silence of the courtiers, therefore, does not imply power-lessness. It constitutes rather the wiser option on their part in their con-frontation with evil and ignorance: 'Do not get up and leave an insolent fellow, lest he lie in ambush against your words' (Sir. 8:11; cf. 20:1-8). The interplay between the courtiers and the king in this situation is in harmony with the expectations of good governance in a time of prosper-ity (Isa. 32:1-8).

36:22-37:2 The third dialogue scene transports us from the city walls to the palace of the king and the temple of YHWH. The courtiers behave in an exemplary way, not only by reporting the Assyrian's bragging to Hezekiah (mentioned here from the Assyrian perspective without the ti-tle 'king'[39]), but also by adopting the appropriate attitude of mourning while doing so: 'with their clothes rent' (v. 22). The king is evidently aware of their gesture (v. 1) which he echoes by adding a further gesture of mourning: 'he covered himself with sackcloth' (v. 1; cf. v. 2). Both mourning rituals express dismay and sorrow concerning something which has either already happened or something which is to be expected ('to rend clothes': Gen. 37:34; Josh. 7:6; 1 Sam. 4;12; 2 Sam. 1:2,11; 13:31; 15:32; 2 Kgs 2:12; 6:30; Job 1:20 and Num. 14:6; Judg. 11;35; 1 Kgs 21:27ff.; 2 Kgs 5:7ff.; 22:11 respectively; 'to cover with sackcloth': Gn. 37:34; 2 Sam 3:31; 1 Kgs 20:31ff.; 21:27; Isa. 15:2; Ezek. 7:18; 21:31; Amos 8:10; Lam. 2:10; Esth. 4:1 and 1 Kgs 20:31ff.; 2 Kgs 6:30; Isa. 20:2; Jer. 4:8; 6:26; 48:37; 49:3; 1 Chr. 21:16 respectively).[40] In the present episode, the display of sorrow can refer to the Assyrian's blasphemous words against YHWH as well as to the pending devastation which now faces Jerusalem.

Hezekiah's reaction stands in sharp contrast to that of his father Ahaz to the news that Aram and Ephraim were preparing a campaign against Jerusalem (ch.7). Instead of panic and desperation (7:2,4), we now en-counter mourning and penitence (37:1). While Ahaz spent his time checking the water reserves and only met with Isaiah on God's initiative (7:3), Hezekiah dresses in penitent's clothes and goes to the temple on his own initiative to seek contact with the prophet (37:1-2; for the first time in BI, and only in these narratives, Isaiah is referred to as 'prophet'; cf. 38:1; 39:3).

3-4 The contrast is continued in the words of king Hezekiah. While Ahaz rejected a sign from YHWH because he considered it a factor bereft of political significance (7:12), Hezekiah asks Isaiah to intercede before

[39] Revell 1996: 124: 'as if already dethroned'.
[40] *TWAT*, VII, 190ff., 851f. (W. Thiel).

YHWH (37:4) and confesses his faith in him by referring to him as 'the living God'. This term is often found in polemical contexts involving foreign nations and alien gods (Deut. 5:26; 1 Sam. 17:26,36; Josh. 3:10; Jer. 5:2; 10:10; 23:36; Hos. 2:1; Ps. 42:3; 84:3; Dan. 6:27).[41] At the same time, Hezekiah does not ask directly for Jerusalem's deliverance but rather for the punishment of the Rabshakeh's blasphemous words.

The king begins by informing the prophet of the seriousness of the situation in the language of the psalms, basing his request for intercession thereon ('day of distress' [צרה]: Ps. 20:2; 50:15; 77:3; 86:7; Jer. 16:19; Ob 12,14; Nah. 1:7; cf. 'time of distress' in Isa. 33:2). Scholars are divided on the question of the identity of the subject and the object of the following actions: 'chastisement' (תוכחה) and 'rejection' (נאצה). Our own explanation below will assume that both terms have YHWH as subject and the Assyrian as object. The traditional imagery of unsuccessful childbirth which follows is in keeping with such an assumption (cf. Isa. 26:17f.; 66:7ff.). The vehicle of the comparison, the absence of 'strength', provides the basis for the 'distress' and calls for a punishing intervention against the Assyrian who had earlier spoken with pride of his possession of 'strength' (36:18-20: 'my hand'; cf. 10:13: 'the strength of my hand'). The first line of the message intended for Isaiah thus constitutes an introduction to the prayer requested by Hezekiah: the distress in which the people find themselves calls for YHWH's intervention against the oppressor.

According to some, the 'distress' is brought about by YHWH, thus suggesting that he 'chastises' and 'rejects' his own people.[42] Others are of the opinion that 'chastisement', as well as 'distress', refer to the actions taken by the Assyrian against Hezekiah and Jerusalem, while 'rejection' refers to his treatment of YHWH.[43] A third option explains 'chastisement' as the action YHWH will take against Assyria because it has treated God with 'rejection, blasphemy' (Watts, 34).

Elsewhere in the Old Testament the rare term תוכחה signifies a 'chastisement' brought about by God (Hos. 5:9; Ps. 149:7). It is methodically unjustified to introduce meanings from the related noun תוכחת at this point and to assume that תוכחה refers to Sennacherib's offensive imputations ('rebuke') with respect to Hezekiah. On the contrary, the king of Judah points out to the prophet that the time has come for YHWH to punish Assyria. With respect to the term 'rejection', the noun in question, נָאָצָה (only here), should not be derived from the *piel* root which can mean 'to blaspheme' (cf. Ezek. 35:12; Neh. 9:18, 26), but rather

[41] *THAT*, I, 554 (G. Gerleman).

[42] Hitzig, 421; Alexander, 53; Duhm, 264; Dillmann-Kittel, 317; Feldmann, 423; Procksch, 446; Oswalt, 645.

[43] Hirsch, 262; König, 305.

from the *qal* root which never has God as its object and, where God is the subject, always signifies an act of repudiation (Deut. 32:19; Jer. 14:21; Lam. 2:6).[44]

In v. 4 the king expresses his hope that YHWH will pay attention to the words of the Rabshakeh ('perhaps' as a term of expectation: Gen. 43:12; Exod. 32:30; Josh. 9:7; Job 1:15; Lam. 3:29; 'to hear' in the sense of 'listening' rather than 'sensory apprehension': v. 17; 1 Sam. 25:24; 26:9; 2 Sam. 15:3; 20:17; Isa. 33:15; Amos 5:23; Prov. 13:1; Eccl. 7:5). At the same time he exposes the true intention behind the partly political, partly religious address of the Assyrian: 'to mock the living God' (חרף: 1 Sam. 17:26,36; Isa. 65:7; Ps. 69:10; 74:10, 18, 22; 79:12; Prov. 14:31; 17:5; 2 Chr. 32:17). In this way he expresses his concern that YHWH be properly acknowledged and turns the Assyrian's blasphemy into a motivation for YHWH's intervention. Nevertheless, the prayer for God's intercession itself is left to the prophet. The expression 'to lift up a prayer' belongs to the terminology of prophetic mediation (נשא תפלה: Jer. 7:16; 11:14; cf. פלל *hitp.* in Gen. 20:7,17: Abraham; Num. 11:2; 21:7; Deut. 9:20: Moses; 1 Sam. 7:5; 12:19: Samuel; 2 Kgs 4:33; 6:17f.: Elisha). The term for prayer as such does not necessarily imply a prayer of appeal in time of distress, although it is frequently found as such in the context of the lament genre (תפלה in collective lament: 1 Kgs 8:28f., 45,49; Isa. 1:15; Ps. 80:5; 90:1; Lam. 3:44; Dan. 9:3,17,21; Neh. 1:6, 11).

Isaiah's prayer must be of benefit to 'the remnant (to be found)'. While the term שארית renders the post-exilic vision of the Jewish community in Jerusalem, it fits, nevertheless, within the intention of the narrative since it is stated at the beginning that Sennacherib had captured all the cities of Judah (36:1). The term is characteristic of the actualising strategy of the redaction of BI which has reinterpreted an originally negative concept (remnant as symbol of destruction: 7:3; 17:1-6) in a more positive manner (remnant as a new beginning: 1:9; 4:3; 10:20-23; 11:11,16).[45]

5-7 Isaiah's response to the king follows the pattern of a priestly oracle of salvation. The element 'do not be afraid' does not single out the military threat directed against Jerusalem but rather 'the words with which the lackeys of the king of Assyria have reviled me' (v. 6). This corresponds to Hezekiah's own formulation which presented the 'mocking of the living God' as the actual 'distress' facing him and his people.

[44] Dillmann-Kittel, 317; *TWAT*, V, 131 (L. Ruppert).
[45] *TWAT*, VII, 942f. (R.E. Clements); Pfaff 1996: 114ff.

God, however, employs a different term, 'to revile' (גדף), to that used by
Hezekiah ('to mock' [חרף]). The verb 'to revile' predominantly means
'to insult with words' (v. 23; Num. 15:30; Isa. 43:28; 51:7; Ezek.
5:15; 20:27; Zeph. 2:8; Ps. 44:17; Sir. 48:18).[46]

The element of God's intervention in v. 7 follows the classical formulation (הנני with participle): 'Behold, I will put a spirit in him, so that he
shall hear a rumour, and return to his own land. And I will make him fall
by the sword in his own land'. Scholars usually explain this announcement as an anticipation of v. 9: 'He heard concerning Tirhakah' and v.
37f.: 'He returned.. His sons slew him with the sword'. With respect to
the first realisation, 'he heard concerning Tirhakah', however, Sennacherib did not in fact withdraw when he heard the news concerning
Tirhakah. On the contrary, he increased the pressure on Hezekiah by
sending him a message (v. 9). Commentators who consider Tirhakah's
advance to be too insignificant as a strategic fact to bring about the cessation of Sennacherib's campaign against Judah (Kaiser, 300), presume
that the 'rumour' referred to political difficulties in Assyria in line with
those which confronted Sennacherib on his accession to the throne. Such
an option, however, lies far from the strategy of the narrative.

It seems more appropriate to envisage also the 'rumour' which was to
follow YHWH's intervention as actualised at the conclusion of the narrative (Leene 1983). After the carnage which takes place among the
Assyrian troops in front of the gates of Jerusalem, the Assyrian king returns to his own land (vv. 36f.). Although it is not stated explicitly that
Sennacherib has heard a 'rumour' concerning this event, the narrative
appears to presume this nevertheless since the king is engaged in battle
at Libnah at the moment of the slaughter (v. 8). The rather vague term
'rumour' invites the reader to locate the realisation of this prophecy
within the narrative.

The 'spirit' which YHWH gives to the king should be understood in the
same way.[47] Some commentators understand the 'spirit' to be one of
folly and panic, brought on perhaps by the advance of the hostile army
from Tirhakah (v. 9). This does not square, however, with the sequence
'spirit – rumour'. In addition, the narrative makes no particular effort to
portray the campaign of the Ethiopian king as much of a threat. It would
seem more appropriate, therefore, to understand the 'spirit' at this point
in the narrative to be indeterminate. A spirit of boundless self-overesti-

---

[46] TWAT, I, 957 (G. Wallis): 'Verbalinjurie' as opposed to 'Realinjurie'. In the Dead
Sea Scrolls, גדף has become a technical term for 'to slander' (DCH, II, 320f., 326f.).

[47] For a 'spirit' from YHWH which brings about misfortune and ruin, cf. Judg. 9:23; 1
Sam. 16:14ff., 23; 18:10; 19:9; 1 Kgs 22:21ff.; Isa. 19:14; 29:10.

mation, however, is becoming more and more evident where Sennacherib is concerned. The reader will be able to draw this conclusion for
himself. By explaining this arrogance and the threat to Jerusalem which
is its consequence as ultimately stemming from YHWH, God is evidently
determined to relieve Hezekiah's distress. The Assyrian's blasphemy
will not go unpunished. Indeed, Sennacherib's sin will ultimately result
in his downfall at the hands of YHWH.

If we are correct in assuming that v. 7 anticipates the conclusion of
the narrative, then its vague formulation permits us to consider the return
of the Rabshakeh and the news concerning Tirhakah (vv. 8f.) as an initial fulfilment of Isaiah's prophecy. The behaviour of Sennacherib's
servant caricatures that of his master, in the same way as the mourning
of Hezekiah's courtiers caricatured that of their king (36:22-37:1).

8-13   The fourth dialogue scene introduces a number of events
whereby the connection is not immediately clear (vv. 8-9). It is for this
reason that a number of exegetes consider the second source of the narrative to begin with v. 9b (cf. 'Essentials and Perspectives'). Reference
to the fact that the Rabshakeh returned without achieving anything (cf.
36:21), sought out the king and gave him his report, only to be followed
up by messengers who speak exclusively in Sennacherib's name (vv. 8-
9), fits well within the dynamics of the narrative. Notice of the fact,
however, that the Assyrian king, in the meantime, has transferred the
battle from Lachish to Libnah, the location of which is unknown, remains both syntactically (see below) and semantically unclear. The notice would appear to serve two possible aims. Should the removal of the
battle front to Libnah suggest that the last but one of Judea's strongholds
has fallen, then the notice could be intended to increase the tension with
respect to the fate of Jerusalem. On the other hand, if Sennacherib has
withdrawn without taking Lachish, unsettled by the report of the approaching Tirhakanian army (v. 9: 'he had heard'), then the notice
serves as a primary indication that Sennacherib's dominant position is
beginning to weaken. The Assyrian king, however, refuses to recognise
any such weakening. This comes to the fore in his next step, the des-
patch of messengers with an even more brutal message for Hezekiah
(vv. 9b-13). This non-functional ambiguity in the narrative, which is
otherwise well-structured, can be explained as a consequence of the
amalgamation of two sources.

The syntactic problem is located in the unclear opening of v. 9. While the
subject of 'he had heard' clearly has to be the king since the message ('He
[Tirhakah] has gone out to fight against you') is addressed to him, the inter-
change of subject is not indicated and must be determined from the preceding

subordinate clause (v. 8b: 'he [the king] had left Lachish'). Furthermore, it is far from clear whether one should understand וישמע in v. 9a as a pluperfect ('he had heard'; Oswalt, 648) or as a simple past tense ('he heard'; Watts, 31,35). In the first instance, the report concerning Tirhakah provides Sennacherib with a reason to strike camp at Lachish, in the second to send messengers to Hezekiah. One is left with the impression that v. 9 sets out to connect both interpretations via the verb וישמע of the second half of the verse. It seems unlikely, therefore, that וישמע in v. 9a serves as an explanation for Sennacherib's departure from Lachish. As historical information, the report concerning Tirhakah has no further role to play. (His campaign, moreover, took place at a later date; cf. 'Essentials and Perspectives'.)

According to several scholars, Sennacherib's message to Hezekiah constitutes a repetition of his previous message (vv. 10-13). This fact provides a second argument in support of the theory that a new source begins with v. 9b (cf. 'Essentials and Perspectives'). More recently, however, exegetes have come to recognise that this latter message forms a climax with respect to its predecessor: it is not Hezekiah who is accused of treachery but YHWH himself (cf. v. 10 with 36:14,18). Sennacherib thus endeavours to alienate Hezekiah from his God, just as the Rabshakeh had done with the people (36:18-20; Smelik 1986: 81f.).

The present message differs from the former message in a variety of additional ways. The pretension of Assyrian supremacy is even stronger: 'the kings of Assyria' (v. 11: plural) and 'my fathers' (v. 12) instead of 'the king of Assyria' (36:18,20: singular) and 'my hand' (36: 19f.); 'all the lands' (v. 11) instead of 'his, these, their land(s)' (36:18,20). The threat itself is similarly more acute, 'destroying them utterly' (v. 11) having no counterpart in the previous address. Furthermore, given that the questions: 'Shall you be delivered?' (v. 11: singular) and 'Where is the king of...?' are not posed in the preceding address, it is clear that the message itself is addressed to Hezekiah personally. The address as such, therefore, need not necessarily suggest a new source. Should there be two sources at work here, care has evidently been taken that the king of Assyria's new message should not be considered a repetition of the first.

14-15 The fifth dialogue scene (vv. 14-35) takes place between Hezekiah and YHWH. The king of Assyria has no longer the chance to speak. Without response from Hezekiah and with only an indirect answer from YHWH, Sennacherib stands alone and seems to have been rejected by both. His messengers hand over his letter but do not speak on his behalf as the Rabshakeh had done. Hezekiah also stands without courtiers or priests (cf. 36:22; 37:2), not even the intermediary presence of the prophet stands between him and YHWH. He goes alone to the temple, spreads open the letter sent by Sennacherib before YHWH and turns to him in prayer (פלל *hitp.* does not carry the nuance of 'intervention' here; cf. 38:2; 45:20; 1 Sam. 1:26; 8:6; 2 Sam. 7:27; 1 Kgs 8:33; Jer. 29:12; Jon. 2:2; 4:2; Ps. 5:3; 32:6; Neh. 2:4).

16 Hezekiah opens his prayer with a hymnic invocation employing three divine titles. He thereby appeals to YHWH's presence in the temple ('YHWH of hosts'; see 28:5), more specifically above the ark ('enthroned above the cherubim': 1 Sam. 4:4; 2 Sam. 6:2; Ps. 80:2; 99:1; 1 Chr. 37:2) and to his solidarity with his people ('God of Israel': Isa. 17:6; 21:10,17; 24:15; 29:23). The space and time in which Israel had come to experience her God continue to serve as the location for a new encounter with him. Two confessions (twice 'You' [אתה]) extend the exclusive territory of divine influence: first to 'all the kingdoms of the earth', whereby Assyria is dethroned as overlord and placed under the authority of YHWH, and then to 'heaven and earth'. The God of history is the creator of the cosmos. The foundation is thus laid for a prayer in which Hezekiah will call upon YHWH to show in reality, and in favour of the people in whose midst he dwells, that his power extends beyond that of the mightiest empires.

17 Hezekiah's prayer for divine attention addresses YHWH twice under his own name, calling upon him 'to see' (cf. 1:15f.; 3:8; 38:3) and 'to hear' (cf. 1:15; 30:19; 37:4; 38:5). The most important element, the prayer to be heard, surrounds the prayer as such, the second time mentioning the object: 'all the words of Sennacherib, which he has sent to mock the living God'. The expression 'to mock the living God' (cf. 37:4) is found here in the immediate context of the personal name Sennacherib (without the title 'king' since it is addressed to God),[48] whereby a wordplay is created between the second half of the name, חרב-, and the term 'to mock' (חרף) together with the term 'to lay waste' (חרב) in the following verse.[49] Sennacherib is thus made to embody the true significance of Assyria: contempt for Israel's God and destruction of the world.

18-19 The logic of the prayer is as solid as a rock. Although Sennacherib's message (vv. 10-13) forms more of a threat for Hezekiah and his land than an affront to YHWH, the pious king limits himself to the latter element, the blasphemy of the message being his greatest concern.

While Hezekiah begins by recognising the historical fact upon which Sennacherib bases his claims, namely that the kings of Assyria have

---

[48] Revell 1996: 151.

[49] The terms employed by Sennacherib himself for the destruction of the nations do not engage in the same allusion to his name (cf. v. 11: חרם *hiphil;* v. 12: שחת שׁ *hiphil*)! Struss 1983 (281-5) refers to further word-play on the name Sennacherib, even on the first part thereof (-סנ).

been able to subdue all the nations because their gods were powerless (vv. 11-12), he does not do so before the Assyrian king himself but rather before God: 'Of a truth, YHWH' (אמנם can introduce a concession in a discussion: Job 9:2; 12:2; 34:12; 36:4; Ruth 3:12). These verses thus constitute a rejection of alien gods, whereby the one praying confesses his faith in YHWH. At the same time, the rejection serves as an explanation of Assyria's expansion into a world power: 'For they were no gods, but the work of human hands' (v. 19b). The mighty Assyria is thus robbed of its fear inspiring and superhuman character and is reduced to a quite transparent phenomenon.

Moreover, Hezekiah portrays the powerlessness of the gods in terms of Israel. While Sennacherib was only aware that the gods of the nations were unable to save their people from the hand of the Assyrians (v. 12), Hezekiah insists that they, i.e. their images, were thrown into the fire and destroyed, thus reducing them to lifeless material, something quite opposite to 'the living God'. The reference to the material construction of the images serves this purpose ('wood and stone': Deut. 4:28; 28: 36,64; 19:17; Ezek. 20:32). Is the narrator here presenting the Assyrians, in spite of themselves, as an example of how one can keep the law of Moses without running the risk of having to face the revenge of the gods (cf. Exod. 32:20; Num. 33:52; Deut. 7:5,25; 9:21; 12:3; 1 Chr. 14:12)? The fact that they are merely 'the work of human hands' gives Sennacherib's argument something of an Isaianic tint (Isa. 2:20; 17:8; 31:7; 41:29; 44:9-20; 46:6). Rhyme between the terms for 'human' (אדם), 'stone' (אבן) and 'they have destroyed them' (ויאבדום) further underlines the expression.

20 The prayer for salvation builds upon the argument developed so far ('So now' [ועתה]). The same logic which led to the destruction of the nations also leads to the salvation which the king expects from YHWH for his people. YHWH, after all, is not simply one among 'the gods' (v. 20). Hezekiah invokes YHWH once again, this time under the title 'our God' (cf. v. 16: 'God of Israel').

The prayer itself is terse and to the point ('save us from his hand'), relating if only in part to Sennacherib's message. While the Assyrian always employed the term 'to deliver' (נצל hiphil: 36:14f.,18ff.; 37:11f.; cf. 44:17!), Hezekiah speaks of 'to save', a term in BI which is characteristic of God's salvific action (ישע hiphil: 19:20; 25:9; 30:15 [see there]; 33:22; 35:4; 38:20; 43:3,11f.; 45:15,17,21f.; 49:25f.; 59:1,16; 60:16; 63:1,5,8f.; 64:4; for the noun 'salvation', see 33:2). Does the narrator hereby wish to portray the king as a disciple of Isaiah?

Hezekiah also takes up Sennacherib's topic of the nations and their kings (vv. 11-13) although he gives it a completely different twist. In the first place, they appear to him to have survived! Secondly, he anticipates a new future for them in the recognition of YHWH's matchlessness. The conventional concluding formula of many oracles of salvation is thus provided with a unique content.[50] Not only those who experience salvation are to come to a new degree of knowledge of YHWH, this knowledge is intended for all peoples precisely because his kingdom ultimately extends over the heavens and the earth (Exod. 7:5,17; 8:6,18; 9:14; 10:2; 1 Kgs 8:43; 18:36f.; Isa. 45:5f.; Ezek. 30:26; 36:23,36; 37:28; 39:7; Ps. 59:14; 67:3; 98:2; 109:26f.; Neh.6:16).

21 Hezekiah receives YHWH's response through the mediation of Isaiah (referred to once again at the beginning of the new scene as 'the son of Amoz'; cf. 37:2,5). The messenger formula speaks of YHWH as the 'God of Israel', the title which Hezekiah used as the basis of his appeal (v. 16). God's message concerning Sennacherib is clearly introduced as an answer to Hezekiah's prayer: 'Because you have prayed to me'.

22-29 Although the 'taunt song' fits well within the dynamics of the narrative it exhibits characteristics which point to an independent literary origin. 'Zion / Jerusalem' thus constitutes Sennacherib's earthly antagonist (next to YHWH, the primary antagonist) rather than Hezekiah. In addition, while the prophet (or Zion) speaks about God (3rd person) in vv. 22-25, God speaks about himself (1st person) in vv. 26-29, a transition which is not marked by a messenger formula.

The two segments of the taunt song exhibit an analogous structure. Rhetorical questions (v. 23 and v. 26a´) are followed in the first half by a quotation of Sennacherib (vv. 24-25), in the second half by the revelation of YHWH's plan in his regard which functions as a response (vv. 26a´´-27). Sennacherib's boasting and YHWH's purpose with him constitute a complete contrast. In addition, just as the first half opens with the derision scene (v. 22b), so the second half closes with an accusation and a judgement speech (vv. 28-29a, 29b).

22 The derision scene opens in a somewhat surprising fashion, characterised phonologically by significant rhyming (the words of v. 22b´ begin with the letters b, l, l, l, b, b, while the dominant vowel sound is a). This opening serves to introduce 'Zion / Jerusalem' which, although forming the décor as it were of these chapters (36:2) as well as the object of Assyria's threats (36:12,15,20; 37:10), takes the stage at this

---

[50] Zimmerli 1954.

point as an actant. The double appellation serves to underline her presence (2:3; 4:3f.; 10:12,32; 24:23; 30:19; 31:4f.,9; 33:20), as does the double interpolation 'daughter'. The latter is found nowhere else in BI ('daughter of Zion' only: 1:8; 10:32 [only here with 'Jerusalem']; 16:1; 52:2; 62:11; 'daughter of Jerusalem' is not found in BI). The term 'daughter', just as the term 'virgin' (בתולה), serves to personify the city ('virgin daughter': Isa. 23:12: Sidon; 47:1: Babylon; Jer. 14:17: 'my people'; 46:11: Egypt; Lam. 1:15: Judah; 2:13: Zion).[51]

The derision of Zion is first rendered by the general term 'to despise' (בוז or בזה in ethnic context: Isa. 49:7; Jer. 22:28; Ob 2; Dan. 11:21; Neh. 2:19), followed by a term which characterises the image of an oppressor in the eyes of an oppressed people: 'to scorn' (לעג; cf. 28:11: 'strange lips'; 33:19: 'stammering language'). The third term, 'to wag the head' (הניע ראש), envisages a situation of suffering and humiliation (Ps. 22:8; 109:25; Job 16:4; Lam. 2:15), although the locative 'behind you' (cf. Isa. 30:21; 38:17) suggests that Zion cannot yet allow herself to show the Assyrian king any open sign of disdain. The derision thus appears to constitute a prophetic anticipation.

23 The literary genre of accusation employing rhetorical questions with 'Who?' appears to be borrowed from DI. It suggests a personal confrontation in which the accused is forced to the wall and condemned to silence (similar questions with respect to God: Isa. 23:8; 36:5,20; 40:12ff.,26; 41:2,4,26; 42:24; 44:7; 45:21; 46:5; 48:14; 63:1). In the course of the interrogation the terms of accusation against Sennacherib already applied by Hezekiah and YHWH through the prophet return ('to mock': 37:4,17; 'to revile': 37:6; see there). Two further expressions (with anthropological components) further elaborate the accusation: 'to raise the voice' (רום קול: Gen. 39:15,18; Deut. 27:14; Isa. 13:2; 40:9; 58:1; Ezek. 21:27; Hab. 3:10; Job 38:34; Ezr. 3:12; 1 Chr. 15:16; 2 Chr. 5:13) and 'to lift the eyes on high' (נשא עין: Isa. 40:26; 49:18; 51:6; 60:4). The term 'on high' is characteristic of human arrogance in Isaiah (Isa. 22:16; 24:4,21; 32:15; 33:5; 38:4; 57:15; 58:4). The response to the rhetorical question is expressed in the form of a climax: 'Whom... against whom... against the Holy One of Israel',[52] thus referring to YHWH with the term preferred by BI (29:19,23; 30:11f.,15; 31:1).

---

[51] TWAT, I, 868f. (H. Haag), 875 (M. Tsevat).
[52] The syntactic pattern of v. 23 runs as follows: ABB (v. 23a′) / ABC (v. 23a′′); BAC (v. 23b′) / A (v. 23b′′), whereby A stands for the interrogative element and the answer, B for the verb and C for the direct object.

24 The accusation 'you have mocked the Lord' is supported by a quotation taken from Sennacherib's boasting. It is a fairly common prophetic procedure to expose the leaders of nations (10:8,13 [the king of
Assyria]; 14:13 [the king of Babylon]; 29:15f.; 30:10,16; 36:4,14) and
evil-doers (5:19f.; 7:12; 8:19f.; 9:8; 19:11; 28:15) by quoting them in
their own words. A variety of style figures provide the Assyrian king's
bragging with a greater degree of intensity. The divine title 'Lord' (אדני:
28:16,22; 29:13; 30:15,20; 38:14,16)[53] contrasts phonologically with
the emphatic 'I' (אני here and in v. 25; cf. 10:14), while the Assyrian
military force, 'my many chariots', is given first position in the clause
(רב: 1:11; 16:14; 31:1; 36:2; רכב: 22:6f.; 30:16; 31:1; 36:8f.;
43:17).[54] Sennacherib's boasting, however, exhibits one single binding
theme. The speaker has literally exceeded everything considered 'high':
he has penetrated to the highest places of the highest mountains and has
cut down the highest trees (cf. 14:8). Thus the expression 'on high'
(מרום) of v. 23 does not only make a double return here ('height'), it
constitutes the very core of a semantic field ('to go up' [עלה]: 7:6; 8:7
[Assyria]; 14:8; 36:1,10; 'mountains': 2:14; 'far recesses': 14:13,15;
'Lebanon': 2:13; 10:34; 14:8; 29:17; 60:13; 'tallest cedars': Isa.
10:33; Ezek. 19:11; 31:5).

25 The second topic of the quotation forms a distinct contrast with the
first, descending from the highest peaks to the wells and waters under
the ground and to the lowlands of Egypt's streams. These too fall under
the absolute authority of the Assyrian king. Additional elements further
underline Sennacherib's boasting. The verb 'to drink' often functions in
a context of presumptuousness (Isa. 5:22; 21:5; 22:13; 24:9; 29:8;
36:12 [contrast],16),[55] in contrast to God's concern that his people have
water to drink (Isa. 41:17; 61:8f.; 65:13). In his arrogant claim to have
walked on the arch-enemy Egypt's soil and to have dried up its life-line,
the Nile, the king's words are amplified from boasting to blasphemy. As
creator of the world, the Great King pretends to have water and drought
at his disposal (חרב in the sense of 'to dire up': Isa. 19:5f.; 44:27;
50:2; 51:10; Jer. 51:36; Hos. 13:15; Nah. 1:4; Ps. 106:9).

26-27 In the face of Sennacherib's pretensions, YHWH (from now on in
the 1st person) presents his own explanation of Assyria's spectacular
rise to power. This was brought about by YHWH's own decision and not

---

[53] This title occurs with lesser frequency in chs. 28-39 than in the remainder of PI.

[54] The titles 'Great King' and 'Rabshakeh' also fall within the range of expressions
associated with the term 'many' (רב).

[55] The reading 'strange waters' from 1QIs[a] is an adaptation to 2 Kgs 19:24 ('strange'
is not found in Sym, Vg, Syr and Tg).

by the personal efforts of the Assyrian kings. The explanation is in keeping with a familiar genre from DI: proof from prophecy (Isa. 41:21-29;
43:8-13; 44:6-8; 45:20-22; 46:8-11). One of the (post)exilic themes of
DI is the presentation of the catastrophe of 587 BC as something which
YHWH had predicted, thereby laying the foundations for the announcement that YHWH is planning to make a new beginning with his people.
The three temporal indicators at the beginning of each clause carry the
whole: 'from long ago', 'from days of old' and 'now'. God has set
things in motion a long time ago and now he has let it happen. Although
the text lacks a verb of 'announcement', this is contained in the statements: 'I have determined it / I have planned it', since the rhetorical
question: 'Have you not heard?' implies the accusation that Sennacherib
could have known.

The statement does not restrict YHWH's concern for Israel to present
events – the siege of Jerusalem and the advance of Sennacherib. Rather
it sets the emergence thereof far in the past: 'from long ago / from days
of old', following the general line of PI in this regard because the fact of
YHWH's concrete intervention is a recurring theme therein (God as subject of עשׂה, 'to make', here translated as 'to determine': 5:5; 9:6; 10:
23; 12:5; 17:7; 25:1,6; 28:21; 33:13; 37:32; 38:7,15; parallel with
יצר, 'to form', here translated as 'to plan': 22:11; 27:11; 29:16; God as
subject of בוא hiphil, 'to bring to pass': 5:19; 7:17; 31:2). It is only
here that the verbs 'to determine', 'to plan' and 'to bring to pass' are
used to indicate God's design of the course of events and the fulfilment
of God's plan.

What YHWH has brought about is not mentioned in detail until vv.
26b-27 (prior to this three times 'it'). Sennacherib's destiny is to destroy
cities and bring their inhabitants to ruin. The verse employs formulations
taken from Isaiah's account of call (6:11: 'to ruin' [שׁאה hiphil], 'cities'
and 'inhabitants'), from an oracle against those who place their trust in
Egypt (20:5: 'dismayed and confounded') and from DI's portrayal of
the situation after judgement ('plants of the field / tender grass'; cf.
40:7: 'grass / flower of the field'; cf. Ps. 90:5f.; 103:15f.), although
applied in the present instance to the situation of Jerusalem, a city with
houses (cf. Ps. 129:6). Sennacherib's historical, God given assignment
is thus described in terms reminiscent of Israel's progress through history.

28-29 The portrayal of Sennacherib's destiny as part of YHWH's plan
flows seamlessly over into an accusation and an announcement of judgement. There is nothing negative in the statement: 'I know your rising up
and sitting down, your going out and coming in' (cf. 'Notes'). The verb

'to know' expresses God's ability and right to scrutinise and to judge the comings and goings of human persons (Gen. 20:6; Exod. 32:22; Deut. 8:2; 13:3; Judg. 3:4; 1 Sam. 3:2; Isa. 29:15; 48:4; Jer. 12:3; 15:15; 18:23; 48:30; Ezek. 11:5; Amos 5:12; Ps. 40:10; 44:22; 69:6,20; 94:11; 139:23f.; Job 23:10; 31:6; Prov. 24:12; Neh. 9:10). The two word-pairs 'to rise up and to sit down' and 'to go out and to come in' form a merism for the entirety of human behaviour, the latter pair occasionally referring to military action (2 Kgs 19:27; Ps. 139:2; Lam. 3:63 and Deut. 28:6,19; 31:2; Josh. 14:11; 1 Sam. 18:16; 29:6; 2 Sam. 3:25; 1 Kgs 3:7; 15:17; 2 Kgs 19:27; Ezek. 46:10; Zech. 8:10; Ps. 121:8 respectively).[56]

Given, however, that YHWH surveys all that human persons undertake, he is also aware of Sennacherib's 'raging against me' (רגז *hitp.*). This word-group appears in two places, at the end and at the beginning of v. 29 (the style-figure of *anadiplosis*) and is thus given emphasis.[57] The verb expresses violent physical reaction and is sometimes used in the context of 'anger' (אנף [here embodied in the term 'nose']: 2 Sam. 22:9; Isa. 5:25; 13:13; Mic. 7:18; Job 9:5; Sir. 5:6).[58] 'To rage' in the present verse is placed on the same level as 'arrogance' (שאנן), the illusionary certainty and nonchalance which accompanies hubris and characterises those whose power and well-being is not under any form of threat (cf. Isa. 32:9,11; Amos 6:1; Zech. 1:15; Ps. 123:4; Job 12:5).[59] In the clause: 'Your arrogance has gone up to my ears', which suggests distance between YHWH and Sennacherib, one can read a correction of the king's boastful words in v. 24: 'With my many chariots I myself have gone up to the heights of the mountain' (cf. 36:10).

The verdict consists of a succinct fact which anticipates the ultimate outcome of Sennacherib's campaign: 'I will turn you back on the way by which you came' (v. 29b, cf. v. 37; in contrast with v. 24: 'I came to its remotest height'), and of a mythical representation thereof: 'I will put my hook in your nose and my bit in your lips'. This latter expression portrays the defeated king as an imprisoned wild animal (Isa. 30:28; Ezek. 19:4; 38:4; Ps. 2:2-4; Job 40:24-26; 2 Chr. 33:11), a topic familiar to Assyrian iconography[60] and annals. King Esarhaddon (681-669), for example, gloried in the fact that he had transported king Asuhili of

[56] Krašovec 1977: 109ff., 140.

[57] *pace* J. Gray, *I and II Kings* (OTL), London 1964, 690; Kaiser, 296: dittography. On the other hand, Barthélemy (259) shows that the omission of v. 29a′ in 1QIsᵃ is due to haplography.

[58] *TWAT*, VII, 328 (G. Vanoni).

[59] *TWAT*, VII, 939f. (W. Thiel).

[60] *ANEP*, 154, nr. 447; Keel 1972: 280f.

Arza to Nineveh and had exhibited him at the city gate together with a
bear, a dog and a pig.[61] The terms employed in the description of
Sennacherib's humiliating enforced withdrawal ('nose' en 'lips') provide a contrasting allusion to his initial rage (cf. 36:5).

30 With the promise of a sign, the prophet now turns to Hezekiah,
who has also been present in YHWH's thought throughout this speech
concerning and addressed to Sennacherib (vv. 21-22a). The opening
words: 'But for you, this...' (וזה לך) rhyme with those of the first segment: 'She despises you' (בזה לך). Both phrases thus serve to mark off
segments vv. 22-29 and vv. 30-32. At an earlier point in BI a sign was
already given to king Ahaz, the father of Hezekiah, in spite of the
former's unwillingness to receive it (7:10-14). Just as the tradition assigned, among other things, the notion of disaster for the cultivated land
to the Immanuel sign (7:23-25), so the redaction of BI has placed the
sign offered to Hezekiah, which announces the restoration of the cultivated land (37:30f.), as a pendant prior to the great transition from PI to
DI.

In similar fashion to a comparison, the sign (אות) consists of a vehicle
and a tenor (cf. Isa. 7:14 and 15-16; 8:16 and 17-18; 19:19 and 20;
20:3 and 4). The vehicle in the present instance is not purely imaginary
(v. 30), since it presumes the devastation of the land which fits well with
the siege of Jerusalem. The three year temporal scheme, however, appears to be a literary convention (2 Sam. 13:38; 24:13; 1 Kgs 10:22;
22:1; 2 Kgs 17:5; 18:10; Isa. 20:3). A literal interpretation of the
scheme tends to lead to speculative calculations concerning the duration
of the siege and the re-commencement of agricultural activity.[62] In addition, the idea that the population would be able to survive on what the
soil perchance might produce (in the first and second years) is far from
realistic, certainly no more so than the suggestion that a vineyard can
produce fruit in a single season (cf. Lev. 19:23ff.; Deut. 20:6; Isa. 5:2).

The idea 'to eat' dominates the vehicle of the comparison (אכל encloses v. 30a''-b).[63] Within a period of three years the produce of the
land will improve from 'what grows of itself' through 'what springs
from that' to the regular produce of sowing and planting. The difference

---

[61] *TUAT*, I/4, 397; other texts with Wildberger, 790f.

[62] *pace* Delitzsch, 381f.; Oswalt, 664f.

[63] The infinitive absolute ואכל at the end of the verse continues the preceding form,
i.e. the imperative ונטעו (J-M, §123 x). The imperatives of this verse are equivalent to a
future with energic nuance (J-M, §114 p). 1QIs[a] also employs the imperative 'plant' in
the form of an infinitive absolute, indeed several commentators do the same with the imperatives 'sow and reap' (*BHS;* Wildberger, 1419). Such co-ordination, however, tends to
undervalue the possibility of linguistic variation.

between the first return and the second is artificial (*Nachwuchs* and *Wildwuchs*). The proposal that the first return is the result of discarded grains of seed and the second of forgotten roots remains nothing more than a guess since the first word has almost no parallels (cf. Lev. 25:5,11f.) and the second is a *hapax legomenon*. The distinction serves a conventional three part scheme for the laborious yet relentless restoration of life in a fertile land, a restoration exemplified by the word-pairs 'to sow and to reap' (Lev. 25:11; Jer. 12:13; Hos. 8:7; 10:12; Amos 9:13; Mic. 6:15; Ps. 126:5; Job 4:8; Prov. 22:8; Eccl. 11:4) and 'to plant and to eat' (Lev. 19:23; Deut. 6:11; Jer. 29:5,28; Amos 9:14; with 'vineyards': Deut. 28:39; Josh. 24:13; Isa. 65:21f.). Such word-pairs are at home in the semantic field of blessing and curse which characterise life in the land granted by God.

31-32 The tenor of comparison of the sign refers to Judah (v. 31) and Jerusalem (v. 32), the fate of both being a constant preoccupation of PI (1:1; 2:1; 3:1,8; 5:3; 7:1; 22:21; 36:7,10; Judah only: 7:6,17; 8:8; 9:20; 11:12f.; 19:17; 22:8; 26:1; 36:1). The explicit association with the vehicle is found in the word 'fruit' (v. 30: 'eat their fruit'; v. 31: 'shall bear fruit'); the term 'to take root' also has a pertinent equivalent in the terms 'to sow' and 'to plant' there. The first application, however, is connected to the preceding vehicle by *weqatal* (v. 31), while the second application is given particular attention through the macro-syntactic כי (v. 32).

In contrast to v. 32, v. 31 gives the impression of being overloaded, especially since the words 'those who survive' and 'the remnant' are not spread over the two halves of the verse, as in v. 32, but concentrated rather in the first half. One is left with the impression that a later hand has applied both terms to Judah.[64] The original form of v. 31 would then have been: 'The house of Judah shall again take root downward, and bear fruit upward', and have exhibited the same metrical pattern (4+3) as v. 32a. The promise includes a healthy vegetative foundation which, with favourable conditions, will lead to genuine fertility ('root' and 'fruit' occur together in Isa. 11:1; 14:29; Jer. 12:2; 17:8; Ezek. 17:9; Hos. 9:16; Amos 2:9). It is possible that the verse makes reference to the song of the vineyard (5:7).

With the application of the sign to 'Jerusalem / Zion' the promise touches on the main issue of the entire story (v. 32a; cf. 36:4,15,20; 37:10,22). The terminology, however, steps outside the narrative frame-

---

[64] The proper name 'Judah' appears elsewhere with both פלט and שאר in Neh. 1:2, with שאר only in what are for the most part later texts (2 Kgs 17:18; 25:22; Jer. 24:8; 39:10; 40:11,15; 42:15,19; 43:5; 44:7,14,28; Zeph. 2:7; 2 Chr. 30:6; 34:9,21).

work since 'remnant / band of survivors' are post-exilic concepts[65] which presuppose the destruction of the city, while in the outcome of the present narrative she remains unharmed. Likewise, Hezekiah did not pray for the opportunity to make a new beginning after the disaster (v. 20). Indeed, the outcome would appear to leave us with the remnant of the Assyrian army! While the original version clearly contained a guarantee for Zion on behalf of YHWH (vv. 33-34), the formulation of the sign reveals that the tradition or redaction has read the narrative against the background of the later destruction of the city.[66] Jerusalem's liberation from the threat of being overpowered by Sennacherib in 701 serves as a sign that the ruined Jerusalem of 587 would ultimately have its population restored. (The term 'to go forth' [יצא] continues the predominantly vegetative imagery of the vehicle [Gen. 1:12,24; Deut. 14:22; 28:38; 1 Kgs 5:13; Isa. 11:1; 61:11; Hag. 1:11; Ps. 104:14; Job 5:6; 14:2; Sir. 38:4].) The renewed occupation of Jerusalem exhibits something of the aspirations of Ezra and Nehemiah (the terms 'to remain' [שאר] and 'band of survivors' [פליטה] are also found together in Ezra 9:8,15; Neh. 1:2).[67]

Within PI the announcement of salvation in v. 32a resumes the programmatic promise found in the early chapters (4:32: '...the fruit of the land shall be the pride and glory of the survivors of Israel. And he who is left in Zion and remains in Jerusalem will be called holy...'). Against the background of PI the word 'Mount' in the locative 'Jerusalem / Mount Zion' also receives a special function: it is the place where YHWH dwells (Isa. 8:18; 10:12; 18:7; 24:23; 31:4f.). The foundations are thus revealed for the fact that Jerusalem will have its population restored. This is made more explicit in the concluding sentence: 'The zeal of YHWH of hosts will accomplish this'. In the self-understanding of the exiles, 'the zeal (קנאה) of YHWH' is the mainspring from which he brings about changes in the course of history. Having visited his people with his wrath he now punishes the enemies thereof (Isa. 59:17; 63:15; Ezek. 35:11; 36:5; 39:25; Joel 2:18; Zeph. 1:18; 3:8; Zech. 1:14; 8:2; Ps. 79:5).[68] YHWH's intervention thus reveals itself to be superior to that of the Assyrian kings ('to accomplish' [עשה]: cf. vv. 16,26 with v. 11).

---

[65] Stohlmann (1983: 168-75), in contrast, sees evidence in v. 31 that the prophets of the 8th century already saw the future of Judah – after the deportation of 701 of which the Rassam cylinder speaks (151-7) – in the remnant *in* the land.

[66] Clements 1996: 46ff.

[67] Pfaff 1996: 117-20.

[68] *TWAT*, VII, 61f. (E. Reuter).

33-35 YHWH himself speaks once again in the judgement speech concerning Sennacherib. The first part thereof is surrounded by quotation formulae (vv. 33-34). The opening clause: 'He shall not come into this city' is restated at the end, here accompanied by the parallel statement: 'By the way on which he came, he shall return', thus forming a second internal inclusion. The first part contains a guarantee of the safety of Jerusalem while in the second, YHWH (1st person) bases this guarantee on his own person and on his bond with David (v. 35). This verse may be a later addition given that the David motif has no further role to play in the narrative, but it is clearly part of the design of the redaction of PI.

33-34 Sennacherib's bragging is countered with a fivefold 'no' on the part of YHWH: in spite of all his advanced siege techniques ('arrow', 'shield' and 'mould') he shall not enter the city. Although he boasts of the fact that there is no territory between heaven and earth which does not lie open to him ('to come' [בוא]: 36:17; 37:24; cf. 'to go up' [עלה]: 36:10), he shall nevertheless be unsuccessful in his efforts to enter the city of YHWH's protection. Empty handed he shall return by the way he came.

35 The guarantee of Jerusalem's military security in the face of Assyrian attack is based on YHWH's bond with David. By means of the promise 'to shield' (גנן; cf. 31:5) the city, God places himself between Jerusalem and the invader (v. 33: 'shield' [מגן]). With the promise 'to save' (הושיע) her, he gives a positive answer to Hezekiah's prayer as well as to an expectation which runs throughout BI (see at v. 20).

The motivation 'for my own sake and for the sake of my servant David' clearly echoes the redaction of BI. On the lips of YHWH, the expression 'for my own sake' is only found elsewhere in DI (43:25; 48:11; cf. 49:7; 55:5), where it also serves as a motif for God's action on behalf of his people. The expression 'for the sake of (my servant) David' is at home in the Deuteronomistic theology (1 Kgs 11:12f.,13,32,34, 36,39; 15:4; 2 Kgs 8:19; Zech. 12:7; 2 Chr. 21:7). The association of both terms is unique to the present verse (parallel in 2 Kgs 19:34; 20:6) but integration of idioms from various literary corpora is characteristic of the exile. The great value attached to David here, however, is not out of place within the various traditions which coincide in BI (7:2,13; 9:6; 16:5; 22:9, 22; 29:1; 38:5; 55:3).

36 'The messenger of YHWH' provides Jerusalem's relief. It is in fact the only time that this figure appears in BI (cf. 63:9: 'the messenger of his face'; other figures are referred to in 42:19; 44:26). He is placed in contrast to the 'messengers of Sennacherib' (37:9,14) and of other nations who cannot negotiate liberation (14:32; 18:2; 30:4; 33:17). After

YHWH has spoken, it is 'the messenger of YHWH' who carries out his sentence concerning Sennacherib by destroying the Assyrian army. This is in harmony with 'the principle of double representation'. The transcendental aspect of a theophany, expressed in the form of a divine voice which judges and issues orders, is reserved for YHWH in person while the visual, active dimension of the theophany is ascribed to 'the messenger of YHWH'.[69] Although the term 'messenger of YHWH' is missing from the account of Isaiah's call, the same pattern is evident there: one of the seraphs purifies Isaiah's lips but it is the voice of YHWH who calls him (Isa. 6:6-8; cf. Gen. 16:7-13; 28:12-13; Judg. 6:12-14,20; 13:2-20).

The fact that the 'messenger' strikes the army, should not be seen as a form of revenge, but rather as in harmony with the message of the prophet which states that YHWH punishes his adversaries and subdues them (נכה *hiphil*: Isa. 1:5; 5:25; 9:12; 10:20; 11:15; 27:7; 30:31; 53:4; 57:17; 60:10). While it may appear unjust that the Assyrian king himself is not put to death, in the design of the narrative he is obliged to witness the loss of his 'undefeatable' forces and experience the shame of powerlessness. Questions surrounding the accuracy of the 185.000 dead extend perhaps from a belief that all the numbers in the Scriptures have to be historically reliable. Such questions have already found their own answer (Oswalt, 669f.). The opinion that the figure of 185.000 is not improbable within the horizon of the concrete narrative, is supported by the fact that the Hebrew word for 'thousand' does not always mean this number. It often stands for a military force of uncertain if always significant dimensions (אלף: Num. 31:5; Josh. 4:13; Judg. 3:29; 1 Sam. 4:2; 2 Sam. 6:1; 1 Kgs 10:26; 2 Kgs 13:7; Isa. 30:17; Ps. 60:2; 91:7; Sir. 16:10).[70]

The expression 'to arise early in the morning' marks the beginning of a new activity,[71] often in the context of events brought about by God (Gen. 19:27; 21:14; 22:3; 26:31; 28:18; 32:1; Exod. 8:16; 9:13; 24:4; 30:4; Num. 14:40; Josh. 3:1; 6:12; 7:16; Judg. 6:28; 1 Sam. 1:19; 5:4; 15:12; 2 Kgs 3:22; Job 1:5; not in Isa. 5:11). The expression adds to the miraculous character of the ruin of the Assyrian army. This is primarily determined by the fact there was no personal intervention on the part of Hezekiah or his army or the inhabitants of Jerusalem.

---

[69] Polak 1998: 15*: 'From a narrative point of view, the paradox is strictly functional: the symbiosis between the invisible divine presence and the physical appearance of the messenger increases the concrete power of revelation, whilst preserving the divine authority of the message'.

[70] *DCH*, I, 298.

[71] *TWAT*, VII, 1333f. (R. Bartelmus).

Both king and people simply have to establish the slaughter (cf. Judg. 6:28; 1 Sam. 5:3f., where the miraculous event is likewise introduced by 'behold' [הנה]).[72] The term 'dead bodies' also connotes a dimension of God's verdict (Lev. 26:30; Num. 14:29,32f.; Isa. 34:3; 66:24; Jer. 33:5; Amos 8:3; Nah. 3:3; Dan. 12:2). – It is possible that for the redaction of PI this outcome served as the fulfilment of the prayer for salvation in the morning pronounced in 33:5.

37 The narrator lets the facts speak for themselves. A series of three verbs portrays the end of Sennacherib's expedition: 'he broke camp, went home and returned', just as God had announced (37:7,29,34). Each of these verbs calls to mind a variety of texts elsewhere in PI, providing a background or contrast in association with this humiliating withdrawal ('to break camp' [נסע]: 33:20; 37:8; 'to go' [הלך] with regard to Assyria: 8:7; 20:2; 'to return' [שוב]: 35:10; 36:9). The occurrence of the title 'king of Assyria' underlines the painful character of the departure. The second announcement, 'He remained at Nineveh', makes it clear that Sennacherib's desire for conquest is suppressed once and for all (ישב: 37:27 [14:13]; cf. 6:1; 32:18).

38 After losing his army and his power, Sennacherib now forfeits his life in the most humiliating way possible: neither in battle, nor at the hand of 'the messenger of YHWH' – there is never direct contact between Sennacherib and God –, but at the hands of his two sons. 'They slew him' (הכהו) as the messenger of YHWH slew the Assyrian army (v. 36). While Sennacherib's powerlessness is clear from the fact that his sons were able to escape, it is all the more evident from the fact that he was killed while he 'was worshipping' (משתחוה) his god Nisroch (most likely the same as Ninurta, the Assyrian god of war)[73] in the latter's 'house'. His perfidious interpretation of Hezekiah's reform of the cult is thus fittingly punished: 'Is it not he whose high places and altars Hezekiah has removed, saying to Judah and to Jerusalem: Before this altar you shall worship?' (36:7). Similarly the prayer of Isaiah is fulfilled: 'They bow down to the work of their hands, to what their own fingers have made. So man is humbled, and men brought low – forgive them not!' (2:8-9).

The outcome of the narrative contrasts Sennacherib with Hezekiah, who went up to the house of YHWH in his hour of need (37:1,14) and

---

[72] The 3rd person plural of 'they arose early in the morning' is unspecified (De Regt 1999: 56) but refers, according to the pattern of actants in the story as a whole, to king Hezekiah and the people of Jerusalem.

[73] The name 'Nisroch' is not found in Assyrian texts. It is probably a textual corruption of 'Nimrod', a name which refers to the god Ninurta. This Assyrian war god can serve as 'the god of Sennacherib' (DDD, 1186-90).

found a God there who differed from the mute god of Sennacherib: a God who listened and responded, a God who promised salvation (37:30-35) and brought it about (v. 36). The Assyrian king's provocative question: 'Where are the gods of...?' (36:19f.; 37:12f.) now turns back on his own self.

THE SECOND STORY: KING HEZEKIAH'S RECOVERY FROM ILLNESS (38:1-22)

TRANSLATION

1   In those days Hezekiah fell ill and was at the point of death.
Then Isaiah, the son of Amoz, the prophet, came to him,
and said to him:
> Thus says YHWH:
>> 'Set your house in order;
>> for you shall die,
>> you shall not recover'.

2   Then Hezekiah turned his face to the wall,
he prayed to YHWH,

3   and said:
> 'Please, YHWH.
> Remember now,
> how I have walked before you
> in faithfulness and with a whole heart,
> and have done what is good in your eyes'.

And Hezekiah wept bitterly.

4   Then the word of YHWH came to Isaiah:

5   Go
and say to Hezekiah:
Thus says YHWH, the God of David, your father:
> 'I have heard your prayer,
> I have seen your tears.
> Behold, I will add fifteen years to your days.

6   Out of the hand of the king of Assyria,
> I will deliver you and this city
> and I will defend this city'.

7   This is the sign to you from YHWH,
that YHWH will do this thing that he has promised:

8   'Behold, I will make the shadow cast by the declining sun
> on the staircase of Ahaz' upper chamber turn back ten steps'.
So the sun turned back on the staircase the ten steps
by which it had declined.

9   A writing of Hezekiah king of Judah,
    when he fell ill and recovered from his illness:

10   'I myself said:
       In the quiet time of my days I must go
    I am consigned to the gates of Sheol
       for the rest of my years.
11   I said: I shall not see YHWH,
       YHWH in the land of the living.
    I shall look upon human beings no more
       among the inhabitants of transitoriness.
12   My dwelling is plucked up and removed from me
       like a shepherd's tent.
    Like a weaver I have rolled up my life.
       He cuts me off from the loom.
    From day to night you deliver me up,
13   I am laid up until morning.
    Like a lion he breaks all my bones.
       From day to night you deliver me up.
14   Like a swallow (a crane) I chirp,
       I moan like a dove.
    My eyes are weary with looking on high.
       O Lord, I am oppressed; be my security!
15   But what shall I say? For he has spoken to me,
       and he himself has done it.
    I walk slowly all my years
       because of the bitterness of my soul.
16   O Lord, by these things people live,
       and in these is all the life of my spirit.
    Oh, you want to restore me to health – make me live!
17   Lo, it is for my peace that I had great bitterness.
    But you have attached yourself to my soul
       (keeping me) from the pit of destruction.
    Truly, you have cast behind your back
       all my sins.
18   Truly, Sheol does not praise you,
       death does not extol you.
    Those who go down to the pit do not hope
       for your faithfulness.
19   The living, the living, he praises you,
       as I do this day.

The father makes known to the sons
    your faithfulness.
20   YHWH is at hand to save me,
    and we will sing to stringed instruments
all the days of our life,
    at the house of YHWH'.

21 Now Isaiah said:
    'Let them take a cake of figs,
      and apply it to the boil, that he may recover'.
22 Hezekiah said:
    'What is the sign
      that I shall go up to the house of YHWH?'.

NOTES

8a 1QIsᵃ reads במעלות עלית אחז את השמש instead of MT במעלות אחז
בשמש. Although the LXX reading of this verse differs considerably from
MT and 1QIsᵃ, it agrees with the latter in reading τοῦ οἴκου τοῦ πατρός
σου as the equivalent of עלית אחז ('upper chamber of Ahaz'; cf. 2 Kgs
23:12). Therefore, haplography in MT is more probable than dittography in 1QIsᵃ. LXX's reading τὸν ἥλιον also agrees with 1QIsᵃ (את
השמש) and not with MT (בשמש). (MT is followed in this instance only by
Vg.) The object את השמש would appear to belong to the verb משיב and
to clarify the masculine noun צל which may have been conceived
secundum sensum as identical with the feminine noun for 'sun' (שמש)
since the feminine verb form ירדה refers to it.
For some scholars, nevertheless, the lack of agreement between the
feminine verb form ירדה, 'has declined', and the always masculine noun
צל, 'shadow', remains a problem. This leads Althann (1988) to the explanation that ירדה refers to מעלות, to be parsed as singular with a
Phoenician ending, in other words: 'the staircase which goes down'. It is
hard to understand, however, what the purport of this relative clause
could be, whereas lack of agreement between subject and predicate,
ירדה, can be accepted.[1]

---

[1] According to GKC (§146a) and J-M (§150 n), the verb form sometimes agrees, in
respect of number and gender, not with the *nomen regens* but with the *nomen rectum* of a
compound subject. This means, with regard to v. 8, that the verb form ירדה could follow
צל with regard to number and מעלות with regard to gender. Cf. also J. Levi, *Die Inkon-
gruenz im biblischen Hebräisch*, Wiesbaden 1987.

On the basis of this text-critical situation it seems advisable to follow the Qumran version instead of MT (see the translation; Iwry 1977; Barthélemy, 261ff.; Catastini 1983).[2]

9 Since Delitzsch (390) the first word of the heading מכתב ('writing') is often emended to read מכתם, a term without clear significance found in the titles of a number of psalms (Psalms 16; 56-60; cf. the survey of discussions in Wildberger, 1458). The versions, however, do not support this emendation (with the possible exception of LXX: προσευχή).

10a The words בדמי ימי (RSV: 'in the noontide of my days') are unclear. While it is evident from Ps. 63:6f.; 83:2 that the expression means 'in the quiet time of my days', a number of commentators are of the opinion that this refers to the conclusion of a typical human life while the context speaks clearly of premature death. LXX interprets: 'in the height' (ἐν τῷ ὕψει; also Begrich 1926: 20ff.: ברם), Vg and Syr have read: 'in the midst' (cf. Jer. 17:11; Ezek. 16:38; Ps. 54:24; 102:25; also Wildberger, 1442; *HALAT*, 217; *DCH*, II, 450). The RSV's 'in the noontide of my days' might be an attempt to harmonise both interpretations. There is insufficient reason to emend the first word or to ascribe a meaning to it other than the traditional one: 'quiet' (*pace* De Boer 1951: 178f.: 'in my fear of death', *b^edummi* [root *dmm*]). It would appear to be a metaphor for the period in a person's life which is free of turbulence (Delitzsch, 390; Oswalt, 683; for a variety of alternative explanations cf. Alexander 80f.).[3] – The construct state generates the metrical pattern 2 + 3, an apparent variation on the predominant *qinah* meter (3 + 2).

11 Several translations emend the last word, חדל, 'cessation', to read חלד, 'world' (RSV), by analogy with Ps. 49:2 and in agreement with Syr, a number of rabbinic and (predominantly) modern commentators (Delitzsch, 391; Duhm, 280; *BHS*). 1QIs^a follows MT. While LXX, Aq, Th and Vg do the same with respect to the root חדל, they appear to have read a verb form. From the text-critical perspective, therefore, the emendation of MT remains unjustified (Dahood 1971). It is more probable that the text represents an example of Isaianic word-play in which the author, instead of using the expected term, employs a term which is related thereto in both form and meaning (cf. Isa. 13:22; 38:17; 41:14, 24,29; 48:10; 51:16; 63:14; 64:6; Barthélemy, 264f.).

---

[2] In addition, Catastini does not interpret אחז as a personal name but rather as a verb form (*yiqtol* 1st person singular): 'I will draw back the sun'. This explanation is speculative and is not based on text-critical foundations; cf. Ognibeni 1992 and the continuing discussion between Catastini 1993 and Ognibeni 1993.

[3] While Gesenius (987f.) associates the 'rest' with the peaceful governance of Hezekiah, there is no further indication that the one praying is speaking as king.

13 Almost all the translations emend MT שׁוִּיתִי ('I have stilled, sc. my soul'; cf. Ps. 131:2 [BDB, 1000]) to read שׁוַּעְתִּי (RSV: 'I cry'). Some, however, follow 1QIsᵃ: שׁפותי (TOB: 'Je serai reduit à rien'). An additional proposal renders the text: 'I shall be devastated' (Nyberg 1974: 92: a denominative of שׁוא; likewise Watts, 56; for a survey, cf. Wildberger, 1443; *HALAT*, 1335). The versions do not appear to offer a solution. Should one uphold MT and presume the root שׁוה I ('to make like'), the second half of v. 13a would then constitute the object of the first: 'Je m'imaginais que, jusqu'au matin, tel un lion, il aurait brisé tous mes os' (Barthélemy [267], following Luzzatto and Buber), but this results in a somewhat laboured clause construction. One can also uphold MT and presume the root שׁוה II ('to lie, be laid up'; Seybold 1973: 151: 'als ein willentlicher Akt, und zwar des niedergebeugten Daliegens und Wachens und d.i. von der bewegungslosen Haltung des Büßers zu verstehen').

14 The word 'crane' (עגור) is probably a gloss from Jer. 8:7, intended to distinguish the Hebrew word for 'swallow', סוס, from the homonymous word meaning 'horse' (Barthélemy, 268f.).

The reading of MT עָשְׁקָה־לִּי (the first word is a noun or according to some scholars, a *qatal* feminine singular), translated by RSV as: 'I am oppressed', is emended in terms of root and form by several commentators to read עֻשְׁקָה־לִּי, 'pay heed for me' (imperative; REB; Cheyne, 231; Duhm, 281; *BHS*). The complex history of the explanation of the *meteg* in this word-group leads one to the conclusion that MT should be maintained and the first word should be treated as a feminine abstract noun (Barthélemy, 269ff.; König, *Lehrgebäude*, I, §13, 1.c.α [99]; Delitzsch, 393; Begrich 1926: 39; Wildberger, 1444; *pace* Nyberg 1974: 93: feminine verb form; cf. 1 Sam. 30:6; Isa. 7:7,14, 24; Jer. 7:31). Furthermore, the roots עשׁק and ערב can be found as a contrasting word pair in Ps. 119:122: 'Be surety for your servant for good; let not the godless oppress me'. The terms in question are take from the context of money lending.

15a Instead of MT ואמר לי (RSV: 'For he has spoken to me'; also Aq, Vg and Syr) several versions and commentators read ואמר לו, 'and what shall I say to him?' (likewise 1QIsᵃ, Th and Tg; Duhm [281] together with the majority of German commentators; Begrich 1926: 41; Barré [1995: 398f.] maintaining לי: 'What can I say on my behalf?' *BHS*). This reading, however, is an adaptation to the preceding verb form (אדברה) and should not be followed.

15b 1QIsᵃ (followed more or less by Syr; also RSV) reads אדודה (from נדד, 'to flee') instead of MT אדדה (from דדה *hitp.*, 'to move slowly'; only here and in Ps. 42:5). The variant reading is based on Gen.

31:40; Esth. 6:1. Begrich (42) emends to read אֹדֶךָ ('I shall praise you all my years, in spite of the bitterness of my soul'; also Wildberger, 1444). Yet, such a thanksgiving element would be premature. The versions have clearly struggled with the problem and opted for a variety of solutions. Barthélemy (273) upholds the reading of MT. With respect to the meaning of דדה *hitp.*, he does not refer to Ps. 42:5, where it signifies a festival ritual, but to the application found in the Talmud. The latter associates the verb with birds which have had their wings tied together: 'to advance slowly or with (short) leaps'.[4] In this way, the meaning of Isa. 38:15: 'I walk slowly, all my years', would be appropriate as a metaphor expressing defectiveness in a description of distress. This explanation (cf. Aq: προβιβάσω) is followed by *HALAT*, 205; *DCH*, II, 416; Watts, 56.

16 The interpretation of the first two cola is highly contested and has led as such to textual emendation (for a survey, cf. Wildberger, 1444f.; a far-reaching reconstruction of vv. 16-17a can be found in Barré 1995), although MT is confirmed by the versions. Basically, the translation of the RSV is maintained here. The word בהן, however, is considered an intervening element in a construct chain, כל חיי רוחי (Barthélemy, 275), such that the translation runs: 'in these is all the life of my spirit' (cf. 'Exegesis by Verse').

17 RSV: 'Thou has held back my soul' follows the emendation of חשק (MT: 'to be attached to') to read חשׂך ('to withhold'), according to some exegetes, in harmony with LXX and Vg (although this is doubtful) and based on the fact that חשק always constructs the object with a preposition. It is probable, however, that we are dealing here with a word-play similar to that found in v. 11 (חדל and חלד). While the author employed חשק, he constructed it in the fashion of חשׂך in order to include the significance of the latter verb (Barthélemy, 275f.).

19 The preposition אל associated with the last word, אמתך, is unusual. Some translations follow 1QIs[a] which replaces אל with אלוה, 'God', at least in the repetition of v. 19, included in v. 20 (REB). It is more likely, however, that we are dealing here with an example of the style-figure *epiphora*: v. 19 ends with the same words as v. 18 (likewise v. 12 and v. 13; Barthélemy, 276f.).

ESSENTIALS AND PERSPECTIVES

The explanation of ch.38 is burdened with the questions which were raised in connection with the whole complex of chs. 36-39 and their par-

---

[4] J. Levy, *Wörterbuch über die Talmudim und Midraschim*, Berlin 1924[2], I, 378.

allel version in 2 Kings 18-20 (and to a lesser extent in 2 Chr. 32:24-26). The differences between this narrative and its pendant (2 Kgs 20:1-11), however, are more significant than was the case with the first narrative. 'The writing of Hezekiah' (Isa. 38:9-20), for example, is absent from 2 Kings 20 while Isaiah's second message (vv. 4-6) has a different character. In addition, Hezekiah's therapy follows the sign in Isaiah 38 (vv. 21-22 after vv. 7-8; cf. 2 Kgs 20:7 and 8-11) where there is no mention of the fact that the king was actually healed (2 Kgs 20:7), nor of his request that the sign be made irrefutable and of the report of YHWH's compliance therewith (2 Kgs 20:10-11). These differences invite us to interpret the present narrative as much 'in its own right' as we did the first.

Such an approach, however, need not suggest that the history of this chapter's emergence is unimportant.[5] The traditional and still honoured position maintains that the version of 2 Kings is the more original of the two, based largely on the fact that the fifteen year prolongation of Hezekiah's lifetime appears to be borrowed from the broad temporal schema of 2 Kings (cf. 2 Kgs 18:2 and 13)[6] and that Hezekiah's prayer is lacking therein. It is suggested, therefore, that the Isaiah redaction inserted this latter segment in the context of the idealisation of the king,[7] such words being at home on the lips of a pious invalid who either hopes for or has received healing (cf. Psalm 6; 32; 38; 39; 41; 88; 102; 103). Moreover, the conclusion to Hezekiah's prayer, the topic of the restoration of the community around the temple (v. 20), would appear to be out of place in the Deuteronomistic History, yet at home in BI.[8] It is likewise suggested that the redaction of BI was responsible for correcting the 'illogical sequence' of healing and sign found in 2 Kings 20. Although this reorganisation placed v. 22 in a somewhat strange position, the redaction seems to have been unwilling to omit this element of 2 Kgs 20:8.

In recent years, however, the very opposite position has been proposed, namely that the Isaiah version is older than that of 2 Kings. The theory is based primarily on the insight that ch.38 plays an important role in the coherence of BI as well as sharing a number of notable themes with PI. Furthermore, Hezekiah's prayer to one side, the version of 2 Kings is longer and touches on themes which exhibit the character of an expansion (2 Kgs 20:4-5: God answers and heals very quickly; v.

---

[5] In so far as the genesis of ch.38 constitutes a part of that of chs. 36-39, see the exegesis of chs. 36-37.

[6] Gonçalves 1986: 336, 345.

[7] Watts 1992 (118-31) has elaborated this carefully.

[8] Williamson 1994: 203.

5: Hezekiah's piety is directed to the temple v. 6: God's motives for acting as he does; vv. 10-11: the sign is indisputably miraculous;[9] vv.
4,8,11: the prophet plays a more significant role). In addition, the arrangement of the material seems to support the idea that BI is the original setting. From the perspective of chronology, chs. 38-39 belong together (cf. 39:1), both narratives having their place prior to the siege of
Jerusalem in chs. 36-37 (cf. 38:6). According to their actual arrangement, however, they are loosely connected with the first narrative (38:1:
'In those days'; 39:1: 'At that time'). To conclude, ch.39 constitutes a
prediction of the Babylonian captivity thus serving to connect PI with
ch.40. Such an arrangement clearly does not serve the structure of 2
Kings where it can only be understood as a borrowed text.[10]

The discussion continues to the present day,[11] giving rise to partly
overlapping and partly divergent opinions. It would be impossible, however, to provide an adequate survey thereof in the present instance. Nevertheless, the fact that both positions sometimes employ the same arguments,[12] might suggest that the narrative originally enjoyed an independent existence[13] which, after complex adaptation, found its way into both
2 Kings and BI, and that both versions ultimately influenced one another
thereafter.[14]

One valuable result of the discussion has been to clarify the extent to
which the Isaiah version now fits down to the smallest units within the
broader framework of the entire book. Within the core of the narrative,

[9] Ruprecht 199: 40. In addition, the sequence of healing followed by sign in 2 Kings
20 may echo the sequence 'I will heal you' and 'you shall go up to the temple' (v. 5); cf.
Vermeylen 1997: 104-7.

[10] Ackroyd 1974 and 1982; Smelik 1986: 73f.; Seitz 1991: 162-82; Mathews 1995:
171-8. Nevertheless, objections have been made to this argument (cf. Williamson 1994:
208 and the authors to whom he refers).

[11] The classical position has been defended of late by Camp 1990: 53-61; Williamson
1994: 202-8; Sweeney, 496-502. The more recent position has been forwarded again by
Vermeylen (1997: 104-8) who also introduces new modifications.

[12] The same tendencies – such as the swiftness of God's response to Hezekiah's
prayer of entreaty and the idealisation of the king – have been ascribed to both versions.
Sweeney (496f.), for example, ascribes these tendencies to the Isaiah version, while
Vermeylen (1997: 105f.) ascribes them to 2 Kings. Seitz (1991: 160f.) has correctly
pointed out that both versions idealise Hezekiah, albeit in different ways.

[13] The original form of the prophetic legend would appear to be most recognisable in
the version of 2 Kings 20, within the inclusion formed by v. 1 ('Hezekiah fell ill') and v.
7 (he recovered').

[14] Research into the pre-Masoretic text forms (especially the *kaige* recension) of 2
Kings 18-20 / Isaiah 36-39 has led Konkel (1993) to the conclusion that these narratives
existed in a form which preceded that of BI. According to him, the insertion of
Hezekiah's prayer into ch.38 together with the shortening and rearrangement of the narrative forms part of the same process with the same theological aims which realised the integration of these chapters into BI (Konkel 1993).

the fifteen years with which Hezekiah's life is prolonged are exemplary
of the respite offered to Jerusalem (vv. 5-6). By way of a number of
metaphors which are also to be found in Jeremiah and Lamentations, the
prayer of Hezekiah interprets the king's illness as the exile which was
the consequence of Israel's sins and which brought the people to the
edge of destruction. Similarly, the healing of the king serves as an image
of the restoration of the community around the temple (Ackroyd 1974).
Finally, the rather unusual fig therapy serves as a symbol for the purification process embodied by the exile (vv. 21f.; Hoffer 1992).

The motif-historical integration of ch.38 into BI as a whole does not
take away from the fact that the story exhibits a solidly narrative form,
something which redaction-historical research is in danger of losing
sight of. The first part of the chapter contains a distinct plot: illness and
announcement of death (v. 1), prayer and response (vv. 2-5), promise of
a sign and the fulfilment thereof (vv. 7-8). It would be incorrect, however, to treat Hezekiah's subsequent prayer (vv. 9-20) as an interpolation
which disrupts the dynamic flow of the narrative from sign to healing
(vv. 21-22). As a psalm of thanksgiving which *anticipates* healing and,
as such, looks back retrospectively to the experience of life-threatening
illness, the prayer quite appropriately embodies the king's faith-filled response to the sign.[15] As a 'writing', the prayer constitutes an example of
the Ancient Near Eastern custom whereby princes and rulers publicly
revealed themselves as faithful servants of their respective gods by way
of prayers which took the form of letters or inscriptions.[16] In other
words, the prayer-letter serves to illuminate the personal and public piety of the king, a characteristic which distinguishes him considerably
from his father Ahaz (ch.7). While the various semantic and thematic associations with the surrounding narrative ('death' and 'life', 'days' and
'years', 'faithfulness' and 'to descend') show that this happened in a
highly polished literary fashion, the prayer also exhibits awareness of
other elements which, of necessity, are left behind by the narrative, elements such as the experience of suffering and mortality, sinfulness and
forgiveness, as well as the motivation behind God's salvific deed.

Although the primary actant in both the narrative and the prayer,
Hezekiah, continues to exhibit the same character,[17] the very theme of
the forgiveness of sins (v. 17b), which is present in the prayer but absent
from the preceding narrative, makes him all the more fitting as an exam-

---

[15] This function of the prayer is wrongly interpreted in the RSV's use of pluperfects in
v. 9: 'after he had been sick and had recovered'.
[16] This literary genre can be found in Sumerian and Akkadian literature (Hallo 1976).
[17] Watts 1992: 118-25.

ple for the exilic community. As such, the portrayal of the king's person which becomes apparent in his prayer relativises the high expectations concerning Jerusalem's security set up by chs. 36-37, with a view to the later destruction of the city and deportation of her population by the Babylonians. The present narrative thus introduces the notion that the end of Sennacherib's campaign offers no hard and fast guarantee of a future.[18]

Because of the location and quantitative imbalance of the prayer with respect to the healing scene (vv. 21-22), Hezekiah's illness loses in significance in favour of a faithful expectation of healing. The function of the illness as a metaphor for exile is thus reinforced. Hezekiah's concluding question (v. 22) does not refer back to v. 7, but refers rather to the therapy prescribed by Isaiah (v. 21). 'What is the sign?' means: 'What positive changes in the fig-treated boil point to a cure?'. The healing is thus formulated, not according to its physical value, but rather according to its religious significance: healing has to make it possible 'to go up to the house of YHWH'. In this way the narrative plays a role in the structure of BI in which the sinfulness of the people is presented as an illness which YHWH himself will heal (1:5-6; 6:10; 30:26; 33:24; 53:3).[19] Since the request for a sign remains unanswered, the narrative remains open-ended, allowing it to function well in the perspective of the exile with its hoped for return to and ascent to a refurbished temple (cf. 2:2-5; 37:30-32).[20]

SCHOLARLY EXPOSITION

Introduction to the Exegesis: Form and Setting

A prophetic legend clearly lies at the foundations of the present chapter.[21] While there are several narratives in existence which deal with the prophetic healing of an individual suffering from a deadly illness (1 Kgs 17: 17-24; 2 Kgs 4:31-37; 5:1-14) or speak of a fatal diagnosis (1 Kgs 14:1-18; 2 Kgs 1:1-18; 8:7-15), the present narrative distinguishes itself in the fact that the healing itself has more to do with the pious prayers of the sick king (vv. 3,9-20) than with some form of prophetic intervention. Although the prophet acts here, as elsewhere in PI and particularly in chs. 36-37, as the intermediary of a divine oracle (twice in

---

[18] Clements 1980: 100ff.; Coetzee 1989: 13f.,24.
[19] Hoffer 1992: 75.
[20] Sweeney, 499f.
[21] Cf. Rofé 1974: 145-53 and the critical remarks of Hoffer 1992: 72-5.

vv. 2,5-8) and, at the end of the narrative, of a healing therapy (v. 21), his intervention exhibits little of the character of a miracle. The narrative is dominated by the confession of Hezekiah and his faith in YHWH, so much so that the therapy is only spoken of at the last moment and without mention of its favourable outcome. The healing as such is shifted to the second half of BI, to the restoration of Israel and the re-occupation of Jerusalem. The topic of Hezekiah's exemplary behaviour serves to relate the narrative firmly with the preceding narrative. This relationship is expressed in the affiliation of the promise of fifteen more years of life with the salvation of Hezekiah and the city (vv. 5-6).

Such details are of little help in historically situating the narrative.[22] If Hezekiah died in 697 BC, the narrative would have to be located around 712 BC, at the time when the Assyrian king Sargon II put down a revolt among the independent Palestinian states and annexed the southern coastal region around Ashdod (Isa. 20:1), thus more than ten years prior to Sennacherib's advance treated in chs. 36-37. It is unlikely that the narrator had such calculations in mind. The undetermined dating 'in those days' invites the reader to associate the present narrative with the preceding one. The origin of the narrative must be sought, therefore, in the context of its literary setting.

Little can be said concerning the genesis of ch.38 within BI. The sign (vv. 7-8) does not compete with the therapy (v. 21) and as such need not be viewed as a later and inappropriate interpolation,[23] since it is designed to inspire Hezekiah to have faith. The king expresses this faith in his prayer (vv. 9-20) upon which the therapy follows. The character of the sign is not out of place in a prophetic legend. At the same time, there is no need to insist on a degree of tension between v. 22 and v. 21 if one avoids viewing the former as a reference to the sign of vv. 7-8 and considers it a request for a sign that the fig therapy will be successful (cf. 'Exegesis by Verse').

The narrative itself is a tightly wrought composition consisting of a long series of verb forms whereby the various actions are connected: 'Hezekiah fell ill... Isaiah came and said (v. 1)... Hezekiah turned... prayed... said (v. 2-3)... the word of YHWH came (v. 4)... the sun turned back (v. 8)... ().)... Isaiah said (v. 21)... Hezekiah said (v. 22)' (once *qatal* and ten times *wayyiqtol* in the first position). The spoken word is evidently important at this level of the narrative. Indeed, the only actant which does not speak is the sun! The significance of the latter's involvement is made clear in Hezekiah's 'writing'.

[22] Cf. the discussions of Alexander, 75; Feldmann, 446f.; Penna, 352f.; Oswalt, 674f.
[23] *pace* Vermeylen 1997: 106.

It would be incorrect to view the psalm as an alien element in the narrative. Of course, the king's prayer stands outside the series of events and does not elicit any new action, but its association with the context is established by the fact that it is addressed to YHWH (vv. 12-19) and to a third party (vv. 10-13,20). The first level of addressation anchors the psalm in the narrative, in which YHWH is an actant, while the second associates it with the readers of BI. It constitutes a commentary *(metatext)* on the promise and the guarantee of the sign given and as such it contains the key to the meaning of the entire event.[24] The abrupt and for some commentators grotesque swing from death to life in the prophet's two messages (v. 1: 'you shall die'; v. 5: 'I will add fifteen years to your life') is explained in the psalm by the king himself (v. 19: 'The living, he thanks you'; cf. the root חי in vv. 9, 11f.,16). He turns the audience into participants in what he has experienced (vv. 10f.: 'I said'; v. 15: 'What can I say?'). He points out to them that the deepest foundation of this event constitutes the 'faithfulness' of YHWH (vv. 18f.: אמת), who does not leave his own without response (v. 3). He likewise renders significance to the sign – God's authority over 'the decline' of the sun (v. 8: ירד) – stating that YHWH allows those who are doomed 'to go down to the pit' (v. 18: ירד), to return in order to praise him (vv. 18f.). The petitioner thus involves his audience in his now ongoing praise of YHWH (v. 20: 'we will sing... all the days of our life at the house of YHWH').

In addition, the outcome of the narrative does not turn out to be farcical after the prayer-letter, at least if one does not consider vv. 21-22 to be a 'flash back' (in spite of several translations which render the verb forms as pluperfects).[25] It is difficult to imagine what the narrator had in mind in placing the therapy after the prayer of thanksgiving if he considered the therapy to have taken place before the thanksgiving. On the contrary, it is possible that the narrator placed the prayer of thanksgiving before the healing in order to highlight the extent of Hezekiah's faith in YHWH's salvation.

Finally, what might the narrator have had in mind by mentioning at the end that Hezekiah had asked for a sign (v. 22) which had already been given him in vv. 7-8?[26] If one accepts, however, that Hezekiah's request was for a *new* sign, then it would appear that the king is express-

[24] Watts 1992: 120f.

[25] The classical term for a 'flash back' would appear to be *'anachoresis'*: 'a return to the original subject after a digression' (Bullinger 1993[17]: 913).

[26] That temporal perspective seems to make sense in 2 Kgs 20:8-10 since there Hezekiah asks for a sign which goes beyond any doubt.

ing his belief that he only considers himself to be really cured when he can 'go up (עלה) to the house of YHWH'. With this end in view, the king has already thanked God in advance for his healing, including those who are witness to his prayer in his thanksgiving: 'We will sing all the days of our life, at the house of YHWH' (v. 20). It is the psalm, therefore, which supplies the narrative with the open end of a further sign. The fulfilment of this expectation appears to be given – against the background of other associations between chs. 36-39 and ch.40 – in the summons of 40:9: 'Get you up (עלי לך) to a high mountain, O Zion, herald of good tidings'. Zion here is the continuation of 'you and this city' (38:6), as well as of the 'we'-group, who in the expectation of Hezekiah shall praise YHWH in his house (v. 20).

The prayer itself (vv. 9-20) conforms to the literary genre of the thanksgiving song of the individual in which elements of lament are retrospectively incorporated. After the superscription (v. 9) follow the retrospective reference to the prayer in time of distress (vv. 10-17a) and the anticipatory narrative of salvation which ends in a statement of faith and a vow (vv. 17b-20). Although these two segments are not sharply distinguished – due in part to the vague formulation of v. 16 and to v. 17a which looks forward to a time of well-being –, the division appears to be determined by the emphatic personal pronouns at the beginning of each part: 'I' (v. 10: אני) and 'But you' (v. 17b: ואתה).[27]

The usual topics of the lament are present in the first segment, although they likewise lack clear demarcation. An initial 'I'-lament which stretches from v. 10 to v. 12b´ then develops into a lament concerning God (vv. 12b´´-13: 'he' and 'you') only to return to an 'I'-lament with a direct prayer for protection (v. 14). A 'doxology of judgement' rounds off the first segment (vv. 15-17a; Coetzee 1989: 21f.). A genre-critical delimitation of this first segment is difficult to establish. There is evidence of an act of acquiescence in the will of God (v. 15a), a new 'I'-lament (v. 15b), the doxology of judgement itself (v. 16a-b´) and a petition for salvation (v. 16b´´), which runs over into the ascertainment of being saved (v. 17a).

The second segment begins with the account of rescue and forgiveness, explicitly presented as deeds of God: 'But you have held back... Truly, you have cast...' (v. 17b). A meditation follows on the godforsakenness of the underworld in which it is impossible to praise YHWH or experience his fidelity (vv. 18-19). An expression of faith (v. 20a) and a

---

[27] Coetzee 1989: 22f.; Wildberger, 1464.

promise to sing God's praises in the temple (v. 20b) conclude with reminiscences of the anticipatory character of the prayer-letter.

Chapter 38 thus exhibits the following structure:

1-8   account of Hezekiah's illness and prayer / promise of recovery

      1a   Hezekiah's illness

      1b   first message of Isaiah: 'prepare for death'

      2-3   Hezekiah's prayer

      4-8a   second message of Isaiah: '15 years more and a sign'

            4-5a   command for Isaiah to inform Hezekiah

            5b-6   message: life and rescue from Assyria

            7-8a   sign confirming the message

                  7   announcement of sign

                  8a   sign proper

      8b   report of sign given

9-20 the writing of Hezekiah

      9   inscription and occasion

      10-14 account of distress

            10-12b´ first 'I' complaint (death) with a simile

            12b´´-13 complaint about God (illness) with a simile

            14   second 'I' complaint

                 14a   simile

                 14b   description of distress, call for attention and protection

      15-17a doxology of judgement

            15a   act of acquiescence in the will of God

            15b   third 'I' complaint

            16a-b´ doxology of judgement proper

               16b´´ petition for salvation

               17a   conclusion of being helped

      17b-20 account of salvation

            17b   God's intervention: preservation from the grave

            18-19   reflection on the godforsakenness of Sheol

               18   dead do not praise God

               19   living do praise God

            20   act of confidence and vow to praise God

21-22 account of Hezekiah's healing process

            21   therapy recommended by the prophet

            22   Hezekiah's request for a sign of recovery and ascent to the temple

Exegesis by Verse

1 The narrative does not begin in one of the specific situations over which the Isaiah was wont to raise his prophetic voice but rather in the context of a broadly human phenomenon, namely the approaching end of Hezekiah's life: 'he fell ill' (חלה in reports: Gen. 48:1; 1 Kgs 14:1; 15:23; 17:17; 2 Kgs 1:2; 8:7ff.; 13:14; 2 Chr. 21:18; 22:6). The very fact that the prophet, unrequested, comes nevertheless to inform the king in God's name that he is going to die, seems inappropriate to the situation. From the perspective of narrative technique, however, the prophet's intervention makes sense. It establishes a sharp contrast between the prophet's two messages: the first announces death, the second life (v. 5). It is thus made clear that YHWH has let himself be mollified by the pious prayer of the king. At the same time, this new course of events is related to the first narrative in which contacts between God and the king take place through the prophet (37:2,6,21; cf. in 38:1 the mention of Isaiah's profession, 'the prophet', whereas the title 'king' for Hezekiah is lacking). YHWH's message, however, is not given in the form of a prophetic accusation or announcement of judgement. YHWH speaks here as the God who ultimately brings an end to all human life. The reason or significance behind Hezekiah's approaching demise is not at stake here. Generations come and go (Ps. 39:14; 103:15f.; 104:29f.; 146:4; Job 10:21; Eccl. 1:4). While the course of every human life is different from that of another, in the hour of dying the final duty of all human beings is the same: 'to set one's house in order' (Gen. 24:1-9; 25:1-6; 27:1-4; 48-49; 50:24-26; Deut. 31:14-30; 33:1; 2 Sam. 17:23; 1 Kgs 2:1-10; 2 Kgs 13:14-21).

By means of the contrast between the theme 'to die' and 'to recover', literally 'to live' (חיה), the first message sets the foundations for both the narrative and the psalm of thanksgiving (vv. 11-12,16-20), while also connecting with the preaching of PI. According to the prophet, life and death are at stake in the context of Israel's ethical choices ('to die' and 'death': 8:19; 14:30; 22:2,13f.,18; 25:8; 26:14; 28:15,18; 37:36; 'to live' and 'life': 8:19; 26:14,19; 37:4,17).

2-3 The king expresses his grief by withdrawing from further human contact ('he turned his face to the wall'; cf. 1 Kgs 21:4)[28] and by praying to God. The prayer itself lacks the solemn opening of his earlier prayer (cf. 37:15) and consists of a simple petition that God recognise ('to remember') his good life. The formulation expresses both personal

---

[28] 'Wall' (קיר) here refers to the wall of the king's room and not that of the temple (*TWAT*, VII, 32 [M.J. Mulder]).

and complete commitment to God ('to remember' [זכר] with God as subject and human persons as object: Exod. 32:13; Deut. 9:27; Judg. 16:28; 1 Sam. 1:11; Isa. 43:25; 63:11; 64:8; Jer. 2:2; 14:10; 15:15; 18:20; 31:20; Hos. 7:2; 8:13; Ps. 8:5; 25:7; 79:8; 115:12; Lam. 5:1); 'to walk [התהלך] before God's face': Gen. 17:1; 24:40; 48:15; 1 Sam. 2:30; Ps. 56:14; 116:9; to walk 'in faithfulness' [באמת]: 1 Kgs 2:4; 3:6; Ps. 26:3; 86:11; 'with a whole heart' [בלב שלם]: 1 Chr. 12:39; 28:9; 29:9; 'to do what is good in God's eyes' [עשה טוב]: Num. 24:13; Deut. 6:18; 12:28; Ezek. 18:18; Ps. 14:1,3; 34:15; 37:3,27; 53:4; 2 Chr. 14:1; 24:16; 31:20). The special mention: 'Hezekiah wept bitterly' appears to be a recognition of his distressful situation (בכה: 16:9; 30:19; 33:7).

4-6 YHWH's response is conveyed to the king by the prophet after an explicit revelation and commission: 'The word of YHWH came to Isaiah: Go and say to Hezekiah' (vv. 4-5). The messenger formula discloses a right to assistance to which Hezekiah did not lay claim: 'YHWH, the God of David, your father' (v. 5). God thus recognises Hezekiah's good life as in harmony with the exemplary life of David, simultaneously stating the motive which moved him to attend to Hezekiah's prayer ('God of David': 2 Chr. 21:12; 34:3; 'David, father of...' as warrant of God's help and moral example: 1 Kgs 2:12,24; 3:3,6f.,14; 6:12; 8:15,20,24f.; 11:4,6,33; 15:11; 2 Kgs 14:3; 16:2; 18:3; 22:2; 2 Chr. 1:9; 8:14; 17:3).

The response consists of a confirmation that YHWH has heard Hezekiah's prayer (v. 5a: 'I have heard... I have seen...'; for 'to hear' followed by 'to see' with God as subject, cf. Exod. 2:24f.; Deut. 26:7; 2 Kgs 13:4; Isa. 37:17; Dan. 9:18) and of a promise (vv. 5b-6). The promise as such contains two elements: the prolongation of Hezekiah's life and the rescue of himself and Jerusalem from the power of Assyria. The syntactic pattern firmly binds both elements together. The main clauses are sequentially connected in the characteristic form of a prophetic announcement of God's intervention: 'Behold, I will add fifteen years' and 'I will defend this city' (הנני יוסף ... וגנותי). The intermediate clause (compound nominal clause) further elaborates the first object of God's concern ('I will deliver you') and prepares the way for the second ('and this city').

Given the fact that Hezekiah did not ask for the salvation of the city, the narrative takes a somewhat unexpected turn at this point. While the connection between the length of the king's life and his liberation from the superior power of Assyria is relatively easy to explain, the mention of 'this city' (not 'your city'!) is rather abrupt. It would appear to be a reference to the primary topic of the preceding narrative, in particular to the conclusion thereof: 'Truly, I will shield this city to save it, for my own sake and for the sake of my servant David' (37:35; cf. 36:15,20; 37:10,33f.). This reference to chs. 36-37 is only anticipated by the opening temporal indicator (v. 1: 'In those days') and the divine title 'the God of David, your father', which includes a guarantee for the Davidic kingship in Jerusalem. Nevertheless, all this suggests that the present narrative has been added to the preceding one whereby it is given a new role to play in the structure of BI (cf. 'Essentials and Perspectives').

7-8 The promise of salvation is confirmed with a sign announced by the prophet himself (v. 7: 'YHWH' 3d person), but presented by him as a 'word of YHWH' (v. 8: 'I' of YHWH).[29] The offer of a sign places the present narrative on a single line with the preceding narrative (37:30) and with the Immanuel sign (7:11f.). While Hezekiah's father, king Ahaz, refused to ask for a sign out of a feigned respect for YHWH which ultimately concealed his lack of faith, a sign is given as a matter of course to Hezekiah, the righteous man who prays for salvation in his distress (otherwise in 2 Kgs 20:8), which he accepts (assuming that v. 22 is not a 'flash back'; cf. 'Scholarly Exposition'). The fact that the sign is to be located in the house of his unbelieving father further serves to underline the contrast.

Confirmatory signs tend to be more significant with regard to their function than their content: the sign guarantees the announcement and invites its recipients to accept in faith (cf. the varied role of signs in Exod. 3:12; 4:8-9; Judg. 6:17 [36-40]; 1 Sam. 2:34; 10:2-9; 1 Kgs 13:3; Jer. 44:29f.).[30] It is for this reason that any questions concerning the precise nature of the present sign must account for the fact that the narrator himself did not require a detailed description of all the ins and outs of the matter. The reversal of the shadow cast by the sun is, on the one hand, an extraordinary sign, even when compared with Joshua's sign at Gibeon when the sun merely 'stood still' (Josh. 10:4). On the other hand, we should not overemphasise the sign's unique character since the sun, in the perspective of the Bible, is subordinate to its Creator (Gen. 1:14-19; Jer. 31:35; Ps. 74:16; 104:19) and as such it plays a servant's role in his global policy (Isa. 13:10; 49:10; 60:19f.; Ezek. 32:7; Joel 2:10; Hab. 4:11; Ps. 19:5-7; Job 9:7; Eccl. 12:2; Sir. 48:23). In light of his prayer which is probably a later insertion, the sign

---

[29] It seems likely that in v. 8 YHWH is speaking, after the term 'the sign from YHWH' in v. 7 and given similar expressions in v. 5 and v. 8: 'Behold, I will add' and 'Behold, I will make turn back' (according to Wildberger [1452] Isaiah is speaking in v. 8).

[30] *TWAT*, I, 199-202 (F.J. Helfmeyer).

receives a symbolic value for Hezekiah. Just as the shadow cast by the sun reverses its descent (ירד) along the stairs, so Hezekiah will thank YHWH that he is not among 'those who go down to the pit' (v. 18: יורדי בור).

An elaborate discussion persists as to whether the sign took place on the exterior stairs of the house built by Ahaz or on a sort of sun-dial (cf. Tg: 'the stone of the hours'; RSV: 'dial'). In the latter case the term מעלות can be understood to refer to specific temporal units rather than stairs. The literary and archaeological evidence is too insubstantial to support the idea that, prior to the exile, Israel was familiar with such a thing as a sun-dial, although similar constructions have been discovered in the surrounding cultures (cf. the discussion in Wildberger, 1452f.).

9 As with the majority of psalms, Hezekiah's prayer also enjoys a title which indicates the type of literature: 'a writing', the author: 'Hezekiah, king of Judah', and the occasion which gave rise to it: 'when he fell ill and recovered from his illness'. The term 'writing' finds its explanation in the Ancient Near Eastern literary genre of the prayer text written by kings on the walls of temples or on pillars (Hallo 1976). In a similar fashion, Hezekiah allows his people to share in his experience of illness and healing and likewise involves them in his faith in YHWH and his anticipated thanks. With respect to the latter, a pluperfect translation seems out of place (RSV: 'when he had been sick and had recovered from his sickness'). In the course of events, the prayer has come to stand in between the sign (vv. 7-8) and the cure (vv. 21-22). Through the public nature of his anticipatory prayer of thanksgiving, the king transfers his personal faith to his people. The redaction clearly had the exiles in mind here since Hezekiah's healing was a symbol for them of their own hopes and expectations.

10-11 By means of a double 'I said' (אני אמרתי) the petitioner situates his lament in his past experience of distress (Jon. 2:5; Ps. 31:23; 41:5; 116:11; Lam. 3:54). The core of the complaint turns around the expression: 'I must go', here a term for 'to die' (הלך: Gen. 15:2; 25:32; Josh. 23:14; 1 Kgs 2:2; Hos. 6:4; 13:3; Ps. 39:7,14; 58:9; 109:23; Job. 14:20; Eccl. 3:20; 2 Chr. 21:20). The context of the narrative sets the expression in contrast with Hezekiah's appeal: 'Remember now, how I have walked (התהלכתי) before you in faithfulness and with a whole heart' (v. 3). It looks as if faithfulness is not rewarded. The prayer itself, however, describes the inevitable death by means of traditional metaphors which do not speak of God as the immediate cause thereof.

The circumstances, expressed in the two laments, determine the king's approaching death as 'bitter'. The first lament (v. 10) thus mentions the prematurity of his death: 'in the quiet time of my days', the loss of 'the rest of my years' (cf. v. 5), 'the gates of Sheol' as his ultimate destination (only here; cf. 'the gates of death' in Ps. 107:18; Job 38:17; Wis. 16:13; Pss.Sol. 16:2; 3 Macc. 5:51) and the assignment to a place under duress: 'I am consigned' (פֻקַּד *qal* in this sense: Num. 1:3,19; 3:10, 15f.; Deut. 20:9; Josh. 8:10; 1 Sam. 11:8; 13:15; 15:4; Jer. 15:3; 51:27; passive participle: Exod. 30:13f.; 38:25f.).[31] There is a climax in the second verse line since the inescapable destination of death is only mentioned at this point.

The second lament describes the sense of deprivation experienced by the dead: the company of YHWH and one's fellow human beings (v. 11). The first line refers to this association with God as 'to see YHWH'. This expression (just as 'to see the face of God') does not imply a direct encounter with the divine, but refers rather to every form of human experience, whether cultic or day to day, in which YHWH reveals himself (Gen. 16:13; 32:31; 33:10; Exod. 24:9-11; Judg. 6:22; Isa. 6:5; 17:7; 30:20; 33:17; Ps. 27:4; 42:3; Job 19:27; 33:26; 42:5).[32] The context of Hezekiah's visits to 'the house of YHWH' (37:1,14; 38:20,22) makes it probable, however, that in this case 'to see YHWH' refers to the king's experience of God's presence in the temple (Coetzee 1989: 18f.). In a restrained and poetic fashion, the double use of the short form of the divine name (יה) thus expresses the immense value attached by the petitioner to his association with God. The intrinsic link between God and life itself is expressed by the locative 'in the land of the living' (or 'of life': Isa. 53:8; Jer. 11:19; Ezek. 26:20; 32:23; Ps. 27:13; 52:7; 116:9; 142:6; Job 28:13).[33]

The second verse line also speaks of the dead's lack of human intercourse in terms of visual perception although a different verb is employed: 'to look upon' (נבט *hiphil*). This term can be used to express everyday perception as well as attentive, involved perception (Gen. 15:5; Exod. 33:8; Num. 21:9; 1 Sam. 16:7; 1 Kgs 18:43; Isa. 5:12,30; 8:22; 22:8,11; 42:18; 51:1f.,6; Hab. 1:5; Zech. 12:10; Ps. 91:8; 92:12; Lam. 1;12).[34] The general term for 'human beings', אדם, is elaborated in the second half of the verse line: 'the inhabitants of transitoriness' (cf. 'Notes'). This latter expression does not refer to the inhabitants of the underworld, as if the petitioner, now dwelling in their

---

[31] The emendation of the *pual* form to read the nominal form פְקֻדָּה is text-critically unwarranted; *pace TWAT*, VI, 721 (G. André): 'für den Rest meiner Jahren wird mein Schicksal in der Scheol sein'.

[32] *TWAT*, VII, 250ff. (H.-F. Fuhs).

[33] *DCH*, II, 387b.

[34] *TWAT*, V, 138f. (H. Ringgren).

midst, would no longer see those dwelling in the world.[35] It refers rather to the living: the petitioner will no longer have his place among the mortal.[36] As such, the expression offers a degree of explanation of the inevitability of death.

12a-b′ The theme of transitory life is continued in two new metaphors: as a tent is folded up and a piece of fabric is removed from the loom. While the first comparison speaks of life being taken away from a person ('removed from me'), the second speaks of both the human individual and God as acting persons ('I have rolled up my life' and 'he cuts me off').

In association with the preceding term 'inhabitants', the first line speaks of the 'dwelling' (דור) of the petitioner.[37] The root of this unusual term suggests a circular form of settlement (2 Sam. 5:9; Isa. 22:18; 29:3; 45:2). In parallelism with 'tent' and in combination with the verbs' to pluck up' and 'to remove' the term signifies a camp made up of a circle of tents (cf. 'tent' as impermanent dwelling: Gen. 12:8; 13:3,5; 26:25; 31:25; 35:21; Num. 2:17; Judg. 4:11; Isa. 13:20; 33:20; 40:22; 54:2; Jer. 4:20; 10:20; Dan. 11:45). The term 'shepherd' underlines the transitory character of human existence (cf. Gen. 31:18; 1 Sam. 16:11; Isa. 40:11; Ezek. 34:14; Amos 7:15; Ps. 23:2; Cant. 1:7).

The imagery of the second line is in harmony with that of the first: after the canvas the fabric on the loom. Two actions bring the weaving process to an end: the cloth is rolled up (קפד) around a wooden shaft and cut loose (בצע) from the loom (cf. Judg. 16:14; perhaps Job 6:9; 27:8).[38] The combination of two different subjects 'I have rolled up' and 'he cuts off', does not constitute a difficulty, either from the perspective of the vehicle of the comparison or from that of the tenor. The vehicle suggests that the weaver himself rolls up the fabric he has woven while another removes it from the loom (Barthélemy, 266). Within the comparison, the human person is both weaver and fabric. The tenor implies that human persons must depart because God has ordained it so.

12b″-13 These verses (and those which follow) refer to Hezekiah's sick-bed as the run up to his death.[39] The complaint as such refers to

---

[35] *pace* Vitringa, 397; Gesenius, 989; Delitzsch, 391; Dahood 1971; Schoors, 215; Watts, 59; *HALAT*, 281; *Ges.[18]*, 326.

[36] Alexander, 81f.; Wildberger, 1460; *DCH*, III, 163; furthermore, all those commentaries which emend חדל to read חלד (cf. 'Notes').

[37] The interpretation of דור as 'generation' is no longer accepted (*pace* Nyberg 1974: 90).

[38] For the technical aspects of the weaving process, cf. Begrich 1926: 30f.

[39] Seybold 1973: 148.

God alone. The topics are quite distinct: rather than the end of life itself, the process of physical deterioration is the focus of attention. The petitioner blames this on God's hostile intervention: 'Like a lion he breaks all my bones'. God has changed from a weaver into a lion (cf. Isa. 31:4; Jer. 49:9; Hos. 5:14; 13:7f.; Amos 1:2; 5:19; Ps. 50:22; Job 10:16; Lam. 3:10f.)! He assails the petitioner's physical and personal vigour by attacking his 'bones' (עצם plural: Jer. 23:9; 42:11; Hab. 3:16; Ps. 6:3; 22:15; 31:11; 32:3; 38:4; 42:11; 102:4; Job 4:14; 19:20; 21:24; 30:30; 33:21; Prov. 3:8; 15:30; 16:24; Lam. 1:13; 3:4; 4:18).[40] At the same time, however, the petitioner accuses God for paying no attention to him, directly addressing the divinity via the inclusion 'You deliver me up'.[41] Metaphors of aggressivity and neglect thus keep each other in balance. The temporal categories 'from day to night' (only here; cf. in laments: Ps. 22:3; 32:4; 42:4; 77:3; 88:2; Isa. 28:19) and 'until morning'[42] indicate that the petitioner's experience of abandonment is unremitting

14 Just as the petitioner compared the God who has overwhelmed him with a lion (v. 13), he now compares himself, God's victim, with two anxious, wailing birds: 'a swallow' and 'a dove'. Of these birds, the 'dove' (יונה) alone has metaphorical significance (Cant. 2:14; 5:2,12; 6:9). Its characteristic gentleness is strongly highlighted here by its now shrieking lament ('to moan' [הגה]: Isa. 59:11; Ezek. 7:16; Nah. 2:8; the metaphor of 'chirping' [צפף pilpel:] is found only in PI: 8:19; 10:14; 29:4).

The second half of the verse continues the prayer with additional literary forms of a lament: a description of distress combined with a call for attention (v. 14b′) and a petition for protection (v. 14b″).

The first statement: 'My eyes are weary with looking on high' constitutes a constructio praegnans, a fixed expression which unites two clauses by omitting one verb which is rendered in translation by 'with looking' (cf. Ps. 22:22: 'You have answered me from the horns of the wild oxen').[43] 'Eyes' frequently constitute the physical seat of sor-

---

[40] TWAT, VI, 331 (K.-M. Beyse).

[41] Although Seybold (1973: 151) interprets שלם hiphil here as 'to force capitulation (peace)', the meaning 'to deliver up, abandon' (LXX: παρεδόθην) seems more probable. Wagner considers the terms an Aramaism (1966: 114f., nr.310; likewise Wildberger, 1440; HALAT, 1421; TWAT, VIII, 98f. [K.-J. Illman]). Eisenbeis (1969: 326-31), in contrast, has criticised this interpretation and suggested the colloquial meaning 'to finish off'.

[42] 'Until morning' means the entire day until the following morning, i.e. 'all day' (cf. Exod. 16:21; 1 Kgs 18:26; Jer. 20:16; Ps. 55:18; TWAT, I, 750 [Ch. Barth]).

[43] The phenomenon is also referred to as brachylogy or ellipsis (Gerber 1885: II, 207ff., with many illustrative examples; Bullinger, 47-51; Watson 1984: 303-6).

row (Deut. 28:63; 1 Sam. 2:33; Jer. 8:23; 9:17; 13:17; 31:16;
Zech. 11:17; Ps. 69:4; 116:8; 119:82,123; Job 11:20; 16:20; 17:5;
Lam. 2:11; 3:49; 4:17), as well as that of expectation (Isa. 17:7;
33:17; Ezek. 18:6; Ps. 25:15; 119:148; 121:1; 123:1f.; 141:8;
145:15; Job 16:20; Lam. 2:18; Dan. 4:31), and in PI of pride (Isa.
2:11; 3:8; 5:15; 17:7; 37:23). The term 'to be weary' (דלל) is found
in the lament form's description of distress (Ps. 79:8; 116:6; 142:7;
cf. Judg. 6:6; Isa. 17:4; 19:6; Nah. 1:4). While its actual meaning
is 'to be low, weighed down', it is constructed here as a verb of motion
with a contradictory direction: 'on high' (an Isaianic term: 24:18,21;
32:15; 33:5; 37:23f.; 40:26; 57:15; 58:4). A ground of petition
and a wordless prayer for attention are thus combined in a single sentence.

The second statement contains a rather terse description of distress
and an appeal for protection (v. 14b''). The vocative: 'O Lord' is the
first invocation of YHWH in Hezekiah's present prayer. It fits well at this
high-point of the first segment. The situation of distress is described
with the term 'oppression', עשקה, which signifies a variety of forms of
social exploitation (Lev. 5:23; Deut. 24:10; Isa. 30:12; 59:13; Jer. 6:6;
22:17; Ezek. 18:18; 22:7,12; Amos 4:1; Zech. 7:10; Ps. 62:11; 73:8;
119:134; Prov. 14:31; Eccl. 5:7; 7:7). On only one occasion do we find
God accused of עשקה (Job 10:3). In a certain sense, the same accusation
applies here since God is responsible for the approaching end of the petitioner's life. At the same time, however, the primary meaning of the
clause is to characterise this fate as an injustice in itself without pointing
a finger at the instigator thereof.

Although the petition for protection employs an unusual metaphor, 'to
stand surety for', this has its roots in the same semantic field as the lament: 'I am oppressed' (cf. Ps. 119:122). Israel, like its neighbours, was
familiar with the legal form by which individuals stood as guarantor or
were taken as such (ערב: Gen. 43:9; 44:32; Job 17:3; Prov. 6:1;
11:15; 20:16; 22:26; 27:13; with other verbs: Lev. 25:39,47; Deut.
15:2,12; Neh. 5:2 [corr.],5).[44] By applying these metaphors borrowed
from the legal order to the fact that he is destined to death, the petitioner
endeavours to gain YHWH as an ally in his struggle to stay alive. Victory
over death thus begins to emerge in this implicit confession of YHWH as
guarantor of justice.

15-17a The suggestion that these verses are a source of difficulty can
only be affirmed in part. The fact that they clearly do not contain any

---

[44] *TWAT*, VI, 350-5 (E. Lipiński).

familiar idiom has led some to propose emendations. The segment becomes less problematic, however, if one recognises therein the literary
genre of the 'doxology of judgement' which leads from 'the account of
distress' (vv. 10-14) to 'the account of salvation' (vv. 17b-20). The references to the narrative in which the psalm is located, moreover, have
the effect of weakening the presence of the idiom of the language of
prayer.

In v. 15a the petitioner asks what he should now say. Following the
double 'I said' (vv. 10-11) his question must imply: is 'the account of
distress' to be continued? The petitioner asks this question against the
background of the fact that YHWH has spoken to him and has put what he
had said into effect. This can only refer to the preceding narrative: the
announcement of his death, the promise of recovery and the sign (vv. 1-
8; cf. 'to say' in vv. 1,5 and 'to do' in v. 7).

The petitioner once again describes his situation of distress: 'I walk
slowly all my years because of the bitterness of my soul' (v. 15b). It is
not immediately clear whether this general idiom has its roots in the lament genre, perhaps with an application to the situation of a sick person,
or whether it specifically refers to the framing narrative. Does 'all my
years' refer to the 'mere' fifteen years granted by God to the king (v. 5)?
This seems unlikely, given the fact that the narrative never suggests
God's promise to be a meagre one. The expression would appear rather
to be in line with v. 10b: 'I am consigned to the gates of Sheol for the
rest of my years'. From the perspective of impending death or, in other
words, from the perspective prior to Isaiah's transmission of God's
promise of recovery (vv. 4-6), the years remaining to the petitioner
would have to be seen by him as years of physical weakness and sorrow.

V. 16ab' is held to be an 'exegete's nightmare', so much so that some
either leave the line untranslated (Wildberger, 1440 [with survey of
opinions, 1444f.]) or emend it beyond recognition (Watts, 54-7). From a
text-critical perspective, however, such an approach cannot be defended.
Due attention, therefore, ought to be given to the explanation of MT
(Barthélemy, 274f.).

A linguistic interpretation should take the following into account:
(1) The expression 'to live by' can be found both as חיה על (Gen. 27:40;
Deut. 8:3) and as חיה ב (Prov. 16:15), even in parallelism with 'to die for'
(Ezek. 33:18f.: עליהם יחיה / ומת בהם). Given this fact, the parallelism in v. 16
בהן חיי רוחי / עליהם יחיו is fully acceptable. The progress represented by the parallelism is related to the subject of 'to live / life': from a vague 'people' (impersonal 3rd person plural) to 'my spirit'.
(2) The fact that a masculine suffix and a feminine suffix are parallel to one
another (בהן / עליהם), can be categorised under the phenomenon whereby alter-

nation of gender sometimes serves to express entirety (cf. Isa. 3:1; 16:6; Prov. 8:13; GKC, §122 v; König, 322; Airoldi 1973: 256).[45]

(3) The sequence ולכל בהן חיי רוחי can be explained as a construct chain with an intervening element (בהן), several examples of which are now known.[46] The prefix ל thus introduces the new subject, כל חיי רוחי, with a degree of emphasis (cf. 32:1).

With the confession: 'O Lord, by these things people live, and in these is all the life of my spirit' the petitioner recognises that his experiences, amply portrayed in the preceding verses, are for him in fact the way towards life. The preposition על establishes a connection between 'the bitterness of my soul' (v. 15: על מר נפשי; cf. 22:4; 24:9; 33:7) and 'these things' (v. 16: עליהם). The king thus justifies God's actions in a doxology of judgement. The new invocation: 'O Lord' is quite fitting in this context. Moreover, the following aspects of formulation are worthy of note:

(1) The petitioner does not consider himself to be an exceptional case. He is aware, rather, that 'people' gain life through such events. The 'we' of the following words of praise (v. 20) is thus prepared for in advance.

(2) The inversion of 'by these things' draws attention to the experiences which have prepared the way for the petitioner's confession.

(3) After 'the bitterness of my soul' in v. 15, the expression 'all the life of my spirit' can be read as an affirmation of the fact that the experiences the petitioner has undergone have increased the quality of his life.

In the final line, the prayer for salvation and the astonished apprehension of being heard are almost inextricably linked (vv. 16b´´-17a). The verbal clause: 'You want to restore me to health' consists of an indicative (yiqtol), the verbal clause: 'Make me live' consists of an imperative and the statement: 'Lo, it is for my peace that I had great bitterness' is a nominal clause.[47] Prior to an imperative, the first clause can have the same meaning,[48] although a volitive value cannot be completely ruled out.[49] At the point of transition between the doxology of judgement and the account of salvation, the margin between prayer of petition and experience of salvation is a small one. Within this constellation, the prayer

---

[45] According to Airoldi (1973: 257ff., with an appeal to S.D. Luzzatto), the masculine suffix in עליהם would refer to 'eyes' in v. 14 and the feminine suffix in בהן to 'my bones' in v. 13: '...che rivivano in essi (occhi) e per tutto in esse (ossa) le vitalità del mio spirito'. This interpretation, however, makes the text improbably complicated.

[46] The phenomenon occurs in various realisations (cf. Dahood, Psalms III, 381-3).

[47] The interpretation of מר לי מר as a stylistic redoubling (cf. יה in v. 11 and חי in v. 19) deserves preference over the strictly grammatical interpretation whereby the second מר is read as a verbal form.

[48] J-M, §113 m: cf. Ps. 71:2; Job 17:10.

[49] J-M, §113 n: cf. 1 Sam. 21:10; 30:15; Ruth 1:11; 3:13.

of petition takes the form of a prayer for *fullness* of salvation which is
expressed in the progression from 'health' (חלם: Job 39:4; Sir. 15:20;
49:10) through 'life' (the key word *par excellence* which unites both
narrative and prayer: vv. 1,5,10,12f.,19f.) to 'peace'. Although the last
word implies personal well-being in the present context (Gen. 37:14;
Exod. 18:7; Deut. 29:18; Judg. 18:15; 1 Sam. 17:18; 2 Sam. 11:7;
20:9; 2 Kgs 5:21; Ps. 38:4; Job 5:24), there is also an echo of the
promise of 'peace' for the house of David (Isa. 9:6; 26:3,12; 27:5;
32:17f.; 33:7 [contrast שלום and מר]).

17b The account of salvation places God ('But you') in the central
position, in the present lines as the one who has brought salvation, in vv.
18-20 as the one to whom the praise of the living is due, now and forever.

Salvation is presented in the first instance as an act of association
('You have attached yourself to my soul') – as is also found between
human beings (חשק: Gen. 34:8; Deut. 7:7f.; 10:15; 21:11; Sir. 40:19) –
which has resulted in protection against ultimate downfall: '(keeping
me) from the pit of destruction'. In this verse 'the pit' (שחת) can signify
both 'grave' (Isa. 51:14; Ps. 103:4; 107:20; Job 33:18) and 'underworld' (Ezek. 28:8; Jonah 2:7; Ps. 16:10; 30:10; 55:24), in preparation
for the following verse which places the latter meaning in the foreground.

In the second instance, salvation is referred to as the forgiveness of
sins. The mention of Hezekiah's sins at this point is a source of surprise
to some scholars who note that neither this nor the previous narrative
make any mention of a misdeed on the part of the king. While it is a familiar biblical conviction that sickness and death are the result of sin
(Ps. 7:4f.; 38:4ff.; 39:9,12; 40:13; 51:3ff.; 55:24; 90:7ff.; 103:3;
Mic. 6:13), we should not picture Israel's conceptual world to ourselves
as ruled by strict causality. When YHWH attaches himself to human beings to protect their lifes, every form of destructive force, sickness and
death, impurity and sin let go of their hold on such persons because
these powers cannot continue to exist in his presence (cf. Isa. 1:18; 6:7;
31:6f.; 33:14; 43:25; 44:22; 59:2,12; for the imagery of 'you have
cast behind your back my sins', cf. Ezek. 18:31; Mic. 7:19; for the opposite, cf. Jer. 16:17; Hos. 7:2; Ps. 90:8; 109:14f.).[50]

18-19 The familiar topic from the psalms which maintains that only
the living and not the dead can praise YHWH (Ps. 6:6; 30:10; 88:11-13;
Sir. 17:27f.), is known traditionally as a motive for God's saving inter-

[50] Lindström 1994.

vention on behalf of the petitioner. The question arises, however, as to whether the topic in question functions in this way, at least here. The praise of YHWH is associated with the expectation of his 'faithfulness' (v. 18b; 'to hope for' [שׁבר]) God's support: Ps. 104:27; 119:166; 145:15; 146:5) and with the felicitous task of passing this conviction on to the next generation (v. 19b). Nevertheless, a summing up of the assets and liabilities of YHWH, should he not intend to save the petitioner, does not seem to be the most appropriate framework for understanding these verses. The petitioner describes 'Sheol' as the place where 'death' has its dominion, as the 'pit' which closes over those who descend therein, robbing them of everything which gives 'life' (cf. the descriptions in which these terms occur: Isa. 5:14; 8:19; 14:9-15; 24:22; 26:14; in satirical contrast: 28:15-19). Included among these life-giving things is association with YHWH, which arises from the expectation of God's fidelity and the praise of his deeds. The petitioner does not speak of Sheol in order to remind YHWH that his power does not extend thus far, but to remind himself of what he would be missing if that were to become his dwelling place. While the petitioner's meditation on his own fate has its place in the context of the praise of God (2nd person singular), its ultimate purpose is not to confront YHWH with what might be to the latter's advantage. It places the existence of the petitioner in a new perspective, because he no longer holds up his own 'faithfulness' to God as a motivation for intervention (v. 3). Rather he discovers God's 'faithfulness' as the horizon of his own life.

In a gradual development of his thoughts, the petitioner takes the task upon himself 'to praise YHWH': 'not Sheol' (v. 18)... 'the living, the living' (חי; in agreement with the twofold 'YHWH' [יה] in v. 11)... 'as I do' (v. 19a). The initiative to such praise, however, is not restricted to the person of the petitioner alone. As a 'father' he will 'make known to the children your faithfulness' (v. 19b; cf. 'to know' [ידע] in similar positive context: Isa. 12:4f.; 29:24; 37:20; in negative context: 1:3; 5:5,19; 6:9; 9:8). Research has come to affirm that these chapters offer a portrayal of Hezekiah in contrast to his father Ahaz. Rooted in his lack of faith, the latter refused to ask YHWH for a sign 'deep as Sheol or high as heaven' and thereby gave 'the house of David' bad example (7:10-13,17). Hezekiah, the son granted to him as a sign in spite of his unwillingness, received a prophetic name, 'Immanuel', i.e. 'God with us', the truth of which he came to recognise in being rescued from Sheol. He now propagates his name in his praise of YHWH. Within PI, Hezekiah thus stands in the same line as the prophet Isaiah, who set the example for his readers in offering anticipated thanksgiving to YHWH. Indeed, Hezekiah is the prophet's first disciple (ידה hiphil: 12:1,4; 25:1).

20 In the final line, the petitioner comes to the realisation that his salvation is an ongoing guarantee which leads him to extend his praise to include his entire life. Now that God has saved him, he knows that YHWH will always do so: 'YHWH is at hand to save me'.[51] Such praise, moreover, will not be a matter for the petitioner alone. It will include those to whom he now proclaims YHWH's deeds, according to the preceding verse his descendants: 'We will sing to stringed instruments'. At the same time, the praise of YHWH will endure 'all the days of our life'. Therefore Sheol, which once threatened to rob him of his life, is not to be his dwelling place but rather 'the house of YHWH'. The song of praise thus ends with a new perspective, opposite to that with which it began. The petitioner is now aware that he has not been exiled to Sheol and thereby prevented from associating with God and his fellow human beings (vv. 10f.). His dwelling is the house of YHWH where together with 'the living' he will sing God's praises.[52]

21-22 The conclusion to the narrative is so open that it hardly deserves to be called a 'dénouement'. The prophet charges the king to apply a determined medical treatment (v. 22), revealing for the first time the particular ailment from which the king is suffering: a 'boil' (שְׁחִין: Exod. 9:9ff.; Lev. 13:18ff.; Deut. 28:27,35; Job 2:7). It remains unclear whether this term, according to modern diagnostic expertise, refers to one specific symptom or to a variety of symptoms.[53] The therapy itself has the unusual character of being prescribed by the prophet himself. He behaves here, to a certain extent, as a thaumaturge, as someone who knows how to bring about healing thanks to his relationship with God (vv. 4-8). This aspect of the prophet's skill, however, is not given further elaboration here.[54] Figs were commonly used for their medicinal properties in the Ancient Near East and not as a miracle cure.[55]

Strikingly enough, in contrast to 2 Kgs 20:7, there is no mention here of the fact that Hezekiah took advantage of the fig cure and was ultimately healed. In expressing his hope that the king 'may recover' (וְיֶחִי; cf. Ezek. 37:9; Ps. 49:10; 69:33), however, the prophet conforms with the concern which has dominated the entire chapter ('to live': vv.

---

[51] This is the tenor of the unusual construction of לְ with the infinitive הוֹשִׁיעֵנִי; cf. Ewald, §296 c; GKC, §114 i; König, 322f.: 'Der Ewige ist darauf gerichtet, mich zu retten'.

[52] Hauge 1995.

[53] Wildberger, 1448; HALAT, 1354. An elaborate discussion is offered by J. Preuss, Biblical and Talmudic Medicine (trl. F. Rosner), New York 1978, 339-46.

[54] Hoffer 1992: 72-75.

[55] Wildberger, 1454. The Scriptures are familiar with fig-cakes as a source of energy (1 Sam. 25:18; 30:12).

1,9,11f.,16,19). The question of the effectiveness of the fig therapy is thus left unanswered, postponed, as it were, to be answered in the restoration of Zion in the second half of BI (cf. 'Essentials and Perspectives').

The king's question underlines the narrative's open-endedness in two ways (v. 22). On the one hand, he asks for a sign that the therapy will be truly effective, on the other hand, he places his recovery on a par with his 'going up to the house of YHWH'. He thereby makes the connection with what he declared in his prayer to be the essential disadvantage of an existence in Sheol: 'I shall not see YHWH' (v. 11), together with his stated resolution: 'We will sing at the house of YHWH' (v. 20). The king thus speaks of his physical recovery in terms of its religious significance.

Given the fact that there is no mention of recovery, attention is drawn to the healing process as such which clearly enjoys metaphorical significance. It would appear that the redaction of BI has transformed the illness of Hezekiah and the recovery promised him into an example for the people in exile. In the introduction to the book, the prophet offered the diagnosis that Israel was sick 'from the sole of the foot to the head' and that her wounds were not being tended (1:5f.). At the moment of the prophet's vocation, YHWH equated conversion with healing (6:10) and far-reaching devastation of the land with the necessary path to renewed growth of the stump (6:13). Moreover, the healing of Israel is to be found elsewhere in a cosmic perspective: it will coincide with an unprecedented explosion of light from the sun and the moon (30:26). Similarly, the healing of Hezekiah is preceded by a sign whereby the laws governing the movement of the sun are suspended (v. 8). Finally, in ch.33, which constitutes a bridge between PI and DI, it is already announced that 'illness / iniquity' will not longer afflict the people of Jerusalem (33:24). The redaction has clearly actualised the narrative of Hezekiah's illness for the needs of the exile by grafting it onto the theme of Israel's illness, or in other words, her sinfulness (root חלה in this context in BI: 1:5; 17:11; 33:24; 38:1,9; 39:1; 53:3f.,10). In the same context, the redaction has evidently accentuated the process of the king's recovery as *a therapy applied by the prophet* which ultimately led the sick king to look forward to his 'going up to the house of YHWH'.

Against the background of the laws of purity, the conclusion of the present narrative gains further significance. In making him impure, Hezekiah's sickness prohibited his entrance into the temple (Lev. 13:18-23 deals with 'boils'). The law required the inspection of the sick person's skin by the priests who would then proclaim judgement as to the ritual purity or impurity of the patient (Lev. 13:6,17, 23,28,34,37,39ff.). Just as the ritual prescribed that the priest should inspect the sick person's skin for developments, so Hezekiah asked for a sign which would herald a positive development in his illness and thereby allow him to go up to YHWH's house.

The metaphorical dimension of the fig therapy may conceal a more subtle significance.[56] Rashi speaks here of a 'miracle within a miracle' (נס בתוך נס), since in contrast to having therapeutic value such a fig-paste would even have impaired healthy tissue.[57] The Mekhilta echoes Rashi in its explanation of Exod. 15:25.[58] R.Simon b. Gamaliel has a problem with the fact that wood, something bitter, was used to make bitter water sweet. He compares the procedure, designated by God, with Isa. 38:21 as follows: 'He puts a thing that spoils on a thing that has been spoiled, so as to perform a miracle therewith'. Taken together, both events serve to underline the conviction that God's ways are different from our ways.

Should the fig-paste's negative effects on body tissue be among the assumptions of the narrative itself, then the metaphorical value of the therapy becomes even excruciating. The king's illness is not helped by the fig-compress, a basically simple therapy, in spite of the fact that the prophet recommends it. The point of the conclusion would then be that only an apparently contradictory procedure of breakdown can bring recovery, both for Hezekiah and for those to whom he serves as an example: the community of the exile. In this interpretation, Hezekiah's request for a sign of impending recovery is given greater relief. In the midst of ruin, it comes to embody the community's hope-filled longing for purification which will re-open access to YHWH's house.

---

[56] Hoffer (1992: 79-82) deserves the honour for unearthing the following data.
[57] Rosenberg, 309f.
[58] *Mekilta De-Rabbi Ishmael* (trl. J.Z. Lauterbach), Philadelphia (1933) 1976, II, 92f. (Vayassa', I, 115-30).

THE THIRD STORY: THE WORD ABOUT THE KING OF
BABYLON IS GOOD (39:1-8)

1 At that time
   Merodach-baladan the son of Baladan, king of Babylon,
   sent (envoys)
   with letters and a present for Hezekiah,
   for he heard that he had fallen ill and had recovered.
2 Hezekiah welcomed them
   and he showed them his treasure house, the silver, the gold,
   the spices, the precious oil,
   his whole armoury, all that was found in his storehouses.
   There was nothing in his house or in all his realm
   that Hezekiah did not show them.
3 Then Isaiah the prophet came to king Hezekiah,
   and said to him:
        'What did these men say?
        And whence did they come to you?'
   Hezekiah said:
        'They have come to me from a far country, from Babylon'.
4 He said:
        'What have they seen in your house?'
   Hezekiah answered:
        'They have seen all that is in my house.
        There is nothing in my storehouses that I did not show them'.
5 Then Isaiah said to Hezekiah:
        'Hear the word of YHWH of hosts:
6   "Behold, the days are coming,
             when all that is in your house,
             and that which your fathers have stored up till this day,
             shall be carried to Babylon.
             Nothing shall be left",
        says YHWH.
7   "And some of your sons, who shall issue from you,
             whom you shall beget,
             shall be taken away.
             And they shall be eunuchs in the palace of the king of Babylon".

8   Then said Hezekiah to Isaiah:
      'The word of YHWH which you have spoken is good'.
      He said:
      'Truly, there will be peace and faithfulness in my days'.

NOTES

1 MT does not mention 'envoys', although it presumes these individuals in vv. 2-4. Efforts have been made to solve this problem by introducing סריסים, 'eunuchs' (cf. v. 7; Duhm, 284), or by vocalising ספרים,
'letters', as a *nomen agentis*, 'scribes' (especially since the plural 'letters' is unusual[1]) or by reading a term ספירים which is related to the
Akkadian *šapīru*, 'high officials' (Driver 1937: 47f.). While LXX also
interpolates the missing word (ἐπιστολὰς καὶ πρέσβεις καὶ δῶρα), the
location of the interpolation between 'letters' and 'present' gives the impression that the translators likewise did not find the term in their original. The phenomenon of insufficient information with respect to the dis-
patching of envoys and the execution of their task is not unique. In
37:14 we are informed that the emissaries of Sennacherib carry a letter
for Hezekiah but there is no reference to such a letter when they are dis-
patched in 37:9. It is possible that we have a further example of the phenomenon here in 39:1. Although it is impossible to reconstruct the original form of the text, it is equally clear that the concept 'envoys' is contained therein.

ESSENTIALS AND PERSPECTIVES

Unlike chs. 36-38, ch.39 does not place Assyria in the spotlight as the
major source of threat but Babylon (vv. 1,3,6f.), thus preparing the
reader for the second half of BI.[2] While it is true that the name of this
city only appears beyond this point in 43:14; 47:1 and 48:14,20, the
power it represents is present everywhere in the announcement of salvation contained in chs. 40-48. From the redactional perspective, ch.39 is
connected with chs. 37-38 by means of the modifier 'at that time', and at

[1] Ehrlich 1912: 141: cf. 36:3; 37:2; Crown 1974: 368f. According to most commentators.
[2] Ch.39 is not the first place in BI where Babylon is mentioned. Prior to this we find
references in 13:1,19; 14:4,22; 21:9; 23:13 ('Chaldeans'). In a sequential reading of PI,
the reader of ch.39 is thus already well-informed of the tyrannical character and contemptible end of this world power (Begg 1989: 123f.; Höffken 1998: 249).

the level of content primarily with ch.38 by means of the mention of Hezekiah's illness and recovery (v. 1). Ch.39, however, places the king in a different light and does not raise the question of the fate of Jerusalem.[3] Hezekiah's welcome and familiar treatment of the Babylonian envoys does not enjoy Isaiah's approval and provokes an announcement of divine punishment (vv. 6-7). The manner in which the prophet interrogates the king betrays a degree of political opposition which has its proper place in the former's rejection of alliances with foreign kings against Assyria (Isa. 30:1-7,15-17; 31:1-3). The pious behaviour of the king, so evident in chs. 36-38, is only recognisable here in his reaction to the announced judgement (v. 8).

It is difficult to escape the impression that the narrative has been reworked. The king's display of all his possessions to the Babylonian envoys, more than likely a demonstration of his power (v. 2), is hardly an appropriate reaction to their felicitations upon his recovery (v. 1). From the narrative perspective, the suggestion that the king's wealth will one day be carried off (v. 6) may well be apt in the context of Hezekiah's mistaken gesture, but the idea that Babylon will be its destination and not Assyria points to a *vaticinium ex eventu*, since the prophet usually gives warning that foreign kingdoms with which Judah desires to establish an alliance against Assyria will be unable to extend their power (7:4-7; 14:28-32; 20; 30:3-5; 31:3). The fact that Hezekiah's sons will one day be carried off to serve in the Babylonian court (v. 7), while the king himself will be spared (v. 8), constitutes an additional strange element in the narrative. Furthermore, in the related narrative of ch.7 it is the king who is punished (vv. 17-20), while his successor expects salvation (vv. 15-16; cf. 22:15-19 and 20-24).[4] Thus the deportation and employment of Hezekiah's sons in the Babylonian court would also appear to be a *vaticinium ex eventu* (cf. Dan. 1:3-5; Neh. 2:1). Finally, the location of the framing formula, 'says YHWH', after v. 6 and not after v. 7, leaves the impression that v. 7 is an addition.

It is probable that the narrative originally refers to a conflict between the prophet and the king concerning the sympathetic reception given to the Babylonian envoys who had come to negotiate an alliance. The king mentioned here, Merodach-baladan of Bit-Yakin, reigned over Babylon from 721 to 710 BC, when the Assyrian king Sargon II ousted him, and later from 704 to 703 BC, during the first turbulent years of Sargon's successor, Sennacherib.[5] According to the sources Merodach-baladan always opposed Assyria's efforts to gain superior power.[6] The suggestion that this was the purpose of the alliance can also be found in Flavius

Josephus: 'The king of Babylon, named Baladas, sent envoys bearing gifts to Hezekiah and invited him to become his ally and friend' (Ant. XX, II, 31-32). It is possible that Isaiah had warned that an alliance with Babylon would bring little advantage against Assyria, and that, counter to expectations, Hezekiah would be forced to pay tribute to the latter (cf. 2 Kgs 18:14-16).

In the context of the later actualisation of the narrative, the announcement of an Assyrian levy may have been replaced by the plundering of Jerusalem by the king of Babylon, more than likely Nebuchadnezzar (v. 6), and expanded with an announcement of the deportation of the sons of Hezekiah which reflects upon the fate of the dynasty (v. 7).[7] This *vaticinium ex eventu* probably refers to the first plundering and deportation of 597 BC (2 Kgs 24:13-17), rather than the second of 587 BC, since the sons of Hezekiah were killed at the time of the second deportation and the city and temple were destroyed (2 Kgs 25: 7-17). This latter fact is a fundamental datum to which the prophecy does not allude.[8]

At the same time, the redaction of BI has transformed the illness and recovery of Hezekiah into an occasion for the visit of the Babylonian envoys (v. 1). This need not necessarily suggest a lack of historical sense or literary taste since the Ancient Near East was quite familiar with the practice of sending envoys to sympathetic royalty to inquire after their health.[9] The present narrative was thus able to link up with the preceding narrative and thereby serve a variety of purposes. The most important of these was the fact that the Babylonian captivity, albeit restricted to

---

[3] Seitz (1991: 182-91) must be given priority for having drawn attention to the various tendencies of ch.38 and ch.39. According to him, chs. 36-38 came into existence in the context of BI from which they were taken over to 2 Kings 18-20. Ch. 39, on the other hand, came into existence in the context of 2 Kings from which it was taken over into BI in order to correct the prophecy of Zion's inviolability (chs. 36-37) and the continuation of Hezekiah's dynasty (ch. 38).

[4] *pace* Ruprecht 1990: 43f. This author refers to v. 7 as a *vaticinium ante eventum*, since it exhibits too little agreement with the historical events as given in 2 Kgs 24:12.

[5] Delitzsch (397f.) provides a detailed history of Merodach-baladan.

[6] It is difficult to determine what the most probable setting for this narrative might be: the end of Merodach-baladan's first reign, when Ashdod in the west was the motivating force behind an anti-Assyrian coalition in Syria and Palestine (cf. Isaiah 20; Rofé 1988: 95f.; Ruprecht 1990: 41), or his short second reign, when the military threat was greater for both him and Hezekiah (Brinkman 1965; Dietrich 1970: 1-3).

[7] Höffken 1998.

[8] Clements 1980: 63-71. Sweeney (509f.), by contrast, postulates the second capture of (587) as a date since king Jehoiachin has no role to play in BI.

[9] Ruprecht (1990: 40f.) mentions two texts. In the first king Burraburias II of Babylon complains to Pharaoh Amenophis IV that he had not sent a message of comfort during his serious illness (*EAT*, I, 1915: 78ff.). In the second, Esarhaddon of Assyria makes a similar complaint concerning a son of Merodach-baladan.

Hezekiah's sons, was given mention prior to the beginning of the second part of BI in which it was to be assumed as a historical fact. This intention seems to have determined the form of the chapter to a significant extent.[10] A further aim appears to have been the provision of an explanation for the fact that YHWH did not maintain Hezekiah's descendants on the throne, in spite of his portrayal as the ideal king in chs. 36-38.

SCHOLARLY EXPOSITION

Introduction to the Exegesis: Form and Setting

The narrative constitutes a diptych: the arrival of the legation from Babylon (vv. 1-2) and the discussion between Isaiah and Hezekiah (vv. 3-8).

The first half introduces the apparently sympathetic king of Babylon, his initiative to send Hezekiah his congratulations and his reason for doing so using two verbal forms (v. 1: 'he sent' and 'he had heard'), which is then followed by Hezekiah's reaction, also employing two verbal forms (v. 2: 'he welcomed them' and 'he showed them'). The latter element is further elaborated in an inclusive catalogue, presented in both positive ('all that was found') and negative ('there was nothing') terms. Hezekiah's open display of his treasures prepares the reader by way of contrast for the announcement of the loss thereof in v. 6.

In the second half it is the prophet who leads the discussion. He twice interrogates the king (v. 3 and v. 4), and then delivers the word of YHWH (vv. 5-7), to which the king reacts in twofold fashion(v. 8).

The first of the prophet's questions consists of two parts: 'What did these men say?' and 'Whence did they come to you?', but the king only responds to the second part: 'from Babylon' (v. 3). The prophet does not return to the first part of his question, but poses a further question, one which reflects his primary concern: 'What have they seen in your house?' In response the prophet gets more information than he had asked for: the envoys have seen everything in Hezekiah's house and storehouses and the king himself has shown it them (v. 4). This rhetorical procedure of concealment followed by a minimal question with a maximal response provides the short narrative with a dynamic development.

The word of YHWH constitutes an announcement of judgement with a double focus: 'all that is in your house' will be taken as booty (v. 6) and 'some of your sons' will be carried off to Babylon as servants (v. 7).

[10] Becker 1997:221f.

One can assume a redaction-historical seam between both elements (cf. also the framing formula 'says YHWH'), Indeed, v. 7 can be considered an addition since, in contrast to v. 6, it does not enjoy any element of preparation in the preceding text.[11] V. 7 thus transforms a narrative of an incident relating to Isaiah's criticism of Hezekiah's foreign policy into a prophecy concerning the end of the dynasty. While it cannot be proven with any certainty, it is probable that this expansion coincides with the re-focusing of the narrative from an Assyrian military expedition to a Babylonian one.

At the same time, should v. 7 constitute an expansion of v. 6, it is clear that both elements are well attuned since the words 'house' (בית) and 'son' (בן) are semantically related (Gen. 16:2; 30:3; 1 Sam. 2:35; 2 Sam. 7:1-17; 1 Kgs 11;38; Ruth 4:11). The end of the dynasty is now in view. Hezekiah's descendants will not only be robbed of the possessions, and thereby power, amassed by their forefathers, his own sons will be forced to serve in a function (v. 7: 'eunuchs') which precludes the very possibility of further descendants.[12]

Hezekiah's reaction to the announcement of judgement is twofold (v. 8). He accepts the sentence of YHWH delivered by Isaiah. Obedience to the prophet forms an integral part of the image of this king (cf. Jer. 26:18f.). As such, he re-assumes the exemplary role which he played in chs. 36-38. In these chapters he accepted the prophet as God's emissary (37:2,21; 38:1,4) and continued to have faith in YHWH and in Jerusalem's ultimate liberation in spite of the apparent invincibility of the Assyrian forces (37:15,18,20; 37:4,10,20). There also he praises God for saving him from his deadly illness, in recognition of his sins and with a 'doxology of judgement' (38:15-17). In the same way, he now accepts the announcement that his possessions and sons will be taken into captivity as something 'good'. Such a qualification can only refer to the fairness of God's actions if it also concerns the actual outcome thereof.[13] Given the fact that we are not told how the exile can be seen as something good, Hezekiah's remark thus provides the narrative with an open end.

V. 8b has long been a source of exegetical difficulty.[14] Nevertheless, the repetition of the introductory 'he said' after a direct discourse of only

[11] Höffken 1998: 247.

[12] According to *TWAT*, V, 950-4 (B. Kedar-Kopfstein), the term סריס should be understood here in the physical sense of 'eunuch' (cf. 2 Kgs 9:32; 23:11; 24:15; Isa. 56:3f.; Jer. 29:2; 38:7; 41:16;:Esth. 1:10ff.; 2:3,14f.; 4:4) since the alternative 'high official' cannot be considered a punishment.

[13] *TWAT*, III, 332 (I. Höver-Johag).

[14] This is already evident from the fact that LXX and Vg employ the volitive form here. For what follows, cf. Ackroyd 1974: 335-8.

one sentence (v. 8a) need not necessarily imply that v. 8b is an unattached interpolation, lacking any connection with the narrative as such. Similarly, the absence of the determinative '(He said) to Isaiah', need not imply that Hezekiah's remark ('Truly, there will be peace and faithfulness in my days') constitutes a self-interested side reflection which the king conceals from the prophet (RSV: 'For he thought').[15] The phenomenon of 'resumptive אמר within direct discourse' is frequent in the Hebrew Bible and can have a variety of functions and antecedents.[16] It can only be explained from case to case. The statement of v. 8b may have been provided with a second introduction in order to indicate that it deals with a completely different topic, one which has a much broader significance than the narrative context of the discussion with the prophet allows (Alexander, 92).[17]

The statement certainly need not imply that what will happen later is of no concern to the king (cf. 1 Kgs 21:29; 2 Kgs 22:20; Job 21:21; contrast in Jer. 31:15). Generally speaking, such an idea does not tally with the Ancient Near Eastern tradition that prosperous descendants keep a person's name alive (Ps. 112:1-3; 115:14; 128; Job 5:25-27). Furthermore, the suggestion that Hezekiah thus endeavoured to conceal the forthcoming disaster from himself (cf. 2 Sam. 18:24-33) is too psychological for this part of BI. Indeed, on the threshold of DI one would expect a statement in harmony with the latter's theology of the exile, as is the case with Hezekiah's first statement.

The following explanation would seem to be the most fitting. Over Isaiah's head, as it were, the king addresses himself to those for whom the words and deeds of the prophet are being preserved. These addressees need not necessarily be identified with the post-exilic readers of BI, one might also identify them with the pre-exilic circles which gave rise to the transmission of Isaiah ben Amoz' words and deeds, the same circles we encountered with some frequency in our analysis of chs. 28-32. The king bears witness to his conviction that 'peace and faithfulness' continue to form the horizon of his existence and that the same is possible for those whose lives have been marked by the threat or indeed the fact of the exile. This is what he expects from YHWH and it is to

---

[15] The history of the interpretation of this verse is a classic example of scholarly bias (cf. the survey of Alexander, 92). Echoes of Duhm's commentary: 'Indessen überschreitet diese Gottergebenheit und Zufriedenheit auf Kosten anderer und sogar der eigenen Nachkommen das Maß erlaubter Naivität' (286) continue to resonate (cf. Watts, 66; Oswalt, 697; Motyer, 297; otherwise Penna, 394).

[16] Meier 1992: 73-81.

[17] LXX does not translate the second ויאמר.

this that he commits himself (in agreement with his policy of reform, the memory of which is preserved by the tradition; cf. 2 Kgs 18:4; Jer. 26:17ff.; 2 Chronicles 29-31). The conclusion of the narrative thus upholds the image of the pious king. In his acceptance of the prospect of deportation to Babylon, Hezekiah adheres to his expectation of 'peace and faithfulness' from God and to his own loyalty to these values (Sweeney, 509f.).

In light of the evidently integral function of v. 8 for the narrative within the overall design of BI, the structure of ch.39 can be established as follows:

1-2 Merodach-baladan's embassy to Hezekiah
    1   their purpose
    2   their reception: Hezekiah shows his wealth
3-8 dialogue between Isaiah and Hezekiah
    3   first interrogation and answer: where the embassy have come from
    4   second interrogation and answer: what they have seen
    5-7 announcement of punishment
        5   messenger formula
        6   first notice: Hezekiah's wealth will be carried off
        7   second notice: Hezekiah's sons will be carried off
    8   Hezekiah's reaction
        8a first response: doxology of judgement
        8b second response: expectancy of peace and faithfulness

Exegesis by Verse

1 While the narrative opens with a new actant, 'Merodach-baladan, king of Babylon', it harks back simultaneously to the preceding narrative via the latter's interest in Hezekiah's illness and ultimate recovery. In contrast to earlier references to Babylon (13:1,19; 14:4,22; 21:9) the much-feared world power appears here as a friendly instance: 'with letters and a present for Hezekiah'. The term employed here for 'he had recovered', ויחזק, makes allusion to the king's name, 'Hezekiah' (root חזק, 'to be strong'), although it differs from the term used in ch.38 (חיה: vv. 1, 9,16,19,21). This variant word-play tends to support the independent character of this prophetic narrative. From the narrative perspective, it underlines Hezekiah's position as a mighty king, further evidence of which is soon to be revealed (Josh. 14:11; 17:13; Judg. 1:28; 2 Sam.

10:11; 1 Kgs 16:22; 20:23,25; Ezek. 30:22; Dan. 11:5; 2 Chron. 11:17).[18]

2 The fact that Hezekiah proudly exhibits his possessions to the Babylonian envoys (ראה *hiphil*) is not only a matter of political power display, it may also have a juridical connotation. While there is clearly no question of transferring right of possession[19] there may be a suggestion here that Hezekiah is making his wealth available to a possible alliance or coalition of powers (ראה can have a variety of juridical functions; cf. Gen. 13:14; 41:41; Num. 27:12; Deut. 1:8; 2:24; 3:27; 32:1,49; 34:1; Josh. 6:2; 1 Kgs 9:12; Jer. 40:4; Ps. 35:21; Job 8:18).[20]

The survey of Hezekiah's treasures covers three locations: (1) 'his treasure house',[21] in which capital goods were stored: 'silver and gold, spices and precious oil' (cf. 1 Kgs 10:10; Ezek. 27:17,22; Hos. 12:2; Esth. 2:12); (2) 'his whole armoury', a term without parallel and thus undetermined;[22] (3) 'his storehouses' (אוצרות), a term which can signify both 'depot' (Deut. 28:12; Jer. 10:13; Joel 1:17; Mic. 6:10; Mal. 3:10; Ps. 33:7; Neh. 13:12f.; Sir. 39:17) and 'treasury' (Josh. 6:19,24; 1 Kgs 7:51; 15:18; 2 Kgs 12:19; 14:14; 16:8; 18:15; Isa. 45:3; Jer. 38:11; Ezek. 28:4; Zech. 11:13; Prov. 8:21; Dan. 1:2; Ezr. 2:69). It seems reasonable to assume that the first storage place formed a part of the royal palace while the two other stores were probably located elsewhere. The negative formulation of v. 2b appears to repeat the locations referred to in v. 2a: 'nothing in his house or in all his realm' (cf. 1 Kgs 14:26).

The emphatic, all inclusive survey provides a glimpse of Hezekiah's material capacity as well as the naiveté of his political disposition. This forms the basis of the remainder of the narrative. At the same time there is a clear echo of the negative evaluation of 'gold and silver' in PI (Isa. 2:7,20; 13:7; 30:22; 31:7).

3-4 The rhetorical development of these verses (cf. 'Introduction to the Exegesis') illustrates the personal authority with which the prophet engages in dialogue with the king, an element which is also evident in the preceding narratives (37:21; 38:1). From a genre-critical perspective this is in harmony with the fact that in classical prophetic announcements of judgement, especially those directed against an individual, the element of accusation is often given in the prophet's own name and not

---

[18] *TWAT*, II, 848ff. (F. Hesse).

[19] *pace* Ackroyd (1974: 339) with reference to D. Daube, *Studies in Biblical Law*, Cambridge 1947, 24ff.

[20] *TWAT*, VII, 244f. (H.-F. Fuhs).

[21] בית נכתה is a Babylonian loan-word which is only found here (/ 2 Kgs 20:3).

[22] According to Wildberger (1476) this was 'the House of the Forest' of Isa. 22:8.

placed under a messenger formula (2 Sam. 12:1-7; 2 Kgs 1:3f.; Isa. 1:21ff.; 28:7-13; Jer. 28:15).[23] Furthermore, the king responds in all sincerity and does not attempt to conceal his behaviour. As such he is presented as the opposite of those sinners whose behaviour constitutes a clear rejection of the prophet's and indeed God's concerns (28:9-15; 29:15; 30:10f.,16).

The segment makes a further contribution to the chapter's function as prefatory to DI by referring to Babylon as 'a far country' (with inversion in first position). The term 'far' (רחוק) plays an important role in the topic of the exile (Isa. 5:26; 6:12; 33:13; 43:6; 46:11; 49:12; 57:19; 60:4,9; Jer. 27:10; 31:10; 46:27; 51:50; Ezek. 11:16; Mic. 4:3; Zech. 6:15).[24] In terms of information provided by Hezekiah in response to the prophet's question the expression appears to be redundant. As an allusion to the concrete horizon of the exiles, however, it actualises the narrative on their behalf: Babylon is a land far removed from the place they consider to be their home (cf. Ps. 137:1-6).

5-6 The first announcement of judgement is given particular gravity by way of the repeated introduction of the two actants ('Then Isaiah said to Hezekiah'; cf. v. 3). The direct discourse as such opens with a summons to listen to God's word, a characteristic form element of BI (1:2,10; 7:13; 28:14,23; 32:9; 33:13; 34:1; 42:18; 44:1; 46:3,12; 47:8; 48:1,12,16; 49:1; 51:1,7,21; 55:2f.; 66:5). The title 'YHWH of hosts', so frequent in PI (see 28:5), sets the prophecy in a long series of announcements of judgement, both against the prophet's own people (1:24; 2:12; 3:1; 5:9; 9:18; 13:13; 22:5, 12,14f.,25; 28:22; 29:6) and against alien nations (10:16,23,26,33; 14:22-24,27; 17:3; 19:4,16f.; 23:9; 24:21; 34:2; 47:4). The segment thus exhibits an Isaianic character while simultaneously offering a clear reflection of the concerns of the redaction.

The expression: 'Behold, the days are coming' is not employed here in a 'transitional' manner (introducing redactional supplements) but rather as 'integral' (organical within compositional units; cf. 1 Sam. 2:31; Jer. 7:32; 19:6; 48:12; 49:2; 51:47,52; Amos 4:2).[25] The temporal perspective belongs to the message itself. In the king's perspective, the announced event is a continuation of the present ('remote future'),[26] with a vague suggestion that he himself will experience it ('your house', 'up till

[23] Westermann 1960: 92-106.
[24] Ackroyd 1974: 338f.; *TWAT*, VII, 494 (L. Wächter).
[25] De Vries 1995: 74-7.
[26] Of course it is 'a past in the composer's experience and observation'; cf. De Vries 1995: 81.

this day'). Only in v. 8 (to some degree in v. 7) do we find that the temporal juncture of the announced event has shifted to the time of his descendants.

The formula 'Behold, the days are coming' differs from the related formula 'Behold, I will...' (הנה with a 1st person suffix referring to God followed by an active participle) to the extent that the event announced here is not presented as YHWH's own work, his direct intervention, but as a worldly event, something which is simply going to happen. Such a formulation leaves undisclosed the identity of those responsible for carrying Israel into exile, a question dealt with in DI (Isa. 43:18-25).

The summation of Hezekiah's property differs from that of v. 2 in that it focuses less on its location ('in your house' as opposed to 'his treasure house... his armoury... his storehouses... his house... his realm') and more on its temporal character: 'that which your fathers have stored up till this day'. This is in line with the temporal reference 'the days are coming' and with the verdict which follows: 'some of your sons who are born to you' (v. 7). The announcement of judgement thus calls to mind the passage of the Davidic dynasty through time.

The punishment of the removal (cf. Isa. 8:4; 30:6) of *all* of Hezekiah's treasures ('Nothing shall be left')[27] corresponds with the king's offence of revealing *all* his possessions to the Babylonian envoys (vv. 2,4). The terminology employed in the announcement is more in harmony with the facts of the first deportation in 597 BC (2 Kgs 24:13) than with those of the second in 587 BC (2 Kgs 25:13-17), since the latter report only speaks of the treasures in 'the house of YHWH' (and primarily, moreover, of the bronze objects found therein). V. 6, in contrast, does not speak of the treasures found in 'the house of YHWH', as is the case in 2 Kgs 24:13. On the basis of these literary facts, a precise conclusion with respect to the date of origin of the narrative cannot be sanctioned. Since the destruction of Jerusalem (2 Kgs 25:8-10) is not mentioned, however, the period of the first deportation would appear to enjoy greater credibility.

7 The second announcement of judgement refers to Hezekiah's sons. In light of the concluding formula 'says YHWH' in v. 6 this announcement is considered an interpolation. While the removal of Hezekiah's property rests on an offence committed by the king himself (vv. 2,4, 6), this is clearly not the case with respect to the deportation of his sons. It is probable that the redaction was striving for completeness here, since the respective historical reports concerning Nebuchadnezzar's expedi-

---

[27] The term 'to remain over' (יתר) is only used elsewhere in PI of persons (1:8f.; 4:3; 7:22; 30:17).

tions against Jerusalem in 597 and 587 BC refer to the plundering of the royal palace and the temple coupled with the deportation of the court and those of social standing (2 Kgs 24:12-16; 25:11-17). Agreement with these reports, however, is only partial, given that the report of the first deportation does not speak explicitly of the king's sons (2 Kgs 24:15) while the second states that they were killed (2 Kgs 25:7).

The contention that the deportation of Hezekiah's sons because of the sin of their father tarnishes the image of the punishing God with suggestions of injustice is much too facile an allegation. The *vaticinium ex eventu* clearly endeavours to explain the course of history. The sons of Hezekiah are expressly referred to as the king's descendants with whom they form an ethical unity and not as individuals with their own responsibility (cf. Isa. 14:21; 45:10; 51:2). The double expression 'who shall issue from you' and 'whom you shall beget' draws attention to the dynasty as such.[28] The first term, 'who shall issue from you', can refer to immediate as well as more remote descendants (יצא מן: Gen. 15:4; 17:6; 46:26; 2 Sam. 7:12; 2 Kgs 20:18), the second, 'whom you shall beget', only to immediate descendants (ילד *hiphil*: Gen. 5:3f.; 11:11; 25:19; Deut. 28:41; Judg. 11:1; Jer. 16:3; 29:6; Ezek. 18:10,14; 47:22; Eccl. 5:13; 6:3; Ruth 4:18-22).[29] The problem of historical referent arises once again at this point. According to 2 Chron. 33:11 the Assyrian military command led king Manasseh, Hezekiah's genetic son, in fetters to Babylon,[30] but he did not serve at the Assyrian court and was later released. It is more likely, therefore, that v. 7 exhibits a sort of 'telescoping' of a number of historical deportations.

The deportation of Hezekiah's sons illustrates how he and his lineage were forced into humiliating service of the king of Babylon. The term 'to take away' does not only imply enforced displacement, it also suggests subordination to the intentions of one who is more powerful (לקח with reference to individuals: Gen. 4:19; 6:2,11; 11:29; 12:19; 14:12; 42:24,36; 43:18; Num. 8:16; 23:11; 1 Sam. 20:31; 25:43; 2 Kgs 4:1; 23:34; Job 40:28; Esth. 2:7,15). The king of Babylon lives in a 'palace' (היכל), a word which suggests affluence (cf. 1 Kgs 21:1; Isa. 13:22; Hos. 8:14; Joel 4:5; Amos 8:3; Nah. 2:7; Ps. 45:9,16; 144:12; Prov. 30:2; Dan. 1:4; 2 Chron. 36:7), certainly in the context of the removal of Hezekiah's treasures, while the dwelling of the latter is referred to simply as 'his house' (vv. 3,4,6). The greatest humiliation, however, lies

---

[28] Ackroyd 1974: 335.

[29] *TWAT*, III, 637, speaks of 'horizontale und vertikale Genealogie' (J. Schreiner).

[30] For the historical reliability of this report, i.e. of a deportation to Babylon by the Assyrian authorities, cf. the commentaries on Chronicles.

in the fact that the sons of Hezekiah were forced to realise their service to the king of Babylon to the point of having to endure the violation of their physical integrity (Deut. 23:2; Isa. 56:3f.; Sir. 30:20), even if it be true that 'eunuchs' could rise to high rank in the royal court (Gen. 37:36; 40:2; 1 Sam. 8:15; 1 Kgs 22:9; 2 Kgs 8:6; 9:32; 23:11; 24:15; 25:19; Jer. 29:2; 38:7; 41:16; Esth. 1:10ff.; 2:3,14f.; 4:4; 1 Chron. 28:1).[31] The ongoing existence of Hezekiah's lineage is sacrificed for the glory of the king of Babylon.

8 Misunderstanding surrounding this verse (cf. 'Introduction to the Exegesis') calls for a careful reading thereof.

While the first expression (v. 8a: 'The word of YHWH which you have spoken is good') clearly implies the king's approval of Isaiah's message employing the customary terminology (cf. Deut. 1:14; 1 Sam. 9:10; 2 Sam. 15:3; 1 Kgs 2:38; 18:24; 22:13; Prov. 15:23), it simultaneously implies the recognition of the prophet as God's messenger. The absence of a further determinative in the form of 'to me' or 'with regard to me' betrays the intended emphasis of the verse segment. Hezekiah accepts Isaiah's message as word of God, even now that it announces the deportation of his sons to Babylon and their service to the Babylonian king.

It is against this background that we are obliged to interpret the second expression: 'Truly, there will be peace and faithfulness in my days'. In the first instance the expression suggests a political prognosis: in Hezekiah's days, in contrast to 'the days (that) are coming' (v. 6) there will be a trustworthy peace, the words 'peace and faithfulness' (שׁלום ואמת) evidently forming a hendiadys (Jer. 14:13; 33:6; Esth. 9:30).[32] In association with the narrative concerning Hezekiah's sickness and recovery, however, a second interpretation is likewise evident. For in that story 'peace' is the outcome of the king's bitter experiences (38:17) and 'faithfulness' the currency of exchange between the king and God (vv. 3,18f.). Moreover, Hezekiah has placed the newly acquired extension of his life under a specific mandate: 'The father makes known to the sons your faithfulness' (v. 19). This statement clearly continues to resonate in 39:8. Even after hearing that his sons are to be deported to Babylon to serve at the court there, the king continues to insist that he expects 'peace and faithfulness' to govern the remainder of his days. Seen in this way, the king plays an exemplary role at the point of transition between PI and DI.[33] For the way in which 'peace' and 'faithfulness' will once

---

[31] Cf. note 12.

[32] *TWAT*, I, 334 (A. Jepsen).

[33] Even from the text-critical perspective v. 8b appears to be a redactional interpolation since the B-text of the LXX of the parallel text in 2 Kgs 20:19 only has the first half

again become reality constitutes a significant theme of the second half of BI (45:7; 48:18; 52:7; 53:5; 54:10,13; 55:12; 57:19; 60:17; 66:12 and 42:3; 43:9; 48:1; 59:14f.; 61:8 respectively).[34]

of the verse (/ Isa. 39:8a), while the Hexapla provides the second half (/ Isa. 39:8b) with an asterisk (Field I, 691; Konkel 1993: 477).

[34] Williamson (1994: 210f.) likewise recognises the prospective role of v. 8 in the design of BI, more specifically in connection with the triple division of the second half (48:22; 57:21).

PRINTED ON PERMANENT PAPER • IMPRIME SUR PAPIER PERMANENT • GEDRUKT OP DUURZAAM PAPIER - ISO 9706

ORIENTALISTE, KLEIN DALENSTRAAT 42, B-3020 HERENT